DICTIONARY
OF
AMERICAN POLITICS

EVERYDAY HANDBOOKS

DICTIONARY OF AMERICAN POLITICS

second edition

EDWARD C. SMITH and ARNOLD J. ZURCHER

BARNES & NOBLE BOOKS

A DIVISION OF HARPER & ROW, PUBLISHERS

New York, Hagerstown, San Francisco, London

PREFACE

This second edition of *Dictionary of American Politics* is a thorough revision of a standard reference book which, for many years, has helped students and the general public toward an understanding of American government and politics. In 1888, Everit Brown and Albert Strauss produced the first *Dictionary of American Politics* which was largely devoted to political issues, slogans, terms used in party and electoral organization, and brief biographies of political figures. In 1924, Edward C. Smith revised the book, incorporating hundreds of new terms that had become current during the Progressive Movement and the beginning of federal expansion, especially during the administrations of Theodore Roosevelt and Woodrow Wilson.

When a third revision was planned in the 1940's, it was evident that a dictionary devoted exclusively to the American political scene would be inadequate because of the increasing involvement of the United States in world affairs. Professor Arnold J. Zurcher was associated with Professor Smith as joint editor, and the assistance of twelve collaborators was obtained in order to prepare definitions, relevant to the American scene, from the fields of comparative government, political theory, constitutional law, international law, public administration, and social welfare. To provide space for new entries, all biographical sketches were eliminated. This revision was published in 1944, and a fourth revision, with many editorial changes and the addition of about 500 entries, appeared in 1949.

In the past twenty years new terms have come into general use reflecting especially the involvement of the United States in world affairs from Truman to Lyndon B. Johnson, the activities of the Warren Court in expanding the meaning of civil rights, the administrative changes following the Hoover Commissions' reports, and the domestic programs of the New Frontier and the Great Society. Many of the older terms have acquired new meanings or have needed restatement. Contemporary methods of research in political science require ever more up-to-date and accurate definitions of terms.

This edition differs from the last one in noteworthy respects: Following good dictionary style, all entries, including abbreviations, are listed in strict alphabetical order. A typical entry begins with a definition, which is often made more explicit by a parenthetical clause showing the application of the word or the phrase to a specific subject. A usage clause is frequently affixed so that the reader may estimate the significance of the term. An etymological clause is provided when the meaning of the term is clarified by a statement of its origin. To save space, separate entries for each State have been eliminated, and the material formerly included there, and more, is presented in the Appendix. Other space was saved by dropping many terms which have passed into what Grover Cleveland called "innocuous desuetude." There is no initialing of entries; the editors assume responsibility for every definition.

The result is a book containing more than 3,800 entries, of which 600 are new. Moreover, definitions of the older terms contain far more information within nearly the same space as a result of eliminating extraneous matter and streamlining the style. We believe that the new and revised definitions are easier to read and to understand in this book than in any previous edition, and that its usefulness to the student and the lay reader has been greatly increased.

E.C.S.
A.J.Z.

ACKNOWLEDGMENTS

We must first express our sincere thanks to the contributors to the 1944 edition—Professor Jesse T. Carpenter, of Cornell University; President George H. Durham, of Arizona State University; Professor John W. Follows, of Hofstra College; President John W. McConnell, of the University of New Hampshire; Professor J. Roland Pennock, of Swarthmore College; Dr. James J. Robbins, of Washington, D.C.; Dr. C. Hart Schaaf, in public service abroad; Professor Elmer E. Smead, of Dartmouth College; and Professor Arthur J. Waterman, Jr., of C. W. Post College; and to the heirs of Dr. James A. Padgett and of Dean Catheryn Seckler-Hudson—for their gracious permission to allow their definitions of terms to be reprinted, in whole or in part, in this second edition. Most of their contributions have endured and have been carried forward with only minor editorial changes. We are grateful to Dr. Samuel Smith, Editor in Chief of Barnes & Noble, Inc., for his encouragement and advice in undertaking this revision. We especially thank Mr. Harvey Graveline, the Editor in immediate charge of this revision, for his keen interest, good humor, and firmness in bringing the project to completion. He has added the expertness of a lexicographer to the work of academicians. We must also thank Mrs. Marion Zeigman, Mrs. Kathleen Pisano, and Miss Hara Seltzer for their skillful typing of the manuscript.

DICTIONARY
OF
AMERICAN POLITICS

A.A.A. Agricultural Adjustment Administration or Acts.

A.&M. College. Agricultural and Mechanical College.

A.B.A. American Bar Association.

abatement. The act of abolishing a nuisance or of doing away with a wrongfully imposed tax.

A.B.C. Powers. Argentina, Brazil, and Chile which have sometimes assumed leadership in Latin-American affairs.

abdication. Renunciation of the privileges and prerogatives of an office. The act of abdication is usually personal and does not affect the existing rules of succession to the office unless so stipulated.

ability theory. A theory that taxes should be levied upon persons in accordance with their ability to pay them, measured either by the amount of property owned or by income received;—opposed to the benefit theory, *q.v.*

abjuration. The renunciation under oath of one's citizenship or some other right or privilege.

Ableman v. Booth. A case involving a State's attempt to release an abolitionist editor held by a federal marshal for violating a federal law. In its opinion, 21 How. 506 (1859), the Supreme Court held that when a person is legally in federal custody for a federal offense and this fact has been made known to State authorities by proper return on a writ of habeas corpus, the State is barred from proceeding further, federal authority being exclusive.

Abolitionist. An extreme opponent of Negro slavery who sought to do away with the institution by propaganda based on moral principles, as William Lloyd Garrison; by force, as John Brown; or by the organization of parties, appeals to Congress, and other political means.

abrogation. 1. The action by the signatory powers in terminating a treaty or international agreement. *Compare* denunciation. 2. Repeal of a statute or other public act.

absentee voting. Participation in elections by qualified voters who, because of serious illness, military service, or absence from home for business or other reasons, are unable to appear at the polls in person on election day. Under the laws of nearly every State, they are permitted to mail their ballots to the proper election officials.

absolute contraband. Arms and munitions of war transported by neutrals in wartime. *See* contraband of war.

absolute majority. More than half of the number of persons entitled to vote on a given question, regardless of the number in attendance or voting. In the Senate, an absolute majority is now 51, an absolute two-thirds vote is 67.

absolute veto. The veto of a bill or resolution by an executive or other authority which is conclusive because of the absence of any constitutional provision for overriding the veto.

absolutism. 1. A system of government in which unlimited and arbitrary power over persons and property is committed to a monarch or dictator. 2. The exercise of political power uncontrolled by effective constitutional or legal provisions.

acceptance speech. *See* speech of acceptance.

accession. 1. The act of taking office or coming to power. 2. The act of entering a confederation or of accepting the terms of a multilateral treaty or convention.

acclamation. Overwhelming approval expressed by cheering, shouting, or handclapping in a party convention or similar body;—usually the characteristic method of voting in the parliaments of authoritarian governments.

accord. 1. A diplomatic entente or international understanding usually of a verbal character. 2. The agreements or compromises reached by previous conflicting groups (as labor and capital) within a country.

accountability. The state of being under the obligation to render a financial statement or otherwise justify one's actions before a superior authority;—sometimes used as a synonym for political responsibility. *See* responsibility 2.

accredit. 1. To send an envoy with credentials. 2. To receive an envoy from a foreign state and allow him to begin his functions.

accretion. The extension of territorial boundaries through a gradual rise of the land surface at the coast line or through the deposit of silt.

accusation. A formal charge before a court or magistrate that a person is guilty of an offense punishable by law.

A.C.L.U. American Civil Liberties Union.

acquisition. The securing of title to a territory either by such legal means as discovery, occupation, purchase, treaty, or peaceful annexation, or by forcible annexation.

acquittal. The dismissal (as by a jury or a court decision) of criminal charges formally brought against an accused person, absolving him from further prosecution for the same offense.

Acting President. The Vice President during the period when, under the provisions of the Twenty-fifth Amendment, *q.v.*, he is discharging presidential powers and duties.

action. A legal proceeding (as in common-law practice) to enforce one's rights against another in a court of justice;—distinguished from suit, *q.v.*

activist. 1. One who is impatient at the slow progress of reform and espouses bold action in new directions. 2. A reformer who, in order to promote his cause, resorts to street demonstrations, sit-ins, and other forms of direct action.

Act of Chapultepec. A declaration by the Inter-American Conference on War and Peace at Mexico City, March 6, 1945, that any attack against the territory or sovereignty of any one of the American states would be countered by the combined forces of all. *See* Rio Treaty.

act of Congress. *In American parliamentary usage:* a statute, *q.v.*, of Congress that originates as a bill introduced by the clause, "Be it enacted, etc." *Compare* joint resolution. Acts of Congress are published after every session in the *Statutes at Large of the United States*, and those in force may be found in the *Code of Laws of the United States* as revised and supplemented.

A.D.A. Americans for Democratic Action.

Adair v. *United States.* A case, 208 U.S. 161 (1908), in which the Supreme Court held that a federal statute outlawing yellow-dog employment contracts, *q.v.*, in interstate commerce violated the due-process clause of the Fifth Amendment. A virtually identical rule was made seven years later in *Coppage* v. *Kansas*, 236 U.S. 1, in which a similar State statute was held to violate the due-process clause of the 14th Amendment. Yellow-dog contracts were outlawed by the Norris-La-Guardia Act, *q.v.*, but the Supreme Court did not completely repudiate its rule in the Coppage case until 1949.

Adams and Clay Republicans. The faction of the Democratic-Republican party which after 1825 supported John Quincy Adams and Henry Clay.

Adamson Act. An act of Congress, Sept. 5, 1916, which gave legal recognition to the eight-hour day for employees on interstate railroads and established a procedure for the solution of pending railroad labor controversies.

Adams-Onis Treaty. *See* Florida purchase.

Adamson v. California. A case, 332 U.S. 46 (1947), in which the Supreme Court held that a California statute permitting judicial comment on the failure of a defendant to take the stand did not violate the Fifth Amendment's prohibition of self-incrimination and, in essence, reiterated earlier rulings, such as *Twining* v. *New Jersey* and *Palko* v. *Connecticut*, *qq.v.*, that the due-process clause of the 14th Amendment does not extend to State courts the procedural limitations of the first eight Amendments.

adhesion. The acceptance by a third state of the general principles or only part of the stipulations of an existing treaty. *Compare* accession 2.

ad interim. Referring to a legislative committee which is authorized to perform functions in the interval between legislative sessions; *also:* referring to an officer who succeeds to an office upon the occurrence of a vacancy and serves until the office is filled.

adjournment. The closing of business for a day, for several days, or indefinitely (*sine die*). Neither house of Congress may adjourn for more than three days without the consent of the other. If the two houses disagree as to the time of adjournment, the President may adjourn them; but he has never had occasion to exercise the power. An adjournment closes the legislative day; a recess does not.

adjudication. The process of settling controversies over legal rights before a court of law or an administrative tribunal.

adjusted compensation. A bonus paid in 1924 to veterans of World War I in the form of paid-up life insurance, the amount being based on length of service, with a premium for foreign service, later (1936) converted to bonds or cash.

adjutant general. 1. The principal administrative officer of the National Guard of a State who is appointed by the governor with the approval of the War Department. 2. The officer of the Department of the Army who is responsible for the army's administrative, statistical, and accounting services, supervises the army's postal service and its communications with the public, and administers the personnel records of the army and the Army Department.

Adkins v. Children's Hospital. An early minimum-wage case, 261 U.S.

525 (1923), in which the Supreme Court declared unconstitutional a federal statute prescribing minimum pay standards for employed women and minors in the District of Columbia. In the court's opinion the legislation established an uncertain yardstick for compensation and discriminated against employers; hence it violated standards of due process under the Fifth Amendment. This decision was subsequently reversed in *West Coast Hotel Co.* v. *Parrish, q.v.*

Adler v. Board of Education. A decision of the Supreme Court, 342 U.S. 485 (1952), sustaining a New York State law which disqualified a person from holding a position in the public schools if he were listed as a member of any organization which the New York Board of Regents, after inquiry, had listed as one advocating overthrow of the Government by unlawful means. The Court held that disqualification of such a person, provided he knew the purposes of the organization when he joined, did not violate the guarantees of free speech and association protected by the due-process clause of the 14th Amendment.

administration. 1. The management of public affairs, the enforcement of law, and the fulfillment of public policy, sometimes differentiated from the executive and legislative functions in its lack of power to determine and declare public policy; and from the judicial function in its ability to arrive at decisions with relative freedom from the formality of procedural rules. Because of the growing complexity of government and the increased social responsibility of the state, these distinctions have tended to disappear. Evidence that they are disappearing may be found in the creation of numerous independent commissions with quasi-legislative and quasi-judicial powers and in the tendency of Congress and the State legislatures to delegate power to administrative officers. The growing importance of public administration is reflected in contemporary emphasis upon the proper articulation of governmental agencies, improvement in the techniques of management, the substitution of trained for amateur personnel, and the increasing prestige of public service. **2.** The whole body of executive officials. **3.** The tenure of a President of the United States or a governor.

administration bill. *In the federal government:* a bill drafted in an administrative department or agency, approved (as to financial implications) by the Bureau of the Budget, and sponsored by friendly senators and representatives.

administrative. Pertaining to management generally, or to the art or function of managing public affairs, or to the agencies or branches of government which perform the task of administration.

administrative courts. 1. Specialized courts in western Europe that are organized in a separate hierarchy, that apply administrative law, *q.v.*, and that have jurisdiction over all cases in which the government or officers of the government are concerned. Sometimes the judges also have some executive functions. Generally administrative courts have a reputation for fairness in protecting the interests of citizens, for rendering speedy justice, for invalidating administrative orders which lack proper statutory authority, and for granting compensation for injuries suffered at the hands of officers or employees of the government.

2. Those courts not created under Art. III of the Constitution which are usually called legislative courts, *q.v.*

administrative law. 1. That part of public law which regulates the conduct of public officials and determines the rights of individuals in their dealings with these officials, including the legal remedies available to individuals for the protection of these rights. **2.** The body of law created by administrative agencies in the form of rules and regulations, administrative orders, and administrative decisions.

administrative lie. A statute passed in response to public demand for moral reform which is purposely made so stringent as to be unenforceable;— the term originated with W. T. Jerome, former district attorney of New York County.

Administrative Office of the United States Courts. An agency created in 1939 which, under the direction of the Judicial Conference of the United States, *q.v.*, prepares budgets, disburses funds, audits vouchers, supervises clerical staffs, examines the state of dockets, prepares statistical information, and, in general, acts as the administrative office for all the federal courts except the Supreme Court.

administrative order. A regulation issued by an administrative officer amplifying and making more specific the provisions of a statute. In the United States the power to issue such an order is normally expressly granted by statute; and when properly issued, the order has the force of law. *See* administrative law.

Administrative Procedure Act. An act of Congress, June 11, 1946, which requires the publication of orders and rules by every agency; notice of every proposed new rule by publication in the *Federal Register* with place and date of hearing, statute involved, and substance of rule proposed; definite procedure for the conduct of hearings; and judicial review for any person suffering a legal wrong as a result of the action of an agency. The courts may compel agency action when it has been unlawfully withheld or unreasonably delayed, and set aside actions that are arbitrary, capricious, an abuse of discretion, contrary to constitutional rights, in excess of statutory authority, without observance of the procedures required by law, unsupported by substantial evidence, or unwarranted by facts.

administrative reorganization. 1. *In the United States:* the effort to promote governmental economy, efficiency, and more effective control by reconstructing and simplifying the administrative apparatus of government. The federal administrative system has been the subject of several extensive surveys since 1911, most thoroughly by the Hoover Commissions, *q.v.* Noteworthy improvements include stricter supervision through the Budget and Accounting Act of 1921, the Government Corporations Control Act of 1945, the Administrative Procedure Act of 1946, the provision of staff services for the President, creation of the departments of Defense, of Health, Education, and Welfare, of Housing and Urban Development, and of Transportation, and numerous consolidations and realignments carried out under temporary grants of authority from Congress by every President since F. D. Roosevelt. **2.** *In the States:* reforms made through constitutional amendment or statute usually embracing the consolidation of numerous administrative agencies into relatively few single-headed, integrated departments under the direct supervision of the governor; the appointment and removal of principal officers by the governor with, or without, the advice and consent of the State senate, and discontinuance of the popular election of such officials; and the investiture in the governor of the preparation of the budget, fiscal controls, and staff services. **3.** *In municipalities:* a reorganization movement strongly influenced by such reforms as the strong-mayor, the commission, and the council-manager types of government.

admiral. 1. A naval officer (as Farragut, Porter, and Dewey) holding the highest permanent rank in the U.S. Navy. **2.** *In World War II:* a flag officer of lesser rank than a fleet admiral who wore a four-star insignia and ranked with a four-star general in the U.S. Army.

admiralty jurisdiction. The authority to try cases arising under maritime law, *q.v.* It is concerned with wartime captures, collisions, piracy and lesser crimes, and torts on the high seas and on navigable lakes and rivers; also with contracts for shipments of goods, insurance, and wages of seamen. It is not concerned with crimes and other incidents committed on board ships while they are in port. Original jurisdiction in admiralty cases is exercised by federal district courts acting as admiralty courts.

admissions tax. An excise tax levied upon patrons of places of amusement or recreation, usually in the form of a fixed percentage of the price of admission.

admission to the Union. An act of Congress which has the irrevocable effect of creating a new State equal in every respect to States already in the Union. Except for Maine, Vermont, Kentucky, Texas, California, and West Virginia, all new States have been elevated from a territorial status. The procedure usually followed is a petition of the territory for statehood, enactment by Congress of an enabling act which authorizes the inhabitants to draft a constitution, and the passing of an act of admission following the acceptance of the proposed State's constitution. Although Congress may make certain conditions in the act of admission, only such conditions are valid as regulate national governmental or proprietary rights. Congress may not admit new States formed out of the territory of an existing State (technically when West Virginia became a separate State in 1863 it secured the consent of Virginia's legislature), or combine two existing States without the consent of the legislatures of the States affected.

ad valorem tax. A tax levied on property or an article of commerce in proportion to its value, as determined by assessment, appraisal, or invoice. For ad valorem customs duties the tax base may be the cost of the article abroad (foreign valuation) or its fair value in the United States (domestic valuation). *Compare* duty 3.

advisory ballot. An official poll, the results of which are not binding, designed to exhibit the voters' preferences and to influence their representatives.

advisory commission. A permanently organized or *ad hoc* body which makes recommendations to a principal and consults with it.

advisory opinion. An opinion rendered by a court as to the constitutional or legal effect of a bill or a statute when no actual case is before it. The Supreme Court has always refused to render such opinions on the ground that it would be engaging in nonjudicial activity. A few States authorize the governor or legislature to ask State courts for advisory opinions but, when rendered, they have no binding force except in Colorado. *See* declaratory judgment.

advisory recall. The attempted extension (circa 1920) of the principle of the recall in North Dakota and Arizona to their Congressmen and local federal judges. The recall under such circumstances, however it may be formulated at the polls, can be interpreted only as an invitation to the officeholder to resign, because his tenure is controlled by national, and not by State, law.

A.E.C. Atomic Energy Commission.

A.E.F. American Expeditionary Force.

aerial domain. Space beginning at the terrestrial surface and continuing outward through the stratosphere into the ionosphere and beyond. For an undetermined distance immediately beyond the terrestrial surface, space is held to fall within the jurisdiction of the state controlling the surface. In the United States preeminent authority over such space resides in the federal government because of its power over interstate and foreign commerce and defense although the States also exert regulatory authority. Beyond what is conceded to fall within the jurisdiction of the surface state, outer space, like the open sea, is not subject to the jurisdiction of any state. Within the past decade several nations have sought to establish a clear delineation between inner or lower space, which is subject to the jurisdiction of the surface state, and outer or upper space, which is free of the claims of national sovereignty but which may be regulated by international treaty.

affirmation. A solemn declaration, made under circumstances normally requiring an oath and legally equivalent thereto, by a person whose moral or religious scruples prevent his taking an oath.

A.F.L.-C.I.O. American Federation of Labor and Congress of Industrial Organizations.

Afroyim v. Rusk. A case (No. 46, Oct. Term, 1966), in which the Supreme Court declared unconstitutional a provision of the Nationality Act of 1940 under which U.S. citizens by certain actions might forfeit their citizenship and reversed its decision in *Perez* v. *Brownell*, *q.v.*, on the ground that the definition of citizenship in the 14th Amendment is binding on Congress and prevents deprivation of citizenship without the individual's own consent.

Agency for International Development. A part of the Department of State concerned with the administration of America's non-military, foreign-aid programs. Such aid includes loans and gifts for developmental purposes in friendly countries and grants to international organizations for economic assistance in underdeveloped areas. The Agency is also responsible for the Alliance for Progress program, *q.v.*, in Latin America.

agenda. Items of business in the program of a public meeting, council, committee, or deliberative assembly.

agent provocateur. 1. An unofficial police agent who associates with politically disaffected groups or persons suspected of crime to win their confidence or encourage them to resist authority and commit illegal acts, and subsequently informs on them. **2.** An undercover man hired by one nation to encourage disaffected elements of another nation's citizenry to commit acts of sabotage, sedition, or treason.

aggravation. 1. Any action or circumstance which increases the magnitude of a crime or its penalties. **2.** Any action or circumstance which intensifies the seriousness of a dispute and makes its solution more difficult.

aggression. The attempt by one state to impair another state's political sovereignty or territorial integrity by forcible means devoid of moral or legal justification.

agitation. 1. An attempt to stir up popular enthusiasm and support for some political nostrum or cause. **2.** Sustained and persistent effort (sometimes considered subversive) that threatens to upset the status quo.

agreement. A mutual arrangement or understanding among two or more parties which, if legally enforceable, is equivalent to a contract. *See* executive agreement.

Agricultural Adjustment acts. Two acts of Congress designed to regulate the production and marketing of certain agricultural products. The first act, May 12, 1933, set up an Agricultural Adjustment Administration and provided that processors of farm products should pay taxes the proceeds of which were to be used to reimburse farmers who voluntarily cooperated with the administration in limiting acreage and the number of farm animals produced. After it was declared unconstitutional (*see United States* v. *Butler*) a second act was passed, Feb. 16, 1938, providing for benefit payments from general funds for farmers who participate in a soil conservation program by diverting lands to pasturage and the production of soil-building crops.

agricultural and mechanical college. A college (often a university) established and operated by a State for instruction in agricultural, engineering, military, and other subjects and supported, at least in part, by funds from the sale of public land provided by the Morrill Act, *q.v.*

agricultural bloc. *See* farm bloc.

agricultural cooperatives. Organizations of farmers to market produce and purchase supplies without the services of middlemen. The national and State governments have encouraged the formation of cooperatives through special incorporation laws, exemption from certain taxes, and cheap credit.

agricultural credit. Financial credit extended to farmers, ranchers, and agricultural cooperative associations for the purchase and improvement of land, for feed, seeds, and fertilizers, and for assistance in marketing crops. The credit is extended under the terms of various acts of Congress beginning with the act of July 17, 1916, which established the federal land banks. The Farm Credit Administration, *q.v.*, administers this credit system.

agricultural experiment station. A center for research in agricultural science, including development of knowledge of nutrition and domestic and industrial use of agricultural products, established by the Department of Agriculture in the 50 States, in territories, and in certain foreign countries, often conducted in cooperation with the States and located at a land-grant university or similar institution.

Agricultural Research Service. An operational unit of the U.S. Department of Agriculture, created in 1953, which conducts research and regulatory functions involving the control of plant and animal diseases, the enforcement of quarantines, human nutritional problems, the industrial uses of agricultural products, and marketing research.

Agricultural Wheel. A farmers' association founded in Arkansas in 1882 and active in politics in the Southwest.

AID Agency for International Development.

aid and comfort to the enemy. An overt attempt by a person owing allegiance to a belligerent state to render material assistance to the government or combatants of an enemy belligerent. In the United States such action, if proved in court, may be punished as treason.

aide-mémoire. A digest or outline of the contents of a treaty or other document.

air space. *See* aerial domain.

Air University. An agency within the Department of the Air Force which supervises the operation and curricula of the Air War College, the senior Air Force school at Maxwell Air Force Base, Ala., the Air Command and Staff College, and other technical training units for Air Force personnel.

"Alabama" claims. Claims by the United States against Great Britain for damages to American commerce by the "Alabama" and other Confederate war vessels and privateers which were built in England in violation of international law and British statutes. By the Treaty of Washington, May 8, 1871, the United States and Great Britain agreed to submit the claims to arbitrators, who later met at Geneva, Switzerland, and awarded the United States $15,500,000.

alarmist. One who attempts to excite popular fears of the consequences of some governmental policy.

Alaskan Boundary Dispute. A controversy between the United States and Great Britain arising from the indefinite terms of an Anglo-Russian treaty of 1825. It had fixed the boundary between Alaska and Canada along the crest of a range of mountains paralleling the coast; but if the

Alaskan Boundary Dispute

crest was not ascertainable, the line was to be drawn not more than ten marine leagues from the coast, following its sinuosities. There was no continuous range of mountains in the position indicated. The United States claimed that the distance of ten marine leagues should be measured from the heads of fiords which deeply indent the coast; Great Britain, that it should be measured from the headlands, thereby including most of the ports. In 1903 a joint commission of three persons from each country fixed a compromise boundary line.

Alaska purchase. The acquisition from Russia of all of Alaska for $7,200,000 by a treaty negotiated by Secretary William H. Seward and signed March 30, 1867;—called "Seward's Folly" by unfriendly critics.

Albany Plan of Union. The proposal of Benjamin Franklin at the Albany Convention of 1754 for a colonial confederation with power to maintain military and naval forces, regulate Indian affairs, and levy taxes. A president-general would be appointed by the Crown, and delegates chosen for three-year terms by colonial assemblies would meet annually. Neither Great Britain nor the colonies approved of the plan.

Albany Regency. A group of politicians, among whom were Silas Wright and William L. Marcy, who controlled the Democratic party of New York from 1821, when Martin Van Buren first became a U.S. Senator until about 1850.

Albertson v. Subversive Activities Control Board. A case, 382 U.S. 70 (1965), in which the Supreme Court declared that provisions of the Internal Security Act and other acts requiring individual Communists to register were void under the self-incrimination clause of the Fifth Amendment, because admission of Communist affiliation exposed the registrant to criminal prosecution. This decision rendered practically inoperative other provisions requiring the registration of the Communist party and Communist-front organizations.

alderman. 1. *Formerly:* a member of a municipal council of higher rank than common councilor. 2. A member of the upper house of a council and often the title of a councilman.

Aldrich Act. An act of Congress, March 4, 1907, which authorized the Secretary of the Treasury to designate national banks as public depositories and fiscal agents of the national government.

Aldrich-Vreeland Act. An act, May 30, 1908, passed after the financial crisis of 1907 which permitted associations of national banks to issue emergency bank notes secured by commercial paper and the securities of States and their subdivisions. A few million dollars of this currency were placed in circulation prior to the inauguration of the Federal Reserve System.

Algeciras Conference. A diplomatic conference at Algeciras, Spain, 1906, called to adjust conflicting interests of Germany, France, and other powers in Morocco. The attendance of American representatives is historically significant as evidence of the growing concern of the United States in world diplomacy.

alien. A person domiciled in a state of which he is not a citizen. Aliens enjoy most of the civil rights and the same measure of protection for those rights that citizens enjoy, especially in the United States, where the federal and State bills of rights expressly extend their guarantees to "persons," whether citizens or aliens. But aliens are often denied the right to own or inherit property, particularly real property, to engage in the exploitation of natural resources, to compete with citizens for certain types of private employment, or to engage in the practice of certain professions. They are usually excluded from the enjoyment of political rights, such as voting, officeholding, and public employment. Sometimes they are allowed to volunteer in the armed forces of the state of their domicile, or they may even be compelled to render military service. In such cases the alien is normally required to make a declaration of allegiance. Moreover, when aliens are drafted into the military service of the state of their domicile, the state of which they are subjects or citizens usually gives its consent by treaty or otherwise. In most states aliens are required to register, giving information as to their origin, their place of domicile, and other pertinent personal data. For moral turpitude or activities detrimental to the integrity of the political institutions of the state granting them hospitality, aliens may be deported. Aliens may become citizens through the process of naturalization, *q.v. Compare* enemy alien.

Alien and Sedition laws. Several acts passed by Congress in 1798 which authorized the President to deport aliens dangerous to the peace of the country, and punished the writing, printing, or publication of any false, scandalous, or malicious writing against Congress or the President.

alienation. The transfer of title to property by a municipality or other unit of government to an individual or to another unit.

Alien Registration Act. An act of Congress, June 29, 1940, which required all aliens domiciled in the United States annually to file a detailed personal and occupational record and a statement of their political beliefs; and made it unlawful for any person to advise disloyalty or to advocate the overthrow of the Government by force and violence or to join any organization knowing that it was engaged in such activity. *Called also* the Smith Act.

¹allegiance. The duty of fidelity and obligation of service owed by a citizen to his state or by a subject to his king. Aliens owe a local allegiance to the state in which they reside in contrast to the natural allegiance of the native-born, or the express allegiance of naturalized citizens or subjects.

²allegiance. *See* oath of allegiance.

alliance. A formal agreement, secret or public, between two or more states in which they mutually pledge military and diplomatic support for the furtherance of a common policy toward another state or states. The publicly avowed purpose of an alliance is usually the defense of the territorial and political integrity of the allied states.

Alliance for Progress. A ten-year, $20 billion program for accelerating the economic and social development of Latin American countries adopted by twenty American states at the Inter-American Economic and Social Conference at Punta del Este, Uruguay, Aug. 17, 1961. The United States pledged a major share of the funds as grants and long-term (50 yr.) loans virtually without interest, the receiving Latin American countries agreeing to speed up social reform and devote an increasingly large share of their resources to their own economic and social development. For the United States the program is administered under the Agency for International Development (AID) of the State Department.

allotment plan. A fiscal practice in some States by which annual lump-sum appropriations for an administrative unit become available to it only when, at intervals of one or three months, a central fiscal agency approves and allocates sufficient funds for anticipated expenditures.

alluvion. An addition to territory resulting from the gradual action of waves and tides or the currents of a river.

alphabet soup. New federal agencies, often referred to by the initial letters of their titles, which proliferated in President F. D. Roosevelt's first administration.

alternate. 1. Any person designated to perform a duty in place of another. 2. A person chosen to attend a party convention and act in place of a delegate who is absent at any time.

A.M.A. American Medical Association.

ambassador. A diplomatic envoy of the highest rank, usually entitled "ambassador extraordinary and minister plenipotentiary," who is sent by the head of a state to serve as his personal representative at a foreign government or court. The United States began to accredit ambassadors in 1893.

Amen Corner. A room in the Fifth Avenue Hotel in New York City where Senator Thomas C. Platt conferred, in his "Sunday school," about 1900, with State officials and politicians.

amendment. 1. A change made or proposed on the floor of a legislative body or in committee by adding to, striking out, or altering the wording of any part of a bill or resolution. Legislative rules usually require that the amendment be germane to the subject matter, but violations are not uncommon. 2. An addition to, or a change of, a constitution or an organic act which is appended to the document rather than intercalated in the text. The Constitution of the United States provides for two methods of proposing amendments: (*a*) by a convention called by Congress on the application of two-thirds of the States; or (*b*) by a two-thirds vote of both houses of Congress. Amendments so proposed may be ratified either by legislatures or conventions of three-fourths of the States. A State legislature which has rejected an amendment may afterward accept it; but, conversely, if it has once accepted an amendment it cannot recall its action. The Supreme Court has held that a legislature must act and not the voters in a referendum, though an advisory referendum has sometimes been employed. In proposing amendments Congress may set a time limit (as seven years) within which they must be ratified or considered to be rejected. Other matters concerning the amending process are deemed political questions to be settled by Congress. Amendments to State constitutions are usually proposed by the legislature; but many States have also authorized proposals by constitutional commissions, constitutional conventions, or initiative petitions. In nearly every State ratification is accomplished by means of a referendum.

amendment limitation. Any restriction upon the process of amending a constitution in the States. It may affect the subject matter of the proposed amendment, or the number of proposals which may be offered within a given period, or the methods of submission or ratification. The federal Constitution also stipulates certain limitations on the amending power, as the proscription of a change in the equal representation of a State in the Senate without the State's consent.

Amerasia affair. The discovery in 1945 of 1,700 stolen confidential documents relating to U.S. Far Eastern policy in the offices of the magazine *Amerasia*. The editors denied that they themselves had stolen the documents or were Communists. Because the discovery had been made in an illegal search, the editors were not subject to prosecution; but the President tightened security measures and Congressional committees intensified their investigations into Communist infiltration in the federal government.

America First Committee. An organization created in 1940 for the purpose of preventing the United States from being drawn into World War II. For a time it enjoyed considerable financial and popular support but quickly disintegrated after the Japanese attack on Pearl Harbor, Dec. 7, 1941.

America for Americans. A slogan of the Know Nothing or American party.

American Arbitration Association. A private organization with headquarters in New York City which provides panels for arbitrating labor and commercial disputes. It publishes the quarterly *Arbitration Magazine*.

American Bar Association. A national organization of attorneys with headquarters in Chicago, Ill. To carry out its program of serving the interests of the legal profession, it is organized in many sections and several committees of members and issues a monthly *Journal*.

American Civil Liberties Union. A national organization with headquarters in New York which, through various educational mediums and representation in legal actions as amicus curiae, seeks to uphold freedom of inquiry and expression, judicial due process, and other civil liberties generally.

American Colonization Society. A society formed Jan. 1, 1817, for the purpose of transporting free Negroes from the United States. It settled Monrovia, Liberia, in 1821.

American Communications Association v. *Douds*. A case, 339 U.S. 382 (1950), in which the Supreme Court upheld paragraph 9(h) of the Taft-Hartley Labor Management Relations Act of 1947, *q.v.*, which denied access to the facilities of the National Labor Relations Board to unions whose officials refused to take oaths that they do not believe in violent overthrow of the Government and that they are not members of the Communist party. Such regulation is permitted Congress under the commerce clause in its effort to discourage obstructions to interstate commerce and is not in conflict with the freedom of speech guaranteed by the First Amendment.

American Expeditionary Force. 1. The American military and air forces sent to France during World War I and popularly referred to as the "A.E.F." **2.** Forces sent to Europe, Australia, Africa, and elsewhere during World War II and during subsequent conflicts.

American Farm Bureau Federation. *See* farm bureau.

American Federation of Government Employees. One of the three principal organizations of federal employees, other than postal workers, organized in 1932 following secession of some units from the parent organization (National Federation of Federal Employees) and affiliated with the American Federation of Labor and Congress of Industrial Organizations.

American Federation of Labor and Congress of Industrial Organizations. An American labor organization formed by the merger in 1955 of the A.F.L. and the C.I.O. The former, composed of craft unions, was founded in 1886 in reaction to revolutionary and industrial unionist policies within the Knights of Labor, *q.v.* The latter was founded in 1935–36 by several dissident A.F.L. unions in order to extend industrial unionism to large-scale mass production industries like steel, motors, and rubber. The combined federation included four-fifths of all organized labor in its 130 or more constituent national and international unions. Reluctant to interfere in the internal affairs of any constituent union, the federation seeks to promote the cause of labor by support in collective bargaining and through pressure-group activities, including lobbying, and publicity concerning the records of State and national legislators and other officials.

American Knights. A Copperhead society founded in 1862.

American Labor party. A minor party in New York, founded in 1936, which usually nominated the same candidates as the Democratic party in national and State elections, but opposed Tammany Hall in New York City. Its organization was captured by Communists in 1944, and it supported Wallace for President in 1948. Shortly thereafter it ceased to exist.

American Legion. A servicemen's organization with various auxiliaries established at Paris in 1919 to protect and defend the interests of veterans of World War I and to promote preparedness, patriotism, and Americanism. Its ranks have been opened to veterans of World War II and later wars.

American Legislators' Association. A body founded in 1925 and composed of the membership of all the State legislatures. Since 1933 its research activities on legislative problems, organization, and methods and its information services for legislative councils, reference bureaus, and individual legislators have been conducted through the Council of State Governments, *q.v.*

American Liberty League. A conservative organization formed in 1934 and dissolved in 1940 which opposed the New Deal.

American Medical Association. A national organization with headquarters in Chicago, Ill., composed of State and regional medical societies, which represents the professional interests of the bulk of American physicians and seeks to establish standards for drugs and therapeutic devices and to influence legislation and opinon on health-care matters.

American Municipal Association. A federation of State leagues of municipalities with headquarters in Chicago, Ill., and Washington, D.C. The local leagues provide consultant services on problems of municipal government and some issue periodicals and other publications.

American National party. A minor party, founded in 1874 mainly to oppose secret societies, which advocated prohibition of liquors, resumption of specie payments, restriction of monopolies, and direct presidential elections. It had presidential candidates in 1876 and 1880.

American National Red Cross. The national Red Cross society of the United States chartered by act of Congress, Jan. 5, 1905, to perform all duties with which each national society is charged by the Geneva Convention, *q.v.*; to furnish voluntary aid to the sick and wounded in time of war; and to provide a system of national and international relief for suffering caused by famine, pestilence, flood, fire, earthquakes, and other calamities. See International Red Cross.

American party. 1. The official title adopted by the Know Nothings. In 1856 they nominated Millard Fillmore for President, who received 874,538 popular and 8 electoral votes. After 1858 the party ceased to exist. 2. A minor party organized in 1887 which advocated 14 years' residence as a prerequisite for naturalization and the exclusion of socialists and anarchists.

American Political Science Association. An organization of political scientists, public officials, and others interested in the art and science of government founded in 1903. It publishes the quarterly *American Political Science Review*.

American Protective Association. A secret anti-Catholic and anti-foreign organization founded in Iowa in 1887.

American Revolution. A war between thirteen British North American colonies and the mother country resulting partly from British acts in imposing taxes and regulations which were regarded as tyrannical in America, and partly from a growing sense of American nationality and power. Hostilities began with a skirmish at Lexington, Mass., Apr. 19, 1775, and virtually ended, after substantial military and naval help had been extended by France, with the surrender of Cornwallis at Yorktown, Va., Oct. 19, 1781. Preliminary articles of peace between the United States and Great Britain were signed at Paris, Nov. 30, 1782, and the definitive treaty, Sept. 3, 1783. It was ratified by Congress on Jan. 4, 1784.

American Samoa. Tutuila and six lesser islands in the Pacific, about 76 sq. mi. in extent, some 4,100 miles southwest of San Francisco, over which the United States assumed control under an agreement with Great Britain and Germany in 1899. The islands were ceded to the United States by the native population in 1900, and Congress ratified the cession in 1929. Although especially valuable as naval and air stations, the islands were transferred by Congress from the control of the Department of the Navy to the Department of the Interior in July, 1951. The governor is appointive; the bicameral legislature is elective.

Americans for Democratic Action. A group founded by intellectuals and Democratic Congressmen in 1947 to advocate continuance of the liberalism of the first two F. D. Roosevelt administrations. In national politics it supported Stevenson and Kennedy.

American Society for Public Administration. A private organization of public officials, educators, research workers, and others interested in fostering the study and art of public administration. It has headquarters in Chicago, Ill., and publishes the quarterly *Public Administration Review*.

American Society of Planning Officials. A private professional organization, with headquarters in Chicago, Ill., which, in cooperation with public and private agencies, seeks to improve administrative practices and policies relating to planning at all governmental levels. It publishes a monthly *News Letter*.

American system. The policy of developing American industry by protective tariffs and a national system of internal improvements, associated with Henry Clay and the Whig party 1824–52.

amicus curiae. A person not identified with either party to a controversy, who is heard by leave of the court or at its request, and who may assist the court on points of law or bring to its attention matters of public concern which are not presented by attorneys for the parties.

amnesty. A general pardon (by act of Congress or by the President as a corollary of his pardoning power) of punishment or legal disabilities usually incurred as a result of political offenses and granted often before trial or conviction. Both President Lincoln and President Andrew Johnson issued proclamations of amnesty for the benefit of persons who had participated in rebellion against the United States.

Ananias club. A supposititious society to which President Theodore Roosevelt nominated several persons whose truthfulness he impugned.

anarchism. A political theory that all government is evil and unnecessary, generally combined with opposition to the institution of private property. As a practical movement anarchism has been chiefly represented abroad by syndicalist parties and in the United States by the Industrial Workers of the World, *q.v.*

anarchist. One who believes in, supports, or advocates anarchism (as by individual or mass violence against the established order). Anarchists vary from the individualism of Godwin and Proudhon to the communism of Kropotkin; and although their philosophy exhibits a high degree of diversity, they generally base their conclusions upon faith in the natural goodness, sociability, and reasonableness of man. Since Bakunin an increasing number of anarchists have advocated violent means to overthrow established order.

anarchy. 1. A society in which government is completely lacking. **2.** The conditions, such as lawlessness, denial of authority, and political disorder, which prevail in the absence of government.

angary. The legal right of a belligerent, under pressure of urgent necessity, to destroy or requisition for his own use ships and other property belonging to neutral states or their nationals. The neutral owner must be indemnified.

Annapolis Convention. A convention called by the Congress of the Confederation to meet at Annapolis, Md., in 1786 to consider means for regulating interstate commerce. The twelve delegates from five States who attended recommended to Congress and the States, at Alexander Hamilton's insistence, the calling of the convention which met at Philadelphia in 1787 and drafted the Constitution of the United States.

annexation. A unilateral act by which sovereignty is formally extended over territory acquired by discovery, occupation, or absorption of the territory of another state. By joint resolution of Congress the republics of Texas and Hawaii were annexed in 1845 and 1898 respectively.

annexationist. One who, after 1830, advocated expansion of the United States by annexing Texas and other territory.

annulment. The act, by competent authority, of canceling, making void, or depriving of all force.

Anthony rule. A rule of the U.S. Senate first used in 1870 and adopted in 1880 which makes it in order to consider unopposed measures during the calling of the Calendar of Bills and Resolutions, with discussion limited to five minutes for each Senator;—so named from Senator Henry B. Anthony of Rhode Island.

anticipatory borrowing. Short-term borrowing for current expenses in anticipation of taxes not yet due;—a device frequently used by American municipalities.

Antidumping Act. An act of Congress, May 27, 1921, which imposes a special dumping duty equal to the difference between the price shown on the invoice and the foreign market value of imported goods, or, if the market value is not ascertainable, cost of production.

Antifederalist. One who, because of particularistic tendencies, fear of centralized power, or other motives, opposed ratification of the Constitution of the United States. In North Carolina the Antifederalists delayed ratification until Nov. 21, 1789, and in Rhode Island, until May 29, 1790. They were numerous in New Hampshire, Massachusetts, New York, Pennsylvania, and Virginia. By 1793, the main body of Antifederalists had become supporters of Jefferson and the Republican party which he led.

Antigag Law. A rider on the Post Office Appropriation Act, Aug. 24, 1912, which guaranteed that federal employees should have the right to organize and to petition Congress individually and collectively; that dismissals should be made only for the good of the service; and that when dismissal was recommended the employee should have a written copy of the charges against him and the opportunity to reply in writing.

anti-Lecompton Democrat. A Northern Democrat who opposed the admission of Kansas under the proslavery constitution drafted at Lecompton, Kas., in 1857.

antilynch bill. Any of various bills introduced in Congress since 1922, most of which would have granted U.S. courts jurisdiction to try persons accused of participation in lynching, and some of which would have made counties in which lynchings occurred financially responsible for damages.

Antimasonic party. A third party which sprang into existence during the intense popular excitement that followed the disappearance of William Morgan, and his alleged murder by members of the Masonic order. It initiated the national convention as a nominating device in 1831. Its candidate for President, William Wirt, received the electoral votes of Vermont and many popular votes, particularly in Pennsylvania and western New York.

Antimerger Act. A law of Congress, 1950, which prohibited a corporation from acquiring the capital stock or the assets of a competing company when the result would be to lessen competition.

Antimonopoly party. A minor party which nominated Benjamin F. Butler for President in 1884 and advocated a federal interstate commerce act, direct election of senators, a federal income tax, and industrial arbitration. It became one of the components of the People's party.

anti-Nebraska men. Northern Democrats opposed to the Kansas-Nebraska Act, 1854, many of whom helped to form the Republican party.

Antipeonage cases. See *Taylor* v. *Georgia*.

Antiquities Act. An act of Congress, June 8, 1906, which authorized the President to designate as national monuments objects of historic, prehistoric, or scientific interest which were on the national domain, and also authorized acceptance of such objects when relinquished to the Government by private owners.

Antiracketeering Act. A law of Congress, June 18, 1934, which made it a criminal offense to interfere with foreign or interstate commerce by violence, threats, coercion, or intimidation.

Antirenters. A group in New York who, between 1839 and 1846, violently agitated for the abolition of semifeudal tenures which had continued from the period of the Dutch colony.

Anti-Saloon League of America. An organization, founded in 1895, which by propaganda and pressures on candidates and officeholders was influential in the prohibition movement that culminated in the 18th Amendment and the national and State laws to enforce it.

anti-Semitism. Hatred for, and legal and social discrimination against, Jews, practiced by many peoples throughout history, and, in modern times, by German National Socialists and their imitators.

Antisnapper. A New York Democrat who favored the renomination of Grover Cleveland and denounced the "snap" convention called by D. B. Hill early in 1892.

antisorehead law. A provision in the primary laws of several States which forbids a person who has been defeated for nomination to become an independent candidate in the ensuing general election.

antitrust. Pertaining to the regulation of cartels, trusts, pools, monopolies, interlocking directorates, and other devices to lessen competition and restrain trade. When large-scale enterprises developed, State control of monopolies under the common law proved ineffective. Congress in 1890 enacted the Sherman Antitrust Act, *q.v.*, but its lack of detailed provisions left much discretion to administrative officers and courts. It was not enforced until the administration of Theodore Roosevelt when it was applied to monopolistic practices in transportation, manufacturing, and labor unions. See *Northern Securities Co.* v. *United States*, and the Danbury Hatters' case. In 1914 the Clayton Act, *q.v.*, prohibited specified business practices and exempted lawful activities of labor unions from the scope of the act. The Federal Trade Commission Act, 1914, provided some administrative enforcement. In 1933 the National Industrial Recovery Act, *q.v.*, suspended for two years the operation of the antitrust laws. The Robinson-Patman Act, *q.v.*, 1936, outlawed special discounts in the pricing of goods, and the Miller-Tydings Act, *q.v.*, 1937, permitted manufacturers to set minimum resale prices for trade-marked articles. The courts have played an especially important role in antitrust policy, often restricting or broadening formal statutory and administrative regulations. The antitrust laws are enforced mainly through the Antitrust Division of the Department of Justice.

Anzus Pact. The defensive alliance signed at San Francisco, Sept. 1, 1951, by Australia, New Zealand, and the United States.

A.P.A. The American Protective Association, *q.v.*

Apex Hosiery Co. v. Leader. A case, 310 U.S. 469 (1940), in which an employer sought to collect damages from a labor union under the Sherman Act because of production losses suffered as a result of a sit-down strike. The Supreme Court held that the losses were not substantial enough to be considered a restraint of interstate commerce and that the Sherman Act was not applicable.

appeal. 1. The transfer of a case from a lower to a higher tribunal for review, usually as to questions of law, with the possibility that the lower court's decision may be modified or reversed. 2. *In legislative procedure:* a challenge by a member of a ruling made by the presiding officer which, if sustained by majority vote, overturns the ruling.

appeasement. *In international relations:* the sacrifice of important national interests, or of an ally or innocent third nation, to propitiate a state or league of states which engages in militant diplomacy or poses a serious military threat, especially when done in violation of a treaty and moral obligations, as in the sacrifice of Czechoslovakia by Great Britain and France in 1938.

appellate. Pertaining to the authority to hear and decide cases or controversies on appeal.

appellate court. A judicial tribunal which reviews cases originally tried and decided by inferior tribunals. The appellate court acts without a jury and is primarily interested in correcting errors in procedure or in the interpretation of law by the lower courts.

appellate jurisdiction. The authority of a court to review the decisions of other courts and uphold, reverse, modify, or return them to a lower court for retrial. *Compare* original jurisdiction. Congress determines the appellate jurisdiction of federal courts.

appointment. The process, which may include both nomination and confirmation, by which a superior authority designates a person to hold an office. In some jurisdictions the issuance of a commission is necessary to complete an appointment. Ambassadors, other public ministers, consuls, and judges of the Supreme Court, together with several thousand others who have been designated by law as "officers," must be confirmed by the Senate. When the Senate is not in session, the President may fill vacancies by temporary appointments which expire at the end of the next session of the Senate. Appointments of "inferior officers" may be made under national laws by the President alone, by the courts, or by heads of departments, independent agencies, and government-owned corporations. Most of them are chosen under civil service rules. In the States gubernatorial appointments generally require confirmation, and those made by heads of departments do not.

apportionment. 1. Determination by law of the number of representatives which a State, county, or other subdivision may send to a legislative body; or by a competent party authority of the number of delegates to a party convention. The Constitution provides for a census every ten years, on the basis of which Congress apportions representatives according to population; but each State must have one representative. No reapportionment was made during the period from 1920 to 1929. In June, 1929, Congress provided that the President, after every decennial census, should submit tables showing the number of representatives to which each State would be entitled. If Congress fails to act, the presidential apportionment becomes effective. **2.** The assignment of one or more representatives to specific areas. *Compare* redistricting.

appraisal. An estimate of the value of imported articles by customs inspectors for the purpose of determining the basis for collecting ad valorem duties, or of the value of property in condemnation proceedings or for other public purposes.

appropriation. The act of appropriating; *specifically:* the setting aside of a sum of money to be expended for a public purpose and in a manner determined by law. An itemized appropriation goes into great detail as to the purpose for which often small amounts may be spent. A lump-sum appropriation allows the executive considerable discretion. By custom, because revenue bills must originate in the House of Representatives, appropriation bills originate there also. The Committee on Ways and Means prepared appropriation bills until 1865, when a committee on appropriations was created. Later eight other committees were authorized to introduce appropriation bills. Since the passage of the Budget and Accounting Act of 1921, *q.v.*, the expenditures recommended in the President's budget message have been referred to the Committee on Appropriations which, through its subcommittees, prepares all appropriation bills. In the Senate, which has power to amend by increasing, decreasing, or eliminating items, the Committee on Appropriations is enlarged by the addition of two or three members of other committees when items falling within their legislative province are under consideration. *See* budget; pork barrel.

approval of bills. The signing by the chief executive of measures passed by the legislative chambers, which is the final step required to make such measures law, except in North Carolina where the governor has no veto. The President may sign a bill or joint resolution within a ten-day period before or after Congress adjourns. Several State constitutions allow the governor an extended period in which to consider an accumulation of bills passed at the end of the legislative session.

arbitrament. 1. The award or decision made by an arbitrator. **2.** The process of judging as by an arbitrator.

arbitrary government. A government conducted according to the caprice of rulers and not according to a constitution, laws, or established precedents.

arbitration. The hearing, investigation, and determination of a controversy by a person or board of arbitration to whom the parties submit conflicting claims, and by whose decision (usually called an award) the parties agree to be bound. (*a*) *In international relations*, the states which are parties select the arbitrators and draw up a compromis, *q.v.*, setting forth in detail the limitations of the case and the rules and principles by which the arbitrator or tribunal of arbitration is to be guided. A permanent panel of judges or umpires, available to states wishing to arbitrate disputes, was provided by the Permanent Court of Arbitration established at The Hague in 1899. (*b*) *In industrial disputes*, usually the employer and the labor union each designate one member, and these two choose the third member of a board of arbitration. About half the States have statutes regularizing the selection of arbitrators and their procedure and have made their awards enforceable at law. *Compare* conciliation; mediation.

A.R.C. *See* American National Red Cross.

Arcadia Conference. A conference which met in Washington, D.C., Dec. 24, 1941, at which President F. D. Roosevelt, Prime Minister Churchill, and their staffs planned the strategy to be followed in World War II. On Jan. 1, 1942, it issued the Declaration of the United Nations (also signed by 24 other nations), stated war aims, and laid the groundwork for a more permanent international organization.

Architect of the Capitol. An official, acting as agent of Congress, who has charge of the structural and mechanical care of the Capitol, the Library of Congress, the U.S. Supreme Court building, the House and Senate office buildings, and certain functions with respect to other buildings in the District of Columbia.

archives. A collection of public records. *See* National Archives and Records Services.

area of the United States. The total area of the fifty States is 3,615,211 square miles. The area of Puerto Rico is 3,435 sq. mi.; of outlying possessions 463 sq. mi.; of the Canal Zone 553 sq. mi.; and of the Corn Islands (leased from Nicaragua), 4 sq. mi. Excluding trust territories (area 8,484 sq. mi.), the total area is 3,619,666 square miles.

Area Redevelopment Act. An act of Congress, 1961, for long-range aid to unemployed persons in regions subject to chronic economic distress.

Argentia Conference. A meeting of President F. D. Roosevelt and Prime Minister Churchill in the harbor of Argentia, Newfoundland, August 10–12, 1941, at which war aims were discussed and agreement was reached on the Atlantic Charter.

aristocracy. 1. A state in which political power is possessed by a minority and especially qualified class (as by its best citizens). 2. A governing body composed of prominent citizens (as a hereditary nobility).

Armageddon. A supposedly decisive struggle (as the Progressive party's campaign in 1912, or World War I) against alleged forces of evil;— from the site of the last battle between good and evil at the Day of Judgment (Revelation 16:14–16).

armament. A state's military equipment, including warships and planes, weapons, armed forces, potential manpower, control of strategic raw materials, weapon-producing capacity, and peacetime plant and equipment and other resources convertible to war needs.

Armed Forces Staff College. An institution for selected officers maintained by the three military services in the Department of Defense to provide advanced training in the joint staff techniques and procedures required by operations in which more than one military service participates.

Arm-in-Arm convention. A convention of Republicans supporting President Andrew Johnson, held at Philadelphia in 1868, at which the delegates from Massachusetts and South Carolina entered arm-in-arm.

armistice. A localized or general cessation of hostilities by an agreement between belligerents, usually signed by the responsible military commanders, and sometimes involving military surrender by one side as a prelude to negotiations for peace. *Compare* truce.

arms race. The struggle among nations to outdo one another in technological improvements and productive capacities, as by creating increasingly effective offensive and defensive weapons and armaments, and thus secure military and political advantages. *See* disarmament.

arm-twisting. *Slang.* Presidential pressure on members of Congress to vote for administration bills; the ultimate sanction might be loss of patronage or of party organization support in re-election campaigns.

army. 1. The entire military force of a state as distinguished from its naval force and sometimes also from its air force. 2. An organized military force trained for land warfare and commanded by a general officer.

Aroostook War. A disturbance along the disputed northern boundary of Maine in 1838, caused by the governor's sending troops to expel Canadian lumbermen.

arraignment. A proceeding in which a prisoner is called to the bar of the court to be identified, to hear the indictment against him, and to make an appropriate plea.

arrest. The legal detainment of a person to answer for criminal charges or (infrequently at present) civil demands upon him. Constitutional limitations prevent detention under false or assumed authority and harassment of persons without warrants properly issued. *See* habeas corpus.

arsenal. A state-owned establishment for the manufacture and storage of munitions of war and equipment for the armed forces.

arsenal of democracy. The significant role of the United States as supplier of munitions to nations opposing the Axis powers in World War II;— from a phrase in a speech by President F. D. Roosevelt, Dec. 29, 1940.

arson. The crime of setting fire to buildings or property with malicious intent or with intent to defraud fire-insurance companies.

Articles of Confederation. The framework of a "perpetual union" drafted by a committee which was appointed by the Continental Congress, June 11, 1776; approved by Congress, Nov. 15, 1777; and effective after the ratification of all the thirteen States, Mar. 1, 1781. Many provisions of the Articles, especially those relating to the obligations of States and the powers of Congress, were later incorporated into the

Constitution of the United States. Congress was made the repository of all legislative and executive authority, but had no power to raise revenue by taxation, and no means to compel the States, which were declared to be sovereign, to pay the amounts apportioned among them for the expenses of the Confederation. Efforts to correct these defects by amendment proved abortive because of the provision requiring ratification by every State. The Confederation Congress ceased to exist on Mar. 2, 1789.

articles of war. Rules for the government of the army enacted by the Continental Congress in 1775, changed by later Congresses as the need arose, and superseded in 1950 by the Uniform Code of Military Justice, *q.v.*

Article X. A provision of the Covenant of the League of Nations that member states "undertake to respect and preserve as against external aggression the territorial integrity and existing political independence of all Members of the League." It was violently opposed in the Senate because of fear that it would involve the United States in future European wars.

Ashcraft v. Tennessee. A case, 322 U.S. 143 (1944), in which the Supreme Court held that a confession obtained by State officers from an accused person by methods "inherently coercive," in this instance by practically continuous questioning for 36 hours, violated the due-process clause of the 14th Amendment.

Ashurst-Sumners Act. 1. An act of Congress, June 6, 1934, which permitted any two or more States to enter into compacts for mutual assistance in the prevention of crime and the enforcement of their criminal laws and policies. **2.** An act, July 24, 1935, which prohibited the interstate shipment of prison-made goods in violation of State laws.

Ashwander v. Tennessee Valley Authority. A case, 297 U.S. 288 (1936), in which the Supreme Court upheld the construction of hydroelectric installations in the Tennessee Valley both under Congress' war power and its power to improve navigation; and also upheld acquisition by the Tennessee Valley Authority of transmission lines for the distribution and sale of its electric power on the principle that, if the government owns property, Congress, acting in the public interest, may determine the manner and conditions of its disposition.

assassination. 1. The murder of a high public official, whether by one person acting alone or in a conspiracy with others. Four Presidents—Lincoln, Garfield, McKinley, and Kennedy—have been assassinated. Since the latter's assassination such an act has been made a federal crime. **2.** Any murder in which the distinguishing feature is resort to treachery or stealth.

assault. The menacing of another's safety by uttering threats of immediate bodily harm or by violent gestures. Assault and battery occurs if a blow is struck.

assay office. A federal laboratory which analyzes ores and determines the content of gold and silver bullion presented for coinage.

assembled examination. The standard written or printed examination for a particular grade or classification in the civil service administered at a particular time and place to qualified applicants on a competitive basis.

assembly. 1. A legislature. 2. The more numerous house of a legislature, as in New York.

assemblyman. A member of the lower house of certain State legislatures, as in New York.

assessment. 1. Determination of the amount of a tax to be paid. 2. An estimate of the value of real or personal property for purposes of taxation, stated in terms of the full market value or a percentage thereof.

assessor. An officer, usually elective in rural areas but appointive in all but a few cities, who fixes the valuation of land and other property for direct taxation.

assimilation. The process of absorbing immigrants of an alien culture by accustoming them to the political ideology and ways of the new community.

assimilative crimes statute. A law of Congress which provides that, in the absence of an appropriate federal penal law, an offense committed on a federal reservation shall be punishable under laws of the State in which the reservation is located.

assistance clause. A provision in the laws of many States by which an illiterate or physically handicapped voter may receive help from an election official or, in some cases, any qualified voter whom he may select to mark his ballot.

Assistant to the President. An official within the Executive Office of the President, *q.v.*, or the White House Office, *q.v.*, who is regarded as the President's personal aide, and whose activity is subject to change at the wish of the President.

Associated Press* v. *National Labor Relations Board. A case, 301 U.S. 103 (1937), in which the Supreme Court upheld, as not a violation of freedom of the press, the action of the National Labor Relations Board in ordering the reinstatement of an editorial writer who had been discharged, according to the record, for labor union activity and for no other reason.

association of states. A league or confederation of sovereign states.

Association, The. Articles drawn up by the Continental Congress of 1774 under which it was agreed that Americans would not import any goods from Great Britain.

assumption of risk. A common-law defense in workmen's compensation cases that persons entering upon an employment know the hazards involved and assume them. Statutes in most States have outlawed this defense.

assumption of State debts. The fiscal policy proposed by Alexander Hamilton as Secretary of the Treasury in 1789 and subsequently approved by Congress, of having the federal government assume responsibility for all unpaid debts contracted by the States for the prosecution of the Revolutionary War. Certain Southern States, notably Virginia, bitterly opposed assumption because they had paid off their debts, but were won over as a result of Hamilton's success in gaining Northern approval for the location of the national capital on the Potomac.

asylum of the oppressed of every nation. The United States, according to the Democratic platform of 1856.

Atlantic Charter. A program of postwar reconstruction announced by President F. D. Roosevelt and Prime Minister Churchill after their conference on the British battleship, "Prince of Wales," in the Atlantic, off Newfoundland, Aug. 14, 1941. The program consisted of eight "points" or declarations pledging the United States and Great Britain jointly to take measures to prevent national aggrandizement, to encourage international trade, and to secure to individuals everywhere "freedom from fear and want." *See* Argentia Conference.

Atlantic States Marine Fisheries Compact. An interstate compact among 12 Atlantic seaboard States which came into force May 4, 1942, and which set up an advisory commission to secure uniform State legislation to regulate and promote the interests of the marine fisheries and seafood industries.

at large. Chosen by the voters of the State as a whole rather than from separate Congressional or legislative districts;—a condition usually resulting from the failure or willful neglect of a legislature to redistrict a State after a decennial census. In many cities, especially those with commission or commission-manager plans, the governing board is chosen by the voters at large.

Atomic Energy Commission. An independent agency, consisting of five commissioners appointed by the President and Senate under the terms of the Atomic Energy Act of 1946, that fosters research and technical developments in the field of nuclear energy; administers public production, ownership and exploitation of fissionable materials in the interests of national defense; encourages private participation in the United States in atomic research and development; and, after adequate international safeguards have been erected, shares, on a reciprocal basis, information relating to the industrial application of nuclear energy.

Atoms for Peace Program. President Eisenhower's proposal, Dec. 8, 1953, that nations with advanced scientific resources should contribute to a pool for the development of the peaceful uses of atomic energy.

attaché. A Foreign Service officer of minor grade attached to the staff of an embassy whose special province may be military, naval, commercial, or cultural.

attainder. The annihilation of all civil rights and privileges which in early English law followed a condemnation for treason or felony. The person attainted forfeited all property and lost all capacity to inherit or transmit property to his descendants; nor could he appear in court or claim the protection of law. In the United States "no attainder of treason shall work corruption of blood or forfeiture except during the life of the person attainted." A bill of attainder, which is prohibited by the Constitution, is a legislative condemnation without the formality of a judicial trial.

attestation. The act of verifying or affirming, orally or in writing, the genuineness or validity of some legal document, such as a will or an affidavit.

attorney-at-law. A practitioner of law whose services are available to the public and who is qualified to practice and represent clients in the law courts; *called also* lawyer.

Attorney General. 1. The head of the Department of Justice and a member of the President's cabinet who gives legal advice to the President and heads of departments, supervises district attorneys and United States marshals, oversees criminal investigations, and has charge of cases in which the Government is involved. He may appear in court, but rarely does so. **2.** The chief legal officer of a State who advises State and local officers, who may appear in cases in which the State is sued by another State, but who usually lacks the power to supervise locally elected prosecutors.

Attorney General's List. A list of organizations, held to be totalitarian, subversive, Fascist, or Communist-controlled, compiled by the Department of Justice in the late 1940's and subsequently extended.

auditor. A State official, usually chosen by the electorate or the legislature, whose duty is to examine the accounts of other officers to determine if expenditures were made in accordance with authorizations by the legislature. Some State auditors also conduct the preaudit, *q.v.*, and periodically examine the accounts of local government officials.

Austinian theory. The doctrine that legal sovereignty resides in a determinate human superior and that law, as distinguished from custom and morality, consists of those rules tacitly or expressly sanctioned by the legal sovereign;—proposed by the analytical school of jurisprudence, of which the English utilitarian jurist John Austin (1790–1859) is regarded as the founder.

Australian ballot. A secret ballot printed by State authority that contains the names of all candidates who have been nominated according to law, with usually a space for voters to write in other names, and is distributed within the polling place by election officials to qualified voters who are required to mark it before leaving. As originally used in Australia it listed the names of candidates without party designations, but since its adoption in the United States, beginning in 1888, it has appeared generally as the Indiana, or party-column, ballot, or the Massachusetts, or office-block, ballot, *qq.v.*

autarchy. The condition of a state which is self-sufficient. In order to conserve foreign exchange or prepare for a possible war, some states have striven for autarchy by limiting imports, encouraging domestic production, and developing substitutes for foreign goods.

authoritarian. Relating to the quality of a political system which exalts the power of the state at the expense of the individual (as in the Prussian monarchy or in contemporary dictatorial regimes); *also:* emphasizing the duty of obedience rather than the rights of individuals;—opposed to democratic, liberal, and constitutional.

authority. 1. The legally established power to issue orders and enforce obedience to them. **2.** A government corporation or similar unit (as the Tennessee Valley Authority). **3. authorities.** All officers concerned with the determination and enforcement of policies of government as a whole or in any of its functions or subdivisions.

authorization. *In legislation:* an act approving a project or program, outlining its purposes and procedures, and usually fixing a maximum amount which can be spent for it;—usually the first step (the second being an appropriation act) in expenditure of public funds by Congress.

autocracy. A state in which one person possesses unlimited political power which is considered as not flowing from any external source.

autonomy. 1. The legal right of self-determination conceded to an organized minority race or people in matters affecting civil government, religion, language, education, culture, or commerce and industry. 2. The degree of independence enjoyed by a locality or group in the exercise of governmental powers. *See* home rule.

avulsion. A sudden and violent change in the course of a waterway from natural or artificial causes; *also:* a violent change in the shoreline. Boundary and property lines remain as they were prior to the avulsion.

award. The judgment of an arbitrator or board of arbitration in a dispute between nations or between individuals or groups.

Axis. The collaboration of the Italian and German dictators Mussolini and Hitler, which began Oct. 25, 1936, developed into a close political and military alliance, and ended in 1943 with the defeat of Italy in World War II;—from the abbreviation of "Rome-Berlin Axis."

B

backdoor spending. Congressional financing of government corporations and other agencies by authorizations to borrow from the U.S. Treasury; —usually used opprobriously;—from the implication that such authorizations receive less careful scrutiny than appropriations made in the regular way.

backlash. That portion of white opposition to candidates or parties supporting civil rights for Negroes which is attributable to Negro rioting and threats of the more militant Negro leaders;—sometimes sufficient, as in Democratic primary elections in Maryland and Georgia in 1966, to secure the success of segregationist candidates.

Bacon's Rebellion. An unsuccessful insurrection in Virginia in 1676 led by Nathaniel Bacon in opposition to Governor Sir William Berkeley's policies concerning taxation and Indian trade.

bad tendency test. A rule enunciated by the Supreme Court in *Gitlow* v. *New York, q.v.,* that a legislative body may suppress speech which tends to spread revolutionary doctrines, even though danger of resulting armed uprising or other violence is remote.

Baghdad Pact. An alliance in 1955 between Great Britain, Turkey, Iran, Iraq, and Pakistan to prevent the spread of Communist influence in Asia, especially in the Persian Gulf region. After the pro-Western government of Iraq was overthrown by pro-Communist riots in 1958, the remaining countries formed the Central Treaty Organization. *See* CENTO.

bail. The person giving surety (also the surety given) that an accused person will appear in court at the proper time. When bailed out the accused is released into the custody of his sureties. Bail is normally refused to persons accused of capital crimes or may be denied altogether. When allowed, it must not be excessive in proportion either to the gravity of the crime or to the resources of the accused.

Bailey v. Drexel Furniture Co. *See* Child Labor cases.

bailiff. 1. A sheriff's assistant who executes writs. 2. A minor officer of the court.

Bakelite Corporation, Ex parte. A case, 279 U.S. 438 (1929), in which the Supreme Court differentiated between the so-called constitutional courts created under Article III of the Constitution and the legislative courts created under Congress' powers in Article I. The jurisdiction of the latter type of courts and the tenure of their judges are not controlled by constitutional provisions but are subject to Congress' discretion.

Baker Island. An atoll in the mid-Pacific occupied by the United States in 1936 as a meteorological station.

Baker v. Carr. A case, 369 U.S. 186 (1962), in which the Supreme Court invalidated a Tennessee legislative apportionment of 1901 which had remained unaltered despite losses of population in many counties and large increases in others. Rejecting what appears to have been a contrary earlier view expressed in *Colegrove* v. *Green*, 328 U.S. 549 (1946), the Court held that the equitable apportionment of voters among districts from which members of the State legislature are chosen is a justiciable, and not a political question; and that, when the apportionment is determined to be inequitable, the courts can provide relief. The decision was followed by other cases questioning the validity of apportionments in many States. *Compare Gray* v. *Sanders.*

balance of payments. The difference between a country's foreign "earnings," which include the value of its merchandise exports and services rendered to foreigners, income from foreign investment, inflow of new foreign capital and the like, and a country's "expenditures," which include its merchandise imports, value of services rendered by foreigners, expenditures of its residents abroad, capital outflow to foreign countries, and earnings paid foreigners on investment. If the earnings of this international account exceed the expenditures, the balance is said to be a "favorable or credit balance"; if expenditures exceed earnings, an "unfavorable or deficit balance" exists. Deficit balances are normally extinguished by the movement of gold and convertible currencies from deficit countries. *Called also* balance of international payments.

balance of power. The policy, especially favored by European diplomatists, which seeks to prevent any state on the European Continent from acquiring a hegemony or from achieving such a position of power and influence as to become a potential menace to the integrity of the remaining states; *also:* the same principle applied to international politics generally.

balance of terror. The unstable equilibrium existing when each of two great powers or leagues of powers possesses nuclear or similar weapons sufficient to destroy the other, and refrains from using them from fear of immediate retaliation and a worldwide holocaust.

balance of trade. A quantitative comparison between a country's exports and imports. The balance is "favorable" if exports exceed imports: "unfavorable" if the reverse is true.

Ballinger-Pinchot controversy. A dispute which began in August, 1909, when Chief of Forestry Gifford Pinchot publicly criticized his superior, Secretary of the Interior R. A. Ballinger, for having reopened for sale certain public lands previously closed. An investigation was ordered, but before it ended Pinchot wrote a letter condemning Ballinger, and was dismissed by President Taft. Theodore Roosevelt's friends sided with Pinchot.

ballot. A method of voting, usually secret, in which voters deposit in an appropriate receptacle written or printed papers designating the names of persons or propositions voted for. The ballot replaced viva voce voting in four of the American colonies by 1776, and in all but three of the States by 1850; but it was not required in British elections until 1872. Before the adoption of the Australian ballot, ballots were usually printed and distributed by agents of each political party and contained only a list, or ticket, of that party's candidates. State legislatures tried with indifferent success to preserve the secrecy of the voter's choice by requiring all ballots to be printed on paper of uniform color, size, and texture. *Compare* Australian ballot; Massachusetts ballot; Indiana ballot.

ballot box stuffing. The clandestine insertion of illegal ballots into a ballot box, either by the use of tissue ballots (as formerly) or when made possible by the carelessness or connivance of election officials.

ballot stub. A detachable portion of an official ballot bearing a number, which may be compared with the number entered opposite the voter's name in the poll book, to identify the ballot as the one which was given to the voter. It serves to prevent the voting fraud known as the Tasmanian dodge, *q.v.*

bamboo curtain. An ideological, military, and political barrier erected by Communist China against diplomatic, commercial, cultural, or other contact with most of the Western world. *Compare* Iron Curtain.

band wagon. *See* climbing aboard the band wagon.

banishment. The expulsion and enforced exclusion of a person from the country or region where he normally resides, as a result of the sentence of a court or the decree of public authorities. *See* deportation.

bank. A financial institution which receives deposits, makes loans, and functions in the circulation of credit. The power to charter a bank, though not expressly granted to Congress, was implied from the borrowing and currency powers and other powers involving the collection of revenue and the transfer of funds from one part of the country to another. The power was used to create the two Banks of the United States, the National Banks established since 1863, and the Federal Reserve System, *qq.v.* State banks have been in continuous operation from the period of the Confederation, though their issuance of bank notes, formerly the principal currency of the country, ceased with the imposition of a tax of 10 per cent on such notes by act of Congress, July 13, 1866. Both State and national banks are closely supervised, and their books are subject to periodical unannounced inspection by examiners. State banks have come under limited national regulation in such matters as membership in the Federal Reserve System, reorganization, and the insurance of deposits.

bank deposits guarantee. Insurance of bank deposits up to a limited amount against bank failure, made available to banks at reasonable rates through the Federal Deposit Insurance Corporation, *q.v.* All federal reserve member banks are required to carry deposit insurance.

bank examiner. An official charged with making periodic unannounced inspections of banks and similar institutions to determine whether their practices are in accord with legal requirements and sound banking policies, and whether the institutions are solvent.

Bank for International Settlements. An institution at Basel, Switzerland, created in 1930 under the Young plan, *q.v.*, for administering German reparations payments, which has since become of major importance in administering international financial operations and as a credit source for European states, particularly for the European Common Market.

Bankhead-Jones Farm Tenant Act. A law of Congress, July 22, 1937, authorizing long-term, low-interest loans to competent tenant farmers, sharecroppers, and farm laborers for the purchase of farms, livestock, farm equipment, and supplies.

bank holiday. The period from Mar. 4 to Mar. 14, 1933, when all banks in the United States were closed by Presidential proclamation.

bank note. A promissory note or bill of credit now issued only by a federal reserve bank, with such security as the law requires, that is payable to bearer on demand and serves as currency. State bank notes were taxed out of existence after the Civil War. *See Veazie Bank* v. *Fenno.* National banks issued bank notes between 1863 and 1935.

Bank of the United States. Two central banks with branches in various parts of the country which were depositaries and fiscal agents of the federal government. The first bank was chartered by Congress for the period, 1791–1811, and the second bank for 20 years in 1816. In 1829 President Jackson expressed the opinion that the second bank should not be rechartered, and the issue was fought out in the election of 1832. The next year President Jackson ordered the removal of all federal deposits, and the second bank ceased to exist in 1836.

bankruptcy. The condition of a person when a court has determined that his property is to be administered for the benefit of his creditors. Under its power to pass uniform laws on bankruptcy, Congress enacted statutes which were in effect 1800–1803, 1841–1843, 1867–1878, and since 1898. When there is no federal law on bankruptcy, the States may legislate providing they do not impair the obligation of a contract. At present a person may file a voluntary petition of bankruptcy, listing his assets and liabilities; or he may be forced into bankruptcy on petition of his creditors. In either case his assets are disposed of by an officer appointed by the court, his creditors are paid pro rata, and he is discharged from further obligation. In 1933 special provision was made by law to facilitate the reorganization of railroads and other corporations which were in financial difficulties.

banks for cooperatives. A central bank and twelve district banks chartered by the Farm Credit Administration, *q.v.*, to make loans at low-interest rates to bona fide farmers' cooperatives.

banner State. The State in which a presidential candidate receives the greatest plurality in the popular vote.

bar. 1. The railing separating the judge, counsel, and jury from the general public. **2.** The whole body of attorneys and counselors who have been admitted to practice in a court. *Compare* bench.

Barbary pirates. Tripoli, Tunis, Algiers, and Morocco, whose governments were engaged in piracy, and to which the United States and other nations were accustomed to pay tribute to avoid depredations on their commerce. Wars with Tripoli, 1801–1805, and with Algiers in 1815 broke up the practice.

Barenblatt v. United States. A case, 360 U.S. 109 (1959), in which the Supreme Court held that the freedom of speech of a college teacher, or academic freedom, under the First Amendment properly appertained to the classroom and did not protect him from the consequences of refusing to answer pertinent questions about his knowledge of Communist influence and his association with Communists on American college campuses, when such questions were asked under the undoubted power of Congress to inquire into alleged Communist infiltration into the field of education.

bargain and corruption. A slogan of Andrew Jackson's followers after Henry Clay's influence had proved decisive in electing J. Q. Adams President, and Adams had appointed Clay Secretary of State in 1825.

Barnburners. Radicals in the Democratic party, 1843–48, who condemned public improvements and corporations, opposed the Albany Regency, and the Hunkers, *qq.v.*, and merged with the Free Soil Party, *q.v.*, in 1848;—from the supposed resemblance of their policy to that of a legendary farmer who burned his barn in order to rid it of rats.

Bar of the House (*or* **Senate**). The space immediately in front of the presiding officer's desk to which are brought persons who have been formally cited for inquiry or for contempt proceedings, or to receive a censure voted by the legislative body.

Barron v. Baltimore. A case, 7 Pet. 243 (1833), in which the Supreme Court decided that the due-process clause of the Fifth Amendment and, by implication, the remainder of the Bill of Rights of the U.S. Constitution, were intended to limit only the federal government and not the governments of the States. *See* Gitlow v. New York; Fourteenth Amendment.

Bartkus v. Illinois. A case, 359 U.S. 121 (1959), in which the Supreme Court reiterated its position that the due-process clause of the 14th Amendment does not automatically apply all the express limitations of the first eight Amendments to State jurisdictions. In this case, conviction of an offense (robbery of a federally insured loan association) in a State court, of which offense the defendant had previously been acquitted in a federal court, was held not to violate due process in the 14th Amendment or raise any valid question of double jeopardy.

base. A fortified location, usually possessing natural defensive advantages, from which hostile operations of a nation's military, naval, or air forces may begin and which serves as a supply and communications center for such forces.

Battle Act. The controversial Mutual Defense Assistance Control Act of Congress, 1951, which provides for the termination of all military, economic, and financial assistance to any nation which knowingly permits shipments of strategic materials behind the Iron Curtain.

Battling Bob. A nickname of the elder Robert M. La Follette.

Baumes Law. An act of the New York legislature, 1926, which made mandatory the imposition of a sentence of life imprisonment upon habitual criminals (persons convicted of four felonies), and since imitated in many other States.

Bay of Pigs. The site (*Bahía de Cochinos*), near Cienfuegos, Cuba, of an unsuccessful attempt, April 15, 1961, by expatriate Cubans trained in the United States to invade their homeland and topple the dictatorial regime of Premier Fidel Castro. Although the attempt was aided by the Central Intelligence Agency, *q.v.*, President Kennedy was unwilling to commit U.S. Armed Forces, especially air power, which, as the event proved, were necessary for the success of the expedition.

Bear Flag revolt. An uprising against Mexican authorities by U.S. citizens who were in California at the outbreak of the Mexican War, 1846. Their flag bore the figure of a grizzly bear and a star.

Beauharnais **v.** *Illinois.* A case, 343 U.S. 260 (1952), in which the Supreme Court upheld an Illinois statute that banned writings or pictures defaming a class or group of persons (in this case Negroes). By thus extending the concept of libel to include "group libel," the Court removed such publications from the protection of the First and (by extension) Fourteenth Amendments.

B.E.C. Bureau of Employees Compensation.

Belknap Scandal. The discovery in 1876 that a considerable sum had been paid annually to the wife of W. W. Belknap, Secretary of War, for securing an appointment to the lucrative trading post at Fort Sill. When an impeachment was threatened, Belknap resigned and his resignation was accepted by President Grant. The Senate failed to convict Belknap apparently because of the belief that an officer who had resigned was no longer subject to impeachment.

belligerency. The international status, and its consequent rights and duties, assumed by a state which wages war against another state. Organized rebels may have the same status if foreign powers recognize them as belligerents.

bench. 1. The seat occupied by the judge in a courtroom. **2.** The body of judges collectively composing a court or courts. *Compare* bar.

beneficial services. Natural and other resources and facilities (as fish and game, educational institutions, hospital service, and public assistance) which a State reserves for the use and benefit of its own residents, and which it may open to residents of other States on limited terms, or not at all.

benefit payment. A payment made by government for compliance with a program of regulation; *also:* a payment made to farmers under the Agricultural Adjustment Act of 1933 for limiting production of certain commodities.

benefit theory. A theory that taxes should be imposed in proportion to the benefit which taxpayers derive from the government, which, though outmoded in general, is still used as a justification for automobile, gasoline, business, poll, and ad valorem property taxes.

benevolent assimilation. The motive assigned by President McKinley for taking over the Philippines and other Spanish possessions in 1898.

Bering Sea Arbitration. The settlement of a dispute which arose from the conviction of Canadian seal hunters for violating American regulations forbidding the killing of seals in the open sea near the Pribilof Islands in the Aleutians. The arbitrators in 1893 denied American claims to property in the seals or to jurisdiction over the Bering Sea. A later agreement with Russia, Japan, and Great Britain provided a means to safeguard the seal herds from destruction.

Bering Sea Arbitration

Berlin blockade. The Soviet closing of all access routes by land to Berlin on June 23, 1948, in retaliation for Allied measures to organize a West German republic. Until May 12, 1949, American and British cargo planes supplied the city with food, fuel, and other necessities.

Berlin Decree. The announcement of a paper blockade of Great Britain and all her possessions in Europe by Napoleon at Berlin, Prussia, Nov. 21, 1806;—partly responsible for the passage of the Embargo Act.

betterment tax. A tax or special assessment levied upon property to pay for a public improvement adjacent to or near the property taxed which is calculated to enhance its capital value.

bicameral. Having two houses in a legislature.

biennial session. The regular session of most State legislatures, usually held in odd-numbered years;—gradually being supplanted by annual sessions as State problems become more complicated.

biennium. A two-year period; *especially:* the period for which appropriations are made in most State legislatures.

big fix. An arrangement between political machines and the underworld for the nonenforcement or partial enforcement of laws relating to bootlegging, racketeering, and other forms of organized crime and vice.

big government. A description of expanded governmental activities, especially at the federal level, of the resulting growth of public service and its intrusion into the daily lives of citizens, and of the diversion of proportionately greater increments of national income into taxes to support public budgets.

big stick. A symbol of Theodore Roosevelt's conduct of diplomacy;—from the proverb, "Speak softly and carry a big stick," which Roosevelt was fond of quoting.

bill. The draft of a proposed law from the time of its introduction in a legislative house through all the various stages in both houses, including reference to committee, consideration and amendment in committee, committee report, debate and amendment on the floor of the chamber or in committee of the whole, passage on three readings, conference, engrossment, enrollment, and approval by the executive or passage over his veto, when it becomes a statute. Bills for raising revenue for the federal government must originate in the House of Representatives, and by usage appropriation bills·must also originate there. Once introduced, a bill may be considered in any session of a Congress, but it dies at the end of a Congress, and its contents must be reintroduced as a new bill if a succeeding Congress is to consider it.

billboard regulation. The prohibition or limitation of outdoor advertising by federal or State statute or by municipal ordinance, which is constitutionally justified for reasons of safety and also, by the courts of some States, for aesthetic reasons.

bill drafting. The art of expressing a legislative idea or proposal in concise legal terms faithfully carrying out the intention of the sponsors, avoiding duplication or unintentional repeal of existing legislation, and, as far as possible, assuring the measure against judicial annulment. Congress has had the services of a bill-drafting agency, known as the Office of Legislative Counsel, since 1918; and most State legislatures maintain such offices either alone or in conjunction with the State Library or commissions for the revision of statutes.

Billie Sol Estes scandal. The rigging of cotton acreage allotments and contracts for storing government agricultural surpluses by Billie Sol Estes, a Texas manipulator. His indictment in 1962 was followed by the resignation of two federal officials, Republican charges of corruption, and his own conviction for swindling. His conviction was later set aside by the Supreme Court in *Estes* v. *Texas*, 381 U.S. 532 (1965), because at the preliminary hearing and, to a lesser degree at the trial, the bright lights, numerous strands of television cable, and activities of representatives of news mediums, which were excessive in relation to the public's interest in the news, had prevented a sober search for the truth and so had denied Estes a fair trial.

Billion Dollar Congress. The 51st Congress (1889–91) which was the first peacetime Congress to make appropriations in excess of a billion dollars.

bill of attainder. *See* attainder.

bill of credit. Any paper money or evidence of indebtedness issued by a government or fiduciary institution and designed to circulate as money. The issuance of bank notes by a bank whose capital was owned by a State was held in *Briscoe* v. *Bank of Kentucky*, 11 Pet. 257 (1837), not to violate the constitutional prohibition against State issuance of bills of credit.

bill of pains and penalties. A legislative conviction similar to an attainder, *q.v.*, except that it imposes a penalty of less than death. It is prohibited in the United States.

bill of rights. A brief statement of certain fundamental rights and privileges which are guaranteed to the people against infringe-Sment by the government. The English Bill of Rights from which some provisions of American bills of rights have been derived is a statute of Parliament passed in 1689. The Virginia Bill of Rights, *q.v.*, 1776, incorporated some common law principles. The first ten amendments to the Constitution of the United States, popularly called the Bill of Rights, were added to the Constitution in 1791 after State ratifying conventions had objected to the absence of such guarantees in the original document. They were originally limitations on the federal government only (*see* Barron v. *Baltimore*). Beginning in 1925, many of the substantive provisions of the federal Bill of Rights have also become limitations on State governments by judicial interpretation (*see* Fourteenth Amendment). A bill of rights is nearly always the first article of a State constitution.

bimetallism. The use of both gold and silver, more or less freely coined in some legally fixed ratio of value, as the standard of value. The United States was on a bimetallic basis before 1900.

Biological Survey. *See* United States Fish and Wildlife Service.

biological warfare. Harnessing the life sciences to military ends; *especially:* the deliberate release in enemy territory of bacteria or germ cultures which are calculated to spread death and destruction in enemy ranks through disease and pestilence.

bipartisan deal. An understanding among opposing party leaders, usually secret and prejudicial to the public interest, regarding the distribution of patronage or other perquisites, or the disposition of pending public issues.

bipartisan foreign policy. The collaboration of many Republicans under the leadership of Senator Arthur H. Vandenberg with the Truman administration in supporting Marshall plan aid to Europe, the Truman Doctrine, and the policy of containing Soviet expansion.

biparty system. *See* two-party system.

bipolarity. 1. A condition in international politics after World War II when the principal states of the world tended to gather into two mutually suspicious alliances headed by the U.S. and the U.S.S.R., in which there is no third force capable of effecting a balance between them, and in which the continued maintenance of peace depends on nuclear deterrents and fear of the consequences that would follow their use. 2. A trend in the direction of a two-party system in any state.

Birchite. A member of, or sympathizer with, the John Birch Society, *q.v.*

birth registration. Legal certification of the birth of an infant which State laws or administrative regulations require the attending physician or midwife to file with local and State registrars of vital statistics.

B.I.S. Bank for International Settlements.

Bituminous Coal Code cases. Two cases in which the Supreme Court reviewed the validity of two separate statutes, the Guffey-Snyder Coal

Act, and the Guffey-Vinson Act, *qq.v.* In *Carter* v. *Carter Coal Co.*, 298 U.S. 238 (1936), the Court held the first Guffey Act unconstitutional because its attempt to regulate wages and working conditions in the mines amounted to a regulation of production and not of commerce. In *Sunshine Anthracite Coal Co.* v. *Adkins*, 310 U.S. 381 (1940), the Court, whose personnel had meanwhile undergone some changes, sustained the minimum price and other features of the second Guffey Act, thereby, in effect, reversing its earlier decision and greatly broadening the judicial view of Congressional power over production.

Black and Tans. A faction of the Republican party in Southern States in which, from the Reconstruction Period, white and Negro voters have participated on fairly equal terms;—opposed to the Lily Whites, *q.v.*

Black Belt. 1. A strip of territory extending south and southwest from eastern Virginia to the Texas border in which the Negro population exceeds the white. **2.** A strip of black alluvial soil 40 to 100 miles wide extending across southern Alabama and Mississippi.

blackbirding. Illegal importation of slaves.

black code. 1. Laws regulating the conduct of Negro slaves. **2.** A name given to statutes enacted in Southern States after the Civil War applying to "persons of color," that is, Negroes. The statutes provided for apprenticeship, enforceability of labor contracts, punishment of vagrancy, and sale of the labor of those convicted to private persons.

Black Horse Cavalry. An epithet applied to some members of the New York legislature, 1875–1905, who conspired to extort money or favors from corporations by threatening to pass regulatory or strike bills, *q.v.*

Black Jack. A nickname of Senator John A. Logan of Illinois, and of John J. Pershing, General of the Armies in World War I.

blacklist. A list of persons or organizations who, because of alleged unfriendly, illegal, or unethical activity, have been singled out for discriminatory action: as (*a*) by an employer against a prospective employee who has been active in labor unions or has been publicly identified as sympathetic to radical or allegedly subversive causes; or (*b*) by labor unions against workmen who have incurred the unions' displeasure.

blackmail. *See* political blackmail.

black market. 1. An establishment which sells goods in violation of rationing and price-fixing regulations. **2.** Traffic in rationed goods or in foreign exchange at less than official rates.

Black Muslim. An American-Negro Islamic cult, officially the "Nation of Islam," established in 1930 in Detroit, Mich., by W. D. Fard, its first "prophet," presently centered in Chicago, Ill., under Elijah Poole, known as Elijah Muhammad, whose members preach Negro racial superiority and oppose integration into the predominantly white community, advocating instead a separate Negro state and culture.

black power. A slogan adopted in 1966 by several of the more militant Negro civil rights groups expressing their intention to do without help from whites, to organize Negro voters into voting blocs or separate parties, and to substitute self-defense, when attacked, for nonviolence; *also:* a program stigmatized by several moderate Negro leaders as "black racism" or "black nationalism."

black propaganda. Announcements, appearing in any medium, that are deliberately ascribed by those responsible to a false source and intended to mislead or deceive the public.

black Republican. A nickname of the Republican party shortly after its founding, apparently bestowed because it espoused the cause of the Negro;—usually used derisively.

Blair House. A thirty-two room mansion, originally owned by the Blair and Lee families, across Pennsylvania Avenue from the White House in Washington, D.C., which served as the residence of President Truman while the White House was being repaired, 1948–52, and now serves as a guesthouse for foreign heads of state and other visiting dignitaries.

Bland-Allison Act. A law of Congress, Feb. 28, 1878, which made the silver dollar of 412½ grains legal tender and provided that the Secretary of the Treasury should purchase from two to four million dollars' worth of silver monthly.

blanket ballot. A printed ballot which lists names of candidates for many elective offices and legislative proposals, and hence discourages the voter from attempting an intelligent and discriminating choice.

blanket code. A popular name for the President's Re-employment Agreement which was signed in July, 1933, by many businessmen engaged in industries for which no codes had been formulated under the provisions of the National Industrial Recovery Act, *q.v.*

blanket primary ballot. A ballot, like that in the State of Washington, in which the names of candidates seeking nominations by all parties for a given office are printed together. The voter has the option of voting for any candidate so listed regardless of his (the voter's) or the candidate's party affiliation.

bloc. 1. A temporary combination of parties in French legislative assemblies who agree upon a common parliamentary policy or to support or oppose a ministry; *also:* similar arrangements in other legislative assemblies. 2. *In America:* a group of Congressmen whose devotion to some common economic interest (as agriculture) often transcends their formal party allegiance. *See* farm bloc.

blockade. The use of force by a belligerent to prevent travel by persons or shipment of goods to or from designated ports, sections of coastline, or other places in the territory of an enemy, for the purpose of depriving the enemy of munitions and foodstuffs or in other ways hampering his ability to wage war. Under international law, a belligerent may seize, detain, confiscate, or destroy the ships and goods of neutrals engaged in running a blockade, provided that (*a*) due notice of the existence of the blockade is given in advance and (*b*) sufficient force is applied to prevent access under normal conditions. A *pacific blockade* is sometimes imposed in peacetime to compel a state to pursue, or refrain from, some course of action (as Russian missile installations in Cuba); but such a blockade is not recognized in international law.

blockade runner. A vessel employed in carrying persons and goods to and from ports under blockade.

blocked credit. Governmental restrictions upon the time and manner in which a debtor may pay obligations to a creditor in a foreign country.

blocked currency. The condition of a national currency when its holders are subject to administrative restrictions or prohibitions in their purchase of foreign exchange.

Block* v. *Hirsh. A case, 256 U.S. 135 (1921), in which the Supreme Court, by a bare majority, upheld State and federal emergency rent laws enacted at the close of World War I. The legislation, which fixed rents and temporarily extended leases, was held to be consistent with due process on the theory that the wartime emergency had clothed the relationship of landlord and tenant with a preponderant public interest and, at least temporarily, had made that relationship subject to the same sort of regulatory power that government was accustomed to exert over the rates and services of public utilities and other businesses.

bloc voting. 1. The tendency among some nationality and economic groups to vote alike in elections. **2.** A similar tendency among some groups of nations represented in the General Assembly of the United Nations.

Bloody Bill. The Force Bill, *q.v.*, of 1833.

bloody shirt. *See* waving the bloody shirt.

B.L.S. Bureau of Labor Statistics.

Blue Eagle. The symbol of the National Recovery Administration, first used in 1933 as an award of merit to be displayed by employers who had signed a code of fair competition or the President's Re-employment Agreement.

blue laws. 1. A puritanical code regulating public and private morality in the theocratic New Haven colony during the 17th and 18th centuries. **2.** Any laws prohibiting athletic contests or the opening of stores and theaters on Sunday, race-track betting, or any similar activity usually regulated by individual conscience. Recently the Supreme Court, as a protection of religious freedom, has exempted businessmen who observe a Sabbath day other than Sunday from the obligation to obey Sunday-closing laws.

Blue Lights. An epithet for the Federalist party dating from 1814, when attempts of an American fleet to put to sea from the harbor of New London, Conn., were said to have been thwarted by blue signal lights displayed at the mouth of the harbor to warn a British blockading squadron.

blue-ribbon jury. A special jury composed of persons belonging to the upper economic and social strata which might be empaneled in New York counties having a population of one million or more. Such juries were abolished by law in 1965.

blue-sky laws. State laws designed to protect investors by requiring the licensing of securities dealers and salesmen and the registration with the appropriate State official of stocks and bonds offered for sale, and detailed information concerning the capitalization, assets, and business of the issuing company;—from the remark of a Kansas legislator in 1911 that some promoters would sell shares in the bright blue sky. *See* Securities Act; Securities Exchange Act.

board. A body of three or more persons charged with some specific func-

tion, such as parole, election, educational, or health or welfare administration. When a board is charged with specific administrative duties, its
functions are generally supervisory, and such duties are delegated to
experts under its direction. When its formal functions are political or
quasi-judicial in nature, the board itself performs them.

board of control. An ex officio board, common in State governments, consisting of the governor, attorney general, and other persons, which must
approve the apportioning of budgeted funds and the settlement of
accounts and claims against the State;—often replaced by a director
of finance or controller.

board of education. 1. A body of laymen, usually elective but sometimes
appointed, which has legal responsibility for establishing and maintaining public elementary and high schools in municipalities, counties, and
other school districts and which, for that purpose, has limited powers
of borrowing money and fixing a tax levy on real estate or general property. 2. A State board with powers ranging from merely advisory to
appointing the State superintendent of schools, establishing minimum
standards, and apportioning State funds to aid local school districts.

board of estimate. A board of a State or municipal government about
1900 with principally budgetary powers. It has continued to exist
in New York City with important controls over city finances, property,
personnel, franchises, planning, and zoning.

Board of Governors of the Federal Reserve System. A board of seven
members which stipulates what reserves shall be maintained by federal
reserve member banks against their deposits; controls the issuance and
retirement of federal reserve notes by the 12 federal reserve banks;
determines the federal reserve bank rediscount rate; examines the condition of reserve banks and member banks; and generally supervises the
federal reserve banking system. Each member of the board is appointed
for a fourteen-year term and serves on the Open Market Committee, *q.v.*

board of higher education. A board that in some States supervises pub-
licly-supported colleges and universities.

Board of Immigration Appeals. A five-member quasi-judicial agency within the Department of Justice which reviews actions of the Commissioner of Immigration and Naturalization in deporting and excluding
aliens and hears appeals from transportation companies penalized for
violating immigration laws.

board of pardons. A State board, having various official designations,
which acts alone or with the governor in granting executive clemency
to criminals or advises the governor in the exercise of that function.

Board of Parole. An eight-man board in the Department of Justice which
grants or revokes all paroles of federal prisoners. If authorized by a
court, the board determines the date of a convicted person's eligibility
for parole.

board of regents. A body of officials appointed to direct and supervise an
educational institution or, as in New York, the educational system of a
State.

board of review. An administrative appeals board which, after hearing evidence, determines whether an assessment, action, or decision of an officer was correct.

Bobby Baker probe. A long-continued investigation by the Senate Rules Committee of the business activities of Robert G. (Bobby) Baker, a former Secretary to the Senate Majority during part of the period when Senator Lyndon B. Johnson was Majority Leader. In an interim report in March, 1965, the Committee found several irregularities in Baker's conduct and recommended for the future that all Senators and Senate officers and employees earning more than $10,000 be required to file confidential reports of their outside income. The Republican committee members filed a minority report calling the majority report a "whitewash."

Bogota Conference. The Ninth International Conference of American States that met at Bogota, Colombia, March 30 to May 2, 1948, and drafted a detailed charter for the Organization of American States, *q.v.*; the Pact of Bogota for the peaceful settlement of international disputes; and an agreement to pay fair compensation whenever property of foreigners is expropriated by any country.

***Bolling* v. *Sharpe*.** See *Brown* v. *Board of Education*.

Bolshevism. Lenin's program, accepted in 1903 by the left wing of the Russian Social Democratic party (later the Russian Communist party), which opposed as ineffective the use of established parliamentary methods, and advocated instead the inevitability of class war, the violent overthrow of capitalist political institutions, and the establishment of a dictatorship identified with the toiling masses.

bolter. One who deserts his party and supports opposition candidates or proposals;—from racetrack argot describing the sudden running away of a horse;—used in a political sense since about 1812.

bond. 1. A pledge of money or assets of value offered as bail by an accused person or his surety to secure the former's temporary release from custody. Bond is forfeited if the conditions of bail are not fulfilled. **2.** An evidence of indebtedness (which may or may not be negotiable), issued to long-term creditors by governments or corporations. **3.** A binding legal claim or covenant.

bondage. 1. Indentured service or slavery. **2.** Any form of political or civil servitude.

Bonneville Power Administration. An agency in the Department of the Interior created by Congress in 1937 to market power generated at the Bonneville and Grand Coulee dams and other federal power projects in the Pacific Northwest. The administration may build transmission lines and substations and is authorized to make power available to the ultimate consumer at the lowest possible rates warranted by "sound business principles."

bonus. 1. Any payment over and above regular compensation for services. **2.** The name given by veterans' organizations after World War I to additional compensation which they demanded of the Government to equalize soldiers' pay with the high wages received during the war by "stay-at-home" workers.

Bonus Army. Numerous veterans of World War I who congregated in

Washington in the summer of 1932 to lobby for immediate payment of adjusted service certificates previously issued as additional compensation for military service. They were expelled from their camp by military force.

boodle. Money accepted or paid for the use of political influence: bribe money. The term originated in New York City about 1883.

Book of the States. A biennial reference volume published by the Council of State Governments, Chicago, Ill., which, with occasional supplements, provides authoritative information on the activities, finances, and constitutional changes of the governments of the fifty States.

boom. 1. A decided advance by a candidate in public favor. 2. Extensive propaganda in favor of a candidate. 3. A period of intense economic activity.

boondoggling. The expenditure of public funds on useless public works;—often used opprobriously;—from a description of the less useful or patently useless works projects by which the federal government sought to provide employment during the depression period of the 1930's.

bootlegging. Illicit traffic in liquors or in any proscribed or heavily taxed commodity, especially in retail distribution.

border ruffian. A resident of Missouri who crossed into Kansas after the passage of the Kansas-Nebraska Bill in 1854 for the purpose of intimidating free-soil settlers and participating illegally in elections.

Border States. 1. *Formerly:* the northern tier of slave States, Delaware. Maryland, Virginia, Kentucky, and Missouri, which were more inclined to compromise and less disposed to insist on Southern rights than the States farther south. Of them, only Virginia seceded; but the western part of the State, now West Virginia, remained loyal to the Union. 2. *In contemporary politics:* the same States, including also West Virginia, Tennessee, and Oklahoma, which have sometimes given their electoral votes to Republican candidates.

Border War. The armed conflict in Kansas between proslavery and antislavery men following the opening of Kansas to settlement under the Kansas-Nebraska Act, *q.v.*, 1854.

boring from within. Opposition tactics carried out by hostile persons who have become formally allied with a group for the purpose of weakening its organization and program.

borough. 1. An incorporated self-governing town or village in England and in certain States of the United States. 2. One of the five subdivisions of the municipal government of New York City since 1898.

borrowing power. The authority of a government to obtain funds for immediate use by issuing bonds, notes, and other evidences of indebtedness payable at a specified time in the future;—used mainly for capital expenditures and during wars, depressions, and other emergencies. The borrowing power of Congress is subject only to self-imposed limitations. Many State constitutions place severe limitations on the amounts and purposes of State and local borrowing, and often require an extra-majority vote of approval from the electorate before borrowing is authorized.

boss. The autocratic and usually irresponsible leader of a political machine in a State, county, or city whose power rests upon devious or corrupt methods of controlling the processes of nomination and election. Because the officers of all branches of the government owe their positions to him, he can dictate appointments by executive officers, votes in the passage of legislation, judicial decisions from the bench, and a great variety of acts and determinations on the part of administrative and law-enforcement agencies.

Boston Massacre. A street encounter in Boston, Mass., Mar. 5, 1770, in which, under serious provocation, British soldiers killed five citizens and wounded six others. The troops were afterward removed to a fort in the harbor.

Boston Police Strike. A strike of the Boston police in September, 1919, as part of a union organization campaign. Governor Calvin Coolidge's statement, "There is no right to strike against the public safety by anyone, anywhere, any time," made him a presidential prospect.

Boston Tea Party. The dumping of 342 chests of tea into Boston harbor, Dec. 16, 1773, by a crowd of citizens, disguised as Mohawk Indians, who were determined to prevent the breaking of a colonial nonimportation agreement.

boundary. The territorial limit of a state or of its political subdivisions, fixed artificially in terms of latitude or longitude, or consisting of some natural barrier, such as a mountain, river, or sea, the latter being more favorable for purposes of national defense. Existing political boundaries often violate economic, cultural, or ethnic considerations.

bounty. A premium offered by public authority for the performance of some service useful to the community, as the production of certain articles, the killing of noxious animals, or, formerly, enlistment in the armed forces.

bounty jumper. A soldier, especially one during the Civil War, who deserted after accepting a bounty for enlisting.

Bourbon. A reactionary Southern Democrat, corresponding to a standpat Republican;—from his supposed resemblance to the later members of a European royal family who could "learn nothing and forget nothing";—especially applied to those who refused to accept the results of the Civil War.

Boxer Indemnity. A compensation paid by China to foreign powers for loss of life, damage to property, and the cost of armed intervention during an uprising of Boxers, an antiforeign, anti-christian secret society which in the summer of 1900 seized the city of Peking, besieged foreign legations, and killed many foreigners. The American share of the indemnity was $24 million of which $13 million was later returned and was used by China for scholarships for Chinese students in American colleges.

boycott. A concerted agreement to refuse to have any dealings with a nation, corporation, or employer with the object of bringing pressure to bear;—usually considered illegal if third parties are coerced into joining;—from Charles Boycott, harsh agent of a landlord, who was severely let alone by the people of County Mayo, Ireland, in 1880.

Boy Orator. A nickname of William Jennings Bryan, who was nominated for the presidency at the age of 36.

brain trust or **brains trust.** A name first used by a New York reporter to describe the small group of professors and other experts who assisted Franklin D. Roosevelt in the campaign of 1932 and who were reported to have had much influence on his early policies as President;—often used in a derogatory sense to identify any body of experts in the public service. *Compare* egghead.

brainwashing. The systematic application of intensive methods of persuasion, including reiteration of slogans and propaganda, and the use of drugs and physical and mental torture, for the purpose of inducing a person to forsake his fundamental beliefs and accept their opposite;—practiced upon some prisoners of war and persons disaffected with their regimes by Chinese Communists and their imitators.

Brannan Plan. The proposal of Secretary of Agriculture Charles F. Brannan in 1949 that storable crops be supported at 90 per cent of parity, but that perishable crops be permitted to rise and fall with the market. Any difference between market price and 90 per cent of parity was to be paid to the farmer by the federal government. The plan was opposed by both the Grange and the Farm Bureau and was never enacted by Congress.

brave. 1. An Indian warrior. **2.** A member of Tammany Hall.

breach of privilege. The use of force against, or of words reflecting upon the integrity of, a legislative body or any of its members. Such interdicted actions are equally culpable whether taken by the body's own members or by outsiders.

breach of the peace. Disturbance of public order and tranquility by an act of violence, or by an act inciting to violence.

break. The point in the proceedings of a nominating convention when, after a deadlock, the switching of a block of votes causes a pronounced trend in favor of the candidate who is eventually nominated.

Bretton Woods Conference. The United Nations Monetary and Financial Conference, consisting of representatives of 44 nations, which met at Bretton Woods, N.H., July 1–22, 1944. The conference's "Final Act" contained the Articles of Agreement for the establishment of the International Monetary Fund, *q.v.*, and of the International Bank for Reconstruction and Development, *q.v.*

bribery. The action of giving, receiving, or offering money or other reward for the purpose of influencing the action of an officer, voter, or any other person entrusted with a public duty;—usually prohibited by law under penalties which in some States may include the disfranchisement of a voter convicted of bribery.

Bricker Amendment. A proposal, in 1952, to amend the U.S. Constitution by requiring that a treaty must be in accordance with the Constitution, and that the treaty could become effective only through legislation that would be valid if there were no treaty. The amendment would have weakened the President's power to make executive agreements and reversed the rule in *Missouri* v. *Holland*, *q.v.* It failed by one vote to receive the two-thirds vote in the Senate required for submission.

Bridges v. *California.* A case which, together with the case of *Times-Mirror Co.* v. *Superior Court of California,* involved the question whether courts could hold persons in contempt who published invidious comments concerning the trial of pending cases. In its opinion, 314 U.S. 252 (1941), the Supreme Court rejected applicable common-law precedents justifying summary contempt proceedings in such cases; asserted that the First Amendment's guarantees of free speech and press precluded a court from banning all public expression on pending matters; and declared that whether or not such publications militated against the impartial administration of justice to a degree justifying contempt citations depended upon the circumstances in particular cases.

brinkmanship. The practice of pressing a threatening situation to maximum limits of safety: allegedly reckless conduct of diplomacy;—derived from criticism of Secretary of State John Foster Dulles in a *Life* magazine interview, Jan. 16, 1956, in which, after commenting on three separate confrontations with Communist nations, Dulles was quoted as saying: "The ability to get to the verge without getting into the war is the necessary art. . . . If you are scared to go to the brink you are lost."

Briscoe v. *Bank of Kentucky. See* bill of credit.

Broad Seal War. A dispute over the election of six Congressmen at large from New Jersey which delayed for two weeks the organization of the House of Representatives in 1839;—so-called because one group was certified under the Broad Seal of the State. In the next apportionment law, 1842, Congress provided, for the first time, that Representatives must be chosen from single-member districts.

Brother Jonathan. The United States;—derived supposedly from Washington's habit of saying, "We must consult Brother Jonathan" (Governor Jonathan Trumbull of Connecticut), when he needed supplies for the Revolutionary army.

brown derby. A personal symbol of Alfred E. Smith, Democratic candidate for President in 1928.

Brown v. *Board of Education.* A decision of the Supreme Court, 347 U.S. 483 (1954), outlawing segregation of Negro students in the public schools. After reviewing the efforts of Southern States to satisfy the equal-protection clause of the 14th Amendment by legally requiring segregated schools for Negroes under the "separate but equal" interpretation given that clause in *Plessy* v. *Ferguson, q.v.,* the Court declared continuance of the Plessy interpretation would in fact result in denying equal educational opportunity to Negro children, because separate facilities in education are "inherently unequal" and their continuance by the State would breach the equal-protection clause of the 14th Amendment. In *Bolling* v. *Sharpe,* 347 U.S. 497 (1954), which arose in the District of Columbia, a similar conclusion was reached on the basis of the due-process clause of the Fifth Amendment. The Court requested further argument concerning the relief to be granted; and, 249 U.S. 294 (1955), it ordered defendants "to make a prompt and reasonable start," and instructed the lower courts to "proceed with all deliberate speed" to end segregation in schools.

Brown v. Maryland. A case, 12 Wheat. 419 (1827), in which the Supreme Court developed the original-package doctrine, declaring that so long as an imported commodity remained in the container in which it had been imported, State tax and police regulations could not apply to it.

Bryan-Chamorro Treaty. A treaty with Nicaragua, signed Aug. 5, 1914, by which Nicaragua granted to the United States the exclusive right to build an interoceanic canal and a site for a naval base in the Gulf of Fonseca.

Buchanan Committee. A special committee of the House of Representatives which in 1949–50 exposed the lobbying activities of various groups and the lax enforcement of laws for the regulation of lobbyists.

Buchanan v. Warley. A case, 245 U.S. 60 (1917), in which the Supreme Court struck down, as a violation of due process affecting property rights under the 14th Amendment, a city ordinance which sought to establish residential separation of whites and Negroes by prohibiting a member of one race from occupying premises in districts in which a majority of the dwellings were occupied by members of the other race. The action encouraged resort to restrictive covenants which were later denied judicial enforcement in *Shelley* v. *Kraemer, q.v.*

Bucklin plan. A scheme of preferential voting invented by James W. Bucklin and first used at Grand Junction, Colo., in 1909, by which a voter expresses first, second, and third choices among candidates. A candidate with a majority of first choices is declared elected. If no one has a majority, the first and second choices are added together, and so on.

Buckshot War. A riot in Harrisburg, Pa., in 1838 caused by an attempt by the Antimasonic party led by Thaddeus Stevens to organize the legislature without admitting Democratic members from Philadelphia. The governor ordered the militia to load with buckshot, and the Democratic members were seated.

Bucktails. A faction of the Democratic party in New York, 1816–26, opposed to the Clintonians;—so-called from a buck's tail worn on the hat as an emblem of the Tammany Society.

budget. A balanced estimate of expenditures and receipts for the next fiscal year or other period for the purpose of planning and effectuating an orderly financial policy. Normally the stages in budget-making are: (*a*) preparation of estimates by departments and other spending agencies; (*b*) correlation and review in the course of hearings by a budget office which may reduce or change estimates in line with expected income; (*c*) approval and recommendation by the chief executive; (*d*) appropriations by the legislature after committee hearings and debates during which items may be reduced, increased or eliminated (sometimes called *budget authorization*); and (*e*) close supervision over expenditures by control and auditing offices (sometimes called *budget execution*). Recent laws and practice emphasize the *performance budget*, which is a listing of work projects to be completed, in contrast to the usual itemization of offices, salaries, and materials. Federal budgets are brought into balance over a period of years, but most State and municipal budgets are balanced annually. In imitation of Great

Britain, where public budgeting began, several States forbid the legislatures to increase or add items. *See* Bureau of the Budget.

Budget and Accounting Act. A law of Congress, June 10, 1921, which for the first time vested in the President the power and responsibility of preparing a budget, and which established the Bureau of the Budget, and the General Accounting Office, *qq.v.*

Buenos Aires Conference. A meeting at Buenos Aires, Dec., 1936, at which President F. D. Roosevelt sought collective action by American nations against possible interference by Germany and Italy in the Western Hemisphere. A permanent committee was set up which could be consulted whenever danger of war should arise.

buffer state. 1. A small state occupying a territory which neighboring great powers may covet for strategic or other reasons, but which none dares to annex because of mutual rivalry or distrust. **2.** A small neutral state which separates great powers whose boundaries would otherwise be contiguous, and which thereby reduces the possibility of diplomatic friction between the great powers and provides a potential military barrier.

building code. A collection of regulations governing the construction of all buildings within a given municipality.

building line. The margin upon a piece of private property beyond which municipal building regulations or the terms of a deed or contract prohibit the owner from building.

building permit. Permission granted by a municipal or local government to build a structure of approved design and materials on a specified site within the corporate limits.

bulldoze. To coerce by threats or violence;—originally used in Louisiana about 1875 to describe the process by which Negro voters were excluded from the polls.

bullionist. An advocate of a metallic currency.

Bull Moose. An emblem of the Progressive Party in 1912;—derived from a statement by Theodore Roosevelt: "I am as strong as a bull moose."

buncombe. Insincere public speech or action; *especially*: speechmaking for the purpose of winning the approval of a constituency;—from the statement of Felix Walker, representing the North Carolina district which included Buncombe County, that he wished "to make a speech for Buncombe" during the later stages of the debate on the Missouri Compromise, 1820, when other members of the House of Representatives were impatiently calling for the question. *Called also* bunkum.

Bund. A confederation or federation;—used during World War II to designate a disloyal group of German Nazi aliens and sympathizers in America.

bunk. *See* buncombe.

Bunting **v.** *Oregon.* A case, 243 U.S. 426 (1917), in which the Supreme Court, virtually reversing *Lochner* v. *New York*, *q.v.*, upheld an Oregon law prescribing a maximum working day (10 hours) in certain industries as a proper exertion of the State's police power and an acceptable limitation of the freedom of contract protected by the due-process clause of the 14th Amendment.

Burchard incident. A statement that the Democrats were the party of "rum, Romanism, and rebellion," which was made by the Rev. S. D. Burchard at a New York political meeting in 1884 and which Blaine, who was present, did not deny. By alienating Catholic voters, the remark is supposed to have cost Blaine the election.

bureau. 1. The basic unit of the hierarchical administrative structure of the French state. **2.** A functional unit of subordinate grade in American public administrative systems. **3.** An administrative establishment (as Bureau of Labor Statistics) in federal and State governments.

bureaucracy. 1. The highly centralized, autonomous, and quasi-military type of administrative system developed in France after the First Napoleon, the principal units of which were called bureaus. **2.** A government dominated by permanent administrative agencies. **3.** The whole body of public officials including the permanent civil service. **4.** A government characterized by slavish devotion to routine, by the application of a set of rigid rules and formulas, and by unresponsiveness to the political authorities of the government and to public opinion.

Bureau of Animal Industry. A unit of the Department of Agriculture, established in 1884, whose research and related activities, such as disease prevention among farm animals and meat inspecting responsibilities, were transferred to the Agricultural Research Service, *q.v.*, in 1953.

Bureau of Customs. A part of the Treasury Department responsible for the assessment and collection of import duties, the prevention of smuggling, the supervision of export controls, and the enforcement of various administrative and fiscal regulations affecting the movement of vessels and aircraft in foreign and coastwise commerce.

Bureau of Employees' Compensation. An agency in the Department of Labor which administers laws providing compensation in case of injury to civilian employees of the U.S. Government, to members of reserve components of the armed forces when on active duty, and to private employees in the District of Columbia and in maritime pursuits, and to certain other persons.

Bureau of Employment Security. An administrative unit of the Department of Labor responsible for securing compliance of State unemployment insurance plans with the standards set in the federal Social Security Act, for manpower utilization plans to relieve unemployment, and for coordinating public and private employment security activities.

Bureau of Engraving and Printing. A part of the Treasury Department responsible for designing, printing, and engraving items of a financial and monetary character issued by the Government, and documents like commissions, permits, and various types of certificates.

Bureau of Family Services. A part of the Social Security Administration of the Department of Health, Education, and Welfare which helps the States develop plans to assist the aged, dependent children, and the blind and determines whether State plans meet the requirements of the Social Security Act for receipt of federal financial aid which the Act authorizes.

Bureau of Federal Credit Unions. A unit of the Department of Health, Education, and Welfare which administers the Federal Credit Union

Act of 1934 and supervises privately-chartered cooperative credit unions that accept savings from, and make small loans to, their members.

Bureau of Indian Affairs. A unit of the Department of the Interior, responsible for the exercise of special guardianship over the economic, educational, and moral welfare of Indians and other American aborigines, which acts as trustee for Indian property, seeking at the same time to encourage and train the Indian owners to exercise direct control, and which assists the Indian when he seeks to leave tribal ways and become assimilated to American culture outside the reservation.

Bureau of International Commerce. A unit of the Department of Commerce, created in 1963, which administers export controls, supplies foreign trade information and service, and stimulates the expansion of American exports and business abroad.

Bureau of Labor Standards. A research and statistical agency of the Department of Labor concerned with raising health, educational, and safety standards in the field of labor relations, both federal and State, and with the improvement of the quality of labor legislation and its administration. It cooperates with the Bureau of International Labor Affairs in an effort to raise international labor standards.

Bureau of Labor Statistics. A unit of the Department of Labor which collects, publishes, and evaluates statistics on wages, hours, prices, cost of living, industrial accidents, number of people employed and unemployed, employment outlook, volume of privately and publicly financed construction, and labor conditions in other countries. Its statistics are the usual standard for measuring cost-of-living increases in industrial wage contracts and for measuring income, employment, and levels of economic activity throughout the country.

Bureau of Land Management. A unit of the Department of the Interior (an outgrowth of the General Land Office) concerned with the survey, multiple-use management, exploitation, conservation, protection and disposition of public lands (about one-third of the area of the United States), and the mineral, water, forest, and grazing resources in such lands.

Bureau of Mines. A unit of the Department of the Interior whose chief activities are to eliminate health hazards and promote safety in mines, provide statistical information on domestic and foreign mineral production and consumption, and support research dealing with the conservation and effective use of various minerals and their adequacy for normal and emergency national needs.

Bureau of Old-Age and Survivors Insurance. A unit of the Department of Health, Education, and Welfare responsible for the administration of the old-age, survivors and disability insurance provisions of the Social Security Act. It was abolished in 1963 and its duties were transferred to the Social Security Administration, *q.v.*

Bureau of Public Roads. A bureau in the Department of Transportation which, as the principal road-building agency of the federal government, administers federal grants-in-aid and other federal appropriations for the construction and maintenance of arterial highways and, in cooperation with other federal agencies, constructs national park and forest roads.

Bureau of Reclamation. A unit of the Department of the Interior which constructs and operates numerous public works designed to furnish water for irrigation and other purposes, to generate electric power on Bureau projects, and to control floods. Most of its projects are located in the western part of the United States.

Bureau of the Budget. An agency placed nominally in the Department of the Treasury when it was created in 1921, but since 1939 a part of the Executive Office of the President. Its head, the Director of the Budget, prepares the budget, *q.v.*, under the immediate supervision of the President. Other responsibilities include efforts to improve administrative and financial management in the executive branch of the Government, coordination and improvement of the Government's statistical services, the review of all legislative proposals prepared in Government departments and offices, and assistance in developing the President's legislative program.

Bureau of the Public Debt. An administrative unit of the Treasury Department which prepares, issues, and retires bonds and other federal public debt issues, allocates and accepts subscriptions to new offerings of such issues, and controls transactions in these securities by fiscal agents of the Treasury Department.

burgess. 1. A member of the colonial assembly of Virginia. **2.** The principal officer of a borough in Pennsylvania. **3.** A member of a board governing a borough in Connecticut.

Burlingame Treaty. A treaty negotiated by Anson Burlingame, an American citizen acting as minister plenipotentiary for China, at Washington, July 28, 1868. The United States and China reciprocally guaranteed to citizens of each other liberty of conscience and worship and rights of residence and travel, as accorded to the most favored nation.

Burr Conspiracy. Various schemes to detach Louisiana from the Union, or to seize and colonize Texas, hatched by Aaron Burr, former Vice President of the United States, and communicated to many persons in the course of his Western travels in 1806. Burr was indicted for treason but acquitted for want of proof.

business affected with a public interest. A virtually abandoned concept of American constitutional law in accordance with which the government may fix the prices charged by certain businesses for commodities or services and subject them to regulations which if imposed upon ordinary business would be deemed inconsistent with due process of law. The businesses thus set apart have never been fully defined; but they are supposed to be monopolistic in character or traditionally regulated callings like that of innkeeper. Public utilities constitute the bulk of the class.

business cycle. Alternating periods of prosperity and depression in an economic system, or of intense business activity followed by a perceptible decline, a phenomenon explained by many and often conflicting theories, some of which, more popular a generation ago than today, suggest that the cycle is a product of forces beyond human control, whereas contemporary economists express hope of overcoming or "flattening out" the cycle by private and public planning and by appropriate use of fiscal and monetary policy.

butternut. 1. A backwoodsman who wore clothing dyed with butternut bark. 2. A Confederate soldier. 3. A resident of the Middle West who sympathized with the Confederacy.

Buy-American Act. An act of Congress, 1933, which required federal procurement officers to give preference to American producers if their prices exceeded those of foreign producers by not more than a reasonable amount (normally 6 per cent); and allowed a greater margin of preference on account of national security or relief of local unemployment.

by-election. 1. A special election held in Great Britain to fill a vacancy in the House of Commons occurring within the life of a Parliament. 2. *In the United States:* a special election to fill an unexpired legislative term.

bylaw. A regulation adopted by a corporation for the government of its own internal affairs which must be in accord with the terms, strictly interpreted, of the federal and State constitutions and statutes, and of the corporation's charter.

Byrd Machine. The regular Democratic party organization in Virginia which was tightly controlled by Harry Flood Byrd, U.S. Senator, 1933–65, who on his retirement transferred his position to his son, Harry F. Byrd, Jr., thus beginning a "Byrd Dynasty."

Byrnes Act. An act of Congress, June 24, 1936, which prohibited the interstate transportation of strikebreakers with intent to interfere with peaceful picketing.

C

C.A.B. Civil Aeronautics Board.

cabinet. 1. A council composed of heads of departments and other high officers (as the Vice President, Ambassador to the United Nations, Director of the Budget), whom the President may summon to give him information and advice, discuss problems, and receive oral instructions. The cabinet has existed continuously since Washington's administration, though some Presidents have relied on it more than others. Cabinet meetings are held once a week or oftener. The sessions are secret and informal, and no minutes are kept. Only rarely is a vote taken, because a vote could not bind a President, who must take personal responsibility for every decision. 2. *In England:* an executive and policy-making body, consisting of the heads of the principal administrative departments, with perhaps a few ministers without portfolio, which under the leadership of the Prime Minister directs the administration and exercises political leadership in legislation.

cabinet government. *See* parliamentary system.

Cable Act. A law of Congress, Sept. 22, 1922, which, as amended, provides that an alien woman shall no longer automatically acquire American citizenship by marriage with an American citizen, but may acquire it within a minimum period of one year through naturalization. Conversely it provides that an American woman marrying an alien retains her citizenship unless she formally renounces it.

Cactus Jack. A nickname of John Nance Garner, Vice President of the United States, 1933–1941.

Cairo Conference. A conference between President F. D. Roosevelt, Prime Minister Churchill, and Generalissimo Chiang Kai-shek of China held at Cairo, Egypt, Nov. 20, 1943, at which plans were concerted for bringing about the unconditional surrender of Japan.

calamity howler. 1. One who predicts that certain governmental policies will lead to disaster. 2. A Populist.

calendar. 1. A list of cases pending in a court of justice. 2. A list of bills, resolutions, or other items, in the order of their presentation for action by a committee or a legislative house as a whole, which usually serves as a convenient order of business. The Union and House calendars of the House of Representatives, however, are merely records of the order in which financial and other public measures are reported from committee, and give no clue as to the order in which they will be called for consideration.

Calendar of Bills and Resolutions. The Senate's legislative calendar, which contains bills and resolutions reported from committees, notices of motions, matters on the table, and unfinished business. When the calendar is called, items may be considered in turn under the five-minute rule. Otherwise by motions or unanimous consent separate items may be brought to the floor for unlimited debate.

Calendar Wednesday. Wednesday of each week in the House of Representatives when committees, as they are called in turn, may bring up unprivileged bills from the House or Union calendars; but no committee may ordinarily occupy more than one Wednesday until all have been called. The rule was adopted to obtain a hearing for public non-financial bills which could not be passed under unanimous consent, suspension of the rules, or special orders. Calendar Wednesday is rarely observed at present.

call. A document issued by a national party committee in December or January preceding a presidential election which fixes the date and place of the convention, the number of delegates to which each State is entitled, the method of choice, and the procedure in case of contesting delegations.

call of the House. A roll call of members of the House of Representatives in alphabetical order to determine the presence of a quorum.

call of the States. A roll call of the States in alphabetical order in a national nominating convention for the purpose of making nominations or voting.

Calvo Doctrine. The principle advanced in 1887 by Carlos Calvo, Argentinian publicist, that a state should never resort to armed or diplomatic intervention to enforce pecuniary claims of its citizens sustained as a result of mob violence, insurrection, or civil war in another state. *Compare* Drago Doctrine.

Cameron-Quay-Penrose Dynasty. Simon Cameron, his son James Donald, Matthew Stanley Quay, and Boies Penrose, all of whom were U.S. Senators and bosses of the Republican party in Pennsylvania for a half century after 1861.

campaign. The contest of rival candidates for a particular office, or for primary designations, and of their respective political organizations to win the support of voters at the polls. The methods used are limited only by the law and the ingenuity and financial resources of the contestants and their supporters; but much reliance is placed upon platform speeches, television appearances, printed appeals for support sent through the mails, the distribution of posters, placards, buttons, and similar materials, parades and other spectacles, and personal solicitation.

campaign fund. The total monetary resources at the disposal of a candidate or party committee used to win a nomination or an election. National party funds, despite strenuous efforts to obtain many small contributions from the rank and file, have mostly been made up of large contributions. In many State and municipal elections, money is raised by assessments upon officeholders and candidates. Funds are used to maintain headquarters and to pay for radio and television time, newspaper advertising, billboard space, posters, handbills, lithographs, pamphlets, special trains, rental of halls, and expenses of precinct workers. Expenditures of national committees tend to be concentrated in a few large doubtful States. Laws have been passed to regulate the amounts, sources of income, and objects of expenditure of campaign funds by corrupt practices acts, q.v., passed by Congress and the States. Congress in 1966 provided for limited public support of campaign expenses by allowing income tax payers to designate $1.00 to be paid into a fund which at four-year intervals would be shared equally by the major parties, but repealed the provision in 1967.

campaign textbook. A pocket-sized volume issued by each party in a presidential campaign for use of party speakers, editors, and workers. It contains the party platform, biographies of candidates, and other pertinent information.

Canal ring. A corrupt collusion of politicians and contractors for repair of the Erie Canal which was exposed by Governor Samuel J. Tilden of New York in 1875.

Canal Zone. A tract of land (area 553 sq. mi.) extending five miles on either side of the Panama Canal which the United States leased from the Republic of Panama by the Hay-Bunau-Varilla Treaty, signed Nov. 18, 1903. By a supplementary treaty, Jan. 25, 1955, the United States agreed to increase the rental and granted important economic ad-

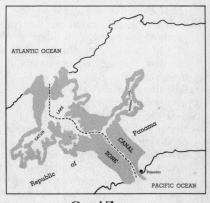

Canal Zone

vantages. Following serious anti-American riots in the Zone in 1964, President Johnson proposed a new treaty to settle all outstanding issues. The governor of the Canal Zone, under the supervision of the Department of the Army, is charged with the civil government, including health, sanitation, and protection.

candidate. A person who seeks public office through the established procedures of nomination and election.

Cannonism. Despotic control over the process of legislation by Joseph G. Cannon, Speaker of the House of Representatives, 1903–11.

Canton Island. One of the Phoenix group in the mid-Pacific, which, with Enderbury Island, *q.v.*, has been jointly administered by the United States and Great Britain since April, 1939. It is valuable as an air transit and communications post.

Cantwell* v. *Connecticut. A case, 310 U.S. 296 (1940), in which the Supreme Court held for the first time that the due process clause of the Fourteenth Amendment applies to the States the First Amendment's guarantees of religious freedom; these included an absolute freedom of belief and a qualified freedom of action. In reversing the convictions, under Connecticut law, of three Jehovah's Witnesses, the Court declared that a permit was not necessary for an effort to proselytize on the streets; nor did a breach of the peace result from the playing of a phonograph record which insulted another religious faith.

canvass. 1. Solicitation for votes and political support. **2.** Reexamination of election returns.

canvassing boards. State, county, or municipal boards, often ex officio, which review the work of precinct election officials, determine the validity of the votes cast, and certify the official returns.

capital. 1. Wealth saved from income which is being, or may be, utilized in the production of goods and services. **2.** The city in which the seat of government is located.

capital budget. A separate budget used by some States and cities (but not by the federal government) to provide for nonrecurring expenditures in the construction of public buildings and public works.

capital gains tax. A federal tax levied on profits from the sale or exchange of assets not ordinarily involved in the owner's business or profession, and normally administered as part of the individual or corporate income tax at rates which are the same as for incomes from salaries, interest, dividends, and rents, when the assets have been held for six months or less, but half as much when assets have been held for longer than six months.

capitalism. An economic system in which the ownership and management of productive wealth is in the hands of private enterprisers who hire labor and compete with one another in providing goods and services for profit.

capital punishment. The death penalty by electrocution, lethal gas, hanging, or shooting. It has been abolished in numerous foreign countries and in eleven States. Most of the other States exact it only on conviction of murder in the more heinous degrees or circumstances, though several apply it for rape, treason, arson, or kidnapping. Under various federal statutes capital punishment may be exacted for the crimes of treason, murder in the first degree, rape, kidnapping, or the assassination of the President or of certain other high officials.

capitation tax. *See* poll tax.

Capitol. 1. The building occupied by the United States Congress. **2.** The building and offices of an American State government; *called also* Statehouse.

capitulation. 1. The act or agreement of surrender by a belligerent force or nation; *also:* the agreement containing the terms of such surrender. **2.** A convention or treaty in which certain nations of the Near East once granted rights of a sovereign character to Occidental powers.

captive. A prisoner or prize of war.

Caracas Declaration. A resolution of the Tenth International Conference of American States voted in March, 1954, that the domination or control of any American State by the international Communist movement would constitute a threat to the sovereignty and political independence of the American States, and would call for a meeting to consider appropriate action in accordance with existing treaties.

card-carrying Communist. One who has joined, and pays dues to, the Communist party;—distinguished from others who, without formal affiliation with the party, sympathize with Communist principles and objectives. *Compare* fellow traveler.

career service. Government employment which provides opportunity for a career. The minimum requirements for such a service are: employment based on tested fitness; promotion according to merit; the possibility of advancing to the highest ranks in the service; and tenure secure against dismissal for reasons unrelated to performance.

Carey Act. An act of Congress, Aug. 18, 1894, granting desert land to States for irrigation and sale to farmers.

Caribbean Organization. A multilateral international agency, first established in 1942 as the Caribbean Commission, which seeks to improve the economic and social well-being of the peoples of the Caribbean area. Puerto Rico and the Virgin Islands each have representation on the agency.

"Caroline." An American steamer fitted out to aid Canadian insurgents in 1837 which was destroyed in American territory by Canadian authorities, with the result that war was threatened between the United States and Great Britain.

Caroline Islands. *See* Trust Territory of the Pacific Islands.

carpetbagger. An adventurer who seeks wealth and power by political manipulation and office-holding in a State or section other than his own;—applied to wildcat bankers in frontier areas and to Northerners who went to the South after the Civil War with no more property than could be carried in a carpetbag (a cheap valise of the time).

cartel. 1. An informal association of businessmen in similar industries in one or various countries who agree to control the amount and method of production and sale of their products or services;—found chiefly in Europe. **2.** An agreement between belligerents for the exchange of prisoners, the treatment of the wounded, the use of flags of truce, and methods of communication.

Carter v. Carter Coal Co. *See* Bituminous Coal Code cases.

Casablanca Conference. A conference between President F. D. Roosevelt and Prime Minister Churchill held at Casablanca, French Morocco, January 14–24, 1943, at which military plans were concerted to compel the unconditional surrender of the Axis powers in World War II.

case. Any suit, action, or other proceeding in law or equity contested before a court of justice.

cash and carry. A policy of the United States, 1939–41, which required foreign belligerents when purchasing supplies within the United States to pay cash for them on delivery and transport them abroad in non-American bottoms.

casting vote. 1. The vote of a Vice President or lieutenant governor to break a tie when the votes of members of the chamber are equally divided. **2.** The vote of the Speaker, who is also a member of the House, either to break a tie or, if there is a difference of only one vote on a motion, to create a tie and thus cause the motion to be lost.

casus belli. An incident or series of incidents provocative of war or used by one state as an excuse to make war on another.

categorical assistance program. Funds which the federal government grants to the States under social security laws to be paid to four categories of persons: the needy aged, the blind, dependent children, and the totally and permanently disabled. Relief for other classes of persons remained a responsibility of State and local governments.

caucus. 1. A secret meeting of party leaders to agree upon candidates or to arrange compromises. **2.** The primary or mass convention of voters in townships or wards;—used especially in Western States. **3.** A closed meeting of all the members of one or both legislative houses who belong to the same political party for the purpose of making nominations to offices and committee posts, choosing party leaders, and agreeing on concerted action on pending legislation. The decision of the Democratic House caucus, if made by a two-thirds vote, is binding on all members of the party unless they are excused because of previous pledges, instructions of constituents, or conscientious scruples concerning an interpretation of the Constitution. *See* Congressional caucus.

caveat. A legal notice directed to a public officer requiring him to delay a contemplated action until the party filing the notice has had an opportunity to express formal opposition to the action.

C.C.C. Civilian Conservation Corps, or Commodity Credit Corporation.

C.E.A. Council of Economic Advisers.

cease-and-desist order. An order issued by an administrative agency to an individual, firm, or corporation requiring that a particular fiscal or business practice be discontinued, and continuing in effect until reversed by a court of competent jurisdiction;—commonly used by agencies charged with the regulation of business, as the Federal Trade Commission or a State public service, or railway, commission.

censors. *See* council of censors.

censorship. Examination by a public authority of any printed matter, telephonic or telegraphic dispatch, wireless dispatch or broadcast, or dramatic or similar spectacle, prior to publication or transmission, with a view to making such deletions or revisions as the preservation of military secrets, public morality, the interests of religion, or some other consideration may require. Except in time of war or national emergency, governmental agencies in states with an English common-law background rarely exert a censorship over printed matter or over instrumentalities for transmitting intelligence. In this respect they differ sharply from the governments of many contemporary states and particularly from authoritarian governments under which censorship is constant and universal. Liberals have always regarded the absence of public censorship as a basic condition for the exercise of the twin rights of freedom of speech and the press, and as necessary to the maintenance of popular government.

censure. The formal resolution of a legislative, administrative, or other body reprimanding an administrative officer or one of its own members for specified conduct.

census. An official count of the population instituted primarily to establish a basis for the periodical apportionment of representatives and direct taxes among the States, and within the States to reapportion the representatives in the legislature. The national census, which has been taken decennially since 1790, has increasingly listed a great variety of social and economic data. The census office, formerly set up *ad hoc* and then disbanded, has developed into a bureau of the Department of Commerce engaged continuously in collecting and compiling statistical information on population, housing, agriculture, manufacturing, wholesale and retail trade, and transportation. On some matters it issues monthly, quarterly, and annual reports supplementing more elaborate compilations published at intervals of several years.

Center. Political parties or groups of moderate views;—so-called because in Continental European legislative chambers they are seated directly facing the presiding officer between the Right and the Left.

CENTO. The Central Treaty Organization (so-called after the withdrawal of Iraq from the Baghdad Pact, *q.v.*, Aug. 21, 1959). An alliance of the United Kingdom, Turkey, Iran, and Pakistan which forms a link between NATO and SEATO for the containment of Communist aggression. The United States, though not a member, is associated with individual members through bilateral pacts or understandings and is represented at meetings by observers.

Central Intelligence Agency. An agency created by the National Security Act of 1947 to coordinate intelligence services of federal agencies, to evaluate and interpret intelligence relating to national defense, and to make such intelligence available, when appropriate, within the Government. It operates under the direction of the National Security Council, *q.v.* The agency's operations both within and outside the United States are rarely submitted to public scrutiny and its expenditures are legally exempt from the kind of detailed audit to which public expenditures are normally subject. *Called also* C.I.A.

centralization. 1. The shifting of political authority from local governmental bodies to or toward the central government. 2. The transfer of
authority from the legislature to the executive.

centralized purchasing. The procurement of supplies, material, and
equipment by a central purchasing agency, which has become an increasingly common procedure in State and municipal governments, in
order to eliminate waste and duplication, to secure the advantages of
large-scale purchasing, and to provide more effective control over the
spending departments of the government.

Central Valley Project. A system of irrigation works to carry surplus
water from northern California to the semiarid upper reaches of the
San Joaquin River in southern California.

certificate. 1. A document which formally establishes the existence of a
fact or set of facts. 2. A record of proceedings filed by one court with
another.

certificate of election. An official certificate issued by a governor, a board
of elections, or other competent authority that the person or persons
named therein have been duly elected.

certificate of public convenience and necessity. A license issued by the
public service commission of a State permitting an individual or corporation to engage in a particular kind of business. Statutes withholding the right to do business without such a certificate first applied to
common carriers, but now apply to many businesses. The purpose of
such certificates is to prevent duplication of plants and services, when
such duplication is not in the public interest.

certification of eligibles. The act by which a civil service commission or
equivalent agency supplies names (usually three) of qualified applicants for a position to an appointing authority which then normally
chooses one of the applicants so certified.

certiorari. A writ issued at the discretion of a higher court calling upon a
lower court or an administrative agency to hand over the record of a
stated case for review;—usually the means by which most cases are now
brought before the Supreme Court when at least four justices concur in
granting certiorari; *called also* writ of certiorari.

cession. The act of transferring territory from the sovereignty of one state
to that of another; *also:* the territory thus transferred.

chain store tax. A graduated license fee levied by 16 States on stores in
excess of a certain number when operated under one ownership, management, or common agreement.

chain voting. Another name for the Tasmanian dodge, *q.v.*

chairman. The presiding officer of a party convention, legislative committee, administrative board, or other body whose powers may include, in
addition to maintaining order in the proceedings, practical control over
the selection of business that may come before the body or chief responsibility for administering its functions.

challenge. 1. An allegation that a vote or decision is invalid or that a
voter at the polls is not legally qualified to cast his ballot. 2. An objection entered against the service of a prospective juror.

chamber. 1. One of the houses of a bicameral legislature. 2. *In Romance* *states:* the first or lower house (as Chamber of Deputies) of the national parliament. 3. An arm of the sea, partly enclosed by headlands.

Chamizal Treaty. A treaty with Mexico, 1963, by the terms of which the United States restored to Mexico the Chamizal area, part of the business district of El Paso, Texas, which, by action of river currents since 1849 had come to be on the northern side of the Rio Grande; and provided for other exchanges of territory and the stabilization of the course of the Rio Grande.

Champion v. *Ames.* A case, 188 U.S. 321 (1903), in which the Supreme Court widened the judicial concept of the police power of Congress by declaring that the power to regulate interstate commerce includes the power to prohibit interstate traffic in lottery tickets.

chancellor. In some States, the presiding judge in a court of chancery or equity.

chancery. *See* court of chancery.

Chandler Act. A general revision and consolidation of the bankruptcy laws of the federal government, June 22, 1938.

change of venue. The removal of a case from one locality (as a county) to another for trial, when a condition of public excitement or prejudice in the locality in which the offense was committed renders it improbable that the defendant will receive a fair trial there.

chapel meeting. A meeting of employees called by union leaders during working hours, as in negotiations with the New York *Daily News* in 1967.

Chapultepec. *See* Act of Chapultepec.

Charcoals. A Unionist faction in Missouri, 1863–65, that wished to abolish slavery in the State;—opposed to the Claybanks, *q.v.*

charge. A statement of the law governing a case and other instructions given by a judge to the jury at the conclusion of a trial.

chargé d'affaires. 1. The head of a diplomatic mission, of lower rank than a minister resident, accredited to the ministry of foreign affairs rather than to the chief of state. 2. An officer placed temporarily in charge of an embassy or legation in the absence of the ambassador or minister.

Charles River Bridge v. *Warren Bridge.* A case, 11 Pet. 420 (1837), in which the Supreme Court modified substantially the rule in the Dartmouth College case, *q.v.* The public interest and common-law rules of construction, said the Court, required that franchises granted to private corporations be construed strictly and that they afford their holders no implied protection against legislative action which might injure the value of the franchise. The rule of strict construction, thus affirmed, applies to all corporate franchises.

charter. 1. A formal document issued by authority of a government granting rights and privileges to act in a corporate capacity and imposing conditions and obligations. The charter of a corporation, whether public or private, is to be strictly construed; that is, no privileges may be assumed to exist without specific grant of power. 2. The basic law of a municipal corporation which describes its governmental apparatus and defines its powers and responsibilities. 3. The fundamental statute of an international organization, as the United Nations.

charter colony. A colony (as Connecticut or Rhode Island) governed under the terms of a charter granted by the Crown and usually exempt from all but incidental control by royal officials.

Charter-of-Democracy Speech. An address by Theodore Roosevelt at Columbus, Ohio, Feb. 11, 1912, in which he stated his personal platform for the coming presidential campaign.

Charter of the United Nations. The multilateral international treaty that created the United Nations, *q.v.*, which was drafted by the representatives of 50 nations at the San Francisco Conference, *q.v.*, and which consists of a preamble stating the general purpose of the United Nations and some 111 articles defining the structure, powers, and procedures of the various United Nations agencies. The Charter was signed June 26, 1945, by the nations participating in the constituent conference, became effective Oct. 24, 1945, when ratified by 29 states, and was amended in important particulars in 1965.

chauvinism. Excessive patriotism verging on jingoism and bellicosity;—from Nicolas Chauvin, a French soldier who was ridiculed for his fanatical devotion to Napoleon I and exaggerated militant patriotism.

checkoff. The collection of union dues through the employer, who deducts them from wages due to members of the union.

checks and balances. A system of "so contriving the interior structure of the government as that its several constituent parts may, by their mutual relations, be the means of keeping each other in their proper places" (*The Federalist*, No. 51). While recognizing the principle of separation of powers, *q.v.*, among the legislative, executive, and judicial departments, this system seeks to protect each of them against the others, and the people against all, by requiring the approval by one department of certain acts of another;—also used to describe certain aspects of the relations between States and national government, and the requirement of concurrent action by both houses of a legislature.

cheeseparing. Niggardliness in making appropriations.

chemical warfare. The application of the products of chemical science to combat tactics in warfare, especially the military use of toxic or lethal gases and incendiary materials.

Cherokee cases. Two cases which arose over efforts of the State of Georgia to gain jurisdiction over lands held by the Cherokee Indians under treaties with the United States. In *Cherokee Nation* v. *Georgia*, 5 Pet. 1 (1831), the Supreme Court held that it had no jurisdiction to hear a case brought against a State by an Indian tribe because it was a "domestic dependent nation."

Boundaries of the Cherokee Nation in 1831

In *Worcester* v. *Georgia*, 6 Pet. 515(1832), it was held that the Cherokee Nation was a distinct community over which Georgia could not exercise jurisdiction except with the assent of the tribe or under the terms of a treaty between the United States and the tribe.

Cherokee Outlets. Two rectangular tracts of land, one in the southeastern corner of Kansas, purchased by the United States from the Cherokee Indians in 1866, and the other in northern Oklahoma, purchased from the same tribe in 1893. *See map, p. 191.*

Cherokee Strip. A narrow belt within the southern Kansas border ceded by the Cherokees to the United States in 1872.

Chicago Sanitary District. A special district created by the State of Illinois in 1890 to dispose of sewage without contaminating water supplies which were drawn from Lake Michigan. The upper portion of the South Branch of the Chicago River was deepened and connected by a canal with the Desplaines River so that the sewage of Chicago could be carried to the Mississippi watershed. Today the District provides sewage services for an area of 500 square miles, produces fertilizer and electricity, and provides facilities for navigation.

chief justice. The official head of a collegially organized court of justice. The Chief Justice of the Supreme Court of the United States presides over the hearing of cases and over meetings of justices for the purpose of reaching decisions; assigns the writing of opinions to different justices who voted with him in making up the majority in deciding a case, himself taking his turn; appoints members of the Court to consider revisions of the rules of procedure; and, performs other administrative duties. He presides over the Senate when the President or Vice President is impeached. His salary is $40,000, only $500 more than the salary of an associate justice. The following named jurists have held office: John Jay, 1789–95; John Rutledge, 1795–96; Oliver Ellsworth, 1796–1800; John Marshall, 1801–35; Roger B. Taney, 1835–64; Salmon P. Chase, 1864–73; Morrison R. Waite, 1874–88; Melville W. Fuller, 1888–1910; Edward D. White, 1910–21; William Howard Taft, 1921–30; Charles E. Hughes,-1930–41; Harlan F. Stone, 1941–46; Fred M. Vinson, 1946–1953; and Earl Warren, 1953–

chief of state. A king, emperor, or president whose powers are mostly dignified and ceremonial or, who, like the U.S. President, may in addition be the chief executive in fact;—distinguished from the head of government (prime minister, chancellor, premier) who has the principal responsibility for governing.

child labor. The gainful employment of children below a legal or traditional age by persons other than their parents, often subject to abuse because of the greed of both employers and parents. Nineteenth century reforms included laws requiring minimum periods of school attendance, elimination of work at night or near dangerous machinery, gradually higher minimum ages, and lower daily or weekly hours of labor. Uneven success in securing State legislation, especially in the South, caused reformers, early in the 20th century, to seek and obtain federal legislation under the commerce and taxing powers. The Supreme Court declared two successive acts unconstitutional (see Child Labor cases). In 1924 Congress submitted to the States a proposed amendment to the Constitution which would have authorized Congress to limit, regulate, or prohibit the labor of persons under eighteen years of age. It was never ratified by the requisite three-fourths of the States. The need for the amendment virtually ceased when Congress passed the Fair Labor Standards Act, q.v., 1938, fixing the minimum age for employment in industries engaged in interstate commerce at sixteen (eighteen in hazardous occupations), and the Supreme Court, reversing earlier decisions, upheld it in *United States* v. *Darby Lumber Co.*, q.v. On farms and in very small industrial establishments, the protection of child labor depends on the State laws in force.

Child Labor cases. Two cases in which the Supreme Court declared unconstitutional two separate attempts by Congress to regulate child labor. In *Hammer* v. *Dagenhart*, 247 U.S. 251 (1918), the Court held that an act prohibiting the interstate transportation of goods made in factories employing children was not a bona fide regulation of commerce among the States but an effort to control the conditions of employment and manufacture within the States. In *Bailey* v. *Drexel Furniture Co.*, 259 U.S. 20 (1922), the invalidated statute sought to levy a federal tax of 10 per cent on the net profits of any establishment knowingly employing minors under certain ages. The Court insisted that this was not a bona fide revenue measure but a police regulation which violated the 10th Amendment. The Court has since reversed its position. See *United States* v. *Darby Lumber Co.*

Children's Bureau. A unit of the Department of Health, Education, and Welfare created in 1912, which investigates child life and welfare, administers grants and other aids to local agencies in support of programs for children and adolescents, and enforces federal laws relating to child and maternal welfare.

Chinese exclusion. Denial of permission to all but a few excepted classes of Chinese nationals, such as merchants, students, and travelers, to enter the United States, which began with the act of Congress of May 6, 1882, annulling provisions of the Burlingame Treaty, q.v., and ended by act of Congress, Dec. 17, 1943. See exclusion.

Chisholm v. *Georgia.* A case, 2 Dall. 419 (1793), in which the Supreme Court ruled that, under Art. III of the Constitution, it might take jurisdiction over a suit against a State of the United States brought by a citizen of another State. The decision led directly to the adoption of the Eleventh Amendment, q.v.

chosen freeholder. A member of a county board in New Jersey.

C.I.A. Central Intelligence Agency.

Cincinnatus of the West. A nickname of William Henry Harrison.

C.I.O. See American Federation of Labor and Congress of Industrial Organizations.

circuit court. A State court of record whose jurisdiction may extend over several small counties in each of which a judge holds court at intervals of a few months.

Circuit Court of Appeals. See United States Circuit Courts.

citizen. A member in full standing of a political community. As a citizen, a person owes the state allegiance, that is, the obligation of fidelity, the duty of compulsory military service, and the faithful performance of such other duties as the state imposes upon its members. Within his own state a citizen normally secures no greater protection from the laws than is accorded to noncitizens; but the citizen alone usually enjoys whatever privileges of popular participation in government may be accorded by the constitution and laws of the state, and laws extending economic privileges and regulating professional status may discriminate in his favor. Under international law the state is regarded as responsible for safeguarding the rights of its citizens when they travel or reside abroad. In the United States national citizenship was regarded as incidental to citizenship in one of the States until the adoption of the 14th Amendment which confers national citizenship directly upon all persons born or naturalized in the United States and "subject to the jurisdiction thereof"; and recognizes a secondary citizenship in the member State of the Union in which a person resides. The qualifying phrase, "subject to the jurisdiction thereof," excludes from citizenship children born to members of diplomatic entourages and natives of certain dependencies, and originally excluded Indians belonging to the tribal community. The American citizenship of all persons born of United States citizens abroad is recognized by law, subject to the qualification that the state in which such persons are born may have a prior claim to them as its citizens or subjects *jure soli*. A child born abroad to parents one of whom is a citizen is also a citizen provided that the parent has resided in the United States for at least ten years, half of that period after having reached the age of 14. To retain his citizenship, such a child must come to the United States before the age of 23 and must reside in the United States at least five years between the ages of 14 and 28. Laws and usages governing the acquisition and renunciation of citizenship vary greatly. European states have normally applied the doctrine that the children of citizens are also citizens even though born abroad and remaining outside the immediate jurisdiction of the state which thus claimed them, and they have until recently been loath to recognize any personal right of expatriation. *See* naturalization. An American citizen may voluntarily relinquish his citizenship or he may lose his citizenship if, without United States consent, he serves in the army of a foreign country or as an officer of its government.

citizens' military training camps. Camps at Plattsburgh, N.Y., and other places where civilian volunteers received military training as part of a preparedness movement before World War I.

citizens' tickets. Independent nonpartisan nominations, generally for local or municipal offices.

Citizens' Union. A good-government association founded as a political party in New York City in 1897, but which since 1905 has made recommendations to voters concerning the records of candidates nominated by political parties.

city. 1. An urban center chartered as a public corporation with its own system of municipal government, and with an extensive municipal administrative apparatus to provide a variety of public services. **2.** In many States, the highest grade of municipal corporation.

city council. The principal deliberative body of a municipal corporation with power to pass ordinances, levy taxes, appropriate funds, and generally oversee city government. *See* council-manager plan; *compare* commission plan.

city court. A court which tries persons accused of violating municipal ordinances and has jurisdiction over minor civil or criminal cases, or both.

city manager. An official employed, usually for an indefinite term, by a commission or by a mayor and council to be in charge of the enforcement of ordinances and the construction, maintenance, and administration of all municipal works and services. *See* council-manager plan.

city planning. Preparing and keeping in adjustment a comprehensive plan locating streets, parks, playgrounds, terminals, rapid transit lines, schools, other public buildings, and zones for single residences, apartment houses, retail and wholesale business, and manufacturing in order to provide for the orderly future development of a city. The original plan for Washington, D.C., drawn by the French engineer, Pierre Charles L'Enfant, is an example of early city planning in America. Recently planning has become a permanent function in many city governments and metropolitan areas; and currently it covers social, as well as physical, aspects of urban growth.

civic center. An area within a city or town in which all of the principal public buildings are located.

Civil Aeronautics Board. An independent federal agency created in 1938 and consisting of five members appointed for six years, which regulates rates and accounting practices of air carriers; controls mergers between civil aviation companies and cooperative practices among them; and issues certificates of convenience and necessity to domestic air carriers and permits to foreign carriers to do business between the United States and foreign countries. The Board's former power to stipulate safety standards and practices for air transport was transferred to the Federal Aviation Agency, *q.v.*, in 1958.

civil case. A judicial proceeding to enforce a private right or to obtain compensation for its violation;—distinguished from a criminal case, *q.v.*

civil commotion. A serious and prolonged disturbance of the peace not sufficient to amount to insurrection.

civil defense. *See* Office of Emergency Planning.

civil disobedience. The collective application against the government of the techniques of passive resistance and non-cooperation, such as picketing, boycotting, refusal to pay taxes, and peaceable demonstrations. Its most extensive development occurred in India under the leadership of Mahatma Gandhi.

civil embargo. *See* embargo.

civilian complaint review board. *See* police review board.

Civilian Conservation Corps. A federal unit which, from 1933 to 1942, managed work programs, as in reforestation, flood control, and soil conservation, for 17- to 25-year-old youths of needy families.

civil law. 1. The law of Rome, or law derived therefrom. **2.** The law applicable to civil disputes.

civil liberty. 1. Liberty as defined by law; *specifically:* personal security and the peaceful enjoyment of property and other lawful rights which result from the existence of organized government, as distinguished from the supposed liberty of a state of nature. **2.** Freedom from interference or exactions of government officers which violate the constitution or laws of the country. *See* civil rights.

civil list. 1. A register of officeholders in the civil service. **2.** *In Great Britain and other monarchies:* the public appropriations annually made, at an amount normally fixed at the beginning of a reign, for the personal and household expenses of the royal family.

civil office. An elective or appointive office in any part of a government except the armed services.

civil rights. Those liberties possessed by the individual as a member of the state; *especially:* those liberties guaranteed to the individual against encroachment by his government. In this latter sense, civil rights are enumerated in the bills of rights of federal and State constitutions and include both substantive rights, such as freedom of speech, press, assembly, or religion; and procedural rights, such as protection against unreasonable searches and seizures or against punishment without a fair trial. The most important civil right is embodied in those clauses in State and Federal Constitutions which prohibit government from depriving anyone of life, liberty, or property without due process of law. Twice found in the Federal Constitution, this clause imposes a limitation upon the States as well as Congress. Of somewhat less importance is the equal-protection clause of the 14th Amendment which limits State action. By its interpretation of these two clauses the Supreme Court of the United States largely determines the scope of civil rights in America. Recently interest in civil rights has been directed toward legislation by Congress and State legislatures to secure certain liberties of the individual against encroachment by other individuals and groups, and to prohibit discrimination by them on account of race, color, religion, or membership in labor unions.

Civil Rights cases. Five cases, 109 U.S. 3 (1883), in which the Supreme Court held void the Civil Rights Act of 1875 insofar as it forbade proprietors of public conveyances, hotels, restaurants, and places of amusement to refuse accommodations to a person on account of his race, color, or previous condition of servitude. The prohibitions of racial discrimination in the equal-protection, and the due-process clauses, *qq.v.*, of the 14th Amendment were thus confined to State action and were not extended to invasions of private rights by individuals.

civil rights legislation. Laws designed to protect the Negro and other minorities in the exercise of their civil rights, especially legislation to prevent discrimination at the polls, in law courts, schools, hotels and places of amusement, and in matters affecting employment and professional advancement; and to establish penalties for those who deny such rights. Congress enacted legislation in 1957, 1964, and 1965 to assure minorities, especially the Negro, of equal access with others to places of entertainment and hospitality, and of equal employment opportunity, and to eliminate discriminatory practices in educational institutions. Congress also sought to overcome legal obstacles to Negro registration and voting in certain Southern States by requiring the use of federal registrars and election inspectors and restricting the application of literacy tests. *See* Voting Rights Act. Regulations of the U.S. Office of Education deny federal aid to schools which fail to carry out desegregation, *q.v.*, orders. The Department of Justice enforces most federal civil rights legislation. A six-member Federal Commission on Civil Rights, created in 1957, appraises enforcement of existing legislation and recommends new legislation; and various presidential agencies study discrimination in such areas as employment and housing and make appropriate recommendations.

civil service. 1. The whole body of appointed officers and employees of a government, who are not members of the armed services, and who rank below the principal administrative and judicial officers. 2. Government service in which members acquire positions by examinations rather than by political patronage or by appointment by the President and Senate.

Civil Service Assembly of the United States and Canada. A professional organization of representatives of civil service commissions and other public personnel agencies with headquarters in Chicago, Ill., that serves as a reference center and information clearinghouse and promotes research in public personnel problems. It publishes the quarterly *Public Personnel Review*.

civil service reform. The transformation of government service from office holding based on patronage or party spoils to a professionalized service chosen on the basis of ability and free from fear of partisan interference, begun by the Pendleton Act of 1883 which established a bipartisan Civil Service Commission of three members and provided for a rudimentary system of selecting civil servants by examination; subsequently extended by increasing the number of positions included, improving recruitment facilities and examination procedures, instituting efficiency ratings for promotions, and providing retirement allowances. Progress in State and rural local governments has tended to lag behind federal standards. No country unqualifiedly concedes the right of public servants to strike against the government, but all permit professional associations; in the United States such associations may affiliate with labor unions. Statutes protect civil servants against political exploitation and define the degree of political neutrality which they must observe.

civil suit. Legal process before a court, historically in equity, to recover property, maintain a right or privilege, or satisfy a claim.

civil war. An armed conflict within a state arising from two or more factions fighting for control of the government, or from a community within a state seeking by force of arms to gain its independence;—distinguished from insurgency or banditry. Civil war demands that the competing forces possess the qualifications of belligerents, such as maintaining some form of government over the territory they control and supporting organized armies in the field capable of holding out prospects of ultimate success.

Civil War. The armed conflict, otherwise known as the War of the Rebellion and as the War for Southern Independence, between eleven seceded Southern States, calling themselves the Confederate States of America, and the United States of America, which began at Fort Sumter, S.C., Apr. 12, 1861, and ended with the surrender of Kirby Smith in Texas, May 26, 1865. Extensive operations were conducted on several land fronts and on the high seas, and more than 2,000 separate engagements were fought. The victory of the Union forces resolved the long-standing controversy between advocates of State sovereignty and of national supremacy in favor of the latter principle, and effectively ended Negro slavery.

Civil Works Administration. A federal unit which, from November 1933 to March 1934, provided remunerative work for unemployed people.

claim. 1. To assert possession, as of territory. **2.** To assert a privilege, as under the patent, pension, or homestead laws. **3.** To demand as due. Contractual claims against the national government are decided by the Court of Claims, *q.v.*, others in limited amounts are settled by departments or other agencies. For many years the sole recourse of most claimants was to appeal to Congress for the passage of a private bill in their behalf. In 1946 the Federal Tort Claims Act, *q.v.*, provided for judicial settlement of most claims, thereby greatly narrowing the possibility of private legislation.

Clark Distilling Co. v. Western Maryland Ry. Co. A case, 242 U.S. 311 (1917), in which the Supreme Court sustained the constitutional power of Congress to divest alcoholic beverages, transported in interstate commerce, of their interstate character, thereby in effect permitting the States to determine the admissibility of interstate liquor shipments notwithstanding the original-package doctrine in *Leisy* v. *Hardin*, *q.v.*

class. A group differentiated from numerous others in a society on the basis of wealth (as the upper class), occupation (as the working class), or political power (as the ruling class).

classification. 1. The establishment of categories (as of municipalities, taxpayers, or property), to which certain legislation applies unequally from category to category. The courts tend to uphold the classification as long as it is reasonable and the law applies equally to all persons or things within a category. **2.** The grouping of civil service positions according to duties performed.

classification of cities. The practice of many State legislatures of grouping cities into three or more classes according to their populations, and providing general legislation or charters for each class.

classified service. That portion of the civil service to which entrance is gained by some form of examination, and which affords promotional opportunities and tenure free from ordinary political influence with removal only for cause. By the Classification Act of 1949 Congress established eighteen grades in the General Schedule including professional and scientific, subprofessional and clerical, administrative, and fiscal positions; and ten grades in the Crafts, Protective, and Custodial Schedule.

classified tax. A system of taxation used in various States under which different rates are levied upon various types of property, and certain property is classified as exempt from taxation;—occasionally used for other than property taxes.

class legislation. Laws passed for the benefit of a particular group at the expense of, or contrary to the interests of, society as a whole.

class struggle. The supposed hostility of economic classes toward one another in capitalist society, especially the Marxian concept of the inevitable and increasingly bitter conflict between owners and proletariat, the militancy of workers against owners being regarded as a prime factor in hastening the eventual development of a classless society and the withering away of the state.

Claybanks. A Unionist faction in Missouri, 1863–65, which placed the preservation of the Union above the slavery issue;—opposed to the Charcoals, *q.v.*

Clayton Act. A law of Congress, Oct. 14, 1914, which clarified and strengthened the Sherman Antitrust Act, *q.v.*, by forbidding rebates, tying contracts, price discriminations, price cutting to restrain trade, the ownership of stock in competing companies, and interlocking directorates in banks and large businesses. Officers of corporations were made personally responsible. Competitors when injured were allowed to use the injunction and to offer evidence unearthed by the Government. Labor and agricultural organizations not conducted for profit were exempted from the provisions of the act.

Clayton-Bulwer Treaty. A treaty between the United States and Great Britain, Apr. 14, 1850, which provided that neither nation should control a proposed interoceanic canal in Central America by fortification or the occupation of adjacent territory, but that such a canal should be neutralized and open on equal terms to all nations.

clean bill. A bill, prepared after extensive marking up, *q.v.*, by a standing legislative committee, in which all the committee amendments are intercalated in the new text so that, when presented in the chamber, it can be debated and voted on as a whole and not by separate consideration of each amendment.

clean sweep. The removal of all, or nearly all, subordinate administrative employees belonging to a faction or party opposed to that of a newly elected executive head of a government, as a preliminary to his filling their positions under the spoils system, *q.v.*

clearance. Permission given by an agent of the Bureau of Customs to vessels or aircraft to discharge passengers or cargo or to leave port or landing field.

clear-and-present-danger rule. A rule of constitutional interpretation formulated by Justice Holmes in *Schenck* v. *U.S.*, 249 U.S. 47 (1919), that in prosecutions for seditious utterances in which statutory encroachment on freedom of speech is pleaded in defense, the question which the court must decide is "whether the words used are used in such circumstances and are of such a nature as to create a clear and present danger that they will bring about the substantive evils that Congress has a right to prevent."

clerk. An official of the House of Representatives who has the care and custody of the records and papers of the House and the keeping and printing of the journal; who attests the passage of bills and joint resolutions, makes contracts, keeps accounts, and performs other duties of a clerical nature; *also:* a similar official of somewhat lesser stature in the Senate or in State legislatures.

clerk of bills. A subordinate of the clerk of a legislative chamber who keeps track of the progress of all bills and resolutions introduced.

clerk of court. A popularly elected county official who records the proceedings and issues the processes of courts of record sitting in the county, and whose office is sometimes combined with that of the county clerk, *q.v.*

climbing aboard the band wagon. Giving one's support to the candidate or proposal that appears to be winning.

Clintonians. A faction of the Republican party in New York, 1812–20, with strong support upstate, but opposed by Tammany Hall.

closed primary. A primary election in which participation is limited to members of a particular party, as determined by enrollment, challenge, or declarations by voters of their past affiliation with the party or of their intentions to vote for its candidates.

closed rule. A special order of the Rules Committee of the House of Representatives proposing a limited time for the consideration of a bill, but prohibiting, or limiting the number of, amendments from the floor.

closed sea. A gulf, bay, or other arm of the ocean, the shores of which are under the exclusive jurisdiction of one state.

closed services. Certain establishments of the federal government in which higher positions in the civil service are filled only by promotions of men already in the service.

closed shop. An industrial establishment in which only union members may be employed;—distinguished from a union shop, *q.v.*

closure. The halting of debate and amendment and the bringing of a question to a vote. In the House of Representatives and in most State legislatures it is accomplished by a mere majority vote on a motion for the previous question. In the Senate it is accomplished by written petition of sixteen Senators followed by a two-thirds vote of the Senate on roll call, after which each Senator may speak for only one hour. *See* filibuster.

club. *See* political club.

coalition. A temporary alliance or union of parties for the purpose of promoting a common legislative policy or electing candidates.

Coast and Geodetic Survey. One of the oldest services of the U.S. Government, known by its present title since 1878 and now a part of the Department of Commerce. It surveys and charts coasts and coastal waters to facilitate navigation and compiles and distributes topographical, gravitational, seismological, oceanographic, and astronomical observations of value to mariners, aviators, cartographers, and surveyors.

Coast Guard. *See* United States Coast Guard.

coasting trade. Water-borne commerce between ports of the same state, usually restricted by law to vessels of the state's own registry.

code. 1. *In Roman-law countries:* a systematic statement of the body of the law enacted or promulgated by the highest authority of the state, on which all judicial decisions must immediately be based. **2.** *In the United States:* a private or official compilation of all permanent laws in force consolidated and classified according to subject matter. Such compilations of national laws are the *Revised Statutes of the United States,* first enacted in 1874, and *A Code of the Laws of the United States,* *q.v.* Many States have published official codes of all laws in force, including the common law and statutes as judicially interpreted, which have been compiled by code commissions and enacted by the legislatures. American codes lack the permanence and authority of European codes because of the volume of new statutes and of judicial decisions, each of which, under common law principles, constitutes a precedent for the decision of later cases.

code authority. Representatives of a particular industry who, in 1933–35, formulated codes of fair competition, subject to governmental approval, and assisted in their administration under the National Industrial Recovery Act, *q.v.*

Code Napoleon. The codification of French private substantive law prepared at the instance of Napoleon Bonaparte. It became widely accepted as a model among Latin peoples.

coercion. 1. The use of force to compel performance of an action. **2.** The application of sanctions or the use of force by government to compel observance of law or public policy.

coexistence. *See* peaceful coexistence.

Cohens* v. *Virginia. A case, 6 Wheat. 264 (1821), in which the Supreme Court held that, though State courts may exercise final authority in cases which fall entirely within their jurisdiction, they are subject to the appellate jurisdiction of federal courts if their judgments involve the construction of federal laws, treaties, or the Constitution. The Court also declared that review by a federal court of a judgment secured by a State against a defendant in its own courts does not constitute a suit against a State such as is prohibited by the 11th Amendment.

coinage. The act or process of stamping metal into pieces of a stated value for purposes of exchange. In the United States the coining of money is a monopoly of the federal government. The first coins issued by the United States in 1794 had a stated value approximately equal to the intrinsic value of the gold, silver, or copper which they contained. Variations in metal prices have often led to hoarding and melting down of coins. In 1853 the weight of subsidiary coins was substantially reduced. By law of 1965 the silver content of half-dollars was reduced to 40 per cent, and of quarters and dimes to a thin shell over an alloy of base metals. The coinage of gold ceased in 1933, and no silver dollars have been coined since 1935.

Coin's Financial School. A pamphlet written by W. H. ("Coin") Harvey and used in the 1896 presidential campaign to win votes for Bryan.

Cold War. Military confrontations and diplomatic deadlocks which characterized the relations between the Soviet Union and Western Powers after World War II. In violation of agreements the Soviet Union refused or delayed withdrawal from occupied territory until Communist regimes had been established, and provided money and arms for subverting other governments. The United States provided economic and military assistance and took the lead in forming alliances, such as NATO, SEATO, CENTO, to contain Communist aggression.

Colegrove v. *Green. See Baker* v. *Carr.*

Coleman v. *Miller.* A case, 307 U.S. 433 (1939), in which the Supreme Court declared that a State legislature might ratify an amendment to the Federal Constitution even though the same State had previously rejected the proposed amendment; that the political departments of the federal government, and not the courts, had power to determine the validity of ratifications; that the time permitted the States for ratifications was to be determined by Congress; and that a pending amendment must be presumed valid until Congress ruled otherwise.

collective bargaining. Negotiation between an employer and organized employees as distinguished from individuals, for the purpose of determining by joint agreement the conditions of employment. The right of workers employed in industries engaged in interstate commerce to bargain with the employer collectively through representatives of their own choosing is protected by a series of federal statutes, beginning with the Railway Labor Act of 1926 and including especially the National Labor Relations Act of 1935, *q.v.* Similar legislation for intrastate employees has been enacted in numerous States.

collective naturalization. Naturalization by legislative act or treaty of persons not individually named, but described as those who are natives of a particular territory or who possess a particular status. *See* naturalization.

collective representation. The theory that a member of a legislative assembly represents the interests not merely of his immediate constituency but of the state as a whole.

collective security. Formal agreement among the states of the world or a substantial portion thereof to maintain international peace through the instrumentality of a league or confederation of states endowed with power to compose international differences and to use force against potential aggressors.

collectivism. Any social system or movement in which independent individual control of land or other capital goods and productive effort, and sometimes personal property, is systematically subordinated to collective or group action, the instrumentality being either the state or some private organization having power over the property of its members. The concept includes nonrevolutionary socialism and cooperative action.

collector of customs. An official of the Bureau of Customs of the Department of the Treasury who collects import duties levied upon goods entering the United States and enforces laws and regulations to prevent smuggling and frauds against the Treasury.

collector of taxes. A county or other local official, often elective, charged with the collection of certain taxes, especially property taxes.

Collector v. Day. A case, 11 Wall. 113 (1871), in which the Supreme Court held that Congress may not tax the salary of a State judicial officer and, by implication, may not levy a tax on any instrumentality used by the States in carrying out their powers under the Constitution. The ruling is a concession to the States analogous to that conceded to the federal government in *McCulloch v. Maryland, q.v.* Compare *Helvering v. Gerhardt.*

collusive bidding. A fraud consisting of the submission of prearranged bids by ostensibly competing firms.

colonial agent. The agent of a colony who represented its special interests at the seat of government of the mother country. Benjamin Franklin was probably the best known American colonial agent.

colonialism. 1. Advocacy of the settlement of the people of a country on sparsely-settled portions of the earth's surface in order to relieve population pressures at home, to exploit sources of food, minerals, and other raw materials, to develop foreign markets, or to obtain strategic advantages. **2.** The practice, by certain strong nations, of holding weaker nations or peoples in a state of economic and political subjection;— usually used in a derogatory sense. *See* colonial system; colonization.

colonial system. The maintenance by a great power of colonies, spheres of influence, or other politically subject areas, primarily because of the economic advantages derived from them.

colonization. 1. The occupation and permanent settlement of undeveloped or newly acquired territory by the nationals of a state under the political control of that state;—sometimes used to denote the extension of sovereignty by an imperialist power over the peoples and lands of weaker nations. **2.** The illegal introduction of nonresident voters into a doubtful electoral area for the purpose of carrying an election.

colony. A politically subject area inhabited by persons who have migrated from the country exercising sovereignty and by their descendants; *also:* such an area inhabited by people who have been forcibly subjected by the colonizing power.

Colorado River Compact. An interstate compact, 1922, entered into by Wyoming, Utah, Nevada, New Mexico, Colorado, Arizona, and California, which sought to secure their respective interests in the contemplated exploitation of the waters of the Colorado River and its tributaries, and which was an essential preliminary to the construction of the Hoover Dam and other works in the Colorado basin. Under a 1963 decision of the Supreme Court, implemented by the Pacific Southwest Water Plan of the Department of the Interior (1964), five of these States will receive stipulated amounts of Colorado River water, and the revenues from water service and attendant production of electricity will be used for research on water resources and their development in the basin.

Colossus of Debate. A nickname of John Adams.

Columbia River Compact. An interstate compact, 1925, entered into by Washington, Idaho, Oregon, and Montana, which provided for their respective rights in the contemplated exploitation of the Columbia River and its tributaries and led subsequently to the construction of the Grand Coulee and Bonneville dams. *See* Bonneville Power Administration.

Columbus Day. A legal holiday in several States commemorating the first landfall of Christopher Columbus in the New World at Watlings Island in the Bahamas, Oct. 12, 1492.

combat area. The area of hostile operations of belligerents; *also:* the area so defined by proclamation of one belligerent.

combination in restraint of trade. An agreement or understanding between two or more persons, in the form of a contract, trust, pool, holding company, or other form of association, for the purpose of unduly restricting competition, monopolizing trade and commerce in a certain commodity, controlling its production, distribution, and price, or otherwise interfering with freedom of trade without statutory authority. Such combinations within a State were prohibited by State constitutions and statutes after 1870; and in interstate commerce by the Sherman Antitrust Act, 1890, and later statutes.

Cominform. The international Communist party information bureau which was officially established, Oct. 5, 1957, by Communist party leaders from the U.S.S.R. and eight Soviet satellite states and was, in effect, a revival of the Comintern which had been officially dissolved in Moscow in July, 1943. The Cominform's headquarters, originally in Belgrade, Yugoslavia, were subsequently removed to Bucharest, Rumania. The growing cleavage between the Soviet Union and the People's Republic of China over their respective policies of coexistence, *q.v.*, and world revolution has prevented any viable international organization of the various national Communist movements.

Comintern. *See* Third International.

comity. 1. The recognition which one nation gives within its territory to the legislative, executive, or judicial acts or decisions of another. 2. The cooperative spirit which sometimes prompts a nation to return a fugitive from justice or render favors to another state when not required by treaty stipulations. The statement in the Constitution that "the citizens of each State shall be entitled to all privileges and immunities of citizens in the several States" is sometimes called the comity clause.

commander in chief. 1. A general in supreme command of military forces engaged in operations against the enemy. 2. The position of the head of a state who has the supreme administrative control, in time of peace and war, of all the combat forces of the state.

commerce. The exchange of commodities and commercial intercourse and traffic, including navigation, the transportation of goods and persons, and the transmission of messages. The meaning of the term is not confined to the instrumentalities in existence at the time of the adoption of the Constitution, but extends immediately to every new invention to facilitate transportation and communication. The regulatory powers of Congress, which extend over foreign and interstate commerce and commerce with the Indian tribes, is considered not to include bills of exchange. Since 1937 the Supreme Court has upheld Congressional statutes regulating manufacturing, wages and hours, farm production, mining, and related industries under the commerce power. Commerce begins when goods are delivered to the depot or warehouse of a common carrier and ends when goods are delivered to the consignee and are broken up into convenient lots for sale. Almost every aspect of water-borne commerce is under the control of Congress because of its specific constitutional powers over navigation. The States retain the power to regulate intrastate commerce; but their regulations are not enforceable if they adversely affect the free flow of interstate commerce. On the other hand, the States may make certain regulations which may affect the instrumentalities of foreign or interstate commerce if such regulations have a reasonable relation to the protection of public health, safety, morals, or convenience.

Commerce. *See* Department of Commerce.

Commerce Court. A federal court created in 1910 and abolished in 1913 which had power to review and enforce determinations of the Interstate Commerce Commission.

commercial treaty. An international agreement regulating trade in specified products, establishing reciprocal tariff reductions or trading privileges, or providing means for the settlement of commercial claims. *See* treaty.

commissary. *Formerly*: a branch of a military establishment that procured supplies for troops.

commission. 1. A warrant, usually issued by the chief executive, which confers the powers and privileges of an office upon a person newly appointed to it. 2. A body of three or more officials who collectively discharge the duties of an administrative agency.

commissioned officer. 1. An Army, Air Force, or Marine Corps officer of the rank of second lieutenant or above. 2. A Navy officer of the rank of ensign or above.

commissioner. 1. A member of certain independent federal agencies, of certain State boards, of the principal county board, or of the governing board of a city under the commission form of government. 2. Part of the title widely used for heads of national bureaus (as Commissioner of Accounts), and State and municipal departments.

commission of inquiry. A board (as the Commission on Government Security) composed of members of the legislature, administrative officials, nonofficial members, or a combination of two or more of these groups, appointed to investigate and report on a particular problem.

Commission on Civil Rights. A federal agency of six members, established by law on September 9, 1957, which investigates and reports upon charges that citizens, and especially minority groups, have been deprived of their civil and political rights and of equal protection of the laws, or that they are being discriminated against by other citizens and by public authority. The commission makes recommendations to Congress and the President to remedy such conditions.

Commission on Organization of the Executive Branch of the Government. *See* Hoover Commission.

commission plan. A form of municipal government, first adopted at

Galveston, Tex., in 1901, in which executive and legislative powers are combined in a commission of, usually, five or six members each of whom administers a department of municipal government subject to the control of the whole body. It was widely adopted elsewhere, but is now being rapidly superseded by the council-manager plan, *q.v.*

commitment. 1. An order to imprison a person. 2. Reference of a bill to a legislative committee.

committee. An organized body of members of a legislative assembly that gives special and detailed consideration to pending or prospective legislative business. In American legislatures a *standing committee,* essentially a permanent body, considers all bills, resolutions, and other items of legislative business falling within the category of matters over which it has been given jurisdiction. A *special* (or *select*) *committee* investigates and reports on a specific matter and expires when that service has been rendered. *Joint committees* are appointed by the two houses. Membership and rank on standing committees are largely determined by the seniority rule, and the chairman is usually the majority party member of longest continuous service on the committee. The formal choice of committeemen is a function of each house of Congress, but the actual choice is made by committees of the party caucuses. Majority and minority parties secure membership on a committee approximately in proportion to their strength in a house. Minority members have the right to make a formal minority report. The power and influence wielded by standing committees in Congress and State legislatures is probably greater than that wielded by comparable bodies in any other legislative assembly. They may hold open or secret sessions, invite outside testimony, and compel the attendance of witnesses. They may organize subcommittees for special phases of their activities and have considerable power to initiate legislation. All bills and resolutions introduced in one or the other house are referred to them and most of them die in committee. Such as are reported back may be amended or emasculated beyond recognition. In the British House of Commons the legislative leadership of the cabinet has prevented the standing committees from assuming positions of importance. They number five at present, are composed of a numerous personnel, and have little power to emasculate, sift, or initiate legislation. Special committees are created to improve the details of bills after the general principle has been decided in the Commons acting as a plenary body or as a committee of the whole. *See* committee of the whole; party committee.

committee of correspondence. 1. A committee of a colonial legislature appointed to correspond with the agent of the colony in London and with other legislatures. 2. One of a hierarchy of citizens' committees created after 1772 in all colonies, and extending into counties and towns, to exchange information and arouse resistance to British policies.

Committee of Forty-Eight. A liberal Socialist group formed in 1919, and representative of each of the States, which helped to found the Farmer-Labor party in 1920.

committee of the whole. The entire membership of a legislative house sitting under modified rules with its own chairman to consider a specific measure or class of measures. In the House of Representatives its quorum is 100 and its sessions are divided into general debate and the consideration of amendments under the five-minute rule without record votes. All revenue and appropriation bills must be, and other bills may be, considered in committee of the whole. To become effective its conclusions must be approved by the House in formal session.

committee on accounts. A standing legislative committee charged with the duty of determining whether or not funds appropriated have been expended in accordance with the law.

committee on committees. A committee of a party caucus which nominates and, in effect, determines the assignment of members to committee posts in the House of Representatives. Because of the seniority rule its discretion is normally limited to filling vacancies. The Democratic committee consists of the Democratic members of the Ways and Means Committee; the Republican committee consists of one member from each State having Republican representation, and he has as many votes as his State has Republican representatives.

Committee on Political Education. *See* COPE.

Committee on Rules. A committee of the House of Representatives with power to propose modifications in the general rules and to propose special rules for the consideration of individual bills out of turn with limitations on the time for consideration and the number and scope of amendments; it may even forbid any amendment to a bill. Except during the brief periods when the Twenty-one-Day Rule, *q.v.*, has been in effect, the Committee on Rules has prevented legislation from coming to the floor of the House except on its own terms. *See* open rule; closed rule.

committee stage. A step of legislative procedure in which (*a*) a standing committee invites or requires testimony from government officers or the general public, and (*b*) in closed session discusses, debates, and amends a bill.

Committee to Defend America by Aiding the Allies. An organization of leading American citizens, created after the fall of France in 1940, which originally advocated measures short of war and, subsequently, American involvement in the war, if necessary, to save Britain. It supported the Lend-Lease Act, naval convoys for American supply ships to Britain, and the recruitment of American volunteers for Allied armies.

Commodity Credit Corporation. A six-member agency of the Department of Agriculture, created in 1933, and having a federal charter since 1948, which makes loans on agricultural commodities and buys, stores, and sells such commodities with a view to supporting and stabilizing farm prices. It has a capital of $100 million and a borrowing capacity that exceeds $14.5 billion.

Commodity Exchange Act. An act of Congress, June 15, 1936, which regulates transactions on commodity futures exchanges, limits short selling, and curbs manipulation.

Commodity Exchange Authority. An agency set up in the Department of Agriculture in 1947 to regulate trading and competitive pricing on various commodity exchanges and otherwise supervise such exchanges in order to maintain fair and honest practices. Its authority is derived from the Commodity Exchange Act of 1936 and earlier legislation.

common carrier. A proprietor (as of a railroad, ship, airplane, pipeline, bus, or taxicab), who undertakes to carry goods or persons of a general class for hire, and whose business is affected with a public interest because of public dependence upon his service, and may be regulated extensively through legislation.

common council. 1. *In the Colonial Period:* an elective unicameral body which, with an appointed mayor presiding, adopted bylaws and administered a municipal government. **2.** *In the 1800's:* the lower ·house of many municipal legislatures.

common law. The basic law of Anglo-Saxon countries which originated from decisions of judges based on customary law in different parts of England and later became common to the realm through regular conferences of judges and the writings of commentators. It rests on judicial precedent, "the fruit of reason ripened by experience." As unusual cases arose the law was gradually broadened in scope. During the Colonial Period the doctrine associated with Lord Chief Justice Coke that the common law was fundamental and afforded protection against oppressive acts of government found acceptance in America. After the American Revolution practically all the common law continued to be the principal law in the States. Under the decisions of different courts common law has tended to vary somewhat from State to State. Common law may be repealed or modified by statute and much of it has been converted into statute law by legislative revisions or codifications.

Common Market. The customs and economic union of six European states, Belgium, France, German Federal Republic, Italy, Luxembourg and The Netherlands, created by the Treaty of Rome, March 25, 1957; called officially the European Economic Community.

common market. Any agreement of sovereign states to establish a customs union, *q.v.*

Common Sense. A pamphlet written by Thomas Paine in 1776 which helped to crystallize popular sentiment in favor of American independence.

commonweal army. May-Day demonstrators, including Coxey's Army, *q.v.*, before the national Capitol in 1894.

commonwealth. 1. The body of a politically organized people that forms a state. **2.** The official designation of certain States (as the Commonwealth of Pennsylvania).

Commonwealth. The United Kingdom of Great Britain and Northern Ireland, the Dominion of Canada, the Commonwealth of Australia, and about twenty other independent countries, formerly a part of the British Empire, which continue a loose affiliation, their principal ties being the Queen, occasional meetings of Prime Ministers, committee sessions, economic interests, and sentimental attachments.

Commonwealth preference. The practice among members of the Commonwealth of applying lower than prevailing duties to United Kingdom imports, which became essentially reciprocal between the United Kingdom and the rest of the Commonwealth after the Ottawa Conference of 1932, and which occasionally includes bilateral preferences among Commonwealth countries in which the United Kingdom is not involved.

Communism. 1. The political and social theory and institutional apparatus of the U.S.S.R., the People's Republic of China, and other states within the orbit of these two powers which are derived from the teachings of Marx, Lenin, and of more recent theoreticians and rulers of Communist states, such as Stalin and Khrushchev of the U.S.S.R., Mao of China, and Tito of Yugoslavia. The theory, however tempered by such doctrines as peaceful coexistence, *q.v.*, emphasizes implacable opposition to private capitalism and plural politico-social organization and insists instead upon the eventual revolutionary transition from private capitalism to social ownership of capital, state direction of production and distribution, a totalitarian discipline of society, and a form of government which, though nominally expressing the will of the enfranchised masses, is in reality a closely knit authoritarian oligarchy verging on a dictatorship. **2.** A theory advocating the abolition of private property and substitution of social or common ownership of wealth.

Communist Control Act. An act of Congress, Aug. 24, 1954, outlawing the Communist party as the agency of a hostile foreign power and subjecting its members to control and possible prosecution under the provisions of the Internal Security (McCarran) Act of 1950.

Communist front. An organization with professedly humanitarian and liberal aims which is secretly controlled and directed by hardcore Communists.

Communist Manifesto. A proclamation of the principles of Marxian Socialism drawn up and published in London in 1848 by Karl Marx and Friedrich Engels.

Communist Party of America v. *Subversive Activities Control Board.* A case, 367 U.S. 1 (1961), arising out of the effort to compel the American Communist party to register under the terms of the Internal Security Act of 1950. The Supreme Court accepted the Congressional conclusion that Communism was a movement dominated by a particular foreign country, which was dangerous to the United States and its free institutions; that, hence, requiring the Communist party in the United States, as part of this world movement, to shed its secrecy and legally imposing limitations on the privileges of the members of that party, does not violate freedom of expression and association protected by the First Amendment. A bare majority of the Court also ruled against the party's contention that the Act was directly aimed at it, and was so obviously intended to punish and destroy it that the Act was, in effect, a bill of attainder and hence unconstitutional. *See Albertson* v. *Subversive Control Board; United States* v. *Brown.*

Communist Party of the U.S.A. A minor party in the United States allied, or having aims in sympathy, with the Third International (Moscow, 1919). It was organized in 1919 by consolidation of the Communist and Communist Labor parties. Its largest vote in a presidential election, 102,991, was cast in 1932. The Communist Control Act of 1954 deprived it of all the "rights, privileges and immunities attendant upon legal bodies" because of its role as the agent of a hostile foreign power, and required it to register under the Internal Security Act of 1950, *q.v.*

community. 1. Any group of individuals having some identity of interests, especially a group inhabiting a defined area; *also:* the area containing such a group. 2. A union or association of nations (as the European Economic Community, *q.v*), having defined political or economic objectives.

community property. Common ownership by husband and wife of property acquired by either spouse after their marriage;—a legal principle in effect in some of the southwestern States where the annual income of either is regarded as common income. Since 1948 federal income tax laws have permitted all married couples to file joint returns in which the income of either or both may be treated as common income.

commutation. The alteration of a punishment to one which is less severe, which may be granted only by the officer or body exercising the pardoning power.

compact. 1. A contract or covenant; *also:* a fancied or actual agreement among a large number of persons (as the Mayflower Compact), by which political society is brought into being. *See* contract theory; governmental contract. 2. An agreement among two or more States regulating matters of common concern, such as the diversion of waters from a common river system, which usually requires the ratification of Congress in order to be valid.

companion bills. Identical bills introduced in both houses of a legislature.

company union. An employee organization limited in membership to the employees of one plant or employer. Federal and State labor relations acts, while not outlawing such unions, seek to prevent their domination, control, or maintenance by the employer.

compensating duty. A duty levied upon an imported commodity in order to compensate for an internal tax levied on the commodity when grown or produced within the importing country.

compensation. 1. The pecuniary award made by a tribunal to the owner of property condemned under the power of eminent domain, *q.v.* 2. Money paid to an employee or his beneficiaries from a state insurance fund because of injury or death sustained in the course of employment. 3. Payments or restitution for acts or omissions which have caused loss or injury.

competitive system. 1. Rivalry among producers or distributors under a regime of free enterprise to capture a larger share of the available market by offering lower prices or better terms, lowering costs of production, or improving the quality or increasing the desirability of goods or services. 2. The recruitment of civil service employees through examinations open to all persons having minimum qualifications in competition with one another.

complimentary vote. Scattered votes cast by delegates at a political convention for a person whom they wish to honor but who is not an avowed candidate and who is not seriously considered for a nomination.

compound duties. The combination of specific and ad valorem duties levied on the same article.

compromis. A written statement, agreed to by states in controversy, as to the rules and principles to be followed and the limitations to be observed when a question is submitted to arbitrators for an award.

compromise. The adjustment of differences through mutual concession by the parties involved; *also:* any agreement secured through mutual concession. Compromises are a normal part of the action of arbitral tribunals and of deliberative political assemblies and are essential to the functioning of a democratic polity in which divergent views must be reconciled in order to reach a decision.

Compromise of 1850. A compromise arranged by Henry Clay and enacted in five separate bills which provided for the admission of California as a free State, the organization of Utah and New Mexico territories without reference to slavery, the assumption by the United States of the debt of the former Republic of Texas and a settlement of its boundaries, abolition of the slave trade (but not slavery) in the District of Columbia, and a more effectual law for the return of fugitive slaves.

compromises of the Constitution. Adjustments of many conflicting interests and points of view in the Convention of 1787. The most important were the Connecticut compromise and the three-fifths compromise, *qq.v.*, and the one which gave Congress power to regulate foreign and interstate commerce, but prohibited it from stopping the importation of slaves before 1808.

Compromise Tariff. The tariff law of 1833 which provided for the gradual reduction of duties over the following ten years.

comptroller. An official who examines and audits public accounts; *called also* controller.

Comptroller General. An officer created by the Budget and Accounting Act of 1921 who heads the General Accounting Office, *q.v.*, who is appointed by the President and the Senate for a term of 15 years and can be removed only by impeachment proceedings or joint resolution of Congress.

Comptroller of the Currency. An official of the Department of the Treasury since 1863 who is responsible for the execution of the laws relating to national banks, and whose approval is required for the organization of new national banks and the merger of banks when the survivor is a national bank. Through frequent examinations, his staff determines the financial condition of national banks and the soundness of their management.

compulsory arbitration. A proposed requirement that all international or industrial disputes must be submitted to an arbitral tribunal whose decision would be binding. It has been used for labor controversies with equivocal success in New Zealand. A law of Kansas requiring arbitration in specific industries was declared unconstitutional by the Supreme Court in 1923. *See* arbitration.

compulsory military service. Service in the armed forces of a state enjoined by law upon those capable of bearing arms. *See* draft; Selective Service System.

compulsory process. The means employed to compel the attendance in court of a person wanted as a witness.

compulsory school attendance. The policy of compelling young people, usually to age 16 years except those attending a private school, to attend a public elementary or high school for at least part of an academic term or for a minimum number of days each year; in effect in every State since 1918.

compulsory vaccination. Immunization from smallpox required by law in many States, usually as a prerequisite to admission to elementary schools. The power of a State legislature to determine the general necessity for it was upheld in *Jacobson* v. *Massachusetts*, 197 U.S. 11 (1905). The United States and certain other countries normally require proof of vaccination for smallpox before admitting foreigners seeking entrance or permitting the re-entry of citizens who have been abroad.

compulsory voting. A legal requirement that qualified voters cast ballots at every election or suffer penalties provided by law. It exists nowhere in the United States, though one or two State constitutions authorize the legislature to provide for it. Experience in a few other countries indicates that such laws, though increasing participation in elections, have had little effect on the results of elections.

Comsat. The Communications Satellite Corporation created and partly financed by the United States in 1963 for the development of a world system of electronic communication by the use of space satellites. Capital stock is mostly owned in equal portions by private communication companies and by the general public, each group appointing six directors and the President of the United States appointing three. Under international agreements, more than fifty nations share in the control and benefits of the system but delegate management to Comsat.

concentration. The tendency to centralize all power of decision in the head of an administrative establishment, thereby decreasing the discretionary authority of subordinates.

concentration camp. A place for the incarceration or detainment, usually without any process of law, of persons who oppose an existing political regime or are otherwise politically suspect.

concert of powers. A loosely defined diplomatic agreement, especially among the great European powers in the 19th century, to preserve peace and the international status quo.

concession. A privilege or right, usually economic, granted by a government to another government or to individuals.

concession theory. The legal doctrine in England and the United States that the power of a person or a group to act as a corporation exists only by express legislative authority.

conciliation. Counsel by a friend common to the parties to a dispute, accompanied by an attempt to reach a compromise acceptable to them. There is no submission of an agreed issue, as in arbitration, *q.v.*, nor consent by the parties to be bound by the mediator's judgment. Labor disputes are often settled by permanent national and State conciliators.

concordat. An agreement between the Roman Catholic Church and the authorities of a state which regulates the position of the Church and its hierarchy within the state. Concordats may deal with the exemption of ecclesiastical property from taxation, public financial support of the Church, and the Church's authority over marriage and morality.

concurrent jurisdiction. Authority shared by two or more legislative, judicial, or administrative officers or bodies to deal with the same subject matter.

concurrent majority. A majority made up by the coincidental agreement of two or more sectional or interest-group majorities each separately recorded;—sometimes advocated in order to guard against the tyranny of a numerical majority. *See* concurrent voice.

concurrent power. The power of either Congress or the State legislatures, each acting independently of the other, to make valid regulations of the same subject matter, as under the 18th Amendment. An older use of the term referred to valid State police regulations over subjects committed to Congress, but on which Congress had not acted.

concurrent resolution. An action of Congress passed in the form of a resolution of one house, the other concurring, which expresses the sense of Congress or accomplishes some purpose of common interest to the houses, with which the President has no concern. It is not submitted to the President for his signature and does not have the force of law. In statutes delegating powers to the President, Congress has sometimes stipulated that the delegation may be terminated or that action taken by the President (as in reorganizations of the executive branch) may be disallowed by the passage of a concurrent resolution.

concurrent voice. The expression of political opinion by the different divisions and interests of society each separately recorded, and each entitled to be counted in determining a concurrent majority;—from a phrase associated with John C. Calhoun who insisted that, in matters which might injuriously affect any group, the group affected must either agree to the enactment of laws or have a veto over their execution in order to protect itself from the possible tyranny of a numerical majority of the whole society.

concurring opinion. A separate opinion delivered by one or more judges which agrees with the decision of the majority of the court but offers different reasons for reaching that decision.

condemnation. 1. A judicial proceeding in which private property is taken for public use under the power of eminent domain, *q.v.*, and compensation to the owner is determined. **2.** The judgment by which property seized for violation of revenue or other laws is declared forfeited to the state. **3.** The determination of a court that a ship is unfit for service, or was properly seized and held as a prize.

conditional contraband. *See* contraband of war.

condominium. The exercise of sovereign power jointly by two states over a colony or politically dependent territory, as the joint sovereignty exercised by Egypt and Great Britain over the Sudan prior to 1953.

Confederate States of America. A government established provisionally at Montgomery, Ala., Feb. 4, 1861, by delegates from South Carolina, Mississippi, Florida, Alabama, Georgia, and Louisiana. Within a few months Texas, Arkansas, Virginia, North Carolina, and Tennessee were added, and the number of States became 13 when minority provisional governments were recognized in Missouri and Kentucky. Under a constitution adopted in the fall of 1861, the President was to be elected for six years, but was ineligible for reelection; cabinet members might speak but not vote on the floor of Congress; an extramajority vote was required to pass appropriations not requested by the heads of departments, and the President was given an item veto; internal improvements and protective tariffs were practically prohibited; and any three States could compel Congress to call a constitutional convention.

confederation. An association of sovereign states usually possessing a central political or administrative organ to which is delegated power to act on matters of common concern. *See* Articles of Confederation.

conference. 1. A meeting of managers appointed by each of the houses of a legislature to adjust differences when a bill passed by one house is amended by the other and the first house refuses to accept the amendment. In a *simple conference* managers act under instructions; in a *free conference* they may make compromises within the limits of difference between the houses. The number of managers appointed by each house is usually three, but it may be more. A majority in each group is necessary to reach an agreement. Though the houses must each vote on the agreement, it is customary for them to accept it. **2.** An open meeting of members of a legislative body belonging to one party, in contradistinction to a secret caucus.

Conference for Progressive Political Action. A meeting of various labor and agrarian organizations in 1922 which paved the way for the independent candidacy of Robert M. LaFollette for President in 1924.

Conference of Commissioners on Uniform State Laws. A body of lawyers appointed by the several States which, since 1892, has drafted model laws and worked to secure their enactment by State legislatures.

confirmation. The ratification or approval of executive acts by a legislature or one house. In order to be valid, Presidential appointments of important officers of the United States require approval by a majority of the Senate, and treaties must be approved by two-thirds of the Senate. Most gubernatorial appointments in the States require approval by the upper house of the legislature. Legislative confirmation of executive appointments weakens the administrative control of the executive over his appointees; it is also responsible for the practice which allows members of the confirming body unofficially to select many of the appointees, the appointing authority being obliged to nominate such selections by the tacit threat of the confirming body to withhold approval of all executive nominations. Confirmation of treaties is logically more defensible since treaties are political instruments and directly affect the normal sphere of activity confided to legislative bodies.

confiscation. The seizure of private property by the government without compensation to the owner, often a consequence of conviction for crime or participation in rebellion, or because possession of the property was contrary to law, or because it was being used for an unlawful purpose.

conflict of interest. The situation that arises when an officer, in the discharge of his public duties, has to administer, decide, or vote on some matter in which he, or a member of his family, has a private pecuniary interest. Anticipating such a situation, high public officials, upon being elected or appointed, sometimes divest themselves of stock or other forms of ownership in private companies or place their property in the hand of trustees. Legislation regulating conflict of interest has been little developed.

conflict of laws. 1. Different provisions of two or more laws, each of which may properly govern a particular situation. 2. Private international law, *q.v.*

congress. A formal assembly of heads of states, ministers, and envoys (as Congress of Westphalia, Congress of Vienna).

Congress. The legislature of the national government, which consists of the Senate and the House of Representatives. With the exception of the executive power to ratify treaties and appointments which belongs to the Senate, the sole right of initiating revenue bills which is reserved to the House, and different roles in impeachments and the election of the President and Vice President, the two houses are legally coordinate. Congress may legislate on all subjects expressly granted by the Constitution, or reasonably implied from specific grants, or resultant from the general constitutional structure, subject to certain limitations in the Bill of Rights and elsewhere in the Constitution. The houses are reasonably free from procedural limitations. Each must have a majority present in order to do business, must keep a journal, and must take a record vote whenever one-fifth of those present demand it or when reconsidering a bill after a Presidential veto. A two-thirds vote is required in certain matters, such as the passing of a bill which has been vetoed, the expulsion of a member, a decision on the President's disability, and, in the Senate, judgment in impeachments and the ratification of treaties. Otherwise each house is free to adopt any rules it chooses. Each elects its own officers (the Vice President presides over the Senate), determines the elections and qualifications of its members, and may punish for disorderly behavior. Speeches made in either of the houses of Congress may not be called in question outside it, and members are free from arrest, except in the most extreme circumstances while attending the sessions and in traveling to and from them.

congressional campaign committee. A party committee first created in 1866 to conduct the reelection campaigns of Radical Republican Representatives who feared to trust the national committee. The Democratic committee began in 1882. Both committees have been active in off-year elections, *q.v.*, and have recognized their subordination to the national committees in presidential years. Each party caucus chooses one member, nominated by the State delegation, for each State having party representation in Congress.

Congressional caucus. Members of Congress belonging to either of the two parties (Federalist or Democratic Republican) who met in secret session in election years from 1800 to 1824 to choose the party's candidates for President and Vice President. The practice broke down because of protests of candidates and popular fear of Congressional domination of the executive. *See* caucus.

Congressional Directory. A volume published annually or oftener containing biographies of Congressmen, maps of Congressional districts, and valuable information on the organization of Congress, courts, and executive agencies.

Congressional district. A division of a State for the election of one member of Congress. A law of Congress, in effect from 1842 to 1929, required compactness and contiguity of territory and equality of population in each district; but partisan majorities in State legislatures often violated all these principles by redrawing boundaries with an eye to party advantage. *See* gerrymander. Recent decisions of the Supreme Court require that the Congressional districts within a State be as nearly equal in population as possible.

Congressional Medal of Honor. *See* Medal of Honor.

Congressional Record. An official publication of the debates and proceedings of Congress established in 1873, superseding the *Congressional Globe* which was privately published after 1830. Members of Congress are allowed to edit their speeches which appear in it and may insert material never spoken by securing from their respective houses leave to print or to extend their remarks.

Congressional Revolution of 1910–11. The action by progressive Republicans and Democrats of stripping the Speaker of the House of Representatives of his power to appoint standing committees and their chairmen, removing him from the Committee on Rules (he had been its chairman), and restricting his power of recognition; thus entrenching the seniority rule, *q.v.*, and enhancing the powers of the chairman of standing committees, the majority floor leader, and whips. *See* speaker.

Congressman. A member of Congress; *especially*: a member of the House of Representatives.

Congressman at large. A member of the House of Representatives, elected by the voters of the whole State and not from a district, who is chosen when a State is entitled to increased representation after a census and the legislature does not care to disturb existing district boundaries, or when the legislature ignores the principle of the single-member district.

Congress of Industrial Organizations. *See* American Federation of Labor and Congress of Industrial Organizations.

Congress of Racial Equality. *See* CORE.

Connally Reservation. An amendment, by the addition of the words quoted below, to the resolution, 1946, for United States adhesion to the Statute of the International Court of Justice, which excludes from the jurisdiction of the Court matters within the domestic sphere "as determined by the United States";—named for Tom Connally, who at the time was Chairman of the Senate Foreign Relations Committee.

Connecticut compromise. An arrangement promoted by Connecticut delegates to the Convention of 1787 by which the desire of small States for equal representation in Congress was satisfied by the creation of the Senate, and the large States were satisfied by representation in the lower house according to population. *See* compromises of the Constitution.

conquered territory. Territory which, by reason of invasion by the armed forces of a hostile power, has temporarily come under the immediate control and jurisdiction of the commander of such forces. Such territory may ultimately be permanently assimilated to the territory of the conquering power; but international usage normally requires a treaty or formal cession or proclamation of annexation to transform the mere fact of conquest into a right of sovereignty. In conquered territory the authority of the conqueror supersedes that of the existing government; but civilian rights normally remain in statu quo except that the commander of the invading forces may make such requisitions on the property of individuals as the usages of war permit. In the United States, the interim power of governing conquered territory is vested in the President as commander in chief, and Congress may provide for the permanent government of such territory.

conquest. The territorial expansion of a state through war; *also:* a permanent territorial acquisition resulting from a victorious war or aggression.

conscience money. Funds paid into a public treasury by persons who feel that they have cheated the government in tax payments or otherwise.

Conscience Whigs. Antislavery Whigs who disapproved of several provisions of the Compromise of 1850, especially the part relating to the return of fugitive slaves.

conscientious objector. One who, because of religious or moral convictions, refuses to engage in combat service and who may be assigned to noncombatant duties, as in the Medical Corps, a military band, or in an office; *also:* one who for similar reasons refuses to perform any military service and who may be assigned to a hospital, welfare institution, or approved nonprofit social service agency.

conscription. The forced enrollment and induction of men into one of the armed services. *See* draft; Selective Service System.

consent calendar. A calendar of the House of Representatives for expeditious consideration of noncontroversial bills from the Union calendar or the House calendar, *qq.v.*, and usually called on the first and third Mondays of each month. When a bill on this calendar is first called, one objection postpones its consideration for two weeks. At the second call, if less than three members object, the bill is considered at once, but if three or more members object, the bill is struck from this calendar.

conservation. The preservation, protection, and planned use of natural resources, such as waterpower, land, mineral wealth, and scenic beauty. Begun tardily in America, the conservation movement has rapidly progressed, as in the development of State and national forest and game preserves and park systems, the Tennessee Valley and many other reclamation and flood control projects, efforts to stem pollution of lakes and streams, control of the output of crude oil, legislation to encourage crop rotation and prevent soil erosion, and in the passage of the Wilderness Act, 1964.

conservatism. 1. General and uncritical opposition to change of any sort. 2. A reasoned philosophy, associated with the English writer Edmund Burke, directed toward the control of the forces of change in such a way as to conserve the best elements of the past by blending them into an organic unity with new elements in an ever-evolving society.

conservative. 1. One who follows the philosophy of conservatism, *q.v.*, 2. A supporter of President Andrew Johnson's administration, 1865–69, who opposed the Radical Republicans. 3. A member of the Conservative party, *q.v.*

Conservative Coalition. The informal cooperation of Republican and Southern Democratic members of both houses of Congress which, during the administrations of Truman, Eisenhower, and Kennedy, often defeated, delayed, or watered down legislative proposals of Northern Democrats.

Conservative Party. A minor party in New York State formed in 1962 by Republicans who opposed the reelection of Governor Nelson Rockefeller and Senator Jacob Javits.

consolidated fund. The pooled receipts of all State revenues, except those marked for a special purpose, from which withdrawals are made to defray the general expenses of government. *Compare* general fund.

consolidated laws. A compilation of all the laws of a State in force arranged according to subject matter. *See* code.

consolidation. The process of combining two or more administrative or territorial units of government to form a single entity, as the consolidation of several administrative agencies to form a single department or the consolidation of school districts, counties, or counties and cities, within a State.

conspiracy. A combination of two or more persons to do an unlawful act or accomplish some lawful purpose by illegal means.

constable. The elective peace officer of a town or township.

constituency. The inhabitants of an electoral district; *also:* the electoral district.

constituent power. 1. The power officially to propose or ratify a new constitution or amendments. 2. The body, or groups of persons, authorized to revise or amend a constitution. *See* amendment 2.

constitution. The fundamental law of a state, consisting of: (*a*) the basic political principles which ought to be followed in conducting the government; (*b*) the organization of government; (*c*) the vesting of powers in the principal officers and agencies; (*d*) limitations on the extent of, and methods of exercising, these powers; and (*e*) the relationship between the government and the people who live under it. The constitution may be simply an uncollected body of legislative acts, judicial decisions, and political precedents and customs, like that of the United Kingdom; or, at the other extreme, a single document drafted and promulgated at a definite date by an authority of higher competence than that which makes ordinary laws, like constitutions in the United States. It may be enforced by the courts as superior to statutes which conflict with it, as in the United States and a few other countries; or its preservation may be entrusted to the political authorities. In the latter case, which is still the usual one in Europe, a written constitution stands as a convenient standard by which the people may judge the conduct of their government and the degree of its respect for their liberties. Constitutions are sometimes classified as *written* or *unwritten*, according to whether or not their written material is presented in consolidated and systematic form; or as *flexible* or *rigid*, according to whether they can be amended by legislative enactment or require a more complicated procedure of proposal and ratification by different authorities. See Constitution of the United States; State constitution.

constitutional. Authorized by a written constitution, or not in conflict with its terms; in conformity with the usages of a constitution.

constitutional amendment. See amendment 2.

constitutional convention. A unicameral body which in an earlier period in the history of the United States was conceived to represent the people in their sovereign capacity, with the power to promulgate new constitutions, adopt ordinances of secession, and even, as in Missouri in 1861, to depose the governor and legislature and assume authority to govern directly. A contrary view that the convention was an agent whose action must be ratified by the principal was expressed in Massachusetts where the constitution of 1780 had to be approved by the people before being proclaimed. This view gained rapid acceptance in the North and later spread throughout the country. A few State legislatures are required to submit the question of calling a new convention to the voters at relatively frequent intervals but not many constitutional conventions have been called since 1900. Arrangements as to the date of meeting and the election and compensation of members are made by the legislature. A convention usually has about as many members as the State legislature. It appoints committees to consider separate articles or subjects and to make recommendations for approval by the whole body, and may submit a new constitution to the people or follow the growing practice of submitting several amendments piecemeal in order to avoid the possibility that its whole work may be negatived because of the unpopularity of one or two provisions. The Convention of 1787 has been the only national constitutional convention.

constitutional court. 1. A court created by or under a specific authorization of a constitution. 2. *In the federal judicial system:* a court, established under Article III of the Constitution, whose judges are entitled to tenure during good behavior and to salaries that can not be decreased. The U.S. Supreme Court, Courts of Appeals, and District Courts were created as constitutional courts, and the same rank was accorded by Congress in 1946 to the Court of Claims, the Court of Customs and Patent Appeals, and in 1956 to the Customs Court, all three of which previously had been legislative courts, *q.v.*

constitutionalism. The doctrine that the power to govern should be limited by definite and enforceable principles of political organization and procedural regularity embodied in the fundamental law, or custom, so that basic constitutional rights of individuals and groups will not be infringed.

constitutional law. The body of legal rules and principles, usually formulated in a written constitution, which define the nature and limits of governmental power as well as the rights and duties of individuals in relation to the state and its governing organs, and which are interpreted and extended by courts of final jurisdiction exercising the power of judicial review, *q.v.*

constitutional limitations. Provisions and judicial interpretations of constitutions which restrict the powers of government, especially of the legislative branch. In most States the legislature may exercise all powers not prohibited to it or assigned to another branch by the State or the U.S. Constitution. The Constitution of the United States contains numerous limitations on both national and State organs, and by implication all branches of the national government are limited to the powers delegated to them by the Constitution.

constitutional officer. A State official whose office was created and whose tenure is determined by a State constitution;—distinguished from an officer whose position has been created by the legislature.

Constitutional Union party. One of the four parties contesting the election of 1860, which was composed chiefly of former Whigs and Know-Nothings in the South, and whose candidates, John Bell and Edward Everett, received the electoral votes of Virginia, Kentucky, and Tennessee.

Constitution of the United States. The fundamental law of the American federal system drafted by the Convention of 1787, *q.v.*, and submitted by the Confederation Congress to conventions in the States, Sept. 28, 1787. Shortly after the ratification of the ninth State (*see* Art. VII), the Congress determined that the Constitution should go into effect, Mar. 4, 1789, and congressional and presidential elections were held; but the inauguration of Washington was delayed until Apr. 30. The ratifications by several State conventions were conditioned upon the adoption of a Bill of Rights; and so the first ten amendments, which were speedily proposed by Congress and ratified in 1791, may be regarded as part of the original Constitution. Additional amendments since 1791 brought the total to 25 in 1967, although actually the 21st repealed the 18th. All unrepealed amendments are in full force and effect as if they were parts of the original Constitution. The Constitution is a grant of powers to the national government, which are definitely enumerated (most of them are in Art. I, Sec. 8), or which may reasonably be implied from express grants, or which result from the constitutional structure as a whole. Some powers, such as those over the army and navy, foreign affairs, currency, and coinage, were expressly forbidden to the States; and others were expressly forbidden to both the national government and the States. When a limitation is expressed in general terms, as in the first ten amendments, it was originally held to apply only against Congress. But since 1925, decisions of the Supreme Court under the due-process and equal-protection clauses of the Fourteenth Amendment, *q.v.*, have applied many of the same limitations against the States. Since its adoption the Constitution has become more and more national in character through the processes of formal amendment, judicial interpretation, statutes, and usages or customs.

construction. The determination of the meaning of a constitution or statute by taking into account the intention of the framers, as shown in committee reports and debates, or the circumstances which brought it into being;—distinguished from interpretation, which is the process of determining the meaning of an instrument from an analysis of its terms. In the early history of the United States heated debates were frequent as to the proper construction of the Federal Constitution. *Liberal,* or *loose, construction* recognizes implied and resultant powers under the theory that the framers intended to establish a government with adequate powers to carry out its proper functions. *Strict construction* constitutes a denial that the framers had any other intentions than were expressed in the language they used.

consul. A public official stationed in a foreign industrial or commercial city to foster the economic interests of his government and look after the welfare of his government's nationals who may be traveling or residing within his jurisdiction. United States consuls form a part of the Foreign Service and are of various grades: consul general, consul, vice consul, and consular agent, *qq.v.*

consular agent. A consular officer of the lowest grade, who is sometimes a foreign resident or national.

consular immunity. Inviolability of archives and other privileges granted by a state to foreign consular officers under the provisions of applicable treaties.

consulate. 1. The residence or official quarters of a foreign consul. 2. *Historically:* the office or period of incumbency of Roman or French executive officers called consuls.

consul general. A consular officer of the highest rank stationed in a commercial metropolis whose duties may include supervising consulates located in other cities of the same geographical area.

consumers' advisory boards. Boards intended to represent the interests of consumers when codes of fair competition were being formulated under the National Industrial Recovery Act, *q.v.*, of 1933; also created under later agricultural and defense programs.

containment. The policy, attributed to George Kennan, of trying to prevent the spread of Communist power and influence by a system of alliances (as NATO, CENTO, and SEATO, *qq.v.*), the creation of bases near the periphery of Communist-controlled territory, and the dissemination of propaganda explaining and defending the Western way of life. After 1947 containment became a cardinal principle of American foreign policy. *See* Truman Doctrine.

contempt of Congress. Interference with the proper functioning of a house of Congress or one of its committees by refusal to testify or produce documents, interruption of proceedings, or attempts to bribe a member. The power of either house to punish for contempt extends to proceedings for impeachment or for the expulsion of a member and, most frequently, to investigations by select or standing committees. Such investigations, however, "must be related to, and in furtherance of a legitimate function of Congress," and relevant provisions of the Bill of Rights limit this discretion. In 1857 Congress provided that persons who refused to appear before a committee or answer questions should be subject to indictment and prosecution in the courts. *See* investigative power; *Kilbourn* v. *Thompson; Watkins* v. *United States.*

contempt of court. Willful disregard for, or disobedience to, a court committed in its presence (*direct contempt*) or so near thereto as to impair its authority (*constructive contempt*). It is *criminal contempt* when directed against the court itself, since the proceeding is between the court and the defendant, whereas mere failure to carry out the court's orders for the benefit of the other party to a civil action is *civil contempt*. Both are punishable by fine and imprisonment. If the contempt was not seen or heard by the judge, punishment for criminal contempt requires notice, representation by counsel and, when required by Congress (as in labor disputes), trial by jury. The President may pardon those convicted of criminal, but not of civil, contempt.

contested election. An election the result of which is contested by two claimants before the authority which is empowered to admit a person to an office. Legislative houses settle such contests through investigations by committees on elections whose recommendations must be approved by a majority of the house. Often the vote follows party lines. Contests for nonlegislative offices are settled by the courts.

contesting delegations. Groups of delegates to a nominating convention, each of which claims to be the rightful representative of the party membership.

Continental Congress. The de facto body first organized by the delegates of the 13 American colonies at Philadelphia in 1774 to petition the British government for redress of grievances. The second Continental Congress, which met in 1775, adopted measures of resistance against the British government and became the responsible political agency for carrying on the Revolution against Great Britain. The Continental Congress met at intervals until the adoption of the Articles of Confederation in 1781.

contingent expense. An incidental or unforeseen expenditure usually of a petty nature.

contingent fund. A fund created in anticipation of incidental or unforeseen expenditures. As systematic accounting, budgeting, and expenditure controls are developed, such funds tend to become formalized, and questionable manipulation is minimized.

continuous voyage. A doctrine traditionally applied by British and American prize courts that merchandise ostensibly bound for a neutral port but intended to be transshipped either in the same carrier or another to an enemy port is in continuous voyage from the consignment point to belligerent destination, and subject to the law of contraband.

contraband of war. Commodities which neutrals have no right, under the rules of international law, to supply to belligerents. The Declaration of London, 1909, classified neutral goods as *absolute contraband*, or goods exclusively used in war; *conditional contraband*, or goods used in both war and peace; and *free goods*, or goods of no use in war. A belligerent may exercise the right of visit and search, *q.v.*, on neutral vessels and confiscate absolute contraband *en voyage* to the enemy as well as goods which are conditional contraband if it is apparent that the latter are destined for the enemy's military establishment.

contract. A legally enforceable agreement between two or more parties under the terms of which, for valid consideration, the parties agree to perform some act or refrain from performing some act.

contract clause. A clause (Art. I, Sec. 10), in the U.S. Constitution which forbids a State legislature to enact any law impairing the obligation of a private contract. In the Dartmouth College case, q.v., the force of this clause was extended by the Supreme Court to include charters or franchises granted by public authority to individuals or corporations, but this ruling was substantially restricted in *Charles River Bridge* v. *Warren Bridge, q.v. See* obligation of a contract.

contract labor. Immigrants brought to the United States under contract to work for persons who advanced their passage money. Since 1885, such contracts have been forbidden by law.

contract settlement. *See* Office of Contract Settlement.

contract theory. A class of theories which strive to explain the origins of, and the existing obligation to conform to, social and political institutions. *Compare* social contract; governmental contract.

contractual rights. Property or other rights secured under a contract. The courts afford protection for such rights, an action for damages being available to an injured party under a contract against the other party or parties thereto who have failed to fulfill their covenanted obligations. Equity also offers remedies, such as a writ of specific performance, to secure the fulfillment of contractual rights. Contracts, and rights thereunder, are protected by the contract clause, q.v., of the U.S. Constitution as well as by the due-process clauses of the Constitution against impairment by State legislatures; but contractual rights are safeguarded no more than other rights against the exercise of a State's prerogatives of eminent domain, taxation, and the police power. *Compare* freedom of contract.

contribution. *See* campaign fund.

contributory negligence. An old common-law rule that any lack of care on the part of an injured employee relieves the employer of liability for damages, which has been modified by statute in most States in favor of a rule of comparative negligence by which the employer is relieved of responsibility only in proportion to the relative negligence of himself and the employee.

controller. *See* comptroller.

controversy. A civil proceeding in a court of law or equity.

convention. 1. An agreement between states relating to trade, finance, the administrative details of international intercourse, or other matters considered less important than those usually regulated by a treaty. 2. An extraordinary assembly, conceived to possess the full powers of sovereignty, which is convoked to consider sweeping changes in the constitution, as the Convention Parliament of 1660 which recalled Charles II, or of 1689 which placed William and Mary on the throne; or the French National Convention, 1792–95. 3. A unicameral body convoked at irregular intervals to draft constitutional revisions for the approval of the electorate. *See* Constitutional convention; Convention of 1787. **4.** A meeting of voters belonging to one party in a town, township, ward, or other minor division, or of delegates in larger areas, which nominates candidates, formulates a platform, adopts rules of party organization, and appoints a committee to advance the interests of the party during the interval between conventions. Until the advent of the primary election the convention system was based on mass meetings of voters which elected delegates to county conventions, which in turn elected delegates to the next higher convention, and so on to the national convention. State party conventions have survived chiefly to formulate platforms and reconcile differences among factions.

Convention of 1787. A convention, composed of 55 delegates from all the States except Rhode Island, which met in secret session from May 25 to Sept. 17, 1787, on the call of the Congress to revise the Articles of Confederation, and which drafted the Constitution of the United States, *q.v.* Its discussions, which were not known in detail until the publication of Madison's *Journal* in 1840, were devoted mainly to compromising differences between the advocates of a strong central government and of a weak confederation; between large States and small States; between North and South; between commercial and agrarian points of view; and between advocates of a strong and a weak executive. Some provisions were altered several times before the Constitution was ready to be put into final form by a committee on style and submitted to State conventions for ratification.

conversations. Exploratory conferences between diplomats of two or more states to determine whether, and in what manner, a pending issue may be adjusted.

convict. 1. A person found guilty of a felony or other serious offense. **2.** A person sentenced for a long term to a penal institution.

convict labor. Work performed by inmates of penal institutions either under contract with private parties or directly for the State, the products of which were forbidden in interstate commerce by an act of Congress effective in 1934.

Conway Cabal. A plot, 1777–78, to remove Washington from the command of the Continental army and appoint General Horatio Gates in his stead.

Coodies. New York Federalists who favored the vigorous prosecution of the War of 1812;—derived from "Abimalech Coody," the pseudonym of Gulian C. Verplanck.

Cooley v. Board of Wardens. A case, 12 How. 299 (1852), in which the Supreme Court developed the doctrine that the commerce power of Congress is not exclusive but that, on the contrary, where a uniform national rule is not required, the States may apply their own regulations to foreign and interstate commerce (as in local pilotage regulations), which remain valid until such time as Congress may decide to supersede them.

cooling-off period. 1. The interval after the beginning of a dispute during which states which have ratified conciliation treaties agree not to resort to war. **2.** A similar period in labor disputes during which the parties may not resort to strikes or lockouts.

cooperative federalism. Theory and practice which emphasize the mutually helpful aspects of federal-State relationships, as in law enforcement, the exchange of information, and financial grants-in-aid to the States, made possible by the virtual abandonment by the Supreme Court of the concept of dual federalism, *q.v.*

Co-operative Marketing Act. An act of Congress, July 2, 1926, which set up a division in the Department of Agriculture to acquire and disseminate economic, legal, and financial information regarding cooperatives here and abroad; to make surveys of the accounts and business practices of cooperative associations on their request and report the result to them; to advise groups of producers who desire to form a cooperative; and to make economic surveys and analyze market data for cooperatives.

cooperatives. *See* agricultural cooperatives.

COPE. An acronym for Committee on Political Education, a special agency of the American Federation of Labor and Congress of Industrial Organizations, *q.v.*, which raises funds and engages in activities to secure the election of Congressmen and other public officials "friendly to labor";—known earlier as Political Action Committee. *See* Labor's League for Political Action.

Coppage v. *Kansas*. *See Adair* v. *United States.*

Copperhead. A Peace Democrat, member of a disloyal secret society, or other Northerner (especially active and numerous in Illinois, Indiana, Ohio, and New Jersey) who opposed the Civil War and advocated a negotiated peace restoring "the Union as it was";—from the venomous copperhead snake which strikes without warning.

copyright. An exclusive right granted by law to an author or artist to publish or reproduce his work for a term of years. Holders of copyrights may protect themselves against infringement in the courts. In the United States a copyright runs for 28 years and may be renewed for another 28 years; thereafter the copyrighted work is held to be in the public domain. An international convention to which most of the states of the world adhere prevents infringement by the nationals of one state of the copyrighted productions of nationals of another state. *See* Library of Congress; *compare* patent.

CORE. An acronym for the Congress of Racial Equality, a civil rights organization founded in 1942 which, through sit-ins and like demonstrations in the 1960's, sought to focus national attention on the Negroes' demand for civil equality.

Cornerstone Speech. An address of Alexander H. Stephens at Savannah, Ga., Mar. 21, 1861, in which he declared that the cornerstone of the Confederacy "rests upon the great truth, that the Negro is not equal to the white man; that slavery . . . is his natural and normal condition."

Corn Islands. Two islands, Great Corn Island and Little Corn Island (total area, 4 square miles) off the eastern end of an interoceanic canal route, leased in 1916 from Nicaragua by the United States.

coroner. A local government official who is required to hold an inquest, assisted by a jury, over the body of every person who is supposed to have met a violent death. In many States the coroner has been supplanted by the medical examiner, who must be a physician.

corporal punishment. Flogging or other forms of physical chastisement, once inflicted as punishment for crime or violation of discipline, now nonexistent in the United States except in Delaware.

corporation. An artificial body created by law under a charter or act of incorporation, that has a special name and certain legal capacities separate or distinct from those of the natural persons composing it, such as perpetual succession, the power to make contracts, to sue and be sued as an individual under a corporate name, to have a common seal, and to make and repeal bylaws. All corporations derive their legal capacities from State or national constitutions or statutes. Their powers are strictly construed. In issuing charters to private corporations the State usually sets a time limit and reserves the right to modify or repeal the charter. Even without such stipulation, the corporation is subject to the police power and eminent domain. *See* municipal corporation; contract clause.

corporation court. A court in a Virginia city with jurisdiction similar to that of a county court.

corporation tax. A special tax levied on the grant of a charter, the admission of a corporation to the privilege of doing business in another State, the amount of capital stock, the value of a franchise and other intangibles, or on corporate income as distinguished from other forms of income taxes.

corporative state. The systematic organization of the whole social and economic life of a state into a limited number of corporations or estates which have extensive authority over persons and activities within their respective jurisdictions, functionally rather than territorially defined, and are in turn supervised and controlled by state organs.

correction. Activities of judicial and administrative officers for the reformation of young delinquents.

corruption of blood. The legal consequence, under the old common law, of conviction of treason or felony, according to which the person so convicted could neither possess nor transmit by inheritance any property, rank, or title.

corrupt practices act. A statute defining crimes against the purity of elections and prohibiting under penalties the purchase of votes, bribery, personation or the procurement of personation, treating, betting on elections, payment of naturalization fees or taxes by persons other than the voter, excessive campaign expenditures, campaign contributions from corporations, any campaign contribution above a maximum set by law, failure to report campaign expenditures, or other acts tending to bring undue influence upon the electorate.

cosmopolitanism. A philosophy or way of life which tolerates and attempts to understand other ideals and institutions in addition to one's own, and which rejects intense local attachments and narrow patriotism in favor of more general, and even universal, cultural and political values.

cost-plus contract. A government contract which provides for the payment not of a definite sum but of the cost of labor and materials plus a fixed percentage or a fixed fee.

Cotton is king. A Southern slogan in 1861 based on the belief that both the English government and Northern manufacturers would prevent war because of their dependence on cotton.

Cotton States. The Carolinas, Tennessee, Arkansas, Georgia, and the States bordering on the Gulf of Mexico whose politics have in the past often been dominated by cotton-growing interests.

Cotton Whigs. Northern Whigs who supported the Mexican War, the Compromise of 1850, and "our country however bounded." *Compare* Conscience Whigs.

council. 1. A municipal legislature, or its lower house. *See* common council. **2.** An official body created for the purpose of performing or assisting in the performance of work which is essentially administrative in nature. *See* executive council; judicial council; legislative council.

councilman. A member of a city council, originally elected from a single ward, now often with others at large.

council-manager plan. A system of municipal government that originated in Staunton, Va., in 1908 but received its first important application in Dayton, Ohio, in 1913, in which ordinance-making powers and the determination of general policy repose in a small council whose members are sometimes elected by proportional representation. Responsibility for the entire administration of the municipality is usually given to a city manager who is appointed by the council and serves at its pleasure. The plan contemplates that the manager shall be an expert administrator and that he shall be chosen for his demonstrated abilities and without reference to political affiliation or place of residence. Some of the nation's largest cities, including Dallas, San Antonio, and San Diego now operate under the plan, and more than a thousand medium-size cities and smaller communities prefer it to either the mayor-council or commission plans. A few American counties use a similar plan. *Called also* city-manager plan.

Council of Appointment. The governor and four State senators of New York who from 1777 to 1821 appointed State and local officials.

council of censors. A board provided for in the first constitutions of Pennsylvania and Vermont to report on the conduct of government and propose constitutional amendments.

Council of Economic Advisers. Three principal economists who, under the Employment Act of 1946, operate as part of the Executive Office of the President, advising the President on measures for promoting the economic equilibrium of the nation, and whose findings may be incorporated in an economic report which, according to the terms of the same act, the President is directed to prepare and submit annually to Congress.

Council of National Defense. A council created in 1916 to mobilize the country for World War I, which remained in existence between wars, and was reactivated just before World War II. Numerous agencies evolved from it, all but two being units of the Office for Emergency Management. The Council is now inactive.

Council of Revision. A body consisting of the governor, chancellor, and judges of the supreme court of New York which had the power to veto acts of the legislature, 1777–1821.

Council of State Governments. A joint agency, founded in 1925 as the American Legislators' Association, which is maintained by the States as a research center and permanent secretariat for associations of State officials, and which publishes the monthly *State Government* and a biennial *Book of the States*.

counsel. *See* right to counsel.

counselor. A lawyer who gives advice on legal matters and who may be concerned in the preparation of cases and the management of a client's interests before a court.

counselor of embassy. A foreign service officer ranking just below the head of an embassy.

counselor of legation. A foreign service officer ranking just below the head of a legation.

counterfeit. A spurious coin or piece of paper money in imitation of one issued by public authority.

counterpart funds. Funds in the currency of a foreign country which are equal in official exchange value to the dollars which that country has received under the Marshall, and other plans, and from which advances are made to private persons and local units for economic, and other forms of, development. Generally, the funds are managed by treasury officials of the foreign country, subject to the veto of American representatives.

counterrevolution. 1. Organized opposition to a revolutionary political movement on the part of those who wish to preserve the status quo. 2. The reaction which follows a political revolution, reversing the revolutionary trend and producing institutions antithetical in form and spirit to those which the revolution has established.

countervailing duty. An additional duty or surtax levied upon an imported commodity in order to neutralize bounties and other favors granted the producer or exporter of that commodity by the country of origin.

counting board. A board of three or more members which counts the votes cast at an election precinct.

counting out. The illegal rejection of some ballots by a partisan election board in order to secure the election of a fellow partisan.

country. 1. The territory of a nation. 2. The land of birth, citizenship, residence, or origin of a person;—often used interchangeably with "state" or "nation."

county. The most important unit of local government in the United States except in Alaska and Connecticut where it does not exist, and in other New England States where it exists mainly for judicial administration. In Louisiana, the equivalent unit is called a parish. The county is the principal local unit for judicial administration and the enforcement of the criminal law of the State; the assessment and collection of State and local taxes; the selection of polling places, appointment of election officials, and canvassing of votes; the construction and repair of roads and bridges; indoor and outdoor relief and assistance; and often for the administration of schools and libraries. In nearly every State counties are governed by boards, either of supervisors or county commissioners, and by numerous officials, nearly all elective, of whom the most important are the sheriff, prosecuting attorney, coroner, assessor, and recorder.

county agent. A field agent of the U.S. Department of Agriculture, partly supported from State and county funds and stationed in an agricultural county in the United States, who informs farmers and ranchers about improvements in production methods, marketing possibilities, and public agricultural credit and other facilities, and who operates in conjunction with a land-grant college or State university.

county clerk. A popularly-elected county official who supervises registration of voters, prepares ballots, records land titles, mortgages, and liens, issues licenses, and performs miscellaneous other duties.

county commissioner. A member of a board of usually from three to seven members which administers the affairs of a county, determines tax rates, appropriates funds, manages property, and appoints minor officials and employees.

county court. A body formerly composed of all the justices of the peace within a county which was both the chief county administrative board and a court inferior to the circuit court. At present it may have purely administrative, or purely judicial functions, or combinations of both, depending on the laws of particular States.

county manager. The executive head of a few American counties which have been reorganized on the analogy of the council-manager plan for cities, who often lacks supervisory power over the entire administration of the county.

county seat *or* **county site** *or* **county town.** The town or city in a county where the principal offices of the county government are located.

coup d'état. A sudden attempt by a faction or band of conspirators to overthrow an existing government by violence or stratagem.

court. A tribunal which administers justice by enforcing laws, maintaining the legal rights of persons against impairment by government officials and private parties, and adjudicating controversies between individuals. *See* judiciary.

courtesy of the Senate. *See* senatorial courtesy.

court house. The building at the county seat, *q.v.*, which houses the principal offices of county government and provides quarters for courts.

court-martial. A tribunal in one of the armed services composed of officers and enlisted men, which tries armed forces personnel or other persons accused of violating military law. A *general court-martial* of five or more persons, a judge advocate, and a defense counsel may try any offense. *Special* and *summary courts-martial* have limited jurisdiction. In the American armed services, a court-martial verdict may, in some instances, be appealed to the U.S. Court of Military Appeals, which is composed of civilian judges, but not to the civil courts.

court of appeals. A judicial tribunal whose jurisdiction is usually limited to the consideration of points of law in cases already tried and decided by courts of original jurisdiction. In New York, Kentucky and Maryland it is the name of the highest State court. In about one-fourth of the States and in the federal judicial system it is the name of an intermediate court, *q.v. See* United States Courts of Appeals.

court of chancery. A court having jurisdiction in equity cases.

court of claims. A special federal or State court with jurisdiction to hear and decide cases concerning certain carefully defined classes of pecuniary claims against the Government. *See* United States Court of Claims.

court of record. A court which exists independently of the magistrate who presides over it, which keeps a permanent record, which may punish contempt by fine or imprisonment, and to which writs of error or certiorari may be directed. Courts of justices of the peace, and municipal, police, and probate courts are not of record unless so designated by statute.

court-packing plan. A proposal by President F. D. Roosevelt, Feb. 5, 1937, for the appointment of one additional federal judge or justice for each incumbent judge of a lower court or justice of the Supreme Court who failed to retire after reaching the age of seventy; provided that the number of Supreme Court justices at any time should not exceed fifteen. Congress refused to approve the plan.

Court Proctor Act. An act of Congress, Aug. 7, 1939, which created the Administrative Office of the United States Courts, *q.v.*

covenant. A solemn contract between two or more parties.

Covenant of the League of Nations. That part of the Treaty of Versailles, 1919, which formed the constitution of the League of Nations, *q.v.*

Covenant with the People. The introductory portion of the platform of the Progressive party in 1912.

Cowboy President. A nickname of Theodore Roosevelt.

Coxey's Army. A group of unemployed persons led by "General" Jacob S. Coxey which, on May 1, 1894, went to Washington, D.C., to present a "petition-in-boots" to Congress for economic relief.

Coyle v. Smith. A case, 221 U.S. 599 (1911), in which the Supreme Court upheld the power of Oklahoma to change its capital, contrary to a condition imposed by Congress when Oklahoma was admitted to the Union, because the location of the capital was a political question, *q.v.*, for State authorities to determine. *Compare Stearns v. Minnesota.*

Cradle of Liberty. Faneuil Hall in Boston, used as a meeting place for patriots at the beginning of the Revolution.

craft union. A labor union with membership limited to workers in a particular trade or craft. *Compare* industrial union.

Crandall v. Nevada. *See* privileges and immunities clause.

Crawford County system. An early name for the direct primary election; —derived from Crawford County, Pa., where the delegate convention was first abolished by party action.

credentials committee. The committee of a party convention which examines the credentials of delegates, holds hearings when contests occur, and recommends appropriate action.

credibility gap. A phrase applied in 1966 to public skepticism or disillusionment resulting from official estimates that did not prove correct, official denials of reports that afterwards were proved true, and contradictory announcements concerning foreign and domestic policies.

Crédit Mobilier. A Pennsylvania corporation which in 1867 became the instrument by which officials of the Union Pacific Railroad transferred property of the railroad to themselves. Fearing an investigation they attempted in 1872 to bribe members of Congress.

creeping socialism. The suggestion that government construction and maintenance of projects like the Tennessee Valley Authority and others of a kind traditionally reserved for private enterprise are part of a gradual evolution toward a socialistic state;—from an address by former President Hoover.

Creole case. An incident arising from the freeing of slaves on board the American vessel "Creole" by the authorities of the Bahama Islands, where the vessel had been run into port by mutineers while *en voyage* from Virginia to New Orleans. On protest by the United States, Great Britain paid an indemnity to the owners of the slaves.

crime. A serious offense (a felony or a misdemeanor) which violates the law of the state. Minor trespasses and violations of local ordinances are not considered crimes.

Crime against Kansas. A speech by Charles Sumner of Massachusetts in the U.S. Senate, May 19 and 20, 1856, in which he cast reflections on the methods of Southerners in trying to secure the admission of Kansas to the Union under the Lecompton Constitution, *q.v.* After its delivery Representative Brooks of South Carolina assaulted Sumner with a heavy cane.

Crime of '73. A nickname for the act of Congress of Feb. 12, 1873, which discontinued the coinage of silver dollars.

criminal. A person who habitually violates the law and who suffers punishment as a consequence after trial and conviction; *also:* a person who commits an offense punishable by death or imprisonment.

Criminal Appeals Act. An act of Congress, Mar. 2, 1907, which allows the United States to appeal to the Supreme Court in a criminal case when a lower court, without having placed the defendant in jeopardy, has held that a federal statute is unconstitutional.

criminal case. A case prosecuted on behalf of the state against an individual accused of violating the law.

criminal identification. The recording of significant physical characteristics of individual criminals, especially fingerprints, for rapid and permanent identification.

criminal law. The branch of jurisprudence which deals with offenses committed against the safety and order of the state.

criminal syndicalism. The advocacy of sabotage, violence, terrorism, or other unlawful methods for revolutionary purposes. Statutes imposing severe penalties for such advocacy, directed mainly against the Industrial Workers of the World, but enforced against Communists and others, were enacted in most States between 1917 and 1920.

crisis government. The temporary substitution of an emergency governmental device or process for the normal constitutional processes. The substitution may involve a violation of the written constitution, such as the unwarranted interpretations given Article 48 of the Weimar Constitution both by Hitler and by certain of the Chancellors who preceded him in the German government; or it may involve processes which, under certain conditions, are regarded as consistent with the written constitution, as martial law, a state of siege, or extensive delegations of discretionary power to the executive. The classic illustration of crisis government is the constitutional dictator of the ancient Roman republic.

critical material. A material essential to national defense, the procurement of which in wartime poses a less difficult problem than that of a strategic material, *q.v.*, either because it is less essential, or is obtainable in more adequate quantities from domestic sources.

Critical Period. The period between the close of the Revolutionary War and the adoption of the Constitution.

Crittenden Compromise. A proposal of Senator John J. Crittenden of Kentucky, 1860–61, to restore the Missouri Compromise line, allow new States to decide the question of slavery for themselves, maintain interstate commerce in slaves, and provide federal compensation to owners of slaves freed by violence.

cross-filing. The procedure by which a person may become a candidate for nomination to an office in the primary elections of more than one party.

Cross-of-Gold Speech. An address by William Jennings Bryan at the Democratic national convention at Chicago, July 9, 1896, which ended with the words: "You shall not crucify mankind upon a cross of gold" [the gold standard].

cross-voting. The act of voting for candidates of more than one party, equivalent to splitting one's ticket.

cruel and unusual punishment. An inhumane punishment, as torture, lingering death, or breaking on the wheel; *also:* any punishment which is disproportionate to the offense, or which outrages the sensibilities of the community. Death by electrocution, unusual when introduced, is not within the category prohibited by federal and State constitutions; nor is a second attempt at electrocution following a mechanical failure at the first attempt. *See Louisiana* ex rel. *Francis* v. *Resweber.*

Cuba. A republic in the West Indies whose freedom from Spain was secured with the aid of the United States by the Treaty of Paris, Dec. 10, 1898. Following a period of American occupation, Cuba was set up as an independent republic in 1902, although under the Platt Amendment, *q.v.*, which Cuba was required to attach to its constitution, the United States reserved the right to intervene in Cuban domestic affairs to maintain order. The United States relinquished this right by treaty May 29, 1934. Though challenged repeatedly by the Communist government of Premier Fidel Castro after 1960, the United States has retained a naval and air base at Guantánamo Bay under a nominal rental.

Cuba missile confrontation. An international diplomatic crisis in 1962 in which the principal events were: secret construction by Russian engineers of emplacements for launching intermediate ballistic missiles, materials for which Russia had sent to Cuba; photographing of the emplacements by U.S. reconnaissance flyers; the announcement by President Kennedy, Oct. 22, 1962, that ships approaching Cuba would be stopped and inspected in order to prevent further landing of such material in Cuba; support of the United States' policy by other Latin American nations, Uruguay alone abstaining; reversal of course by some Russian ships en route to Cuba; and finally an agreement whereby Russia promised to withdraw its missiles from Cuba under U.S. aerial inspection, and allow on-site inspection in Cuba, and the United States promised to discontinue reconnaissance over Cuba and to refrain from invading Cuba. The Cuban government refused to allow on-site inspection, and so aerial reconnaissance was resumed.

Cumberland Road. A national highway projected and partly completed between Cumberland, Md., and the West, for which Congress appropriated $6,821,246 between 1806 and 1822.

Cummings v. Missouri. See test oath.

cumulative voting. A system of minority representation which has been used since 1870 for the election of members of the lower house of the Illinois legislature. Each voter has three votes which he may plump on one candidate or distribute among two or three candidates as he chooses.

curative statute. A law, retrospective in effect, which is designed to remedy some legal defect in previous transactions and validate them.

currency. 1. Any medium of exchange which is received everywhere throughout a country, whether it be coin or paper or,

For State Senator, 28th District,
JOSEPH W. FIFER.

For Representative, 28th District,
THOMAS F. MITCHELL, 1½ votes.

GEORGE B. OKESON, 1½ votes.

For States Attorney,
ROBERT B. PORTER.

Cumulative Voting—Part of Republican ballot in Illinois, 1880

sometimes, only paper money. The currency of the United States in circulation consists principally of federal reserve notes, *q.v.*, and subsidiary coins of silver and base metals. In addition there are smaller amounts of silver certificates, national bank notes, federal reserve bank notes, and treasury notes, issued under various laws, all of which are being retired from circulation. In 1933, gold coins and gold certificates were called in by the Treasury, and no silver dollars have been coined since 1935. The issuance of currency is a function of the federal government. The States are forbidden to issue bills of credit. 2. The proceeds of bank loans subject to withdrawal by check which, until retired, constitute an addition to the regular currency and a substantial part of the nation's money supply; *called also* deposit or check currency.

current expenses. Ordinary or regularly recurring expenses.

current tax payment. The payment of income taxes by deductions from salaries and wages on the payment dates; *also:* the payment in quarterly installments of an estimated tax on income derived from other sources.

custody. 1. The placing under guard of accused persons awaiting trial, or material witnesses whose testimony is wanted in the trial of a criminal case. **2.** The temporary guarding of valuable articles by the police. **3.** Authority to act in the capacity of guardian over minors.

customary law. Law derived from long-established usages and customs; —distinguished from written law.

customhouse. A public establishment for the inspection and assessment of duties on merchandise imported from other countries.

customs. Taxes levied on imported goods at the time they enter a country.

Customs. *See* Bureau of Customs.

customs and patent appeals. *See* United States Court of Customs and Patent Appeals.

Customs Court. *See* United States Customs Court.

customs union. An agreement between two or more nations to abolish tariffs and other restrictions on trade between them and to adopt a common commercial policy toward other nations.

C.W.A. Civil Works Administration.

czar. 1. The former absolute monarch of Russia. **2.** A nickname of Thomas Brackett Reed, whose rulings as Speaker of the House of Representatives, 1889–91 and 1895–99, greatly limited the powers previously enjoyed by the minority.

D.A. district attorney.

damages. Compensation, usually in money, awarded in a court of law for an injury inflicted upon person or property by another's wrongful action or failure to act.

Danbury Hatters' case. A case, *Loewe v. Lawlor*, 208 U.S. 274 (1908), in which the Supreme Court held that a nation-wide boycott instituted by employees against the products of an employer was in restraint of trade under the Sherman Antitrust Act. The ruling of this decision was nullified by the Clayton Act, *q.v.*, (1914) which exempted labor unions from the operation of the Sherman Act.

Daniel Ball, The. A case, 10 Wall. 557 (1871), in which the Supreme Court declared that navigable waters of the United States included all rivers and other natural waterways which are navigable in fact and which are used, or are susceptible of being used, as highways of interstate and foreign commerce.

Danite. An administration (Buchanan) Democrat who opposed Douglas in the Illinois senatorial campaign of 1858.

dark horse. A man who is unexpectedly nominated after a long course of futile balloting has resulted in a deadlock among the leading avowed candidates. Among presidential dark horses were Polk, Pierce, Garfield, and Harding.

Dartmouth College case. *Dartmouth College* v. *Woodward*, 4 Wheat. 518 (1819), in which the Supreme Court decided that an act of the New Hampshire legislature altering the charter of Dartmouth College without its consent was in violation of the clause of the U.S. Constitution forbidding a State to impair the obligation of a contract; a decision afterwards applied in favor of nonacademic (business) interests. Later the Court ruled that corporation charters must be strictly construed, and not in opposition to the public interest. *See Charles River Bridge* v. *Warren Bridge.*

Davis-Wade Manifesto. A paper issued by Representative Henry Winter Davis and Senator Benjamin F. Wade impugning President Lincoln's motives in failing to sign a bill for the reconstruction of seceded States in July, 1864.

Dawes Act. *See* Indian.

Dawes plan. A comprehensive plan, prepared by a committee of American and European experts headed by Charles G. Dawes, which fixed the total of German reparations payments to the Allied and Associated Powers of World War I and indicated the methods by which such payments were to be made. The plan was accepted and placed in operation, Sept. 1, 1924, but was later superseded by the Young plan, *q.v.*

day in court. The opportunity afforded a person to seek relief from injustice or to defend his rights in a competent judicial tribunal.

D.C. District of Columbia.

dead-letter office. A depository maintained by the U.S. Post Office Department which receives all undeliverable letters and valuable parcels to be disposed of according to law.

deadlock. The refusal of parties engaged in a controversy (as the two houses of a legislature, the executive and the legislature, the supporters of rival candidates in a party convention, or states engaged in diplomatic negotiations) to make any further concessions or compromises.

deal. A secret bargain or understanding among politicians for the exchange of influence, support, appointment to public office, or other advantage not in the public interest.

death penalty. *See* capital punishment.

death-sentence clause. A nickname for a provision in the federal Public Utility Holding Company bill of 1935, as first drafted, which would have outlawed public utility holding companies. As enacted, the law authorized the dissolution by legal proceedings of all but single integrated holding companies.

debasement. The practice of reducing the weight of gold and silver coins of standard value or of increasing the amount of alloy in such coins.

[1] **debate.** The examination, by means of argumentation and discussion, of

any measure and the resolution of attendant issues in a legislative assembly or other public deliberative body. Legislative rules are designed to secure adequate opportunity for discussion, and equal time is usually given to those for and against the measure. Nevertheless, to expedite discussion and reach a decision, most contemporary legislatures have had to limit the time of participants and the total time allotted for discussion by means of closure rules and similar regulations.

² debate. *See* freedom of debate.

Debs, In re. A case, 158 U.S. 564 (1895), in which the Supreme Court declared that the federal government has authority to protect its interests in the mails and the flow of interstate commerce and that such authority includes the discretionary power of its officers to secure injunctive relief from the courts.

debt limit. 1. The maximum amount fixed by Congress from time to time beyond which the Secretary of the Treasury may not raise the public debt by borrowing even though existing statutes may authorize him to borrow. **2.** The maximum amount of indebtedness fixed by a State constitution which a legislature may authorize and which may be either an absolute figure or a certain percentage of the assessed valuation of taxable property. The borrowing power of a municipality may be limited in a similar manner by its charter or by law.

debt service. The allocation of funds in the annual budget or appropriation bills for the payment of legally required sums into a sinking fund, for the immediate amortization of such portions of the outstanding indebtedness as policy or the law may require, and for the payment of interest on outstanding debt.

decentralization. Division or dispersion of powers previously centralized in one place or under a single authority.

decision. The determination of a legal controversy or issue upon the law and facts involved by a judicial or similar tribunal.

declaration. 1. A document formally proclaiming the principles and aims of some public body and recommending, approving, or adopting a specific program of action. **2.** An inventory of personal effects, currency, and merchandise in the possession of travelers crossing frontiers, often required in the administration of customs and frontier regulations.

Declaration of Havana. A statement by a meeting of foreign ministers of American states at Havana, Cuba, July, 1940, that "any attempt on the part of a non-American state against the integrity or the inviolability of the territory, the sovereignty, or the political independence of an American state should be considered an act of aggression against the states which sign this declaration." The effect was to declare hemispheric support for what the United States had tried to accomplish under the Monroe Doctrine, *q.v.*

Declaration of Honolulu. Statements issued jointly by South Vietnam and the United States, Feb. 8, 1966, affirming their intention to resist Communist revolution and aggression, eradicate social injustice, hunger, ignorance, and disease, establish a viable economy, build a true democracy, and press for peace in Vietnam "in every forum." *See* Vietnam War; *compare* Manila Summit Conference.

Declaration of Independence. A document drafted by a committee consisting of Thomas Jefferson, John Adams, Benjamin Franklin, Roger Sherman, and Robert R. Livingston in response to a resolution presented in the second Continental Congress, June 7, 1776. The draft, which was almost wholly the work of Jefferson, was reported from committee on June 28, and was adopted July 4, 1776. It consists of an enumeration of tyrannical acts by the King and Parliament of Great Britain, a justification for resistance to these acts on the basis of theories of natural rights and governmental contract, and a declaration that the colonies "are, and of Right ought to be, Free and Independent States; that they are Absolved from all Allegiance to the British Crown, and that all political connection between them and the State of Great Britain is, and ought to be, totally dissolved." Though the Declaration forms no part of the law of the land, the sentiments expressed in it of natural liberty, inalienable rights, and self-government have continued to exert a profound influence on American political thinking.

Declaration of Interdependence. A phrase in an address delivered by President John F. Kennedy at Philadelphia, July 4, 1962, in which he emphasized the desirability of a partnership between an eventually united Europe and the United States, describing such a partnership as the keystone of "an eventual union of all free men."

Declaration of Lima. A statement by the Eighth Inter-American Conference at Lima, Peru, 1938, which reaffirmed the principle of hemispheric solidarity and the sovereignty of American republics against all foreign intervention or activity that might threaten them.

Declaration of London. A code of rules on naval warfare signed in London, Feb. 26, 1909, by representatives of the United States, Japan, and the chief European states, but not ratified by any of them. The code nevertheless influenced the conduct of belligerents in both World Wars.

Declaration of Paris. An agreement concluded by European powers in 1856, and since accepted by most states, that privateering "is and remains" abolished; that enemy goods on neutral ships and neutral goods on enemy ships (except contraband) are exempt from seizure; and that a blockade must be effective to be binding.

Declaration of the Presidents of America. The official statement of an "action program" released at the conference of heads of state and of government of 20 Western Hemisphere countries at Punta del Este, Uruguay, April 13, 1967, the principal feature of which is a plan to create, after 1970, a Latin American common market with which would eventually be integrated the existing Latin American Free Trade Association and the Central American Common Market, and which the United States promised to encourage with appropriate commercial policies and economic assistance.

declaration of war. A formal declaration by a belligerent state which has the effect of bringing into execution many statutes previously passed to govern conditions in time of war and of canceling or modifying the effect of certain other statutes. Some countries, in order to avoid the legal disadvantages of formal belligerency (as arms embargoes), have dispensed with a declaration of war altogether. In the United States only Congress may declare war.

declaratory judgment. A judicial declaration in an actual controversy of the existing rights of parties under a statute, contract, will, or other document, without executory process granting relief, but binding upon the parties. It is not necessary to show that any wrong has been done, as in action for damages; or that any is immediately threatened, as in injunction proceedings. In most States and territories, and in federal courts since 1934, this remedy has been made available by statute as a means of ascertaining the rights of parties without expensive litigation, though the courts tend to construe these statutes narrowly.

declaratory statute. A statute designed to remove doubts as to the meaning of the law on some particular subject.

dedication. A donation of property for public use (as for a street or sidewalk) which precludes the owner from ever claiming it again as his private property.

de facto. 1. Actually: in fact. **2.** Pertaining to a condition of affairs actually existing. *Compare de jure.*

de facto segregation. Separation of people of different races resulting from social or economic causes rather than legal discrimination. In order to alleviate effects of de facto segregation in schools, educational authorities in some Northern cities have redrawn district lines and have provided for the transportation of children to schools in neighborhoods other than those in which they reside.

Defender of the Constitution. A nickname of Daniel Webster.

defense. *See* national defense; Department of Defense.

deficiency supply bill. An appropriation bill to provide additional funds for agencies during the current fiscal year, or for urgent projects authorized by law after the budget has been submitted. *Compare* supplemental appropriation.

deficit. The difference between income (revenue) and expenditure when expenditure is greater.

deficit financing. Stationary or increased appropriations in the face of a sharp decline in public revenues; characteristic especially of the 1930's when certain economists successfully urged that the Government should borrow for public works to speed up general economic activity, claiming that the burden of added debt would be more than offset by the resulting rise in national income. In recent years deficit financing and resulting inflation have been recommended by some economists as instruments of fiscal policy.

deflation. A fall in prices; *specifically:* an increase in the value of the unit of a currency in terms of the commodities it will purchase or in terms of its exchange value with units of other currencies in an uncontrolled or unregulated international money market with a resulting decline in demand, and hence in production, usually producing significant unemployment.

degressive tax. A tax levied at a uniform rate on wealth or income at or above a certain (high) level, and at successively decreasing rates on amounts within lower tax brackets.

de jure. 1. By right: according to law. 2. Pertaining to a situation which is based on law, or right, or previous action. *Compare* de facto.

delegate. 1. One who is selected by a constituency and authorized to act for it at a party or State constitutional convention. 2. A representative of a territory who has the right to speak but not to vote in the House of Representatives. 3. A member of the lower house of the legislature, as in Maryland, Virginia, and West Virginia.

delegated legislation. General rules having the validity of law (as in making detailed regulations to fit specific circumstances), formulated and put into effect by an agency which has been authorized by the legislature to act for it.

delegation. 1. The body of delegates from a State to a national nominating convention or from a county to a State or other party convention. Each delegation elects its chairman who is required to poll the delegates before announcing their votes. 2. All the members of Congress from a particular State. 3. Authorization by a superior to an inferior officer to exercise powers which are normally exerted by the superior officer. *See* delegation of powers.

delegation of powers. The transfer of authority by some organ or branch of government in which such authority is vested to some other organ or branch or to administrative agencies. Relying on the principle of *delegata potestas non potest delegari,* the courts have consistently denied that Congress can delegate legislative power; but increasingly they have upheld statutes in which Congress has outlined broad policies or fixed certain limits of action, leaving to administrative officers or boards a large rule-making authority. *See Field* v. *Clark; Schechter Poultry Corp.* v. *United States.*

De Lima v. *Bidwell. See* Insular cases.

delinquency. 1. Minor infraction of the law or neglect to perform specific obligations established by law. 2. Vicious or criminal conduct or ungovernable character on the part of a child.

delinquent taxes. Taxes unpaid after the stated date for collection. The taxpayer may suffer monetary or other penalties for delinquency, and in cases of long neglect to pay taxes on property, the property may be sold at auction or may revert to the state through foreclosure proceedings.

demagogue. A politician who lacks moral scruple and who attempts to gain popular favor by flattery, false promises, and appeals to the prejudices or passions of the mob.

demilitarization. The proscription of military activity within a designated area, involving usually the removal of all garrisons, armament, and military equipment and the razing of existing fortifications.

demobilization. The wholesale reduction of a nation's military establishment following a war or other national emergency, effected chiefly by discharging conscripts and reservists from active service. The sudden return to civilian life of millions of discharged servicemen may disturb the national economy, already seriously dislocated by the sudden stoppage of wartime demands.

democracy. Rule by the people. In practice this means that power to determine the major issues of public policy must reside in the bulk or majority of the community and that in the making of such decisions, the vote of each individual shall count for one and none for more than one. Hence democracy may be described as government by consent and political equality. The people exercise power either directly (as in referendums or town meetings), or indirectly through representative institutions in which the popular role is confined to using the ballot to enforce responsibility upon those to whom authority is entrusted. Since political democracy is based on the concept of equality, the term is often extended to cover institutions necessary to the preservation of the substance of such equality. Thus in a democratic system elections must be held with reasonable frequency and regularity, the ballot must be secret, and the individual must be secure against arbitrary arrest. Likewise there must be freedom of speech, of the press, of assembly, and of petition, as well as equality before the law. Democracy in its political sense seems to have come into modern usage in connection with a broad social ideal of which democratic government formed only a part. This broadened concept is apparent in the Puritan Revolution, and in the French revolutionary slogan of "Liberty, Equality, and Fraternity." The relative stress placed on each of these terms, and especially on the first two, has varied from time to time. As long as the major threat to both liberty and equality was to be found in the autocratic state and a feudal social system, the potential conflict between the ideals of liberty and equality did not become evident. When these elements had been swept away, however, it appeared that some of the reformers were more interested in individual liberty than in equality, and others in the reverse. The fact emerged that complete liberty of the individual permits the development of serious inequalities of wealth and power, and that complete equality of political power is likely to result in action inimical to individual liberty, while economic equality can be achieved only at the expense of the liberty of the individual in certain respects. This conflict was somewhat mitigated by the interpretation of political democracy to include the protection of certain minority rights. It is through an interpretation of the third of the basic concepts, fraternity, that a reconciliation is best achieved, because it contains within it both the notion of equality and that of liberty, and because rights are protections against invasions of liberty. "Equality of opportunity" and "equality of consideration" are other phrases used to convey the same idea. The basic notion is that each individual is an end in himself, and that as such he is entitled to a certain presumption of equality with other human beings. Logically then, if not historically, the demand for equality of political power is based upon the conviction that in practice this is essential to equality of consideration in the long run; that without such equality, the "essential dignity of man" suffers. Social democracy entails the denial of all special privileges, political or social, not based upon merit and provides equal access to all forms of public accommodation and recreation without regard to irrational bases of discrimination like color or national origin. Those who lay their major emphasis upon the equalitarian aspect of democracy frequently insist that it involves a substantial degree of economic equality, and apply the term "economic democracy" to this ideal. This phrase implies public efforts to establish minimal educational opportunities for the entire population and advancement to all who can qualify.

Democratic party. A major party which traces its origin from the Republican party of Jefferson, but which may be said to have arisen from the personal following of Jackson in the campaign of 1824 and the Democratic-Republican party of 1828. In that period it stood for frontier democracy, equality, the abolition of special privileges, and the discontinuance of centralizing and loose-construction tendencies. It won all but two presidential elections before 1860. During the slavery controversy it gained strength in the South but alienated Northern support. In 1860 it split into Northern and Southern Democratic parties. During the Civil War period it lost the support of War Democrats, who were only in part replaced later by the adherence of Liberal Republicans; but it became the "white man's party" in the South where it soon disposed of Negro and carpetbag opposition. It has been rather more inclined than the Republicans to favor the common man, and less disposed toward the promotion of private enterprise. It opposed imperialism, a completely centralized banking system, and, until 1928, high protective tariffs. On the currency question it has been divided between advocacy of cheap and sound money. It won the elections of 1884, 1892, 1912, 1916, 1948 and 1960 by close votes, and those from 1932 to 1944 inclusive and 1964 by large majorities. In and out of power it has been hampered by conflicts among its Southern, Northern urban, and Western agrarian supporters.

Democratic-Republican party. 1. The Republican party of the Jeffersonian period. 2. The party which supported Jackson in the election of 1828. 3. For many years the official title of the Democratic party.

democratic societies. Organizations widely established in America, 1793–94, which expressed sympathy for the French Revolution, criticized Washington's foreign policy, and agitated for a wider suffrage.

Democratic Study Group. The caucus of liberal Democrats in Congress.

demonetization. Withdrawal of a metal from use as money, thus depriving it of a standard or legal value and making it a commodity.

Demonstration Cities Act. An act of Congress, 1966, authorizing expenditures of $1.3 billion for 80 per cent of the cost of renewing core areas and constructing mass transit, sewerage, and water-supply facilities in 60 or more cities which were expected to participate in the program.

Dennis v. United States. A case, 341 U.S. 494 (1951), in which the Supreme Court upheld the conviction of eleven leaders of the American Communist party under the Smith Act's, *q.v.*, prohibition of willfully advocating and teaching overthrow of the government of the United States by force and violence. Relying on Judge Learned Hand's interpretation of Justice Holmes' "clear-and-present-danger" rule, whether the "gravity of the evil, discounted by its improbability, justifies such invasion of free speech as is necessary to avoid the danger," the Court decided that the danger here justified the modification of the freedom of speech guaranteed by the First Amendment.

denunciation. The act of giving notice of the termination of a treaty. The right of one party to terminate a treaty is usually defined in the treaty itself although, in international law, such a right is sometimes asserted in the principle of *rebus sic stantibus, q.v.* Congress may fail to pass legislation to enforce a treaty municipally or pass legislation which contradicts the terms of a treaty. The treaty, however, is still binding internationally unless formally denounced. The power to denounce a treaty resides constitutionally in the President alone or in the President and the Senate.

department. 1. One of the three great branches (as legislative, executive, and judicial) into which governmental authority is divided. 2. One of the major administrative divisions of the federal government usually headed by an officer of cabinet rank. Other large administrative units, as the three subdivisions of the Department of Defense (Air Force, Army, and Navy), have been officially designated as departments, but their heads are not of cabinet rank. 3. The most important administrative subdivision of a State or municipal government. 4. *In France:* a territorial division presided over by a prefect.

Department of Agriculture. A department of the federal government, created May 15, 1862, enlarged and given cabinet rank, Feb. 9, 1889, which conducts research in the management of soils, the production, industrial use, and marketing of farm animals and crops, human nutrition, and home economics, and makes results available through publications and extension work in cooperation with the States. It fixes commodity standards, inspects meat and poultry, seeks to eradicate plant and animal diseases, administers the nation's forests, enforces many regulatory acts to protect farmers and consumers and to improve the economic position of farmers and ranchers, makes loans to farmers when credit is not available from private or other public sources, and tries to improve the standards and conditions of rural living. 2. An administrative unit in many States which independently, or in cooperation with the federal Department of Agriculture, engages in research and dissemination of information, promotes the welfare of farmers, and enforces laws enacted under the State police power to compel the observance of sanitary regulations, to eradicate plant and animal diseases, and to maintain marketing standards.

Department of Commerce. A department of the federal government, created Mar. 4, 1913, as part successor to the Department of Commerce and Labor which was created Feb. 14, 1903, whose purpose is to promote the commerce and industry of the United States. Its principal divisions are the Maritime Administration, the Business and Defense Service Administration, the Coast and Geodetic Survey, the Patent Office, the Offices of International Commerce, Business Economics, and Foreign Commercial Services, the Weather Bureau, and the Bureaus of the Census and of Standards. Departments or other units with similar objectives are maintained by State governments.

Department of Defense. A department of the federal government, successor to the National Military Establishment, created in 1949, which includes the Departments of the Army, the Navy, and the Air Force, *qq.v.*, the Joint Chiefs of Staff, the Joint Staff, and other staff offices responsible for research and engineering, weapons systems evaluation, installations and logistics, supplies, international security affairs, personnel and manpower, communications, intelligence, together with institutions for advanced training. The Secretary of Defense is of cabinet rank, responsible directly to the President, and is authorized to direct and control, but not to merge, the three military departments and to hold responsible the commanders of unified and specified commands for the accomplishment of their missions.

Department of Health, Education, and Welfare. A cabinet department, created 1953, which supervises a miscellany of services including the Public Health Service, the Office of Education, the Social Security Administration, the Food and Drug Administration, the Vocational Rehabilitation Administration, and Saint Elizabeths Hospital. The department's budget is one of the largest in the Government outside the military establishment. The federal government's interest in education, health research, and the fostering of civil rights has expanded the department's significance;— often abbreviated HEW.

Department of Housing and Urban Development. A cabinet level department, created Sept. 9, 1965, which assumes responsibility for coordinating the functions of the Housing and Home Finance Agency, the Federal Housing Administration (a relatively autonomous unit), the Public Housing Administration, and the Federal National Mortgage Association. The department contains a unit for "urban program coordination" which is concerned with programs of community development;—often abbreviated HUD.

Department of Justice. The legal department of the federal government, created by a law of June 22, 1870, expanding the office of the Attorney General, *q.v.*, which furnishes legal advice and opinions to the President and heads of other federal departments and represents the Government in legal matters concerning taxes, lands, monopolies and trusts, immigration and naturalization, civil rights, internal security, and other civil and criminal proceedings. The Department directs and supervises the work of the Federal Bureau of Investigation, the U.S. Marshals and District Attorneys, the federal penal institutions, the Pardon Attorney and the Parole Board and conducts all suits in the Supreme Court in which the United States is a party.

Department of Labor. A department of the federal government created in 1913 primarily in order to introduce a representative of organized labor into the President's cabinet, and consisting of the bureaus of Labor Statistics, Labor Standards, Apprenticeship and Training, Employees' Compensation, Employment Security, International Labor Affairs, and the Women's Bureau; the Labor-Management Services Administration; the Wage and Hour and Public Contracts divisions; the Office of Manpower, Automation, and Training; the Employees' Compensation Appeals Board; and the Neighborhood Youth Corps.

Department of State. 1. A department of the federal government, created as the Department of Foreign Affairs, July 27, 1789, and given its present title and some duties of a domestic character on Sept. 15, 1789, which advises the President in determining foreign policy, supervises the Foreign Service, conducts negotiations with foreign governments, promotes friendly relations with other countries in trade, international development, and cultural exchanges, and issues passports and visas. There are bureaus on African, European, Inter-American, Far Eastern, and Near Eastern and South Asian affairs. Other offices conduct foreign intelligence research, foreign information services, and relations with the United Nations, NATO, and other international organizations. The Department is now almost exclusively concerned with foreign affairs. The influence of its head, the Secretary of State, varies widely under different Presidents. **2.** A department of State government which has the custody of the State seal and control of other functions, usually including the administration of election laws, the issuance of charters to corporations, and the admission of corporations chartered in other States.

Department of the Air Force. A security department within the Department of Defense, created under the National Security Act of 1947 (as amended in 1949), which exercises administrative responsibility for the U.S. Air Force under the Secretary of the Air Force, who is without cabinet rank and who is subordinate in most matters to the Secretary of Defense.

Department of the Army. A security department within the National Military Establishment during 1947–49 and the Department of Defense since 1949, succeeding to most of the functions of the Department of War (first created August 7, 1789), which controls the organization, training, and equipment of the land forces, and develops weapons, tactics, and techniques for combat and service forces and civil defense. It is responsible for the construction, maintenance, and care of the Panama Canal; for river, harbor, flood control, hydroelectric power, and shore protection installations; and for issuing permits for the construction of piers, dams, bridges, and other works which may affect navigation.

Department of the Interior. A department of the federal government, created Mar. 3, 1849, which is the custodian of the nation's natural resources, as public lands, minerals, oil and gas, water, hydroelectric power, fisheries and wild life, national parks, and scenic and historic sites. It provides services for Indians, most of whom live on reservations, and for residents of the territories and of the Trust Territory of the Pacific Islands. Its principal divisions are power administrations, the Geological Survey, the National Park Service, the Office of Territories, and the Bureaus of Mines, Indian Affairs, Land Management, Reclamation, and Territories.

Department of the Navy. A security department of the federal government created by act of Congress, Apr. 30, 1798, to administer the Navy and the Marine Corps, part of the National Military Establishment during 1947–49, and since 1949 a part of the Department of

Defense. The Secretary of the Navy, formerly of cabinet rank, is now subordinate to the Secretary of Defense.

Department of the Treasury. A department of the federal government, created Sept. 2, 1789, which superintends and manages national finances and is especially charged with improvement of public revenues and public credit. It analyzes taxing policies, collects customs duties and internal revenue taxes, is responsible for borrowing, paying off, and refunding long- and short-term debts, continually studies the flow of funds into and out of the United States and the effects of international lending, enforces export controls, registers and licenses vessels engaged in foreign and domestic commerce, administers the narcotics laws, coins money, prints paper money and postage and other stamps, suppresses counterfeiting and violations of the revenue laws, investigates thefts of government property, and, through its Secret Service Division, protects the person of the President.

Department of Transportation. A department of the federal government, created Oct. 15, 1966, to which were transferred the Federal Aviation Administration (formerly independent); the Bureau of Public Roads and other units concerned with transportation (except the Maritime Administration) from the Department of Commerce; the Coast Guard (in time of peace) from the Treasury Department; the safety functions of the Civil Aeronautics Board and the Interstate Commerce Commission whose other regulatory functions were left intact; and the newly created National Transportation Safety Board. The Secretary of the Department is responsible for developing a coordinated national transportation system.

Department of War. *See* Department of the Army.

dependency. An outlying possession subject to the sovereignty of a state but not incorporated into it. *Compare* incorporation 2.

deportation. Forcible removal of an alien to his country of origin, resorted to in the United States in the case of aliens who enter illegally, or commit a serious crime or engage in subversive activities.

Deportation Act. An act of Congress, May, 10, 1920, which provided for the deportation of aliens found guilty of seditious conspiracy and the violation of any of several security acts of the United States.

depositary. A treasury, bank, or vault where public monies are deposited and records are stored for safekeeping.

deposit bank. A State bank in which federal funds were deposited after having been withdrawn from the Bank of the United States on President Jackson's orders (1833).

deposition. Testimony taken on oath in writing outside the courtroom to be used as evidence. The deponent may be cross-examined by the adverse party.

depressed area. Any defined area in which economic activity and employment are at a noticeably lower level than elsewhere and which, therefore, may be considered eligible for assistance under legislation to combat poverty and blight.

depression. One of the several phases of the business cycle, marked by deflation, business stagnation, low prices, and mass unemployment.

deputy. 1. Any person commissioned to represent another or to act in his behalf, the scope of such representation being either comprehensive and embracing all the principal's interests, or limited to specified interests. **2.** A person who acts either as the agent or substitute for a public official (as deputy prime minister, deputy sheriff). **3.** A member of the lower house of the legislature in some European countries.

deputy sheriff. An assistant appointed by a sheriff who serves writs, aids in law enforcement, and in some States may act in place of a sheriff.

desegregation. Any effort to overcome racial separation or imbalance in schools, housing, and places of accommodation, amusement, and employment, including efforts to repeal legislation which enforces separation of races and to discourage racial discrimination by individuals and private organizations.

Deseret. A provisional territory, organized by Mormons (members of the Church of Jesus Christ of Latter-Day Saints) in 1849, which included all the Mexican cession between the Rockies and the Sierra Nevada range. A petition to Congress for recognition as a State was disregarded, and Utah Territory was created in 1850.

desertion. 1. Abandonment of duty in any of the armed services without leave and without intention of returning. **2.** Abandonment of one of the partners in marriage by the other without prior arrangement for the discharge of responsibilities, such as financial support or the care of the home and children.

Des Moines plan. A commission form of city government originating in Des Moines, Iowa, in 1907 which provided for nonpartisan nominations, the initiative and referendum, and the merit system in appointments. *See* commission plan.

despotism. A political system in which the power to govern is concentrated in a ruler whose authority is uncontrolled by customary or formal constitutional limitations.

Destroyer deal. An executive agreement, September, 1940, between President F. D. Roosevelt and the British government under the terms of which the United States exchanged fifty overage destroyers in return for ninety-nine-year leases of several sites on British island and continental territory in the western Atlantic to be developed into American naval and air bases.

Destroyer Deal—Bases secured from Great Britain

detente. Relaxation of military and diplomatic international tensions.

detention. *See* house of detention.

deterrence. A strategic concept which emphasizes superiority in armament as the best security against aggression;—applied especially to contemporary nuclear armament because its destructive capabilities deny the aggressor a quick and easy victory and make aggression unprofitable.

devaluation. 1. Reduction in the gold or silver content of the basic monetary unit. 2. The repeal of an existing privilege of converting paper money into metallic currency of a standard weight and fineness or the equivalent in uncoined metal. The American dollar was devaluated, Jan. 31, 1934, from 23.22 grains to about 15.24 grains nine-tenths fine, or to 59.06 per cent of its former value in gold. 3. The reduction of the value of one country's currency in relation to another's. 4. Fixing the legal value of a currency at a lower level.

Development Loan Fund. A fund established by Congress in 1957 from which loans may be made on liberal terms to foreign countries which are unable to borrow from private investors, from the World Bank, or from the Export-Import Bank; administered after 1961 by the Agency for International Development, *q.v.*

devolution. Allocation or delegation of powers by a central governmental authority to several local or regional authorities or to functional groups.

D.F.C. Distinguished Flying Cross.

dictatorship. 1. Absolute power vested in one or two persons (as in ancient Rome) for a strictly limited period during a crisis. 2. Absolute power over a state granted to, or seized by, a leader without effective constitutional limitation.

diehard. One who is unwilling to compromise: an irreconcilable.

Dies Committee. *See* Un-American Activities Committee.

differential duty. A duty, roughly equivalent to the difference between the market value of an imported article in the country of origin and its cost to an importer, which is added to the normal duty on such an article, and which is designed to discourage dumping or to overcome advantages accruing to an exporter because his country has devaluated its currency.

dilatory motion. A parliamentary motion made for the purpose of delaying action on a legislative proposal, disrupting the time schedule of the majority party, and forcing it to make concessions to the minority.

Dillon Round. Tariff negotiations conducted under the General Agreement on Tariffs and Trade which culminated, Jan. 16, 1962, in an agreement between the United States and the European Economic Community for a partly reciprocal reduction of duties on certain manufactured goods and a guarantee of continued entry, duty free, of about two-thirds of American farm exports. American negotiators were headed by C. Douglas Dillon, Secretary of the Treasury. *See* Kennedy Round.

Dillon's Rule. The judicial principle enunciated by Judge John F. Dillon of the Iowa supreme court in 1868 to the effect that municipal corporations possess only powers expressly granted by charter or law and implied from, or incident to, the expressly granted powers necessary to accomplish the declared purpose of the municipal corporation. It was afterwards adopted by the courts of all the States.

Dingley Act. A high protective tariff law, July 24, 1897, named for Nelson Dingley, of Maine, chairman of the House Committee on Ways and Means.

diplomacy. The art and practice of conducting negotiations between sovereign states for the attainment of mutually satisfactory political relations. Diplomacy, which embraces international relations of a political, but not of an administrative, nature, is normally based on considerations of national interest or expediency, and directed toward the maintenance or increase of national power and prestige. Early stages of diplomatic negotiations are conducted through ambassadors and other diplomatic agents, *q.v.*, but increasingly, as the technology of travel and communication improves, heads of state meet in summit conferences, *q.v.*, to complete negotiations on important questions.

diplomatic agent. An agent sent by one state to the seat of government of another to conduct negotiations and serve as an intermediary in international intercourse. He observes and reports political events of importance, adjusts claims, and seeks to protect the citizens and nationals of his state against wrongful acts by officers of the state to which he is sent. If his conduct is unsatisfactory, he may be recalled on the demand of the state to which he is sent or in extreme cases he may be dismissed. Diplomatic agents rank as follows: (*a*) ambassadors, legates, and nuncios, who represent the person of the head of the state; (*b*) envoys and ministers, accredited to the sovereign; (*c*) ministers resident, who are of lower rank than ministers but are accredited to the sovereign; (*d*) chargés d'affaires, accredited to the head of the office for foreign affairs.

diplomatic corps. The whole body of foreign diplomatic agents residing at the capital of a state.

diplomatic immunity. The exemption under international law of a foreign diplomat, his entourage, and the premises they occupy from taxation, civil suit, criminal process, searches and seizures, and the obligation to appear as witnesses in court in the state to which the diplomat is accredited or through which he may be traveling.

direct action. Resort to intimidation or violence (as a sit-in, street demonstration, or riot), in order to overawe the authorities, seize power, or obtain some other political objective.

direct democracy. Institutions, such as the initiative, referendum, recall, and primary, *qq.v.*, intended to facilitate more immediate control of government and public policy by the voters.

direct initiative. *See* initiative.

directive. An order or instruction issued by a superior to a lesser administrative official.

direct legislation. Participation by the electorate in the process of lawmaking, as in the initiative and referendum, *qq.v.*, or in town meeting.

direct nomination. The nomination of a candidate for public office by means of a petition circulated among voters or through the direct primary.

direct primary election. *See* primary.

direct tax. A tax the burden or incidence of which cannot readily be

shifted from the person or the property upon which it has been formally levied. The Constitution requires Congress to apportion direct
taxes among the States according to population. At first only property
and poll taxes were considered direct; but after the Supreme Court in
1895 brought income taxes within this category, the 16th Amendment
was adopted, 1913, permitting Congress to levy income taxes without
apportionment. *See Pollock* v. *Farmer's Loan and Trust Co.*

Dirksen Resolution. A proposed constitutional amendment, sponsored by
Senator Everett M. Dirksen, which would have permitted a State to
apportion one house of its legislature on a basis other than population
and thus would have qualified the Supreme Court's decision in
Reynolds v. *Sims, q.v.* It failed in 1965 to receive a two-thirds vote.

disability. 1. Legal incapacity which may result from infancy, insanity, or
some act in contravention of law. 2. Lack of legal qualifications to hold
office, such as want of sufficient age or period of residence, the holding
of an incompatible office, foreign citizenship, and, for the presidency,
foreign birth.

disallowance. 1. The power of the government of a metropolitan state to
reject or annul acts of a colonial legislature; *specifically*: the power once
exercised by the British Crown to annul American colonial legislation.
2. The power of Congress to annul legislation of territories and dependencies. 3. A power of rejection or annulment wielded by the
Dominion government over some legislative acts of Canadian provinces.

disarmament. The limitation of the size of the world's armies, navies, and
air forces and the reduction of the amount and caliber of their armament and equipment. Many efforts in this direction, usually abortive,
were made in the period between the two World Wars. Efforts since
World War II, under the aegis of the United Nations, have sought
especially to reduce the threat of thermo-nuclear weapons. The Nuclear
Test Ban Treaty which prohibits atmospheric and underwater nuclear
arms testing was signed by the United States, the Soviet Union, and
the United Kingdom on August 5, 1963. Since 1961 the United States
has had a special agency, known as the United States Arms Control and
Disarmament Agency, to formulate disarmament policy and conduct
disarmament negotiations with other states.

disaster area. A region affected by a hurricane, flood, drought, fire, or other
natural calamity which, if designated as such by Presidential proclamation, is entitled to federal financial assistance.

disbarment. Deprivation of the privilege of an attorney to practice his
profession.

discharge. 1. The release of an individual from custody, from legal
obligations, or from the jurisdiction of some tribunal. 2. The release of
a committee from further consideration of a matter submitted to it by
a legislative body which has the effect of bringing a matter to the floor.
3. Separation from military service.

discharge calendar. A special calendar of the House of Representatives
containing measures awaiting House action after the requisite number
of members has petitioned for discharge from further committee consideration.

discipline. 1. The maintenance of order and decorum in any organized public body. 2. The maintenance of the authority of an administrative superior over a subordinate.

discovery. *See* right of discovery.

discrimination. Unfair treatment or denial of normal privileges to persons because of their race, color, nationality or religion. Discrimination may be by private persons, or by public authority in unequal statutes or partiality in law enforcement. Its worst manifestations have occurred in employment, education, housing, transportation, and access to public accommodations. Antidiscrimination laws are designed to create equality of treatment and to remove legal protections (as in housing) from agreements to continue private discriminations. *See* civil rights legislation.

disengagement. A proposal in 1963, advanced by George Kennan and others, that the United States and the Soviet Union recede from their extreme military and other positions in Central Europe.

disfranchisement. 1. State action depriving a designated class or an individual of the privilege of voting, as by imposing new requirements, such as a literacy test; or as a consequence of conviction for felony or bribery; or because of the neglect or refusal of election officers to register otherwise qualified voters. 2. Any act of discrimination or intimidation by private persons which has the practical effect of preventing exercise of the suffrage;—usually used colloquially.

disgruntled. Disappointed or dissatisfied with nominations, party policies, or because of failure to obtain appointive office.

dishonorable discharge. Dismissal from military service for undignified, shameful, or disgraceful conduct involving moral turpitude.

dismissal from office. Removal from office either summarily or after a hearing.

disorderly conduct. An act legally interdicted as an offense against public morals, peace, or safety.

dispensing power. The right to abrogate statutes which was formerly claimed by certain English kings;—sometimes used by critics to characterize Presidential acts in removing positions from the merit system or in refusing to enforce certain laws.

displaced person. A refugee; *especially*: a person uprooted and made stateless by World War II who was housed in special camps by the occupation authorities in Germany and elsewhere and who became a charge of the International Refugee Organization, *q.v.*, and often was subsequently admitted as an immigrant to the United States or to another country.

disputed election. An election which both leading candidates claim to have won and which differs from a contested election, *q.v.*, in that no regular provision has been made by constitution or statute to determine the result. The presidential election of 1876, which was finally decided by an electoral commission, was a disputed election.

disqualification. Inability to hold public office or employment, or to continue in such office or employment, or to exercise some public privilege, such as voting, because of mental or physical incapacity, or the commission of a crime, or lack of positive legal qualifications.

dissenting opinion. A statement by one or more members of a tribunal of their reasons for disagreement with the majority in the disposition of a case. Such opinions sometimes foreshadow changing rules of the law.

Distinguished Flying Cross. A decoration, identical for the Army, Navy, Marine Corps, and Coast Guard, which is awarded for heroism in the air.

Distinguished Service Cross. A decoration, second only to the Medal of Honor, awarded to a person who, while serving in any capacity in the Army or the Air Force, distinguishes himself by extraordinary heroism. The Navy Cross is an equivalent award.

Distinguished   *Distinguished*   *Distinguished*
Flying Cross   *Service Cross*   *Service Medal (Army)*

Distinguished Service Medal. A decoration presented by the President for exceptionally meritorious service to the United States in a duty of great responsibility. The medal has separate designs for the Army, Navy, Air Force, Coast Guard, and NASA.

district. A territorial area of a nation, State, county, city, or other unit delimited by law for judicial, electoral, or administrative purposes.

district attorney. A locally elective State official who represents the State in bringing indictments and prosecuting criminal cases; *called also* the prosecuting attorney or State's attorney. *See* United States Attorney.

district court. *See* United States District Courts.

district director of internal revenue. An official of the Internal Revenue Service, *q.v.*, who, in one of the Internal Revenue districts of the United States, immediately superintends the collection and deposit of federal taxes other than customs duties, and who is responsible for initial determinations of assessments and investigations of violations of most internal revenue laws.

district leader. The boss or leader of a political party in an assembly district or ward.

District of Columbia. The seat of government of the United States over which Congress may exercise "exclusive legislation in all cases whatsoever." It originally embraced 100 sq. mi. ceded by Maryland and Virginia, but in 1846 the Virginia cession was returned, leaving an area of about 62 sq. mi. Its 1960 population was 763,956. Two municipal corporations, Washington and Georgetown, existed until 1871 when Congress set up a government resembling that of a territory. By a temporary law, 1874 (made permanent in 1878), Congress made the District a municipal corporation and itself assumed sole legislative authority, even to the passing of laws resembling local ordinances elsewhere, and three commissioners, appointed by the President, performed the usual functions of a municipal executive. In 1967 the District government was placed under a single executive with a council of nine members appointed by the President. Congress retains power to control appropriations. The federal government pays a portion of the expenses of the District. The people are guaranteed all civil rights under the Constitution, and adult residents may vote for President and Vice President (with three electors), and for members of the board of education.

diversity of citizenship. The condition which exists when the parties in a judicial case are citizens of different States of the United States or of a State of the United States and a foreign state. The U.S. Constitution provides (Art. III) that federal courts may have jurisdiction (though not exclusive jurisdiction) in cases between citizens of different States. In disposing of such cases the federal courts normally apply State law as determined by the latest applicable decision of the supreme court of the State.

divided sovereignty. A condition in which, in a federal system, the separate states and the general government are each presumed to possess supreme and unlimited power within their respective fields of authority; *called also* dual sovereignty. *See* dual federalism.

divine right. The right of a monarch to rule because of the divinity of his person, or the divine origin and authority of his office, or inheritance of the right from ancestors who were divinely appointed to rule.

division. 1. A subordinate administrative unit ranking in most cases below a bureau. **2.** A method of voting in an assembly by which members for and against a motion alternately stand and are counted by the presiding officer, as in the United States, or pass in two files before tellers, as in the United Kingdom.

division of powers. The strict allocation of governmental authority between the States and the national government. *Compare* separation of powers.

divorce. *See Williams* v. *North Carolina; Haddock* v. *Haddock.*

Dixie. The States south of the Mason and Dixon line.

Dixiecrats. A nickname of Democrats, formally known as States' Rights Democrats, from several Southern States who opposed their party's nomination of President Truman in 1948 because of his civil rights stand and who subsequently held a convention of their own and nominated Governor J. S. Thurmond of South Carolina for the presidency.

Dixon-Yates controversy. A dispute which began when advocates of public power proposed the construction of additional steam generating facilities for the Tennessee Valley Authority to avert a threatened crisis in the electrical supply of the city of Memphis, Tenn., resulting from increasing use of T.V.A. power by the Atomic Energy Commission. Refusing to include an appropriation for the proposed T.V.A. plant in the budget, President Eisenhower instead encouraged the Atomic Energy Commission to contract, Nov. 11, 1954, with Dixon-Yates interests for the construction of a large generating plant at West Memphis, Ark. The contract was attacked as over-generous to the company, and one of the Government's advisers in formulating its terms was accused of having a conflict of interest. When the mayor of Memphis proposed the construction of a municipal generating plant, the Government cancelled the Dixon-Yates contract incurring a penalty of $1,-500,000.

docket. A list of cases pending before a court or similar tribunal, with brief minutes of all proceedings thereon.

doctrinaire. 1. Applying some logical system of thought, abstract philosophy, doctrine, or dogma, with little or no regard for practical or empirical considerations. **2.** Pertaining to a political program that is idealistic and abstract.

doctrine. A systematic statement of principles or beliefs especially in the formulation of public policy, as in the Monroe Doctrine.

document. An official paper, deed, manuscript, or any other written or inscribed instrument which has informational or evidentiary value.

dollar. Originally a Spanish coin, widely circulated in America, which, as divided into 100 cents, was adopted as the basic monetary unit of the United States by the Confederation Congress, July 6, 1785, and by the Federal Congress, Apr. 2, 1792. The United States mint first coined silver dollars in 1794. Some other countries have a coin or note of the same name. *See* coinage.

dollar-a-year man. A business executive or other person who, during World War I, served in the administrative establishment of the federal government in return for the minimum salary required by law to be paid.

dollar diplomacy. A nickname for the foreign policy of Philander C. Knox, Secretary of State, 1909–13, which was designed to expand American investments and trade abroad and lessen the dependence of Latin America on European bankers.

dollar gap. The amount of the deficit in the nation's balance of payments, *q.v.*

domain. 1. Territory (including air space) over which sovereignty or public authority is exerted. **2.** A landed estate.

domestic corporation. A corporation created under the laws of the State in which it does business.

domestic relations court. A judicial tribunal of inferior grade, usually part of a system of municipal courts, the jurisdiction of which extends typically to matters concerned with family support and the care of children.

domestic violence. Extensive disorder within a State of the Union. Under the Constitution and an act of Congress of 1795 the legislature, or, when it is not in session, the governor may apply to the President for military intervention to suppress domestic violence; but the President may act without such application in order to enforce national law.

domicile. The permanent place of residence of a person or the place to which he intends to return even though he may actually reside elsewhere. The legal domicile of a person is important since it, rather than the actual residence, often controls the jurisdiction of the taxing authorities and determines where a person may exercise the privilege of voting and other legal rights and privileges.

domination. The exercise of sovereignty or controlling authority without constitutional or moral restraints.

Dominican Republic. A Spanish-speaking nation, formerly called Santo Domingo, on the island of Hispaniola in the West Indies. A treaty to annex it was negotiated by President Grant, 1869, but failed of ratification in the Senate. By executive agreement in 1905 and by treaty in 1907, the collection of customs duties and the debt service of the Dominican Republic were for a time in charge of a receiver appointed by the President of the United States. In 1965 the United States sent troops to the country to protect property and facilitate return to constitutional government.

dominion. 1. One of the self-governing nations of the Commonwealth, as the Dominion of Canada. 2. Sovereignty or governmental supremacy over territory.

donkey. A symbol for the Democratic party originated by the cartoonist Thomas Nast in 1874.

doorkeeper. An employee of a legislative chamber who has charge of furniture and equipment and enforces rules governing the admission of persons to the floor or galleries.

Dorr Rebellion. A violent but bloodless incident in the manhood-suffrage movement in Rhode Island. In 1842 Thomas W. Dorr was elected governor under a constitution framed by an unofficial "people's convention" and ratified by an unofficial popular vote. When President Tyler supported the legitimate government, Dorr fled the State and his followers disbanded.

Dorr v. United States. See Insular cases.

double jeopardy. Putting a person on trial for an offense for which he has previously been properly indicted and a jury has been empaneled and sworn to try him, provided that the jury has not disagreed or been discharged because of the illness of a juror or other sufficient reason;— prohibited by the Fifth Amendment. The purpose of the prohibition is to prevent repeated harassment of an accused person and reduce the danger of convicting an innocent one. A federal prosecutor may not appeal from a verdict of not guilty, but a State may make such an appeal if substantial errors are shown (*see Palko v. Connecticut*). There is no double jeopardy when a convicted person appeals to a higher court; nor when State and federal governments prosecute separately for different offenses arising from the same act.

double standard. The coinage of two metals at the same time, both having a standard value and both being legal tender.

double taxation. 1. The action of a single taxing authority (national, State, or municipal) in levying twice, within a particular taxing period, upon what is essentially the same thing. 2. *Colloquial:* the levy of taxes on the same base by both national and State, or by two or more State or local, governments within the same taxing period.

doubtful State. Any State where the voting strength of the major parties is so evenly divided that the outcome in a presidential election is unpredictable, or where experience has demonstrated that the candidate of no one party consistently obtains a plurality.

doughface. One easily influenced to forsake principles, as—according to John Randolph of Roanoke—a Northern member of Congress who voted with Southern members when the Missouri Compromise was under consideration.

dove. A critic of President Lyndon Johnson's policy in the Vietnam War who advocates the cessation of bombing by American planes in North Vietnam and other de-escalation procedures in order to induce the Vietcong and North Vietnam to consider a negotiated peace. *Compare* hawk.

Downes v. Bidwell. See Insular cases.

D.P. displaced person.

draft. Originally the selection of men from the organized or unorganized militia for compulsory active service with the armed forces. Under present laws members of the organized militia (National Guard) may be drafted into the federal service. Other individuals may be inducted under a selective service system, *q.v.*

draft riots. Violent disorders in protest against the draft law of 1863 which were especially serious in New York City, July 13–16, where 1,000 persons were killed and property damage was estimated at more than $1,500,000.

Drago Doctrine. A principle formulated in 1902 by Luis M. Drago, foreign minister of Argentina, that "a public debt cannot give rise to the right of intervention, and much less to the occupation of the soil of any American nation by any European power." In 1907 the Hague Conference endorsed the doctrine in the modified form that intervention should not be used in the collection of debts unless the creditor nation had proposed, and been refused, arbitration.

drainage district. A political subdivision created for the purpose of reclaiming marshy land and promoting public health at public or private expense.

drawback. A rebate of customs duties paid when articles on which they were levied are re-exported either in their original or a manufactured form.

Dred Scott v. Sanford. The case, 19 How. 393 (1857), of a Negro slave who had resided with his master for several years in the free State of Illinois and at Fort Snelling, which was in a territory that had been made free by the Missouri Compromise. On being returned to Missouri, Scott sued his master, a citizen of New York, for his freedom. The Supreme Court held, Justices Curtis and McLean dissenting, that Scott was not a citizen and therefore had no standing in court under the diversity-of-citizenship clause of the Constitution; that national citizenship was determined by State citizenship; and in *obiter dicta,* that the Missouri Compromise was unconstitutional because Congress had no right to prevent citizens from carrying their slaves into a territory or to impair the protection which should be given to property while it is in a territory.

Droop quota. A quota, devised by H. R. Droop in 1869 and normally used with the Hare system of proportional representation, which may be found by dividing the total vote cast for all candidates by the number of seats to be filled plus one, disregarding fractions, and adding one to the quotient.

dry. One who advocates prohibition of the manufacture, sale, or use of intoxicating liquors.

D.S.C. Distinguished Service Cross.

D.S.M. Distinguished Service Medal.

dual citizenship. 1. *In the United States:* possession of both State and national citizenship. **2.** Simultaneous possession of citizenship in two countries resulting from diversity of nationality laws or the unwillingness of one country to permit the expatriation of a citizen or subject who has been naturalized in another.

dual federalism. A doctrine, occasionally maintained by the Supreme Court, especially 1836–64, that the powers of the national and State governments are separate and distinct, and that the powers delegated to the national government are limited by the powers reserved to the States under the 10th Amendment. *Compare* divided sovereignty.

dual officeholding. The holding of two public offices simultaneously, often prohibited when one office is membership in a legislative body.

dudes and pharisees. Republicans who were accused of overscrupulousness because they refused to support Blaine for the presidency in 1884.

due process. Legal restrictions confining the government "within the limits of those fundamental principles of liberty and justice which lie at the base of all our civil and political institutions," *Hurtado* v. *California,* 110 U.S. 516 (1884); practically equivalent to the English term law of the land. Originally derived from the common law and directed in England to restraining the executive from using arbitrary methods of depriving persons of life, liberty, and property, its later development has been nearly parallel to changes in popular attitudes concerning the importance of individual liberties. In America many of the restrictions were embodied in separate articles of State and federal bills of rights. The phrase "due process" appears in the Fifth Amendment as a limitation on the federal government and in the Fourteenth Amendment as a limitation on State governments, and its meaning has been expanded by judicial interpretation to include both procedural limitations and limitations on the substance of the laws themselves. *Procedural due process* was defined by Daniel Webster as a procedure "which hears before it condemns, which proceeds upon inquiry, and renders judgment only after trial"; it governs both judicial and administrative procedures. *Substantive due process,* developed by the Supreme Court since 1856, means that the courts will refuse to enforce arbitrary or unjust provisions of statutes under which a person is tried. The court has used the due-process clause both to strengthen other guarantees in the Constitution and as a reservoir of fundamental principles of liberty and justice from which it has at different times drawn such widely different concepts as freedom of contract, *q.v.*, the unconstitutionality of continuing to segregate Negro and white school children in the District of Columbia, *Bolling* v. *Sharpe*, 347 U.S. 497 (1954), and the assimilation of most of the first eight amendments to the Constitution into the Fourteenth Amendment, thereby prohibiting the infringement of their provisions by State authorities. Some decisions under substantive due process have led to criticism in some quarters that the Supreme Court has usurped the functions of the legislature.

Dumbarton Oaks Conference. Conversations held at Dumbarton Oaks, Washington, D.C., during 1944, by representatives of the United States, U.S.S.R., the Republic of China, and the United Kingdom to explore plans for a world organization to succeed the defunct League of Nations. At the conclusion of the conference on Oct. 7, it issued the so-called Dumbarton Oaks Proposals for a General International Organization which became one of the principal sources of the Charter of the United Nations formulated at the San Francisco Conference, *q.v.*

dumping. The disposal of a national surplus of a given commodity by selling it abroad at or below cost of production for reasons that may include limitation of the home supply to maintain a price level, production at capacity to reduce unit cost, and the destruction of competitors by underselling them in their best markets.

duty. 1. An obligation imposed by law on an officer or private person. 2. A moral obligation upon a citizen, subject, or voter. 3. A tax on imported goods.

Dyer Act. An act of Congress, Oct. 29, 1919, which made it a criminal offense to transport stolen motor vehicles in interstate or foreign commerce.

earned income. Income (as wages, salaries, profits, or fees) derived from labor, professional practice, or entrepreneurship;—opposed to income derived from invested capital (as rents, dividends, interest, gifts, or the returns from trust funds).

easement. A privilege or liberty of use without right to profits which one person enjoys in the property of a neighbor, and which may arise by deed or prescription, *q.v.*;—distinguished from complete ownership or a revocable license to use.

Eaton affair. A tempest in Washington society caused by the refusal of the wives of high officials to recognize the wife of John H. Eaton,

Secretary of War, in defiance of President Jackson's wishes. Martin Van Buren, a widower, is sometimes supposed to have won his advancement through conspicuous gallantry toward Mrs. Eaton.

Economic and Social Council. One of the principal organs of the United Nations consisting, after 1965, of representatives of twenty-seven member states, nine of whom are elected annually for three-year terms by the General Assembly. The Council seeks to improve living standards, particularly in the underdeveloped regions of the world, and its economic and related research often results in recommendations and draft conventions for the UN and member states. The Council also approves the creation of specialized agencies of the United Nations (or authorizes such a status for agencies which may already exist), and coordinates their activities.

Economic Cooperation Administration. *See* Marshall Plan.

economic council. A body composed of representatives of economic interests (as banking, mining, and the food industry) or from broad economic categories, such as labor, management, and the professions, which may advise the legislature and the administration on economic and social policies and, in some countries, has power to initiate economic legislation.

economic determinism. The theory, especially popular with Marxian Socialists, that in every historical epoch the prevailing mode of economic production and exchange determines the form of social and political organization and explains the political, intellectual, and moral history of the people. *Called also* economic interpretation of history.

economic nationalism. The policy of a state in imposing protective tariffs, quotas, and other trade barriers, establishing exchange controls, monopolizing raw materials by embargoes, creating cartels to control foreign trade, or acquiring colonies or other controlled sources of strategic raw materials to assure economic self-sufficiency and protection against other states.

economic planning. *See* planning.

economic report. The review of the economic condition of the United States, based on the findings and recommendations of the Council of Economic Advisers, *q.v.*, and submitted annually to Congress by the President.

economic royalists. The members of the Liberty League and other business men who opposed President F. D. Roosevelt's policies;—the epithet was used by President Roosevelt in a speech delivered in June, 1936.

economic warfare. The use of any means, ranging from blockade to preclusive buying of strategic or critical materials in neutral countries, blacklisting, and pressures upon neutral states, which is designed to hamper an enemy's ability to obtain munitions or cripple his domestic economy.

E.D.C. European Defense Community.

Edge Act. A law of Congress, Dec. 24, 1919, which permitted the national chartering of corporations to engage in trade or financial operations abroad.

Edmunds Act. A law of Congress, Mar. 22, 1882, prohibiting polygamy in the territories under severe penalties.

education. *See* Office of Education; public education.

educational qualification. A requirement that a person must be able to read and write in order to vote; *specifically:* a requirement that a voter must have successfully pursued studies through a certain grade in school. Since it rests on presentation of a diploma or educational records, it is less susceptible to unfair discriminations than the literacy test, *q.v.*

Edwards v. *California.* A case, 314 U.S. 160 (1941), in which the Supreme Court invalidated a California law, making it an offense to transport indigent nonresidents into the State, on the ground that the law imposed an unconstitutional local burden upon interstate commerce.

E.E.C. *See* Common Market.

egghead. An academic scholar; *also:* any pretentious intellectual;—often used derisively.

Eighteenth Amendment. An amendment to the U.S. Constitution, proclaimed Jan. 29, 1919, which prohibited the manufacture, transportation, and sale of alcoholic beverages and granted Congress and the States concurrent powers to enforce these prohibitions;—later repealed, Dec. 5, 1933, by the 21st Amendment.

Eighth Amendment. One of the Bill of Rights of the U.S. Constitution which, as interpreted by the Supreme Court, prohibits the fixing of bail in an amount greater than is reasonably required to insure the appearance of an accused person at his trial; and also prohibits cruel and unusual punishments which, in addition to torture and lingering death, include penalties that may result in the destruction of the individual's status in organized society. *See Trop* v. *Dulles.*

eight-hour law. A law fixing the length of the normal working day at eight hours with provision for extra pay for additional hours of labor;— an early goal of organized labor achieved in the Adamson Act, *q.v.*, (1916) for railway employees and in the Fair Labor Standards Act, *q.v.*, (1938) for employees of other businesses engaged in interstate commerce.

Eisenhower Doctrine. President Eisenhower's policy, after the Suez Crisis, *q.v.*, of rendering economic and military assistance (as in the dispatch of air-borne troops to Beirut in 1958 at the request of the Lebanese government) to any Middle Eastern country threatened by Communist aggression.

Eisenhower Library. The collection of public papers and memorabilia of the administration of President Dwight D. Eisenhower housed in a special building at Abilene, Kan., under the supervision of the General Services Administration, *q.v.*

elastic clause. The 18th clause of Art. I, Sec. 8 of the U.S. Constitution which grants Congress power to make all laws necessary and proper for carrying into execution all other legislative powers committed to it. Chief Justice Marshall in the case of *McCulloch* v. *Maryland, q.v.*, gave this clause a liberal interpretation, declaring that if no other motive for its inclusion in the Constitution could be suggested, a sufficient one was found "in the desire to remove all doubts respecting the right to legislate on that vast mass of incidental powers which must be involved in the constitution if that instrument be not a splendid bauble." *Called also* the necessary-and-proper clause.

elastic currency. A monetary system in which the standard currency unit does not have a constant value in terms of a certain weight and fineness of some precious metal, administrative authority being competent to change the value ratio from time to time within legal limits; *also:* a monetary system in which the exchange value of the standard currency unit can be deliberately increased or decreased by administrative authority.

election. A choice, by persons qualified to vote, among candidates for a public office;—distinguished from referendum, *q.v.* In the United States the administration of elections is under State authority, subject to the provisions that qualified voters may not be denied equal access to the polls and that, in the election of members of Congress and presidential electors, the regulations contained in federal voter-registration and corrupt practices acts must be observed. Federal officers may be assigned to register voters, attend the polls, and prevent fraud, intimidation and other irregularities. The preparation of ballots, including the determination of the validity of nominations, is usually a function of a State secretary of state. Locally appointed bipartisan boards, clerks, and other officers conduct the polling in the precincts. The results of elections are ascertained by examining voting machines or counting votes in the separate precincts. At various times, States or cities have experimented with a central count of votes in order to reduce fraud or as a procedure in proportional representation.

election board. A board, usually bipartisan, and consisting of three inspectors or commissioners and two clerks appointed in each election precinct by county authorities, which determines whether individual voters are qualified, supervises the polling, and often ascertains and reports the results.

election certificate. *See* certificate of election.

election district. 1. An election precinct. **2.** An area from which one or more officers are chosen by popular vote.

electioneering. A candidate's activities in canvassing for votes or political support prior to a primary or general election.

election precinct. A compact area (the smallest unit for election administration and party organization) which usually includes from 150 to 1,000 voters and in which there is established one polling place.

elective franchise. The privilege of participating in the selection of public officers which is conferred by public authority upon persons possessing stated qualifications.

elector. 1. Any person who is entitled to vote. **2.** A member of an electoral college, *q.v.*

electoral college. Any body of electors, limited in number, meeting in one place to choose an official. For the formal election of President and Vice President the Constitution provides for fifty electoral colleges, or one in each State, constituted as the legislature of the State may provide. Today the laws of every State require that electors shall be popularly chosen. In addition, under the 23rd Amendment, the District of Columbia is entitled to choose electors, the number of whom shall not exceed those of the least populous State. All the colleges meet at the same time in their respective State capitals and ballot separately for President and Vice President. Since 1796 members of the colleges have nearly always cast their ballots for the presidential and vice-presidential candidates nominated by their respective party caucuses or conventions. But in 1820 a New Hampshire elector voted for John Quincy Adams instead of President Monroe; and since 1948 there have been other examples of electors not voting for their party's choice in Tennessee, Virginia, Mississippi, Alabama, and Oklahoma.

Electoral Commission. A body consisting of five Senators, five Representatives, and five Justices of the Supreme Court created by act of Congress, Jan. 29, 1877, to resolve the deadlock between the two houses of Congress as to the proper method of counting the disputed electoral votes in that year. It decided the disputes by a strict party vote of eight to seven, thus insuring the election of the Republican candidate, Rutherford B. Hayes.

Electoral Count Act. An act of Congress, Feb. 3, 1887, which provides that disputes concerning the election of presidential electors shall be settled by a judicial or other authority designated by law within each State six days before the date set for the meeting of the State's electors. If two or more returns are submitted by different authorities within a State, the decision is to be made by the two houses of Congress voting separately. If they disagree, the returns certified by the governor under the seal of the State are to be accepted.

electoral quota *or* **electoral quotient.** The smallest number of votes which will suffice for election under a system of proportional representation. *See* Droop quota.

electorate. The body of persons who are legally qualified to vote.

electric voting. A device used in some State legislatures by which votes may be flashed to the clerk by pressing different buttons at members' desks, thus saving time in roll calls.

elephant. A symbol for the Republican party originated by the cartoonist Thomas Nast in 1874.

Eleventh Amendment. An amendment to the Constitution, proclaimed Jan. 8, 1798, which provides that the judicial power shall not be construed to extend to any suit in law or equity commenced or prosecuted against one of the United States by citizens of another State or by citizens or subjects of a foreign country, and which was proposed after the Supreme Court had accepted jurisdiction in a suit, 2 Dall. 419 (1793), brought by one Chisholm, a citizen of South Carolina, against the State of Georgia.

eligibility. Fulfillment of the qualifications legally required for election or appointment to some public office, for the enjoyment of some civic privilege (as voting), or for the performance of some civic duty (as jury service). Citizenship, the possession of one's mental faculties, and the absence of a criminal record are practically the only qualifications for elective office universally required of adult persons. Special minimum age and residential requirements are established for Representatives, Senators, and certain State officials. To be eligible for the office of President or Vice President, a person must be a natural-born citizen, at least 35 years of age, and a resident in the United States for at least 14 years prior to election.

eligible list. A list of qualified persons drawn up by a civil service commission or equivalent agency from which are supplied candidates to fill vacancies in the civil service.

elite. A group which, by reason of intelligence, education, or specialized experience is considered by some writers as the actual or potential formulators of public opinion and determiners of policy; *especially:* civil servants in a bureaucracy or the inner circle (whether or not officers) of a political party organization.

elitism. Belief in government by an elite, *q.v.*

Elkins Act. An act of Congress, Feb. 19, 1903, which strengthened the Interstate Commerce Act by prohibiting rebates and other forms of preferential treatment to large shippers; by making departure from published transportation rates the sole test of discrimination; and by making corporations, as well as individuals, liable for violations of the law.

Elliot's *Debates.* The standard source for the debates of State conventions ratifying the U.S. Constitution, in four volumes edited by Jonathan Elliot. The first edition was published in 1827–30.

emancipation. The act of freeing a slave. All the Northern States passed acts of absolute or gradual emancipation between 1774 and 1804, and there was an active emancipationist movement in all the border slave States until about 1850.

Emancipation Proclamation. A proclamation issued by President Lincoln, Jan. 1, 1863, after 100 days' preliminary notice, which declared all slaves free in the States then in rebellion except Tennessee and the parts of Virginia and Louisiana occupied by Union troops. It did not affect slavery in the loyal slave States, and was justified as an act of military necessity under the President's powers as commander in chief.

embargo. 1. An order issued by a state prohibiting the arrival or departure of vessels in ports that it controls, usually as an act of reprisal or coercion against another state. A *hostile embargo* is a seizure of foreign ships, which may become permanent if war follows. A *civil embargo*, such as the Embargo Act of 1807 (repealed in 1809), prevents the departure of vessels or goods belonging to the state which declares it and sometimes also closes ports to vessels of the offending state. **2.** An order forbidding the export of arms and munitions of war often issued by several nations in concert to prevent aggression.

embassy. 1. The official residence of an ambassador. **2.** The mission, function, or business of an ambassador. **3.** The entourage of persons attached to an ambassador's staff.

embezzlement. The fraudulent appropriation of funds or illegal diversion of funds to the personal use of an employee to whom such funds have been entrusted. *Compare* larceny.

emergency measure. 1. Action by a President or Governor in cases of war, insurrection, civil commotion, or natural disaster, usually under some constitutional power or under the authority of a statute. **2.** A State law which is urgently required for the preservation of the public peace, health, or safety, and which becomes effective immediately, rather than at the end of the 60-day, or other waiting period, required by the laws or the constitution in States which have provided for the referendum. Sometimes legislatures have declared ordinary laws emergency measures as a subterfuge to prevent their submission to a referendum. *Compare* emergency powers.

Emergency Planning. *See* Office of Emergency Planning.

emergency powers. 1. Powers conferred upon the executive for a limited time or until withdrawn by the legislature. **2.** Powers (as the war powers), granted in the Constitution but not used in ordinary times. **3.** Powers sometimes claimed by a President to justify extraordinary actions in time of national peril;—as some of Lincoln's acts after the beginning of the Civil War which were validated retroactively by Congressional statute, July 4, 1861; or Truman's steel seizure which was declared unconstitutional because not authorized by existing law; *see Youngstown Sheet and Tube Co.* v. *Sawyer*. In *Wilson* v. *New* and in *Home Building and Loan Association* v. *Blaisdell, qq.v.*, the Supreme Court held that, although an emergency may not create a power, it may furnish the occasion for the exercise of a power already in existence.

Emergency Price Control Act. An act of Congress, Jan. 30, 1942, which authorized rationing of supplies and fixing of ceiling prices for many goods and for rents, to insure a fair distribution of available goods and prevent a runaway price inflation during World War II. Its operation was a responsibility of the Office of Price Administration, abolished 1946.

emigrant aid societies. Organizations in the North which aided antislavery men to settle in Kansas, 1854–61.

eminent domain. The paramount right of the sovereign to take over, or use, private property which is exercised by national and State governments, but only for a public purpose and on payment of just compensation. "Public purpose" includes the power to confer the right upon public service companies. "Just compensation" means a monetary award which is determined by judicial proceedings, often with a jury, in which an owner of property has a right to be heard.

emolument. The salary, fees, or perquisites of an office or employment.

Employees' Compensation. *See* Bureau of Employees' Compensation.

Employees' Compensation Appeals Board. A three-man board in the Department of Labor which may review decisions in workmen's compensation cases made by the Bureau of Employees' Compensation.

employer's liability law. Any law, as those passed by practically all the States since 1910, which modifies common-law rules respecting an employer's responsibility for accidents and occupational diseases and requires him to make compensation through a State insurance fund or otherwise. Except in a few States, it does not provide compensation for farm laborers, domestic servants, or employees in very small establishments.

Employment Act of 1946. An act of Congress, Feb. 20, 1946, which seeks to encourage the maintenance of high levels of employment, production, and purchasing power. It authorizes the President to make an annual economic report to Congress outlining the economic condition of the nation and making appropriate recommendations for legislative action. To assist the President in preparing the report and to make a continuous study of economic conditions, the act creates a Council of Economic Advisers, *q.v.*

Employment Security. *See* Bureau of Employment Security.

Employment Service. *See* United States Employment Service.

enabling act. 1. A legislative act authorizing an executive or administrative official, an organ of local government, or a corporation to exercise some unusual power. **2.** An act of Congress authorizing the people of a territory to call a constitutional convention or take other steps preparatory to admission to statehood.

enacting clause. An indispensable clause at the beginning of every statute which states the authority by which it is made. For an act of Congress the clause is: "Be it enacted by the Senate and House of Representatives of the United States of America, in Congress assembled"; for a joint resolution: "Resolved by, etc."; for an act in New York: "The people of the State of New York, represented in Senate and Assembly, do enact as follows."

enactment. The action, usually completed by the signature of the chief executive, by which a legislature develops a statute from a bill.

Enderbury Island. One of the Phoenix group in the mid-Pacific which, with Canton Island, *q.v.*, has been jointly administered by the United States and Great Britain since April, 1939, and which is a communications and air transit station.

endless chain. The monetary crisis of 1894–95 during which the U.S. Treasury repeatedly sold bonds to replenish the gold reserve, which continued to be drawn upon by persons who feared for the stability of the dollar;—usually used colloquially.

endless chain fraud. *See* Tasmanian dodge.

enemy. *In warfare:* a military foe.

enemy alien. An alien residing or traveling in a state which is at war with the state of which he is a national. Enemy aliens may be interned or restricted as to place of residence, freedom of travel, possession of arms and equipment for sending or receiving messages, or otherwise.

enemy property. Any property used in illegal trade with a public enemy, even if owned by a neutral or a citizen of the state which seizes such property.

enforcement. An action or process to compel observance of law or the requirements of public policy.

enfranchise. To confer the privilege of voting upon classes of persons who have not previously possessed it.

Engel v. Vitale. The case, 370 U.S. 421 (1962), in which the Supreme Court invalidated the publicly prescribed use in the public schools of a prayer formulated and recommended by the New York Board of Regents (the so-called Regents' prayer), such prescription being held to violate the First Amendment's prohibition of laws establishing a religion, as applied to the States through the due-process clause of the Fourteenth Amendment. The decision appears to conflict with the view enunciated in *Everson v. Board of Education, q.v.* The rule of the Engel case was extended by subsequent cases, especially *School District of Abington Township v. Schempp*, 373 U.S. 203 (1963), which outlawed compulsory Bible reading and the recitation of the Lord's Prayer in the public schools. The majority opinion in these cases held that the First Amendment requires the government to maintain "strict neutrality, neither aiding nor opposing religion."

engrossment. The drafting of an authoritative copy of a resolution or bill just prior to the final vote upon it in a legislative house.

enlistment. The action of entering voluntarily one of the armed services.

Enoch Arden law. A statute granting permission to remarry without fear of legal penalty to a person whose spouse has been absent usually for seven successive years (in New York, five) and is presumed to be dead.

enrolled bill. The final copy, printed or written in permanent form, of a bill or joint resolution which has passed both houses of a legislature and is ready for signature.

enrollment. 1. The action of registering or recording a document, or of preparing an enrolled bill, *q.v.* 2. The official listing of vessels engaged in fisheries or limited domestic commerce which, because they do not engage in foreign commerce, are not entitled to registry. 3. The act of registering one's affiliation with a political party in order to participate in a closed primary election.

ensign. 1. A national flag. 2. A flag or banner indicating the nationality of a ship at sea. 3. The lowest commissioned rank in the navy.

entail. The transmission of the ownership of land by inheritance in accordance with a predetermined order of succession, the one holding the land at any given time being legally forbidden to change the order of succession to ownership or to alienate the property. Entail has been abolished in the United States.

entangling alliance. A treaty with a foreign state which would obligate the United States to participate in some future action in circumstances over which it may have no control or real interest;—from a phrase used by Jefferson in his first inaugural address, and often repeated by isolationists.

entente. A general understanding reached by two or more states to compose all outstanding differences and to pursue a policy of reciprocal aid and diplomatic solidarity in their relations with other states. An entente is broader in scope and less explicit than an alliance although it may embrace a tacit alliance.

enumerated powers. 1. The 18 powers specifically given to Congress in Art. I of the U.S. Constitution. 2. The powers specifically delegated by the Constitution to some branch or authority of the national government, and which are not denied to that government or reserved to the States or to the people.

envoy. A diplomat of the rank of minister or ambassador sent by a state to an international conference or to the government of a foreign state to execute a special mission or to serve as a permanent diplomatic representative.

EPIC plan. The social welfare program which Upton Sinclair advocated while an unsuccessful candidate for governor of California, 1934;—from an acronym of the slogan, "End Poverty in California."

E Pluribus Unum. A Latin motto, meaning "one out of many," appearing on the obverse of the Great Seal of the United States and on many pieces of currency.

equality. The principle stated in the Declaration of Independence and similar public documents which asserts the fundamentally similar worth of every human being. It is a cardinal premise of democracy and provides the logical and moral justification for such democratic institutions as universal suffrage, rule by popular majorities, equal representative districts, equal treatment before the law, equal treatment in places of public accommodation and entertainment, such as hotels, restaurants, theaters, and transportation facilities, and equal educational opportunities.

equalization fee. A fee collected from all prospective beneficiaries of a project in order to compensate a few participants who may suffer a loss from its operation. See McNary-Haugen Bill.

equalization of assessments. The action of a board or other administrative authority in revising valuations made by assessors for direct property taxation, in order to secure a more equitable distribution of the tax burden among taxpayers of a particular locality, or among counties or other taxing districts in a State.

equal protection. A requirement of the 14th Amendment that States must give equal treatment under the law to all persons. For many years the Supreme Court sharply limited the effectiveness of this clause. In the Civil Rights cases, q.v., 1883, it held that the clause prohibited only discrimination by State action and not discrimination by private individuals and groups. In Plessy v. Ferguson, q.v., 1896, the Court approved the segregation of different races if equal accommodations were provided; but until the 1930's it rarely reviewed lower court decisions to determine if separate accommodations were in fact equal. In Brown v. Board of Education, q.v., it held that segregated schools were inherently unequal. Other decisions voided State laws discriminating between persons in employment, transportation, housing, and access to public accommodations and places of amusement. But in matters not concerned with race or nationality, classifications may still be made by State legislatures if they are reasonably adapted to the accomplishment of proper governmental objectives (as protection of health, safety, morals, or general welfare), and if all persons falling within a given class are treated alike. Thus State laws may discriminate between men and women in conditions of employment, between residents and non-residents in access to State privileges, between chain stores and department stores in the rate of taxation, and between residential and commercial districts in zoning regulations because of a reasonable relation to the State's police power. To prevent discrimination by private persons several States have enacted civil rights laws requiring equal treatment for all persons regardless of race, color, creed, or nationality in employment, lodging houses, conveyances, amusement centers, and other places of public accommodation.

Equal Rights party. 1. Another name for the Locofocos, *q.v.* 2. A minor party of the 1800's advocating women's rights.

equity. A branch of remedial justice which arose perhaps by the 12th or 13th century in England, when petitions to the King for relief from the positive and rather inflexible rules of the common law were referred to the Lord Chancellor; hence the name "chancery" which is used for an equity court. Much of the substance and procedure of equity was derived from civil and canon law. Abstract principles of justice, or natural law, guided the judge in deciding each suit. In time equity developed its own precedents. Procedure in equity is relatively simple. An attempt is made to present the whole case, with all possible grounds for decision, to a court; and for that purpose all individuals having an interest may be summoned as parties even after the beginning of a case. The court has a considerable choice of remedies in "commanding what is right and prohibiting what is wrong." The most important are the requirements of specific performance, and preventive justice by means of the injunction. Separate equity courts, once the general rule, now exist in only a half dozen States. In most States both common law and equity are administered by the same judge in the same case; but in others separate proceedings must be held for law and equity cases, even though the same judge may preside over both.

Era of Good Feelings. The period in American politics during the presidency of James Monroe when, because of the virtual extinction of the Federalist party, partisan differences tended to disappear. It was none the less a period in which personal rivalries and factional dissensions flourished.

Erdman Act. An act of Congress, June 1, 1898, which set up machinery for the mediation and arbitration of labor disputes between railroad companies and their trainmen and switchmen, and outlawed the yellow-dog contract and discriminatory discharge by employers.

Erie Canal. A canal constructed by the State of New York between Albany and Buffalo, 1817–25, which is still in operation as a barge canal.

Erie Railroad v. Tompkins. A case, 304 U.S. 64 (1938), in which the Supreme Court held that the law to be applied in diversity of citizenship cases is the law of the State where the dispute arises; and "whether the law of the State shall be declared by its Legislature in a statute or by its highest court in a decision is not a matter of federal concern. There is no federal general common law." This decision reversed the long-standing rule in *Swift v. Tyson*, 16 Pet. 1 (1842), which held that when there were no State statutes governing diversity of citizenship cases, the federal courts were free to exercise an independent judgment as to what the common law of the State is, or should be.

E.R.P. *See* Marshall Plan.

error. *See* writ of error.

escape clause. A provision in a tariff law which authorizes the President, on recommendation of the Tariff Commission, to impose quotas or rescind tariff reductions already made whenever competition from foreign imports threatens serious injury to domestic industry.

Esch Act. An act of Congress, Mar. 4, 1907, which made it unlawful for any common carrier in interstate commerce to require or permit an employee to remain on duty more than 16 consecutive hours or to go again on duty until he had had 10 consecutive hours of rest.

Esch-Cummins Act. *See* Transportation Act 1.

escheat. The reversion of land to the state, as the original and ultimate proprietor, by reason of failure of heirs.

Escobedo v. *Illinois.* A case, 378 U.S. 478 (1964), in which the Supreme Court held that the refusal of police to honor an accused's request to consult an attorney, their informing him they had convincing evidence against him, their obtaining a confession from him, and the admission of the confession as evidence against him by a State court constituted a denial of due process of law. *Compare Miranda* v. *Arizona.*

Espionage Act. An act of Congress, June 15, 1917, imposing severe penalties for uttering statements deliberately intended to impede the operations of the armed forces. It was strengthened by the Sedition Act and the Alien Registration Act, *qq.v.*

Essex Junto. A group of leaders in Essex County, Mass., who opposed Governor John Hancock, 1780–89, and sided with Hamilton in opposing President Adams, 1798–1801. The name was later applied to all Federalists.

establishment. A group which has acquired the power, under laws, legislative rules, precedents, or customs, to determine public policies or the fate of legislation;—probably from the establishment, continuously since the reign of Elizabeth I, of the Church of England as the state church.

estate tax. An indirect tax levied on the entire estate of a deceased person. *Compare* inheritance tax.

Estes v. *Texas.* *See* Billie Sol Estes scandal.

estimates. Statements of anticipated expenditures for the next fiscal year furnished by spending agencies to budget-making authorities.

Euclid v. *Ambler Realty Co.* A case, 272 U.S. 365 (1926), in which the Supreme Court upheld a comprehensive zoning ordinance restricting and regulating the location of businesses, industries, and various types of dwellings. Despite the loss sustained by many property holders in the zoned areas, the Court reconciled the ordinance with the due-process clause of the 14th Amendment as a reasonable exercise of the police power, *q.v.*, of the State.

European Defense Community. A plan to pool forces, weaponry, and defense strategy by the six European nations which subsequently formed the Common Market, *q.v.* It failed of adoption when, in August 1954, the French parliament rejected it.

European Economic Community. *See* Common Market.

European Recovery Program. *See* Marshall Plan.

European state system. A concept, that the power of the sovereign national states of Europe should be kept in balance by a system of shifting alliances so that no state, or group of states, would feel strong enough to wage aggressive war. Balance-of-power concepts were generally accepted from the Peace of Westphalia (1648) to the Treaty of Versailles (1919), and perhaps later.

Evans v. Gore. A case, 253 U.S. 245 (1920), in which the Supreme Court held that the constitutional doctrine of the separation of powers and the clause in Art. III, Sec. 1 of the Constitution which guarantees a federal judge's salary against diminution during his tenure prevent the levying of a federal tax upon a federal judge's salary if the tax was enacted after the judge assumed his office.

ever-normal granary. Equalization of the supply of basic farm products during years of good and bad harvests, the objective being a continuous and stable supply. Surpluses may be accumulated by the government as collateral for loans to growers, and may be reduced and disposed of through other than normal trade channels, by means of school-lunch programs, aid to relief agencies, and foreign aid.

Everson v. Board of Education. A case, 370 U.S. 421 (1947), in which the Supreme Court upheld the public payment of the cost of transporting children to religious schools as a means by which parents can "get their children, regardless of their religion, safely and expeditiously to and from accredited schools." The Court insisted that the wall between church and state had not been breached by this decision.

every man a king. The slogan used by Huey P. Long in his "share the wealth" crusade during the considerable period of his dictatorial control over Louisiana.

evidence. Legally admissible information submitted to a court or investigating body, either orally, in writing, or as an exhibit, in order to determine the truth of any matter in issue.

exaction. A tax or contribution assessed or collected with undue severity, or in excess of powers, or by abuse of official discretion. *Compare* extortion.

excepted positions. Three categories of positions in the civil service which it is impracticable to fill by competitive examinations in the usual form, such as (*a*) those for which no suitable written examination can be prepared; (*b*) those requiring persons whose competence is best attested by experience, previous publications, and letters of recommendation from competent observers; and (*c*) those of a confidential or policy-determining character.

excess condemnation. The taking of private property by right of eminent domain in excess of what is absolutely necessary for immediate public use. Though urged by city planners on aesthetic and fiscal grounds and regularly used in Europe, it is legally possible in only a few States of the Union.

excess profits tax. A graduated tax on business profits in excess of a fixed percentage of invested capital or of average profits over a given period.

exchange controls. Public regulation of the buying and selling of foreign exchange, often intended to prevent foreign travel and export of capital by a state's own citizens, or to give preference to imports of certain goods over others, as capital goods over consumer's goods.

exchange stabilization fund. A fund with a book value of $2 billion from the profits of dollar devaluation placed at the disposal of the Secretary of the Treasury by the Gold Reserve Act, 1934, for the purchase of gold, foreign exchange, and similar instruments of credit, thereby to promote equilibrium between the value of the dollar and foreign currency.

excise. An indirect tax levied on goods produced, manufactured, sold, used, or transported within a country, or upon various privileges;—in current usage the term has been extended to include various license fees and practically every internal revenue tax except the income tax.

exclusion. The policy of denying admission into a state of the nationals of a foreign state, or classes of such nationals. The United States has passed various exclusion acts directed against the immigration of Oriental peoples. After World War II, however, minimum immigration quotas were assigned to nationals of all Asian countries. *See* quota.

exclusive committee. Any one of the more important standing committees of the House of Representatives, service on which is presumed sufficient to occupy most of the time which a member can devote to committee work. He may not be assigned to a second exclusive committee, but may be assigned to one or more nonexclusive committees.

exclusive power. A power which, under the federal system of the United States, is deemed to fall wholly within the jurisdiction either of the federal government or of a State.

execution. 1. A judicial writ directing an officer to carry out the judgment of a court of law. 2. Enforcement of the judgment, especially of the death penalty following conviction of a capital crime and sentence by a court of law. 3. Rendering valid a legal document by signing and delivering it.

executive. The officer or officers (as President, governor, mayor, chief of state, cabinet, and council of ministers) who, individually or collectively, are responsible for the enforcement of the laws and the fulfillment of public policy. The principal executive powers are supervision of civil administration, the appointment, direction, and removal of subordinate officers and employees, the command of the armed forces, the conduct of relations with other governments, and the issuance of pardons and reprieves. In the United States, executives have been granted the veto and other legislative powers, and the effectiveness of a chief executive is increasingly being measured by his leadership of the legislature and of public opinion rather than by his administrative accomplishments. In parliamentary forms of government the cabinet formulates the legislative program and usually has control of sufficient legislative time to guide it to passage.

executive agent. A personal representative of the President entrusted with special missions to foreign governments or heads of state. He is to be distinguished from a regular diplomatic official, although he is often accorded the privileges and immunities, and even the rank, of regular diplomats.

executive agreement. An agreement between heads of state or governments. The President may make such agreements without senatorial ratification by virtue of his position as commander in chief or of his constitutional authority over foreign relations, or under specific statutory authority. An executive agreement usually deals with administrative matters or with matters of policy less portentous than those normally incorporated in the more enduring international treaties and conventions.

Executive Calendar. The Senate's calendar which lists presidential nominations for appointive offices, drafts of proposed treaties, and other executive documents. *Compare* Calendar of Bills and Resolutions.

executive council. An executive cabinet, or a body of advisers of a chief executive, such as the governor's council of colonial America. It survives in Maine, New Hampshire, and Massachusetts.

executive department. *See* department 2, 3.

executive discretion. The choice of means which an executive possesses in carrying out all except his mandatory powers.

Executive Office of the President. The various agencies under the immediate direction of the President, so placed under the terms of the Reorganization Act of 1939 and subsequent legislation, which include personal assistants of the President, the White House Office, and agencies like the Council of Economic Advisers, the Bureau of the Budget, the National Security Council, the Central Intelligence Agency, the Office of Economic Opportunity, and the Office of Emergency Planning.

executive order. Any rule or regulation issued by the President or some administrative authority under his direction for the purpose of interpreting, implementing, or giving administrative effect to a provision of the Constitution or of some law or treaty. An order may relate to the organization and procedure of an administrative agency or it may have general applicability as law. To be valid, orders must be published in the *Federal Register*. The practice of delegating discretionary powers to the executive by statute has greatly increased the use of executive orders. *See* administrative order.

executive session. 1. A session devoted to executive business, as approval of treaties and presidential appointments, which the United States Senate formerly considered in secret session. **2.** *Colloquial.* A session of a committee or other body from which the press and members of the public are excluded; *also:* any secret session.

exemption. Immunity from certain legal obligations, as jury duty, military service, or the payment of taxes. The latter immunity is usually extended to charitable, religious, and educational institutions.

exequatur. A document issued to a foreign consul or consular agent by the government to which he is accredited permitting him to take up his residence and perform his official duties.

ex officio. By virtue of office or official position.

expansion. The process of enlarging a state's territory by annexing unoccupied territory, or through purchase, acts of aggression, or wars of conquest.

ex parte. Pertaining to a proceeding where there is no adverse party; or where the adverse party is absent or without opportunity to be heard.

expatriation. 1. The action of an individual in renouncing his allegiance to the state of which he has been a citizen or subject. Most contemporary states recognize the right of their citizens or subjects voluntarily to expatriate themselves and become the naturalized citizens of other states. 2. Forfeiture of citizenship because of the commission of illegal acts for which such forfeiture is a penalty. *See Perez* v. *Brownell.* 3. *Historically:* banishment of a citizen or subject by a state.

experiment station. *See* agricultural experiment station.

export. Pertaining to commodities, merchandise, money, or credit sent out of a country.

Export Control Act. An act of Congress, Feb. 26, 1949, which, as amended, embargoed direct shipments of goods to Communist-dominated countries and provided for selective control over exports to other countries in order to prevent strategic goods or materials from reaching Communist-dominated countries.

Export-Import Bank of Washington. A United States government corporation, established by executive order in 1934 and given a statutory basis and added powers by Congress in 1945 and 1947, which guarantees private loans or makes loans directly when private credit sources are not available, in order to finance expanded trade between the United States and its possessions and with foreign countries. Its authorized capital is $1 billion and its obligations, either in the form of loans, guarantees, or insurance, are limited to $9 billion.

export tax. A duty levied upon merchandise shipped out of a country. Such a tax is prohibited by the U.S. Constitution, Art. I, Secs. 9 and 10.

exposition. 1. The action of clarifying or providing a detailed commentary upon some theme. 2. A fair or exhibition usually supported in whole or in part by public funds.

ex post facto law. A retroactive criminal law which is unconstitutional when it declares an act a crime which was not a crime when it was done; or, with retrospective effect, increases a crime or a penalty; or alters the rules of evidence to the disadvantage of an accused person; or in other ways decreases the protection which the law previously afforded to him.

Expounder of the Constitution. A nickname of Daniel Webster.

express powers. Powers specifically granted to the national government or one of its branches by the U.S. Constitution.

expropriation. 1. The action of a state under the civil (Roman) law in taking private property;—somewhat similar to eminent domain under the common law. In some countries the compensation paid to foreign investors has often been only a fraction of the true value of their property. At the Bogota Conference, *q.v.,* the American Republics agreed that fair compensation should be paid whenever the property of foreigners is expropriated. **2.** Nationalization, especially of industrial or other productive property.

expulsion. Enforced withdrawal of a person from a country or society or from some public body such as a legislative assembly. By a two-thirds vote, either house of Congress may expel a member.

expunge. To strike out or rescind entries in a permanent record, as by writing the word "Expunged" across lines in the Senate Journal, or "Rescission" in the House Journal.

extension of remarks. The printing in the *Congressional Record*, by permission of either house, of material not spoken in debate. If in continuation of remarks on the floor, such material follows the reported speech in the body of the *Record*; otherwise it is printed in the appendix.

Extension Service. An agency of the U.S. Department of Agriculture which, in cooperation with the staffs of the land-grant colleges, makes available to the rural population of the country the results of departmental and related research on agricultural problems and rural life. Its service is rendered chiefly through county agricultural, home-demonstration, and 4-H club agents throughout the country.

external loan. A loan obtained by a country from foreign private or governmental sources.

extortion. The crime of obtaining something of value by the use of force or threats.

extraconstitutional. 1. Not expressly or impliedly provided for by a written constitution. **2.** Prohibited by a constitution. **3.** Unconstitutional.

extradition. The delivery of fugitives from justice by the authorities of the state where such fugitives have sought asylum to the authorities of the state from which they fled. Extradition may be demanded in accordance with applicable provisions of international treaties, and such provisions normally do not call for the surrender of fugitives charged with political offenses. Among the States of the Union the return of fugitives is more properly called rendition, *q.v.*

extralegal. Outside or beyond the scope of law.

extramural. Pertaining to activities or works of a municipal corporation (as water supply) which are conducted outside the corporation's boundaries.

extraordinary session. A legislative session, called usually by the executive, which meets in the interval between regular sessions. In a majority of the States such sessions are limited to the consideration of matters specified in the governor's call.

extraterritoriality. The right of a state to exercise its authority outside its own territory, as on its public vessels or on its merchant vessels on the high seas, or over the residences of its diplomats abroad;—sometimes used to describe the immunity enjoyed by public ministers from the laws of the state to which they are accredited.

F

F.A.A. Federal Aviation Administration.

faction. 1. A wing of a political party; *also:* a personal clique within such a party. **2.** Any loosely knit group of politicians, with or without defined leadership, who seek to aggrandize themselves by pursuing opportunistic policies or by promoting dissension within the ranks of an organized political party or within the state at large. **3.** Divisive or tumultuous political activity.

Fair Deal. The legislative program, proposed by President Truman in his address to the 81st Congress, 1949, that included an increase in minimum wages and social-security benefits; repeal of the Taft-Hartley Labor-Management Relations Act, *q.v.;* extension of federal aid in slum clearance, housing, and urban renewal; adoption of the Brannan Plan, *q.v.,* for supporting agricultural prices; strengthening of civil rights; and provision for health insurance and aid to education.

fair employment practice measure. State legislation, such as the Ives-Quinn law passed by the New York legislature in 1946, the executive orders placed in effect by President F. D. Roosevelt during World War II, or civil rights legislation and administrative regulations, especially those of the Kennedy-Johnson administrations, which seeks to eliminate discrimination in employment based on race, creed, color, or national origin.

Fair Labor Standards Act. An act of Congress, June 25, 1938, which set a minimum standard wage of 40 cents an hour (increased by later statutes) and a maximum work week of 40 hours in industries engaged in interstate commerce, and prohibited the labor of children under 16 in most employments, and under 18 in dangerous occupations.

Fair Play Amendment. An amendment to the rules of the Republican national convention, adopted in 1952, which made delegates whose seats were contested (unless put on the temporary roll by a vote of more than two-thirds of the national committee) ineligible to vote on the question of seating themselves or any other contested delegate. Adoption of this amendment assured the nomination of Eisenhower over Taft.

fair return on a fair valuation. A principle of rate-fixing set forth, but not carefully defined, by the Supreme Court in *Smyth* v. *Ames, q.v.*

fair-trade laws. Statutes passed in most States which prohibit merchants from selling goods at prices lower than those set by the manufacturers. *Compare* antitrust.

fairway. The most navigable or most generally used channel of a river or bay;—sometimes used interchangeably with thalweg, *q.v.*

fait accompli. An action which is regarded as completed and therefore not subject to further negotiation.

false imprisonment. 1. Detention under false or assumed authority or because of a miscarriage of judicial procedure. **2.** Any unlawful restraint of a person's liberty.

family of nations. 1. *Formerly:* the Christian states of Europe. **2.** *In contemporary politics:* the aggregate of sovereign states which recognize

143 FASCISM

certain obligations toward one another under international law and custom; *called also* the international community.

Family Services. *See* Bureau of Family Services.

Fannie Mae. *See* Federal National Mortgage Association.

F.A.O. Food and Agriculture Organization.

farm bloc. A bipartisan group of Senators and Representatives from agricultural constituencies first organized in 1921 to secure legislation favorable to the farming class by the usual methods of minorities, including dilatory tactics and refusal to support other legislation until the farmers' demands were satisfied.

farm bureau. A local organization of farmers first created about 1915 for the purpose of bringing pressure to bear on county boards, for the employment of county agricultural agents and for cooperative activities. Bureaus were later combined into State federations and an American Farm Bureau Federation which maintains a lobby to promote legislation favorable to the more prosperous agricultural interests.

Farm Credit Administration. An independent agency of the executive branch of the federal government which supervises and coordinates the federal land banks, intermediate credit banks, production credit corporations, and banks for agricultural cooperatives located in each of the 12 federal farm credit districts into which the United States is divided. The system provides short- and long-term credit to farmers and ranchers.

Farmer-Labor party. 1. A minor party with socialistic tendencies which in 1920 cast 265,000 votes for Arthur Christensen for President and in 1924 joined the LaFollette Progressives. 2. A third party in Minnesota which grew out of the Nonpartisan League, *q.v.*, and, after successfully electing several of its candidates to important offices, was merged with the Democratic party in 1936.

Farmers' Alliance. 1. A secret farmers' organization founded in Texas in 1874 which, after absorbing other groups, attempted to capture the Democratic party in the South about 1890. 2. A non-secret organization founded in the Northwest in 1880 which, after sponsoring third-party tickets in State elections, was instrumental in forming the Populists, *q.v.*

Farmers Home Administration. An agency of the U.S. Department of Agriculture that makes agricultural loans on favorable terms to veterans and to low-income farmers, especially tenant farmers, sharecroppers, and farm laborers, for the purchase of land, stock, equipment, and supplies; for building and improving homes and other farm buildings; and for family subsistence. It also makes loans to improve community water facilities and for rural renewal programs, and may insure private loans for the purchase of farm land.

fascism. 1. The authoritarian political system and totalitarian social regime evolved by Benito Mussolini and his followers of the Fascist party in Italy between 1922 and 1943; *also:* any regime like that of the German Nazis or the Spanish Falangists inspired by the Italian model or comparable to it. 2. Any program which advocates the destruction of democratic parliamentarism, personal liberty, and a pluralistic social order and demands instead the institution of a political dictatorship supported by a single hierarchically organized party, the regimentation of all forms of social and economic activity under a regime of totalitarian governmental control, and the extensive use of force, violence, and arbitrary power in the process of government. Although similar in many respects to totalitarian communism fascism has historically been more sympathetic toward private capitalism and has received support from the conservative Right and the middle classes rather than from the Marxist Left. Fascist ideas have had no great currency in the United States although they were advocated by the Silver Shirts and the German-American Bund before World War II and, afterward, by the American Nazi party and similar organizations.

fat cat. *Political slang.* A man of wealth from whom a party expects liberal campaign contributions.

fat frying. Bringing pressure to bear on business interests which have benefited from a party's policies to contribute to its campaign fund.

Father Abraham. A nickname of President Lincoln.

Father of His Country. An appellation of George Washington.

Father of the Constitution. A nickname of James Madison.

Father of the House. The oldest member in point of service in the House of Representatives.

Father of the Revolution. A nickname of Samuel Adams.

Fathers, The. *See* Founding Father.

favorite, the. The candidate who, before a convention or in its early stages, has the most pledged delegates or appears to have the best chance of nomination.

favorite son. An aspirant for a Presidential nomination who has little or no support beyond an instructed delegation from his own State.

F.B.I. Federal Bureau of Investigation.

F.C.A. Farm Credit Administration.

F.C.C. Federal Communications Commission.

F.D.A. Food and Drug Administration.

F.D.I.C. Federal Deposit Insurance Corporation.

featherbedding. The practice of requiring employers by law or under conditions prescribed by a labor contract to hire more workmen for a given operation than are necessary to perform the operation satisfactorily, or to hire workmen whose skills have become superfluous because of technological change.

federal. 1. Pertaining to the division of public powers in a state between one central government with authority to legislate on certain subjects and to enforce its will upon individuals, and numerous regional governments each having authority in other matters within its restricted territorial jurisdiction, the division being established and maintained by a constituent authority legally superior to both the central and the regional governmental areas. 2. *In common usage:* pertaining to an officer or establishment of the national government in the United States.

Federal Advisory Council. A body consisting of one representative from each of the 12 federal reserve districts which makes recommendations on economic and general business conditions to the Board of Governors of the Federal Reserve System, *q.v.*

federal aid. Any form of national subvention or grant-in-aid to States and local governments to finance in whole or in part approved local projects or activities. *See* grant-in-aid.

Federal Aviation Administration. A federal agency, created in 1958, and placed under the Department of Transportation in 1966, which performs functions such as the promulgation of air safety standards and regulations; inspection of aircraft; investigation and determination of the probable causes of airplane accidents; ratings of aircrew personnel; direction of a cooperative private industry-federal government program to design and develop supersonic transport aircraft; construction and maintenance of various landing devices on airfields; installation of safety devices; and prescription of air traffic rules and regulations. It also administers federal appropriations for the construction of airports and federal legislation to encourage cooperation with foreign nations and the International Civil Aviation Organization, *q.v.*

Federal Bureau of Investigation. A bureau of the Department of Justice, established 1908, which investigates and makes arrests for violations of federal law (except violations of currency, customs, internal revenue, postal and anti-narcotics laws which are within the purview of other federal agencies). Because criminal activities are increasingly interstate, the bureau is often called into cases which formerly were wholly within the jurisdiction of State and local police and prosecuting authorities.

Federal Communications Commission. An independent regulatory agency, consisting of seven members, established by Congress in 1934 to administer the Federal Communications Act of that year. It regulates interstate and foreign communications by telephone, telegraph, cable and wireless, including the regulation of rates and accounting practices. It also supervises radio and television networks and stations, assigns frequencies, and conducts engineering research on the more effective use of electronic communication and the improvement and standardization of electronic equipment. By means of wire and wireless communication, the commission seeks to promote safety at sea.

Federal Credit Unions. *See* Bureau of Federal Credit Unions.

Federal Crop Insurance Corporation. A public corporation in the Department of Agriculture which insures growers of wheat, cotton, tobacco, and about twenty other crops against loss by drought, flood, insects, and plant disease, and damage resulting from inability to obtain labor and other essentials.

Federal Deposit Insurance Corporation. A government corporation, created 1933, which insures depositors' bank accounts up to $15,000, and is managed by the Comptroller of the Currency and two directors appointed by the President. The Corporation may act as receiver of closed banks, take steps to avoid unsound banking practices, purchase the assets of a bank which finds itself in difficulties in order to facilitate its merger with another bank, supervise consolidations of insured and uninsured banks, and examine insured banks not members of the Federal Reserve System. The Corporation is supported by assessments on insured banks and its own investment income.

Federal Emergency Relief Administration. A unit which, from 1933 to 1938, dispensed federal funds outright to the poorer States, and on a matching basis to others, to assist them in relieving poverty.

Federal Extension Service. An agency of the Department of Agriculture which, in cooperation with the staffs of the land-grant colleges, makes available to farm and home the results of research on agriculture and rural life and provides information on marketing and consumer problems. Its service is rendered chiefly through county agricultural, home-demonstration, and 4-H club agents throughout the nation.

Federal Farm Loan Board. One of the first agencies (created 1916) to provide credit facilities to farmers, whose functions have now been transferred to the Farm Credit Administration, *q.v.*

Federal Firearms Act. A law of Congress, June 30, 1938, which forbids any unlicensed person to ship firearms or ammunition in interstate commerce and subjects such shipments to numerous restrictions.

federal government. *In the United States:* the Government which, from its capital in the District of Columbia, directly legislates, administers, and exercises jurisdiction over matters assigned to it in the Constitution and exerts considerable influence, by means of grants-in-aid and otherwise, over matters reserved to the State governments. *Called also* general government; national government.

federal home loan bank. One of 12 federally chartered regional banks which provides credit reserves and insures liquidity of resources for member savings, home financing, and insurance institutions. The member institutions own all the stock of each regional federal home loan bank. Bonds and notes of the home loan banks are not directly guaranteed by the U.S. Government.

Federal Home Loan Bank Board. An independent corporation of the federal government, consisting of three members, which supervises the 12 federal home loan banks, *q.v.*, the Federal Savings and Loan Insurance Corporation, *q.v.*, and federal savings and loan associations, *q.v.*

Federal Housing Administration. A unit created in 1934, now part of the Department of Housing and Urban Development, which provides insurance on loans and mortgages of various kinds in order to improve housing standards and encourage home ownership.

federal intermediate credit bank. A federal bank created in each of 12 farm-credit districts in 1923 to make loans to, and discount obligations of, agricultural credit cooperatives and similar institutions making short-term loans (not more than 12 months) to farmers. These banks are under the Farm Credit Administration and obtain their loanable funds from the sale of short-term debentures (not guaranteed by the U.S. Government) to the general public.

federalism. A principle of political organization which permits former independent states to combine under a common central government while retaining some portion of their former power and identity. The principle may also be used to decentralize an existing unitary state. *See* federal 1.

Federalist. 1. An advocate of a confederation or of a federal form of government. 2. An advocate of the adoption of the Constitution of the United States, 1787–89. 3. A supporter of the Federalist party, *q.v.*

Federalist, The. A series of 85 essays contributed by Alexander Hamilton, James Madison, and John Jay to New York newspapers in the fall and winter of 1787–88 with the object of securing the ratification of the Constitution. They have been reprinted in several editions and constitute one of the best sources for the construction of the Constitution and for the study of federal government.

Federalist party. The first of the national parties in the United States. Alexander Hamilton was its principal leader until his death in 1804. The party was somewhat authoritarian in its political theory, nationalistic in its foreign policy, and liberal in its interpretation of the national government's powers under the Constitution. It dominated the administrations of Washington and the elder Adams. Its later decline was caused partly by its lack of effective popular organization, partly by its factious opposition to measures of Jefferson's and Madison's administrations which appealed to the judgment and patriotism of the people. It disappeared from national politics after 1816, though its organization continued in Delaware until 1828.

federal kidnaping statute. *See* Lindbergh Law.

federal land bank. One of 12 banks created by Congress in 1916 to make loans to farmers, ranchers, and agricultural cooperatives for the purchase of land and equipment. Loans are secured by mortgages on land and appurtenances and are financed by the sale of consolidated federal farm loan bonds to the public. The 12 federal land banks are wholly owned by the cooperative farm loan associations and are under the jurisdiction of the Farm Credit Administration, *q.v.*

federal land bank association. A group of ten or more farmers or ranchers who form a local cooperative which, under the Federal Farm Loan Act of 1916, can make long-term loans to its members with funds supplied by a federal land bank, taking in exchange the member's mortgage which the association endorses and which serves as security for the loan. There are several hundred of these land bank associations, all stock being owned by farmer-members. The associations, in turn, own all the stock of the 12 federal land banks, *q.v.*

Federal Maritime Commission. An independent federal agency, successor in part to the U.S. Maritime Commission, which is composed of five members appointed for 4-year terms by the President and Senate, and which regulates rates and services of common carriers by water, licenses freight-forwarders by ship on the high seas, and enforces various statutes and regulations applying to water carriers.

Federal Mediation and Conciliation Service. An independent agency, created by the Taft-Hartley Labor-Management Relations Act, *q.v.*, of 1947 as successor to the U.S. Conciliation Service, that lends its good offices in efforts to bring about adjustments of labor disputes, especially during cooling-off periods which the act prescribes in the case of certain types of labor disputes.

Federal National Mortgage Association. A U.S. Government corporation which, since 1965, has been part of the Department of Housing and Urban Development. The association's primary purpose is to increase liquidity for mortgage investments and to make loans, secured by first mortgages, to private companies and public agencies for the construction of low-rental dwelling units. *Called also* Fannie Mae.

Federal Open Market Committee. *See* Open Market Committee.

Federal Power Commission. An independent commission of five members, established by Congress in 1920 and set up in its present form by the Federal Power Act, June 30, 1930, which issues licenses for the construction of works to develop hydroelectric power and protect navigation at nationally-owned power sites and on navigable waters; issues certificates to gas companies to construct and extend facilities for the transport of natural gas interstate and for resale locally; determines wholesale rates for electric power conveyed and sold interstate; controls the issuance of securities by companies engaged in such activity; and supplements and strengthens State regulation of utilities furnishing electricity and natural gas.

Federal Prison Industries, Inc. A public corporation with six directors, operating under the Bureau of Prisons of the U.S. Department of Justice, which has charge of industrial enterprises and vocational training in federal penal institutions.

federal question. Any matter in a case in law or equity which involves a right or privilege claimed under the Constitution or a valid law or treaty of the United States.

federal range. Approximately 153,000,000 acres of United States public land in ten Western States suitable for grazing and range purposes. Issuance of grazing permits, leasing, and other exploitation of this land is controlled by the Bureau of Land Management, *q.v.*

Federal Register. An official daily publication, begun May 14, 1936, which contains proclamations and executive orders of the President and general and special orders, rules and regulations, and notices of hearings issued by executive departments or agencies.

Federal Regulation of Lobbying Act. Title III of the Legislative Reorganization Act of Aug. 2, 1946, which requires lobbyists to register with the clerk of the House and the secretary of the Senate, and to state the names and addresses of the persons employing them and the amount of salary and expense allowances which they receive. Lobbyists are further required to make quarterly reports of all money received and paid by them for the purpose of influencing legislation and to state the names of publications in which they have caused articles or editorials to be printed.

federal reserve bank. *See* Federal Reserve System.

federal reserve bank notes. Currency formerly issued in small amounts by individual federal reserve banks and normally based on certain issues of United States bonds.

Federal Reserve Board. *See* Board of Governors of the Federal Reserve System.

federal reserve notes. The principal currency of the United States issued in various denominations by the federal reserve banks. The notes are based on collateral consisting chiefly of commercial paper discounted by a bank and U.S. Government bonds and notes. Federal reserve notes are direct obligations of the United States.

Federal Reserve System. A decentralized banking and credit system, established by the Federal Reserve Act of 1913, composed of 12 mutually independent quasi-public banks one of which is located in a principal city of each of 12 federal reserve districts into which the United States is divided, namely Boston, New York, Philadelphia, Richmond, Atlanta, Dallas, Cleveland, Chicago, St. Louis, Minneapolis, Kansas City, and San Francisco. The 12 banks operate under the general supervision

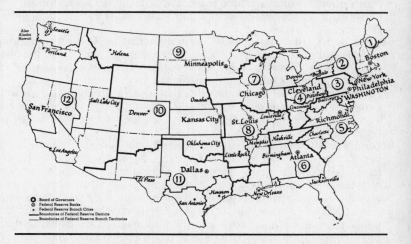

Federal Reserve System—Federal Reserve Districts and Branches

of the Board of Governors of the Federal Reserve System, *q.v.* The stock of each bank is owned by the member banks of each district, and they include all national banks and such private State-chartered banks and trust companies as have been admitted to the system. The member banks elect a majority of each reserve bank's board of directors. The minority are appointed by the Board of Governors of the Federal Reserve System. The reserve banks, which are "bankers' banks," deal directly with banks and rarely with the general public. They rediscount commercial paper, hold reserves for member banks, assist in the transfer of funds, issue notes, act as fiscal agencies for the federal government, and hold government funds on deposit. Under the direction of the Board of Governors, operating through an Open Market Committee, *q.v.*, the reserve banks buy and sell bankers' acceptances and government securities. The system also includes a Federal Advisory Council, *q.v.*

federal savings and loan association. One of approximately 2,000 private building and loan or savings and loan associations chartered and supervised since 1933 by the Federal Home Loan Bank Board.

Federal Savings and Loan Insurance Corporation. A credit corporation which insures savings in private building and loan associations under the supervision of the Federal Home Loan Bank Board.

federal state. A state in which the powers of government are divided between one general government with jurisdiction over certain matters wherever they occur throughout the extent of the state, and a number of other governments in States, provinces, or cantons which exercise a relatively independent jurisdiction over other matters within their particular areas, the extent of powers of both central and component governments being defined in a written constitution, and jurisdictional disputes usually being settled by a permanent court provided for in the constitution. In such a regime sovereignty usually resides in the authority which is legally capable of amending the federal constitution. *Compare* unitary state.

Federal Tort Claims Act. Title IV of the Legislative Reorganization Act of Aug. 2, 1946, which gives to administrative agencies of the national government authority to settle claims of $1,000 or less growing out of negligent or wrongful acts or omissions of employees of the United States while on duty; and provides that U.S. District Courts, sitting without a jury, may render judgment for any such claim for money only, subject to appeal to the Court of Claims or to a U.S. Court of Appeals.

Federal Trade Commission. An independent quasi-judicial commission of five members, created by act of Congress, Sept. 26, 1914, which promotes fair competition by preventing illegal combinations in restraint of interstate trade, unlawful price-fixing or price-discrimination agreements among distributors of goods or services, or other agreements among producers or distributors essentially monopolistic and not in the public interest. Included among prohibited practices are exclusive dealings, "tying" arrangements and illegal brokerage, and corporate mergers and interlocking directorates which substantially lessen competition or foster monopoly. The commission seeks to prevent fraudulent or deceptive advertising of foods, drugs, cosmetics and therapeutic devices, and may enjoin unfair advertising practices by instituting an appropriate action in a U.S. District Court. In cases of unlawful conspiracies or combinations to restrain or divert trade, the commission, after a hearing, may issue a cease-and-desist order, *q.v.*, which can only be set aside by a United States Circuit Court after an appeal from the commission's ruling, and which becomes final if not appealed within 60 days. The commission often secures voluntary agreements among companies to terminate competitive or trade practices which are of questionable legality.

federal war ballot. A ballot authorized by act of Congress in World War II which contained blank spaces in which a member of the armed forces might write in his choices for President, Vice President, Senator, and

Representative in Congress. Soldiers' voting had been permitted in the Civil War election of 1864. *See* absentee voting.

federation. 1. The act of two or more states which, while retaining exclusive control over most public affairs, create a federal government with exclusive control over other affairs, the arrangement being maintained under a juridically superior authority such as a written constitution. **2.** The act of two or more states in forming a league or a confederation, *qq.v.*

fee. A fixed charge required by law to be paid by a person to defray all or part of the expense of some public action which confers a special benefit on the payer and also involves the enforcement of a public policy.

fellow-servant doctrine. A common-law doctrine or rule, now generally abrogated by workmen's compensation legislation, that in an action for damages brought against an employer by an injured employee the employer may plead that the negligence of another employee was partly or wholly responsible for the accident resulting in the injury and, by proving such negligence, reduce or extinguish his own liability.

fellow traveler. A person who, though not a member of the Communist party, belongs to one of its auxiliary organizations, or sympathizes with its aims, or actively supports its program.

felony. A grave crime at common law or under statutes in many States which is punishable by death or by imprisonment in a penitentiary; a graver offense than a misdemeanor.

F.E.R.A. Federal Emergency Relief Administration.

Fess-Kenyon Act. An act of Congress, June 2, 1920, to aid the States on a dollar-for-dollar basis in vocational rehabilitation.

fetcher. *Slang.* A bill introduced and supported for the purpose of collecting legislative blackmail, *q.v.*

Few die and none resign. A paraphrase of Jefferson's comment, July 12, 1801, on vacancies in the national civil service: "Those by death are few; by resignation, none."

F.H.A. Federal Home Administration, or Federal Housing Administration.

F.H.L.B.B. Federal Home Loan Bank Board.

fiat money. Paper money (as U.S. Civil War greenbacks) issued by a government without provision for convertibility into other forms of currency, or for redemption in precious metals, or backed with other forms of wealth, but usually declared to be legal tender.

field service. That part of public administration which is conducted through local branch offices or traveling representatives.

Field v. Clark. A case, 143 U.S. 649 (1892), which involved presidential authority under the Tariff Act of 1890 to suspend that act's free list in the case of countries that imposed duties upon American products which were "reciprocally unequal and unreasonable." The act had been attacked as an unconstitutional delegation of law-making power. The Supreme Court affirmed the principle that legislative power cannot be delegated, but asserted that no such delegation had occurred in this case since the contingency when the discretionary power of the President was to take effect had been "named" and nothing involving the "expediency or just operation" of the statute had been confided to the President. The case is a landmark in judicial accommodation to the delegation of legislative discretion to the President and administrative agencies.

Fifteenth Amendment. An amendment to the Constitution, proclaimed Mar. 30, 1870, which forbids a State to deny the suffrage to any person because of race, color, or previous condition of servitude. Several Southern States have circumvented it by imposing literacy, taxpaying, and other qualifications and through discriminatory administration of election laws by registration and polling officials. Some provisions of civil rights acts are designed to enforce the 15th Amendment against State and private action.

Fifth Amendment. An amendment to the Constitution, proclaimed Dec. 15, 1791, which restricts the powers of the national government by requiring presentment or indictment by a grand jury before judicial trials for "capital or otherwise infamous" crimes; and prohibits double jeopardy, compulsory self-incrimination, the deprivation of life, liberty, and property without due process, and the taking of private property for public use without just compensation. These limitations protect every "person," including corporations and noncitizens within the jurisdiction of the United States and incorporated territories.

Fifth Amendment Communist. A person who pleads the Fifth Amendment's protection against self-incrimination rather than answer questions before congressional committees investigating allegedly subversive activities;—from a derogatory term applied by Senator Joseph R. McCarthy.

fifth columnist. An actual or potential traitor in wartime;—derived from a remark made during the Spanish Civil War of 1936 by a rebel general who, in advancing with four columns upon the loyalist capital of Madrid, declared that a fifth column of rebel sympathizers existed within the city.

fifty-four forty or fight. A slogan which appeared in the press in 1846 demanding that the Oregon Country, then jointly occupied by the United States and Great Britain, should be included in the United States to its full extent northward, that is, to 54° 40', the southern boundary of Alaska. *See* Oregon Country.

file. A list of documents arranged for reference, especially in relation to a case pending in a judicial or investigative tribunal.

filibuster. 1. An adventurer who leads a military expedition against some country with which his own country is at peace. 2. Long-continued speechmaking by a member, or members, of a legislative body, or other delaying tactics deliberately intended to compel the majority to abandon part of its legislative program. It is of fairly common occurrence in the U. S. Senate, where the rules until recently have made closure almost impossible.

filibusterer. A legislative obstructionist.

filing. Announcing one's candidacy for nomination by a political party in a primary election, which must be done before a fixed date in the office of a designated State or local public official. In many States payment of a filing fee at the same time is required as an earnest of good faith.

Finality Men. Northerners who, 1850–61, regarded the Compromise of 1850 as a final settlement of the slavery issue and wished to avoid its further discussion.

Finance Committee. A committee of the U. S. Senate with jurisdiction similar to that of the Ways and Means Committee of the House.

finance committee. The committee concerned with taxation in many State legislative bodies.

finding. A conclusion of fact certified after inquiry by a judicial or other body.

fine. A sum of money which a court exacts from a person as punishment for a proved violation of law.

fire department. An administrative department of municipal or local government which is charged with the prevention and extinguishment of fires and the enforcement of local fire ordinances.

fire-eater. A violent advocate of Southern interests, constitutional rights, and secession in the decade of the 1850's.

fire limits. The periphery of closely congested districts of cities within which the use of flammable materials for construction is prohibited by building codes.

fire marshal. A State or local officer charged with the enforcement of fire inspection laws, the elimination of fire hazards, and the investigation of the causes of fires, especially those in which arson or incendiarism is suspected.

fireside chat. An informal radio or television broadcast addressed to the people;—derived from a term applied by the press to President F. D. Roosevelt's periodic radio reports to the nation.

First Amendment. An amendment, the first of the federal Bill of Rights, adopted Dec. 15, 1791, which prohibits an establishment of religion, requires the separation of church and state, and guarantees freedom of worship, of speech, and of the press, and the right of peaceable assembly, association, and petition. Originally a limitation only upon the federal government, it has been extended to State governments under the due-process and equal-protection clauses of the 14th Amendment by numerous judicial decisions beginning in 1925 with *Gitlow* v. *New York, q.v.* Though some Justices hold that First Amendment freedoms are absolute or occupy a "preferred position," the majority of the Supreme Court has generally held that they are subject to modifications on account of conditions or circumstances. *See* clear-and-present-danger rule.

First International. An organization of socialist and labor leaders, officially known as the International Workingmen's Association, formed in London in 1864 by Karl Marx and others. Divergent views of various national contingents distracted its councils from the outset, and personal animosities and doctrinal conflicts of various leaders, in particular of Marx and the anarchist Bakunin, led to a struggle for control which was climaxed by Bakunin's expulsion at The Hague in 1872. The Marxian wing, left in control, moved the headquarters of the International to

New York, and the First International was disbanded at a final congress at Philadelphia in 1876.

First in War, First in Peace, and First in the Hearts of His Countrymen. An appellation of Washington which originated in the funeral oration by Richard Henry Lee.

First President of the Southern Confederacy. A title bestowed on John C. Calhoun by a posthumous medal struck by the State of South Carolina. Actually the first (and only) President of the Confederate States was Jefferson Davis.

First War Powers Act. An act of Congress, Dec. 18, 1941, authorizing the President to redistribute functions among federal agencies, including the power to consolidate or abolish agencies except the General Accounting Office; to make defense contracts without competitive bidding, except that no contract should be for cost plus percentage of cost, or in violation of laws fixing profits; to embargo exports of coin; to control property in which a foreign country or one of its nationals has an interest; and to institute a censorship of communications with any foreign country which the President should specify.

fiscal policy. Any action by government involving a change in tax policy especially the form, incidence, or rate of taxation, or the scale of public appropriations, including decisions as to whether to endure a surplus or deficit, the objective in any case being the reversal of an existing or anticipated deflationary or inflationary trend and the promotion of economic stability.

fiscal year. The twelve-month period beginning at any fixed date during which annual appropriations are to be spent, taxes collected, and accounts kept. The fiscal year of the United States begins July 1.

Fish and Wildlife Service. *See* United States Fish and Wildlife Service.

fishing expedition. *Slang.* An investigation by a legislative committee or by an administrative agency or officer, primarily inspired by the hope of discovering evidence of wrongdoing that can be used for partisan advantage or as a basis for criminal prosecution. The courts usually condemn such searches.

five-minute rule. A rule of the House of Representatives, applying only in committee of the whole, which limits the proposer of an amendment to five minutes in which to explain it, after which "the Member who shall first obtain the floor shall be allowed to speak five minutes in opposition."

Five-Power Treaty. The Washington Naval Limitation Treaty of Feb. 6, 1922, signed by the United States, Great Britain, Japan, France, and Italy, which fixed capital-ship ratios among the signatory powers and limited replacement tonnage.

five-to-four decision. A decision of the U. S. Supreme Court in which the result is sometimes said to be determined by one of nine Justices. Criticism of such decisions in important constitutional cases has occasionally led to a demand that at least six Justices be required to concur in holding a statute unconstitutional.

Flag of the United States. A standard carried by troops and war vessels and displayed over public and private buildings. It was adopted by the

Continental Congress, June 14, 1777. From 1795 to 1818 it had fifteen stripes and fifteen stars; but since the latter date it has had thirteen stripes and a number of stars equal to the number of States in the Union.

Flag-Salute cases. Two cases involving the power of State authorities to exclude children from the public schools for their refusal, on religious grounds, to salute the American flag during school exercises. In *Minersville School District* v. *Gobitis*, 310 U.S. 586 (1940), the Supreme Court supported a State's requirement of a salute as a means of inculcating loyalty in youth to an orderly political society, holding that such requirement did not interfere with religious freedom. In *West Virginia State Board of Education* v. *Barnette*, 319 U.S. 624 (1943), the earlier decision was reversed, the Court declaring that any official effort to prescribe orthodoxy in politics or religion, or to force citizens against their will formally to profess adherence to such orthodoxy, is a violation of the Fourteenth Amendment which incorporates the substance of the First.

fleet admiral. *See* admiral.

***Fletcher* v. *Peck*.** A case, 6 Cr. 87 (1810), which grew out of the Yazoo Land Fraud, *q.v.*, and an attempt of the Georgia legislature to repeal a land grant corruptly made by the preceding legislature. The Supreme Court held that the action of one legislature in rescinding a former grant was void because, although legislative acts may be repealed, rights vested under prior acts cannot be divested. The Court also held that the original grant was in the nature of a contract the obligation of which, under the Constitution, cannot be impaired.

flexible constitution. A constitution (as the British Constitution) which can be formally changed or amended by legislative action;—originally used by James Bryce, Viscount Bryce, in his *The American Commonwealth* (1888). *Compare* rigid constitution.

flexible price support. A government support price which, under provisions of federal legislation in 1954, can be adjusted by administrative action to the supply and the market price of certain farm products.

flexible tariff. A tariff law which permits the President, upon ascertaining the existence of certain legally defined conditions, to raise or lower duties within prescribed limits; for example, the discretion confided to the President in the Trade Expansion Act, *q.v.*

floater. 1. A purchasable voter. 2. A person who, giving false or fictitious addresses, registers and votes illegally in several precincts at one election.

floating debt. That portion of a public debt in the form of treasury bills or other short-term obligations which has not been funded;—distinguished from funded debt, *q.v.*

flood control. The erection of dikes, levees, and similar works along rivers and other bodies of water to prevent overflow; and the construction of dams, canals, and similar installations to permit the regulation of the flow and volume of water in lakes and streams. Systematic flood control also embraces reforestation and afforestation, conversion of some tilled land to pasturage, contour farming, and activities designed to regulate drainage, prevent flash floods, and reduce erosion. Flood control is carried on by the Corps of Engineers of the Army, the Soil Conservation

Service of the Department of Agriculture, and by various other federal and State agencies and international agencies like the International Boundary and Water Commission, United States and Mexico, *q.v.*

floor. 1. The main part of a legislative hall reserved for the use of members, as distinguished from galleries. 2. The exclusive privilege of a member to address a legislative house at a given time.

floor leader. A member designated by his party caucus to take charge of party interests during legislative sittings. He may plan the course of debate, defend his party from attack, determine the order in which members of his party may speak, and, through the whips, strive to maintain party solidarity. The floor leaders of the two major parties in the Senate usually decide when debate shall be closed and a vote taken.

Florida purchase. The purchase of the whole of East Florida from Spain for $5,000,000 by the Adams-Onis Treaty signed at Washington, Feb. 22, 1819. Spain also relinquished all claim to West Florida, *q.v.*, agreed to a settlement of the boundary between her Mexican possessions and the Louisiana Purchase and ceded her claims to the Oregon country to the United States.

F.M.C. Federal Maritime Commission.

F.M.C.S. Federal Mediation and Conciliation Service.

F.N.M.A. Federal National Mortgage Association.

Foggy Bottom. A nickname for the Department of State;—from the rather marshy location of the Old State Department Building in Washington.

Fong Yue Ting v. United States. A case, 149 U.S. 698 (1893), in which the Supreme Court held that in matters affecting foreign affairs, Congress and the President, as the political departments of the national government, exercise what amounts to an inherent sovereign power determined by international public law and usage to exclude or expel aliens, in this case certain Chinese laborers who had not secured certificates of residence as required by law.

Food and Agriculture Organization of the United Nations. One of the specialized agencies of the United Nations, which is concerned with raising nutritional standards, improving rural life, and promoting a better balance between production and distribution of agricultural commodities throughout the world. To attain its objectives the agency makes appropriate recommendations to its member states.

Food and Drug Administration. A division of the Department of Health, Education, and Welfare which is charged with the enforcement of federal pure food, drug, cosmetic, and other laws and for this purpose maintains an inspection service to detect adulterated or misbranded goods. If those charged with violations of the law fail to desist voluntarily, the agency may cite them for prosecution to the Department of Justice. The agency also conducts research to determine the effect of new drugs and to protect consumers against toxic or other potentially dangerous ingredients in foods, drugs, cosmetics, pesticides, and other articles of commerce.

food-stamp plan. A plan whereby relief clients who purchased stamps redeemable for food at designated stores would receive 50 per cent additional in free stamps good for items of food declared surplus by the Department of Agriculture;—in use prior to World War II.

Foraker Act. An act of Congress, April 12, 1900, creating a civil government for the newly acquired island of Puerto Rico under an appointive governor and council and a locally elective lower house of the legislature. *See* Puerto Rico; *compare* Jones Act.

Force Act. An act of Congress, May 31, 1870, directed at the "reconstructed" South, which authorized the President to use military force to support civilian law enforcement agencies in order to protect Negroes' civil and political rights under the 14th and 15th Amendments against interference by States or individuals.

Force Bill. 1. An act of Congress, 1833, which gave the President authority to use the army and navy to enforce the tariff laws of the United States. 2. Any of several bills introduced in Congress, 1871–90, providing for national supervision of elections in order to strengthen or implement the Force Act, *q.v.*

Fordney-McCumber Tariff. A tariff law, Sept. 21, 1922, which increased the duties on many articles and in which for the first time was introduced the principle of the flexible tariff, *q.v.*

foreign corporation. From the point of view of a State of the Union, any corporation chartered in a different State. Such corporations can do business within the State only with its express approval, but it may not prescribe conditions for entry which deny such corporations the right to resort to federal courts or to engage in interstate commerce. They are not citizens with constitutional privileges and immunities; but they are artificial persons protected by the due-process and equal-protection clauses of the 14th Amendment.

foreign policy. A relatively consistent course of conduct pursued by a state over an appreciable period in its relations with other states. American foreign policy has been largely determined by precedent and tradition, international treaties, moral and legal obligations, national interest, and physical circumstances. During most of its course it emphasized neutrality, freedom of navigation and trade, noninvolvement in European affairs, and resistance to foreign encroachments on the Western Hemisphere. Involvement in World War I interrupted the main trend. After World War II American foreign policy emphasized cooperation with the United Nations in the peaceful solution of world problems, Marshall Plan aid to Europe and similar assistance to underdeveloped countries, a system of alliances (as NATO, SEATO, CENTO) for the containment of Communist aggression, and direct military confrontation of Communist aggressors (as in Korea, Vietnam). The President formulates foreign policy with the aid of the Secretary of State, specialists in the State Department, and confidential advisers. The Senate and House committees on foreign affairs wield great influence because of the necessity for obtaining the Senate's consent to treaties and congressional acts authorizing projects and appropriating money.

Foreign Securities Act. An act of Congress, Apr. 13, 1934, which prohibited buying or selling within this country of the bonds or other securities of any nation which was in default of its obligations to the United States. *Called also* Debt Default Act and Johnson Act.

Foreign Service. The career service of the State Department established by the Rogers Act, *q.v.*, 1924, which combined the previously separate diplomatic and consular services. The Foreign Service has a separate service for recruitment, examination, and promotion. Its officers are classified in three groups as Foreign Service officers, Foreign Service Reserve Officers, and Foreign Service staff. They may be assigned in Washington as well as abroad.

Foreign Service Institute. An agency in the Department of State which provides instruction and training in foreign and international affairs for foreign service personnel, State Department employees, and certain other federal employees.

Foreign Service officer. An officer of the U. S. Foreign Service whose rank, when he is assigned abroad, is ordinarily ambassador, minister, counselor of embassy, attaché, diplomatic secretary, consul general, consul, or vice consul.

foreign-trade zone. A special policed area adjacent to a port of entry where goods from foreign countries may be stored and prepared for re-shipment without the payment of customs duties and without being subjected to most customs regulations. Such zones, operated as a public utility, are authorized in the United States by the Foreign Trade Zones Board consisting of the Secretaries of Commerce, the Treasury, and the Army.

foreign valuation. The cost or fair market value in the country of origin of goods imported into the United States which is the basis used by U. S. Customs authorities for levying ad valorem duties.

Forest Service. A unit in the Department of Agriculture, created in 1905, which controls the use and development of national forests, comprising some 181,000,000 acres in 39 States and Puerto Rico, guards them against fire and disease, conducts research in scientific forestry and wild-life resources, and seeks to develop forests commercially and for various public purposes including recreation.

forfeiture. The loss of property as a punishment for some wrongful act or negligence on the part of the owner.

forgotten man. A person (or group) who merits more attention than he receives;—derived from the writings of the sociologist William Graham Sumner and applied by President F. D. Roosevelt in 1932 to middle-class and labor elements in the population which the previous Republican administrations had allegedly neglected.

forty-niner. One who participated in the extensive migration to California in 1849 following the discovery of gold in that region.

forty-shilling freehold. Real property yielding an annual income of forty shillings, ownership of which was required of every voter in a county constituency in England from 1430 to 1832. This requirement, either in its original form or as capitalized according to value or acreage, was usual in the suffrage laws of the Colonial and early Federal periods in the United States.

forty thieves. The members of the Board of Aldermen of New York, about 1850, who distinguished themselves by corrupt grants of franchises;—usually considered opprobrious;—also applied to certain statehouse rings in other States.

Founding Father. A statesman of the Revolutionary and Confederation periods; *especially:* a member of the Convention of 1787.

four freedoms. Freedom of speech, freedom of worship, freedom from want, and freedom from fear which were the chief objectives of American and Allied policy summarized by President F. D. Roosevelt in his message to Congress, Jan. 6, 1941.

4-H Club. A unit in a youth program conducted by the Extension Service of the Department of Agriculture in cooperation with State and local authorities to stimulate achievement and excellence among farm youth.

Four-Power Treaty. A treaty signed at Washington, Dec. 13, 1921, by which France, Great Britain, Japan, and the United States pledged respect for one another's possessions in the Pacific and agreed to settle controversies relating to such possessions by conference or joint discussion.

Fourteen Points. President Wilson's proposal for a peace settlement, as presented in a speech to Congress, Jan. 8, 1918. The most important points were: open covenants openly arrived at; freedom of the seas; removal of economic barriers; reduction of armaments; consideration for colonial populations; evacuation of territory occupied by Germany; readjustment of Italian frontiers; autonomy for people of Austria-Hungary and Turkey; independence for Poland; and a general association of nations to guarantee independence and integrity to large and small states.

Fourteenth Amendment. An amendment to the Constitution, proclaimed July 28, 1868, which superseded the rule of the Dred Scott decision by defining as citizens of the United States and of the States in which they reside "all persons born or naturalized in the United States, and subject to the jurisdiction thereof"; restricted the powers of the States in relation to such citizens and other persons; ordered the reduction of a State's representation in Congress wherever the right of suffrage of adult males was denied; disqualified from office former officeholders who had engaged in rebellion; and validated the war debt of the United States while voiding the war debts of rebellious States and claims for loss or emancipation of slaves. The restrictions on State powers, broadly phrased in the due-process, equal-protection, and privileges-and-immunities clauses, *qq.v.*, though designed primarily to protect freed Negroes, were judicially interpreted most frequently as constitutional limitations upon State taxing power and State social legislation, especially attempted regulation of economic activity. Since 1925 the Supreme Court has expanded the meaning of the Fourteenth Amendment so as to include the whole of the First Amendment and selected portions from the Fourth to the Eighth Amendments of the federal Bill of Rights. Thus States may not abridge the freedoms of speech, press, religion, assembly, or petition; make searches and seizures which unduly infringe on personal privacy; keep people of a different color or nationality off jury lists; use physical coercion or prolonged questioning to obtain confessions; require excessive bail; deny an accused person an opportunity to cross-examine a hostile witness; deny counsel to an accused person at any stage of police questioning or judicial proceedings; or unduly speed up or delay a trial.

fourth estate. The journalistic profession, or the press;—derived from a reference to the reporters' gallery of the British Parliament whose influence on public policy was said to equal that of Parliament's three traditional estates, the clergy, nobility, and commons.

Four-Year-Tenure Act. An act of Congress, May 15, 1820, which limited the terms of most appointive officers of the federal government to four years in order to facilitate the retirement of superannuated employees. It was later used to secure rotation in office under the spoils system.

F.P.C. Federal Power Commission.

fractional currency. 1. Coins or notes the face value of which is less than that of the standard monetary unit. **2.** Any coin or note of a face value less than one dollar in U. S. currency.

franchise. 1. A special privilege granted by public authority to an individual or corporation, especially the privilege of using streets or other public property for gas mains, electric or telephone wires, and public transportation, or permission to a railroad or public utility to acquire rights of way by proceeding under eminent domain. After the decision in the Dartmouth College case, *q.v.*, public authorities have usually limited franchises to a term of years and to minutely specified conditions. Franchises are always strictly interpreted. *See Charles River Bridge v. The Warren Bridge.* **2.** The privilege of voting. *See* suffrage.

franking privilege. The privilege of sending mail, relating strictly to official business, within covers bearing actual or facsimile signatures of members of Congress and certain other persons, including widows of former Presidents, who have been authorized by law to send mail free of charge.

Franklin. The name of a new State which people residing in what is now Tennessee hoped to form in 1784 from the western part of North Carolina.

fraud. An action characterized by deceit, cunning, or misrepresentation.

fraud order. An order issued by the Postmaster General which directs the return to sender of all mail addressed to persons against whom there is evidence of use of the mails for fraudulent purposes. Misuse of mails for lotteries may result in a similar lottery order.

Frazier-Lemke Act. An act of Congress, Aug. 28, 1935, which established a three-year moratorium on farm mortgage foreclosures, required the owner to pay rental during the period of the moratorium, and provided for the sale of the property at auction after reappraisal at the expiration of the moratorium if the mortgagor had not been previously satisfied. It superseded an earlier law of the same name which had been declared unconstitutional.

Fredonian Republic. A government independent of Mexico prematurely proclaimed by American settlers in Texas in 1826.

free coinage. The public policy of accepting unlimited amounts of monetary metal for coinage.

free conference. *See* conference 1.

Free Democracy. The name adopted by the antislavery faction of the Democratic party in New York which nominated Martin Van Buren for President in 1848. Later in the same year the Free-Soil party also nominated him as its candidate.

Freedmen's Bureau. A Bureau in the War Department created by Congress, March 3, 1865, which provided work relief in devastated areas, protection of Negro labor from exploitation, and educational opportunities for Negroes. Its discontinuance in 1869 resulted partly from charges that many of its activities were directed toward organizing the Republican party in the South.

freedom march. A demonstration in which participants, often proceeding much of the way on foot, converge on centers (as a capital city) to protest violations of the civil rights of minorities and segregation practices. *See* March on Washington.

freedom of assembly. *See* right of assembly.

freedom of association. *See* right of association.

freedom of contract. A concept formerly used by courts in declaring unconstitutional State and federal labor legislation, by upholding the right of an adult person to accept employment at longer hours, lower wages, or in different terms than provided in the law, unless the prosecution could prove that such employment would have a deleterious effect on his health, safety, or morals. *See Lochner* v. *New York.*

freedom of debate. The right, essential to representative government, and guaranteed by the U.S. Constitution, Art. I, Sect. 6, of a legislative body to consider any matter it chooses and to discuss, deliberate, and act under rules of its own making unhampered by the other branches of the government; and of individual members to state their opinions freely without fear of arrest or punishment anywhere, or of being called in question by any authority other than that of the house of which they are members.

freedom of religion. The rights of religious belief and of conscience which are absolute, and the rights of worship, preaching, and the organization of religious congregations which are subject only to the condition that actions inimical to morals and public order may be punished. Freedom of religion is guaranteed from interference from federal or State authorities by the First and Fourteenth Amendments.

freedom of speech and press. A right guaranteed in American federal and State constitutions to speak or write freely on any subject, provided the speaker does not slander or libel another person or affect adversely some superior interest of the state, such as protection of society against obscene literature or advocacy of enemy causes in time of war. The sedition statutes of 1798 and 1918 and the Smith Act of 1940, enacted in the exercise of national war powers, and State criminal syndicalism laws, enacted under the police powers to promote the public safety and welfare, all imposed limitations on the right to criticize the government.

Judicial opinion concerning them has varied, sometimes holding that Congress may suppress speech or writing which has a "tendency" toward overthrow of the government, while at other times the Court has insisted that First Amendment freedoms occupy a preferred position. Currently justifiable restrictions begin only at the point where the spoken or written statement creates a clear and present danger that words will result in unlawful acts. Because freedom of speech and press are guaranteed in order to foster the communication of ideas, mere profanity and abuse are not under its protection. Under the Fourteenth Amendment, the First Amendment's guarantees are applied by the federal judiciary to protect speech and press against action by a State government. Historically the guarantee of free speech and press was aimed at the institution of direct censorship, but now it protects against subsequent punishment as well as previous restraint and covers such indirect attempts at invasion as a special tax on publishers or the enactment of ordinances prohibiting the distribution of handbills to prevent littering the streets. With the development of new mediums for conveying ideas, the scope of the right of free expression has been expanded to include the stage, the cinema, the phonograph record, radio, television, the employer's leaflet, and the laborer's placard in the picket line.

freedom ride. An organized tour to protest against segregation in public accommodations or to test civil rights under desegregation legislation.

freeholders' charter. A municipal charter drafted by a locally appointed charter commission, or board of freeholders, and submitted to the voters of a municipality or urban area for approval under constitutional or legal provisions for home rule.

free list. That part of a tariff law which contains an enumeration of articles which are exempt from duty.

freeman. 1. A person who is not a serf or a slave. 2. One who, in the Colonial period, was admitted to the privileges of a public corporation and who thereby secured certain economic and civil rights, including the suffrage.

free port. A foreign-trade zone, *q.v.*

Freeport Doctrine. The doctrine announced by Stephen A. Douglas in 1858 at Freeport, Ill., during his famous debates with Lincoln in which he attempted to reconcile the opinion of the Supreme Court in the Dred Scott case with his own principle of territorial or squatter sovereignty. Douglas conceded that neither Congress nor a territorial legislature could expressly abolish slavery in a territory but insisted that a territory could effectively prevent the existence of slavery by failing to support it with local police regulations or by passing unfriendly legislation.

free silver. The unrestricted coinage of standard silver dollars.

free soil, free speech, free labor, and free men. A slogan of the Free-Soil party in 1848 and of the Republicans in 1856.

Free-Soil party. A minor party opposed to the extension of slavery to the territories which was active in the elections of 1848 and 1852.

free trade. International trade conducted without legal limitations designed to protect domestic producers; *especially:* such trade conducted in the absence of tariffs except those solely intended to raise revenue.

free trade and sailors' rights. An American slogan before and during the War of 1812.

Free World. *Colloquial.* Those states which are not under Communist domination; *also:* those states which are opposed to Communism.

French spoliation claims. Claims by American citizens against France for the seizure of ships and goods, 1791–1815. By agreements with France in 1800 and 1803 the United States relinquished prior claims in return for national advantages; but it was not until 1885 that Congress made fully satisfactory arrangements to compensate private claimants. Claims for losses incurred after 1803 were settled by France in 1831.

friar lands. Lands in the Philippines owned by religious orders but put into the possession of farmers by insurgents about 1896. The United States later extinguished the friars' title by purchase.

Fries' Rebellion. Concerted resistance led by John Fries to the national tax on houses which occurred in eastern Pennsylvania in 1799. Until suppressed by military force, the rebels poured scalding water on officers engaged in measuring houses for tax purposes; *called also* Hot Water War.

frontier. 1. Land near the boundary separating two states. 2. The extreme limit of a civilized or inhabited area.

front porch campaign. A "stay-at-home" political campaign, such as that conducted by McKinley in 1896 when he made addresses to visiting delegations of citizens from the front porch of his home while his opponent was engaged in extensive speaking tours.

Frothingham v. *Mellon.* See *Massachusetts* v. *Mellon.*

F.R.S. Federal Reserve System.

F.T.C. Federal Trade Commission.

Fugitive Felon Acts. Acts of Congress, 1932 and 1934, which make it a federal offense to travel in interstate or foreign commerce in order to avoid (*a*) prosecution, (*b*) confinement after conviction, or (*c*) giving testimony, where under the laws of the State, the offense charged is a felony (or in New Jersey, a high misdemeanor).

fugitive from justice. 1. A person who has fled from the State in which he is accused of having committed a crime in order to avoid arrest and punishment. 2. A person who has fled from a State in order to avoid giving testimony in a criminal prosecution. *See* extradition.

fugitive slave laws. Acts of Congress, the most important of which were passed in 1793 and 1850 to secure the return of runaway slaves to their masters. Attempts to enforce them in Northern States sometimes resulted in incidents which exacerbated sectional feelings.

Fulbright Act. An act of Congress, 1946, which provided that funds from the sale of surplus U. S. war property abroad were to be used to finance research and graduate study by American scholars and students in foreign countries and "to promote the exchange of students and professors and other educational projects"; supplemented by the Fulbright-Hays

(Mutual Educational and Cultural Exchange Act) of 1961 which invites sharing of costs by other interested countries and provides other sources of funds.

full dinner pail. A Republican slogan in the campaign of 1896 designed to appeal to the laboring classes.

full employment. The condition of an economy in which, after allowing for "frictional unemployment" and the application of restraints to prevent excessive inflation, the number of job vacancies is never far below the number of those seeking employment (circa 2 per cent). The attainment of this condition is a national objective under the Employment Act of 1946, *q.v.*

full-faith-and-credit clause. Art. IV, Sec. 1 of the Constitution, which makes it obligatory on a State to recognize and give effect to the legislative acts, public records, and judicial decisions of other States when attested according to the forms prescribed by Congress. This provision makes it unnecessary for a person to re-establish his rights under deeds, wills, and contracts, in every State where he has property interests. Judgments of courts in divorce cases are, however, not binding upon other States unless one of the parties had a bona fide domicile in the State in which the decree of divorce was granted. *See Williams* v. *North Carolina.*

full powers. A document which empowers an envoy to negotiate in behalf of his government.

functional consolidation. The creation by, or on behalf of, two or more local government units of a single agency to administer some common function, as health, welfare, water supply, or parks.

functional representation. Representation in which constituencies are composed of groups of people defined according to occupation or economic status rather than apportioned among different territorial districts.

fund. Money in a public treasury earmarked for normal expenditures (general fund), or for certain special classes of expenditures.

fundamental law. 1. The constitution; *also:* organic statutes or laws which are intrinsically superior to the ordinary law of a state or which the courts regard as law of superior obligation. 2. Natural law, *q.v.*, which is sometimes deemed to be morally if not juridically superior to positive law.

funded debt. Debt in the form of bonds or other long-term obligations.

funding. The process of converting existing debt into interest-bearing bonds or equivalent long-term obligations, or of creating a sinking fund for the extinction of debt at maturity.

Fur Seal controversy. *See* Bering Sea Arbitration.

Furuseth Act. *See* La Follette Seamen's Act.

fusion. A temporary coalition of two or more parties or organized political groups to support a common ticket.

G

Gadsden Purchase. A tract of nearly 30,000 square miles, lying south of the Gila River, now included in Arizona and New Mexico, which was purchased for $10,000,000 from Mexico by a treaty negotiated by James Gadsden and ratified Dec. 30, 1853.

Gadsden Purchase

gag law. Any law abridging freedom of speech, or of the press, or the right of petition.

gag rule. A rule adopted by the House of Representatives in 1836 (repealed 1844) which provided that petitions and papers relating in any way to slavery should be laid on the table without further opportunity being given to consider them; *specifically:* any special closure rule adopted by a legislative body; *called also* gag resolution.

galleries. Portions of a legislative chamber separated by a railing from the floor where the general public and representatives of the press may sit and listen to the debates and discussions.

Galveston plan. The commission plan, *q.v.,* of municipal government which originated in Galveston, Texas in 1901.

game and fish department. A division of State government which engages in research for the conservation of wild life, maintains game refuges, bird sanctuaries, and fish hatcheries, determines open and closed seasons for hunting and fishing, and employs game wardens to enforce conservation laws.

G.A.O. General Accounting Office.

Garrisonians. Radical abolitionists, 1831–61, who denounced the Constitution and government of the United States because they countenanced slavery;—named from William Lloyd Garrison.

gasoline tax. An excise tax upon each gallon of gasoline sold, levied in all States and by the national government to defray the capital expense and maintenance cost of motor roads and highways and often continued as an important source of general revenue.

GATT General Agreement on Tariffs and Trade.

gavel rule. Exercise of power by the presiding officer of a legislative body in contravention of the rules or in violation of the rights of individual members or the minority.

general. One of the higher ranks in the army, air force, or marine corps, corresponding to the rank of admiral in the navy. The highest of all military ranks is "general of the armies" held by only one man in American history, General John J. Pershing, after his retirement. The rank of "general of the army" has been held by several officers either temporarily during active service or permanently after retirement.

General Accounting Office. An independent auditing office of the federal government, created by the Budget and Accounting Act of 1921, which settles all claims in which the United States is a creditor or debtor and investigates all matters pertaining to the receipt, disbursement, and use of public funds. It renders binding opinions as to the legal power of disbursing officers of the government to make payments and prescribes uniform accounting procedures for all government departments and establishments. *See* Comptroller General.

General Agreement on Tariffs and Trade (GATT). A multilateral agreement, 1947, among various nations, chiefly from the industrialized areas of the world, which sought to reduce trade barriers and stimulate multilateral trade. In 1964 the participants in GATT began consideration of a so-called Kennedy Round of additional proposed reductions of industrial tariffs. *See* Dillon Round; Kennedy Round.

General Assembly of the United Nations. The principal political organ of the United Nations consisting of delegations from all member nations each of which has one vote. The Assembly has general supervision of budgetary matters and of the various administrative and specialized agencies, *q.v.*, affiliated with the United Nations. It also develops policies and makes recommendations for the promotion of world peace and welfare. Meetings are held once each year and special meetings may be called.

General Bridge Act. Title V of the Legislative Reorganization Act of Aug. 2, 1946, which gives blanket consent to the construction of bridges over navigable waterways if the location and plans are approved by the Chief of Engineers and the Secretary of the Army before construction is commenced; grants the power of eminent domain; and requires that tolls charged shall be just and reasonable.

general court. The official title of the legislature in Massachusetts and New Hampshire.

general election. 1. An election held in the state at large. 2. A regularly recurring election to select officers to serve after the expiration of the full terms of their predecessors.

general fund. Monies at the disposal of fiscal officials which can be drawn upon to cover legislative appropriations for normal operating expenses of government;—distinguished from special funds, *q.v.*

general law. A statute expressed in general terms and affecting all places, persons, or things within the territory over which a legislature has power to act, but which may include reasonable classifications or categories, provided that all places, persons, or things within each category are treated alike;—distinguished from local legislation and special legislation, *qq.v.*

general pair. An agreement for an indefinite period between two members of a legislative house to have their names recorded on opposite sides of a question when one or both are absent.

general property tax. A tax levied on both real and personal property at a uniform rate according to valuation; once the principal source of State and local revenue but now, chiefly as a real property tax, providing a third of State, and less than half of local, revenues.

General Services Administration. An independent agency of the federal government which is responsible for the management of government property, construction and maintenance of public buildings, procurement of supplies, management of government transportation and communication, stockpiling of critical and strategic materials, preservation of records, publication of new constitutional amendments, statutes, and executive orders, and other housekeeping services.

general staff. A group of high-ranking officers, associated with a chief of staff, who immediately direct the administration of a state's military forces and are responsible for planning military strategy.

general strike. Work stoppage by the employees of the chief industries in a country or district in order to gain some economic or political advantage or to overthrow the existing political and economic system.

general ticket system. Any electoral system in which voters choose more than one person for the same office at a given time. It is used for the selection of presidential electors, for Representatives in Congress from a few States (where more than one is chosen at large), for members of the lower house of the Illinois legislature, and for members of the municipal council in many cities.

general-welfare clause. A clause in Art. I, Sec. 8 of the Constitution which says that Congress may use its taxing power to "pay the debts and provide for the common defense and general welfare of the United States." Strict constructionists once argued that Congress may levy taxes only to promote functions specifically granted to it by the Constitution or properly implied from them. Others held that it enables Congress to make appropriations for any subject deemed to affect the public welfare; this interpretation prevails today.

general will. 1. According to Rousseau, the collective will of the people which, if purged of purely selfish or individual interests, should constitute the true collective interest or common good of the state and society. **2.** In English idealism, the moral quality of the state which is said to be the principal reason (rather than force) for political obedience. **3.** The consensus of an association's membership as to its ultimate objectives.

Geneva Award. *See* "Alabama" claims.

Geneva Convention. An international agreement for the conduct of belligerents drafted in 1864 and ratified by nearly every country. It provides that a belligerent shall give proper care to enemy sick or wounded in its power, that the Red Cross shall be the emblem of the sanitary service; and that hospitals and ambulances with their personnel shall be respected and protected. Revisions in 1906 and 1949 brought the convention of 1864 into accord with newer scientific discoveries and methods of warfare. *See* International Red Cross.

genocide. The systematic killing of members of a political, racial, or cultural group, or causing such a group bodily or mental harm, or deliberately inflicting conditions of life calculated to bring about their destruction, or imposing measures intended to prevent births within a group, or forcibly transferring children from one group to another group; as defined by the United Nations General Assembly, Dec. 11, 1946, in a convention designed to prevent, for the future, horrors like Hitler's anti-Jewish program.

gentlemen's agreement. 1. An informal understanding or engagement; *especially:* an informal diplomatic agreement arranged by an exchange of notes between the foreign offices of two or more governments or by conversations among heads of state or their emissaries. **2.** The agreement between the United States and Japan, Feb. 18, 1908, in which Japan outlined an informal policy of curbing emigration of her nationals to the United States. More definite commitments as to such policy were made by Japan in 1911 and the agreement continued until 1924 when the United States barred Japanese immigration by law. *See* Orientals' exclusion.

geographic determination. The theory that climate, the physical features of the earth, the distribution of natural resources, and other geographic phenomena exert a profoundly important, if not controlling, influence in molding human institutions and shaping human culture. Jean Bodin and the Baron de Montesquieu were among the first modern writers to give serious attention to this theory. A number of recent writers have examined with special care the role which geography has played in fostering national and colonial expansion, national maritime power, imperialism, and war.

geography. *See* political geography.

Geological Survey. A unit of the Department of the Interior which engages in geologic and related research, investigates mineral and water resources and their availability, classifies public lands for exploitation, conducts topographic surveys, and prepares the maps of the United States and possessions of the National Topographic Map series.

Georgia county unit system. A method of weighting votes in Democratic primary elections in Georgia by which populous counties were grossly discriminated against in favor of sparsely populated rural counties. Each of the 159 counties was assigned 2, 4, or 6 units. The candidate who had a plurality in a county was credited with all its units, and the candidate with the most units (but frequently *not* with the most popular votes) was declared the party nominee. This system was invalidated by the Supreme Court in *Gray* v. *Sanders, q.v.*

German Alliance Insurance Co. v. Lewis. A case, 233 U.S. 389 (1914), in which the Supreme Court upheld State regulation of the rates of fire-insurance companies on the ground that fire insurance is a semimonopolistic business and presents a justification for public regulation not unlike that of public utilities.

German Saboteurs case. The case, *Ex parte Quirin,* 317 U.S. 1 (1942), of seven German spies who landed on American shores during World War II to commit military sabotage and who were tried and sentenced by a military commission. The U.S. Supreme Court declared that the military commission had been properly constituted; that the seven spies were subject to its jurisdiction as "unlawful belligerents" under the laws of war; and that the guarantee of a jury trial in the Sixth Amendment was not applicable to the case since that guarantee applies only to federal civilian courts and not to military tribunals.

gerrymander. A redistricting of a State for the election of congressional or legislative representatives which violates the principles of compactness, homogeneity of popular interests, and, before the decisions in *Baker* v. *Carr* and *Gray* v. *Sanders, qq.v.*, equality of population in order to secure the future advantage of the party or group in control of a State legislature. The term is said to have arisen when an artist added wings, claws, and teeth to the map of a sprawling district created in Massachusetts in 1812 and suggested that it be called a salamander, and a Federalist editor changed the title to Gerrymander after Governor Elbridge Gerry.

Gettysburg Address. A brief commemorative address, delivered by President Lincoln, Nov. 19, 1863, at the dedication of a cemetery on the battlefield at Gettysburg, Pa., which contains the definition of democracy as a "government of the people, by the people, for the people."

ghetto. A generally squalid urban slum inhabited almost exclusively by people of a minority race or ethnic group who, because of poverty and social or political discriminations, find it practically impossible to move to a different section;—from the section of a medieval Italian city in which Jews were segregated from others. *See* de facto segregation.

Gibbons v. *Ogden.* A case, 9 Wheat. 1 (1824), in which the Supreme Court declared that Congress' power to regulate foreign and interstate commerce embraced every species of commercial intercourse between the United States and foreign nations and every commercial transaction that was not wholly carried on within the boundaries of a single State; that in the case of interstate commerce, its power did not stop at the boundary line of any State but was applicable within the interior of a State; and that the term "commerce" included navigation.

G.I. Bill of Rights. The Servicemen's Readjustment Act, June 22, 1944, which provided for hospitalization, vocational rehabilitation, and education for veterans; a guarantee of loans up to $4,000 for the purchase of homes, farms, and business property; a readjustment allowance of $20 per week for one year for veterans who are unemployed; together with provisions for job counseling and employment placement. Similar measures have been enacted for the benefit of veterans of the Korean and Vietnam Wars.

Gideon v. *Wainwright.* A case, 372 U.S. 335 (1963), in which the Supreme Court included among the fundamental rights of persons guaranteed by the Fourteenth Amendment the right under the Sixth Amendment to be represented by counsel when a person is being tried for a crime in a State court, including the right of an indigent defendant to have counsel assigned by the court.

gift tax. A tax on the transfer of property by gift, designed chiefly to prevent evasion of inheritance tax laws, and normally assimilated administratively to inheritance or income tax systems. Under federal laws an individual may make total donations of $30,000 during his lifetime which are tax free to donor and recipient and may give not more than $3,000 to any one individual, tax free to donor and donee, during any one year. Federal gift tax rates are steeply graduated, from 2¼ to 57¾ per cent.

Gilbert Islands. *See* Trust territory of the Pacific Islands.

Ginzberg v. *United States.* A case, 383 U.S. 463 (1966), in which the

Supreme Court held that publications created and advertised solely in
order to appeal to prurient interests in sex had the characteristics of
illicit merchandise and could not claim the protection of freedom of the
press, though in a different context (as by sale to physicians) their
distribution might not have been challenged.

Gitlow v. New York. A case, 268 U.S. 652 (1925), involving a criminal
anarchy statute of New York in which the Supreme Court established
standards for judicially acceptable legislative restrictions of free expression in peacetime. Noteworthy was the express statement in the Court's
opinion that freedom of speech and of the press, which are protected
against impairment by Congress in the First Amendment, are also protected against impairment by the States by the due-process clause of
the Fourteenth Amendment.

Glass-Steagall Act. An act of Congress, June 16, 1933, also known as the
Banking Act of 1933, which established the Federal Deposit Insurance
Corporation, *q.v.*, and required the separation of commercial and invest-
ment banking.

G-Man. An agent of the Federal Bureau of Investigation.

G.N.P. Gross National Product.

gobbledygook. The verbose style and stilted jargon which is often characteristic of government directives, reports, and documents;—a word
coined by Representative Maury Maverick of Texas in 1944.

gold certificate. A piece of paper currency formerly issued in denominations of $10 and up which certified that an equivalent amount in gold
had been deposited in the Treasury of the United States; and circulating freely until 1934 when called in and exchanged for other currency.
Only the $10,000 certificates are still in use to settle balances among
Federal Reserve Banks.

Gold Clause cases. Five cases, the principal ones being *Norman v. Baltimore and Ohio R.R. Co.*, 294 U.S. 240, and *Perry v. United States*,
294 U.S. 330, in which the Supreme Court in February, 1935, held that
Congress may invalidate clauses in private contracts calling for payment
in gold but may not invalidate gold clauses in U.S. bonds. Holders of
such bonds may not recover, however, if the government refuses to pay
in gold unless they can show actual economic loss. Congress outlawed
suits for recovery.

Gold Democrats. Democrats who, refusing to support Bryan and free
silver, *q.v.*, in 1896, formed the National Democratic party and nominated a separate ticket.

Gold Hoarding Act. An act of Congress, Mar. 9, 1933, which confirmed
acts and proclamations of the President relating to banks and currency
during the previous five days, and which authorized the Secretary of
the Treasury to call in all gold coin, gold bullion, or gold certificates,
exchanging for them an equivalent amount of any other form of currency or coin issued by the United States.

Gold Reserve Act. An act of Congress, Jan. 30, 1934, under the terms of
which the United States bought all gold on deposit with the Federal
Reserve banks, which had previously been called in from circulation,
and established it, with other gold authorized to be purchased, as a

permanent reserve for outstanding paper money and for other legal purposes. Most of the gold stock is stored in the Gold Bullion Depository at Fort Knox, Ky.

gold standard. A monetary system in which every form of currency is convertible on demand into its legal equivalent in gold or gold coin. The United States adopted the gold standard in 1900 and abandoned it in 1934.

Gomillion v. Lightfoot. A case, 364 U.S. 339 (1960), in which the Supreme Court invalidated an Alabama law redrawing the city boundaries of Tuskegee so as to exclude all but a few Negro inhabitants. The Court declared that the law was obviously designed to disfranchise Negro citizens, constituted a denial of suffrage because of race, and was barred by the 15th Amendment.

good behavior. 1. Proper performance of duties, which is a condition of tenure of office. **2.** Faithful observance of prison regulations, which is often rewarded by reduction in the time to be served by a prisoner.

good-government association. A nonpartisan organization devoted to the improvement of government, usually at the city or county level, that presents information and recommendations at meetings of legislative committees, city councils, and other authorities, publicizes the records of office-holders, recommends electoral action on bond issues and other referendums, and sometimes expresses preference among party candidates for public office.

good-neighbor policy. The policy adopted by the United States toward other American states in the administration of President F. D. Roosevelt. Its principal aims were hemispheric diplomatic solidarity and a common system of hemispheric defense. It rejected any suggestion of political domination by the United States and stressed the triple concepts of equal partnership, friendly collaboration, and mutual assistance.

good offices. The expediting of communication between the parties to a dispute by a third, neutral party without suggesting any form of settlement or compromise.

G.O.P. Grand Old Party.

governance. The method or manner of exercising public or other authority.

government. 1. The organization of a state which normally consists of the executive, the legislative, and the judicial branches in addition to administrative agencies. **2.** The political and administrative activities of the organized state by means of which its powers are exerted and its ends are secured. **3.** *In parliamentary states:* the heads of departments and principal ministers who collectively assert political leadership and determine public policy;—used interchangeably with "ministry" or "cabinet."

governmental contract. A supposititious contract between a sovereign and his subjects whereby the sovereign promises to rule justly, and the subjects promise to obey his lawful commands. Violation of the contract by either party is held to absolve the other from the obligations of the contract. In the Middle Ages governmental contract theories were the favorite starting point for debating, explaining, and defining the limits of governmental authority and were most fully developed as a justification for resistance to absolute monarchy in France, the Low Countries, and the British Isles during the 16th and 17th centuries, and for the American Revolution in the 18th century. *See* Declaration of Independence; *compare* social contract.

government by injunction. The injunction in labor disputes which before 1932 was often abused by being issued against strikers in general terms or without due notice, sometimes prohibiting acts which were entirely legal, and with long delays before final judicial determination of the legality of the injunction;—used opprobriously. *See* Norris-LaGuardia Act.

government corporation. A device first used extensively by the federal government during World War I, and continued since, for the administration of functions which are essentially business enterprises. Its corporate stock is wholly owned by the government. It is financed by congressional appropriations and by bond issues sold to private investors. Incorporation permits administrative and financial autonomy and superior means of handling contracts with private parties. *See* Government Corporations Control Act.

Government Corporations Control Act. An act of Congress, Feb. 24, 1945, which provided for extensive, but not complete, control by the Budget Bureau and the General Accounting Office over the financial operations of government corporations, *q.v.*; required their personnel procedures to conform more nearly with those of civil-service laws; and provided that henceforth only Congress could create a government corporation. Those previously chartered under State laws were liquidated.

Government Printing Office. An agency, created in 1861 and controlled by Congress, which provides printing and binding service for all branches, departments, and establishments of the national government and distributes and sells at cost government publications. It also furnishes stationery supplies to government agencies.

governor. The chief executive of an American State. Originally elected or controlled by the State legislature, he has acquired practical independence through successive constitutional revisions. His administrative power, however, still must often be shared with other popularly elected officers whose mandate from the people is as good as his own, and with boards a majority of whose members may have been appointed for long terms before his inauguration. Since 1917 a movement to make the governor the real head of the State administration has made considerable progress. *See* administrative reorganization. His legislative powers have increased. He has the veto power except in North Carolina; the item veto of appropriations in 41 States; and he may reduce items in 6 States. The frequent provision that he may have from six to thirty days in which to sign or veto a bill after the legislature has adjourned tends to make his veto absolute. In calling special sessions of the legislature he may often limit them to the consideration of subjects which he specifies. Through appeals to the people he may compel unwilling legislators to accept his legislative program. His term is two or four years, with an increasing tendency toward the longer term. Several State constitutions prohibit his succeeding himself in office.

governors' conference. A meeting of governors held annually since 1908 for the exchange of experience on common problems and the promotion of uniform action by States.

governor's council. *See* executive council.

G.P.O. Government Printing Office.

gradualism. The reliance of radical parties or political movements upon piecemeal legislative and administrative reforms and upon evolutionary social trends instead of upon violent revolution for the ultimate realization of their programs.

graduated tax. A tax (as upon incomes, estates, inheritances, or the number of stores in a chain) which is levied at progressively higher rates increasing more rapidly than the increase in the tax base.

graft. Money or valuable privileges gained at the expense of the public or of the public interest, usually by officeholders, employees, or persons who possess political influence, and obtained through actions ranging from downright theft to morally reprehensible acts for which there is no legal penalty.

Grain Futures Act. An act of Congress, Sept. 21, 1922, which empowered the Department of Agriculture to register brokers in grain and other commodity futures transactions, regulate the amount and duration of their transactions, and prohibit corners in staples, market manipulation, and the dissemination of false information designed to influence commodity prices.

grandfather clause. A clause contained in several of the post-Civil War suffrage laws of Southern States which exempted persons who had voted or whose progenitors had voted prior to 1867 from the fulfillment of educational tests and property qualifications required of other voters. The clause discriminated in favor of whites and against Negroes and because of this was declared void by the Supreme Court. *See Guinn* v. *United States.*

grandfather's hat. A tall hat of the style of 1840 which was a Republican emblem in 1888, in allusion to the fact that Benjamin Harrison, successful Republican presidential candidate of that year, was the grandson of William Henry Harrison who had been elected President in 1840.

Grand Junction Plan. Another name for the Bucklin plan, *q.v.*

grand jury. A body of from 12 to 23 persons at common law who are summoned to a court to hear witnesses presented on behalf of the state and, after deliberating in secret and by a majority vote, to return indictments or make presentments against all persons whom they find just cause to hold for trial. It may also act concerning nuisances, the prevalence of crime, and neglect of duty by officials. In federal courts, trial for a crime punishable by imprisonment in a penitentiary must be after indictment by grand jury; but in more than half the States, information, *q.v.*, may be substituted for indictment, and the grand jury may be infrequently called.

Grand Old Party. A phrase applied by Republican orators to their party in 1880 and since used by others, sometimes in a derisive sense, to designate that party;—often abbreviated G.O.P.

Grange. The Patrons of Husbandry, a secret farmers' organization founded in 1867, which by 1874 had 750,000 members and exerted great influence over State legislation. It continues as the National Grange.

granger legislation. Laws favoring agricultural interests and named for the Grange, but not necessarily sponsored by it, which were passed, 1870–90, in many Western States. They fixed rates and imposed stringent regulations on railroads, grain elevators, and warehouses.

grant. 1. A tract of land, franchise, monopolistic privilege, or sum of money given by governmental authority to a private person or corporation. 2. A gift to another country under a foreign aid program.

grant-in-aid. An appropriation made by Congress to assist the States, or by a State legislature to assist local government units, in the maintenance of schools, construction of public works, provision for relief, or other public purposes. Its payment may, or may not, be conditioned upon the maintenance of certain standards fixed by the granting authority; but the temptation to utilize it for regulatory purposes has been almost irresistible. Grants-in-aid are usually made to supplement appropriations made by the State or locality, and may be conditioned upon such appropriations. *Compare* subsidy.

grass roots. The origin or basis of something;—used especially by Republican party orators, to identify the allegedly spontaneous or popular origin of party nominations or policy.

Graves v. New York ex rel. *O'Keefe.* A case, 306 U.S. 466 (1939), in which the Supreme Court upheld the application of the New York State income tax law to the salary of employees of the Home Owners' Loan Corporation, an agency of the federal government. The Court thus modified the rule, derived from *McCulloch* v. *Maryland, q.v.,* that the salary of federal employees is immune from State taxation.

Gray v. Sanders. A case, 372 U.S. 368 (1963), in which the Supreme Court invalidated the Georgia county unit system, *q.v.* The Court held that, under the equal protection clause of the 14th Amendment, every individual's vote, regardless of his place of residence, is equal to every other vote and must be counted as such in determining the results of primary contests for nomination of U.S. senators and State officials.

Great Pacificator. A nickname of Henry Clay, author of the Missouri Compromise, the Compromise Tariff, and the Compromise of 1850.

Great Seal of the United States. A device for authenticating signatures and other writings, adopted by the Congress of the Confederation, June 20, 1782, and by the Federal Government, Sept. 16, 1789. It is in the custody of the Secretary of State, and it is affixed to all civil commissions of officers appointed by the President either alone or with the consent of the Senate; to all documents signed by the President and countersigned by the Secretary of State; to proclamations; to ratifications of treaties; and to certain other instruments of international relations.

The Great Seal of the United States

Great Society. A slogan of President Lyndon Johnson in 1964 advocating greater educational and job-training opportunities for American youth, the preservation of natural beauty, redevelopment of housing in the cities, better medical care for the aged, and measures for the alleviation of poverty. *Compare* Square Deal, New Freedom, New Nationalism, New Deal, Fair Deal, New Frontier.

greenback. A U.S. note, a form of irredeemable or fiat paper currency issued as legal tender by the United States in 1862 to help finance the Civil War, which quickly depreciated in value, but began to rise as the end of the war approached, and which reached par value in 1878. *See* legal tender.

Greenback Labor Party. A minor party, formed by a merger of the Greenback Party with other groups in 1878, which advocated fiat money, the income tax, federal regulation of railroads, and the eight-hour day;— officially entitled the National Party.

Greenback Party. A minor party formed in 1874 to advocate the continued emission of greenbacks and merged with other groups into the Greenback Labor Party in 1878;—officially entitled the Independent Party.

Green v. Frazier. A case, 253 U.S. 233 (1920), in which the Supreme Court recognized the right of North Dakota to operate grain elevators, banks, and other business establishments which had the sanction of the State's courts, legislature, and people. Taxes levied for this program were not to be construed as for a non-public purpose.

Gresham's Law. The observed tendency, when coins of the same nominal value are minted from different metals, for coins of the metal of less intrinsic value to remain in circulation while coins in the metal of greater intrinsic value are hoarded, melted down, or exported;—named for Sir Thomas Gresham, English 16th century financier. A contemporary application has been noticed in inconvertible currency systems and expressed as "bad money drives out good money" because debtors pay debts in the most depreciated and least wanted available legal tender and withhold more acceptable currency from general circulation.

grievance. A ground for complaint or remonstrance against the government resulting from abuses, unpopular acts, or neglect to remedy an unsatisfactory condition. The right to petition the government for redress of grievances is guaranteed by the First Amendment to the Constitution.

groom for office. To attempt to create a widespread and favorable impression of a potential candidate for office by having him appear frequently in public and by securing publicity for him in newspapers, magazines, and radio and television broadcasts.

gross income. 1. The total income of a person or business from every source before expenses are deducted. **2.** The total income before allowable deductions under income tax laws.

Grossman, Ex parte. A case, 267 U.S. 87 (1925), in which the Supreme Court, relying upon earlier British and American practice, ruled that criminal contempt of a federal court is an offense against the United States and, as such, comes within the pardoning power of the President.

gross national product. The value at market of all finished goods and services produced by a nation's economy. Included are private purchases of goods and services and income in kind, government purchases of goods and services (with certain exceptions), gross private domestic investment, and net foreign investment. In 1964, gross national product in the United States reached a total between $625 and $650 billion. Subtraction of an appropriate sum for capital consumption or depreciation yields the "net" national product.

group pressure. Influence exerted by or on behalf of members of a group upon officers of the government either directly or through political parties or mediums of communication.

Grovey v. Townsend. See Texas Primary cases.

G.S.A. General Services Administration.

Guam. The largest of the Marianas Islands, lying in the Pacific Ocean about 1,589 miles east of Manila, which the United States acquired at the end of the Spanish-American war in 1898. It is administered by the Department of the Interior under the terms of an organic act passed in 1950. A governor is appointed for a four-year term by the President. Considerable autonomous power resides in the local Congress elected biennially by the permanent residents. Most of the inhabitants are citizens of the United States. The capital is Agaña.

guano islands. Various barren islands, rocks, and keys, including Jarvis, Baker, and Howland islands in the mid-Pacific, which were once important because of their deposits of guano, a source of fertilizer. By act of Aug. 18, 1856, Congress extended American jurisdiction over such places while the deposits were being worked by American companies. Occupation under this act is a basis for territorial claims over these islands subsequently asserted by the United States.

Guantánamo. A United States naval station on a bay of the same name in Oriente Province in southeast Cuba originally leased July 2, 1903, under the terms of the Platt Amendment, *q.v.*

guarantee of deposits. See bank deposits guarantee.

guerrilla warfare. 1. Warlike acts by individuals or groups not immediately under orders of responsible military authorities. Such guerrillas or partisans are not always accorded the rights of regular armed forces of a belligerent. **2.** Irregular warfare, including demolition of military installations, economic sabotage, propaganda, and intelligence activities, carried on by small detachments of regular forces behind enemy lines or during special missions in areas where the battle lines of belligerents are not clearly drawn.

Guffey-Snyder Coal Act. An act of Congress, Aug. 30, 1935, which provided for a bituminous coal code-making authority to fix maximum and minimum prices. This act was declared unconstitutional.

Guffey-Vinson Act. An act of Congress, Apr. 26, 1937, which set up a national Bituminous Coal Commission with power to fix minimum and maximum prices and rules for marketing coal, and which placed a tax on coal sold or consumed. *See* Bituminous Coal Code cases.

guideline. A presidential or other official suggestion to business men, labor unions, and others concerning prices and wage rates which are supposed not to exceed productivity rates or result in inflation.

guild socialism. A brand of socialism which advocates public ownership of the means of production, control of production by industrial unions or guilds in each industry, and functional representation in legislative bodies;—found principally in Great Britain about 1900.

guilt by association. The idea which has sometimes been embodied in statutes that a person's guilt is prima facie determined by his membership in an organization stigmatized as criminal or subversive regardless of his knowledge of the aims and activities of the organization, or of his own active involvement.

Guinn v. United States. The case, 238 U.S. 347 (1915), in which the Supreme Court, acting under the 15th Amendment's prohibition of laws abridging the right to vote on account of race, held discriminatory against Negro citizens, and hence invalid, an Oklahoma electoral law which prescribed literacy tests for voters unless they met the requirements of a grandfather clause, *q.v.*

gumshoe campaign. Unobtrusive efforts of a candidate to secure the support of political leaders and delegates to a party convention.

habeas corpus. The "great writ of liberty"; a writ directed to a sheriff, jailer, or anyone else holding a person under detention, requiring him to bring the prisoner into court and state the time and the cause of the arrest. If the cause is deemed sufficient the prisoner may be admitted to bail when the offense charged is ordinarily bailable. If the cause is insufficient he is at once unconditionally released. The importance of the writ is that, by guaranteeing judicial intervention and review, it prevents arbitrary imprisonment. It does not apply under martial law or to persons subject to military law. The privilege of the writ may be suspended only when, in times of rebellion or invasion, the public safety requires suspension. Although President Lincoln suspended it on his own authority several times, the best opinion holds that his action, without prior Congressional authority, was unconstitutional.

habitual offender. A persistent violator of law; *also:* an incorrigible criminal. In certain States, under habitual offender acts or so-called Baumes laws, *q.v.*, persons convicted of a certain number of felonies, usually four, are sentenced to imprisonment for life.

Haddock v. Haddock. A case, 201 U.S. 562 (1906), in which the Supreme Court held that the State of the marriage domicile need not give full faith and credit to a divorce granted one spouse by another State if the second spouse continued in the marriage domicile and had not appeared in the divorce proceedings but had been notified by publication;—overruled in 1942.

Hague Conferences. International conferences at The Hague in 1899 and in 1907 to promote disarmament and international peace, which drafted several conventions to regulate warfare and promote the settlement of disputes by arbitration.

Hague v. Committee of Industrial Organization. A case, 307 U.S. 496 (1939), in which the Supreme Court struck down as a violation of the rights of association and of freedom of speech an ordinance of Jersey City, N.J. The ordinance, ostensibly designed to prevent disorder, prohibited any organization (in this case a labor union) from hiring a hall to air grievances or from distributing handbills in the streets without a permit, application for which had, in fact, been denied.

Half-breeds. A faction of the Republican party, 1876–84, which opposed a third term for Grant and supported the conciliatory policy of Hayes toward the South and the nomination of Garfield in 1880. They were opposed by the Stalwarts, *q.v.*

Halifax Fishery Commission. A joint American and British commission created under the Treaty of Washington, 1871, which sat at Halifax, Nova Scotia, and in 1877 determined that the United States should pay Great Britain $5.5 million for certain privileges granted by the treaty to American fishermen in Canadian and Newfoundland waters and ports.

Hammer v. Dagenhart. See Child Labor cases.

Hampton Roads Conference. A futile meeting of Lincoln and Seward with three Confederate commissioners at Hampton Roads, Va., Feb. 3, 1865, to discuss terms of peace and end the Civil War.

Hansard Society for Parliamentary Government. A private agency with a worldwide constituency, created in 1944, with headquarters in London. By means of its quarterly periodical, *Parliamentary Affairs*, books, and pamphlets, it seeks to promote understanding and support of parliamentary government. The Society is an associate member of the International Political Science Association.

Hard Cider Campaign. The presidential election of 1840 when a jug of hard cider was one of the Whig emblems.

hard money. 1. Metallic currency or specie;—the term originated before the Civil War when the circulating medium included only nominal amounts of such money, the principal currency being notes of State banks. **2.** Any money of relatively stable value, especially in international exchange.

Hards *or* **Hard-shells.** The regular organization of the Hunker, *q.v.*, faction of the Democratic party in New York, 1852–60.

hardship post. *Foreign Service slang.* A foreign service assignment in which the officer is entitled to extra remuneration because of the difficulty and expense of obtaining proper housing, food, and medical services.

Hare plan. The single-transferable-vote system of proportional representation favored in the United States. Either the Droop quota, *q.v.*, or a fixed quota may be used. All candidates whose vote equals the quota are declared elected. Surplus votes of winning candidates are transferred according to the next choice expressed by the voters. The lowest candidates are then successively eliminated and their votes are transferred until the required number of candidates have received the electoral quota or have been declared elected because no others can possibly receive it.

Harper v. Virginia State Board of Elections. A case, 383 U.S. 663 (1966), in which the Supreme Court declared unconstitutional a State law requiring payment of a poll tax as a prerequisite for voting in State and local elections, because wealth and taxpaying have no relation to ability to exercise the suffrage, and because the imposition of a fee, however small, discriminates arbitrarily, contrary to standards established by the equal-protection clause of the 14th Amendment. This decision gave the final blow to the poll-tax requirement. *See* Twenty-fourth Amendment.

Harter Act. An act of Congress, Feb. 13, 1893, designed to promote safety in commerce at sea, which relieved the owner of a vessel from liability for loss provided he had exercised due diligence in equipping, manning, and supplying a vessel to render her seaworthy, and which voided all contracts between owner and shipper for transportation under conditions less than the minimum established by the law.

Hartford Convention. A meeting of delegates from the New England States in secret session at Hartford, Conn., from Dec. 15, 1814 to Jan. 5, 1815, which proposed seven amendments to the Constitution, considered measures for the better defense of New England, and agreed that States ought to interpose for the protection of their citizens against an allegedly ambitious and inept administration of the national government.

Hatch acts. Two acts of Congress, Aug. 2, 1939 and July 19, 1940, which limited the annual expenditure of any political committee to $3 million and an individual annual contribution to any candidate or committee in an election for national office to $5,000; prohibited a federal government or a State employee, partly or wholly paid out of federal funds, from using his position to influence political conduct; outlawed coercion of voters in national elections; prohibited solicitation of funds from employees on public relief projects; forbade efforts to secure political support by the promise or denial of employment on any project made possible by federal appropriations; and, in effect, compelled States to adopt the merit system for all projects supported in part by federal funds.

hat in the ring. *Slang.* Announcement of candidacy for elective office.

Hawaii annexation. A movement sponsored by American cane sugar growers in Hawaii that overthrew the native dynasty in 1891 and, when President Cleveland refused to support their plea for annexation to the United States, established the Republic of Hawaii. After the outbreak of the war with Spain, Congress adopted a joint resolution annexing Hawaii, July 7, 1898.

Hawaii v. Mankichi. See Insular cases.

Hawes-Cooper Act. An act of Congress, Jan. 19, 1929, which removed the protection of the Supreme Court's original-package doctrine, *q.v.*, from prison-made goods shipped in interstate commerce.

hawk. A critic of President Lyndon B. Johnson's policy in the Vietnam War who advocates escalating the war, or "fighting to win," in order to force the Vietcong and North Vietnam to the conference table. *Compare* dove.

Hawke v. Smith. A case, 253 U.S. 221 (1920), in which the Supreme Court ruled that a State may not substitute the decision of its voters in a referendum for that of its legislature when acting upon a proposed amendment to the U.S. Constitution.

Hawley-Smoot Tariff. The latest (or last) full-scale legislative tariff revision. As enacted June 17, 1930, its rates were extremely high. More recent policy, formulated in the Trade Agreements Act, *q.v.*, of 1934, as periodically renewed, and executive agreements with foreign countries, has sought to lower tariffs on the basis of reciprocity.

Hay-Bunau-Varilla Treaty. A treaty signed Nov. 18, 1903, by which Panama, for a consideration, ceded sovereign rights in a ten-mile-wide strip across its territory to the United States to permit it to construct and operate a canal. *See* Panama Canal.

Hayden-Cartwright Act. An act of Congress, June 16, 1936, which provided funds for the construction of secondary roads without the requirement that States should match the federal appropriation.

Hay-Herran Treaty. A draft treaty signed Jan. 22, 1903, providing for lease of land by Colombia to the United States for constructing the Panama Canal, *q.v.* Failure of Colombia to ratify led to Panama's secession from Colombia.

Hay-Pauncefote Treaty. A treaty signed Nov. 18, 1901, by which Great Britain relinquished rights under the Clayton-Bulwer Treaty, *q.v.*, to participate in the joint construction of a trans-Isthmian canal and waived objections to United States acquisition of a canal route in Central America and sole operation and control of a canal when built, providing that the canal be open to all nations on equal terms.

H-bomb. A hydrogen or thermonuclear bomb in which explosive energy is produced in accordance with Einstein's equation $E = mc^2$, but by fusion rather than by fission of matter. The United States exploded the first H-bomb in 1952 at the Eniwetok Pacific proving area. The bomb's technology is now generally known.

Head Money cases. A series of cases, 112 U.S. 580 (1884), in which the Supreme Court ruled that, if the terms of any self-executing treaty to which the United States is a party conflict with the terms of a statute subsequently enacted by Congress, the courts will enforce the statute, the treaty notwithstanding.

head tax. 1. A tax on aliens landing at any port of the United States, first levied in 1882. **2.** A poll tax.

Health, Education, and Welfare. *See* Department of Health, Education, and Welfare.

health research. *See* National Institutes of Health.

hearing. 1. A procedure in equity. **2.** A preliminary examination in a criminal case. **3.** An opportunity granted by an administrative body or a legislative committee to present evidence before it.

hearing officer. An officer in an executive department or quasi-judicial agency who hears evidence and arguments on some controverted matter and makes reports and recommendations to his superiors for appropriate action.

heeler. A party worker who runs errands for a district or precinct leader, distributes literature, canvasses for votes, and gets out the vote on election day.

hegemony. 1. The ascendancy of one state over others acquired by diplomacy or military victory. **2.** The position of leadership or superior influence enjoyed by an individual in the government, or by one branch or office of government over others.

Helderberg War. Armed resistance to civil authority by antirenters, *q.v.*, in Albany County, N.Y., in 1839.

Hell 'n' Maria. A nickname of Vice President Charles G. Dawes.

Helvering v. *Davis.* *See* Social Security cases.

Helvering v. *Gerhardt.* A case, 304 U.S. 405 (1938), in which the Supreme Court sustained the application of the federal income tax law to employees of the Port of New York Authority, a State instrumentality. *Compare Collector* v. *Day; Graves* v. *New York* ex rel. *O'Keefe.*

henchman. A faithful lieutenant or active supporter of a political boss.

Hepburn Act. An act of Congress, June 29, 1906, which increased the jurisdiction of the Interstate Commerce Commission to include oil pipelines and sleeping-car and express companies; prohibited free passes to other than employees; forbade common carriers to transport any products, except timber, in which they had an interest; and required joint tariffs by carriers and a uniform system of accounts.

Hepburn v. *Griswold. See* legal tender.

Hero of Appomattox. A nickname of Ulysses S. Grant who forced Lee to surrender at Appomattox Court House, Va., April 9, 1865, thus effectively ending the Civil War.

Hero of New Orleans. A nickname of Andrew Jackson, who won a decisive victory over the British at New Orleans, Jan. 8, 1815.

H.E.W. *See* Department of Health, Education, and Welfare.

H.H.F.A. Housing and Home Finance Agency.

Hickory Pole Canvass. The presidential election of 1828, when the Democratic emblem was a hickory pole in honor of the party's presidential candidate, Andrew Jackson, whose nickname was "Old Hickory."

high commissioner. 1. The representative of the sovereign at the seat of a colonial or other dependent or associated government; *specifically:* the representative of the executive authority of the United States in the Philippine Islands during the period of the Philippine Commonwealth, 1935–46. **2.** A diplomat sent by one (British) Commonwealth country to another.

high crimes and misdemeanors. Offenses against law sufficiently grave to warrant impeachment by the House of Representatives.

higher-law doctrine. 1. The concept of a law of nature intrinsically superior to positive law. **2.** A declaration that "there is a higher law than the Constitution," made by Senator William H. Seward of New York, an abolitionist spokesman, March 11, 1850, during the debates on the Compromise of 1850, *q.v.*

high license. Regulation of the liquor traffic by means of high license fees designed to drive less responsible saloon and tavern keepers out of business.

high seas. 1. The open ocean; *especially*: those portions of the ocean which are not enclosed within headlands or recognized as being within the territorial limits of any state. **2.** The ocean beyond the distance of three miles from the shore. The Supreme Court held in *U.S. v. Rodgers,* 150 U.S. 249 (1893), that for the purpose of enforcing criminal laws, the open waters of the Great Lakes are high seas.

highway patrol. A special State force, known by various names, which enforces motor vehicle and other laws in those States which have not established a State constabulary invested with general law-enforcement powers.

Hinds' Precedents. A digest of Speakers' decisions and actions of the House of Representatives interpreting the rules of the House, compiled by Asher C. Hinds and first published in 1907, and revised by Clarence Cannon in 1935.

His Excellency. A courtesy title used in referring to the governor of a State.

His Honor. A courtesy title sometimes conferred on the mayor of an American city.

Hiss trials. Two trials, the first ending in a disagreement of the jury, 1949, the second in a conviction for perjury, Jan. 21, 1950, and sentence to five years in prison of Alger Hiss, formerly a high official of the State Department, who was accused of passing secret documents to a Communist spy ring. Because the President and others had expressed confidence in Hiss, some members of the public believed that the Roosevelt and Truman administrations had been unaware of, or indifferent to, the danger of Communist subversion. *See* McCarthyism.

His Superfluous Excellency. A title humorously suggested in 1789, for the Vice President of the United States because of his lack of power.

Hobbs Act. An act of Congress, July 3, 1947, designed to curb labor racketeering, which imposed penalties on persons found guilty of robbery or extortion when these acts have the effect of obstructing, delaying, or otherwise affecting interstate commerce.

holding company. A corporation which owns stocks of one or more companies (subsidiaries); *especially*: a corporation whose activities are confined to the ownership of stock, control of management through boards of directors, and the receipt of dividends, interest payments, and management fees from subsidiary companies.

holdover. A member of the U.S. Senate, or of the upper house of a State legislature, whose term continues into a new Congress or legislature.

hold-up bill. A measure introduced and supported in a legislative body for the purpose of extorting money or favors from corporations or other interests which would be adversely affected by its passage.

Holman rule. A rule of the House of Representatives, adopted in 1876 and revived in 1911 after long disuse, which forbids the insertion in a general appropriation bill of any provision changing existing laws except such as, being germane to the subject matter of the bill, would have the direct effect of retrenching expenditures. *See* rider.

Holy Alliance. An alliance in 1815 of Russia, Austria, Prussia and, later, other Continental states, to apply Christian principles to the relations of rulers with their subjects and with each other, which subsequently became identified with the effort to maintain the reactionary political and territorial settlement established by the post-Napoleonic peace treaties, including the reconquest of Spain's colonies in the New World that had achieved independence. To counter its efforts the Monroe Doctrine, *q.v.*, was announced.

Holy Wednesday. *Slang.* Wednesdays in the House of Representatives, formerly devoted to bills reported by standing committees. *See* morning hour.

Home Building and Loan Association* v. *Blaisdell. A case, 290 U.S. 398 (1934), in which the Supreme Court upheld a State statute extending a mortgagor's right to redeem foreclosed property two years beyond the time stipulated when the mortgage was made. The Court held that the contract clause of the Constitution, Art. I, Sec. 10, was not breached since existing contracts are subject to regulation in the public interest under the State's police power, exertion of which in this case was justified by an emergency resulting from an economic depression.

home rule. The partial autonomy enjoyed by cities and counties which have adopted their own charters under permissive provisions of constitutions or statutes in many States. Such charters are drafted by locally elected charter commissions and ratified by popular referendums. They must conform to the general laws of the State. The degree of local autonomy under home rule varies greatly; often severe limitations with respect to taxation, finance, law enforcement, and education are imposed on home-rule cities and counties by State constitutions and laws.

home-rule charter. *See* freeholders' charter.

homestead. Real estate occupied by the owner as a residence which, up to a certain fixed value or acreage, is exempted under constitutional and legal provisions in various States, from taxation, or from forced sale to pay the owner's debts. The latter exemptions do not apply when the debt has been contracted before the constitutional or legal provisions went into effect.

Homestead Act. An act of Congress, May 20, 1862, which permitted any citizen to settle on 160 acres of public land and to receive title to it at the end of five years' actual residence or by paying $1.25 per acre six months after taking possession.

honest graft. Unethical gains which do not render the recipient liable to legal penalties, such as those resulting from buying up property about to be taken for a public purpose and profiting from its subsequent appreciation in value;—a phrase popularized by W. L. Riordan, *Plunkitt of Tammany Hall.*

Honolulu. *See* Declaration of Honolulu.

Hoover Commissions. A non-partisan body of experts, known officially as the Commission on Organization of the Executive Branch of the Government, chosen from business and professional life and headed by former President Herbert Hoover, which was created by act of Congress in 1947 to examine the structure and practices of the executive branch and make recommendations for its reorganization and improvement. More than 250 formal reports relating to every principal executive agency and recommending structural and procedural changes were issued during 1949. Each commission report was usually supplemented by a more extensive report of a special committee or task force of experts appointed by the commission to study each major subject on the commission's agenda. Between 1949 and 1955 more than half of all the recommendations were accepted and put into effect, either by executive order or by Congressional action. A second Hoover Commission was appointed by President Eisenhower in 1953 to carry on the work of reorganization.

Hoovercrat. A Southern Democrat who supported Hoover in the presidential campaign of 1928.

hopper. *Slang.* A receptacle on the clerk's desk in which a member places a bill by way of introducing it in the House of Representatives.

hot line. The teletype circuit linking the White House communications center, the Pentagon, and a Russian communications center, probably in the Kremlin, which was established Aug. 30, 1963, designed to avoid action resulting from military miscalculations, and first used in a period of crisis by Premier Aleksei Kosygin and President Lyndon B. Johnson during the Arab-Israeli War of 1967.

Hot Oil cases. Three cases, the principal one being *Panama Refining Co. v. Ryan,* 293 U.S. 388 (1935), in which the Supreme Court held that Congress had unconstitutionally delegated legislative powers to the President by authorizing him in 1933 to prohibit the shipment in interstate and foreign commerce of oil in excess of the amount permitted to be produced or withdrawn from storage under the laws of any State.

hot pursuit. A principle of international law justifying pursuit and arrest of vessels that have infringed the laws of a state, provided such pursuit begins within the territorial waters of the offended state and is continued without interruption. The right of pursuit ceases when the vessel reaches the territorial waters of another state.

Hot Water War. Another name for Fries' Rebellion, *q.v.*

House calendar. A calendar of the House of Representatives listing, in the order of their report from a standing committee, all bills of a public character which do not raise revenue or directly or indirectly appropriate money or dispose of public property. *Compare* union calendar.

House-Divided Speech. An address by Lincoln accepting the Republican nomination for U.S. Senator in June, 1858, which contained the statement, "A house divided against itself cannot stand. I believe this government cannot endure permanently half slave and half free. . . . It will become all one thing or all the other."

housekeeping function. Auxiliary administrative activity (as personnel administration, purchase and handling of supplies, or provision for transportation) which is essential to the functioning of a government unit, though not part of its main operations.

House of Commons. The lower house of the Parliaments of the United Kingdom, of Northern Ireland, and of the Dominion of Canada.

House of Delegates. The lower house of the legislature in Maryland, Virginia, and West Virginia.

house of detention. A building maintained by local governments to house lost or abandoned children, juvenile delinquents awaiting trial, and youthful material witnesses, when in custody of the police.

House of Lords. The second chamber of the British Parliament, no longer coordinate in power with the House of Commons.

House of Representatives. 1. The more popular chamber of the Congress of the United States. Each State is guaranteed at least one seat, and additional seats are distributed after each decennial census according to the method of "equal proportions" which guarantees representation approximately in proportion to population. Since 1910 the total membership has been 435 (temporarily 437 in 1959–61) and the ratio of representatives to population is now one for more than 400,000. Though a few members are elected from a State at large, the great bulk are chosen from single-member districts which, in accordance with the principle of "one man, one vote" in recent Supreme Court decisions, must be nearly equal in population within each State. The House of Representatives has the sole powers of impeachment and of initiating revenue bills. When no candidate has received a majority of the electoral votes, it may elect a President from the three candidates standing highest in the electoral college vote; voting in the House is by States, and the Representatives from a State collectively have one vote. **2.** The lower house of many State legislatures.

Housing and Home Finance Agency. A constituent unit of the Department of Housing and Urban Development, *q.v.*

Housing and Urban Development. *See* Department of Housing and Urban Development.

Howland Island. One of the guano islands in the mid-Pacific, near the equator, occupied by the United States in 1936 for use as a meteorological station.

H.R. House of Representatives.

H.U.D. *See* Department of Housing and Urban Development.

Hull-Alfaro Treaty. A treaty between the United States and Panama, 1939, by which the United States relinquished the right to intervene in

Panamanian affairs and acknowledged Panama's equal right and obligation to defend the Canal.

Hull trade agreements. *See* reciprocal trade agreement.

human rights. *See* Universal Declaration of Human Rights.

Hunkers. The conservative faction of the Democratic party in New York, 1845–52, which cooperated with slaveholders and which was said to have no principles except to hunger, or "hunker," for office.

Huron Portland Cement Co. v. City of Detroit. A case, 362 U.S. 440 (1960), in which the Supreme Court sustained the application of a municipality's smoke-abatement ordinance to ships in its port, operating in interstate commerce, whose boilers and equipment had been federally inspected and licensed. The Court held the local regulation valid because it looks to the health of the local community and imposes no discriminatory burden on interstate commerce, whereas federal regulation looks to maritime safety and has not preempted the field to the exclusion of local police regulation. *Compare Pennsylvania v. Nelson.*

Hurtado v. California. A case, 110 U.S. 516 (1884), in which the Supreme Court ruled that the protection of the life and liberty of the person afforded by the due-process clause of the 14th Amendment does not require a State to use an indictment or presentment of a grand jury in prosecutions for murder or other offenses but permits the State, after examining and committing the accused through a magistrate's court, to substitute an information for such indictment or presentment.

hustings court. The name of certain local courts in Virginia.

hyphenates. Americans of foreign birth or descent whose sympathy with the countries of their origin led them to oppose, or give only half-hearted support to, the policies of the United States in World War I.

I.A.D.B. Inter-American Defense Board.

I.C.C. Interstate Commerce Commission.

ice patrol. A service, known officially as the International Ice Patrol, maintained in the North Atlantic by the United States and other governments to destroy icebergs or warn merchant ships of their presence and to collect data of value to oceanographers.

idealism. A theory that reality is discoverable through ideas, thought, and insight rather than apprehended through the senses. German idealists, as Fichte, Hegel, Treitschke, and the National Socialists idealized the state and affirmed that, through it, the individual could reach his highest development. English and American idealists, like T. H. Green, Bosanquet, and Royce, while holding to the liberal tradition, emphasized the interdependence of individuals and the social community of which they are a part.

I.F.C. International Finance Corporation.

I.L.O. International Labor Organization.

"I'm Alone," The. A rum-running vessel of Canadian registry, but owned by Americans, which was sunk by a U.S. Coast Guard cutter Mar. 22, 1929, when about 200 miles from shore. A joint commission determined that the United States should apologize and pay indemnity to Canada and to the crew; but the United States refused to compensate the owners.

I.M.F. International Monetary Fund.

immigration. Entrance into a country for the purpose of establishing a permanent residence or obtaining employment. The federal government, which has exclusive control over the subject under the Constitution, made no attempt to limit immigration until 1882 when it prohibited the entrance of paupers, lunatics and idiots, and Chinese laborers. Later statutes debarred other Orientals, contract laborers, diseased persons, those convicted of crimes involving moral turpitude, prostitutes, white slavers, anarchists, professional beggars, illiterates, and those likely to become a public charge. Beginning in 1921, Congress limited the total number of immigrants from the Eastern Hemisphere and, by setting quotas for each country, drastically reduced the flow of immigration from southern and eastern Europe. After World War II, additional numbers, principally of displaced persons and war brides, were admitted. In 1965 Congress abolished the quota system entirely, but continued to limit the number of immigrants from the Old World and for the first time limited Western Hemisphere immigration. Preference in admission is to be given to near relatives of persons already in the United States, artists, scientists and professional people, skilled labor, unskilled labor to fill shortages, and refugees from Communist countries.

Immigration Appeals. *See* Board of Immigration Appeals.

immunity. 1. Exemption of a person from a duty, obligation, service, or penalty (as presidential or diplomatic immunity from judicial process), imposed by law on all others not similarly situated. 2. Exemption from prosecution which is sometimes promised by a prosecutor to a person accused of crime who agrees to "turn state's evidence";—usually used colloquially.

Immunity Act. An act of Congress, 1954, which provided that, in matters of national security, witnesses could be compelled to testify before Congressional committees if, on request of a federal district attorney approved by the Attorney General, immunity from prosecution had been granted by a U.S. district judge. *See Ullmann* v. *United States.*

immunity bath. The exemption from prosecution of an excessive number of accused persons, or of principal defendants;—the term originated in 1906 when 16 defendants alleged to have been implicated in a beef trust were exempted from prosecution because they had aided the Government in obtaining evidence against others.

impacted area. A community in which federal military or other installations are extensive and in which, in order to lighten the burden on local taxpayers, the federal government supplies most of the funds for the maintenance and operation of the schools.

impeachment. A formal written accusation by the lower house of a legislature sent to the upper house for the purpose of removing a civil officer (other than a member of the legislature) for treason, bribery, or other high crimes and misdemeanors. The House of Representatives has the sole power of impeachment of national officers, and through a committee it presents evidence and manages the prosecution. The Senate must try all impeachments; and before the trial Senators must be placed on oath or affirmation. If the President is tried the Chief Justice of the Supreme Court of the United States presides over the Senate. A two-thirds vote of the Senators is required for conviction. The penalty which the Senate may impose on conviction is limited to removal from office and disqualification to hold any office of honor, trust, or profit under the United States. A convicted person, however, remains liable to trial and punishment in a court of law. The President's pardoning power does not extend to impeachments. Since 1789 only a dozen officers have been impeached by the House of Representatives, and of these only four (all judges) were convicted. In the States, where similar provisions exist, governors and other officers have occasionally been removed from office after conviction on impeachment.

imperialism. The policy of extending the sovereignty or dominion of a state; *especially:* the acquisition of distant territory which is inhabited by an alien race and is not suitable for extensive colonization by the state's own people.

implied powers. Powers not granted in express terms but existing because they are necessary and proper to carry into effect some expressly granted power. Though such powers had been exercised by the national government almost from its beginning, the Supreme Court first gave them a broad scope in its decision in the case of *McCulloch* v. *Maryland, q.v.,* when Chief Justice Marshall declared: "Let the end be legitimate, let it be within the scope of the Constitution, and all means which are appropriate, which are plainly adapted to that end, which are not prohibited, but consist with the letter and spirit of the Constitution are constitutional."

import duty. A tax levied upon foreign goods imported into a country at their arrival at a port of entry and before they have become commingled with domestic goods.

impost. A financial or other payment imposed by public authority, probably, historically, in addition to other taxes.

impressment. The impressing or drafting of men into the navy for the defense of the state;—a royal prerogative in Great Britain frequently exercised before 1815. The stopping of American vessels for the impressment of Americans alleged to be British subjects was one of the causes of the War of 1812.

imprisonment. Confinement in a penal institution for a fixed or indefinite period in accordance with the sentence of a court following conviction of a crime.

imprisonment for debt. Detention on civil process for debt, formerly universal but since 1823, when Kentucky abolished it, prohibited or restricted by constitutional provisions in the States. Where it exists it is mostly applied against absconding debtors or those who have deliberately entered into a contract without means of fulfilling their obligations.

inalienable rights. Rights which inhere in a person and are incapable of being transferred. Such rights have been claimed under natural law.

inauguration. The ceremony of inducting a President, governor, or other chief executive into office, the primary features of which are administering the oath of office and the inaugural address.

incapacitation. Inability to hold office or discharge some public duty because of physical or mental infirmity or legal disqualification.

incidence of taxation. The financial burden of paying a tax which, as in the case of a poll tax, may be borne by the person who first pays it, or, as in the case of most other taxes, be shifted in varying degrees to other persons.

income tax. A tax levied upon wealth as it is being acquired, in the form of salaries, wages, commissions, rents, royalties, interest, dividends, business profits, or increases in capital actually realized. Income taxes were twice levied by Congress in the Civil War period and were upheld by the Supreme Court in 1881; but the income tax provisions of a law passed in 1894 were declared unconstitutional on the ground that a tax on the income from land was indistinguishable from a tax on the land itself, and therefore was a direct tax which must be apportioned among the States according to population. The 16th Amendment, proclaimed in 1913, empowered Congress to lay and collect taxes on incomes "from whatever source derived." During World War I the income tax became the principal source of revenue of the federal government and has remained so. It is levied on both individuals and corporations. A small amount of income is exempted from taxation. Higher incomes are taxed at steeply progressive rates on the principle of ability to pay. Income taxes are also levied by a majority of the States and by some municipalities.

incompatible offices. Two or more offices, one of which is ordinarily membership in a legislative body or a court, which, according to law, may not be held simultaneously by the same person.

incorporated territory. A territory of the United States which Congress, either expressly or by implication, has recognized as a part of the United States, to which all provisions of the Constitution, both procedural and substantive, apply in full force as if it were a State. At present there are no incorporated territories. *Compare* organized territory; unincorporated territory.

incorporation. 1. The creation of a corporation by act of Congress, or by the authority of the legislature of one of the States of the Union. 2. The action of Congress or the treaty-making power in bringing a territory within the full protection of all provisions of the U.S. Constitution.

incrimination. The disclosure of facts that render one liable to criminal prosecution. The accused cannot be compelled to be a witness against himself in a criminal case, but he may waive the privilege and take the stand voluntarily. A witness is immune from being required to incriminate himself in any proceeding, including a Congressional investigation, but he may not withhold facts that merely impair his reputation, nor even incriminating facts if he has been promised immunity from prosecution under the law. *See* unreasonable searches and seizures; Immunity Act.

indemnification. Compensation for loss or damage sustained because of improper or illegal action by public authority.

indemnity. 1. Monetary or material compensation for an injury or loss. **2.** A legislative act canceling specific debts to a government, assuming personal financial obligations incurred in the public service, or legalizing actions which were illegal when done.

indentured servant. A person bound to service for a specified number of years to pay off indebtedness. Early American immigrants often paid the cost of passage by indenturing themselves.

Independence party. A minor party, the outgrowth of the Independence League, founded by William Randolph Hearst in 1905 which in 1908 nominated a national ticket and polled 83,562 votes.

independent agency. 1. A division of the federal administrative establishment (as a regulatory commission or a service agency) which is not incorporated into any of the executive departments. **2.** A quasi-judicial body not subject to executive control.

independent nomination. The nomination of one or more candidates for office by petitions signed by voters;—distinguished from nomination by organized parties through the regular procedures of conventions or primary elections.

Independent party. The official title of the Greenback party, *q.v.*

independent treasury. *See* subtreasury system.

independent voter. 1. A voter who is not affiliated with any party. **2.** One who, though enrolled in a party, is accustomed to vote in general elections according to his judgments as to public affairs, or his prejudices, dislikes, or reactions to the personalities and campaign methods of candidates.

indeterminate permit. An exclusive right or franchise granted to a public utility company for an indefinite period but subject to the right of a governmental authority to take over the enterprise on payment of just compensation.

indeterminate sentence. A sentence of imprisonment the duration of which is not fixed by the court pronouncing sentence but is left to the determination of responsible penal administrative authorities within minimum and maximum time limits fixed by the court or by law.

Indian. A person of an aboriginal American race. Formerly, an Indian born within a tribe was not a citizen of the United States, and could become so only under the explicit terms of a treaty or statute providing for the collective or individual naturalization of members of certain tribes. Under the terms of the Dawes Act, Feb. 8, 1887, Indians who accepted allotments of land, lived on them apart from their tribes, and became assimilated culturally might be naturalized after 25 years. By act of June 2, 1924, all Indians born within the United States were declared to be citizens.

Indiana ballot. A form of secret ballot in which names of candidates of different parties are printed in separate columns under the party name and party circle, and sometimes the party emblem.

Indian Affairs. *See* Bureau of Indian Affairs.

Indian nation. A separate and distinct body of Indians. Though such nations were never recognized as having sovereignty, but were declared to be "domestic dependent nations," *Cherokee Nation* v. *Georgia,* 5 Pet. 1 (1831), the United States conducted relations with them by treaty until 1871 and regarded them as capable of managing their internal relations subject to the paramount legislative authority of Congress. The national government has sole power to regulate commerce with them and exercises guardianship over their economic activities. *See* Indian.

Indian reservation. A tract of land to which an American Indian tribe retains its original title to ownership or which has been set aside for its use out of the public domain. Indian reservations are under the control of the Bureau of Indian Affairs, *q.v.*

Indian Territory. A district nearly coterminous with the present State of Oklahoma which was set aside by Congress in 1830 as a permanent home for Cherokees, Creeks, Seminoles, Choctaws, Chickasaws, and other tribes removed from the eastern part of the United States. In 1866 the tribes were forced to retrocede their western lands to the United States in consequence of aid they had given to the Confederacy during the Civil War, though the Cherokees, part of whom had aided the Union, were allowed to retain a western "outlet." The lands thus retroceded were assigned to western Indians, except a portion around Guthrie and Oklahoma City which were opened to white settlement in 1889 and became the nucleus of

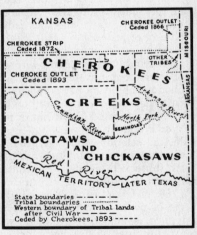

Indian Territory

the Territory of Oklahoma. The Indian Territory was never organized by Congress. Each of the Five Civilized Tribes named above was completely self-governing under a constitution and laws of its own making.

indictment. A formal written accusation, drawn up by the prosecuting officer of a state and returned as a true bill by a grand jury duly summoned and sworn, which charges one or more persons with having committed a serious offense against the law. *Compare* information; presentment.

indignation meeting. A mass meeting called to protest against some public act or policy.

indirect initiative. A form of the initiative, *q.v.*, in which a petition must be submitted to the legislature for action and is placed on the ballot for popular approval if the legislature rejects it.

indirect tax. An excise, customs duty, or other form of taxation the burden of which may be readily shifted to persons other than those upon whom the tax is levied.

individualism. The theory that the individual man, with his reasoning ability, his awareness of his own interests, and his desire for happiness and improvement, constitutes the foundation for political society and the basis for determining the limits within which government should operate. The theory is especially associated with Hobbes, Locke, and the Utilitarians. In the United States it is usually equated with frontier democracy and laissez faire.

indoor relief. Maintenance within public institutions of persons who have become public charges. *Compare* outdoor relief.

industrial accident. An injury arising out of or in the course of employment which causes temporary or permanent disability or death. State laws require safety devices, screening of dangerous machinery, fire escapes, adequate lighting, detailed procedures in hazardous operations, protection against dangerous radiation, and, for many occupations, the passing of tests for general health, vision, and technical competence as a condition of employment. Every State requires employers to insure against industrial accidents through State compensation insurance funds or accredited private insurance companies, or else provide proof of financial ability to pay compensation. *See* workmen's compensation.

Industrial Congress. A convention of workingmen in Philadelphia in 1848 which nominated Gerrit Smith for President and William S. Waitt for Vice President.

industrial relations court. A panel of judges empowered to decide labor disputes under compulsory arbitration, established in 1920 by a Kansas law subsequently declared unconstitutional.

industrial revolution. 1. *Historically:* the invention in England, about 1750, of labor-saving devices in manufacturing and transportation, the use of power-driven machinery, and the substitution of the wages system for handicraft production, with resulting unprecedented economic expansion which has continued to this day. **2.** Technical and scientific progress, as in nuclear fission and fusion, space propulsion, and computerization, which has resulted in revolutionary changes in industry in the 20th century.

industrial union. A labor union open to all workers in an industry regardless of their trades, crafts, or skills. *Compare* craft union.

Industrial Workers of the World *or* **I.W.W.** An organization of workingmen in the United States in the early 1900's which endeavored to organize all workers into one big union for the purpose of gaining absolute control of economic activity. They employed strikes and violence to gain their ends and ignored political activity. *Called also* Wobblies.

ineligibility. The condition of not being qualified to be chosen for an office.

infamous crime. Any crime punishable by death or incarceration in a penitentiary (maximum security institution) or imprisonment at hard labor, and often resulting in the loss of civil and political rights.

infant industry. A newly established industry for which the claim is made that, if temporarily protected from foreign competition by high tariff duties, it will attain self-sufficiency through the development of large-scale production.

inferior officer. Any officer of the national government whose appointment is vested by law of Congress in the President alone, a court, or the head of a department. Under the Constitution, Congress could probably put any officer into this category except ambassadors, other public ministers and consuls, and judges of the Supreme Court.

inflation. Rapid and extensive increase in the amount of money or credit in circulation, in comparison with the actual needs of trade, which causes prices to rise. Inflation may result from new discoveries of gold, large emissions of paper money, overexpansion of credit, acceleration of governmental expenditures for military or civilian purposes, or sudden decrease in the available supply of consumers' goods.

information. A written accusation before a magistrate, made upon oath by a prosecuting officer, which charges one or more persons with having committed a felony or a misdemeanor. In more than half the States it may ordinarily be substituted for indictment by a grand jury.

infringement. Unauthorized production, sale, or use of an article or process protected by a patent or of a publication protected by copyright.

inherent powers. 1. Powers originating from the nature of government or sovereignty. 2. *In the United States:* powers over and beyond those explicitly granted in the Constitution or reasonably to be implied from express grants (as powers which are conceded to the national government because it alone is competent to act in international affairs). *See United States* v. *Curtiss-Wright Export Corporation.*

inheritance tax. A tax or excise levied ad valorem upon the share of the estate of a deceased person which an heir receives;—distinguished from estate tax, *q.v.*

initiative. A procedure whereby the electorate may formally propose statutes and amendments to State constitutions. A petition containing the private draft of the measure is first signed by the requisite number or percentage of the electorate. In the form of the *direct initiative* the measure must be submitted to a popular referendum at a special, or the next general, election. In the form of the *indirect initiative* (required in a few States) the measure must first be submitted to the legislature and is referred to the electorate only if the legislature rejects it or proposes a substitute measure. The initiative for statutes may be invoked in 20 States and for constitutional amendments in 13, most of which are west of the Mississippi River. In any form the initiative is designed to afford a remedy for legislative opposition or inertia.

injunction. An order issued by a court of equity commanding a person to do, or to refrain from doing, an act which would injure another by violating his personal or property rights. A *mandatory injunction* commands the specific performance of an act; a *preventive injunction* orders a person to desist from an act already commenced or contemplated; a *preliminary*, or *interlocutory*, *injunction* may be issued when a danger is immediately threatened and there is inadequate opportunity for a court to determine finally the rights of the parties; and a *permanent injunction* is the final decree of the court. The violation of an injunction is a contempt of court and may be punished by fine or imprisonment.

innocent passage. *See* right of innocent passage.

inquest. A legal inquiry to establish some question of fact; *specifically*: an inquiry by a coroner and his jury into a person's death where accident, foul play, or violence is suspected as the cause.

in-service training. Specialized training offered employees by various administrative agencies (as the programs of the Department of Agriculture and of the Bureau of the Census) similar to management courses offered by business corporations to their employees.

insolvency. The inability to pay debts when due even though assets may exceed liabilities.

inspection laws. Federal or State laws or local ordinances authorizing or requiring various public services to (*a*) inspect buildings, machinery or equipment, and particularly to (*b*) investigate and maintain surveillance over the preparation, packaging, and labeling of foods and drugs in order to insure qualitative standards and purity, and to (*c*) inspect plants and animals in order to control human, animal, and plant diseases and parasites. Any fees charged by State inspection officials at State boundaries, which exceed the cost of maintaining the services, must be paid into the U.S. Treasury.

instruction. 1. A resolution of a State legislature, town meeting, or other public body directing representatives to support or oppose a certain measure. 2. A resolution of a party convention directing delegates to a nominating convention to vote for specified candidates. Whether such an instruction is binding on only a few ballots or until the delegates are released by the candidate for whom they were instructed to vote is a matter of frequent dispute. 3. Directions given by a judge to a jury.

Insular cases. A group of cases, including *De Lima* v. *Bidwell*, 182 U.S. 1 (1901); *Downes* v. *Bidwell*, 182 U.S. 244 (1901); *Hawaii* v. *Mankichi*, 190 U.S. 197 (1903); and *Dorr* v. *United States*, 195 U.S. 138 (1904), in which the Supreme Court distinguished between incorporated and unincorporated territories and held that in the latter only the fundamental guarantees of the Constitution were binding upon Congress; but not those, like equality in taxation or indictment and trial by jury, which were "procedural, remedial, or formal."

insurance. Provision against some contingency through a contract in which, for a consideration, one party agrees to indemnify another against specified risks. Long regarded as exclusively the subject of State regulation, insurance contracts when made interstate were brought within the scope of federal regulation in 1944. *See United States* v. *South-Eastern Underwriters Association.*

insurgency. Rebellion against a government of such scope and effectiveness that the rebels merit quasi-diplomatic recognition from foreign states and acquire limited belligerent rights. *Compare* belligerency.

insurgent. 1. A member of an organized group who resorts to arms against governmental authority. 2. A person who, while formally retaining his membership in a party, acts in opposition to its decisions and policies; *specifically:* a Republican Congressman who rebelled against Cannonism in 1909–10, or who acted independently after 1921.

insurrection. Organized armed rebellion against established political authority.

intangible property. Bonds, stocks, mortgages, and other paper titles to wealth, or even less corporeal values such as goodwill.

integration. Revision of laws and administrative practices so as to abolish racial discrimination in the armed services, schools, public and private offices and workshops, and places of public accommodation or amusement.

intelligence. Information, usually collected secretly, concerning the armament, manpower, training, morale, production capabilities, transportation, and other aspects of a declared or potential enemy; *also:* the agencies engaged in gathering such information which in the United States include the Central Intelligence Agency, the National Security Agency, the Defense Intelligence Agency, the intelligence services of the Army, Navy, and Air Force, the State Department's Bureau of Intelligence and Research, the Atomic Energy Commission, and the Federal Bureau of Investigation.

inter-Allied debts. The complex network of intergovernmental debts contracted between Allied and Associated governments during and following World War I for the purchase of war equipment and foodstuffs and for economic stabilization.

Inter-American Defense Board. A permanent international body of defense experts representing 21 American republics, created in 1942 which, within the framework of the Organization of American States, studies and recommends plans for the common defense of the Western Hemisphere.

interest equalization tax. A tax on investments in foreign securities levied by Congress in 1963 primarily to counteract the effects of higher interest rates abroad, and thus help maintain the nation's balance of payments and lessen the drain on U.S. gold resources.

interest group. Persons who, whether closely organized or not, have interests in common in the molding of public opinion or in the passage of legislation. *Compare* pressure group.

interests. *Colloquial.* Men of wealth, corporations, or the capitalist class.

Intergovernmental Maritime Consultative Organization. A specialized agency of the United Nations, with a membership of more than 50 states having maritime interests, which promotes the observance of the Convention for Safety at Sea (signed at London, June 17, 1960), standardizes ship tonnage measurements, and seeks to prevent the pollution of the seas by oil and other contaminants and to discourage discriminatory and restrictive practices in ocean shipping.

interim. The period between legislative sessions.

Interior. *See* Department of the Interior.

interlocking directorates. Boards of directors of competing companies or of closely related financial concerns composed in part of the same individuals;—prohibited by the Clayton Act, *q.v.*, as a device to restrain trade.

intermediate court. A court, known by various names, in a judicial hierarchy falling between the highest, or supreme, tribunal and the trial court. Its jurisdiction is usually appellate, but some States confer original jurisdiction in special cases such as election contests.

internal improvement. A highway, railroad, canal, dredged waterway, air terminal, or other means of transportation or aid to commerce constructed within a country at public expense.

internal revenue. 1. Governmental income derived from domestic taxation. 2. Income of the federal government derived principally from taxes other than customs duties.

Internal Revenue Service. A part of the Treasury Department responsible for the assessment and collection of income and excise taxes, and the prevention of tax frauds.

Internal Security Act. An act of Congress, passed Sept. 23, 1950, over President Truman's veto, which outlawed conspiracies to establish a totalitarian dictatorship in the United States, required the registration of all Communist-front organizations, and created the Subversive Activities Control Board. *Called also* the McCarran Act.

international. 1. Pertaining to relations between or among nations. 2. Referring to private persons and organized groups whose activities extend across national boundaries for purposes of athletic competition, business, cultural exchange, and tourism; *called* also transnational.

international agreement. Any kind of engagement entered into between two or more states, ranging from an informal understanding or administrative convention to a formal treaty.

International Atomic Energy Agency. A specialized agency of the United Nations, established 1957, which maintains nuclear laboratory facilities and collaborates with other U.N. agencies in extending technical assistance and training to exploit peaceful uses of nuclear power. It consists of representatives of some 80 member states, with headquarters in Vienna.

International Bank for Reconstruction and Development. A specialized agency of the United Nations set up under the Bretton Woods Agreement of 1944. Its membership consists of about 100 nations including the United States. The bank promotes the rehabilitation and economic development of member nations by insuring private capital loans or, when necessary, by making loans itself. Working capital is provided by the pledged subscriptions of member nations and this can be replenished by the sale of the bank's debentures to the investing public. In 1960, an auxiliary institution, known as the International Development Association, came into being. This adjunct organization, with a membership of more than 90 countries which have subscribed its capital of approximately $1 billion, provides underdeveloped states with "soft" capital loans, that is, loans which bear less than the going rate of interest and provide long-term repayment schedules, both conditions being designed to reduce the adverse impact of loan repayments upon the recipient country's balance of payments.

International Boundary and Water Commission, United States and Mexico. A binational commission created in 1944 to effectuate existing treaties between the United States and Mexico on boundary and water issues (as construction of storage dams and power plants) and equitable distribution of the waters of the lower Colorado and the Rio Grande.

international boundary commission. A body chosen *ad hoc* by two or more states to determine the location of an international boundary line. Its decision may be based on principles of international law or prescription, or may represent a compromise of conflicting claims.

International Bureau of Weights and Measures. An international scientific organization, created in 1875, with headquarters in Sèvres, France, which has established international standards for the metric system and for measuring units of electricity, has custody of international prototypes of these and other standards, and verifies national standards by comparing them with their international prototypes.

International City Managers Association. A professional organization of city managers and other individuals, organized in 1914, with headquarters in Chicago, Ill., which is interested in the professional status and problems of city managers and in the general improvement of municipal government. Among its publications are the monthly *Public Management* and the annual *Municipal Year Book*.

International Civil Aviation Organization. A specialized agency of the United Nations, created in 1947 to deal with problems of air navigation and civilian air transport, which formulates common technical standards and procedures for international air transport and recommends their adoption by member governments.

international commodity agreement. An intergovernmental agreement to control production, stockpiling, and distribution (hence to control supply and price) of staple products like cotton, wheat, tin, rubber, sugar, and coffee, or to consult on plans for orderly marketing of such products, the principal aim of which is to stabilize international demand and thus assist in promoting economic equilibrium in countries whose economies are especially dependent on the export of one or a few products and hence are vulnerable to variations in demand.

international community. All the states of the world which are presumed to share certain common moral and legal values and social goals (as peace and human welfare) said to be institutionalized in such agencies as the League of Nations or the United Nations, or some auxiliary agency of the latter.

international copyright. An exclusive right to copyrighted literary or artistic property in all states with which the author's or artist's state has agreements pledging reciprocal respect of copyrights.

International Court of Justice. An international tribunal of 15 judges, elected for nine-year terms by the General Assembly and Security Council of the United Nations, which hears and decides justiciable international disputes referred to it by the parties involved and gives legal advice to organs of the United Nations. Its jurisdiction and powers are defined by its statute, to which all member states of the United Nations are parties and to which nonmember states may adhere as determined by the General Assembly and Security Council. The tribunal, with headquarters at The Hague, succeeded the Permanent Court of International Justice, *q.v.*

International Development Association. *See* International Bank for Reconstruction and Development.

International Finance Corporation. An affiliate of the International Bank for Reconstruction and Development (World Bank), established in 1956, which (usually) in cooperation with the Bank and its other affiliate, the International Development Association, and private investors, finances the establishment and development of private manufacturing enterprise and local industrial development companies in various states of the world and especially in underdeveloped areas. The Corporation may purchase the equities of the local companies, make direct loans, or underwrite the loans of others. It has a paid-up capital of $100 million and a membership of some 75 states.

International Joint Commission, United States and Canada. A binational agency of six members, created in 1911 to adjust the interests of the United States and Canada and their nationals in common boundary waters (as the Great Lakes), which exercises quasi-judicial authority over all cases involving use, diversion, or obstruction of boundary waters.

International Labor Organization. A specialized agency of the United Nations, at Geneva, Switzerland, first created as part of the League of Nations by the Treaty of Versailles in 1919, which conducts research and makes recommendations concerning hours, standards of employment, labor of women and children, and workers' health, unionization, and economic condition. The United States joined the original agency in 1934.

international law. An inchoate body of rules, classified as laws of peace, war, or neutrality, which deal principally with relationships between governments or between the government of one state and subjects of another. Although various usages existed in the relations between peoples of earlier civilizations, modern international law is a product of the European nation-state system. Early jurists, such as Gentilis and Grotius, endeavored to derive an interstate legal system from Roman and mercantile codes, contemporary custom, and reason. As international relationships grew more complex, new customary law developed and old rules were elaborated and interpreted in court decisions and studies by jurists. In the past century new rules have been decreed by states meeting in conferences, and in organizations like the League of Nations and the United Nations and their auxiliary agencies, thereby adding written international law to customary law. Controversies over the existence of international law are due partly to the common misconception that international law defines interstate relations as they ought to be and partly to the absence of a common superior to make it uniform and enforce it. Austinian jurists maintain that law must necessarily be handed down by a sovereign authority and be enforced by courts and police, whereas the test of a rule of international law is its universal acceptance by the community of states and their obedience to its mandates. That international law does not always coincide with international ethics is regrettable but technically irrelevant. *See* private international law.

international legislation. Rules of international law expressed in the form of multilateral agreements formulated by international conferences or by the United Nations or its specialized agencies and ratified by the principal states;—distinguished from unwritten customary international law discovered by jurists investigating the practice of states.

International Monetary Fund. A specialized agency of the United Nations set up under the Bretton Woods Agreement of 1944 to stabilize international exchange and promote balanced international trade. The agency has custody of a fund of several billion dollars provided by the subscriptions of its more than 100 members. Any member nation whose balance of international payments is temporarily deranged may draw upon the fund for necessary foreign currency to adjust its balance of payments subject to repayment when the crisis has passed. This privilege is designed to promote liquidity in international financial relations and make unnecessary resort by the member nation to unilateral action, such as depreciation of its own currency, or the imposition of arbitrary trade quotas or exchange controls.

international police forces. Contingents of military forces of member states placed under United Nations control, as authorized by Article 43 of the U.N. Charter, for the purpose of preserving peace and preventing or resisting aggressive actions (as in Korea, the Gaza Strip, the Congo, and Cyprus).

International Red Cross. Two international organizations known respectively as the International Committee of the Red Cross and the League of Red Cross Societies, both with headquarters in Geneva, Switzerland. The first of these is a wholly neutral agency, unconnected with any national society, which attempts to maintain the basic Red Cross principles of the Geneva Convention, *q.v.*; the second agency is a federation of autonomous national Red Cross societies designed to further cooperation among them. Both organizations receive financial support from national societies.

International Refugee Organization. An agency of the United Nations which until liquidated sought to protect, repatriate, and resettle refugees and persons displaced after World War II.

International Telecommunications Union. A specialized agency of the United Nations, consisting of more than 120 nations, successor to the International Telegraph Union (formed 1865) which, through its headquarters at Geneva, Switzerland, provides governments with information on telecommunications and publishes various technical communications, bulletins, and periodicals. In accordance with the Telecommunications Convention signed at Geneva, Dec. 21, 1959, this agency formally approves and records broadcasting frequencies, publishes call letters and other data on the technical aspects of international telecommunication, and makes recommendations on operational and fiscal questions. In 1963 it became concerned with the problem of communication in space.

International Trade Organization. A proposed specialized agency of the United Nations to promote multilateral international trade and domestic employment, eliminate discriminations in trade practices, and assist the economies of less developed states. Although in 1947 a preparatory committee in Geneva, Switzerland, drafted a charter, and the United Nations Conference on Trade and Development, held in Geneva in 1965, recommended its creation, its actual establishment appears remote.

international transit. The passage of ships, trains, automobiles, trucks, and airplanes from one country to, or through, another. International agreements for the navigation of the Rhine and Danube rivers date from the 16th century. Numerous agreements are in force governing other means of transit, especially by air.

International Wheat Council. An international body of representatives of wheat-exporting and -importing countries interested in stabilizing the world's wheat economy including maintenance of minimum and maximum world prices. It is responsible for the execution of periodic international agreements for trading in wheat.

internment. 1. The confinement of enemy aliens or persons suspected of disloyalty in special camps or designated areas. **2.** The custody exercised by a neutral state over the troops, ships of war, or military planes that have sought asylum within its territory or that have violated its neutrality.

Interparliamentary Union. A worldwide association of national groups of legislators, founded in 1889, which, through annual conferences and by other means, promotes such causes as the liberalization of international trade, disarmament, and the peaceful settlement of disputes among national parliaments and governments.

interstate commerce. Commerce among the several States which Congress has the power to regulate under the commerce clause of the U.S. Constitution. It includes traffic, transportation, communication, and intercourse which concern more States than one, and also, especially since 1938, has embraced intrastate operations for the production of goods and services and working conditions which affect interstate commerce in a substantial way. The Supreme Court, holding that "the federal commerce power is as broad as the economic needs of the nation," has limited it in only a few cases since 1938. *Compare* intrastate commerce.

Interstate Commerce Act. An act of Congress, Feb. 4, 1887, which provided that rates charged by interstate railroads were to be reasonable, and which prohibited special rates, rebates, drawbacks, undue preferences to persons and localities, and higher rates for a short haul than for a longer haul over the same line. *See* Interstate Commerce Commission.

Interstate Commerce Commission. An independent commission, created by Congress, Feb. 4, 1887, and now consisting of eleven members, which fixes just and reasonable rates among carriers, regulates pooling and approves consolidations, prescribes uniform accounting practices, evaluates carrier property, approves the issuance and sale of securities under certain circumstances, and decides on discontinuance of interstate railway and ferry service or of intrastate service on interstate railways. Carriers under its jurisdiction include all railway and express companies, oil pipelines, sleeping-car companies, motor carriers operating interstate, and water carriers operating on coastwise, intercoastal, or inland waterway routes. The commission may also determine intrastate rates where necessary to remove discrimination against interstate rates.

interstate compact. An agreement between two or more States made with the consent of Congress and relating usually to boundaries, control and improvement of rivers for irrigation or water power, conservation of natural resources, penal jurisdiction over boundary rivers and lakes, public utility regulation, development of ports, regional educational development, or uniformity of legislation. Many agreements concerning minor matters are made without the consent of Congress.

interstate rendition. *See* rendition.

intervention. Forcible interference by one state in the internal affairs of another to restore order, prevent the commission or continuance of acts which shock the moral sense of civilized peoples, compel a state to fulfill its international obligations, or for more selfish or less worthy purposes. Premature recognition of the independence of insurgents constitutes intervention, but recognition of their belligerency is not so regarded.

intimidation. An offense against the purity of elections which consists of threats of physical violence or of loss of employment or other privileges.

intransigent. Unwilling to compromise on matters of policy; irreconcilable.

intrastate commerce. Trade, transportation, or communication conducted wholly within the boundaries of a single State which is subject to State regulatory authorities; but rates and standards of service fixed by them must not interrupt or burden the free flow of commerce among the States. In practice, this means that regulations of State commissions can be, and often are, made to harmonize with those of national commissions.

investigative power. "An essential and appropriate auxiliary to the legislative function," *McGrain* v. *Daugherty*, 273 U.S. 135 (1927), which enables a legislative body to obtain information by compelling the attendance of witnesses and the production of books and papers, and which subjects recalcitrant persons to punishment for contempt of legislative authority. The inquiry must relate to a subject within the competence of a legislative house, such as an impeachment or the trial thereof, a contested election, or the punishment of a member; or to a subject on which legislation is contemplated; or to a subject in need of remedial legislation. Investigations are usually conducted by joint, standing, or special committees whose scope and powers must be carefully delimited in advance, and whose methods and activities must respect the civil rights of witnesses and persons subjected to investigation.

Investment Advisers Act. An act of Congress, Aug. 22, 1940, which requires investment advisers to register with the Securities and Exchange Commission, and provides that their registrations may be revoked for cause. It prohibits fraudulent or deceitful statements or misrepresentations concerning securities.

Investment Company Act. An act of Congress, Aug. 22, 1940, which requires investment trusts to register with the Securities and Exchange Commission; limits the number of directors of such companies who are affiliated with banking, brokerage, and investment advisory companies; prohibits the purchase of securities in their interest rather than in the interest of stockholders; prohibits pyramiding and unsound methods of accounting; and seeks to protect stockholders when new securities are issued and when the investment company is being reorganized.

Invisible Empire. Another name for the Ku Klux Klan.

invisible government. The rule of a boss who, having secured the nominations and elections of governors or mayors, legislators, and judges, dictates their policies, appointments, acts, and decisions in specific cases.

involuntary servitude. Slavery, peonage, or compulsory labor to work out a debt, all of which are prohibited except as a punishment for crime by the 13th Amendment. Even though a person voluntarily pledged his future personal services in return for a valuable consideration, he cannot be required to perform them. State laws imposing criminal punishments for breaching a labor contract by quitting work have been declared unconstitutional. But the courts have held that policemen, firemen, members of train crews, and seamen are obliged to remain on duty when their presence is required to protect the public safety.

ironclad oath. The oath of office prescribed by Congress, July 2, 1862, which required a person to swear that he had never voluntarily given aid or encouragement to the enemies of the United States. A similar oath was required in 1867 for voters in the States undergoing reconstruction.

Iron Curtain. The symbolic division which, according to Winston Churchill (at Westminster College, Fulton, Mo., Mar. 5, 1946), had "descended from Stettin on the Baltic to Trieste on the Adriatic" as a consequence of Russia's imposing Communist regimes on occupied countries by force in disregard of pledges to hold free elections.

irreconcilable. One who insists on the adoption of the program of his party or group and refuses to make concessions or agree to compromises.

irredentism. Aspirations and activity on the part of a national group to annex territory formerly belonging to their state or inhabited by persons of similar racial or linguistic stock or cultural background or values.

Irrepressible-Conflict Speech. An address by William H. Seward at Rochester, N.Y., Oct. 25, 1858, in which he declared that the slavery controversy was "an irrepressible conflict between opposing and enduring forces, and it means that the United States must and will, sooner or later, become either entirely a slaveholding nation or entirely a free-labor nation."

irrigation district. A special district empowered to borrow money and collect taxes in order to purchase or condemn water rights and to construct and operate works for the distribution and sale of water to private persons for artificial watering of arid and semiarid land.

I.R.S. Internal Revenue Service.

isolation. Aloofness in international politics; *specifically*: refusal to participate with other states in efforts to remove causes of international friction and to secure the peace of the world;—often referred to as the avoidance of entangling alliances. Based on the alleged self-sufficiency and immunity from attack of the United States and its lack of real interest in European affairs, the policy of isolation prevented America being represented at general international conferences before 1900, accession to the League of Nations in 1919, and cooperation in the curbing of aggressor nations until after 1937.

itemized appropriations. Appropriations which stipulate in great detail the specific purposes for which even small sums may be spent in contrast to lump-sum appropriations, which may be allocated by the chief executive to spending agencies or by heads of departments to specific subjects.

item veto. The power which the governor possesses in 41 States to veto items in appropriation bills without affecting any other provisions of such bills. In some of these States the governor may also reduce the amount of items, and in the State of Washington he may veto parts of nonfinancial bills.

I.W.W. Industrial Workers of the World.

J

jackpot. A fund contributed by various private interests and disbursed at the end of a legislative session to "pay-off" members who had voted in support of the "interests."

Jackson Day. The anniversary of the battle of New Orleans, January 8, 1815, a legal holiday in Louisiana, and often celebrated elsewhere by the Democratic party with a fund-raising dinner.

Jacksonian democracy. An equalitarian movement which developed from the rapid advance of the frontier, urban growth, and Andrew Jackson's personal policies, rather than from any significant political theory. It was characterized by the virtual disappearance of the aristocratic tradition in politics; by the belief that the common man is capable of deciding political questions and administering the government; by demands for universal manhood suffrage and rotation in office; by opposition to the Bank of the United States and other monopolies; by racism, as applied to Indians; and by an exaggerated emphasis on the dogma of States rights, though Jackson sternly suppressed nullification.

Jacobin. 1. A radical French revolutionist, 1789. 2. A nickname applied to democratic societies and individuals who opposed the neutrality policies of Washington's administration. 3. Radical Republicans in

Missouri, 1861–65, who wished to proscribe all Southern sympathizers.

Jacobson v. Massachusetts. *See* compulsory vaccination.

JAG Judge Advocate General.

jail. An institution for the detention of suspected persons awaiting trial, and for the imprisonment of persons sentenced to less than one year for petty crimes, misdemeanors, and minor offenses. *Compare* house of detention.

Jarvis Island. A mid-Pacific island immediately south of the equator occupied by the United States because of its value as a meteorological and air transit station.

Jaybird primary. *See* Texas Primary cases.

Jayhawker. 1. A Kansan. 2. A freesoil partisan who, before and during the Civil War, engaged in sporadic warfare with the border ruffians, *q.v.*, of Missouri.

Jay's Treaty. A treaty with Great Britain negotiated by Chief Justice John Jay in London, 1794, which provided for British evacuation of military posts on American territory, judicial settlement of claims for unlawful captures by British ships, and payment to British creditors of private debts contracted by Americans before 1783. Jay's Treaty deepened the rift between political parties in Washington's administration.

J.E.C. Joint Economic Committee.

Jefferson Day. Thomas Jefferson's birthday, April 13, a legal holiday in Alabama, Missouri, and Virginia, and occasionally celebrated elsewhere, especially by Democratic party groups.

Jeffersonian democracy. Principles held by Thomas Jefferson and his associates, including belief in the natural rights to life and liberty, equality of opportunity, minimum interference by government with individual affairs, exact administration of justice, preservation of civil liberties, majority rule, local self-government, and subordination of military to civil authorities. Jefferson feared the effects of urban growth and thought the best hope for democracy was in a literate population composed mainly of small farmers.

Jefferson's Manual. A compilation of rules of parliamentary procedure by Thomas Jefferson for his own use while presiding over the Senate as Vice President, 1797–1801; later adopted as basic rules by both houses of Congress.

Jefferson Territory. A provisional government, 1859–61, for the Pike's Peak mining region of Kansas Territory, now in Colorado.

Jehovah's Witnesses cases. Numerous cases concerning door-to-door peddling without a license, littering the streets, holding meetings in public places without permits, insulting statements about other religions, use of unlicensed sound trucks, and refusal of children to salute the flag, appealed to the Supreme Court by the Jehovah's Witnesses sect, usually with the result of widening the Court's interpretation of religious freedom under the First Amendment.

Jenner Bill. A bill introduced in Congress, 1957, by Senator William E. Jenner which would have excluded from the appellate jurisdiction of the Supreme Court cases concerning Congressional investigations of loyalty or security removals in the civil service, enforcement of State laws to control subversive activities, dismissal of teachers for disloyal activities, and State regulations concerning lawyers and admission to the bar.

jeopardy. *See* double jeopardy.

Jim Crow law. Any statute requiring the segregation of the white and Negro races in education, transportation, places of work and amusement, and public accommodation. Such statutes were formerly upheld by the Supreme Court (*see Plessy* v. *Ferguson*), but are now in nearly every respect unconstitutional.

jingo. A bellicose patriot, given to boasting of his country's readiness for war and willingness to fight for its rights;—from a British popular song (1878):

> We don't want to fight,
> But by Jingo if we do,
> We've got the ships, we've got the men,
> We've got the money too.

John Birch Society. A semi-secret, authoritarian, right extremist organization, founded by Robert Welch, a Massachusetts manufacturer, in Indianapolis, Ind., in 1958, that opposes Communism (its announced purpose), impugns the motives of moderate and liberal leaders, and opposes all forms of internationalism;—named for a Georgia "fundamentalist" missionary preacher who had been killed by the Chinese Communists following World War II.

Johnson Act. *See* Foreign Securities Act.

joint ballot. Members of the two houses of a legislature voting together, each member's vote counting as one.

joint budget. A budget prepared by members of the executive and legislative departments meeting together;—used in only a few States.

Joint Chiefs of Staff. The Chiefs of Staff of the Army and the Air Force, the Chief of Naval Operations, the Commandant of the Marine Corps (on matters directly affecting the Corps) and the Chairman of the Joint Chiefs of Staff who are collectively responsible for strategic and logistic planning and integrated mobilization. As the staff of the Secretary of Defense they furnish him with military and strategic information to be used in planning the needs and responsibilities of the armed forces. The Joint Chiefs also serve as advisers to the President and the National Security Council, *q.v.*

joint commission. 1. A permanent international administrative body, as the International Joint Commission, United States and Canada, *q.v.* **2.** A body consisting of representatives of two nations appointed to investigate and recommend means of settlement of a particular matter in dispute between them.

joint committee. 1. Any common committee of two plenary bodies. **2.** A committee composed of members designated by each legislative house which has the functions of (*a*) investigating a particular matter and rendering a report; or (*b*) administering subjects under direct legislative control; or (*c*) performing all the functions normally entrusted to a standing legislative committee, as in Massachusetts, Maine, and Connecticut.

Joint Committee on Printing. A committee of three Senators and three Representatives, created by act of Aug. 3, 1846, which serves as a board of directors for the Government Printing Office, *q.v.*, and approves standards of materials, contracts, and wage agreements.

Joint Committee on the Library. A combined House and Senate committee, created in 1806, whose functions at present are limited to control of the Botanic Gardens. The House members have certain supervisory functions relating to the buildings, management, and acquisitions of the Library of Congress and the Smithsonian Institution.

Joint Economic Committee. A committee of eight Senators (five from the majority party) and of an equal number of Representatives, similarly divided, which, each year before March 1st, following extensive testimony by economists, offers comments and recommendations (as a guide for legislation) on major aspects of the current annual report of the President and his Council of Economic Advisers on the economic state of the country.

joint hearings. The collection of testimony and examination of witnesses by two or more committees sitting together.

joint rate. The common or joint tariff in effect where the facilities of two or more common carriers are required for completion of a shipment.

Joint Reference Library. A library for reference and research purposes maintained by the Public Administration Clearing House at its headquarters in Chicago, Ill., in cooperation with other agencies interested in problems of government and administration.

joint resolution. A statute which, when passed by both legislative houses and signed by the chief executive or passed over his veto, has the same force as a legislative act, though ranking below it in formal dignity. The enacting clause of a joint resolution of Congress begins: "Be it Resolved by the Senate and House of Representatives. . . ." *Compare* act of Congress; concurrent resolution.

joint return. An income tax return filed by husband and wife together that includes income received by each, and their combined deductions for tax purposes.

joint rule. A rule adopted in identical form by both houses of a legislature, or enacted as a statute, to govern the two houses while they are sitting together for the transaction of business.

joint session. A meeting together of two separate bodies (as legislative houses, or committees) for the transaction of business.

joint-stock association. A business organization, similar to a partnership, whose capital stock is owned by various shareholders any one of whom may transfer his holdings without the consent of the remainder. It does not enjoy the legal personality of a corporation since it can sue and be sued only through some designated officer; moreover, its shareholders do not enjoy limited liability but are individually and collectively responsible for the association's debts.

joker. An obscure provision inserted in the body of a bill for the purpose of nullifying other provisions or giving the bill a meaning different from that avowed by its sponsors.

Jones Act. 1. An act of Congress, Aug. 29, 1916, which made both houses of the Philippine legislature elective, broadened the franchise, provided for extensive self-government, and promised independence as soon as a stable government was assured. 2. An act of Congress, Mar. 2, 1917, which liberalized the government of Puerto Rico by making both houses of the legislature elective, increasing their powers, extending the suffrage to all literate adults, and collectively conferring American citizenship upon Puerto Ricans. *Compare* Foraker Act.

journal. The official record of a legislative house, kept by the clerk and published as directed by the house, which contains minutes of the introduction and reference of bills, reports of committees, motions, votes, and other actions, but which does not report debates.

J.P. Justice of the peace.

judge. The principal officer of a court who alone or in concert with colleagues or with a jury, as the law or the rules of the court prescribe, hears and decides cases and controversies and renders judgments.

judge advocate. A legal officer of a court-martial who acts as prosecutor for the government and may act to protect the rights of the accused.

Judge Advocate General. The chief legal officer of a branch of the military services who has, among other duties, supervision of military justice and of the proceedings of courts-martial and military commissions.

judge-made law. 1. The common law as developed in form and content by judges or judicial decisions. 2. Judicial decisions based on tortured constructions of the Constitution, or on the selection of unusual historical and legal precedents, or on unusual definitions of terms in "discovering" the law applying to a given case;—used derogatively.

judge of elections. One of a board of three or four locally appointed persons which supervises the voting in an election precinct and certifies the result.

Judges Act. The Judiciary Act of 1925, drafted by Justices of the Supreme Court, which greatly reduced the number of cases that could be appealed to the Supreme Court, routing most of them to the Court of Appeals instead; gave the Supreme Court power by writ of certiorari to select the cases it would review; and provided that cases could be appealed from State supreme courts only when a federal question was involved.

judgment. An authoritative determination of the legal rights and duties of the parties to a controversy usually rendered by a court.

Judicial Conference of the United States. The governing body of the entire federal judicial system which supervises the Administrative Office of the United States Courts, *q.v.* It consists of the chief judge of each of the 11 circuits (appellate), one district judge from each circuit elected by the circuit and district judges of the circuit, the chief judges of the Court of Claims and of the Court of Customs and Patent Appeals, with the Chief Justice of the United States as chairman.

judicial council. A continuing body, usually composed of judges, lawyers, and laymen, established in most of the States to study the structure, jurisdiction, and functioning of the courts and to make recommendations to courts and legislatures.

judicial power. The power to hear and decide cases and controversies in accordance with the forms and procedures prescribed by the law of the land and to render judgment consistent with the substantive provisions of law, such judgment being definitive except for the legal right of parties to appeal to a higher judicial tribunal.

Judicial Procedure Reform Act. An act of Congress, Aug. 26, 1937, which empowered the Attorney General to appear before district courts in cases where the constitutionality of a federal statute is questioned; allowed the moving of such cases, when decided against the government, directly to the Supreme Court; and reduced the power of federal judges to delay enforcement of acts of Congress.

judicial review. The examination by the courts, in cases actually before them, of legislative, executive, or administrative acts to determine whether or not they are prohibited by a written constitution or are in excess of powers granted by it; and if so, to declare them void and of no effect. The power was exercised by several State courts in the Confederation period and was declared inherent in the judiciary by the Supreme Court in *Marbury* v. *Madison, q.v.* In general the courts do not inquire into expediency or legislative motives; and in cases of doubt the rule is that the statute or act should be sustained.

judicial self-restraint. The tendency of some judges to interpret narrowly the power of judicial review, as by holding that changes in the law to achieve social goals is a responsibility of the legislative and executive departments; and by questioning and even opposing the transfer of functions from the States to the federal government. As typified by Justices Holmes and Frankfurter, they are inclined to express doubts as to judicial infallibility. Their attitude is opposed to that of judicial activists.

judiciary. A system of courts; *also:* the judges collectively. The federal judiciary consists of a Supreme Court, 11 courts of appeals, 90 or more district courts, a Court of Claims, a Court of Customs and Patent Appeals, and a Customs Court, besides courts in the District of Columbia and in the territories. In the States there is always one supreme court, sometimes called the Court of Appeals, or the Court of Errors and Appeals; a number of circuit courts with varying titles, holding sessions in every county; and minor courts presided over by justices of the peace or magistrates. Many States also have intermediate courts ranking just below the highest court; county courts with limited jurisdiction ranking below the circuit courts; and specialized criminal courts, probate courts, domestic relations courts, and children's, juvenile, and adolescent courts. Formerly separate courts were organized to administer law and equity, but this distinction has disappeared almost everywhere. Such courts have been merged and in most States both legal and equitable remedies may be used in the same case. *See* constitutional court; legislative court.

judiciary committee. A committee in national and State legislative houses which has jurisdiction over bills affecting the organization, jurisdiction, and procedure of courts, or bills which pose a constitutional issue, or raise important questions of private law.

Juilliard v. Greenman. *See* legal tender.

junior management assistant. A professional post which leads to a career in the civil service, usually filled from among college graduates in the social sciences who pass examinations stressing general ability, administrative aptitude, and knowledge of current events.

junket. A lengthy trip or outing at public expense by an individual legislator, or members of a legislative committee, or other public servant, under the pretense of making an investigation at a distance from the seat of government.

juridical. In accordance with law and with due process in the administration of justice; pertaining to the office and functions of a judge.

jurisdiction. 1. The authority of a court to hear and decide cases and controversies concerning persons and subjects. 2. The territorial or other limits within which the authority of a government, court, legislative committee, or labor union may be exercised. *See* aerial domain; maritime jurisdiction.

jurisdictional dispute. A conflict among labor unions for the control of employment in certain types of work or for the exclusive privilege of organizing employees in certain industries or areas.

jurisprudence. 1. The science or philosophy of law. 2. The study of the actual substance of law as found in judicial decisions. 3. The formal analytical study of legal systems after the fashion established by John Austin. 4. A study, employing historical, philosophical, and sociological methods, of the nature of law and its relationship to customs and morals.

jury. A body of impartial laymen residing within the territorial jurisdiction of a court who are properly empaneled and sworn to render a true answer to a question of fact submitted to them. In U.S. courts the petit, or trial, jury consists of twelve persons, whose verdict must be unanimous in both civil and criminal cases; but jury trial is usually waived in civil cases and may be waived in criminal cases by the accused with the consent of the prosecutor and the trial court. For the trial of criminal cases (other than those involving capital crimes) several States employ fewer than twelve jurors or authorize verdicts by three-fourths or some other fraction. For civil cases a greater number of States have relaxed the requirement as to both the size of the jury and the majority necessary for a verdict, and several States provide for no jury except on the demand of one of the parties. A few States make the jury the judge of both the law and the facts of a case. *See* grand jury.

jury wheel. A device for selecting by lot the names of jurors who are to be summoned to attend a particular court.

jus gentium. A body of law developed by Roman jurists for the trial of cases between Roman citizens and foreigners and provincials; subsequently held by medieval jurists to embody principles of right reason applicable to all human relationships; and invoked by Grotius and others as authority for rules of international law.

jus sanguinis. The principle implicit in the nationality laws of most Continental European states that a child's citizenship is determined by the citizenship of his parents.

jus soli. The principle of the nationality laws of the United States, Great Britain, and certain other states that a person's citizenship is determined by the place of his birth. *Compare* allegiance.

just compensation. Compensation which is fair to both the owner and the public when property is taken for public use, the amount being determined by such criteria as the cost of reproducing the property, its market value, and the resulting damage to the remaining property of the owner. *See* eminent domain.

justice. 1. The title of a judge. **2.** The process of adjudication by which the legal rights of private parties are vindicated and the guilt or innocence of accused persons is established. **3.** *In Platonic philosophy*: the condition of harmony that exists among citizens of a state when each member cooperates in the affairs of the state and occupies a place according to his individual merits.

Justice Department. *See* Department of Justice.

justice of the peace. A subordinate magistrate, usually without formal legal training, empowered to try petty civil and criminal cases, and, in some States, to conduct preliminary hearings for persons accused of a crime, and to fix bail for appearance in court. Justices of the peace are usually elective within a minor civil division, although their jurisdiction normally extends throughout a county. Except in a few States, their compensation is derived from fees, with the result that, in many cases, judgment is for the plaintiff.

justiciable question. A matter which a court will consider because it concerns a genuine dispute between parties who have a real interest in its solution. The phrase excludes advisory opinions, friendly suits, and cases brought by persons who have no standing to sue.

juvenile court. A specialized court having jurisdiction in cases of delinquent, neglected, or dependent children which seeks to determine the underlying causes of misconduct and provides for reformation through education, healthful activities, or institutional supervision. Juvenile defendants are entitled to be assisted by counsel and to have all the procedural safeguards that are accorded to adult defendants at all stages of police and judicial proceedings against them.

juvenile delinquency. Antisocial or vicious conduct and ungovernable behavior on the part of a child.

juvenile offender. A person under 16, 18, or (in some States) 20 years of age who has been found guilty of having committed offenses against the law.

Kansas Industrial Court. A court of compulsory arbitration created by Kansas in 1920 with power to settle labor disputes by mandatory awards on hours and conditions of work and minimum wages. The law creating the court was declared unconstitutional by the Supreme Court in *Wolff Packing Co. v. Court of Industrial Relations*, 262 U.S. 522 (1923).

Kansas-Nebraska Act. A law of Congress, May 30, 1854, which organized Kansas and Nebraska territories in the region closed to slavery by the Missouri Compromise of 1820, which it expressly repealed. Either territory might later be admitted as a State "with or without slavery, as their constitutions may prescribe at the time of admission"—a provision which introduced popular, or squatter, sovereignty. The act angered the abolitionists, resulted in the disruption of political parties, and hastened the outbreak of the Civil War.

Kansas and Nebraska Territories

Kansas v. Colorado. A case, 206 U.S. 46 (1907), which involved the distribution of water rights from a river flowing from Colorado into Kansas. In establishing its jurisdiction over this case the Supreme Court held that, in the absence of specific limitations, the federal courts are vested with all the judicial power which the United States as a nation is capable of exerting.

Keating-Owen Act. An act of Congress, Sept. 1, 1916, which forbade shipment in interstate commerce of the products of mines and factories in which children under certain ages (14 or 16) had been allowed to work. The Supreme Court invalidated it in *Hammer* v. *Dagenhart*. *See* Child labor cases.

Kellogg-Briand Pact. A treaty signed in Paris, Aug. 27, 1928, by which adhering states renounced war as an instrument of national policy and declared their intention to seek pacific settlement of disputes arising among them. Nearly every country adhered before World War II.

Kendall v. United States. A case, 12 Pet. 524 (1838), in which the Supreme Court upheld the proposition that, under the doctrine of separation of powers, the President is not answerable to either Congress or the courts; and that, except in cases of impeachment, he is immune from compulsory process against him; but when Congress by law imposes a ministerial duty upon an officer, the duty must be carried out even though the President may have ordered otherwise.

Kennedy Library. The collection of public papers and memorabilia of the John F. Kennedy Administration housed in a special building at Cambridge, Mass., constructed and maintained in cooperation with Harvard University. For certain purposes the Library falls under the supervision of the General Services Administration, *q.v.*

Kennedy Round. Negotiations conducted under the General Agreement on Tariffs and Trade, *q.v.*, 1964–67, which resulted in additional reductions in tariffs averaging about 33 per cent. *Compare* Dillon Round.

Kentucky Resolutions. Ten resolutions drafted by Thomas Jefferson which were passed by the legislature of Kentucky in 1798 and 1799 and sent to the other States. They declared that the national government was a government of delegated powers, created by compact among the States; that whenever it exercised undelegated powers each State, as a party to the compact, might declare the action void; and, in particular, that the Alien and Sedition acts of Congress were "void and of no effect." *Compare* Virginia Resolutions.

Kentucky v. Dennison. A case, 24 How. 66 (1861), in which the Supreme Court held that the duty of a governor to return fugitives from justice from another State is a moral and not a legal duty, and that a writ of mandamus will not issue to compel him to perform it.

Kent v. Dulles. A case, 357 U.S. 116 (1958), in which the Supreme Court held that, since the right to travel is part of the citizen's liberty, denial of a passport by the Secretary of State, in the absence of express regulations by Congress, would be a denial of due process even though the passport applicant was charged with Communist sympathies and had refused, upon request, to supply a non-Communist disclaimer.

Keynesian economics. Theories of John Maynard Keynes, British economist, intended to curb deflationary trends and to promote economic prosperity. He advocated stimulating expenditure and investment in order to equal and possibly exceed savings, slight inflation not being condemned—views which are being increasingly adopted by fiscal and monetary experts who advise governments.

keynote speech. The address delivered by the temporary chairman in opening a national nominating convention.

kidnapping. Abduction, forcible removal, and detainment of a person, a capital crime in some States and under federal laws.

Kilbourn v. Thompson. A case, 103 U.S. 168 (1881), in which the Supreme Court held that the investigative power, *q.v.*, of Congress did not include a general authority to inquire into private affairs.

Kingfish. A nickname for Senator Huey P. Long of Louisiana.

Kitchen Cabinet. A group including William B. Lewis, Amos Kendall, Francis P. Blair, and Duff Green whose advice President Jackson was supposed to have followed for a time rather than that of his regular cabinet.

K.K.K. Ku Klux Klan.

knifing. 1. Political treachery. 2. Secret desertion by a party organization of its own candidates. 3. The pretense of supporting a candidate while actively working for the election of an opponent.

Knights of Labor. A national industrial labor union founded in Philadelphia in 1869 which attained a membership of 600,000 by 1886 and continued to have great importance for a few years thereafter. Its disappearance was attributed to political entanglements, rivalry with craft unions, and internal dissensions.

Knights of the Golden Circle. A secret, semimilitary organization formed in 1855 which during the Civil War became the leading Copperhead organization in the Ohio Valley States, claiming 174,000 members in Ohio, Indiana, and Illinois by 1864.

Know-Nothing party. A secret political party opposed to foreigners which grew out of the Order of United Americans about 1852. Its membership was divided into three classes, the first two of which were alone capable of determining policy or being nominated for party or public office. Members of the third class were pledged to vote the party ticket and to reply "I don't know" to all inquiries. It won the elections in Massachusetts in 1854 and attained great influence in other Northern States. In 1855 its organization was captured by Southerners and its name was changed to American party, *q.v.*

Korean War. A conflict which began June 25, 1950, when North Korean Communist forces invaded the Republic of South Korea. At the insistence of the United States, the Security Council of the United Nations on June 27 called on member nations to repel the attack. Forces of the United States and relatively small contingents from eleven other nations fought a long and bloody war (there were more than 125,000 American casualties) against North Korean and Chinese Communist "volunteer" forces. That it was for limited objectives became evident when President Truman in April, 1951, dismissed General Douglas MacArthur from command of the U.N. forces. President Eisenhower signed an armistice on July 27, 1953, which practically maintained the 38th patallel as the boundary between North and South Korea.

Ku Klux Klan. 1. An organization founded in Tennessee in 1866 to reassert white supremacy in the South. Disguised in white masks and robes, members of the Klan rode at night, terrorizing, whipping, and committing other acts of violence (including murder) against Negroes who persisted in voting and against their white leaders. After Congress in 1871 passed the Ku Klux Klan Act and the Force Act, *q.v.*, the Klan adopted less violent means to accomplish its purpose. 2. A national organization founded in 1915, and directed against Catholics, Jews, and foreigners, as well as Negroes, which was influential in several States for a brief period after World War I. The Klan still exists under several different names.

L

Labor Department. *See* Department of Labor.

labor legislation. Laws concerning wages, hours, and other conditions of work, and labor-management relations enacted by State legislatures under the police power or by Congress under the power to regulate interstate and foreign commerce. The first such laws protected children and women against exploitation. By 1900, laws were being passed protecting men in hazardous occupations, removing common-law impediments to recovery of damages for injuries in the course of employment, and creating State workmen's compensation funds. Federal legislation was limited initially to the regulation of conditions of work on interstate railways, but with the Supreme Court's broader definition of interstate commerce in the 1930's it was extended to industry generally. It then came to embrace maximum hours, minimum wages, outlawry of child labor, insurance against unemployment, retirement benefits, the right of labor to organize and bargain collectively, the protection of members of labor unions from irresponsible acts of their leaders, and some concern for the interest of the public when caught up in the economic struggle between capital and labor.

Labor-Management Relations Act. See Taft-Hartley Labor-Management Relations Act.

Labor Reform Act. The Labor-Management Reporting and Disclosure Act of 1959, designed to remedy evils disclosed by the Senate Rackets Committee. The act forbids convicted felons from holding office in a labor union for five years after their conviction or imprisonment, makes misuse of union funds a federal crime, requires detailed annual reports of union finances and activities, and guarantees to union members free participation and vote by secret ballot in union meetings, and access to union contracts and financial and other records. *Called also* Landrum-Griffin Act. See *United States* v. *Brown.*

Labor Reform party. A minor party formed in 1869 which advocated the exclusive use of greenbacks, *q.v.*, for currency, an eight-hour day on government contracts, abolition of the contract system in prison labor, and Chinese exclusion.

Labor's League for Political Action. An organization created by the American Federation of Labor in 1947 to further the political interests of its affiliated unions, particularly in national and State elections, and financed by special dues levied upon the membership of the local unions.

Labor's Nonpartisan League. A body, created Aug. 10, 1936, to unite organized labor for political action, which aided in the reelection of President F. D. Roosevelt in 1936 and organized the American Labor party, *q.v.*

labor union. An unincorporated association of employees which acts as their agent in bargaining collectively with employers concerning wages, hours of work, fringe benefits, and other conditions of employment. Labor unions are roughly classified as *craft,* or *horizontal,* unions which may include all workers of a particular craft, trade, or skill, wherever they may be employed; and as *industrial,* or *vertical,* unions which may include all workers in a given industry regardless of their craft, trade, or skill.

La Follette-Bulwinkle Act. An act of Congress, May 24, 1938, authorizing the allotment of funds to the States to assist them in the prevention, treatment, and control of venereal diseases.

La Follette Seamen's Act. An act of Congress, Mar. 4, 1915, which regulated wage scales, the payment of wages, conditions of employment, and size of crews on merchant ships and established minimum standards for the victualing and quartering of crews on shipboard; *called also* Furuseth Act.

LAFTA. An acronym for Latin American Free Trade Association, formed in 1960 by treaty among Argentina, Brazil, Chile, Mexico, Paraguay, Peru, and Uruguay (and open to other Latin American countries) for ending, over a twelve-year period, tariffs and other restrictions on trade between members.

laissez faire. A phrase coined by French physiocrats which has come to stand for noninterference by government in economic life except for the purposes of maintaining order and protecting property.

lame duck. A politician who has been defeated.

lame duck session. Before the adoption of the 20th Amendment, the short session of Congress which began in December of even-numbered years and ended the following March 4, in which a number of Senators and Representatives sat who had failed of reelection.

land-grabber. One who obtains public land by fraud, bribery, or collusion with officials, or by taking advantage of loopholes in the laws.

land grant. A gift of public land to an individual, corporation, local government division, or State to aid in accomplishing some public purpose.

land-grant college. An agricultural and mechanical (A. & M.) college, or equivalent parts of a State university, established as a result of the distribution, under the Morrill Act of 1862, of public lands to the States in proportion to their representation in Congress; and supported partly from later federal grants but mainly from State appropriations.

land office. One of several regional offices maintained in the western part of the United States and in Alaska by the Bureau of Land Management, *q.v.*, to receive and act upon applications for private entry on public lands and to keep land-title records. Formerly these offices were important in administering land grants to homesteaders and others.

land patent. An instrument conveying a grant of public land; *also:* the land so conveyed.

landslide. Overwhelming triumph of a party in a popular election.

Lanham Act. An act of Congress, Oct. 14, 1940, which authorized various national agencies to provide housing for persons employed in war plants and to acquire land for the construction of necessary community works and services, as hospitals, schools, streets, and water works.

Lansing-Ishii Agreement. An executive agreement, signed Nov. 2, 1917, and ended by mutual consent Apr. 14, 1923, by which the United States recognized that Japan possessed "special interests," particularly in Manchuria, and Japan assented to the principle of the open door, *q.v.*, in China.

larceny. Theft of personal property.

last-minute lie. A falsehood concerning a candidate's public record or private life circulated on the eve of an election when refutation is impossible.

law. 1. A general rule for the conduct of members of the community either emanating from the governing authority by positive command or approved by it, and habitually enforced by some public authority by the imposition of sanctions or penalties for its violation. **2.** The whole body of such rules, including constitutions, the common law, equity, statutes, judicial decisions, administrative orders, and ordinances, together with the principles of justice and right commonly applied in their enforcement.

Law and Order party. 1. The group supporting the constitution of Rhode Island during the Dorr Rebellion, *q.v.* **2.** The proslavery party in Kansas Territory, 1854–61.

law of nations. *See* international law.

laying pipes. Colonization of voters, especially when they are introduced from other States. *See* colonization 2.

leader. 1. The actual, if not the titular, head of a party organization in a city, county, or other subdivision. Though nominally elected directly or indirectly by party voters, he is often actually chosen by a small coterie or by his immediate party superior. The distinction between boss, *q.v.*, and leader depends largely on method of choice and manner in which power is exercised. **2.** The head of the official party and of the state in the German (Fuehrer) and Italian (Duce) Fascist regimes.

league. An arrangement among two or more states for a limited purpose (usually defense or war) without organization for civil government; *also:* the covenant which binds them.

League of Nations. An organization of most of the states of the world created by the Treaty of Versailles in 1919 "to promote international co-operation and to achieve international peace and security." The League Covenant provided for an Assembly of member states meeting annually for general debate, a Council of larger states devoted to the settlement of international disputes, and a Permanent Secretariat to act as a statistical clearing agency for the member states. Various international administrative and judicial agencies were identified with the League organization. The United States never joined the League although it occasionally cooperated with some of its agencies.

League of Women Voters. An organization founded in 1918 to provide information and instruction for women in public affairs. It maintains a staff for research, publishes bulletins, and conducts study groups.

lease system. The practice of hiring out the labor of inmates of penal institutions to private contractors in return for a stipulated amount in cash, and sometimes board, lodging, and clothing for the inmates;—no longer in use by the federal government or any State.

leave to print. Permission, freely granted by both houses of Congress, to print undelivered speeches of members, or almost any other kind of material, in the *Congressional Record.*

Lea-Wagner Act. The Investment Company Act, or the Investment Advisers Act of Aug. 22, 1940, *qq.v.*

Lea-Wheeler Act. The Transportation Act of 1940, *q.v.*

Lebensraum. Areas especially in Eastern Europe which Nazi propagandists asserted Germany was justified in conquering to satisfy her demographic and economic needs.

Lecompton Constitution. A proposed constitution for a new State of Kansas drafted by a proslavery convention at Lecompton in 1857 which freesoil residents of Kansas abstained from attending. Efforts of Southern Congressmen to admit Kansas under this constitution were assailed by Stephen A. Douglas as a breach of faith.

Left. Groups ranging in opinion from liberals, radicals, socialists, and labor parties to Communists, their common characteristics being advocacy of change, their differences being not only in degree, but in methods of accomplishing change;—so-called because, from the period of the French Revolution, party members belonging to such groups have been seated to the left of the presiding officer as he faces a Continental European legislature.

legacy tax. An inheritance tax; *specifically*: a tax on personal property left by a will.

legal aid society. A private or semipublic organization that provides counsel and advice in matters of law, furnished free or at small charge, to those who cannot afford the services of an attorney.

legal fiction. A condition assumed to be true in law, regardless of its actual truth or falsity;—sometimes used by judges so that a new subject for which no rules of law have been formulated may be embraced within existing rules of law.

legal personality. The legal status accorded a corporation or other artificial person entitling it to hold and administer property, to sue in the courts, and to enjoy many of the rights and assume many of the liabilities of a natural person.

legal sovereign. The person or collective body or bodies (in the United States, both houses of Congress and the State legislatures, or national and State conventions) which is formally endowed with unlimited power to amend the fundamental law, as distinguished from the political sovereign which expresses the public will through the electorate.

legal sovereignty. The finality of legal authority ascribed by John Austin and others to a human superior not accustomed to obey any other human superior.

legal tender. Any kind of money which, under the law of a particular country, a creditor is required to accept when offered in payment of a debt expressed in terms of the monetary unit of that country or forfeit interest and compulsory process for collection. The States are forbidden by the Constitution (Art. 1, Sec. 10) to make anything but gold and silver coin a legal tender. The power of the national government to issue legal tender notes long remained in doubt. The Supreme Court held in *Hepburn* v. *Griswold*, 8 Wall. 603 (1870), that the legal tender provision of notes issued by the federal government during the Civil War could not be applied to debts previously contracted, but the Court, with a somewhat different composition, reversed its position by declaring in the Legal Tender cases, 12 Wall. 457 (1871), that the legal tender provision was constitutionally applicable to all debts, under the power of Congress to adopt necessary and proper means to conduct the war. In *Juilliard* v. *Greenman*, 110 U.S. 421 (1884), the Court conceded the power of Congress to make fiat money legal tender at any time under its currency and borrowing powers.

Legal Tender cases. *See* legal tender.

legation. 1. A diplomatic agent of the rank of minister with his staff, retinue, and servants. 2. The official residence of the envoy in the country to which he is sent. *See* diplomatic immunity.

legislation. 1. The process of lawmaking. 2. Laws made by a legislature or other lawmaking body; *specifically*: statutes passed by representative assemblies or by the electorate by means of the initiative and referendum. Most statutes are in the form of acts, but Congress and about half of the State legislatures also legislate in the form of joint resolutions. The most important statutes relate to new subjects or are periodical revisions of broad categories of law; the most numerous are brief alterations of existing statutes made necessary because of the impossibility of foreseeing all future contingencies, deficiencies discovered in enforcement, or poor draftsmanship.

legislative blackmail. An attempt by one or more legislators to extort money or favors from some person, corporation, or group by threatening to introduce or secure the enactment of unfavorable legislation.

legislative budget. 1. A budget prepared by a committee of a State legislature. 2. A budget which the Legislative Reorganization Act of 1946 required the revenue and appropriations committees of both houses of Congress to formulate jointly, after considering the budget submitted by the President. The requirement, which was designed to compel fixing of maximum expenditures early in the appropriating period, has not been carried out.

legislative council. A body composed of members of the legislature, or jointly of legislators and administrative officers, which in several States meets between legislative sessions to study the needs of the State and to formulate a comprehensive legislative program.

legislative counsel. 1. A lobbyist. 2. An attorney employed by a legislative body to give legal and constitutional advice on proposals for legislation, to draft bills and amendments at the request of members or committees, and in some States to assist in the codification of the laws. A permanent Office of Legislative Counsel has assisted Congress since 1919.

legislative court. A court established by Congress under powers other than those granted in Article III of the Constitution. In creating such courts, Congress is not bound by limitations concerning the tenure and salaries of judges, and may impose duties which are not strictly judicial. The territorial courts and the Court of Military Appeals are legislative courts. The courts of the District of Columbia, in addition to being constitutional courts, *q.v.*, are also legislative courts in the sense that Congress has conferred on them additional powers derived from Article I of the Constitution.

legislative day. The period beginning when a legislative house meets after an adjournment and continuing until the next adjournment. The Senate, by taking a recess (instead of adjourning) at the end of each calendar day, may extend its legislative day over a period of several calendar days, or even weeks, in order to postpone the consideration of routine matters which under the rules are in order at the beginning of each day. In the House of Representatives the legislative day is usually the same as the calendar day.

legislative drafting bureau. A body of technical experts employed by a legislative body to aid in securing precision in stating the legislative intention.

legislative reference library. A specialized library for use by members of a legislature which contains in easily accessible form information on subjects of legislation, codes of laws, and copies of bills introduced in other States.

Legislative Reference Service. A division of the Library of Congress which, under the terms of the Legislative Reorganization Act of 1946, provides Congress and its committees with appraisals and evaluations of pending measures, summaries of committee hearings, and other pertinent data. The service employs a number of senior specialists each of whom is an authority on some broad field of potential legislative action, and who directs a staff in research on his specialty.

Legislative Reorganization Act. An act of Congress, Aug. 2, 1946, which increased Congressional salaries; set up a retirement system for members of Congress; reduced the number of committees in both houses and provided that with minor exceptions no Senator should sit on more than two committees and no Representative on more than one committee; made detailed regulations for committee procedure and records; provided for staff members to assist each committee; strengthened the Office of Legislative Counsel and the Legislative Reference Service, *q.v.*; and provided for a legislative budget, *q.v.*, and for other means of handling many matters which had been the subjects of private bills. Other provisions of the act included the Federal Regulation of Lobbying Act, the Federal Tort Claims Act, and the General Bridge Act, *qq.v.*

legislative supremacy. 1. *In Great Britain:* the doctrine that the legislature is sovereign. 2. *In the United States:* the theory implied in most State constitutions, and upheld by courts in a majority of the States, that the legislature, though less than sovereign, enjoys an undefined residuum of power in contrast to other major branches of government whose powers are constitutionally prescribed and defined.

legislative veto. *Colloquial.* Disapproval by one or both houses of an action (as a change in tariff duties or in the organization of the executive branch) which the President has taken under discretionary authority granted by Congress, when Congress has reserved the right, during a limited period, to disapprove.

legislature. A body of persons invested with power to make, revise, and repeal statutes and other ordinary laws, to determine the amount and rate of taxes, to appropriate funds, and, as corollaries of all these powers, to conduct investigations, and to supervise in greater or less degree the conduct of officers who execute or administer the laws. It usually participates in constitutional revisions and may supervise the election of, or sometimes elect, public officers. Generally, the lower house has the sole powers of impeachment and the initiation of revenue bills; the upper house tries impeachments and consents to executive acts like appointments and treaties. State legislatures are bicameral in every State except Nebraska. Until the series of Supreme Court decisions beginning with *Baker* v. *Carr*, *q.v.*, rural interests were generally predominant in one or both houses. Each house chooses its own officers, except that in many States the lieutenant governor presides over the senate; and makes its own rules of procedure subject, in most States, to numerous constitutional restrictions, such as limited length of sessions, requirement of three readings of bills and roll call on final passage, prohibitions of local and special legislation and of riders on bills, and provisions as to the number of members who must be present or vote on the passage of legislation. Procedure is dominated by the presiding officer and committees to an even greater degree than in Congress. In a majority of the States legislative power is construed to extend to every subject not prohibited by federal and State constitutions. Actually, through the use of implied limitations, State supreme courts have severely circumscribed legislative powers.

legitimacy. The quality of a government which has come into existence through established constitutional procedures (as free elections) or which has been recognized by members of the international community.

Leisy v. Hardin. A case, 135 U.S. 100 (1890), which expressly extended the original-package doctrine of *Brown* v. *Maryland, q.v.*, from foreign to interstate commerce, the Supreme Court declaring that the States could not apply police regulations restricting the liquor traffic to interstate liquor shipments as long as the liquor remained in the packages in which it had been shipped. The Court held that the rule of *Cooley* v. *Board of Wardens, q.v.*, did not apply since interstate shipments required national regulation; and that if Congress had not issued regulations, or expressly permitted the States to make them, it was to be presumed that Congress, by its silence, intended no regulation. *See* Eighteenth and Twenty-first Amendments.

Lend-Lease Act. An act of Congress, Mar. 11, 1941, which authorized the manufacture or procurement of munitions (later amended to include foodstuffs and industrial products) for any country whose defense the President deemed vital to the defense of the United States. It authorized the President to sell, transfer title to, lend, or lease such articles under terms which he deemed satisfactory, such as payment or repayment in kind or in property, or any other direct or indirect benefit.

letter of acceptance. An elaborate statement of campaign issues formerly prepared by a presidential or vice-presidential candidate in accepting his nomination.

letter of marque and reprisal. An authorization formerly granted in time of war by a government to the owner of a private vessel to capture enemy vessels and goods on the high seas. The signatory powers to the Declaration of Paris in 1856 agreed to stop issuing such authorizations.

levee district. A political subdivision charged with the duty of maintaining flood-control works.

levy. 1. A tax or toll; *especially:* a nonrecurring tax on capital. **2.** An exaction of property or the like to satisfy a judgment or the imposition of a money penalty as a fine. **3.** *In Europe:* the calling forth of manpower for military service.

libel. 1. The plaintiff's written statement, which is the first proceeding in an admiralty case. **2.** A defamatory writing, picture, or effigy published without lawful justification which imputes to a person the commission of a criminal act, tends to injure him in his trade or profession, or exposes him to ridicule, contempt, or odium. The injured person may bring action for damages. Where malice is shown, the act of publication may constitute a crime.

liberal. A believer in liberalism, *q.v.*

liberal construction. *See* construction.

liberalism. A philosophy which reflects an attitude favorable to the freest and fullest development of the individual, and to the elimination of laws, institutions, conditions, and beliefs which restrict human development. It holds that men are sufficiently reasonable to be able to modify an older order in favor of more progressive institutions without resort to violence. Thus it stands midway between conservatism and radicalism. In the 19th century liberalism stood both for a form of government and for a governmental policy judged most favorable to individual liberty. The form came to mean constitutionalism, with stress laid upon written constitutions, bills of rights, the separation of powers, and checks and balances. The policy became identified with laissez faire. As it became evident that the chief obstacles to human development were by no means all governmental, liberalism was reinterpreted to allow for a positive program of governmental action to provide the conditions, economic and otherwise, without which mere freedom from restraint would be insufficient for individual development. Similarly, the liberal concept of government is undergoing modification to allow for governmental forms more conducive to positive action than are those of the traditional liberal state.

Liberal Party. A minor party in New York, with principal support from labor leaders in the garment trades, formed in 1944 after Communists had gained control of the American Labor Party, *q.v.* It usually endorses Democratic candidates for national and State offices but shows some independence in municipal politics.

Liberal Republican party. A group of Republicans, opposed to the reconstruction and other policies of Grant's first administration, which in 1872 nominated Horace Greeley for President. The Democrats also nominated Greeley, but the two parties together secured only 66 out of 352 presidential electors.

liberty. The privileges and immunities enjoyed by an individual in the state; *specifically:* the freedom of private action which is protected from governmental interference by the constitution and the laws. *See* democracy; *compare* right.

Liberty League. A minor abolitionist party which nominated Gerrit Smith for President in 1848.

Liberty League, American. *See* American Liberty League.

Liberty party. A minor party in the elections of 1840 and 1844 which demanded the abolition of slavery and the equality of human rights.

liberty pole. An emblem of American patriots before and during the Revolutionary War.

Library of Congress. The national library in Washington, D.C., containing more than 13 million books in various languages, more than 19 million manuscripts, including the personal papers of all but the more recent Presidents, and many other items, such as maps, prints, recordings, and musical scores, which serves Congress, the entire governmental establishment, and the public at large. Only its Legislative Reference Service, *q.v.*, serves Congress exclusively. A division of the Library, the Copyright Office, has had charge of the issuance of copyrights since 1870. Its administrative head, the Librarian of Congress, is appointed by the President and Senate.

Library Services Act. An act of Congress, 1956, which authorizes the expenditure of federal funds to aid States and local governments in providing library services in rural areas.

license. Permission by public authority to perform a certain act (as drive a car) or to engage in a business or profession, often granted only after the passing of a qualifying examination or the payment of a fee, or both; and revocable if the terms of the license or the laws or regulations concerning the conduct of the business or profession are violated. Licensing is an administrative device for expediting maintenance of legally stipulated professional or vocational standards or for correction of violations, without the necessity of bringing prosecutions in the courts. The licensee may, however, appeal to the courts to overturn a ruling of the enforcement officers.

lieutenant governor. An officer in most States who presides over the State senate, serves on numerous ex officio and other boards, succeeds to the governorship when it becomes vacant, and in a few States may perform the governor's duties when the governor is temporarily absent from the State.

Lily-whites. A faction of the Republican party in the South which stood for the exclusion of Negro voters from public office and from membership in party conventions and committees. They were opposed by the Black and Tans, *q.v.*

limitation. *See* constitutional limitations; statute of limitations.

limitation of armaments. Restriction, by international agreement, of the quantity and kind of each nation's war equipment, as under the Five-Power Treaty, *q.v.*, 1922, or reduction in the power of weapons, as under the Nuclear Test-ban Treaty, Oct. 10, 1963.

limited vote. A crude system of minority representation under which a voter may vote only for a certain number of candidates which is less than the total number of seats to be filled, and which has been used occasionally for the election of members of municipal councils.

limited war. A war which, since the invention of atomic weapons, is waged with conventional (non-nuclear) weapons, or restricted in the objectives to be attained, the number of belligerents engaged, the area or theater fought over, or the targets to be attacked.

Lindbergh Law. An act of Congress, May 18, 1934, which, under penalties of death or imprisonment, forbids the transportation in interstate or foreign commerce of any person who has been kidnapped and held for ransom. Failure to release a person within seven days after he has been kidnapped creates the presumption that he has been transported in interstate or foreign commerce.

line. *In public administration:* That portion of the civil service, from highest officials to office employees and field force, which has the responsibility for carrying out the basic functions for which an administrative department is established;—distinguished from staff (planning) and housekeeping (auxiliary) functions.

line of succession. The succession of Secretaries of State to the Presidency after two terms, which was customary in the first quarter of the 19th century.

liquor legislation. Laws regulating the liquor traffic. After the repeal of the Eighteenth Amendment, *q.v.*, such regulation again became primarily a matter of State concern, except that Congress regulates interstate traffic in liquor, including advertising. A few States still impose limitations on the traffic or permit local option, *q.v.*, by counties or towns. Others have established a public monopoly and sell liquor through State-operated dispensaries. Still others license private dispensaries.

list system. A method of proportional representation developed in Europe under which a voter casts a vote for a list of candidates usually without the privilege of marking a preference among individuals on the list. Any seats to which the list is entitled by the balloting are given to persons in the order in which their names appear on the list.

literacy test. A test to prove ability to read and write which is required by law in twenty States (six of them Southern) as a qualification for the suffrage. Because of notorious partiality in enforcement, the Voting Rights Act, *q.v.*, of 1965 suspended such tests in States and counties where less than half the adult population were registered or had voted in the previous election.

Little Assembly. A standing committee of the General Assembly of the United Nations, consisting at the time of its creation of one representative of each U.N. member, established by the General Assembly on Nov. 15, 1947, over the protest of Soviet Russia and certain of its satellite states. It was expected to consider international situations and disputes which might arise between sessions of the parent body but has remained largely inactive.

Little Giant. A nickname of Stephen A. Douglas.

Little Group of Willful Men. A bipartisan group of eleven Senators who, by conducting a five-day filibuster ending Mar. 4, 1917, prevented the passage of a bill for arming American merchant ships;—the phrase was applied by President Wilson.

Little Mac. A nickname of General George B. McClellan.

Little Magician. A nickname of Martin Van Buren.

Little Rock riots. Disorders attending efforts to desegregate the Little Rock, Ark., schools under a court order which, in September 1957, led President Eisenhower to send troops to the city to compel a reluctant governor and citizenry to permit Negro children to attend public schools previously reserved for whites.

littoral state. A state which has a seacoast.

live pair. An agreement between two members of a legislative house to have their names recorded on opposite sides of a question when one is absent and the other present but abstaining from voting.

living wage. A theoretical money income without exact definition which is believed adequate to maintain standards of health and decency prevalent among a certain group or within a given area.

Lloyd-La Follette Act. An act of Congress, Aug. 24, 1912, which provided that employees of the federal government might form unions for the purpose of securing improvements in conditions of work, hours of labor, pay, and leave of absence without fear of dismissal or other disciplinary action, provided that such unions did not employ the weapon of a strike against the government.

Loan Association v. Topeka. A case, 20 Wall. 655 (1875), in which the Supreme Court invalidated a local Kansas tax, the proceeds of which were to assist a private company to locate in the State, on the ground that a tax levied for such a purpose was not within the discretion of any free government. Courts are currently more liberal in applying the constitutional limitations of the 14th Amendment to taxes of this type.

lobby. 1. The main corridor of a capitol frequented by persons interested in the passage or defeat of proposed legislation. **2.** Agents of various interests who seek to influence or bring pressure to bear (as by persuasion or indirect influence) on both executive and legislative branches. Lobbying by either principals or agents is protected by the right of petition for redress of grievances, but the right is often abused. Congress and several State legislatures have tried to curb the sinister aspects of lobbying by public investigations and by laws requiring lobbyists to register and state the specific legislative measures in which they are interested, the names of their employers, the amount of compensation they receive, and the purposes for which money has been spent. Congress requires the filing of quarterly reports. See Federal Regulation of Lobbying Act.

local. A branch of the Socialist party in a geographical area or other constituency; *also:* the basic administrative unit of a labor union.

local government. The regulation and administration of matters, chiefly of local concern, which under general laws or the grant of charters by the State are confided to counties, towns, townships, special districts, or municipalities. Each subdivision is nearly always either a public corporation or a quasi corporation, *q.v.*, which may hold property, levy taxes, sue, and be sued; and it is responsible for torts arising from its acts or from neglect of its duties. Its powers are strictly interpreted. For rural local government the county is the principal division in the South, and the town, in New England. Elsewhere functions are more evenly divided between the county and its minor subdivisions. There is a growing tendency toward State centralization and supervision of matters of State-wide interest formerly left almost exclusively under local control.

local legislation. Statutes of State legislatures applying only to counties, cities, or other places specifically named or clearly described, which impose special duties, grant special authority, create public corporations, or alter the provisions of charters. To mitigate the evil of legislative interference in purely local concerns, local legislation is forbidden by State constitutions, either absolutely or whenever general legislation can be made to apply, in nearly all the States for cities; and in a few

States for counties. One result of such constitutional restrictions has been classification of cities and home rule, *qq.v.*

local option. The determination by popular vote in a county, city, or township as to whether or not saloons or bars may be licensed or dispensaries opened for the sale of liquor within its limits.

***Lochner* v. *New York*.** A case, 198 U.S. 45 (1905), in which the Supreme Court invalidated a New York statute prescribing a maximum working day in bakeries because, in the Court's opinion, the statute interfered unreasonably and arbitrarily with the freedom of contract protected by the due-process clause of the 14th Amendment. This decision was overruled in *Bunting* v. *Oregon, q.v.*

lockout. A weapon of employers in labor disputes which consists of closing shops or mines to prevent unionization, forestall a strike, or hinder union activities.

Locofocos. 1. A faction of the Democratic party in New York opposed to monopolies and the corrupt methods used in chartering State banks. **2.** A nickname of the Equal Rights party organized by this group, later applied to all Democrats. Locofoco was a trade name for the newly introduced friction, or "self-lighting," matches which were used by members of this faction in relighting candles after they had seized control of a Democratic party convention in New York City, Oct. 29, 1835, by plunging the hall into darkness.

Lodge Corollary. A resolution introduced in the Senate by Henry Cabot Lodge in 1911 that the United States would view with grave concern the acquisition by a foreign corporation of any harbor on the American Continent so situated as to threaten the communications or safety of the United States. A Japanese company was then reported to be negotiating for a tract of land in Baja California, in Mexico.

Lodge-Gossett Resolution. A proposed constitutional amendment, 1948, which would have eliminated presidential electors, divided each State's electoral vote among presidential candidates in proportion to the popular vote received by each, and declared elected the candidate who received a plurality, provided he received at least 40 per cent of the electoral vote.

Lodge Reservations. Statements interpreting and limiting the application of fourteen provisions of the League of Nations Covenant which were presented to the Senate by Henry Cabot Lodge, chairman of its Foreign Relations Committee, Nov. 6, 1919, as conditions for the Senate's acceptance of the Treaty of Versailles, *q.v.*, of which the Covenant was a part.

***Loewe* v. *Lawlor*.** *See* Danbury Hatters' case.

Log Cabin Campaign. The presidential election of 1840 in which a log cabin was one of the emblems of the Whig party.

logrolling. Mutual aid by members of a legislative body in passing laws of personal or local interest, especially laws authorizing projects or appropriating funds chiefly beneficial to the members' constituencies.

London Economic Conference. A conference in London, June-July, 1933, to find means to ameliorate the prevailing world economic crisis by stabilizing the principal national currencies. Its failure is sometimes ascribed to President F. D. Roosevelt's statement, announced after the conference had begun its sessions, that internal economic reorganization of the participating states should precede stabilization.

London Naval Conference. A conference of representatives of the United States, Great Britain, Japan, France, and Italy, held in London in 1930, which resulted in a treaty limiting the cruiser-building programs of these states and reducing slightly the battleship, destroyer, and submarine tonnages of their respective fleets.

long-and-short haul. Pertaining to a practice, now illegal, under which railroad companies charged lower rates between points at which there was competition than from intermediate points, under the policy of charging all that the traffic would bear.

Long Convention. The constitutional convention elected in Missouri in 1861 which deposed secessionist State officials, appointed others in their places, and acted as a legislature until 1863.

long session. Before the adoption of the 20th Amendment, the first session of Congress which began in December of odd-numbered years.

loose construction. *See* construction.

lottery. A form of gambling formerly used by several States, cities, and the District of Columbia to finance internal improvements, and now a source of revenue for the States of New Hampshire and New York and some foreign countries. The sending of lottery tickets through the mails and by other instrumentalities of interstate commerce is prohibited by federal law.

lottery order. *See* fraud order.

Louisiana ex rel. Francis v. Resweber. A case, 329 U.S. 459 (1947), in which a convicted murderer who had escaped death due to mechanical failure of the electric chair sought to prevent a second attempt at execution on the grounds of double jeopardy and cruel and unusual punishment. The Court held, 5–4, that Louisiana was not violating these standards in proceeding a second time to carry out sentence of death by electrocution.

Louisiana Purchase. A tract of 885,000 square miles, mostly west of the Mississippi River and extending thence to the Spanish possessions or to the Continental Divide, which was purchased from France for $15 million by a treaty ratified Oct. 21, 1803. Under the claim that the Purchase embraced West Florida, the United States asserted its title to the strip west of the

Louisiana Purchase

Pearl River in 1810 and to the area west of the Perdido River (the present western boundary of Florida) in 1813. The western boundary was fixed at the Sabine River and thence by meridians of longitude and river boundaries irregularly northwestward to the Rocky Mountains by treaty with Spain, Feb. 22, 1819. The northern boundary with Great Britain was fixed at the 49th parallel in 1818. The area had been explored and partly settled by the French and had been ceded to Spain in 1763 at the end of the French and Indian War. Napoleon induced Spain to retrocede it to France. A slave insurrection in Haiti, approaching war in Europe, and need for money are supposed to have led Napoleon to abandon plans for a new French colonial empire and sell the area to the United States.

lower chamber. Usually the more popular house of a bicameral legislature.

loyalist. One of a numerous group who espoused the cause of the King of England and opposed the American Revolution. Because of confiscations of their property and the passage of harsh laws against them by the American States, many loyalists sought refuge in Great Britain, Canada, or the British West Indies. *Called also* Tory.

Loyal League. An organization of Union men formed in the North during the Civil War to combat the activities of Peace Democrats, *q.v.*, and extended to the South in the Reconstruction period.

Loyal Legion. A hereditary organization formed in 1865, membership in which was open to officers of the Union Army and Navy and their eldest sons.

loyalty oath. Any of various oaths to support the Constitution and the laws, coupled with abjuration of un-American ideologies, especially Communism, required of many government employees and beneficiaries of government grants in universities and similar institutions.

Loyalty Review Board. A special unit, created by order of President Truman, which from 1947 to 1953 heard appeals from agency review boards and adjudicated cases involving federal civil servants whose loyalty was questioned.

lulu. *Slang.* A blanket allowance "in lieu of" itemized expenses which is a perquisite of committee chairmen and other legislative officers in New York. It can be spent at discretion and is not subject to accounting. The term is attributed to Alfred E. Smith.

lump-sum appropriation. An appropriation which does not stipulate in detail how funds are to be spent but grants them in lump sum to heads of departments and other major administrative units, permitting them to determine how they shall be allocated for various objects or to subordinate spending agencies. *Compare* itemized appropriations.

lunatic fringe. Adherents of reform movements who refuse to recognize the difficulties of practical administration and insist upon the immediate fulfillment of an extreme program. The term is attributed to Theodore Roosevelt.

"Lusitania." A British passenger liner sunk by the German submarine U-20 off the southern coast of Ireland, May 7, 1915, entailing the deaths of 1,198 persons, including 128 American citizens. The German government refused to disavow the act, and public opinion demanded war; but after President Wilson dispatched three notes, Germany made promises of future good conduct which were accepted.

Luther v. Borden. A case, 7 How. 1 (1848), in which the Supreme Court held that the question whether or not a State of the Union possesses a republican form of government as defined in Art. IV, Sec. 4 of the Constitution, and the related question whether insurrection within a particular State warrants federal intervention as provided in the same Article, are political and not justiciable, and, as such, are to be resolved as they arise by appropriate actions of Congress and the President.

L.W.V. League of Women Voters.

lynch law. The punishment of persons by mob violence without waiting for the orderly processes of law;—the term may have been derived from Charles Lynch, a Virginia justice of the peace, who meted out summary punishment to loyalists during the Revolution; or from John Lynch, a North Carolina planter, who took the law into his own hands against criminals who infested the Dismal Swamp.

M.A. Maritime Administration.

McCardle, Ex parte. A case, 7 Wall. 506 (1869), in which the Supreme Court upheld an act passed by a post-Civil War Congress, which resulted in the removal from the Court's calendar of an appeal (*Ex parte McCardle*), 6 Wall. 318 (1868), from an editor who had allegedly violated one of the early Reconstruction Acts. The Court sustained the act on the ground that, though appellate jurisdiction is conferred on the Supreme Court by the Constitution, Congress may make such exceptions to that jurisdiction as it sees fit.

McCarran Act. *See* Internal Security Act.

McCarran-Walter Act. The Immigration and Naturalization Act of 1952, which codified existing laws on the two subjects, continued the quota system, and introduced new provisions to prevent the admission of subversives and, under certain circumstances, to permit the expulsion of resident aliens and the denaturalization of American citizens.

McCarthyism. A habit of branding all except extreme right-wing ideas as Communistic, of indiscriminately leveling false charges of treason, of making new charges instead of furnishing facts, and of attacking the motives of those who questioned the authenticity of statements;—the term arose from the specious charges of Senator Joseph R. McCarthy of Wisconsin, who undermined public confidence in many public officials and private persons until finally censured by the Senate, Dec. 2, 1954.

McCollum v. Board of Education. One of the so-called released-time cases, 333 U.S. 203 (1948), in which the Supreme Court declared invalid, on principles allegedly in consonance with both minority and majority views in *Everson* v. *Board of Education*, *q.v.*, the arrangement by which Illinois public schools, with parental consent, allowed instruction by "outside" religious teachers on school property during school hours. The Court held this to be an infringement of the "establishment clause" of the First Amendment (applicable to States under the Fourteenth Amendment), because tax-supported schools were used to disseminate religious doctrines and because the compulsory public-education law was used to aid sectarian causes. *Compare Zorach v. Clauson.*

McCray v. United States. *See* oleomargarine tax.

McCulloch v. Maryland. A case in the Supreme Court, 4 Wheat. 316 (1819), which arose from the refusal of the cashier of the Baltimore branch of the Bank of the United States to pay a tax levied by Maryland on the issuance of bank notes. In the opinion which contains the classic exposition of the doctrine of implied powers, Chief Justice Marshall declared that Congress had power to create a bank as a "necessary and proper" means to carry out its financial and other powers; and that Maryland could not tax the operations of the Bank because such a power, in the hands of a State, threatens the supremacy of the national government in matters committed to its jurisdiction. *See* implied powers.

mace. The symbol of the authority of certain legislative chambers. In the House of Representatives it is displayed during all sessions, except in committee of the whole, after a Speaker is elected.

McFadden Act. An act of Congress, Feb. 25, 1927, which permitted the consolidation of State banks with national banks and allowed the latter to engage in investment banking and prohibited them from extending their branches beyond the city in which their main office was located.

McGrain v. Daugherty. *See* investigative power.

machine. A cohesive group controlled by a boss or a small coterie of leaders which subjects party organization and public officials to its will. At its worst it ruthlessly exploits governmental activities of every sort for the private gain of its members.

McKinley Tariff Act. A tariff act, Oct. 1, 1890, which provided protection for numerous "infant" industries, raised rates generally to new high levels, offered a bounty for the production of sugar within the United States, and empowered the President to enter into limited reciprocal trade agreements in order to remove barriers imposed by other countries on the admission of American products.

McLaurin v. Oklahoma State Regents. The case, 339 U.S. 637 (1950), of a Negro who had been admitted as a graduate student to the University of Oklahoma, but who had been segregated from white students as required by State law, by seating assignments in classrooms, library, and cafeteria. The Supreme Court held that these segregations denied him the 14th Amendment's guarantee of equal protection because they impaired "his ability to study, to engage in discussions and exchange views with other students, and, in general, to learn his profession."

McLeod case. An international incident resulting from the arrest of Alexander McLeod, a Canadian deputy sheriff, in New York in 1840 on charges of murder and arson at the time of the destruction of the ship "Caroline," *q.v.* The State authorities refused to release him on demand of the British government supported by United States authorities. He was tried and acquitted. To meet such contingencies in the future, Congress empowered federal courts to issue writs of habeas corpus for aliens held by State courts.

McMahon Act. The Atomic Energy Act of August. 1, 1946.

McNary-Haugen Bill. A bill twice vetoed by President Coolidge, 1927, which proposed to raise farm prices by dumping surplus staples abroad and compensating farmers for losses thus sustained by payments from the proceeds of an equalization fee, *q.v.*

Madison's *Journal.* Extensive notes kept by James Madison of debates and resolutions of the Convention of 1787, first published in 1840 after his death. They remain almost the only source of information concerning the Convention's deliberations which molded the federal Constitution.

Mafia incident. The lynching of eleven Italians, allegedly members of a secret criminal society, by a mob in New Orleans, Mar. 15, 1891, for which Italy demanded an indemnity and the punishment of those responsible; and recalled its minister when informed that only the State authorities had jurisdiction to punish the lynchers. Congress voted an indemnity of $25,000 for the deaths of three victims who were Italian citizens.

magistrate. 1. A public official. **2.** A local official exercising jurisdiction of a summary judicial nature over offenses against municipal ordinances or minor criminal cases.

Magna Charta. The Great Charter wrung by the barons from King John at Runnymede, June 15, 1215, confirming privileges and rights which had been violated by royal order. Though a class document, with guarantees to safeguard only the barons' liberties, phrases in the Charter as "judgment of his peers" and "law of the land" are permanently embodied in legal literature relating to individual liberty both in England and in America.

Magnetic Statesman. A nickname of James G. Blaine.

"Maine." An American battleship sunk in the harbor of Havana, Cuba, Feb. 15, 1898, following an explosion of undetermined cause. The incident hastened the outbreak of war with Spain.

Maine-law prohibition. Prohibition of the manufacture and sale of intoxicating liquors by State constitutional amendment and stringent laws, in effect in Maine, 1851–1934.

maintenance of membership. A provision of some labor contracts, now usually enforced by law, that persons who join a union which represents a majority of workers may be required to remain members during the period of an existing labor contract.

majority. More than one-half. Unless an absolute majority, *q.v.*, is required for a decision, a majority consists of more than one-half of those present and voting.

majority leader. A member designated by the caucus of the majority party to take charge of party strategy on the floor of a legislative house. The Senate majority leader controls the allocation of time and the priority of measures. The House majority leader is the principal assistant to the

Speaker. Both leaders make tactical motions and lead party debate on the floor.

majority rule. A principle of politics that decisions supported by the greater number ought to prevail;—often tempered by advocacy of checks and balances, written guarantees of rights, and other devices to prevent the tyranny of the majority over the minority.

malfeasance. The performance of an illegal act, especially on the part of a public official.

Mallory v. United States. A case, 354 U.S. 449 (1957), in which the Supreme Court held that a confession, obtained from a defendant while being detained by arresting officers for an unnecessarily long time (about 18 hours) before being brought before a committing magistrate, was invalid as evidence in a subsequent trial. *Compare Escobedo* v. *Illinois; Miranda* v. *Arizona.*

Malloy v. Hogan. A case, 378 U.S. 11 (1964), in which the Supreme Court held that the Fifth Amendment's guarantee against compulsory self-incrimination is protected by the Fourteenth Amendment against impairment by the States, and if properly invoked in a State proceeding, is governed by federal standards. This decision overruled *Twining* v. *New Jersey,* and *Adamson* v. *California, qq.v.*

malpractice. Negligent or wrongful practice of a profession resulting in injury to a client or patient.

manageable voter. A voter who is willing to vote as he is instructed in return for money or other consideration.

manager. 1. One who conducts the primary or election campaign of a candidate for elective office. **2.** The administrative head of a city government under the council-manager plan; a city manager. **3.** A member of one legislative house appointed to represent it in a conference, *q.v.,* for the adjustment of differences with the other house.

mandamus. A writ issued by a superior court having jurisdiction and directed to a public officer, corporation, individual, or lower court to compel the performance of an act where there is a clear legal duty to act in a certain way. It may be used to compel a public officer to perform ministerial, but not discretionary, acts.

mandatary. A state which administered a mandate, *q.v.,* under the League of Nations.

mandate. 1. Authority granted to Great Britain, some British Dominions, France, or Japan, after World War I, to establish orderly governments in certain former German or Turkish possessions under the supervision of the League of Nations. Many of these mandates later became trust territories under the United Nations, or were set up as independent states. *See* Trusteeship Council. **2.** An instruction issued by a constituency to its representative in a legislative body.

mandated expenditure. An expenditure which a State requires a municipal government to make, often from locally collected funds, and often without reimbursement from State funds.

mandatory law. A law which imposes a duty upon some public official, agency, or local government body and requires that it be executed without exercise of discretion and in accordance with the express terms of the law.

mandatory referendum. A popular referendum required in nearly every State for the ratification of a constitutional amendment and generally required in cities and other local areas for bond issues, charter amendments, and annexations of territory.

manhood suffrage. Full, free, and equal suffrage granted to all adult male citizens not under a legal disability on account of lunacy, idiocy, or commission of a crime.

manifest destiny. A catch phrase much used by expansionists, 1845–60, to promote the idea that the territory of the United States must eventually include the whole continent of North America.

manifesto. 1. A formal statement of the program and objectives of a political party or similar group. 2. A public proclamation.

Manila Summit Conference. A meeting at Manila, Oct. 24–25, 1966, of heads of state or of government of New Zealand, Australia, United States, Philippines, Thailand, South Korea and South Vietnam, allied in the Vietnam War, *q.v.*, which, while reiterating the policy of resisting North Vietnamese aggression, offered to evacuate all foreign forces in South Vietnam within six months after North Vietnam withdrew its forces and ceased infiltration, and which expressed hopes for peace, reconciliation, and economic and social progress among Asian nations.

Mann Act. *See* White Slave acts.

Mann-Elkins Act. An act of Congress, June 18, 1910, which extended the jurisdiction of the Interstate Commerce Commission to telegraph and telephone lines; authorized it to make reasonable classifications of freight and to fix maximum rates on its own motion as well as after hearings of complaints; and provided that changes in rates might be made only with the approval of the commission.

Mapp v. *Ohio.* A case, 367 U.S. 643 (1961), in which the Supreme Court held that evidence secured without an authenticated search warrant, which would be excluded in a federal prosecution, must also be excluded in a State prosecution (in this instance for possession of pornographic material) since the procedural standards under the "unreasonable search and seizure" clause of the Fourth Amendment are included in the Fourteenth Amendment's guarantee of due process.

Marbury v. *Madison.* The case, 1 Cr. 137 (1803), in which the Supreme Court first elaborated the principle of judicial review. William Marbury applied directly to the Supreme Court, as provided by the Judiciary Act of 1789, for a writ of mandamus to compel Secretary of State James Madison to deliver a commission as justice of the peace for the District of Columbia which had been signed and sealed by the previous Secretary of State. The Court through Chief Justice Marshall declared that under Art. III, Sec. 2 of the Constitution it could issue a writ of mandamus only when exercising appellate jurisdiction; hence the provision of the Judiciary Act authorizing the writ of mandamus in original jurisdiction, on which Marbury had relied, was void. The Constitution, said the Court, was the fundamental law; and in cases of conflict between it and a statute, "it is emphatically the province and duty of the judicial department to say what the law is."

March on Washington. The peaceful demonstration by some 200,000 persons, chiefly Negroes, before the Washington Monument on August 28, 1963, in support of immediate recognition of Negro demands for civil equality with whites. *Compare* Coxey's Army; Bonus Army.

marginal sea. Any waters extending outward from the shore at low water mark to a distance of three miles and including all inlets whose mouths are six miles wide or less, which are under the exclusive jurisdiction of the littoral state, subject only to the right of innocent passage, *q.v.*, by foreign vessels. By prescription, certain bays (as Chesapeake Bay) whose entrances are more than six miles wide, are considered as part of the marginal sea. By international agreement jurisdiction for certain purposes (as drilling for oil) may be extended to a greater distance than three miles.

Marianas Islands. *See* Trust Territory of the Pacific Islands.

Marine Corps. A corps of trained soldiers first created by the Continental Congress, June 25, 1776, and permanently established by act of Congress, July 11, 1798, as a separate unit for amphibious service under the Department of the Navy.

Marine Hospital Service. The oldest health service of the federal government, established in 1798 to provide hospitals for merchant seamen;— its establishment marks the origin of the Public Health Service of which it is now a part.

Maritime Administration. A unit of the Department of Commerce, successor to the U.S. Maritime Commission, which is charged with various responsibilities relating to the design and construction of merchant ships, the disposal of publicly owned ships to private operators, and the determination of ocean routes and services, and of construction and operational subsidies to private shipping companies. *Compare* Federal Maritime Commission.

maritime belt. *See* territorial waters.

maritime boundary. *See* territorial waters.

maritime jurisdiction. The power to try cases arising under national regulations or international usages relating to ships, seamen, or merchants engaged in maritime trade which, in the United States, is vested in the federal courts.

maritime law. The laws governing men and ships engaged in peaceful commerce on the high seas. Its content, derived from usages of all maritime nations beginning with Italian city states of the Middle Ages, has been reinforced and made more certain by national statutes and decisions of national courts. Congress has extended it to navigable lakes and inland rivers.

marking up. The procedure in a standing committee of going through a bill section by section and making amendments. If extensively amended, the text of the bill is abandoned and a clean bill, *q.v.*, is prepared by the committee.

marque. *See* letter of marque and reprisal.

marshal. 1. An appointive officer in each judicial district of the United

States who executes the processes of the court and has law-enforcing authority similar to that of a sheriff. **2.** An officer sometimes attached to a magistrate's court.

Marshall Islands. *See* Trust Territory of the Pacific Islands.

Marshall Plan. A plan for American assistance in promoting European rehabilitation and reconstruction after World War II, originated by Secretary of State George C. Marshall in an address at Harvard University, June 5, 1947. The assistance suggested was conditioned by the requirement that European states act together in estimating their needs and agree to plan their recovery on a cooperative basis. Sixteen European states and the Anglo-American occupied zone of Germany subsequently drew up an inventory of requirements and resources and requested of the United States loans and gifts in excess of $21 billion for the period 1948–52. By December 1951 when the plan, known as the European Recovery Program, was officially terminated, these states had received more than $12 billion allocated through the Economic Cooperation Administration. In diminished volume, aid was continued under the Mutual Security Act, *q.v.*

martial law. 1. Government by military commanders over the civilian population in designated areas during which military decrees may, as far as necessary, supersede ordinary laws, and military tribunals may supersede the civil courts. Martial law may be proclaimed during war or threatened invasion in the vicinity of actual hostilities where the local government ceases to function. **2.** A qualified form of military control ordered by a State governor during a domestic disturbance or natural disaster.

Martin v. Hunter's Lessee. A case, 1 Wheat. 304 (1816), in which the Supreme Court declared that it had power to exercise appellate jurisdiction over State courts whenever cases pending or decided in such courts came within the scope of the judicial power of the United States.

Martling Men. A faction of the Democratic party in New York about 1804, led by Aaron Burr and opposed to Jefferson and George Clinton; —from its meeting place, Martling's Long Room.

Marxism. The politico-economic theories of Karl Marx (1818–83), notably dialectic materialism, economic determinism in the interpretation of history, the inevitability of the class struggle, the decay of capitalism and the elimination of the middle class, the triumph of the proletariat, and the withering away of the state—processes that were to be hastened by revolution. Though developed from Marx's observations of advanced capitalist countries, his theories have been most intensively applied in industrially backward countries like Russia and China.

Mason and Dixon's line. 1. The boundary between Pennsylvania and Maryland which was surveyed, except for the western 36 miles, by Charles Mason and Jeremiah Dixon, 1763–67. **2.** The boundary between free and slave States.

Masons. *See* Antimasonic party.

Massachusetts ballot. The office-block type of Australian ballot in which, under each office, the names of candidates, with party designations, are printed in alphabetical order.

***Massachusetts* v. *Mellon* and *Frothingham* v. *Mellon*.** Two suits, 262 U.S. 447 (1923), one brought by a State and the other by an individual taxpayer, to enjoin the Secretary of the Treasury from disbursing funds under a grant-in-aid to the States for maternal welfare. By means of the grant-in-aid, which required acceptance of its terms by the beneficiary States, the complainant State alleged that Congress was usurping powers reserved to the States under the 10th Amendment. In rejecting jurisdiction of this suit, the Supreme Court declared that the issue raised was political and not justiciable and that, in any case, no State may institute judicial proceedings to protect citizens of the United States against the operation of federal statutes. In dismissing the individual's suit, also for want of jurisdiction, the Court held that the individual's interest as a taxpayer in the funds of the United States was so infinitesimal, and the effect of the projected grant-in-aid upon future taxation was so remote, that the individual had no basis for an appeal for injunctive relief in a court administering equity.

massive retaliation. A plan popularized by Secretary of State John Foster Dulles, to meet an act of invasion or aggression by counterattacking at places and with means of America's own choosing (as with both nuclear and conventional weapons);—an alternative to repulsing local attacks, one by one, wherever an aggressor might choose to strike.

masterly inactivity. A favorite phrase of John C. Calhoun when advising against hasty or ill-considered action.

matching fund. The amount, 50 per cent or less, which a State or local government is usually required to appropriate for a project in order to receive a federal grant-in-aid.

Maximilian. An Austrian archduke, French puppet Emperor of Mexico during the American Civil War, who was executed by a Mexican revolutionary government, June 19, 1867, after French troops had been withdrawn at the insistence of the United States.

Mayflower Compact. A written agreement drawn up by the Pilgrim Fathers in the cabin of the "Mayflower," Nov. 21, 1620, which served as the basis of civil government in the Plymouth Colony until 1691.

mayor. The chief executive of a municipal corporation. In the Colonial and early Federal periods the mayor was generally appointed by the governor or elected by the council, and his powers were hardly more than those of an alderman. By 1850 he had become popularly elective, and in some places had a limited veto over ordinances, the power of appointment and removal of officers with the consent of the council, and supervision over administrative officers. Toward the end of the 19th century the strong-mayor plan, *q.v.*, was introduced in which the mayor had real control over municipal administration. Under the commission and council-manager plans, *qq.v.*, there is sometimes a mayor with duties mainly of a ceremonial nature. In many small municipalities the mayor has judicial powers in cases arising under municipal ordinances.

Mecklenberg County Resolutions. Resolutions adopted at Charlotte, Mecklenberg County, N.C., May 31, 1775, which declared that commissions issued by the Crown were null and void and "the constitution of each particular colony wholly suspended." A later spurious draft was called the "Mecklenberg Declaration of Independence."

Medal of Honor. The highest military decoration of the United States, awarded and presented by the President in the name of Congress to a member of the armed forces for conspicuous gallantry and intrepidity at the risk of his life above and beyond the call of duty. It was formerly called the Congressional Medal of Honor when it was voted in each individual case by Congress. The Navy Medal was authorized Dec. 21, 1861, the Army Medal, July 12, 1862, and the Air Force Medal, May 31, 1966.

Medal of Honor (left to right) Navy and Marine Corps, Air Force, and Army

mediation. Interposition by a neutral party between states or private parties in conflict to promote a settlement, reconsideration, or compromise.

mediation board. A panel established to mediate industrial disputes either as a voluntary service to labor and management, or as a compulsory step in the settlement of railroad labor disputes.

Medicaid. A program of assistance to persons less than 65 years old who are financially unable to pay for adequate hospital care and physician's fees, which was established under the provisions of the federal Medicare law and is administered by the States.

medical examiner. A qualified physician appointed to examine or perform autopsies on the bodies of persons who are supposed to have met violent deaths and to investigate the causes and circumstances of death. In some States he has supplanted the coroner.

Medicare. Various proposals for cooperative or public programs to provide medical care for persons who can not afford to pay their own medical and hospital bills. On July 30, 1965, Congress expanded the Social Security program so as to provide for extended periods of hospitalization, care of inmates of nursing homes, outpatient diagnostic service, and home nursing for persons more than sixty-five years old, to be financed by progressive increases in Social Security taxes; and also provided for voluntary supplemental coverage to pay for doctor's bills, other health services, and supplies for persons in the same age group, to be financed partly from payments of monthly insurance premiums by the persons covered and partly from federal funds.

Megalopolis. A name given by writers on population problems to the almost completely urbanized strip of territory extending from Portsmouth, N.H., southwestward to Washington, D.C., including the whole of Long Island; and to similar areas in the United States and other countries.

melting pot. A phrase descriptive of the assimilation of races and cultures to a common pattern in America;—derived from a play of that name by Israel Zangwill.

member bank. Any banking institution which has purchased stock in, and become affiliated with, one of the 12 federal reserve banks. National banks are required to become members; State banks may do so.

member state. One of the sovereign or quasi-sovereign states of a federation, confederation, or international union or organization.

memorandum opinion. A brief statement by a court or a judge of the disposition of a case, sometimes accompanied by citation of precedents. *Compare per curiam* opinion.

mending fences. Adjustments or improvements in a personal political or party organization in preparation for a forthcoming election campaign.

Mental Health Act. An act of Congress, July 3, 1946, which set up an advisory mental health council and provided for grants-in-aid to universities and hospitals for research, and to States and their subdivisions for the establishment and maintenance of mental health services.

mercantilism. Various policies and practices of European states between the 16th and 18th centuries which were designed to unify and strengthen a state in competition with other states through public control over economic activities, thus securing a favorable balance of trade, exporting commodities and importing specie and gems, building a merchant fleet, extending colonies, and planning the domestic economy to conserve and increase wealth.

mercenary. A soldier who serves for hire in the armed forces of a country other than his own.

merchant marine. The ships and personnel of a state's commercial fleet whether publicly or privately owned.

Merchants-of-Death inquiry. An investigation conducted by a special committee, 1934–37, in which the chairman, Senator Gerald P. Nye, amassed one-sided data designed to show that World War I had been caused by bankers and munition makers for their own profit. The report greatly influenced public opinion in favor of isolation and against preparedness.

merit system. *See* civil service.

Merryman, Ex parte. A case, 17 Fed. Cases 9487 (1861), chiefly noteworthy for the opinion of Chief Justice Taney, when sitting as a circuit judge, that the privilege of the writ of habeas corpus may be suspended by Congress but not by the President; and for President Lincoln's refusal to honor Taney's order for the release of a civilian who, as an alleged Southern sympathizer, had been arrested and was confined in a military prison during the Civil War.

message. A formal communication from the chief executive delivered to a legislative body either in person or in writing.

mess in Washington. A phrase used by Republicans during the 1952 presidential election campaign to draw attention to scandals in the Internal Revenue Bureau, the Reconstruction Finance Corporation, and in the disposition of surplus government property, and to morally improper behavior of officials in accepting gifts from lobbyists which marred the Truman administration.

Me Too. A nickname of Senator Thomas C. Platt of New York because he resigned as U.S. Senator, along with Senator Roscoe Conkling in 1881, in a controversy with President Garfield over federal appointments in New York.

metropolitan area. A large city and the numerous urban communities which surround it and which, though administratively distinct, are physically and economically identified with it. *Compare* standard metropolitan statistical area.

metropolitan district. A special district embracing parts or the whole of several contiguous cities or other areas, created by a State to provide unified administration of one or more functions, as park development, sewage disposal, water supply, and metropolitan transit.

Mexican cession. Land acquired by the United States from Mexico under the terms of the Treaty of Guadalupe Hidalgo, ratified May 30, 1848, which closed the Mexican War. After allowing for the rather extravagant claims of Texas, the cession amounted to 523,802 sq. mi., including the entire area of California, Nevada, and Utah, nearly all of Arizona, and parts of New Mexico, Colorado, and Wyoming.

Mexican Cession of 1848

Mexican War. A war which began Apr. 24, 1846, when Mexican forces attacked a United States army detachment in the area between the Nueces and Rio Grande rivers claimed by both the United States and Mexico; and which ended, after United States troops had entered Mexico City, with the Treaty of Guadalupe Hidalgo, *q.v.*

Meyer v. Nebraska. A case, 262 U.S. 390 (1923), in which the Supreme Court invalidated a Nebraska statute prohibiting the teaching of a foreign language (German) in elementary schools. The court held that the statute unreasonably infringed on the liberty to teach and the liberty of parents to secure instruction for their children in a language other than English, both liberties being among those protected by the due-process clause of the 14th Amendment.

M.H.S. Marine Hospital Service.

Middle-of-the-Road Populists. Members of the Populist party who disliked their party's endorsement of Bryan in 1896, and who nominated separate tickets in 1900 and afterward.

midnight judiciary. A derogatory term applied to the judges appointed in the closing days of John Adams' administration under the Judiciary Act of 1801.

Midway Islands. Two small islands in the North Pacific, acquired by the United States in 1867, which with Kure Island form the westernmost link of the Hawaiian chain, and are used as a site of naval installations and a way station for trans-Pacific airplanes.

migration. Transference of residence from one place to another.

Migratory Bird Act. An act of Congress, July 3, 1918, to enforce a treaty of Aug. 16, 1916, between the United States and Great Britain for the mutual protection of migratory birds which was upheld by the Supreme Court in the case of *Missouri v. Holland, q.v.*

Milan Decree. An order issued by Emperor Napoleon I at Milan, Dec. 17, 1807, ordering the seizure of every ship which had stopped at a British port in compliance with British orders in council.

mileage. An allowance for traveling expenses of members of a legislative body going to and from their homes to attend legislative sessions.

militarism. 1. Maintenance of excessive armaments. 2. Elevation of military men over civil authorities and the substitution of military for civilian institutions and ideals.

military appeals. *See* United States Court of Military Appeals.

military commission. A board usually composed of military officers and civilians which tries persons not subject to court martial, *q.v.*, who are accused of violating martial law or the laws of war.

military government. Temporary government maintained by military forces over conquered or occupied territory, under which regulations of the military commander supersede the civil law.

military indemnity. Money or other valuable property exacted by a conqueror from a defeated enemy.

military intelligence. The acquisition of data concerning the offensive or defensive strength or vulnerability of actual or potential enemies by means of espionage, interception of messages, questioning of prisoners, study of maps, photographs, and documents, aerial observation, "spy" satellites orbiting in space; and the interpretation of such data. *See* intelligence.

military law. The law governing the administration and discipline of the armed forces and pleaded before military tribunals;—formerly embodied in separate articles of war for the army and navy and, since 1950, in the Uniform Code of Military Justice.

militia. 1. All able-bodied male citizens, and resident male aliens between the ages of 18 and 45, whether members of the organized militia (National Guard) or not. The States retain power to appoint officers, to train the militia according to the discipline prescribed by Congress, and to call them out for defense and the preservation of order in emergencies. The federal government may provide for their organization, arming, and discipline, and may call them into the national service in time of war or other emergencies. 2. *Colloquial.* The National Guard.

milk control. Regulation of milk prices in order to maintain an orderly market and assure adequate supplies of a product essential to health. *See Nebbia v. New York.*

Miller-Tydings Act. An act of Congress, Aug. 17, 1937, actually a rider to an appropriation bill, which exempted from the operation of antitrust laws agreements which prescribed minimum resale prices for trademarked goods in interstate commerce whenever such agreements were valid under the laws of the State where the goods were sold.

Milligan, Ex parte. The case, 4 Wall. 2 (1866), of a civilian who was sentenced to be hanged by a military commission sitting at Indianapolis in 1864, and who applied to the U.S. Circuit Court for a writ of habeas corpus. The Supreme Court declared that conviction by a military commission was illegal in any community in which the civil courts were open and their processes unobstructed.

millions for defense but not one cent for tribute. An American rallying cry during the informal war with France in 1798, said to have been the reply of Charles C. Pinckney to a suggestion of agents of the French foreign office that the United States should make a loan to France and a present to the agents before a treaty could be negotiated. *See* XYZ Papers.

Minersville School District v. Gobitis. See Flag-Salute cases.

minimum rates. The lowest rates for any particular service which federal or State regulatory commissions permit a business supplying an essential service to charge, the purpose being to prevent destructive competition.

minimum-wage legislation. Laws passed by State legislatures and Congress forbidding the employment of workers at wages less than those found necessary to maintain an adequate standard of living. The Supreme Court refused to recognize the validity of such laws until the case of *West Coast Hotel Co. v. Parrish, q.v.*

minister. 1. A diplomatic representative ranking below an ambassador. 2. The head of an administrative department in many countries.

ministerial. Pertaining to the executive acts, powers, duties, or responsibilities of a minister, or the whole body of ministers.

ministerial act. A duty which an officer is required to perform in the manner prescribed by law.

ministerial powers. Powers of an administrative official precisely stipulated in the instrument granting the powers which permits of little or no discretion in their execution. The exercise of such powers may be reviewed by the courts. *See Kendall* v. *United States.*

ministerial responsibility. The requirement that the policies of a cabinet and the principal administrative acts of a minister must have at least the tacit approval of the legislative branch or, failing in such approval in votes of confidence or interpellations, the cabinet or minister must resign.

minister plenipotentiary. A diplomatic agent with full powers.

minister resident. A diplomatic agent of lower rank than a minister, who may be accredited to a less important state.

ministry. 1. *In a parliamentary government:* the entire body of ministers and their immediate political subordinates who are likely to lose office with a change in the political complexion of the legislature. **2.** *In Great Britain and elsewhere:* a major administrative department or office.

Minnesota Press case. A case, *Near* v. *Minnesota,* 283 U.S. 697 (1931), in which the Supreme Court annulled a Minnesota statute of 1925 which required the suppression of newspapers publishing malicious or defamatory statements. Such censorship was held to contravene the due-process clause of the 14th Amendment.

Minnesota Rate cases. Several cases, 230 U.S. 352 (1913), in which the Supreme Court first suggested that where intrastate and interstate commerce were so thoroughly commingled as to render segregation impossible or difficult Congress might regulate both in order to make effective its power over interstate commerce; subsequently applied in the Shreveport and the Wisconsin Rate cases, *qq.v.*

minority group. Any racial, religious, occupational, or other group constituting less than a numerical majority of the population whose interests need protection from an overpowering majority controlling the government. National minorities in post-Versailles Europe were protected by treaties, and minorities in the United States are protected by the due-process and equal-protection clauses of the Constitution.

minority report. A separate statement prepared by a minority of the members of a legislative committee or a commission expressing their disagreement with the recommendations or conclusions of the body as a whole.

minority representation. Any electoral or representative scheme (as cumulative voting, the limited vote, or proportional representation) designed to permit minority groups to be represented in a legislature or comparable body.

minor party. A party with only local or widely scattered support that has little influence in an election.

mint. A public establishment for coining money. The Bureau of the Mint supervises the mints at Philadelphia and Denver, the assay offices at New York and San Francisco, and the bullion depositories at Fort Knox, Ky., and West Point, N.Y. *See* coinage.

minuteman. Before the American Revolution, a volunteer ready for military service at a minute's notice from a patriotic committee.

Miranda* v. *Arizona. A case, 384 U.S. 436 (1966), in which the Supreme Court extended the protections of the Fifth and Fourteenth Amendments by declaring that a suspect in the hands of police authorities must be clearly informed *prior* to any questioning that he has the right to remain silent and that everything he says can be used against him in a court of law, that he has the right to the presence of an attorney, and that if he can not afford an attorney, one must be appointed for him.

miscegenation. The marriage or cohabitation of persons of different races. The laws of 15 Southern and border States which prohibited marriages between whites and Negroes or other races were declared unconstitutional by the Supreme Court in 1967 because they violated the equal-protection clause of the 14th Amendment.

misconduct in office. Negligent, improper, dishonorable, or unlawful behavior on the part of an individual holding a position of public trust which may result in removal from office.

misdemeanor. A crime not serious enough to constitute a felony; *especially:* a crime so classified by statute, but usually not including minor violations punishable by summary proceedings.

misfeasance. The performance of a lawful act in an improper or illegal manner, to the detriment of another person.

missile gap. An alleged inferiority of the United States to Russia in missile strength which was exploited by Democratic candidates during the campaign of 1960.

mission. 1. A special embassy or *ad hoc* group of diplomatic representatives sent to a foreign state or international conference or organization to carry on some unusual diplomatic enterprise or to conduct negotiations of a special nature. 2. A permanent embassy or legation, such as the United States Mission to the United Nations.

Mississippi **v.** *Johnson.* A case, 4 Wall. 475 (1867), in which the Supreme Court declared that an injunction could not be issued against the President to prevent him from enforcing allegedly unconstitutional laws, the law-enforcing authority of the President being political and not ministerial in nature.

Missouri Compromise. An agreement in 1820 between members of Congress representing free and slave States under which Maine was admitted as a free State and Missouri as a slave State, and the further existence of slavery in the region north of the parallel of 36° 30′ (the southern boundary of Missouri) was to be forever prohibited.

Missouri ex rel. Gaines **v.** *Canada.* A case, 305 U.S. 337 (1938), which introduced an early modification of the "separate but equal" doctrine as respects educational opportunities for Negroes. The decision sustained a Negro's right to a higher professional education on terms of equality with whites by requiring the Negro's admission to the segregated white law school of a State university at least until a law school for Negroes had been provided. The State's offer to finance the Negro's legal education in an out-of-State university with a tuition grant was explicitly rejected as being less than equal treatment.

Missouri **v.** *Holland.* A case, 252 U.S. 416 (1920), in which the Supreme Court sustained a federal statute to enforce a treaty with Great Britain for the mutual protection of migratory birds as a valid exercise of national power. An earlier federal statute on the same subject, antedating the treaty, had been invalidated by the lower federal courts as a usurpation of the reserved powers of the States.

mixed caucus. A nominating body, early in the 19th century, which was composed of all members of a political party in both houses of a State legislature and, in addition, of delegates elected by party conventions from counties and districts not represented by members of the party in the legislature.

mixed commission. A commission composed of representatives from both sides to a controversy which employs experts to gather facts and is authorized to present them and its recommendations to the countries or parties concerned or to the United Nations.

mobilization. The action of placing armies, fleets, and other public forces in readiness for immediate duty; *specifically*: the process of placing a nation on a war footing, including the establishment of emergency governmental controls over manpower, production, and resources.

Model State Constitution. A recommended plan of State government incorporating certain reform ideas, such as the unicameral legislature, a unified executive and judiciary, and a more integrated administrative structure, revised and republished from time to time by the National Municipal League. The League also drafts and publishes a *Model City Charter.*

moderator. The presiding officer of a town meeting.

modus vivendi. An arrangement or understanding between the foreign offices of two or more countries pending final settlement of an international problem.

monarchy. Any form of polity which vests public powers in a king or other potentate. The kingship may be hereditary or elective although the former type now prevails; if elective, the tenure is for life. Where royal powers are subject to enforceable constitutional limitations or where their exercise is shared with other public organs, such as a parliament, or requires the assent of advisers or ministers responsible to the law or to the people, the monarchy is said to be *limited* in form. In some limited monarchies, the powers of the king have become so circumscribed by law or constitutional practice as to render him little more than a titular head of state. Where limitations are not imposed or where such limitations are merely a form involving no serious restrictions upon the personal discretion of the monarch, the monarchy is said to be *absolute.*

monetary policy. Any action by government relating to currency or credit, such as devaluation or revaluation of the currency or the specie cover, or the expansion or contraction of bank reserves, easier or more stringent credit terms which, according to certain economists, may be expected to foster either an inflationary or deflationary trend, the objective of whatever measure is adopted being the promotion of economic stability.

money. Coins of gold, silver, or other metals or paper certificates to represent coins or a certain value of bullion, or notes of the government or of authorized banks, which serve as a medium of exchange.

money bill. Any bill to raise revenue or appropriate public funds. In Congress such a bill must originate in the House of Representatives.

mongrel caucus. Another name for mixed caucus, *q.v.*

monopoly. Such a degree of control of the supply of a commodity or service by a single seller that he can fix its price without reference to a competitive market and thus release the supply at the most profitable price for him. This power may result from exclusive access to the supply, control of patents, a public franchise, or cooperative action of former competitors which tends to eliminate competition. When a very few sellers control the supply and they enjoy quasi-monopolistic privileges in the market, the condition is called *oligopoly*.

Monroe Doctrine. A cardinal principle of American foreign policy first announced in President Monroe's message to Congress, Dec. 2, 1823, when Russia was extending her settlements southward from Alaska and seemed about to join with other members of the Holy Alliance, *q.v.*, in attempting to force the newly independent Spanish-American republics to return to their allegiance to Spain. President Monroe declared that "we should consider any attempt on their part to extend their system to any portion of this hemisphere as dangerous to our peace and safety. With the existing colonies or dependencies of any European power we have not interfered and shall not interfere. But with the Governments who have declared their independence and maintained it, and whose independence we have, on great consideration and on just principles, acknowledged, we could not view any interposition for the purpose of oppressing them, or controlling in any other manner their destiny, by any European power in any other light than as the manifestation of an unfriendly disposition toward the United States." The principal later applications of the doctrine were (*a*) obtaining the withdrawal of French Imperial troops, 1867, which had established the Emperor Maximilian in Mexico; (*b*) pressure on Great Britain, 1895, to settle the boundary between Venezuela and British Guiana by arbitration; and (*c*) action in 1904 to prevent the forcible collection of debts owed by certain Caribbean countries to European creditors. *See* Roosevelt Corollary. Since the 1930's the United States has followed the policy of collaborating with other American states in preventing foreign intervention in the Western Hemisphere, but has acted alone in securing its own defense. *See* Cuba missile confrontation.

Montevideo Conference. The Seventh International Conference of American States at Montevideo, Uruguay, December, 1933, which, among other things, declared that "no state has the right to intervene in the internal or external affairs of another." *Compare* Stimson Doctrine.

Mooney case. The conviction and imprisonment of Thomas J. Mooney, on evidence increasingly regarded as trumped up, for having caused a bomb explosion in the course of a Preparedness Day parade in San Francisco, July 22, 1916. He was pardoned, Jan. 7, 1939.

moral turpitude. The quality of a crime that characterizes it as *malum in se*, that is, as inherently vicious and depraved or as offensive to public morals. Persons convicted of a crime involving moral turpitude are debarred from entry under U.S. immigration laws.

moratorium. The period during which the stated time for payment of a debt is extended by the creditor or by legislative enactment. *See Home Building and Loan Association* v. *Blaisdell.*

Morgenthau Plan. A proposed disposition of Germany after World War II which would have transferred some of its territory to surrounding nations, destroyed most of the mines and factories, and reduced the economy of the country to an essentially pastoral condition. It was prepared by Harry Dexter White and others under the direction of Henry Morgenthau Jr., Secretary of the Treasury, and was accepted by Roosevelt and Churchill at the Quebec Conference in September, 1944, in spite of vigorous protests by Hull and Stimson, the Secretaries of State and War, respectively. The plan influenced directives to the military during the first stages of the occupation of Germany, but was soon abandoned.

Mormon War. A series of disorders between Mormons and non-Mormons at Nauvoo, Ill., 1844–46, which resulted, after some bloodshed, in the migration of the Mormons to Utah.

morning hour. A period set aside at the beginning of a legislative day for the disposition of regular or routine matters; observed in the Senate after an adjournment but, because of special calendars, special orders, and the priority granted to financial business, rarely observed in the House of Representatives.

Morrill Act. An act of Congress, July 2, 1862, making large land grants to the States for the endowment of agricultural and mechanical colleges.

Morrill Tariff. A tariff law, Mar. 2, 1861, which greatly increased duties and embodied many protective features.

mortgage moratorium. *See* moratorium.

most-favored-nation clause. A provision often contained in commercial treaties by which one country agrees to grant to another all privileges in certain matters that have been, or may in the future be, granted to any other country.

motion. 1. A proposal by a member of a parliamentary body for an action either substantive or procedural. **2.** The application of a party or his counsel in a case at law for a ruling or order from the court.

motion-picture censorship. Review in some States by a board of censors of a motion picture before exhibition for the purpose of eliminating or revising scenes deemed offensive to public morals; invalidated by the Supreme Court when a board refuses a license on the ground that a film is deemed sacrilegious; and increasingly subject to judicial challenge because this, like other censorship, violates freedom of publication guaranteed by the First and Fourteenth Amendments.

Motor Carrier Act. A law of Congress, Aug. 9, 1935, which placed foreign and interstate transportation by motor vehicles under the jurisdiction of the Interstate Commerce Commission.

motor vehicle taxation. A State license tax on motor trucks and passenger cars usually levied according to weight, value, or horsepower. The proceeds are usually paid into a special fund for road construction and maintenance.

Motor Vehicle Theft Act. An act of Congress, Oct. 29, 1919, which

made it a federal offense to transport across a State boundary line a
motor vehicle known to have been stolen.

Mr. Republican. A nickname of Senator Robert A. Taft of Ohio.

muckraker. One who exposes corruption in office and scandalous official
and personal conduct or assails the integrity of public officers. The
term, derived from muckrake, a tool for collecting barnyard filth, was
applied by President Theodore Roosevelt to social and political reformers and sensation-seeking journalists of the early 1900's whose
activities were later recognized as important in promoting the progressive movement.

mudslinging. Offensive injection of personalities into a political discussion.

mugwump. 1. A Republican who refused to support James G. Blaine in
1884. **2.** An independent member of a political party.

Mulford v. Smith. The case, 307 U.S. 38 (1939), in which, for all practical purposes, the Supreme Court overruled its decision in *United States
v. Butler, q.v.,* and sustained the second Agricultural Adjustment Act,
declaring that Congress might constitutionally regulate the flow of an
agricultural commodity to the interstate market in order to foster,
protect, and conserve commerce or "to prevent the flow of commerce
from working harm to the people of the nation."

Muller v. Oregon. A case, 208 U.S. 412 (1908), in which the Supreme
Court upheld an Oregon statute forbidding the employment of women
in certain industries for more than 10 hours in any one day, thus
modifying the decision in *Lochner v. New York, q.v.,* apparently on the
theory that women were less able to endure sustained labor than men
and therefore required legislative protection.

Mulligan Letters. A series of letters between James G. Blaine and Warren
Fisher, Jr., read in the House of Representatives by Blaine in 1876 after
one Mulligan had been ordered to present them before an investigating
committee. They aroused the suspicion that Blaine had used the Speak-
ership for his own financial advantage.

multiple-party system. A condition in which several large parties compete
with each other, in which no party is strong enough by itself to establish and maintain a ministry in office, and in which coalition governments are normal;—found in many parliamentary governments, but
usually not in those of English-speaking countries. *Compare* two-party
system.

municipal. 1. Pertaining to an incorporated city or town. **2.** *In international law:* pertaining to the purely internal affairs of a state.

Municipal Bankruptcy Act. An act of Congress, May 24, 1934, which
provided that municipalities or other taxing districts of a State might
file a petition in a United States court stating that the taxing district
was insolvent and submitting a plan of readjustment which 51 per cent
of creditors had accepted in writing, after which relief might be granted;
declared unconstitutional in *Ashton v. Cameron County Water Improvement District,* 298 U.S. 513 (1936), as an invasion of the rights
of States.

municipal corporation. A subordinate unit of government, created under the authority of the State for convenience in administration in a thickly populated area, which has a corporate name, a charter, and delegated powers, strictly interpreted. It has a dual character: (a) as an agency of the State with responsibility for the fulfillment of public policy; and (b) as a *quoad hoc* private corporation with proprietary rights, powers, and responsibilities. See Dillon's Rule.

municipal court. A minor court authorized by municipal charter or State law to enforce local ordinances and also, usually, to exercise the criminal and civil jurisdiction of a justice of the peace.

municipality. An incorporated city, town, or borough; *also:* the body of officials who govern it. See municipal corporation.

municipal ownership. A term applied to the ownership by municipalities of enterprises normally under private management, particularly electric generating and distributing systems, surface or subway transit facilities, retail markets, docks, and warehouses; *called also* municipal socialism because the policy is advocated by Socialist or Marxist parties.

municipal veto. A veto, usually suspensive in effect, which, in a few places, may be exercised by a city's mayor, governing body, or voters against a State legislature's act applying exclusively to the city.

munition. Any weapon of war, including arms, ammunition, equipment, and military stores.

Munn v. Illinois. The most important of the "granger cases," 94 U.S. 113 (1877), in which the Supreme Court sustained State regulation of grain elevator rates, declaring that the "public has a direct and positive interest" in private businesses like that of the operation of a grain elevator; that they are businesses affected with a public interest, and as such, are subject to public control. The case is an important precedent for judicial support of public regulation of the rates and services of public utilities.

Murchison Letter. A letter stating that Cleveland was more friendly to England than Harrison, which Lord Sackville-West, the British minister, was tricked into writing in September, 1888. He was at once dismissed.

Muscle Shoals. The site of a hydroelectric development during World War I, practically unused until control over it was given to the Tennessee Valley Authority in 1933.

mutiny. Revolt against, or concerted disobedience to, the lawful orders of constituted authority, especially by persons in the armed services or by members of a ship's crew.

mutual mortgage insurance system. A procedure for guaranteeing mortgages, established under the National Housing Act of 1934, as amended, which secures private lenders against losses on mortgage loans for the construction of dwellings for one to four families and for the alteration, repair, and enlargement of existing structures.

Mutual Security Act. An act of Congress, Oct. 10, 1951, which provided for the coordination of military and economic aid to foreign countries with emphasis on military aid.

Myers v. United States. A case, 272 U.S. 52 (1926), in which the Supreme Court upheld the power of the President to remove at pleasure any person appointed by himself and the Senate; since qualified in *Rathbun (Humphrey's Executor)* v. *United States, q.v. See* removal from office.

N

NAACP National Association for the Advancement of Colored People.

Nansen passport. An identity certificate provided by the League of Nations Advisory Commission for Refugees to White Russians and others who lost their nationality during and after World War I.

NASA National Aeronautics and Space Administration.

Nashville Convention. A meeting of delegates from nine Southern States at Nashville, Tenn., in June and November, 1850 which, though called to concert action for secession, adopted conservative resolutions.

nation. 1. A numerous nationality, *q.v.*, which occupies a definite territory and possesses some form of political organization, usually as a state. **2.** A numerous nationality (as the Germans or the Italians in the mid-19th century) which seeks unification within a single state. **3.** A subject nationality (as the Polish people after the extinction of their state in the late 18th century) which aspires to independence and statehood. **4.** A country occupied by one, or (as in Belgium or Switzerland) by more than one nationality.

national. A person who owes allegiance to, and is entitled to protection from, a state, though he may not be a citizen. Natives of certain unincorporated territories are nationals but not citizens of the United States.

National Academy of Sciences. A private scientific agency, incorporated by Congress in 1863, whose principal purpose is to stimulate scientific research and to give assistance and recognition to distinguished scholarship in science. On request by the Government it investigates and advises on scientific problems. In 1916 it created the National Research Council to provide research assistance on matters connected with national defense, and in 1965 it lent its assistance in establishing the National Academy of Engineering.

National Aeronautics and Space Administration. An independent agency created in 1958 which, under the direction of an administrator, (*a*) conducts research on problems of flight within and outside of the earth's atmosphere, (*b*) develops and operates aeronautic and space vehicles, (*c*) explores portions of space with manned and unmanned vehicles, and (*d*) cooperates with other nations engaged in similar activities for peaceful purposes.

National Archives and Records Service. An agency created in 1934, and placed in the General Services Administration in 1949, which preserves government records of historic value and publishes (*a*) presidential and executive orders and administrative regulations daily in the *Federal Register,* (*b*) the *Code of Federal Regulations,* (*c*) the *United States Government Organization Manual,* (*d*) slip laws, separate prints of constitutional amendments and Acts of Congress, and (*e*) the *United*

States Statutes at Large. The agency has general supervision of the separate libraries containing the state papers of all Presidents since Hoover.

National Association for the Advancement of Colored People. An interracial organization founded in 1909 to resist discrimination against Negroes, raise their economic status, and secure full political and economic rights for them. An entirely independent NAACP Legal Defense and Educational Fund frequently resorts to the courts to test and vindicate Negroes' civil rights.

national banks. Commercial banks, chartered under the act of Congress, Feb. 25, 1863, and later acts, which, in addition to carrying on usual banking activities, were empowered to issue bank notes up to 90 per cent (after 1900, 100 per cent) of the par or market value of U.S. bonds that they purchased and kept on deposit with the U.S. Treasury. A monopoly of note issues was assured them by the imposition in 1866 of a 10 per cent tax on the issue of bank notes by State banks; but national bank notes have since been retired from circulation. All national banks are under the supervision of the Comptroller of the Currency and are required to be members of the Federal Reserve System, *q.v.*

National Bureau of Standards. A unit of the Department of Commerce, established March 3, 1901, whose research and testing laboratories establish and maintain all the basic scales and units of reference used for testing and measuring in commerce, industry, science, and engineering. Through its research, it assists industry and the government in applying available technology and promotes technological innovation.

national chairman. The chairman of the national committee of a party, who in campaign years is designated by the presidential candidate and formally elected by the committee. He establishes headquarters, raises and allocates funds, manages the campaign, and promotes the interests of the party between campaigns.

National Civil Service League. A private professional organization, founded in 1881, with headquarters in Washington, D.C., devoted to the extension and improvement of the merit system among civil service employees and the promotion of modernized personnel policies at all levels of government.

national committee. The permanent executive body of a national party composed of one man and one woman from each State and the District of Columbia, and, in the Republican committee since 1952, the State party chairmen in States where the party has recently won victories in elections for President, governor, or U.S. Senator. Members are chosen by the national convention on nomination of the State or other delegation, or sometimes of the voters in a primary election. Its most important duty, the supervision of the presidential campaign, is performed by the national chairman, *q.v.* It determines the place and date of the national convention, issues the call, makes up a temporary roll of delegates, and performs other duties imposed by the convention.

national convention. The highest organ of a national political party, composed of more than 1,000 delegates and an equal number of alternates chosen by primary elections or party conventions in States, territories and other areas, and the District of Columbia. The number of delegates is roughly double that of presidential electors, plus a bonus for party victories in immediately preceding elections. In the Democratic convention votes are apportioned to States, delegates with fractional votes may be seated, and a delegation may be required to follow the unit rule, *q.v.*, in voting. In the Republican convention representation is based on Congressional districts as well as States, each delegate has one vote, and there is no unit rule. Each convention determines the right of delegates to be seated, its own permanent organization, changes in the fundamental rules of the party, the party platform and (after numerous nominating and seconding speeches, noisy demonstrations on the floor and in the galleries, and roll calls of the States in alphabetical order) the nomination of candidates for President and Vice President. All actions of a convention require the approval of an absolute majority of the delegates.

national debt. *See* public debt.

national defense. A broadly conceived effort to prepare a nation successfully to repel actual or potential external aggression. Besides the recruitment and training of appropriate public forces and the manufacture and accumulation of the necessary armament, such an effort requires the stockpiling of strategic and critical materials, the elaboration of plans for civilian defense, and the planned mobilization of resources, human and economic, in the event of war.

National Defense Education Act. An act of Congress, 1958, which, as amended, authorizes (*a*) federal support of college and university loan funds for students; (*b*) fellowships for graduate students in the sciences; (*c*) grants and loans to construct science laboratory facilities and to strengthen elementary and secondary education in science, mathematics, and foreign languages; (*d*) assistance to programs to improve foreign-language teachers and teaching; and (*e*) grants and contractual commitments to improve guidance counseling and testing in the schools and to improve the qualifications of guidance personnel.

National Democratic party. The official title of the Gold Democrats, *q.v.*

national emergency. A condition (as the existence of war or threat of war, or the stoppage of production or the transportation system by strikes) which, when proclaimed by the President under specific authorization of a statute, brings into existence certain summary powers and remedies not normally available to executive officers.

National Farmers Union. An organization, founded in 1902 and composed principally of owners and tenants of small farms in about half the States, which emphasizes rural cooperatives, agricultural education, and militant political action designed to foster the small, family-type farm.

National Federation of Federal Employees. The oldest and largest organization of federal clerical employees (excluding postal employees) founded in 1917. It was chiefly responsible for the classification acts and has worked for the extension of the merit system and improved personnel administration, as well as higher pay scales, in the federal civil service.

National Firearms Act. An act of Congress, June 26, 1934, which restrained the importation and interstate transportation of sawed-off shotguns, machine guns, and silencers for any type of weapon, and placed a tax on dealers in firearms.

national forests. Timberlands throughout the United States but chiefly in the West, in total area larger than the State of Texas, set aside by the federal government to conserve moisture, prevent soil erosion, provide recreational facilities, and produce marketable lumber. Many of the States also possess important forest preserves.

national government. 1. A government whose legal authority and administrative organization extend into every part of the country, as distinguished from the governmental activities carried on by territorial divisions or subdivisions. **2.** The central general government of the United States.

National Guard. The volunteer militia of the States which in 1916 was organized as an auxiliary of the regular army, armed and trained by the federal government, and made subject to federal service in wartime or other emergencies on call of the President. At other times the respective State contingents may be called out by the governor when, in his judgment, the regular police forces are unable to maintain order.

national holidays. The following days set aside by act of Congress: New Year's Day, January 1; Washington's Birthday, February 22; Memorial Day, May 30; Independence Day, July 4; Labor Day, the first Monday in September; Veteran's Day, November 11; Thanksgiving Day, the fourth Thursday in November; Christmas Day, December 25.

national income. The total annual income in all categories of production and service including profits, wages and salaries, dividends, rent, interest, taxes levied on corporate earnings, and certain other items as computed for the United States by the Department of Commerce. National income equals gross national product, *q.v.*, less such items as capital consumption, indirect business taxes, and business transfer payments.

National Industrial Recovery Act. An act of Congress, June 16, 1933, which, for a two-year period authorized the President to approve or formulate codes of fair competition for business and industry and enforce such codes in order to promote national economic recovery. The codes were expressly exempted from the provisions of the antitrust laws. The act was invalidated by the Supreme Court in *Schechter Poultry Corp.* v. *United States, q.v.*

National Institutes of Health. Research units of the Public Health Service within the Department of Health, Education, and Welfare. They include institutes for cancer, heart disease, allergy and infectious disease, arthritis and metabolic disease, dentistry, mental health, neurological disease and blindness, general medical sciences, and child health and human development. The Institutes conduct research in the area of their respective special interests, maintain cooperative research programs with universities and medical schools, and also recommend Public Health Service grants-in-aid of considerable magnitude to universities, hospitals, and similar institutions for research, training, and field investigation.

nationalism. Belief in the concept of the nation, *q.v.*, and that the nation achieves fulfillment in statehood—developed especially in Europe after the 16th century where national loyalty to the state slowly superseded devotion to a personal sovereign whose title to rule was derived from feudal or divine right. For people not already politically united (as mid-19th century Germans and Italians) nationalism was a profound stimulus to unification. Exaggerated nationalism led to emphasis on "master race" theories, mistreatment of minorities and, in many parts of the world, to the balkanization (splintering) of peoples into national states lacking essential resources for separate statehood. In the United States political nationalism has taken the form of shifting power from the States to the federal government.

nationality. 1. A numerous group of people with similar racial background and common language, history, traditions, and customs, who may aspire to, or achieve, statehood; *called also* nation. *Compare* nation. 2. The legal relationship of an individual to a state as citizen, national, or subject which may be acquired by birth or naturalization. 3. An ethnic group (as of recent immigrants in Western Hemisphere countries) which maintains group identity and is only gradually assimilated to the dominant culture.

Nationality Act. A revision and consolidation of the immigration and naturalization laws of the United States enacted by Congress, Oct. 14, 1940, parts of which are still in effect.

nationalization. 1. Acquisition by the state, with equitable compensation to private owners, of land, mineral resources, manufacturing industries, and transportation and communication facilities. 2. Seizure by a state of private property, often under the plea that it was wrongfully acquired or is being used against the best interests of the state, with no compensation or only token compensation in the form of future promises to pay in depreciated currency.

National Labor Relations Act. An act of Congress, July 5, 1935, which established the policy of the United States to mitigate or eliminate obstructions to the free flow of commerce by encouraging the practice of collective bargaining and by protecting workers in the full freedom of organizing. It created the National Labor Relations Board, *q.v.*, and provided for the principle of majority rule in collective bargaining. *Called also* the Wagner, or Wagner-Connery, Act.

National Labor Relations Board. An independent federal establishment of five members, created under the terms of the National Labor Relations Act, *q.v.*, and continued since, which supervises elections among employees to determine union representation and certifies unions for collective bargaining. Examiners of the board hear complaints alleging unfair labor practices by employers or by unions which affect interstate commerce, such as employer interference with employees' rights to organize and bargain collectively, discrimination against employees for union activity, refusal of either employees or employers to bargain collectively, discriminatory or excessive union fees, featherbedding, *q.v.*, by unions, and the calling of jurisdictional strikes. If such practices are found to exist, the board may issue cease-and-desist orders and petition a federal court of appeals to enforce such orders. Actions against employers or unions are instituted by the board's General Counsel (appointed by the President and Senate) who exercises a considerable degree of discretionary authority.

National Labor Relations Board v. Jones and Laughlin Steel Corp. A case, 301 U.S. 1 (1937), in which the Supreme Court upheld the constitutionality of the National Labor Relations Act, *q.v.* Although the defendant steel company was not directly engaged in transportation, the successful conduct of its business depended upon the free flow of interstate and foreign commerce; hence Congress' attempt to mitigate labor disputes among the company's employees was, in the Court's opinion, a proper exercise of the power to promote and protect interstate commerce.

National Mediation Board. A board of three members, appointed by the President and Senate, created by Congress in 1934 to promote collective bargaining between management and employees engaged in interstate rail or air commerce and to mediate disputes affecting employee compensation or working conditions. Disputes growing out of grievances or out of the interpretation of labor agreements may be referred to an appropriate division of the National Railroad Adjustment Board. *See* Federal Mediation and Conciliation Service.

National Military Establishment. The official name of the unified Army, Navy and Air Force from 1947 to 1949 when the name was changed to Department of Defense.

national minority. A numerous group of people with strong racial, religious, linguistic, or cultural affinities domiciled in a country controlled by another nationality. Their protection was an objective of treaties after World War I and of the United Nations Charter.

national monument. A historic or scenic site placed under the protection of the National Park Service, *q.v.*

National Municipal League. A private professional organization, with headquarters in New York City, devoted to improving administrative and governmental standards at the local and State levels. It publishes the *National Civic Review. See Model State Constitution.*

national origins. The proportions of the American racial stock attributable to the settlements, immigration, and natural increase of peoples from foreign countries. The National Origins Act of May 20, 1924, required the Bureau of the Census to calculate national origins as of 1920, and these estimates were the principal basis for assigning quotas for admission of immigrants from various countries from 1928 to 1965.

national park. An area of spectacular natural beauty (as Yellowstone, Grand Canyon, Acadia, Great Smokies, etc.) set aside by the national government for recreation. *Compare* national monument.

National Park Service. A division of the Department of the Interior which administers the national park system, the parks in the District of Columbia, and national monuments and develops parks and recreation areas for public use and enjoyment.

National Park Trust Fund. The capital and income from private gifts for the support of the National Park Service which is administered by a five-man board including the Secretaries of the Treasury and of the Interior.

National party. The Greenback Labor party, *q.v.*

National Recovery Administration. A temporary agency, 1933–35, which supervised the formulation and enforcement of codes of fair competition in industry in accordance with the provisions of the National Industrial Recovery Act, *q.v.*

National Republican party. The followers of Adams and Clay in the election of 1832 which with other groups formed the Whig party in 1834.

National Research Council. *See* National Academy of Sciences.

National Road. The road constructed between 1806 and 1838 by the federal government westward for a distance of 800 miles from Cumberland, Md., and financed partly from the proceeds of sales of public lands near the road; *called also* Cumberland Road.

National Science Foundation. A federal agency, created in 1950, to strengthen and expand scientific research and education. It distributes information on science resources and personnel, awards grants or contracts to universities and nonprofit institutions to support scientific research, finances fellowships, research projects, seminars for teachers in colleges and secondary schools, new curricula, construction or modernization of laboratories, and maintenance of exchange programs with foreign scientists.

National Security Council. An inner cabinet for the Cold War created by statute in 1947 with the President, Vice President, the Secretaries of State and of Defense, and the Director of the Office of Emergency Planning as members. It coordinates domestic, foreign, diplomatic, and military policy for national security. Its importance has varied greatly under different Presidents.

national self-determination. A principle enunciated by Woodrow Wilson and others which found application in the use of plebiscites to determine the boundaries of many European states after World War I and in the creation of many small sovereign national states.

National Silver party. A political party composed of seceders from the Republican party in 1896 who endorsed Bryan and free silver.

National Socialism. The authoritarian, totalitarian, and imperialistic doctrine of German Fascism developed by Adolf Hitler and his followers between 1923 and 1945. *See* fascism.

national sovereignty. An idea sometimes expressed by Daniel Webster and Abraham Lincoln that the Union is supreme because it is older than the States and in fact created them as States. *Compare* State sovereignty.

national supremacy. The doctrine, formally developed by Chief Justice John Marshall in the case of *McCulloch* v. *Maryland*, *q.v.*, that the authority and power of a State cannot be interposed as a bar to the effective exercise of any legitimate power of the federal government.

National Transportation Safety Board. A board of five members in the Department of Transportation created in 1966 which has the duty of determining the cause of transportation accidents and to review on appeal the suspension, amendment, modification, revocation, or denial of a license issued by the Department.

National Union party. The combined party of Republicans and War Democrats in the campaign of 1864.

National Urban League. An interracial group founded in 1910 which is chiefly concerned with improving housing, educational, and employment opportunities for Negroes in metropolitan areas, with relieving racial tensions, and with improving welfare services for Negroes.

National Youth Administration. A federal unit which, from 1935 to 1943, administered funds for the part-time employment of high school and college students, and for vocational training, recreation, and job placement for young people generally.

Native American party. An anti-Catholic minor party which had a brief existence about 1845.

nativism. The idea that the institutions established by Americans of older stock should be protected from the influence of the newer immigrant stock. It was manifested in the Know-Nothing party after 1850, in the Ku Klux Klan after World War I, and in movements to restrict immigration, increase the period of residence required for naturalization, and deprive foreign-born residents of civil and political privileges.

NATO North Atlantic Treaty Organization.

natural-born citizens. A phrase in the Constitution, Art. II, Sec. 1, para. 5, respecting eligibility to be President or Vice President the precise meaning of which has not been resolved. In ordinary legal usage it means any person who, under the provisions of the 14th Amendment, is a citizen of the United States because he was "born . . . in the United States and subject to the jurisdiction thereof." Despite the implications of *jus soli, q.v.,* legislation has extended the concept to children of American citizens engaged in public missions abroad and to the children of other American citizens residing abroad, provided the children subsequently subject themselves to U.S. jurisdiction in accordance with the provisions of the law.

naturalization. The process by which an alien becomes a citizen. In the United States *collective naturalization* occurs when designated groups are made citizens by treaty (as Louisiana Purchase), or by a law of Congress (as in annexation of Texas and Hawaii, or granting citizenship to Indians, or Puerto Ricans, and others). *Individual naturalization* must follow certain steps: (*a*) petition for naturalization by a person at least 18 years of age who has been a lawful resident of the United States for 5 years; (*b*) investigation by the Immigration and Naturalization Service to determine whether the applicant can speak and write the English language, has a knowledge of the fundamentals of American government and history, is attached to the principles of the Constitution (anarchists, communists, fascists, and subversives are barred), and is of good moral character (not a polygamist, criminal, gambler, or habitual drunkard, etc.); (*c*) hearing before a U.S. District Court or certain State courts of record; and (*d*) after a lapse of at least 30 days a second appearance in court when, if all goes well, the oath of allegiance is administered. The requirements are somewhat relaxed for spouses of citizens, soldiers and sailors, and older people of long residence. The naturalization of both parents automatically naturalizes children under 16 who are residents of the United States at the time.

natural law. A set of principles and rules discovered by human reason which, it is supposed, would govern mankind in a state of nature (before positive law existed) or, according to others, would provide rational principles for the government of man in society. It has also been considered a valuable supplement to positive law in setting moral standards by which the conduct of governments may be judged. Natural law theories originated with Stoic philosophers and statesmen. In the 18th century natural law was variously derived from reason, the Bible, and the fundamental principles of the common law.

natural monopoly. 1. A monopoly which results from the possession of virtually the entire supply of some natural resource or control of some strategic location. 2. A business inherently monopolistic in that duplication of its product or service would be economically wasteful.

natural resource. Any material in its native state which when extracted has economic value; *also:* any facility or advantage which nature has provided unaided by man.

natural rights. Individual rights, including those to life, liberty, and the pursuit of happiness, which are regarded as inalienable, and the violation of which by the British government was a justification for the Declaration of Independence.

naval academy. *See* United States Naval Academy.

naval base. An area which serves permanently or temporarily as a focal point for naval operations and has facilities for provisioning, equipping, repairing, or providing protection for naval units.

Naval Observatory. An observatory at Washington, D.C., under the jurisdiction of the Navy Department, which collects and publishes astronomical data and broadcasts signals every hour to establish officially standard time.

Naval War College. The first of the armed-services graduate schools established in 1884 and located at Newport, R.I. It conducts instruction and research on naval tactics and strategy.

navigable waters. Waters capable of bearing useful commerce. The beds of navigable rivers, lakes, and inlets are the property of the State in which they lie. National regulation extends over such as form a continuous highway for the passage of foreign or interstate commerce, or are capable, with the construction of artificial works, of being made navigable. *See Daniel Ball.*

navigation acts. A series of British laws, 1651–1750, designed to stimulate British commerce and encourage British colonial production by tariffs, subsidies, and regulations. They ultimately hurt American interests and were in part responsible for the Revolution.

Navy. *See* Department of the Navy.

N.D.E.A. National Defense Education Act.

Neagle, In re. A case involving a federal deputy marshal who, in the performance of a duty imposed upon him by Presidential order, had killed an assailant and had been indicted for murder by a State court. The

marshal's transfer from the State to a federal court for trial turned upon
the question whether he acted under a "law of the United States." The
Supreme Court, 135 U.S. 1 (1890), declared that the order given
Neagle had been issued under the President's constitutional authority
to see that the laws are faithfully executed and to preserve the peace of
the United States, and, as such, was to be regarded as a "law of the
United States." *See Debs, In re.*

Near v. Minnesota. *See* Minnesota Press case.

Nebbia v. New York. A case, 291 U.S. 502 (1934), in which the Supreme
Court upheld the fixing of minimum and maximum prices of milk by a
New York State board and thus expanded, beyond the limited category
of public utilities, the concept of regulation for the public interest, and
virtually abandoned the concept of "business affected with a public
interest."

necessary-and-proper clause. Art. I, Sec. 8, par. 18 of the Constitution,
which authorizes Congress to make all laws necessary and proper to
carry out the enumerated powers of Congress and all other powers
vested in the government of the United States or any department or
officer thereof;—often used to justify the doctrine of implied powers,
q.v.

negligence. Failure to exercise due care to avoid injury to others, usually
entailing civil liability on the part of the culpable party.

negotiation. 1. Discussion among heads of state or diplomats of two or
more countries with a view to arranging a treaty or arriving at some
international understanding. 2. Discussion among interested parties
(as in a labor dispute) with a view to settlement.

Negro disfranchisement. Deprivation, in the South, of the privilege of
suffrage as provided by the Fifteenth Amendment, at first by intimidation by the Ku Klux Klan and other private groups; and, beginning
about 1890, by constitutional amendments which, avoiding mention of
"race, color, or previous condition of servitude" (*see* Fifteenth Amendment), imposed property, taxpaying, educational, or other qualifications. These, administered unequally between the races, accomplished
the practical exclusion of Negroes from the polls until the recent enactment and enforcement of federal civil rights acts. *See* civil rights legislation.

Nelson Act. A comprehensive statute, July 1, 1898, by which Congress
resumed, after a lapse of twenty years, the regulation of bankruptcy.

nepotism. Favoritism to family members or other relatives (as in the
distribution of appointments or benefits) because of kinship rather
than merit.

net income. 1. That portion of gross income remaining after deducting all
costs of producing it and other legitimate expenses. 2. Income subject
to taxation after allowable deductions and exemptions have been subtracted from gross or total income.

neutralism. A policy or attitude of noninvolvement in contemporary power
struggles for fear of a nuclear holocaust; *specifically:* the policy of certain nations (as former colonies of European powers in Africa or Asia
and a few countries in Europe and Latin America) in avoiding entan-

gling alliances or otherwise identifying themselves with any major power bloc.

neutrality. 1. *In international law:* the position of a state which attempts to avoid even apparent support of any belligerent when a war is being waged among other states. It must abstain from rendering direct aid (as building and fitting out ships of war or recruiting soldiers and sailors) to any of the belligerents; and where indirect aid is permissible (as the limited fueling of warships, repair of storm damage, or export of munitions) it must treat all belligerents impartially. 2. *U.S. history:* a traditional policy of the United States dating from Washington's proclamation of neutrality in 1793 and Jefferson's attitude during the Napoleonic Wars, and extending into the 20th century. In 1935 Congress authorized the President to embargo arms, munitions, and materials to belligerents whenever he determined that a state of war existed; in 1936 it forbade loans to belligerents. In 1937 Congress required belligerents who purchased nonmilitary supplies in the United States to pay cash for them and carry them on their own ships; it also provided for control of the munitions industry in war and peace. In 1939, after the outbreak of the war in Europe, Congress repealed the arms embargo, but continued the cash-and-carry principle and forbade American ships to trade with belligerents or Americans to travel on ships of belligerents.

neutralization. An agreement among the principal states of a region to refrain from invading and to respect the neutral attitude of another state.

Newberry v. United States. A case, 256 U.S. 232 (1910), in which the Supreme Court declared unconstitutional that part of the federal Corrupt Practices Act of 1911 which set a maximum limit of expenditures for a candidate for the Senate in a primary election on the ground that a primary is not an election. This case was practically overruled in *United States v. Classic, q.v.*

New Deal. The reformist social and economic policies of President Franklin D. Roosevelt's administration;—from a phrase used by Roosevelt in his acceptance speech at the Chicago Democratic convention in 1932 to characterize his personal platform as a presidential candidate.

New England Confederation. A league, 1643–84, for offensive and defensive military operations against the Dutch and Indians, composed of the colonies of Massachusetts Bay, Plymouth, New Haven, and Connecticut.

New Freedom. The collection of Woodrow Wilson's campaign speeches published in 1913. The phrase stood for Wilson's policy of purifying and "humanizing" American life and, more specifically, for his program of enforcing competition in business.

New Frontier. The domestic and foreign policy program of President John F. Kennedy's administration;—from a slogan used by Kennedy in his acceptance speech in 1960.

New Hampshire Grants. A former name for the part of New York colony now included in Vermont, in which Governor Benning Wentworth of New Hampshire made extensive land grants.

New Harmony. The site of a Utopian communistic colony in Indiana founded in 1825 by the British philanthropist and social reformer Robert Owen (1771–1858). The experimental community proved unsuccessful and was disbanded in 1828.

New Jersey plan. *See* Paterson plan.

Newlands Act. 1. An act of Congress, June 17, 1902, which authorized the Department of the Interior to construct irrigation and other works for the reclamation of arid and semiarid public lands and sell such improved lands to settlers. **2.** An act of Congress, July 15, 1913, which established a federal board of mediation and conciliation and provided for the arbitration of labor disputes on interstate railways.

New Nationalism. The personal platform of Theodore Roosevelt in the campaign of 1912 which called for the abandonment of extreme laissez-faire in favor of federal regulation of business, protection of workers through compensation for injuries, minimum wages for women, the abolition of child labor, measures to safeguard public health, and the recall of judicial decisions in order to prevent judicial nullification of social legislation.

New Roof. A nickname for the Constitution of the United States, 1787–88, when it was before the people for ratification.

Niagara Falls Conference. A meeting at Niagara Falls, Canada, May 20 to July 2, 1914, under the auspices of the A.B.C. Powers, *q.v.*, at which United States and Mexican delegates sought to find a solution for strained relations resulting from the Tampico incident, *q.v.*

night court. A criminal court which, in certain cities, sits during the early evening hours for the immediate disposition of petty offenses and the granting or withholding of bail in more serious cases.

N.I.H. National Institutes of Health.

nihilism. The doctrine that established institutions have no objective validity, at times accompanied by advocacy of their destruction by any effective means, including "propaganda by deed," terrorism, and violence.

nine old men. The nine justices of the U.S. Supreme Court especially during the late 1930's when President F. D. Roosevelt sought legislation expanding the Court's membership in part because of the advanced age of incumbents;—used contemptuously.

Nine-Power Pact. A treaty, concluded at the Washington Conference in 1922 by the United States, Great Britain, France, Italy, Japan, China, Belgium, Portugal, and the Netherlands, which reaffirmed the open door in China, renounced spheres of influence, *q.v.*, and provided for the relinquishment by France, Great Britain, and Japan of some of their holdings in China.

Nineteenth Amendment. An amendment to the Constitution, proclaimed Aug. 26, 1920, in which the principal provision, that the right to vote shall not be denied because of sex, had the effect of giving the ballot to women on equal terms with men.

N.I.R.A. National Industrial Recovery Act.

Nixon v. Condon. See Texas Primary cases.

Nixon v. Herndon. See Texas Primary cases.

N.L.R.B. National Labor Relations Board.

Noble State Bank v. Haskell. A case, 219 U.S. 104 (1911), in which the Supreme Court upheld a State plan for the compulsory insurance of bank deposits as consistent with the due-process clause of the 14th Amendment. The Court reasoned that the police power extends to all great public needs; that such needs embrace the enforcement of the primary conditions of successful commerce; and that the guarantee of bank deposits, upon which the security of check currency depends, may properly be regarded by a State legislature as a condition of successful commerce.

nolle prosequi. An entry made on the record by a prosecuting officer or a plaintiff that he will not prosecute a case in whole or part.

nolo contendere. A plea made by the defendant in a criminal action that, without admitting guilt, he does not contest conviction. Such a plea makes possible denial of guilt in case he is faced with the same or similar charges in a related or collateral proceeding.

nominating convention. *See* convention 4; national convention.

nomination. 1. The designation by a party of a candidate for elective office, as historically in the United States, by secret caucus, committee of correspondence, legislative or Congressional caucus, mixed (or mongrel) caucus, convention, direct primary election, or petition. **2.** Part of the process of appointment, which consists in an executive officer's submitting the name of an appointee for confirmation by the Senate or other body.

noncombatant. A civilian or a member of the armed forces (as a chaplain or medical attendant) not authorized to bear arms.

noncooperation. A form of civil protest against government measures consisting of refusal by individuals or groups to pay taxes or perform normal civic duties.

Nonimportation Act. A law of Congress, Apr. 18, 1806, which prohibited the importation of certain commodities from Great Britain or the British Empire.

nonimportation agreement. Any of several agreements by residents of American colonies or towns, 1768–74, not to import goods from Great Britain.

Nonintercourse Act. A law of Congress, Mar. 1, 1809, prohibiting the entry of British or French ships or goods into the territorial waters or ports of the United States.

nonjusticiable. Pertaining to matters like political questions, *q.v.*, advisory opinions, friendly suits, or cases brought by persons who have no standing to sue, which the courts consider unsuitable for judicial determination.

nonpartisan ballot. A ballot containing no party designations.

nonpartisan board. A board, usually in reality bipartisan, nominally appointed without reference to party affiliations.

nonpartisan election. An election, usually for local or for State judicial offices, in which the names of national or State parties are excluded from the ballots.

Nonpartisan League. A farmers' organization, founded in North Dakota in 1915, which sponsored State ownership and operation of grain elevators, flour mills, and packing plants. It gained control of several State governments in the Northwest through the Republican or Democratic primaries and the organization, in Minnesota, of the Farmer-Labor party.

nonpartisan primary. A direct primary for the nomination of candidates (usually for local offices), without recognition of parties. The two candidates receiving the highest vote oppose each other in the general election. In some States, if one candidate has a clear majority in the primary, he is declared elected.

nonquota immigrant. Under United States laws from 1928 to 1965, the wife or unmarried child, under 18, of a resident citizen of the United States; an alien, previously lawfully admitted, who was returning from a visit abroad; a visiting professor or minister of two years' standing; a bona fide student; a native of a country of the Western Hemisphere; and others admitted without reference to a quota. *See* national origins.

nonresistance. Individual or organized protests against authority (as of a conqueror) which takes the form of acceptance of such regulations as force or circumstances may dictate but which denies the legitimacy of the authority and rejects any form of uncoerced collaboration.

nonsovereign state. A state whose foreign or domestic policies are controlled by another, though outwardly the puppet state may appear autonomous and independent.

nonviolence. A policy adopted by an opposition group which refrains from the use of overt force as a matter of principle or expediency.

normalcy. A word apparently coined by Warren G. Harding in the campaign of 1920 which later was applied contemptuously to the corruption and reactionary policies of the Harding administration.

Norman v. Baltimore and Ohio R.R. Co. See Gold Clause cases.

Norris Amendment. The Twenty-first Amendment, *q.v.*, to the Constitution, so-called because of Senator George W. Norris' long effort to secure its adoption.

Norris-LaGuardia Act. An act of Congress, Mar. 23, 1932, which outlawed the yellow-dog contract, *q.v.*, and deprived U.S. courts of jurisdiction to issue injunctions in labor disputes except after hearing witnesses in open court or unless unlawful acts were threatened, the commission of which could be expected to result in irreparable injury for which there was no adequate remedy at law.

Norris v. Alabama. See Scottsboro cases.

North Americans. Antislavery men who seceded from the convention of the American party in 1856 and made separate nominations, endorsing the Republican candidate, John C. Frémont.

North Atlantic fisheries. Rich fishing grounds off Newfoundland where Americans had the privilege of fishing and of drying their catch on nearby uninhabited shores by the Treaty of 1783 and a convention with Great Britain in 1818. The privileges of obtaining bait and water in nearby ports were granted by reciprocal treaty, 1854–67, by the Halifax Fishery Commission, *q.v.*, 1877–85, and by arbitration in 1909.

North Atlantic Treaty. A treaty signed at Washington, Apr. 4, 1949, by representatives of Belgium, Canada, Denmark, France, Great Britain, Iceland, Italy, Luxembourg, the Netherlands, Norway, Portugal, and the United States for collective security against aggression. (Turkey, Greece and the Federal Republic of Germany adhered later.) The parties agreed that an armed attack against one or more of them should be considered an attack against them all; and in case of such an attack each of them would assist the party or parties so attacked by taking such action as it deemed necessary including the use of armed force. The North Atlantic Treaty Organization (NATO), was set up to implement the treaty.

Northeast Boundary Dispute. A controversy between the United States and Great Britain concerning the identification of the source of the St. Croix River, of highlands between tributaries of the St. Lawrence and "rivers which flow into the Atlantic Ocean," and of the "Northwestern most head" of the Connecticut River mentioned in the Treaty of 1783. In 1827 the question was referred to the King of the Netherlands for arbitration, but neither country accepted the award. A compromise line was fixed by the Webster-Ashburton Treaty of 1842.

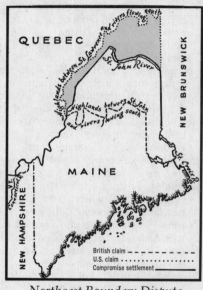

Northeast Boundary Dispute

Northeast Corridor project. Federal research as to the feasibility of high speed trains from Boston via New York and Philadelphia to Washington and the development of prototype trains.

Northern Securities Co. v. United States. A case, 193 U.S. 197 (1904), in which the Supreme Court ordered the dissolution of a holding company controlling northwestern railways on the ground that it constituted a restraint of interstate trade prohibited by the Sherman Antitrust Act, *q.v.*

northwest boundary. The western part of the boundary between the United States and Canada. By the Treaty of 1783, it was to be drawn from the northwest corner of the Lake of the Woods due west to the Mississippi River. After the purchase of Louisiana, and when it was found that the Mississippi did not rise so far north, Great Britain and the United States agreed in 1818 that the line should be drawn south from the northwest corner of the Lake of the Woods to the 49th parallel, and thence westward to the Rocky Mountains. In 1846 it was extended to Puget Sound. *See* Oregon Country. A dispute over the ownership of the San Juan Islands which lie in Puget Sound was settled in favor of the United States by the arbitration of William I, Emperor of Germany, in 1872.

Northwest Conspiracy. A Copperhead plot, exposed in June, 1864, to detach the Northwestern States from the Union.

Northwest ordinances. Three laws passed by the Congress of the Confederation for the organization of the territory between the Ohio River, the Great Lakes, and the Mississippi. The Ordinance of 1784, later repealed, envisaged the admission of nine or ten new States; that of 1785 provided for the survey of all lands in townships six miles square, with one square mile in each township reserved for educational purposes; and that of 1787, for an appointive governor, council, and judiciary, an elective assembly when the population reached 5,000, the abolition of slavery, guarantees of civil rights, and the eventual admission of from three to five new States with minimum populations of 60,000.

notary public. A public officer authorized to authenticate and certify documents such as deeds, contracts, and affidavits with his signature and seal.

note verbale. *In international relations:* an unsigned note summarizing a conversation or a series of events.

notification. A ceremony in which a committee of the national convention officially informs a presidential or vice-presidential candidate of his nomination.

N.R.A. National Recovery Administration.

N.S.C. National Security Council.

Nuclear Test Ban Treaty. An agreement of the United Kingdom, Russia, and the United States, signed July 25, 1963, to refrain from conducting nuclear tests in outer space, in the earth's atmosphere, or at sea. Underground testing which results in little nuclear fall-out was not banned by the treaty.

nuisance. Any establishment or practice which offends public morals or decency or menaces public health, safety, or order which may be summarily abated by a competent police or other administrative officer.

nuisance tax. Any tax of negligible yield which causes undue irritation and annoyance among the taxpayers.

nullification. An alleged right of a State in the American Union, acting in a sovereign capacity through a convention of its people, to declare an act of Congress "null, void, and no law, not binding upon [the] State, its officers or citizens." South Carolina acted in this manner in opposing the tariff acts of 1828 and 1832.

Nuremberg trials. A series of trials conducted by an international military tribunal at Nuremberg, Germany, after World War II, the defendants being party and military officials and other persons intimately associated with the Hitler regime who were accused of violating the laws of war, crimes against humanity, and other international crimes. Trial of the most serious offenders began Nov. 21, 1945, and ended Sept. 30, 1946. Twenty-two defendants were found guilty of whom eleven were sentenced to be hanged.

N.Y.A. National Youth Administration.

O

OAS Organization of American States.

O.A.S.D.I. Old Age Survivors and Disability Insurance.

oath. A solemn appeal to God or a supreme being as to the truth of a statement. A false oath is punishable as perjury.

oath of allegiance. A solemn affirmation or declaration of fidelity to a state on the part of a person who is, or is about to become, a citizen of that state.

oath of office. An oath administered to a person entering public office or employment in the United States, in which he promises to uphold the Constitution and laws of the State or of the nation and to perform faithfully his official duties.

obiter dictum. An incidental opinion by a judge on some point not argued in a case, or not a part of the conclusions necessary to support the judgment, and therefore not binding on the court in later cases.

obligation of a contract. The coercion applied through courts and other agencies of government to compel persons to carry out the terms of agreements they have made with each other. The provision of the Constitution, Art. I, Sec. 10, forbidding a State to impair the obligation of a contract means that the State may not alter the law in effect at the time the agreement was made to the disadvantage of either party or deprive either party of the means of enforcement. A contract made for an illegal or unconstitutional purpose is not enforceable (*see Buchanan* v. *Warley*), and a State may temporarily suspend the operation of a contract in order to afford relief to its people in periods of public emergency. See *Home Building and Loan Association* v. *Blaisdell.*

obstruction. Delay or stoppage of the normal course of legislation (as by repeated quorum calls, demands for record votes, successive procedural motions, or filibustering) deliberately contrived by a minority in order to defeat a measure or upset the legislative program of the majority.

occupational disease. A disease (as silicosis or effects of radium poisoning) resulting from exposure during employment to conditions or substances detrimental to health. Exposure and resulting injury to health were once regarded as necessary, or at least customary, risks of employment. Today regulatory laws try to prevent or reduce exposure, and victims usually receive indemnification under workmen's compensation laws.

occupational representation. *See* functional representation.

occupation tax. A license tax, often for regulatory purposes, levied upon individuals engaged in a particular occupation or profession, or in managing a particular business.

O.C.S. Office of Contract Settlement.

October States. A few States in which gubernatorial and congressional elections during the 19th century were held in October.

O.E.C.D. Organization for Economic Cooperation and Development.

OEP   Office of Emergency Planning.

offense. 1. A felony or misdemeanor, or a less serious violation of the law of a state. **2.** A breach of international law which Congress is authorized to punish (Constitution, Art. I, Sec. 8).

offensive partisan. A holder of a civil service position who engages in political campaigns to an extent contrary to the spirit, if not the letter, of civil service laws.

office. 1. A governmental position which is held by the incumbent by virtue of election, or appointment, or operation of law and not as the result of a contract of employment, and which has legally defined tenure, emoluments, and duties. **2.** An independent agency or the subdivision of such an agency or of a department.

office-block ballot. A form of ballot in which the names of candidates, with or without party designations, are grouped under the offices for which they are contesting. *Called also* Massachusetts ballot.

Office of Economic Opportunity. A unit established in 1964 within the Executive Office of the President which trains and directs the Job Corps, VISTA volunteers, and neighborhood Youth Corps; administers the Urban and Rural Community action programs which mobilize local public and private resources to remove the causes of, and alleviate, poverty; in conjunction with the Department of Health, Education, and Welfare, develops basic education and work experience programs; and, in cooperation with the Small Business Administration, increases the number, strengthens the resources, and improves the management of small business concerns.

Office of Education. A unit of the Department of Health, Education, and Welfare which collects statistics, disseminates information, supervises expenditure of federal grants to support education at all levels, and conducts special studies and programs.

Office of Emergency Planning. A federal agency, in the Executive Office of the President, successor in 1961 to the Office of Defense Mobilization, which advises the President on the use of manpower, materials, transportation facilities, civilian defense, the organization of the national economy, and the continuity of the government in time of war or other national emergency.

Office of Price Administration. An agency created during World War II to enforce legislation authorizing the rationing of goods and services to consumers and the establishment of ceiling market prices and rents. It was abolished in 1946.

Office of Price Stabilization. A federal agency which, during the Korean War, 1951–53, sought to stabilize living and production costs.

Office of Science and Technology. An agency within the Executive Office of the President created in 1962 to advise the President on science and engineering matters, as they may relate to national security and welfare, and to coordinate and integrate national scientific and technological resources.

Office of Tax Legislative Counsel. An agency in the Treasury Department which receives suggestions from the public and other sources on federal tax policy, provides the department with legal advice on tax matters, and formulates tax recommendations which may be submitted to Congress.

Office of Territories. A division of the Department of the Interior which supervises various local services of the federal government in American possessions and seeks to promote the welfare of the local populations.

Office of War Information. An agency created by presidential order in June, 1942, to provide wartime domestic and foreign information services. Its foreign information services were transferred to the Department of State after the office was abolished, Aug. 31, 1945.

official ballot. A ballot prepared by public authority for distribution only within polling places. After being marked by a voter it must be deposited in the ballot box.

offshore oil lands. Oil-bearing areas on the continental shelf under the Pacific Ocean and the Gulf of Mexico which the Supreme Court in 1947 decided were owned by the United States and subject to the control of Congress. By the Submerged Lands Act in 1953, Congress ceded to the States the offshore areas within their historic boundaries extending to ten and one-half miles from the shores of Texas and Florida and three miles from the shores of other States. *Called also* tidelands oil.

off-year election. An election held in any year other than that in which a presidential election occurs.

Ohio Gang. A group of Ohio politicians, chief of whom was Harry M. Daugherty, later Attorney General, who aided in securing the nomination and election of Warren G. Harding as President in 1920 and whose influence, allegedly sinister, continued throughout Harding's administration.

Ohio Idea. A proposal by George H. Pendleton of Ohio in 1868 to pay the national debt in greenbacks.

oil scandal. The transfer in May, 1921, of certain naval oil reservations from the Navy to the Interior Department; the leasing of the Elk Hills reservation in California to interests represented by E. L. Doheny who had made a large loan to Secretary of the Interior Albert B. Fall, on account of which Fall was convicted of bribery in 1931; and the leasing of the Teapot Dome reservation in Wyoming to interests controlled by Harry F. Sinclair, who was later acquitted of the charge of conspiring with Fall to defraud the Government.

Old Abe. A soldiers' nickname of Abraham Lincoln.

old-age security. A public pension system or other form of material aid for persons who, because of advanced age, are no longer capable of gainful employment.

Old-Age, Survivors and Disability Insurance. A broad insurance system (compulsory with minor exceptions) that provides pensions for the nation's retired population, supplies benefit payments to seriously disabled persons who cannot continue gainful employment, and provides income for surviving dependents of the insured. The system is financed by taxes levied on employees and employers (*see* payroll tax) and on self-employed persons. The proceeds of such taxes, invested in government obligations, are credited to a Federal Old-Age and Survivors Insurance Trust Fund and a Federal Disability Insurance Trust Fund. The system thus becomes a creditor of the federal government and the credit and income of the government are the real guarantors of the system's financial integrity. The system is administered by some ten O.A.S.D.I. divisions of the Social Security Administration, *q.v. Compare* Medicare.

Old Bullion. A nickname of Senator Thomas H. Benton of Missouri, a consistent advocate of hard money, *q.v.*

Old Colony. A nickname of the Plymouth Colony, founded 1620.

Old Curmudgeon. A nickname which Harold L. Ickes, Secretary of the Interior, 1933–46, bestowed on himself.

Old Fuss and Feathers. A soldiers' nickname of Winfield Scott.

old guard. A title assumed by delegates to the Republican national convention of 1880 who supported Grant; and since applied to conservative or reactionary Republicans.

Old Hickory. A nickname of Andrew Jackson bestowed because he was said to be "as tough as hickory" or because for some time during the campaign in 1813 against Indians his troops subsisted mainly on hickory nuts.

Old-Line Whig. A member of the Whig party about 1850 who wished to ignore the slavery issue and base political campaigns on economic questions.

Old Man Eloquent. A nickname of John Quincy Adams during his service in the House of Representatives, 1831–48.

Old Public Functionary. A nickname of James Buchanan who was almost continuously a member of Congress or a holder of high executive office from 1821 to 1861.

Old Rough-and-Ready. A soldiers' nickname of Zachary Taylor.

Old White Hat. A nickname of Horace Greeley in allusion to his habitual headgear.

oleomargarine tax. A tax levied by Congress in 1902 on oleomargarine colored to imitate butter. Though attacked as regulative, the Supreme Court, in *McCray* v. *United States*, 195 U.S. 27 (1904), upheld it as being ostensibly a revenue measure.

oligarchy. 1. A government in which authority constitutionally reposes in a few individuals or families. 2. A small coterie of individuals who, because of economic or other power, can measurably influence the policy of government even though they lack formal authority.

oligopoly. *See* monopoly.

Olmstead v. United States. A case, 277 U.S. 438 (1928), in which the Supreme Court ruled that government agents did not violate the prohibition in the Fourth Amendment against unreasonable searches and seizures if they obtained evidence against an accused person by surreptitiously tapping his telephone wire. Under the Federal Communications Act, such evidence is not admissible in federal courts.

O'Mahoney-Ramspeck Act. A law of Congress, June 25, 1938, which extended the classified civil service to include postmasters of the first, second, and third classes.

ombudsman. An official, established in Sweden in 1809 and later in a few other countries, who receives, investigates, and reports upon complaints by private persons about public officials.

omnibus bill. A bill (as the Compromise of 1850 when first proposed) or appropriation measure which combines the provisions of several bills into one.

one man, one vote. A traditional slogan of advocates of universal manhood suffrage and of the abolition of plural voting and rotten boroughs which was revived after the Supreme Court in *Gray* v. *Sanders, q.v.,* had held that every vote was entitled to equal weight with every other vote, regardless of the voter's race, sex, occupation, income, or place of residence. The principle was extended so as to require equal populations in congressional districts in *Wesberry* v. *Sanders, q.v.,* and in State senatorial and representative districts in *Reynolds* v. *Sims, q.v.*

OPA Office of Price Administration.

open court. 1. A court whose sessions may be attended by spectators. 2. A court which is in session for the transaction of judicial business.

open covenants openly arrived at. One of the Fourteen Points, *q.v.,* proposed by President Wilson, Jan. 8, 1918, which would have outlawed secret peace treaties.

open door. A policy providing equal opportunities for commercial and other intercourse for all nations and the abolition of spheres of influence and special rights and privileges;—an extension of the principle of the most favored nation, *q.v.,* first applied to China in Secretary of State John Hay's note to the powers of Sept. 6, 1899, and later applied to all so-called backward countries.

Open Market Committee. A committee of the Board of Governors of the Federal Reserve System and five federal reserve bank representatives which seeks to stabilize the general credit situation by dealing in government and other securities on the open market. *See* Federal Reserve System.

open primary. A primary election open, without any test of party affiliation, to any qualified voter.

open rule. A special order proposed by the Rules Committee of the House of Representatives which would permit amendments to be made when a bill is discussed on the floor.

open sea. Waters in which vessels of all nations may navigate without restriction. *Compare* territorial waters.

open shop. An establishment which hires employees without reference to their union or nonunion status.

open skies plan. A proposal by President Eisenhower at the Geneva Conference, July 21, 1955, to facilitate the international inspection of atomic and other armaments. It included exchange of blueprints and charts showing military installations; construction of isolated airfields in the areas to be inspected; and detailed regulations for the conduct of foreign inspecting aircraft.

operation bootstrap. A program providing for the rapid industrialization of Puerto Rico, begun in 1945, continued by the Commonwealth government, and accomplished principally through favorable concessions to corporations and other private businesses.

opinion. The reasoning by which a court or similar body explains and justifies its decision in a particular case or controversy.

opportunist. One who is inclined to take advantage of circumstances or events for his, or his party's immediate advantage without much regard for long-run consequences or political principles.

opposition. 1. The members of a minority party in a legislature. 2. Members of a party in Congress, whether in a minority or majority, politically opposed to the President and his administration. 3. *In parliamentary governments:* members of the party or partisan coalition who oppose the ruling party.

optional charter plan. A system in use in several States by which cities or counties may select any one of several fully-drawn charters prepared by the State legislature for their local government.

optional clause. A clause in the Statute of the Permanent Court of International Justice which gave that tribunal compulsory jurisdiction over specified classes of disputes among states which had elected to sign the clause. The clause has been continued in the statute of the International Court of Justice, *q.v.*

order. A command or regulation emanating from the executive authority or an administrative officer.

order in council. *In Great Britain:* an executive order issued by the advice of the Privy Council either under the royal prerogative or under the authority of a statute.

order of business. The order in which business before a legislative body is transacted, whether the regular order or an exceptional order which may be substituted under the rules.

Order of the Purple Heart. A decoration established by Washington at Newburgh, N.Y., Aug. 7, 1782, and revived by an order of the War Department, Feb. 22, 1932, as a recognition for soldiers wounded in action or cited for gallantry.

ordinance. 1. A regulation or bylaw of purely local application issued by an American municipal corporation which must be made under authority granted in the corporation's charter and in conformity with national and State constitutions and laws. 2. An act or resolution of a constituent assembly or of a public deliberative body which lacks statute-making authority as normally understood, such as actions of the Confederation Congress or secession, and other ordinances, of State constitutional conventions. 3. *In Great Britain:* an order issued by an authority less than King in Parliament.

Ordinance of 1787. *See* Northwest ordinances.

ordinance power. The authority of the President and certain executive officials or governmental agencies, conferred by the Constitution or the laws, to issue administrative directions or such orders and regulations as may be necessary to apply and enforce the law.

ordinary. A judicial officer who in some States has powers related to probate, guardianship, and the administration of estates.

Oregon Country. The Pacific Northwest extending from the northern boundary of California (the 42nd parallel) to the southern boundary of Alaska (54°40′). The title of the United States to the region was derived from the discovery of the mouth of the Columbia River by Captain Gray in 1792, the explorations of Lewis and Clark, 1803–1805, the settlement of Astoria, 1811, the cession of Spanish claims by treaty signed in 1819, the activities of missionaries after 1834, and numerous settlements after 1840. Great Britain had a claim derived from the voyage of Drake, 1577, the establishment of trading posts by the Hudson's Bay Company, and settlements in what is now British Columbia. A convention in 1818 provided for joint occupation of Oregon by the two countries. In 1846, despite American rallying cries of "Fifty-four forty or fight" and "The whole of Oregon or none," President James K. Polk negotiated a treaty with Great Britain extending the boundary along the 49th parallel from the Rocky Mountains to the Strait of Juan de Fuca and thence to the Pacific Ocean.

Oregon Country

Oregon School case. *See Pierce v. Society of Sisters.*

organ. A partisan newspaper reflecting the views of a politician, a factional group, or a political party.

organic act. An act of Congress creating a territory, conferring powers of self-government, and determining the duties of officers and the rights of individuals.

organic law. The fundamental law or constitution.

organization. The official system of party committees;—sometimes used in the sense of a party "machine."

Organization for Economic Cooperation and Development. Originally an association of Western European states formed in 1948 and located in Paris to plan cooperatively the recovery of such states under the Marshall Plan, and subsequently (1960) given its present name and extended to embrace 20 states, including the United States and Canada. The O.E.C.D. plans stable economic growth, assists in the economic development of emerging states, and seeks an expansion of employment and world trade on a multilateral, nondiscriminatory basis.

Organization for European Economic Cooperation. *See* Organization for Economic Cooperation and Development.

Organization of American States. A regional agency of the 21 republics of the Western Hemisphere the charter for which was signed by the member states at Bogota, Colombia, in 1948, although its origins go back to the founding of the International Union of American Republics in 1890. Its principal organ is a council consisting of one representative with the rank of ambassador from each constituent state. The Pan

American Union, *q.v.*, with headquarters in Washington, D.C., is the principal administrative agency; the latter also serves as the organization's general secretariat for Inter-American conferences, special conferences, and consultative meetings of foreign ministers. The agency seeks to advance political and administrative collaboration among member states and preserve the peace of the hemisphere.

organized reserves. Officers and enlisted men who have received training in the armed services and who, while engaged in civilian pursuits, are subject to call to active duty in time of emergency.

organized territory. A territory with defined boundaries for which Congress has provided a system of laws and a settled government.

Orientals' exclusion. A former policy of the United States of barring immigration from certain Asian countries. Chinese, except for certain classes, were excluded from 1882 to 1943; Japanese were first excluded by law in 1924. Nominally, at least, no discrimination has been directed against nationals of Asian countries in American immigration policy since World War II. *See* immigration.

original jurisdiction. The power of a court to hear and determine cases in the first instance.

original-package doctrine. A rule, first enunciated by the Supreme Court as to foreign commerce in *Brown* v. *Maryland, q.v.*, and as to interstate commerce in *Leisy* v. *Hardin, q.v.*, that as long as the original package remains unsold or unbroken the contents are not subject to State taxing or regulative power. Acts of Congress abrogated the rule as to intoxicating liquors, 1890 and 1913; as to oleomargarine, 1902; and as to goods made by prison labor, 1929; thus allowing the States to prohibit or regulate the entry of such articles in the original package.

Orleans Territory. A territory created by Congress, Mar. 26, 1804, embracing all the present State of Louisiana except the roughly rectangular portion north of Lake Pontchartrain and east of the Mississippi.

orphans' court. A court, so-called in New Jersey, Pennsylvania, Delaware, and Maryland, which has jurisdiction over probate, administration of estates, and guardianship of minors. *Called also* surrogate's court. *See* surrogate.

Ostend Manifesto. A statement by American ministers to Great Britain, France, and Spain at Ostend, Belgium, Oct. 15, 1854, advising the United States to offer to purchase Cuba from Spain, and if Spain refused, to seize the island if its further possession by Spain appeared inimical to American domestic interests.

Our federal union, it must be preserved. A toast volunteered by President Jackson at a Jefferson Day dinner, Apr. 13, 1830, as a slap at John C. Calhoun. *See* nullification.

outdoor relief. Public assistance in the form of food, money, clothing, or medical services rendered to needy persons in their own homes.

outer space. *See* aerial domain.

outlawry of war. The denunciation of war as illegal. Some opinions hold that the Kellogg-Briand Pact, *q.v.*, outlawed war, but the pact did not expressly debar defensive warfare.

Overman Act. An act of Congress, passed during World War I, 1918, which authorized the President to create, coordinate, consolidate, or abolish agencies and bureaus and to transfer funds to accomplish purposes which he thought necessary to win the war.

overseer. A subordinate local officer usually engaged in the administration of charities or charged with the upkeep of roads.

oversight function. The duty imposed by law in 1946 on standing committees of the Senate and House of Representatives to exercise close scrutiny over the enforcement of laws by the executive branch; *called also* the watchdog function.

overt act. An open and manifest act of hostility. The requirement of the Constitution that in prosecutions for treason such an act must be proved by the testimony of two witnesses prevents a person from being convicted merely for hostile words or designs.

oyer and terminer. A court in certain States with jurisdiction over serious crimes;—from the phrase applied in England to the royal order directing judges on circuit to hear and determine certain causes.

P

P.A.C. Political Action Committee.

pacific blockade. A blockade instituted by one nation over some or all of the ports of another for the purpose of obtaining redress for an alleged injury without other hostile intentions.

Pacific Islands. *See* Trust Territory of the Pacific Islands.

pacific settlement. The adjustment of an international controversy by such peaceful means as commission of inquiry, conciliation, or arbitration.

Pacific States Telephone and Telegraph Co. v. Oregon. A case, 223 U.S. 118 (1912), in which a private corporation asked the Supreme Court to invalidate a State tax which had been imposed as the result of a popular initiative, its contention being that resort to the initiative had destroyed the republican (representative) form of government which Art. IV, Sec. 4 of the Constitution guarantees to each State. The Court refused jurisdiction, asserting that the question whether or not a State has a republican form of government is a political and not a justiciable question—one to be decided by Congress, not by the courts.

pacifism. 1. Opposition to war based on religious grounds or on revulsion against the destruction of life, moral standards, and property which war entails. **2.** The belief, often irrational but based on specifically cited historical experiences, that even for the victor the results of belligerency are not worth the cost and likely to be temporary, and that disputes between nations can be settled by arbitration, collective action, or other peaceful means.

pacifist. One who adheres to pacifism or to a policy of nonviolence. *Compare* conscientious objector.

packed caucus. A party primary meeting filled with supporters of a boss or machine, sometimes to the complete exclusion of other voters.

Packers and Stockyards Act. An act of Congress, Aug. 15, 1921, which prohibited unfair, discriminatory, and deceptive practices in the management of stockyards, giving preferences to localities, apportioning supply among packers, and trading in order to manipulate prices and create a monopoly, and which required stockyards to furnish services without discrimination.

pact. An agreement between two or more states usually less elaborate than a treaty but practically equivalent thereto.

pains and penalties. *See* bill of pains and penalties.

pairing. An agreement between members of a legislative body on opposite sides of an issue that in case of the absence of one the other will also be absent or will refrain from voting. Where a two-thirds vote is required two members for a measure may be paired with one against it.

palace guard. The group of advisers and intimates of the President or other influential White House employees. *Compare* kitchen cabinet.

Palisades Interstate Park. Probably the largest bi-State public park system in the United States. It consists of some 61,000 acres including the Palisades on the west bank of the Hudson from Fort Lee, N.J., to Newburgh, N.Y. The system was brought under the jurisdiction of a commission jointly created by New Jersey and New York in 1937 with the consent of Congress.

Palko* v. *Connecticut. A case, 302 U.S. 319 (1937), in which the Supreme Court ruled that the prohibition of double jeopardy, applicable to U.S. courts under the Fifth Amendment, is not included among the procedural limitations enforceable against State courts under the due-process clause of the 14th Amendment. The test of the applicability of procedural rights secured by that clause is never a formal one but, in the words of Justice Cardozo, depends on whether or not the action against a defendant is "so acute and shocking that our polity will not endure it."

Palmyra Island. An island in the Pacific, about 900 miles south of the Hawaiian group, owned by the United States and under the control of the Department of the Interior.

Panama Canal. An interoceanic waterway extending from Colón, on the Atlantic Ocean, to Panama, on the Pacific, a distance of 49 miles. Construction was begun in 1883 by a French company which afterward failed. In 1903 the United States negotiated a treaty with Colombia for a ninety-nine-year lease of a right of way on payment of $10,000,000 down and $250,000 annually, but the Colombian Congress refused to ratify it. Panama then declared her independence of Colombia, Nov. 4, 1903, and was recognized by the United States two days later. She agreed to cede a right of way ten miles wide for the amount previously offered to Colombia. The canal was opened in 1915. In 1921 the United States made a compensatory payment to Colombia of $25,-000,000. *See* Canal Zone.

Panama Congress. A meeting of representatives of several American republics held at Panama in 1826 on the call of the South American general Simón Bolívar to concert plans for an American league. Representatives of the United States were appointed, but were unable to attend.

Panama Refining Co. v. Ryan. See Hot Oil cases.

Pan American Health Organization. *See* Pan American Sanitary Bureau.

Pan-Americanism. 1. Advocacy of the cultural, economic, and political solidarity of the nations of the Western Hemisphere. **2.** The movement, principally sponsored by the United States, for economic, diplomatic, and military collaboration among the republics of the Western Hemisphere.

Pan American Sanitary Bureau. The executive organ of the Pan American Health Organization which provides consultative services and information to the American republics and, in cooperation with individual governments, conducts research relating to sanitation and epidemics.

Pan American Union. The principal administrative agency of the Organization of American States, *q.v.,* which imparts technical and other information and promotes cultural, social, economic, and juridical relations among American states. Among its publications is the monthly magazine *Americas* in English, Spanish, and Portuguese editions.

"Panay" incident. The sinking by Japanese planes of the United States gunboat "Panay" in the Yangtse River, Dec. 12, 1937. Although Japan later apologized and paid reparations, the action was apparently deliberate and part of a campaign directed against American interests in China.

panel. 1. A list of the jurors summoned to attend a court or to assist in trials of cases. **2.** A list of judges of a court, as The Hague Court of Arbitration.

panic. Sudden widespread fright over business conditions resulting in the dumping of securities on the markets, and sometimes in a business depression.

paper blockade. A blockade declared by one country against the ports of another and not enforced, or insufficiently enforced.

paper money. 1. Notes or certificates issued by a government or authorized bank which may be based on specific assets or on the general credit of the issuing authority, usually made a legal tender. **2.** Notes issued by State chartered banks before 1867.

parcel post. A package service of the post office begun Jan. 1, 1913.

pardon. A release from the legal consequences of a crime or a remission of penalties imposed, which may be issued as an act of grace by the competent executive authority before or after indictment or conviction. The President's pardoning power is complete except that he may not remove disabilities imposed as a result of conviction after impeachment. In some States the governor may grant pardons only with the consent of the State senate or council or on recommendation of a pardon board; or the pardon board, of which the governor may or may not be a member, is the pardoning authority. A *conditional pardon* becomes effective on compliance with conditions set forth. A *general pardon,* or amnesty, *q.v.,* applies to a class of persons.

Pardon Attorney. An official of the U.S. Department of Justice who considers all applications for federal pardons and makes recommendations for the exercise of presidential clemency.

pardons. *See* board of pardons.

Paris. *See* Treaties of Paris; Treaty of Paris.

parish. 1. A local government unit in Louisiana corresponding to a county in other States. 2. A minor governmental unit for ecclesiastical and other matters in Great Britain and several British colonies.

parity. 1. Equality such as for naval ships or tonnage of different nations. 2. Equivalence of prices of farm products in relation to those existing at some former date or to the general cost of living. 3. Equality for the standard of money in foreign exchange.

Parkinson's law. The view that any administrative task expands "in importance and complexity in a direct ratio with the time to be spent"; *specifically:* that work can be expanded almost without limit and hence provide employment for a constantly increasing staff;—formulated (with tongue in cheek) by C. Northcote Parkinson, Professor of History at the University of Malaya.

parliamentarian. 1. A supporter of parliamentary or responsible government. 2. One versed in the rules of a representative assembly. 3. An assistant who advises the presiding officer of a legislature on points of parliamentary law and usage.

parliamentary government. *See* parliamentary system; cabinet.

parliamentary procedure. The transaction of business in a deliberative body in accordance with established rules, usages, and precedents.

parliamentary system. 1. A government (as in the United Kingdom or in the Dominions of the Commonwealth) in which the executive, consisting of a prime minister and ministerial colleagues in a cabinet, directs the administration and exercises political leadership on condition that it shall at all times command the support of a majority of the legislature or parliament. Withdrawal of such support necessitates the resignation or reconstitution of the executive. 2. A similar regime on the European Continent and elsewhere in which, whatever the variations from the British system, the tenure of the executive depends on maintaining a supporting majority in the legislature.

parlor caucus. A secret meeting of party leaders for the purpose of agreeing on candidates or policies.

parochial school. An elementary or high school conducted under the direction of a religious organization. Under the First Amendment such a school may not receive direct public financial support.

parole. 1. A conditional release, generally under supervision of a parole officer, of a prisoner who has served part of the term for which he was sentenced to prison, which may be revoked if he fails to observe the conditions. 2. Release of a prisoner of war on his promise, approved by his government, not to bear arms against his captors.

Parole. *See* Board of Parole.

particularism. Devotion to the special interests of a state, section, group, or special interest rather than to the country as a whole.

partisan. 1. Pertaining to party rivalries and struggles; *especially:* denoting excessive devotion to party, as opposed to public, interests. 2. An adherent to a party or cause. 3. A member of a guerrilla band which conducts hostilities against its own government or harasses an invading force.

party. A body of voters organized for the purpose of influencing or controlling the policies and conduct of government through the nomination and, if possible, the election of its candidates to office. In some States a party is legally defined as a group which cast a certain number or percentage of votes at the last election for President or governor. A party is distinguished from other groups by its nomination of candidates and its tacit willingness to assume responsibility for the whole conduct of public affairs. Parties provide a means by which public sentiment may be expressed and ascertained and the policies of various branches of the government may be made consistent.

party affiliation tests. Various conditions in State laws, imposed as a prerequisite to participation in a closed primary, which require a voter to declare that he has generally supported the candidates of a party in past elections, that he intends to do so in the future, or that he has not voted in the primary of a different party within a given period.

party circle. A circle at the top of a party column on some ballots which a voter may use, by marking a cross in it, to vote a straight party ticket.

DEMOCRATIC PARTY	REPUBLICAN PARTY	SOCIALIST PARTY	SOCIALIST-LABOR PARTY	PROHIBITION PARTY
○	○	○	○	○
For President and Vice-President— FRANKLIN D. ROOSEVELT HENRY A. WALLACE	For President and Vice-President— WENDELL L. WILKIE CHARLES L. McNARY	For President and Vice-President— NORMAN THOMAS MAYNARD C. KRUEGER	For President and Vice-President— JOHN W. AIKEN AARON M. ORANGE	For President and Vice-President— ROGER W. BABSON EDGAR V. MOORMANN
For Senator in Congress— HARRY S. TRUMAN	For Senator in Congress— MANVEL H. (Cap) DAVIS	For Senator in Congress— W. F. RINCK	For Senator in Congress— THEODORE BAEFF	For Senator in Congress—
For Governor— LAWRENCE McDANIEL	For Governor— FORREST C. DONNELL	For Governor— JED A. HIGH	For Governor— WILLIAM W. COX	For Governor—
For Lieutenant-Governor— FRANK G. HARRIS	For Lieutenant-Governor— WM. P. ELMER	For Lieutenant-Governor— A. M. DEMAREE	For Lieutenant-Governor— MICHAEL L. HILTNER	For Lieutenant-Governor— WILLIAM J. CADY
For Secretary of State— DWIGHT H. BROWN	For Secretary of State— LOYD (Boots) MILLER	For Secretary of State— HENRY SIROKY	For Secretary of State— HENRY W. GENCK	For Secretary of State—
For State Auditor— FORREST SMITH	For State Auditor— J. T. WADDILL	For State Auditor— HELEN NICHOLS	For State Auditor—	For State Auditor—
For State Treasurer— WILSON BELL	For State Treasurer— SCOTT PETERS	For State Treasurer— LUCY HENSCHEL	For State Treasurer—	For State Treasurer—
For Attorney-General— ROY McKITTRICK	For Attorney-General— RAY MABEE	For Attorney-General— EDWARD J. FLYNN	For Attorney-General—	For Attorney-General—

Party Column Ballot—Showing party circle and party emblem and presidential short ballot (Missouri Ballot of 1940)

party column. A vertical division on the Indiana type of ballot in which are printed, under the name of a particular party, the names of all the candidates nominated by it for office.

party committee. A group chosen by a party convention or by voters in a primary election in practically every area in which one or more executive, legislative, or judicial officers are popularly elected. It assists in conducting an election campaign, and between sessions of the convention, it serves as a general executive committee for the party.

party convention. *See* convention 4; national convention.

party emblem. A device (as the Democratic Statue of Liberty or the Republican elephant) printed at the top of the party column or opposite the names of candidates on some ballots and voting machines to assist voters in identifying candidates of their party.

party finance. *See* campaign fund.

party line. 1. The policy of an authoritarian political organization to which all spokesmen for the organization must subscribe. **2.** The line across the face of a voting machine occupied by names of candidates of one party.

party organ. A newspaper which reflects the official or dominant views of a party.

party politics. Political activity concerned with advancing the program or interests of a party; *especially:* such activity directed toward securing offices and spoils.

party vote. A vote in a legislative assembly, committee, board, or other group more or less strictly according to party affiliations.

Passenger cases. Cases, 7 How. 283 (1849), in which the Supreme Court declared unconstitutional statutes of New York and Massachusetts imposing on shipmasters a head tax on each passenger brought into ports, the revenue to be used to assure the State against the passenger becoming a public charge or to provide the passenger with health services. These are the earliest cases recognizing that Congress has exclusive power over immigration.

pass examination. A noncompetitive civil service examination to determine whether or not the applicant possesses minimum qualifications.

passive resistance. Direct but nonviolent opposition to action of the government by a group of people which may take the form of mass civil disobedience, the disruption of traffic by crowding thoroughfares and entrances to public buildings, and the sit-in.

passport. An official document issued by competent authority of a government (in the United States, the Secretary of State) to a citizen or national, identifying him, permitting him to leave the country and travel abroad, and requesting protection for him from foreign states.

paster. A strip of paper bearing a candidate's name which a voter may paste on a ballot in some States as an alternative to writing in a name.

patent. An official document issued to the inventor of a new and useful process, machine, article of manufacture, or variety of plant entitling him to the exclusive right for a limited period (17 years in the United States) to control its production and sale. *See* land patent.

Patent Office. A federal agency, headed by a Commissioner of Patents, established in 1790 and since 1925 in the Department of Commerce, which examines applications for patents to determine if they are new and useful. Applications which are denied may be appealed to the office's Board of Appeals and then to the Court of Customs and Patent Appeals or to a U.S. district court. More than three million letters patent have been issued since 1790. Certain divisions of the office hear and decide upon applications under federal law for trademark registration.

paternalism. The practice of a government of intervening in affairs ordinarily deemed to be of private interest, as for the protection of persons from the consequences of their own ignorance; *specifically*: the supplying of economic and social services on the theory that they would not be supplied at all, or supplied as well, by private initiative.

Paterson plan. A series of nine resolutions to amend the Articles of Confederation by giving Congress more power, submitted to the federal Convention of 1787 by William Paterson of New Jersey. They were designed to counter the Virginia plan, *q.v.*, which the smaller States considered too nationalistic.

Pathfinder. A nickname of John C. Frémont, discoverer of new transcontinental routes, and first Republican presidential candidate, 1856.

patronage. The power to make appointments to office, when not governed by civil service laws or rules, or to grant contracts and various special favors.

Patronage committee. A committee appointed by the majority party caucus in each house of Congress to insure the equal distribution among members of patronage in appointments of Congressional employees.

Patrons of Husbandry. *See* Grange.

***Paul* v. *Virginia*.** A case, 8 Wall. 168 (1869), in which the Supreme Court held that insurance is not commerce and thereby effectively excluded it from the regulatory power of Congress under the interstate commerce clause. This decision was overruled in 1944. *See United States* v. *South-Eastern Underwriters Association*.

***Pax Brittanica*.** The concept that, like ancient Imperial Rome, Great Britain, with her far-flung empire and naval supremacy in the 19th century, was responsible for keeping the peace and maintaining international equilibrium from the end of the Napoleonic Wars to World War I.

pay-as-you-go plan. Provision for meeting extraordinary expenses, such as for capital projects (school buildings and highways) or during wartime, by increasing taxes rather than by borrowing.

Payne-Aldrich Tariff. A strongly protectionist tariff law, 1909, which was an important cause of the Progressive revolt of 1912.

payola. An indirect payment or bribe to an officer or employee.

payroll patriot. A civilian of military age who is employed by the government or in an essential industry during wartime;—used opprobriously.

payroll tax. 1. A federal tax of 3.1 per cent levied on most employers hiring four or more persons, the amount being calculated on total wages up to a maximum of $3,000 yearly for each employee. A credit of as much as 90 per cent is allowed employers for taxes they have paid to a State unemployment insurance system. The tax was purposely designed to induce States to establish such systems. 2. A similar tax levied by all States, but often embracing more employees and firms than the federal tax, and reducing tax liability of employers with records of furnishing steady employment. 3. A federal tax, scheduled to reach $4\frac{5}{8}$ per cent by 1968, on all wages up to a certain maximum a year (and colloquially also, a like amount deducted from employees' wages) as compulsory contributions to finance federal old-age, survivors and disability insurance for employees.

P.B.S. Public Buildings Service.

peace. A condition of domestic tranquillity within a state and of normal relations with other states.

peace conference. A meeting of representatives of belligerents to discuss and formulate terms of peace.

Peace Corps. An agency of the State Department, created in 1961, which recruits, trains, and assigns volunteer men and women for service abroad as teachers, agricultural workers, etc., primarily in developing nations. Payment is nominal, and volunteers are expected to live and work directly with the people whom they are assisting.

Peace Democrat. A Copperhead or a Northern Democrat who during the Civil War opposed the continuance of hostilities and proposed a settlement by conference between the sections.

peaceful coexistence. A doctrine, popularized by former Chairman Nikita Khrushchev of the Soviet Union, which, though insisting that the historical triumph of Communism and the extinction of capitalist society are inevitable, still maintains that capitalist and Communist societies can exist side by side indefinitely, engage in peaceful economic and ideological competition, and avoid military confrontation or nuclear war.

peaceful penetration. The acquisition of influence by a strong state over a weaker one by means of public and private loans, financial, military, and technical advisers, colonization, or other nonbelligerent activities.

peace offensive. Propagandist efforts by one belligerent expressing its devotion to peace and intended to cast the burden for continuing hostilities upon its enemy.

peace officer. A sheriff, deputy sheriff, marshal, constable, policeman, or other officer charged with maintaining public order.

Peace Ship. The ship, "Oscar II," chartered by Henry Ford, in which he and other peace advocates left New York, Dec. 4, 1915, on a voyage to Copenhagen and The Hague in an abortive attempt to persuade European leaders to end World War I.

peace without victory. A much criticized phrase in President Wilson's address to the Senate, Jan. 22, 1917, when he hoped to end World War I by mediation and avoid American participation in it.

peanut politics. Attention to trivial matters, to the neglect of urgent public business, for the purpose of winning votes.

Pearl Harbor. A primary American naval base in the Pacific with adjacent army installations situated near Honolulu, Hawaii. It was the objective of the surprise Japanese naval and air attack, Dec. 7, 1941, which brought the United States into World War II.

pear tree. *See* shaking the pear tree.

peculiar institution. *Slang.* Negro slavery.

peer. 1. An equal. A trial jury must be composed of persons who are peers (members of the general class) of the accused. **2.** A member of the British House of Lords.

Peerless Leader. A nickname of William Jennings Bryan.

penal administration. The maintenance and management of institutions and programs (as probation and parole) for the punishment and correction of criminals. The personnel of such an administration consists of prison and parole boards, wardens, guards, medical, pedagogical, and psychiatric staffs, and probation and parole officers.

penalty. A punishment by fine or imprisonment, or both, inflicted for violation of a law.

Pendleton Act. The civil service reform act passed by Congress, Jan. 16, 1883. *See* civil service.

penitentiary. A State or federal maximum-security institution designed for the punishment and correction of adult criminals serving terms of more than one year;—usually accepted as a synonym for prison.

Pennsylvania v. *Nelson.* A case, 350 U.S. 497 (1956), in which the Supreme Court reversed a conviction under a State sedition law on the grounds (*a*) that Congress, in passing the Smith Act, *q.v.*, and other acts, had evinced an intention to occupy or reoccupy the field of anti-seditious legislation; (*b*) that the federal interest is dominant and pervasive; and (*c*) that a State program in this area might conflict with federal aims. *Compare Uphaus* v. *Wyman.*

pension. A stated allowance paid at regular intervals to a former soldier or sailor or to a retired employee from a general fund; *also:* a fixed income to a disabled or retired employee or aged person from that portion of an insurance fund which was derived from public funds.

Pentagon. A five-sided office building in Arlington, Va., which houses the Department of Defense;—often used as a symbolic reference for the armed forces high command.

peonage. A condition of servitude which consists of compelling persons to perform labor in order to pay off a debt;—prohibited by the 13th Amendment. See *Pollock* v. *Williams*; *Taylor* v. *Georgia.*

people's lobby. One of several voluntary organizations formed for the purpose of combatting, in the interests of the general public, the activities of special-interest groups.

People's party. The official name of the Populists, *q.v.*

People's Power League. An organization in Oregon about 1900 which worked for the adoption of direct legislation, the primary election, and other governmental reforms.

per capita. For each inhabitant;—used to express the statistical ratio between the whole population of a community and some community resource or liability, such as wealth, tax burden, or public debt.

per curiam **opinion.** A brief announcement of the disposition of a case by a court not accompanied by a written opinion of one of its members. *Compare* memorandum opinion.

peremptory challenge. The right of counsel in a trial to reject a prospective juror without specifying any reason.

Perez v. *Brownell.* A case, 356 U.S. 44 (1958), in which the Supreme Court held that Congress contravened no provision of the Constitution when it stipulated, in the Nationality Act of 1940, that a native-born citizen who had voluntarily tried to expatriate himself (to avoid military service) and who had participated in a significant political election in a foreign state had forfeited his citizenship. Reversed by a five-to-four decision in *Afroyim* v. *Rusk* (No. 46, Oct. Term, 1966) on the ground that the 14th Amendment's definition of citizenship is binding on Congress and prevents deprivation of U.S. citizenship without the individual's own consent, as by naturalization in a foreign state. *Compare Trop* v. *Dulles.*

performance budget. A budget expressed in terms of the total cost of specifically enumerated works to be done or services to be provided, rather than in the usual form of itemizing salaries of employees and costs of different materials and services.

performance test. A test of an applicant's ability to do the tasks required in a position under actual or simulated conditions of employment.

periodic registration. Registration of voters before every election or at designated intervals of a few years.

Period of Personal Politics. The decade between 1820 and 1830, so-called because, after the disappearance of the Federalist party, the chief contests were among rival Republican leaders like Jackson, Adams, and Clay; *called also* Era of Good Feelings.

permanent appropriation. An appropriation for a public institution or a fixed expense which does not require re-enactment every year, but continues in effect until repealed.

Permanent Court of Arbitration. *See* arbitration 1.

Permanent Court of International Justice. An international tribunal, established at The Hague in 1920 under the auspices of the League of Nations, which had jurisdiction, if the states concerned gave their consent, in justiciable controversies, like the interpretation of a treaty or the obligations of states under international law. It was superseded in 1945 by the International Court of Justice, *q.v.*

Permanent Joint Board on Defense—United States and Canada. A joint American-Canadian board of ten members, set up by the President and the Canadian prime minister, Aug. 17, 1940, to study and correlate common measures for the defense of the northern half of the Western Hemisphere.

permanent registration. A system of registration of voters under which a completely new registration is made only at long intervals and the list is kept continuously up-to-date.

permissive powers. Powers conferred by a State legislature upon a municipal corporation or other local agency which may be exercised at its discretion;—distinguished from mandatory powers so conferred which must be exercised.

permit. An official paper identifying a person as one who is entitled to exercise some privilege under the law; *also:* a license.

perquisite. An emolument supplementing the regular salary of an official and acquired in the course of duty; *especially:* some form of supplementary income in kind, such as the use of an official car.

Perry* v. *United States. *See* Gold Clause cases.

persecution. A persistent attack of a prejudiced dominant group in a community upon a weaker group, usually because of national, racial, or religious differences, or economic rivalry.

persona grata. An acceptable diplomatic or consular officer.

persona non grata. A diplomatic or consular official not acceptable to the country to which he is sent.

personal liberty laws. Laws passed after 1850 by the legislatures of several Northern States which, by securing to fugitive slaves the privilege of the writ of habeas corpus and trial by jury, and by denying the use of jails to their pursuers, impeded the enforcement of federal fugitive slave laws.

personal politics. *See* Period of Personal Politics.

personal property. Money, chattels, and other movable goods or things separable from real estate.

personal union. The relationship between nations which share the same sovereign but have independent governments.

personation. An offense against the law which consists in acting under the title or name of another, as casting, or attempting to cast, a vote under the title or name of a registered voter or impersonating an officer.

personnel. The whole body of employees in the public service, in any division or branch thereof, or in any specified governmental or private enterprise.

personnel division. A part of a federal, State, or city civil service authority which prepares classification standards for the public service, assigns positions to particular services, classes, and grades, and promotes the development and more effective utilization of employees.

pet bank. A bank in which public funds are deposited as a result of official favor. The term originated in 1833 when President Jackson removed U.S. funds from the Bank of the United States to State-chartered banks.

petition. A formal written request addressed to some governmental authority. The right of the people to petition for redress of grievances is guaranteed by the First Amendment. Petitions signed by a certain number or percentage of voters are often required (*a*) to place the name of a candidate on a primary or general election ballot, (*b*) to initiate, or invoke the referendum on, legislation, or (*c*) to invoke the recall.

petition jobbing. Professional solicitation of signatures to electoral, referendum, or recall petitions.

Petition of Right. A declaration of the rights of the English people presented by Parliament to King Charles I and signed by him on June 7, 1628.

petit jury. A body at common law of twelve disinterested and impartial men, chosen from the community in which the trial is held, who render a verdict on questions of fact submitted in the trial of a case, later modified in many States by the introduction of women jurors, reduction in number of jurors, especially in civil cases, and provisions for less than unanimous verdicts except in the trial of persons accused of capital crimes;—so-called because fewer in number than a grand jury; *called also* trial jury.

Philippines. A group of more than 7,000 islands lying off the southeastern coast of Asia with a land area of 114,830 sq. mi., which were acquired by the United States at the end of the Spanish-American War. They were governed under military authority until 1901; under a governor and appointive commission, 1902–16; under a governor general appointed by the President and Senate and a popularly elected bicameral legislature, 1916–34; and by the Philippine Commonwealth, a protectorate, 1934–46 (government in exile at Washington during the Japanese occupation). They have been the fully independent Philippine Republic since 1946. By treaty the United States is permitted to maintain certain bases in the Islands.

PHS Public Health Service.

physical valuation. The worth of the tangible assets of a property arrived at by some recognized standard of appraisal, such as reproduction-cost, original-cost, replacement-cost, or prudent-investment-cost,—used as a basis for rate making.

picketing. 1. Carrying placards in a public place in order to protest against some policy of government. **2.** Patrolling the entrance of a factory or business establishment by members of a labor union in order to inform other employees and the public of the existence of a strike and to influence or deter them from entering.

Pick-Sloan Plan. A compromise plan of 1944 devised by General Lewis W. Pick of the army engineers and W. Glenn Sloan of the Bureau of Reclamation for the development of navigation, flood control, hydroelectric power, and irrigation in the Missouri River valley.

pie. *Slang.* Patronage or the spoils of office.

pie in the sky. The benefits that are supposed to accrue in the distant future as a result of accepting a Communist or other ideology.

Pierce v. Society of Sisters. A case involving an Oregon law that required all children between certain ages to attend a public school, thus preventing attendance at a private school. The Supreme Court, 268 U.S. 510 (1925), invalidated the law as a denial of the liberty of parents to direct the education of their children, a liberty protected by the due-process clause of the 14th Amendment.

pigeonholing. The practice of Congressional and legislative committees in most States, of withholding and failing to report out bills referred to them of which they disapprove.

Pinckney's Treaty. A treaty negotiated by Thomas Pinckney at San Lorenzo, Spain, Oct. 27, 1795, by which Spain relinquished her claim to territory north of the 31st parallel, opened the Mississippi River to free navigation by American citizens, granted them the right to deposit produce at New Orleans for a period of three years with the privilege of renewing the right either at New Orleans or another port, and agreed to make compensation for spoliations of American commerce.

pipe laying. *Slang.* Colonization, *q.v.*, of voters.

Pipe-Line cases. A series of cases, 234 U.S. 548 (1914), in which the Supreme Court held that the transportation of oil by pipeline across State boundaries was interstate commerce and therefore subject to Congressional legislation.

piracy. An act of violence committed at sea by individuals or armed vessels not acting under the authority of a state or of a belligerent or insurgent government.

pitiless publicity. A phrase used by Woodrow Wilson in his gubernatorial campaign in New Jersey in 1910. He promised to give the people full information of public affairs regardless of the effect on private interests.

pivotal State. A doubtful State having a large number of electoral votes. In a closely contested presidential election its vote may decide the result.

plank. A section of a party platform referring to a particular subject.

planning. A comprehensive study of present trends and of probable future developments, together with recommendations of policies to be pursued by governments. It embraces such subjects as population growth and distribution, social forces, availability of land, water, minerals, and other natural resources, technological progress, probable future revenues, expenditures, financial policies, and the international situation. Planning must necessarily be flexible and attuned to rapidly changing conditions. In federal, State, and metropolitan governments planning is provided for on a permanent basis.

platform. A statement of principles and of policies to be followed concerning a number of public questions, adopted by a party convention as a basis for the party's appeal for public support. Platforms nearly always result from compromises among conflicting sectional and economic interests and contain phrases designed to appeal to many different interests. Platforms are regarded as of less importance than candidates' campaign statements.

platoon system. The division of policemen or firemen into shifts, or platoons, each of which is on duty during certain hours of a twenty-four-hour day.

Platt Amendment. A rider on the army appropriation bill of Mar. 2, 1901, subsequently appended to the Cuban constitution and embodied in a treaty between Cuba and the United States, May 22, 1903, which provided that Cuba would not make an agreement with a foreign power that would impair her sovereignty, or contract an excessive public debt, and would allow the United States to intervene to preserve Cuban independence and maintain order, continue sanitary improvements, and grant land for naval bases to the United States. The Platt Amendment was abrogated by a treaty signed May 29, 1934.

Platte Purchase. The northwestern corner of Missouri which the United States purchased from the Pottawatomie Indians in

Platte Purchase

1836 and added to Missouri by an act of Congress, Mar. 28, 1837.

pleadings. Formal statements made in court by parties or their counsel to establish the issue of a controversy.

plebiscite. 1. *In Europe:* a vote of the people, usually by universal manhood or adult suffrage, on an issue submitted by the head of a state or a constituent assembly. **2.** A vote, usually administered by an international authority, of the inhabitants of a geographical region to determine to which of one or more adjacent states they prefer to be annexed.

plenary session. A meeting of all members of a deliberative body, as distinguished from a meeting of a committee of the same body.

plenipotentiary. A diplomat with full powers to negotiate (subject to ratification) on behalf of his state with the government of another state or to participate as a member of an international conference.

Plessy v. Ferguson. A case, 163 U.S. 537 (1896), in which the Supreme Court, with only one dissent, upheld a Louisiana law requiring "separate but equal" accommodations for white and Negro passengers on trains.

plum. A desirable appointment or political reward.

Plumb Plan. An abortive plan for government ownership of the railways, with private operation under lease, proposed to Congress in 1919 by Glenn E. Plumb, attorney for the railway brotherhoods, during hearings prior to the enactment of the Transportation Act, *q.v.*, of 1920, and the termination of wartime control and management of the railways under William G. McAdoo, Director General of the Railroads.

Plumed Knight. A nickname of James G. Blaine.

plumping. Giving all one's votes to one candidate, as under the system of cumulative voting used in Illinois.

plunderbund. A corrupt combination of politicians, contractors, and other economic interests that exploits the public.

pluralism. The doctrine that governmental authority within a community should be distributed among various functional groups and neither monopolized nor (according to some writers) shared in some matters by a sovereign power in the state.

plurality. The number by which the leading candidate's vote exceeds that cast for the next highest candidate, usually sufficient for election to office. *Compare* majority.

plural voting. The system formerly in effect (*a*) in several European countries by which voters were permitted to cast two or more votes when qualified by superior education or ownership of property; or (*b*) in some of the United States where a man was qualified to vote in every election precinct in which he owned land.

plutocracy. A government dominated by men of wealth; *also:* the political power of concentrated wealth.

pocket borough. An electoral area in England controlled by the influence of one man;—applied to certain constituencies in the United States.

pocket veto. The failure of the President to sign a bill passed by Congress within ten days before the adjournment of a session. Such an unsigned bill does not become law. **2.** Failure of a governor to sign a bill within the period specified in the State constitution.

Point Four Program. Appropriations for technical assistance, both with trained personnel and with production goods, to improve education, health, sanitation, agriculture, power resources, transportation, and manufacturing in underdeveloped countries;—proposed by President Truman as the fourth point in his inaugural address, Jan. 20, 1949, and implemented by acts of Congress beginning June 5, 1950.

point of order. A question raised by a member of a deliberative body as to the propriety of a motion or proceeding under the rules. The presiding officer is required to rule on it immediately, and his ruling is subject to appeal to the floor.

police. An organized body of municipal, county, or State officers engaged in maintaining public order, peace, and safety, and in investigating and arresting persons suspected or formally accused of crime.

police court. A municipal tribunal which tries those accused of violating local ordinances or acts as a tribunal for the preliminary examination and commitment of those accused of graver offenses, and is essentially equivalent to the criminal court of a justice of the peace in rural communities.

police jury. The administrative board of a parish in Louisiana, equivalent to a county board elsewhere.

police power. The power of the State to place restraints on the personal freedom and property rights of persons for the protection of the public safety, health, and morals or the promotion of the public convenience and general prosperity. It is a residuary power of the States. It extends over a multitude of subjects, and may involve taking or destroying property (as in the abatement of a nuisance) or debarring a person from pursuing a trade, or forcing him to submit to vaccination; and it may affect the movement of interstate commerce through quarantine regulations, requirements of proper safety devices on trains, and adequate service to a community. The police power is subject to limitations of the federal and State constitutions, and especially to the requirement of due process, *q.v.* The need of the general public for legislation must be relatively great; the inconvenience to the individual must be relatively slight; and the restraints imposed must be adapted to secure the end in view. In balancing these principles, court decisions tend to vary with the judge's knowledge of the social situation which a statute is designed to improve and the probable burden of the restraint on the individual.

police review board. A board set up in some cities to investigate complaints by individuals, and especially by minority groups, of discourteous, brutal, or illegal treatment by police officers engaged in making arrests or keeping the peace, and when warranted, to make appropriate recommendations to the head of the police department.

police state. A state (as a totalitarian state or one operating under a dictatorship) which confers special powers over the rights of individuals upon its ordinary or secret police, or military, vesting them with discretion to arrest, detain, incarcerate, and sentence individuals without formal trial or forms of law, and which refuses to be bound by established canons of due process, or by the principle that the rights of individuals shall be adjudicated in established courts of justice.

police station. A local command post in a police department.

policy committee. The executive committee of each major party's caucus (or conference) in each house of Congress, which coordinates the work of party members on standing or special committees, plans party strategy on the floor, directs a permanent research and planning staff, and, though responsible for developing a legislative program for the party, has no real power to impose such a program.

Political Action Committee. An organization created and financed by the Congress of Industrial Organizations during World War II to promote the political interests of the latter's affiliated unions in primary and general elections. Reputedly nonpartisan, it usually endorsed and supported Democratic candidates, especially Presidents F. D. Roosevelt and Truman, and was succeeded by COPE, *q.v.*

political assessment. A levy, usually in proportion to salary and collected every payday, which is sometimes imposed by a political organization on holders of appointive positions under an implied threat of dismissal or delay in promotion. Such levies are forbidden by civil service laws.

political bargain. An agreement between two factions or parties, as for the withdrawal of a candidate in consideration of a division of appointments or other spoils of office.

political blackmail. The corrupt exploitation of political influence or official position by a member of a legislature, public officer, or political boss in order to extort money or other favors from private citizens or corporations.

political clearance. The influence and support of party leaders, including letters and endorsements from county or local chairmen, commonly required as a prerequisite for appointment to unclassified or "spoils" positions but contrary to the spirit of civil service reform.

political club. A local organization which engages in various social, educational, and charitable activities for the purpose of winning votes and which is usually controlled by the recognized local party leader.

political departments. The executive and the legislature. *See* political question.

political disability. Any condition, such as physical or mental incapacity, minority, conviction of crime, or lack of citizenship, which disqualifies a person from holding public office.

political geography. A branch of geography concerning frontiers, boundaries of States, counties, municipal corporations, and other units for regional or local administration, and the location of principal administrative centers within the units.

political liberty. The privileges accorded citizens of a free government to participate in that government's operations and, through the elective franchise and otherwise, to influence and control public policy and the conduct of public affairs.

political offense. An offense against public security committed for the purpose of changing the form of government, or the persons in office, or altering the laws by illegal means. It is usually not extraditable.

political party. *See* party.

political prisoner. A person held in custody for a political offense who usually cannot be extradited under existing treaties.

political question. An issue which the U.S. Supreme Court abstains from resolving primarily because it would be trespassing on the authority of one of the political branches (legislature or executive) or would involve the Court in serious problems of enforcing its decisions. Presidential assertions concerning the boundaries or property rights of the United States (*Foster* v. *Neilson*), or the enforcement of acts of Congress in the Reconstruction period (*Mississippi* v. *Johnson*), or Congressional power to determine how long a constitutional amendment may remain before the States for ratification (*Coleman* v. *Miller*), or the power of the President and Congress to determine whether or not a State has a republican form of government (*Luther* v. *Borden*), are political questions.

political right. A privilege or right (as of the suffrage or of representation, or of legislators to speak and vote freely) which is conferred by federal or State constitutions or statutes. Under recent constitutional amendments and Supreme Court decisions, the former distinction between political privilege and civil right has tended to disappear.

political science. 1. The study of the state and its government which, though often speculative, is normally inductive in nature and makes use of disciplined observations, statistics, various interviewing techniques to test opinion, careful comparison of data yielded by different methods, and generalizations based on facts thus obtained. **2.** An academic discipline which includes political theory, analytical and comparative study of government, constitutional law, public administration, international relations, political parties, and public opinion.

political sovereignty. *See* sovereignty.

political theory. The entire body of doctrine relating to the origin, form, behavior, and purpose of the state. This body of doctrine may be classified as follows: ethical, speculative, sociological, legal, and scientific. (*a*) *Political ethics* or *political philosophy* is fundamentally a branch of ethics. It deals with what ought to be in the realm of political matters and its method consists of systematic rational analysis of common-sense notions and relevant data. (*b*) *Speculative political theory* consists of imaginative constructions of ideal or utopian states such as may be found in Plato's *Republic*, More's *Utopia* (1516), and Campanella's *City of the Sun* (1623). (*c*) *Sociological political theory* may be described as a part of the broader theory of society. Its method is analytical and empirical and it seeks to determine the relation of the state to other aspects of society and to analyze the state as a form of social organization. (*d*) *Legal political theory* deals with the nature of law, the juristic concept of sovereignty, and legal situations arising out of the institutions and devices for distributing and controlling the exercise of political power. (*e*) *Scientific political theory* consists largely of empirical observations of political phenomena to ascertain probable trends or generalizations, the equivalent of laws in the empirical sciences. The study of the course and nature of political change, the relative efficiency of various governmental and administrative forms and processes, and the probable effect of given political institutions upon human liberty and social well-being fall into this category. Although there is a vast and rich literature on the subject, political theory is not a well-integrated body of doctrine.

politician. 1. A person versed in public affairs and skilled in adjusting conflicting interests within a state and in the creation and guidance of public policy. 2. A manager of party affairs or a mere manipulator of public sentiment for private gain;—used disparagingly.

politics. 1. The art and science of organizing the state and managing its affairs, both internal and external. 2. The art of controlling, protecting, assisting, and governing individuals and groups in society. 3. The art of developing and guiding public policy. 4. The adjustment and regulation of the complex of relationships among individuals and groups. 5. The organization of political parties and the promotion of candidacy for public office. 6. The policy-forming function of government, as distinguished from administration and law. 7. *In some colleges and universities*: the designation, somewhat more comprehensive than either government or political science, *qq.v.*, for studies of the state. 8. The manipulation, often by resort to intrigue, of public affairs for private or factional advantage;—used disparagingly.

polity. 1. A state. 2. Organization and management of public affairs. 3. The constitution or guiding principles on which the organization and operation of a state are based.

poll. 1. The counting of individual voters as they announce their preference for different candidates. 2. The result of such a count. 3. The election precinct:—usually used in the plural. 4. Privately conducted interviews to ascertain opinion on some question or personality.

pollbook. The register of voters at an election precinct.

Pollock v. Farmers' Loan and Trust Co. A case, 157 U.S. 429 (1894), 158 U.S. 601 (1895), in which the Supreme Court decided that an income tax was a direct tax and that, consequently, the federal income tax law of 1894 was unconstitutional because Congress had not apportioned it among the States according to population; canceled by the 16th Amendment.

Pollock v. Williams. A case, 322 U.S. 4 (1944), in which the Supreme Court laid down the broad proposition that the 13th Amendment prohibited all legislation which would compel a person to perform labor because of a debt. *See* peonage.

pollster. A nickname, popularized by President Harry S. Truman during his campaign of 1948, for one who conducts public-opinion polls, usually implying contempt and ridicule for his methods and findings. Sampling of opinion on major public and political issues, and on the acceptability of candidates for office, has become a major activity since 1948 and, on the whole, is accorded increasing respect by the public.

poll tax. A direct personal tax usually levied at a stated rate on all male persons (and sometimes on women); *called also* a capitation tax. In some States exemptions are granted to war veterans, physically or mentally disabled persons, or paupers. Payment of poll taxes was formerly required in a few States as a prerequisite for voting; but this was prohibited in federal elections by the 24th Amendment, and in State elections by later decisions of the Supreme Court. *See Harper v. Virginia State Board of Elections.*

pooling. An agreement among competitors to avoid the detrimental effects of unhampered competition by fixing common prices, or by allocating available markets or their common income or profits according to a fixed ratio, which are illegal under antitrust legislation in the United States.

poor farm *or* **poor house.** An institution maintained by a local government unit for the shelter of the aged poor, orphans, and sometimes incapacitated or mentally defective persons.

poor man's dollar. The silver dollar, according to advocates of free and unlimited coinage of silver about 1896.

poor relief. Public assistance to needy families or persons, usually financed and administered by local government units.

Poor Richard. A pen name assumed by Benjamin Franklin.

Popocrat. A nickname given by Republicans to a Democrat who, in the campaign of 1896 or 1900, espoused Populist issues.

popular assembly. 1. A meeting of citizens of a local community or of their representatives for the transaction of public affairs. 2. A legislative body consisting of representatives elected by the people.

popular sovereignty. 1. Supreme and unlimited power of the indeterminate mass of the people to create and alter the fundamental structure of a government, an idea asserted by many writers including the Monarchomachs, Rousseau, and the draftsmen of the Declaration of Independence. Several State constitutions declare that all power resides in the people. 2. The power of the people, represented in the territorial legislature, to admit or exclude slavery, such as in the disputes over Kansas.

popular vote. The vote of the qualified electorate, as distinguished from that of the electoral colleges.

population. The total number of people residing in a country, State, political subdivision, or geographical area; and within any of these, further classified according to age, sex, color, birthplace, nationality, and occupation;—used as the basis for the apportionment of Congressional and legislative districts, and important in the allocation of grants-in-aid and provision for governmental agencies and services.

population explosion. The rapid increase in population throughout the world, especially since the end of World War II, which has resulted from greatly improved sanitary and medical facilities, more dependable food supplies, and, in some countries, earlier family formation and increased birth rates.

Populists. Members of the People's party, organized in 1891 by agricultural and labor groups, who demanded the free and unlimited coinage of silver, an increase of $50 per capita in the amount of greenbacks in circulation, public ownership of railroads, telegraphs, and telephones, recapture of lands formerly granted to railroads, and a graduated income tax. In 1892 they cast 1,027,329 popular, and 22 electoral votes for James B. Weaver for President. They disappeared after 1908.

pork. Appropriations, appointments, and favors obtained by a representative for his district.

pork barrel. The federal treasury from which, by logrolling, *q.v.*, Congressmen vote appropriations for river and harbor improvements, public buildings, navy yards, army posts, and government offices which are of special benefit to their districts and to their campaigns for re-election.

port of entry. A place where a customhouse is established.

Port of New York Authority. A self-supporting corporate agency, its income derived largely from tolls, set up jointly by New York and New Jersey under an interstate compact in 1921 to develop and maintain important public works in the Metropolitan New York-New Jersey area. These include the George Washington, Verrazano, and Goethals bridges, the Lincoln and Holland tunnels, La Guardia, Kennedy International, and Newark airports, surface transportation, terminals, and piers. Its administration is under 12 nonsalaried commissioners, an equal number of whom are appointed by the governors of New York and New Jersey.

position classification. The grouping of civil service positions according to the responsibilities which must be assumed, the duties performed, and the qualifications required of the holders.

position paper. A statement on some issue "researched" by members of a volunteer or official staff to provide a basis for a speech by a candidate for office or a public official.

positive law. Law consisting of definite rules of human conduct with appropriate sanctions for their enforcement, both prescribed by a determinate human superior or sovereign;—defined by John Austin and others of the positive school of jurisprudence which owed much of its inspiration to the French social theorist, Auguste Comte.

posse comitatus. 1. The power of the county. 2. The whole body (under the common law all male persons over 15 years of age) which the sheriff may summon to assist him in law enforcement; *also:* the body he summons.

postaudit. Periodic examinations of the financial records of government departments to determine whether their expenditures have been made in accordance with law. *Compare* preaudit.

Post Office Department. A principal administrative department of the federal government which handles the mails and conducts in addition a registry, money order, and parcel post service. It was created a department on June 8, 1872, although its origins can be traced in an unbroken line from the appointment of Alexander Spotswood in 1727 as deputy postmaster general for the colonies. Its head, the Postmaster General, has been a member of the President's Cabinet since 1829.

post road. Any road or other channel of communication designated as a mail route. Whether the phrase "To establish . . . post roads," authorized Congress to build new roads or merely to designate existing roads was for many years warmly debated.

Potsdam Conference. A conference of the "big three," President Harry S. Truman, Prime Minister Clement R. Attlee of the United Kingdom, and Premier Josef Stalin of the U.S.S.R., at Potsdam, Germany, July-August, 1945, which called upon Japan to surrender or face utter devastation and debated reparations and other conditions of peace for a Germany which had surrendered unconditionally.

Powell v. Alabama. *See* Scottsboro cases.

power politics. The use of naval demonstrations, pacific blockades, mobilization of military forces, reprisals, intervention in internal affairs, and threats as instruments of national policy.

power structure. 1. The formal and informal relationships existing among influential leaders, organizations, and groups (as in business, labor, religion, or journalism) within any defined community, which set general limits to political action and persist in spite of changes in factional or party control of elective offices. 2. The groups which possess a practical monopoly of political power in a pluralistic society.

P.R. Proportional representation.

practical examination. A civil service examination which seeks to determine training and fitness of an applicant for a particular position rather than general knowledge and mental aptitude.

preamble. An introductory statement prefixed to a constitution or statute setting forth the circumstances or reasons which led to its adoption or passage. It is not regarded as a part of the law; but in case of ambiguity in the body of the document, the courts may refer to it to ascertain the intentions of the framers.

preaudit. Determination by a comptroller or equivalent officer of the existence of a legislative appropriation for a claim before authorizing its payment. *Compare* postaudit.

precedent. A judicial, administrative, or legislative decision deemed of sufficient weight to be followed in subsequent cases. The conclusiveness of a precedent depends greatly upon the authority and prestige of the body which established it, and upon its adherence to just principles, its reasonableness, and the length of time it has stood unchallenged.

precinct. 1. A minor division for police administration in a city or ward. 2. A county or municipal subdivision for casting and counting votes in elections.

precinct captain. A person appointed by a ward, township, or other party leader who takes charge of the interests of the party in a voting precinct, especially by performing favors for, or otherwise cultivating, the voters in the precinct, influencing doubtful voters, and seeing to it that members of his party are properly registered and go to the polls when an election occurs.

precinct committeeman. A person elected by the party voters in a precinct who performs the same functions as a precinct captain, *q.v.*

preemption doctrine. A canon of constitutional interpretation in accordance with which the Supreme Court has declared State laws invalid if they are in conflict with valid federal laws when Congress has specifically or by implication stated its intention to occupy a field of legislation lying on the border between federal and State jurisdictions. *See Pennsylvania v. Nelson*; national supremacy.

preemption right. Under former land laws, the right of a person who first marked a tract of land to acquire a legal title to it.

preference primary. *See* presidential primary.

preferential shop. An industrial establishment in which preference is given to union men in hiring and layoff, but nonunion men may be hired when members of the union are not available.

preferential tariff. A tariff law permitting goods of one or a few countries to enter at lower rates than are imposed on products of other countries.

preferential voting. A scheme under which a voter marks first, second, third choices, etc., opposite the names of candidates on a primary or general election ballot. If no candidate has a majority of first choices, the second and later choices may be successively added until one candidate has a majority. *See* Bucklin plan; Ware plan.

preliminary canvass. An investigation of the probable outcome of an election conducted by a party organization through its ward, district, and precinct leaders.

preparedness. Readiness, through adequate naval, air, and military establishments and supplies of critical materials, for a possible war.

preprimary convention. A party convention to present platform planks or endorse a slate of candidates held in advance of a primary election.

prerogative. A right inherent in an office which may be exercised without responsibility to any other authority. Certain powers of the President (as in recognizing a foreign government) and of the Speaker of the House of Representatives (as in the recognition of members) are often called prerogatives.

prescription. 1. Acquisition of sovereignty over a territory by reason of continuous and undisturbed possession over a long period. 2. Acquisition of a personal right to use a way, water, light and air by reason of immemorial usage or long-continued enjoyment.

presentment. A written statement by a grand jury, made of their own knowledge or from statements of witnesses, and without a bill of indictment being presented by the prosecuting officer, accusing a person of having committed an offense against the law. *Compare* indictment.

President. The chief executive of the United States. The Constitution vests in the President virtually complete control of the nation's foreign relations, including the conduct of diplomacy, the leadership of the armed forces, the making of international agreements, and, with the consent of two-thirds of the Senate, the making of treaties. His general administrative powers include the appointment, by and with the advice and consent of the Senate, of principal officers of the government; exclusive power to appoint many other officers; general supervision of the executive departments and agencies; and the power to see that the laws are faithfully executed which is implemented by presidential control of law-enforcement agencies and discretionary authority conferred on him by statute. The President may pardon offenses against the United States. His legislative powers include authority to interpose a veto to the enactment of any bill or resolution, a two-thirds vote of each house of Congress being necessary to override the veto; the power to call Congress or either house into special session; and the power to recommend policy to the Congress by message or oral address. The prestige of the office, the President's ready access to information and opinion-molding mediums (as radio, television, and the press), his power to dispense patronage, and his position as leader of his party have all contributed toward making the more recent Presidents the real leaders in legislation and domestic policy. Electoral colleges choose the President by a majority vote from among candidates selected by the major parties at quadrennial conventions, but in practice the electoral colleges are chosen by a plurality of the voters in each State and the District of Columbia. Until 1940 and 1944, when F. D. Roosevelt was elected to additional terms, usage restricted an incumbent President to two terms of four years each. The Twenty-second Amendment, *q.v.*, now restricts a President to two terms. The President's salary is $100,000 per year with many perquisites and allowances. *See* presidential disability; presidential succession; White House Office.

president. 1. The chief of state of a republic whose powers range in different countries from chief executive and leader in legislation to the performance of merely dignified and ceremonial duties, with at times some political influence in the choice of a new ministry after a cabinet crisis. **2.** The chief or presiding officer of many administrative boards and commissions, of a local government body, or of a legislative house.

presidential agent. A personal representative of the President sent to a foreign state in the capacity of observer or adviser or to conduct negotiations on some special subject. Though normally not a regular diplomat, he may be given a courtesy diplomatic status.

presidential disability. A condition of the President's inability to discharge the powers and duties of his office during which he may voluntarily devolve them on the Vice President; or the Vice President, with the approval of a majority of the cabinet or other body designated by law, may take them over until the President by written declaration to Congress resumes them. In case of a dispute between the President and the Vice President and cabinet over the President's inability, Congress must assemble immediately if not in session and decide the issue within twenty-one days; by a two-thirds vote of both houses it may determine that the President is unable to discharge the powers and duties of his office. *See* Twenty-fifth Amendment.

presidential elector. A person chosen within a State (now always by popular vote of the State at large, though formerly sometimes by the State legislature or the voters of a Congressional or other district) who meets with other electors at the State capital and casts one vote for a presidential, and one vote for a vice-presidential, candidate.

presidential government. A system of government in which there is a chief executive, chosen by an authority independent of the legislature, and heads of departments (who are not members of the legislature or subject to dismissal by it for lack of confidence), appointed by the chief executive and exercising powers subject to his direction. *Compare* parliamentary system.

Presidential Medal of Freedom. A special award, established in 1963, that is bestowed by the President, with the advice of the Distinguished Civilian Service Awards Board, upon a civilian for outstanding contributions to the nation's security and welfare, to world peace, or to worthy cultural endeavors.

Presidential Medal of Freedom

presidential primary. A primary election to enable voters to express a preference among candidates for President by voting either directly for a candidate or for delegates to the national party convention who may, or may not, be pledged to vote for a particular candidate. The result is morally, but not legally, binding on delegates. Its use is either mandatory or optional under the laws of about one-third of the States. *Called also* preference primary.

presidential short ballot. A ballot, headed by the names of nominees for President and Vice President, which omits the names of individual candidates for presidential elector and allows a voter, by making only one mark, to vote for all the electors nominated by one party in a State.

presidential succession. The order in which officials succeed to the presidency in case of the removal, resignation, death, or legal disability of the President. The Vice President is next in line. After him Congress at first, by act of 1792, provided for the succession of the President pro tempore of the Senate and then of the Speaker of the House. In 1886 this law was repealed and the succession devolved upon the heads of the seven departments then in existence, nearly in the order of the creation of their offices. A third change was made by Congress in 1947, the succession after the Vice President devolving (in order) upon the Speaker of the House, the President pro tempore of the Senate, the Secretaries of State, the Treasury, and Defense, the Attorney General, the Postmaster General, and the secretaries of the Interior, Agriculture, Commerce, and Labor. The 20th and 25th Amendments provided for the succession to the presidency in certain unusual circumstances.

presidential timber. A person who, because of a wide public following, acceptability to party "regulars," political leadership in a pivotal State, political ability, or for other reasons, is popularly regarded as qualified to be a party's nominee for the presidency.

presidential year. A year in which a presidential election occurs. *Compare* off-year election.

President pro tempore. A member of the Senate chosen by that body to preside over its sessions when the Vice President is absent. The position has been permanent since 1876.

President's clubs. Fund raising organizations of the Democratic party, begun 1962, and open to persons who contribute $1,000 annually, in return for which they may participate in public affairs seminars and eat a free dinner which the President attends.

President's Committee on Administrative Management. A group of three administrative experts who, in 1937, presented a comprehensive *Report with Special Studies* on the reorganization of the executive branch. It was submitted to Congress at about the same time as the President's court-packing plan, *q.v.*, and was largely ignored. *Compare* Hoover Commission.

President's Re-employment Agreement. The blanket code authorized by the National Industrial Recovery Act and signed after July 27, 1933, by nearly all employers of labor who agreed to observe maximum weekly hours and minimum wages for employees, the maintenance of wages and of prices for their products, and the abolition of child labor.

press. *See* freedom of speech and press.

press gallery. That portion of the gallery of a legislative chamber reserved for representatives of various news mediums.

pressure group. An organization which promotes specific economic, social, moral, or other causes by employing agents or lobbyists to influence legislators and public officials, endorsing candidates nominated by political parties, and conducting systematic educational or propaganda campaigns among the general public.

previous question. A call usually for the original substantive motion which, in the House of Representatives, may be moved for the passage of a bill, an amendment, or a motion or series of motions. It is not debatable. If passed, it has the effect of stopping all debate and amendment and of bringing the question to an immediate vote. If there has been no debate in the House or in committee of the whole when the previous question is moved, each side is allowed twenty minutes before a vote is taken.

price administration. *See* Office of Price Administration; Office of Price Stabilization.

price ceiling. A legally established maximum price for a commodity or service.

price fixing. 1. An agreement among producers or distributors to maintain an arbitrary price for a commodity or service, normally illegal although occasionally countenanced by law. 2. The establishment of a scale of maximum prices for selected commodities or services by legislation or by administrative order, a normal part of a government rationing system or of a public plan to encourage production, distribution, or export of certain commodities such as agricultural staples.

price support. Any action by government to bolster prices to producers or distributors, as by legally prescribed minimum prices; by public loans to enable producers or distributors to keep goods off the market, thereby keeping prices from falling; by government purchases of surpluses to accomplish the same result; or by public subsidies to compensate producers or distributors for the difference between the market price and a legally established higher price.

primary. 1. A mass meeting or primary assembly of voters belonging to one party. 2. A primary election.

primary election. A preliminary election for the nomination of candidates for office or for the choice of party committeemen or of delegates to a party convention, designed as a substitute for party conventions. Primary elections are classified (*a*) as *closed* or *open* depending on whether or not tests of party affiliation are required for participation; (*b*) as *mandatory* or *optional*, depending upon whether the State law requires a primary or leaves to each party discretion to adopt it or not and merely provides machinery for its operation; and (*c*) as *nonpartisan* if party designations do not appear on the primary ballot. The first primary laws, beginning in 1871, were optional. About 1890 the adoption of the Australian ballot prepared by State authority encouraged the passage of mandatory laws, though it was not until 1904 that the first mandatory Statewide law was passed. In a few Southern States the primary election is held under party rules and is optional for parties casting a small percentage of the total vote. *See* presidential primary; runoff primary.

prime minister. The head of the council of ministers in a cabinet or parliamentary system of government.

primogeniture. The right of the eldest son under English law to inherit all real property. It was abolished in America by colonial legislatures or by the States in the Revolutionary or Confederation periods.

prison. An establishment for the incarceration of persons convicted of, usually, the more serious crimes. *See* penitentiary.

prisoner. A person under arrest, held in custody, or imprisoned by lawful authority.

prisoner of war. A member of the armed forces of a belligerent who has been captured by the enemy. The protection of such persons has been the subject of numerous international agreements. *See* Geneva Convention.

prison labor. Work performed by convicts, usually designed to teach useful skills and promote rehabilitation. Products made by prison labor are used principally in government institutions and are debarred by law from interstate commerce.

private bill. A bill for the relief or special benefit of an individual or a locality. Under the terms of the Legislative Reorganization Act, *q.v.*, of 1946, private bills authorizing payment for property damage, for certain torts, and for most types of pension claims, or permitting the construction of bridges across a navigable water or correction of a military or naval record may not be introduced in either house of Congress. Many State constitutions prohibit legislation except by general law.

private calendar. A calendar of the House of Representatives (officially styled the Calendar of the Committee of the Whole House), containing all private bills, which may be called on the first and third Tuesday of each month in numerical order, and unless a bill is deferred by the objection of two members it is immediately considered as a whole under the five-minute rule.

privateer. An armed private vessel formerly authorized by letter of marque and reprisal to cruise against enemy naval or merchant vessels. Privateering was abolished by the Declaration of Paris, 1856, which the United States observed; but not being a signatory, it could not effectively protest against Confederate privateering.

private function. A proprietary function, *q.v.*, in municipal government.

private international law. The usages adopted by municipal courts (i.e., those within a country) in dealing with cases involving private persons whose problems are affected by conflicting national laws or regulations or are subject to the jurisdictions of two or more states; *called also* conflict of laws.

private law. The law which regulates the relations of individuals with each other. *Compare* public law.

private property. *See* property.

private right. A right enjoyed by the individual under law. Many such rights are enumerated in bills of rights of the federal and State constitutions.

privilege. 1. Any favor or exemption granted by law, as to be protected by the government, to enjoy life and liberty, to acquire property, to travel from place to place, or to have access to courts and government offices. 2. The right of freedom of debate in a legislative body and the exemption of its members from arrest for words spoken there.

privileged question. A motion which under the rules of a legislative body has precedence over other motions.

privileges and immunities clause. 1. Art. IV, Sec. 2 of the Constitution which, as interpreted in *Crandall* v. *Nevada, q.v.*, and subsequent cases, guarantees certain rights appertaining to national citizenship which no State may abridge, including the rights of access to the seat of the federal government and to U.S. courts and of participating in federal elections. In *Twining* v. *New Jersey, q.v.*, privileges of national citizenship are identified as those which arise out of "the nature and essential character of the national government, or are specifically granted or secured to all citizens or persons by the Constitution. . . ." 2. A provision of the 14th Amendment designed to protect rights of national citizenship against impairment by the States which was narrowly interpreted in the Slaughterhouse Cases, *q.v.*, and later cases and is not to be compared in effectiveness with the due-process and equal-protection clauses of the same section.

Privy Council. *In the United Kingdom:* An ancient council of the Crown whose membership includes all former and present cabinet ministers, whose formal sanction is essential to the validity of an order in council, *q.v.*, and whose judicial committee, though technically an advisory body, is the highest court of appeal for residents of the British colonies and dependencies.

Prize cases. Four cases, 2 Black 635 (1863), in which the Supreme Court upheld the action of President Lincoln in imposing a blockade of ports in the South controlled by rebels against the United States.

prize court. A tribunal before which the legality of the capture of a vessel or other private property by a belligerent at sea is determined by condemnation, *q.v.*, proceedings.

probate. Proof before the proper judicial officer that a document is the last will of a deceased person. It establishes prima facie that a will is in proper form, and that the testator was competent.

probate court. A court having general supervision over probate of wills, administration of estates, and, in some States, empowered to appoint guardians or approve the adoption of minors. *See* surrogate.

probation. The status of a person who is allowed his freedom after conviction for a crime subject to the condition that for a stipulated period he shall conduct himself in a manner approved by a special officer to whom he must make periodic reports.

probationary period. *Civil service.* The period (usually six months) during which a newly appointed employee learns his duties and becomes adjusted to his job, or may be dismissed without right of appeal or reinstatement.

probe. An investigation by a legislative committee or a grand jury.

procedural law. A branch of law which prescribes in detail the methods or procedures to be used in determining and enforcing the rights and duties of persons toward each other under substantive law, *q.v.*

procedural right. The right of a person to have his case determined before a judicial or administrative tribunal according to the forms set forth in a constitution or law. All procedural provisions of the U.S. Constitution must be observed by federal courts but they are not essential to due process of law in unincorporated territories, *q.v.*, if other methods insuring fairness and impartiality are followed. *Compare* substantive right.

processing tax. A tax levied on millers, packers, and other processors of agricultural products by the Agricultural Adjustment Act of 1933.

proclamation. A published statement by a President, governor, mayor, or other executive officer declaring the existence of certain conditions, announcing a policy, or calling for some public observance.

production credit association. One of several hundred cooperative associations which, under the supervision of the Farm Credit Administration, offer short-term and production credit to farmer- and rancher-members. The associations rediscount members' notes with federal intermediate credit banks. *Compare* federal land bank association.

production tax. A tax levied upon the producer of goods at the time they are sold. *Compare* severance tax.

pro forma amendment. An amendment (as to strike out the last word) proposed for the purpose of allowing a member to continue a discussion in a legislative body.

progressive. One who favors the gradual introduction of political and social reforms by government action.

Progressive Citizens of America. A left-wing organization resulting from a merger of certain liberal groups, Dec. 29, 1946. Allegedly nonpartisan, it later (1948) became the nucleus of a third party that nominated Henry A. Wallace for the presidency.

Progressive Labor party. A socialist party in New York in 1887.

progressive movement. A revolt, beginning about 1890, of middle-class farmers and business and professional men against entrenched privilege with the objectives, among others, of regulating common carriers, controlling financial and manufacturing monopolies, preventing the sale of contaminated meat and other food products, protecting women and other workers, eliminating child labor, reforming municipal government, and securing the adoption of the direct primary, the initiative, referendum, and recall, and the direct election of U.S. senators.

Progressive party. 1. A third party, composed mostly of dissatisfied Republicans, which in 1912 nominated Theodore Roosevelt for President and Hiram Johnson for Vice President, and advocated such reforms as primary elections, direct election of senators, woman suffrage, limited recall of judicial decisions, abolition of the injunction in labor disputes, enactment of child labor, minimum wage, and employers' liability laws, and scientific tariff making. It received 4,119,507 out of a total of 13,900,000 popular votes, and 88 out of 531 electoral votes. **2.** A minor party, 1924, composed of union labor members, dissatisfied farmers, and Socialists, which nominated Robert M. La Follette for President and advocated nationalization of railroads, public development of water power and ownership of utilities, direct popular nomination and election of the President, and Congressional power to overrule decisions of the Supreme Court which declared statutes unconstitutional. It received 4,823,000 popular votes out of a total of 29,000,000, and the 13 electoral votes of Wisconsin. **3.** A minor party, 1948, infiltrated by Communists, which nominated Henry A. Wallace for President and advocated gradual nationalization of basic industries, abolition of segregation, and friendship with Russia. Wallace received 1,156,103 popular votes.

progressive taxation. Taxes, especially those on income and inheritance, levied upon different amounts at percentage rates which increase more sharply than the increase of the tax bases.

¹prohibition. The public policy of entirely forbidding, by national or State law or constitutional amendment, the manufacture, transportation, or sale of intoxicating beverages except for medicinal or scientific purposes.

²prohibition. *See* writ of prohibition.

Prohibition party. A minor party advocating prohibition, and sometimes other reforms, founded in 1869 and in continuous existence since that date, though its highest popular vote for a presidential candidate was 271,058 (1892) and it rarely influenced the outcome of an election.

proletariat. The working class, especially industrial employees.

promotion. *Civil service.* Advancement to a higher rank with duties of greater responsibility usually, but not necessarily, accompanied by an increase in salary. The basic standards for promotion are seniority and ability as measured by efficiency ratings or new examinations. The latter are justified as a means of removing political influence.

promulgation. An executive act by which a law is declared to be in effect.

propaganda. Organized efforts to influence the thoughts, emotions, opinions, impulses, and actions of people collectively and as individuals by means of words, pictures, music, symbols, or public demonstrations. The purpose may include enlightenment, education, increase in patriotic fervor, or destruction of an enemy. Methods run the gamut from careful and thorough presentations of the truth to endless repetitions of lies. The authors of *white* propaganda correctly announce the source when they release the propaganda. In *black* propaganda a false source is announced with intention to mislead. In *gray* propaganda no source is announced.

property. Exclusive possession and enjoyment of something which has economic value including anything tangible or an idea, process, privilege, or interest. The extent of any property right is determined by law.

property qualification. The requirement that a voter must be the owner of real (later personal) property of a certain acreage or value. It existed in all the colonies, but disappeared by 1856, only to be revived by several Southern States after 1890 as an alternative to other qualifications.

proportional representation. A system of minority representation based on the theory that interests, opinions, and party affiliations should be represented in legislative bodies in proportion to their relative strength rather than geographical areas. Large political subdivisions are the units for elections, and each is entitled to three or more representatives as fixed by law or determined by total popular vote. Under the list system voters may express a preference for a whole list of candidates, and representatives are apportioned among various lists according to the number of votes each list receives. Under the single transferable vote, or Hare plan, *q.v.*, a voter has an opportunity to express preferences for individual candidates whether they are party nominees or independents.

proprietary colony. One of several English colonies founded and governed by private individuals or companies under grants by royal authority.

INSTRUCTIONS

Mark Your Choices with NUMBERS Only. (Do NOT Use X Marks.)

Put the number 1 in the square opposite the name of your first choice.

Put the number 2 opposite your second choice, the number 3, opposite your third choice, and so on. You may mark as many choices as you please.

Do not put the same number opposite more than one name.

To vote for a person whose name is not printed on this ballot, write his name on a blank line under the names of the candidates and put a number in the square opposite to show which choice you wish to give him.

CANDIDATES FOR THE OFFICE OF COUNCILMAN

WILLIAM A. CARROLL	Democrat
EUGENE P. CONNOLLY	American Labor
ALAN CORELLI	
BENJAMIN J. M	Communist
S. SAMUEL	Democrat
MEYER C	Republican
STANLEY E.	Republican
LAYLE LANE	Socialist
JOHN P. NUGENT	Democrat
JOHN A. ROSS, JR.	Republican
MORRIS WEINFELD	Democrat
PEARL L. WILLEN	New Deal Committee
SAUL BERGER	

OFFICIAL COUNCILMANIC BALLOT for the GENERAL ELECTION NOVEMBER 2, 1943 CITY OF NEW YORK NEW YORK COUNTY 44 ELECTION DISTRICT 21 ASSEMBLY DISTRICT

Proportional representation ballot formerly used in New York City

proprietary function. An activity of a municipal corporation of the kind normally conducted for profit by a private business enterprise; *especially:* the production of goods and services under government ownership.

prorogation. Deferment or termination of the session of a deliberative assembly by executive authority. It has been unknown in the United States since the Colonial period.

prosecuting attorney. A locally elected officer who represents the State in securing indictments and informations and in prosecuting criminal cases before courts; and who, in some States, also advises local officers and boards concerning their legal powers and duties; *called also* district attorney or State's attorney.

prosecution. 1. The conduct of a criminal proceeding before a judicial tribunal including all steps from the indictment or information to the final decision. 2. The party, usually the State, which conducts a criminal proceeding against an accused person.

protection. 1. Favor granted to economic interests within a country through the imposition of trade or exchange controls or tariffs on imported goods so high as to exclude them from effective competition with domestic products, usually justified for the public reasons of encouraging the establishment of new industries or preserving those in existence, of making a country self-sufficient in case of foreign war, or of maintaining or increasing employment, wages, and the standard of living. 2. Immunity from prosecution granted for partisan or corrupt reasons to criminals or underworld characters engaged in gambling, prostitution, or other illegal transactions.

protective tariff. 1. A rate of duty imposed under the principle of protection, *q.v.* 2. A tariff law containing many protective rates. *Compare* revenue tariff.

protectorate. A state which by treaty has placed itself under the protection of a stronger power, yielding up its control over foreign affairs, but retaining self-government in domestic matters, though the protecting state is usually granted the right to intervene in certain circumstances. A *colonial protectorate* is a district controlled by a state to the exclusion of other states but not claimed as part of its territory.

protest vote. A vote cast against candidates of the voter's own party because of his dislike for a measure or policy pursued by it.

protocol. 1. A memorandum of negotiations or preliminary conclusions arrived at by diplomacy, often serving as a basis for a final convention or treaty. Ratification of a protocol gives it the force of a treaty. 2. Diplomatic or state ceremonial etiquette.

province. A territorial unit in Canada and certain European states.

provisional appointment. An appointment to a civil service position, made prior to the applicant's taking an examination or the certification of the results, which is supposed to be vacated if the applicant does not qualify within a reasonable time.

provisional government. A temporary government set up during, or immediately after, a conquest or a revolutionary overturn of the established order and functioning until a new definitive regime has been provided.

provisional order. An administrative order issued by a British minister or subordinate in anticipation of parliamentary authority which may subsequently be given in an omnibus statute called a Provisional Orders Confirmation Bill.

proxy. 1. A person who casts a vote in place of another, as in a committee. 2. The instrument which authorizes a vote by proxy.

prudent investment theory. A theory used by regulatory commissions in the valuation of public utilities based on the historical cost of property minus the amount represented by imprudent expenditures.

public administration. *See* administration 1.

Public Administration Clearing House. A private professional organization with headquarters in Chicago, Ill., which, through various conferences and information services, seeks to raise the standards of public administration nationally and locally. It publishes a directory of public administration organizations and the weekly *Recent Publications on Government Problems.*

Public Administration Service. An organization with headquarters in Chicago, Ill., jointly maintained by various private or quasi-public professional agencies interested in public administration, whose staff provides consulting services for public bodies, conducts surveys, serves as a source of information on administrative problems, and issues various publications.

public assistance. Aid to the aged poor, children, and handicapped persons under a social security program. *See* categorical assistance program.

public bill. A bill concerning a subject of general public interest to the whole country or State. *Compare* private bill.

Public Buildings Service. A unit of the General Services Administration which supervises the construction, maintenance, and repair of public buildings of the national government.

Public Contracts Act. *See* Walsh-Healey Act.

public corporation. An artificial person (as a municipality or a government corporation, *q.v.*) created for convenience in the administration of public affairs. Unlike a private corporation it has no protection against legislative acts altering or even repealing its charter.

public crib. *Slang.* The payroll of a national, State, local, or municipal government.

public debt. The principal amount and unpaid interest of all outstanding bonds, notes, bills, and other evidences of federal, State, or local government indebtedness resulting from past borrowings, especially during periods of war, national economic crisis, extensive preparations for defense, or construction of highways. *See* Bureau of the Public Debt.

public defender. An official in a few cities and counties of the United States whose duty it is to defend persons accused of crime.

public domain. Lands over which the U.S. Government exercises proprietary rights. The original public domain included western areas ceded to the United States by some of the original States of the Union and all accessions of continental territory after 1800 except Texas. Generous grants of public lands have been made to States for educational purposes, and the liberal homestead policy pursued after 1862 resulted in the transfer of vast areas to private ownership. The public domain now consists of approximately 770 million acres, or about a third of the land area of the 50 States. Of this some 50 million acres have been acquired by purchase for special purposes or in other ways. The public domain includes areas classified as national parks, forests, grazing areas, and Indian reservations, and many military and civilian governmental installations. Most of it is controlled by the Interior and the Agriculture Departments.

public education. Provision for schooling at public expense and under public control. It began early in the Colonial period in New England, but was not in effect in some States until after the Civil War. Elementary and secondary education is administered by district, town, township, city, or county boards of education. State regulations provide minimum requirements for teachers, equipment, length of school terms, and uniform courses of study, textbooks, and achievements for graduation, and are especially effective where State aid to local areas is conditioned upon the maintenance of certain standards. The States maintain universities, junior colleges, training schools, and other institutions of higher education. For many years the federal government has provided financial support for agricultural, engineering, scientific, and vocational education. During the 1960's it became an important source of support for education at every level from kindergarten (Project Head Start) to graduate study.

public enemy. 1. A hostile state, or one of its citizens or subjects. 2. *Colloquial.* A notorious criminal.

public finance. An intellectual discipline lying along the border between political science and economics and partaking of some of the characteristics of both, which deals with governmental expenditures, taxation and borrowing, and public financial policy and administration.

public health laboratory. A laboratory maintained by a State or municipality to produce or test the purity of vaccines and biological products used in the treatment of disease and to conduct research in the prevention of epidemic diseases.

Public Health Service. A service, the origins of which go back to 1798, first known by its present title in 1912, and since 1953 a part of the Department of Health, Education, and Welfare, which engages in research in the causes and prevention of human disease, issues health information to the public, enforces quarantine laws at ports of entry, provides hospitalization for various classes of patients eligible under national laws, cooperates with State and local authorities in public health programs, controls pollution of air and water, grants loans to students training for the health professions, grants funds to States for planning programs for mentally retarded persons, and administers grants for hospitals and sewage treatment works.

public health work. Activities of federal, State, and local governments and of private associations to safeguard and improve the health of the people by such means as collection of vital statistics, research in the causes and treatment of diseases, prevention of water and air pollution, inspection of food and drugs, physical examinations of school children and food handlers, health education, clinics, institutional treatment of the physically and mentally ill, and control of epidemics through quarantines and mass inoculations.

public interest. *See* business affected with a public interest.

publicity laws. National and State laws, such as those requiring the filing by candidates or party committees of statements concerning campaign funds and expenditures, blue sky laws, *q.v.*, and laws requiring lobbyists to file statements of the conditions of their employment, enacted on the theory that publication will alert the public or their representatives to the existence of possible evils.

publicity pamphlet. A pamphlet containing information concerning candidates and party programs, which is prepared and distributed by State authority before a primary or election.

public lands. *See* public domain.

public law. 1. A general classification of law, the principal branches being constitutional, administrative, criminal, and international law, which is concerned with the organization of the state, the relations between the state and the people who compose it, the responsibilities of public officers to the state, to each other, and to private persons, and the relations of states to one another. 2. A statute applying generally to persons and places throughout a state. *Compare* private law.

public nuisance. A condition dangerous to health, disagreeable to the senses, offensive to moral standards of the community, or unlawfully obstructing the public in the free use of highways and public property in violation of legal rights.

public office is a public trust. A statement attributed to President Grover Cleveland which became a slogan of civil service reformers.

public opinion. The attitudes of the people toward political events, policies, programs, and the general state of affairs. Because people are influenced by their previous training, emotions, economic interests, access to information, and response to political leadership, public opinion varies among different classes and groups and over even brief intervals of time. It is measured, as to candidates and perhaps party policies, by elections, and as to individual measures, by referendums. At other times it is often estimated by polling devices.

public ownership. Governmental ownership and operation of a productive enterprise, especially one normally owned and operated as a private business. *See* proprietary function; municipal ownership.

public policy. 1. The principle under which acts of individuals are restricted when they have a tendency injurious to the common welfare. 2. Any governmental policy.

public power. Government ownership and operation of hydroelectric or steam power or of transmission lines.

public purpose. The constitutional requirement that, in order to be constitutionally acceptable, the purpose of any tax, police regulation, or particular exertion of the power of eminent domain shall be the convenience, safety, or welfare of the entire community and not the welfare of a specific individual or class of persons. The distinction between private and public purpose is determined largely either by usage or by the courts.

public roads. *See* road; Bureau of Public Roads.

public school. An elementary or high school established and maintained by authorities of local school districts in accordance with State law and financed by local property and other taxes and by grants from the State and the federal government. *See* public education.

public service commission. An administrative agency of three or more members established by the State legislature to regulate rates and services of electric, gas, telephone, and other public utilities.

public service corporation. A private or a publicly-owned corporation engaged in furnishing essential services to the public. *See* public utility.

public trial. A trial open to the attendance of the public at large.

public utility. A privately owned and operated business whose services are so essential to the general public as to justify the grant of special franchises for the use of public property or of the right of eminent domain, in consideration of which the owners must serve all persons who apply, without discrimination except where such discrimination is required by law. It is nearly always a natural or virtual monopoly. It may be for the production and distribution of a commodity like gas, electricity, water, or steam; for transportation, as a railroad, bus line, taxicab company, ferry, or oil pipeline; for communication, as a telegraph or telephone company; or it may be a dock, wharf, grain elevator, or stockyard. It is subject to a great variety of public regulations regarding its financial structure, the rates it charges, and the standards of its services.

public utility district. A special district which has power to tax and borrow in order to construct generating stations or transmission lines and distribute electricity or gas to the public. Such districts are especially numerous in the Pacific Northwest.

Public Utility Holding Company Act. An act of Congress, Aug. 26, 1935, which placed virtually all gas and electric utility holding companies under the jurisdiction of the Securities and Exchange Commission and gave it authority to bring about geographic and corporate simplification and supervise security transactions, dividends, loans, and contracts between the holding company and its subsidiaries. *See* death sentence clause.

public vessel. A naval vessel or other government-owned ship not used in commerce.

public works. Highways, bridges, levees, and similar undertakings, and major engineering developments, such as irrigation, power, drainage, or navigation projects, financed or undertaken by government for the convenience and welfare of the community.

Public Works Administration. A unit created by Congress June 16, 1933, which until 1943 provided loans and grants for State and local buildings and works to be built by private contractors.

PUD Public Utility District.

Puerto Rico. The easternmost island in the Greater Antilles, with an area of 3,435 sq. mi. and a population of over two million. It was acquired from Spain in 1898 and governed under military law until 1900, and under a governor, commission, and popularly elected lower house from 1900 to 1917. The organic act passed by Congress in 1917 made the people of Puerto Rico citizens of the United States and granted a bill of rights. An amendment to the organic act, in 1947, made the governor popularly elective. In 1951 a convention wrote a new constitution which was approved by the Puerto Ricans and by the U.S. Congress in 1952. Puerto Rico then became a commonwealth voluntarily associated with the United States. Governing power is divided among the bicameral legislature, a Supreme Court, and the Governor who appoints the heads of the executive departments. Puerto Rico is represented in Washington by a resident commissioner who may speak but not vote in the House of Representatives.

Pujo Committee. A special committee created by the House of Representatives in 1912 to determine whether or not there was a "money trust."

pull. *Slang.* Hidden influence with an official or organization that is in a position to grant favors.

Pullman Strike. A strike of Pullman employees in 1894, actively supported by the American Railway Union. Their stoppage of trains in Chicago and consequent interference with interstate commerce and the mails led President Cleveland to send federal troops to the area over the protest of Governor Altgeld of Illinois and to the issuance of an injunction against the strikers by the federal circuit court. Defiance of the injunction by Eugene V. Debs and other union leaders resulted in their conviction and subsequent incarceration for contempt of court. *See Debs, in re.*

pump priming. Huge government expenditures financed mainly by borrowing for the purposes of stimulating production, employment, and general economic activity during the 1930's.

Punta del Este Charter. *See* Alliance for Progress.

Punta del Este Conference. *See* Declaration of the Presidents of America.

purge. 1. *In dictatorships:* the elimination of disloyal or suspected members of the ruling party by officially ordered assassination. 2. *In the United States:* use of executive influence to encompass defeat of non-cooperative fellow partisans in primary or election campaigns.

Purple Heart. *See* Order of the Purple Heart.

pussyfooting. The action of a candidate or official in making general or ambiguous statements, or none at all, on some issue on which a straightforward statement is expected.

PWA Public Works Administration.

qualification. A requirement or condition (as of age, citizenship, residence, character, or education) which an individual must possess before he is eligible for an office or participation in the suffrage, jury service, or admission to practice a profession.

quarantine. 1. The isolation of persons afflicted with, or suspected of having been exposed to, a contagious disease. 2. The stoppage of the travel of persons or the transportation of plants or animals from an infected area. 3. The place where persons under quarantine are detained. Both national and State governments may establish quarantines affecting foreign, interstate, or intrastate travel or commerce.

quartering. The billeting of soldiers or the commandeering of billets for soldiers. The Third Amendment to the Constitution declares that no soldier shall be quartered in any house in time of peace without the owner's consent; nor in time of war, except as prescribed by law.

quartermaster corps. Formerly a branch of an army's organization charged with feeding and clothing personnel and providing transport. The United States Marine Corps still has a Quartermaster General in charge of supply.

quarter sessions. A court with criminal jurisdiction in some States which sits at intervals of three months.

quasi corporation. 1. A local government unit, such as a county, township, or special district. 2. A body of officers of a local government unit (as a school board) which, though not incorporated, has acquired by statute or prescription a corporate personality at least to the extent that it may sue or be sued.

quasi-judicial. Resembling a judicial action or procedure;—applied to the action of an administrative body with limited powers to hold hearings and make decisions affecting the rights of specified persons under the law.

quasi-legislative. 1. Resembling a legislative body or law-making procedure but lacking the general competence of a legislature or the power to act with legislative finality. 2. Pertaining to the delegated rule-making power of an administrative officer or commission.

quasi-public corporation. A private corporation engaged in rendering essential services to the public and therefore given special privileges, as to acquire rights of way under eminent domain.

Quebec Act. An act of the British parliament, 1774, organizing the government of Quebec and extending its boundaries southwestward to the Ohio and Mississippi rivers.

Quebec Conference. 1. A meeting of the American-British Combined Chiefs of Staff at Quebec, Canada, beginning Aug. 12, 1943, which formulated conditions for the surrender of Italy, advanced plans for a postwar United Nations, and adopted a common policy toward the French Committee of National Liberation

Boundaries of Quebec, 1774

which had come under control of General de Gaulle. 2. A meeting in Quebec of Roosevelt and Churchill in September, 1944, which *inter alia* approved the Morgenthau Plan, *q.v.*

question. 1. The chief point of inquiry or discussion. 2. The matter to be decided by a vote.

question of privilege. A matter concerning the privileges of a legislative body or one of its members.

Quids. Members of the Jeffersonian Republican party led, 1804–1808, by John Randolph, who opposed some of Jefferson's policies and favored the nomination of James Monroe to succeed him.

Quirin, Ex parte. *See* German Saboteurs case.

quisling. A sympathizer with a foreign country and potential traitor to his own who may become an actual traitor in wartime;—from Vidkun Quisling, head of the Nazi party in Norway and subsequently head of the German puppet government in that state.

quitrent. A perpetual annual payment originating in the feudal practice of allowing a tenant to pay in money or kind in lieu of furnishing food to, or performing labor for, his lord. Commonly exacted as a condition of holding land in the American Colonies especially from Pennsylvania southward, it was a source of constant friction between the people and their government.

quorum. The number of members who must be present in a deliberative body before business may be transacted. In both houses of Congress a quorum consists of a majority of those chosen and sworn. A smaller number may adjourn from day to day and compel the attendance of absent members. The presence of a quorum is usually ascertained by roll call. In 1890 Speaker Reed instituted the practice of ordering the clerk to add to the roll the names of those present but refusing to answer in the House of Representatives.

quota. *See* electoral quota; immigration.

quo warranto. *See* writ of quo warranto.

rabble-rouser. A politician who uses his oratorical talents to play upon the prejudices and avarice of ignorant and propertyless voters; *also:* a demagogue.

race. A body of people believed to be of common descent, or distinguished from others by common physical characteristics, the most important of which is color.

race discrimination. *See* discrimination; equal protection.

racetrack legislation. State statutes regulating horse or dog racing, usually administered by a State racing commission. Payment of a fee for operating a track or holding a race meeting is usually required, and either betting may be prohibited or (what is more often the case) promoters must share the proceeds of a pari-mutuel pool with the State.

racism. Deeply rooted prejudice which may be expressed in asseverations that one race is superior to another; or in private acts of racial discrimination or repression; or in laws which segregate or in other ways deprive members of a race of civil and political rights and privileges. In varying degrees American Indians, persons of African descent, Chinese, and Japanese have been objects of racism in the United States.

racketeering. Activities of organized gangsters or other criminal elements who systematically extort money from legitimate business enterprise by violence or other forms of intimidation or, by similar methods, conduct illegal enterprises such as gambling, narcotics traffic, or prostitution.

radical. 1. One who advocates immediate and fundamental changes in governments and laws, especially laws relating to economic and social welfare. **2.** A Republican opposed to Lincoln's or Johnson's policy of reconstructing the seceded States, 1864–69.

Radical Democracy. The Republican opponents of President Lincoln who in 1864 nominated John C. Frémont for President. He withdrew Sept. 21, 1864.

radical right. Reactionary extremists in American politics.

Radio Free Europe. Broadcasting stations, operated by a private organization known as the National Committee for a Free Europe, that beam programs to Czechoslovakia, Poland, and other countries behind the Iron Curtain. *Compare* Voice of America.

rag baby. A nickname for greenback currency about 1876.

raiding. Participation by members of one party in the primary elections of another party in order to secure the nomination by the latter of weak or unpopular candidates.

raid on the treasury. A concerted effort to secure large appropriations of public funds for the benefit of localities or special interests.

railroad. A permanent double line of rails on which locomotives and cars operate for the transportation of passengers and goods. Many early railroads were partly financed by subscriptions of stock or bonds by States, municipalities, and other local subdivisions, and (for transcontinental lines) by land grants from the federal government. Railroads are regulated by the Interstate Commerce Commission and, to some extent, by State public service commissions, *qq.v.*

Railroad Retirement Board. A board of three members, appointed by the President and Senate, created by Congress in 1935 to administer retirement pensions, unemployment benefits, and a placement service for railroad employees.

Rail Splitter. A campaign nickname of Abraham Lincoln.

Railway Labor Act. An act of Congress, May 20, 1926, designed to secure the prompt settlement of disputes between railroad companies and their employees. An amendment in 1934 created the National Mediation Board, *q.v.*, and recent amendments have sought to prevent any interruption of railroad service by strikes.

rally. A party mass meeting held before election day for the purpose of getting out a large vote.

Randolph plan. *See* Virginia plan.

rank. Relative standing, especially in the higher positions of the civil service, armed forces, or on a committee, court, or board, usually attained through seniority, appointment, or promotion.

ranking member. The member of a Congressional committee next below the chairman in point of seniority.

ranking minority member. The member of the minority party of longest continuous service on a Congressional committee, and potentially the chairman, if his party gains a majority in the legislative chamber.

rate. 1. The unit cost of a service supplied to the public by a utility which may either be fixed in a utility's franchise or be established by a public service commission or subject to its approval. **2.** *In the United Kingdom:* a tax on property collected by a local government.

Rathbun (*Humphrey's Executor*) v. *United States.* A case, 295 U.S. 602 (1935), in which the Supreme Court declared that the President's power to remove principal officers of the government at pleasure, recognized in *Myers* v. *United States, q.v.,* does not extend to members of administrative commissions vested with quasi-legislative or quasi-judicial powers or to officers not performing an executive function when Congress has specified a different method of removal.

ratification. 1. Confirmation, by the authority in a state competent to make treaties, of an international agreement previously negotiated and signed by the state's diplomatic representatives. **2.** Approval, as by legislatures or conventions in three-fourths of the States, of a constitutional amendment proposed by two-thirds of both houses of Congress. **3.** Approval by the electorate of a proposed State constitution or amendment.

rationing. The policy of reserving to the government such portion of goods and services as may be required in wartime or other emergency and distributing the remainder equitably among the population. During World War II the government limited civilian consumption of particular articles and required the use of ration coupons.

REA Rural Electrification Administration.

reactionary. One who favors a return to an outmoded system.

reading. An essential step in the passage of a bill which formerly consisted in having the clerk read each bill in full on three different days. At present during the second reading in the House of Representatives, or the third in the Senate, legislative proposals may be debated and amendments may be proposed and voted on. The requirement for two other readings in each body is usually met by printing or reading by title only.

Readjusters. A party, formed in Virginia in 1879, which had as its chief issue readjusting, or scaling down, the principal and interest of the State debt. It accomplished its purpose with the help of Republicans in 1882.

reappointment. Renomination, confirmation (if required by law for a particular office), and the issuance of a new commission to an incumbent whose term of office has expired.

reapportionment. A new apportionment, *q.v.,* of seats in the House of Representatives among States "according to their respective numbers" required by Art. 1, Sec. 2 of the Constitution after every decennial census. A similar requirement as to State legislative seats is found in many State constitutions and is now enforced by the Supreme Court. *See Baker* v. *Carr.*

rebate. Part of a stated transportation charge refunded to a shipper. Rebates were forbidden by the Interstate Commerce Act which was passed in 1887.

rebel brigadier. A Southern Democratic member of Congress during the Reconstruction period, so designated popularly because many had been general officers in the Confederate Army.

rebellion. Widespread concerted armed resistance to a government and public defiance of its authority and laws (especially by the people of a geographical section), usually resulting in civil war. Rebels who establish an organized government and de facto control over a considerable territory are entitled under international law to be recognized as belligerents. *Compare* insurrection.

rebus sic stantibus. A controversial doctrine of international law to the effect that treaties remain valid only while "things stand as they are," and that unexpected circumstances, rendering their terms oppressive or obsolete, justify repudiation by one party.

recall. A procedure by which a public officer may be removed from office by vote of the people. After six months of an officer's term has expired, it may be invoked by petition of from 10 to 35 per cent of the qualified voters (usually 25 per cent); and at the election the questions of removal and of the election of a successor may both appear on the ballot. It may be used as to executive and legislative officers in twelve States and as to judges in eight. Many municipal charters provide for it.

recall of judicial decisions. A proposal by Theodore Roosevelt in 1912 that the decision of a court might be prevented from becoming a precedent in the decision of later cases by an adverse vote of the people. It was designed to prevent the courts from annulling social legislation.

recapture. 1. The retaking from the enemy of ships or goods captured by him. Recaptured private property is usually restored to the owner. 2. The taking by the public, under the provisions of a franchise or statute, of the earnings of a public utility beyond a certain fixed percentage of profit.

receiver. A person appointed by a court to manage property in litigation or the affairs of a bankrupt.

recess. 1. An intermission in the session of a legislative body which, unlike an adjournment, *q.v.*, does not end the legislative day. 2. The period between sessions of a court.

recess appointment. An appointment of an officer of the United States made by the President on his sole authority when the Senate is not in session which, unless confirmed by the Senate, expires on the last day of the following session of the Senate.

recess committee. A legislative committee appointed to conduct an investigation in the interim between sessions.

recession. 1. A temporary decline in economic activity characterized by deflationary price trends, and reductions in investment, economic growth rates, and employment. 2. A deflationary period less severe than a depression.

reciprocal legislation. Legislation separately enacted by two or more States which establishes a common policy on some issue or insures a mutually beneficial exchange of some privilege or right.

reciprocal trade agreement. An arrangement between two countries in which one agrees to lower certain tariff rates, buy the other's produce, or supply certain wants in exchange for equivalent favors. The Trade Agreements Act of 1934 as amended, and such subsequent legislation as the Trade Expansion Act of 1962, authorized the President to enter into reciprocal agreements for the reduction of tariffs and other trade barriers and gave him broad authority to raise or lower existing U.S. tariffs. The terms of each agreement apply to all countries to which the United States is bound to extend most-favored-nation treatment.

reciprocity. The mutual granting by two nations of special commercial privileges (as lower tariff duties) which are advantageous to the trade of both.

reclamation. The draining of marshy or swampy land or the irrigation of desert areas, with electric power occasionally an incidental product. *See* Bureau of Reclamation.

recognition. 1. The act of a government in acknowledging the independence of a former colony, or in signifying willingness to enter upon diplomatic relations with a de facto government in another state;— usually accorded by formal agreement, by proclamation, or by sending or receiving an ambassador, and often withheld until the de facto government has reestablished civil order or has shown a disposition to fulfill its international obligations. Premature recognition of an insurgent colony or rebel group is regarded as an unfriendly act by the de jure government. 2. *In legislative procedure:* the act of a presiding officer in granting the floor to a member.

recognizance. An obligation recorded with a court or magistrate guaranteeing appearance of an accused person before a court, or that he will keep the peace under penalties if the obligation is not performed.

recommitment. The action of a legislative body in sending a measure back to a committee with or without instructions. A vote to recommit usually has the effect of killing the measure.

reconsideration. Renewed discussion and vote upon a measure already passed by a legislative chamber, the rules providing that one motion to reconsider, moved by a member who voted with the majority, is in order within a limited time.

reconstruction. The process by which the federal government, during and after the Civil War, reorganized the governments of the seceded States, usually under military authority; forced the adoption of provisions in their constitutions guaranteeing the rights and privileges of their Negro populations and recognizing their obligations to the Union as a prerequisite to readmission; and finally readmitted them.

Reconstruction Finance Corporation. A government-owned corporation, with a capital of $500 million, chartered by Congress in 1932, which, at various times, (a) made emergency or distress loans to banks, insurance companies, railroads, and mortgage companies, taking their stocks, bonds, or other evidences of indebtedness as security; (b) extended credit to public and semipublic cooperative associations; (c) created and capitalized several public corporations which, during World War II, produced, bought, sold, stored, or otherwise dealt in strategic and critical materials; and (d) made funds available for loans by other agencies of the federal government. In the 22 years of its existence, the R.F.C. made about 640,000 loans totaling an estimated $48.8 billion, most of which were repaid by 1954. When in that year it was abolished its assets amounted to $100 million.

record. The official stenographic account of the proceedings of a court of justice or similar tribunal.

recorder. 1. A minor judicial officer in some cities. 2. A local government officer in whose office deeds, mortgages, liens, and other documents are registered.

record vote. 1. A vote in which the response of each individual is recorded, required in both houses of Congress by yeas and nays on roll call on the demand of one-fifth of the members, or when voting on a bill after a presidential veto. 2. An unusually heavy turnout at the polls. 3. A vote for a winning candidate which equals or exceeds that of a previous victor in an electoral contest for the same office.

recruiting. The process by which individuals, influenced by advertising, interviews, and other means, are persuaded to take examinations for posts in the civil service or to enlist in the armed forces.

red. An adherent of orthodox socialism or communism;—derived from the red flag, symbol of international Marxism.

Red Cross. *See* American National Red Cross; International Red Cross.

redemption. The payment of principal and unpaid interest on bonds or other obligations that have matured.

rediscount rate. The rate, fixed from time to time by the Board of Governors of the Federal Reserve System, at which a Federal Reserve Bank can make loans to member banks on the security of commercial paper already discounted by such banks. The reserve rate determines that charged by local banks and thus serves as an economic regulator.

redistricting. The action of a State legislature in abolishing old, and creating new, Congressional districts, or of adjusting the boundaries of existing districts, following a reapportionment of Representatives in Congress or at other times, in order to keep districts approximately equal in population; *also:* similar action with respect to State senatorial, assembly, and judicial districts.

redress of grievances. The correction of abuses in the government of a state. The right of the individual to petition for redress of grievances, one of the oldest of British constitutional rights, is guaranteed in the First Amendment of the Constitution of the United States. Historically such petitions were considered by the British parliament before voting appropriations for governmental services.

red tape. Rigid observance of official routine, including the routing of requests and orders "through the regular channels" and procedures which result in delay and inaction;—so-called from the color of the cotton tape in which official letters and documents were formerly tied together.

re-eligibility. Eligibility for a new election or appointment to an office upon the expiration of a term, or after a certain number of years or terms of service, which is generally assumed to exist unless the contrary is provided by a constitution, statute, or custom.

re-entry permit. Permission given to an alien who has resided in the United States to return after a brief sojourn abroad.

referee. An attorney appointed by a court to hold hearings, take testimony, and otherwise act for it in some aspects of a pending proceeding.

reference. 1. The action of a legislative body, usually by, or at the direction of, its presiding officer, in sending a bill to a particular committee. 2. The action of a court in referring a matter to a referee.

referendum. The act or process of referring to the electorate for approval or rejection the draft of a proposed new State constitution or amendment (*constitutional referendum*) or of a law passed by the legislature (*statutory referendum*). The constitutional referendum is mandatory in all States but one, and often an extramajority vote is required for adoption. The statutory referendum, which is provided for in some 20 States, may be invoked during a period of, usually, 90 days between the passage of a measure and the date it goes into effect by a petition signed by a certain number or percentage (ordinarily 5 or 6 per cent) of the voters. In the general or special election which follows, an adverse majority of the total vote cast on a measure suffices for its rejection. The referendum may not be invoked on laws which the legislature declares to be emergency measures. In many States and municipalities a legislative body may of its own motion refer a controversial measure to a popular vote which is either decisive or is used to ascertain public opinion (*advisory* or *optional referendum*); or the law may provide that certain kinds of measures, like those for the creation of bonded indebtedness, must be submitted (*mandatory referendum*).

reforestation. The scientific replanting of denuded forest lands, an activity carried on in the United States under the supervision of the Department of Agriculture and other federal, State, and local agencies.

reformatory. A penal institution for the incarceration and rehabilitation of young or first offenders or those not deemed incorrigible.

refugee. One who has fled from a country to escape religious persecution or arrest for political activities.

Refugee Relief Act. An act of Congress, 1953, which admitted 215,000 European refugees who had escaped from Eastern Europe by way of Germany, Austria, or NATO countries, or who had lived in Italy, Greece, or The Netherlands, which had suffered great damage during World War II.

refund. The return of all or that portion of a tax or other payment which was found to be in excess of what the law or contractual obligation required.

refunding. The issuance of new bonds to replace previous obligations that are retired, which serves as a means of postponing debt redemption or reducing interest charges on existing debt.

regent. One who assumes the duties of a monarch during the latter's minority, absence, or incapacity.

regimentation. The substitution of legal status for freedom of action and extirpation of individual and group spontaneity in social life resulting from the imposition of a totalitarian regime; *also:* similar results that arise from state socialism or even extensive public regulation of economic life.

regionalism. 1. Any theory of territorial decentralization of power in a state. 2. *In the United States:* the view that the existing 50 States should be superseded by a few (nine or more) great districts or regions.

register. 1. Any officially prepared list relating to official personnel, vital statistics, wills, deeds, or merchant ships. 2. A local official who keeps a record of vital or other statistics; *called also* registrar.

registered bond. A bond the number of which is recorded by the seller in the name of the purchaser and which only the latter, or those legally authorized to act for him, can redeem.

registered mail. Valuable mail given special protection against loss in transmission on payment by the sender of a special fee, a record of which is stamped on the envelope or container.

registrar. *See* register 2.

registration. Official enrollment of persons, with various data concerning them, for the administration of election, compulsory military service, rationing, lobbying, or other laws. Registration of voters is now required in practically all parts of the United States, either by personal appearance of the voter before a board, or by official canvassers. The process may be repeated before each election (*periodic registration*), or lists may be made up at longer intervals and kept up-to-date by a permanent staff (*permanent registration*).

registration area. The part, now comprising nearly the whole, of the United States in which the official recording of births and deaths conforms to standards set by the Census Bureau.

registry. The act of recording; *specifically:* compulsory registration of a ship in the list or record of ships subject to the maritime regulations of a particular country.

regressive tax. 1. A tax levied at rates which increase less rapidly than the increase of the tax base, thus bearing more heavily on poorer than on more wealthy taxpayers. *Compare* progressive taxation. 2. Any tax levied at uniform rates on all taxpayers;—applied as an epithet, especially by opponents of sales taxes.

regular. A voter or officeholder who consistently follows the decisions of his party organization.

regular army. The personnel of all ranks of the U.S. Army on full-time service. Normally it does not include reservists, the National Guard, and conscripted ranks, who, when called to active duty, may be designated members of the Army of the United States.

regulation. A rule made by an appropriate administrative authority; *especially:* an official interpretation of a statute issued by the executive officer charged with its enforcement for the guidance of subordinates. *Compare* executive order.

regulator. 1. A North Carolinian who, 1767–71, engaged in riotous acts against extortionate lawyers and officials. 2. One of a self-constituted band of law enforcers in a frontier community. 3. A bill introduced for the purpose of extorting money from a corporation but ostensibly for regulating it.

rehabilitation. Restoration of a person to productive earning power, or to a position as a useful member of society.

rehearing. Formal presentation of the testimony and pleadings in a particular case before the same tribunal for a second time.

reinstatement. Restoration of a person to an office.

rejection. Refusal (as by the Senate of the United States) to confirm an appointment or to ratify a treaty.

religious establishment. Any religious community or confession which enjoys a preferred position sanctioned and enforced by law and (usually) receiving financial and other support from the state, as the position of the Church of England in Great Britain, or of the Roman Catholic church in Italy;—prohibited in the United States by the First Amendment, *q.v. Compare* freedom of religion.

religious test. A legal requirement that in order to hold an office or exercise some legal privilege a person shall publicly proclaim that he supports a particular religious faith or belief. Such a requirement is specifically prohibited by the Constitution, Art. VI, Sec. 3.

remand. 1. The act of returning an accused person to custody. **2.** The act of returning a case to a lower court or executive tribunal for action.

Remember Pearl Harbor. An American rallying cry in World War II;—from Pearl Harbor, a naval and army base on the island of Oahu, Hawaii, attacked by Japanese naval and air forces on Dec. 7, 1941.

Remember the Alamo. A rallying cry of Texans in their war for independence, recalling the massacre, March 6, 1836, by Mexican forces of a Texan garrison at the Alamo, a mission near San Antonio.

Remember the "Maine." An American rallying cry during the Spanish-American War. *See* "Maine."

Remember the River Raisin. An American rallying cry recalling the murder by Indians of American prisoners who fell into the hands of the British at the battle of the River Raisin, Jan. 22, 1813.

remission. A return of all or part of a fine, or reduction or abatement of some other penalty inflicted by a court.

remonstrance. A formal protest against the policy or conduct of the government or of certain officials and a demand for reform, drawn up and presented by aggrieved citizens or their representatives, as the Grand Remonstrance of 1641 addressed to the Crown by the British Parliament.

removal from office. Dismissal from office by competent authority. The U.S. Constitution makes no specific provision for removal except when an officer is convicted after impeachment. From the beginning of the federal government it was generally conceded that the President was vested with the removal power. But the Tenure of Office Act, *q.v.*, of 1867 (repealed in 1887) and an act of 1876 relating to certain postmasters required the consent of the Senate to the removal of an officer whose appointment was made with its consent. In 1926 the Supreme Court determined in *Myers* v. *United States, q.v.*, that the President alone had power to remove officers appointed with the consent of the

Senate because of the general grant of executive power and as a necessary adjunct to his duty to "take care that the laws be faithfully executed." Under the decision in *Rathbun (Humphrey's Executor)* v. *United States, q.v.,* his power does not extend to members of commissions created by Congress to exercise quasi-legislative and quasi-judicial powers. Congress by law regulates the removal of inferior officers (civil service employees). The provisions of State constitutions and laws rarely grant to the governor an unrestricted power of removal, even of officers appointed by him.

removal of cases. The transfer of cases prior to a decision from a State to a national court, as may be done in a civil case on application of the defendant when the parties are of diverse citizenship or when a federal question is involved, if the amount in controversy is more than $10,000; or in a criminal case if the accused claims that he was acting under color of federal authority.

rendition. The return of a fugitive from justice to the State in which he is accused of having committed a crime, by the order of the governor of the State to which the fugitive has gone. The duty of rendition is imposed by the Constitution, but the courts have found no appropriate means to enforce it. Occasionally governors have refused to grant it. *See Kentucky* v. *Dennison.*

Renegotiation Act. An act of Congress, 1951, which enabled the federal government to secure the return of excess profits from private contractors on certain defense and space projects.

Reorganization Act. An act of Congress, 1949, granting power to the President to make changes in the executive branch of the government unless vetoed by one or both houses of Congress within sixty days. This act was one of the principal means of carrying into effect many proposals of the Hoover Commission, *q.v.*

reparation. Monetary or material compensation for damages done; *especially:* payments exacted by the victor for the expenses of war or damages said to have been committed by the armed forces of a defeated enemy.

repatriation. Restoration of prisoners of war or refugees to their own country.

repeal. The abrogation of a law by the enacting body, either by express declaration or impliedly by the passage of a later act which contains provisions contradictory to the terms of existing law.

repeater. A voter who illegally casts more than one vote.

replacement cost. The amount required to buy new equipment of up-to-date design which would perform the identical function of the equipment already in use.

report. 1. The official printed record of the court reporter of a case or controversy which contains a statement of the principal facts, the opinion, decision, or judgment of the court, and sometimes arguments in counsel's brief. 2. Findings and recommendations of a legislative committee after considering a bill or after an investigation of some subject. 3. A formal statement by an officer or commission concerning its activities or matters under its control which is often required by law to be submitted.

representation. The function of a member of a legislative assembly to speak and act for those who elected him, the acts of a requisite majority of the assembly being binding on the political community. Representation originated in the late medieval period from a desire to obtain the support of townsmen and rural landholders in the royal councils (the ecclesiastical and temporal lords were present in person). During many centuries representation often had a class or corporate basis, and members were given specific instructions by their constituents. The theory that representatives would best serve their constituencies by exercising their own independent judgments concerning the interests of the community as a whole was expressed by Edmund Burke in 1774. This idealized role of the representative as steward of the whole community has won tacit acceptance in England. In most contemporary parliaments, representation is from geographical constituencies and the theory of agency remains strong. The representative is expected to do much "errand running" for his constituents and to secure patronage and appropriations for his State or district. Each organized pressure group adheres to the agency theory in demanding that he vote to advance its interests and to the stewardship theory in demanding that he resist the "selfish" and "unreasonable" requests of other pressure groups. Amid the rivalries of many such groups, the representative attempts a reconciliation of conflicting interests of the groups and of the community interest. *See* minority representation; virtual representation; proportional representation.

representative. 1. One chosen to act for a popular or other constituency in a legislative assembly. 2. A member of the House of Representatives or of a State legislative chamber so named.

representative government. A government in which there is an independent legislature composed of representatives freely elected by a numerous body of the people and endowed with substantial legislative and fiscal powers.

reprieve. A delay for a certain time in the execution of a sentence granted, usually, in order that a convicted person may have an opportunity to prepare and present information in his own behalf.

reprimand. A reproof (*a*) for improper conduct on the part of a member of a legislative house, or (*b*) for inefficiency or dereliction of duty on the part of a subordinate; administered respectively by order of the house or by an administrative superior.

reprisal. A retaliatory act by one country against another for an act allegedly in violation of international law.

reproduction cost. The estimated cost at current market prices and under existing conditions of new equipment which would perform the same function as equipment already in existence;—a basis for rate-making for public utilities.

republic. A government in which the generality of adult citizens determine policies and laws through elected officials and representatives and in which no individual has a vested right to office.

Republican Coordinating Committee. A group established in 1965, and composed of Republican governors, Congressional leaders, and former nominees for the Presidency which periodically issues declarations on party policy.

republican form of government. A government which is administered under the forms of law by responsible officers chosen directly or indirectly by a numerous electorate; *also:* a representative government. The determination as to whether or not a State has a republican form of government within the meaning of the Constitution is a political question. Either house of Congress may refuse to admit members chosen from an irregularly constituted State government, or Congress or the President may determine which of two rival governments in a State is the rightful authority and intervene in its behalf.

Republican party. 1. A major party led by Jefferson and Madison which arose about 1791 in opposition to the assumption of State debts, the chartering of the United States Bank, the excise tax, the foreign policy, and other centralizing and loose-construction tendencies of Washington's administration. It lost the election of 1796 by three electoral votes; but carried all subsequent elections until, by 1820, it had no national opposition. Long tenure in office caused it to relax, in practice, many strict-construction principles on which it had been founded. It was dispersed in 1824 into several personal followings; and in 1828 split into National-Republican and Democratic-Republican wings. **2.** A major party which arose in 1854 out of the widespread dissatisfaction with the Kansas-Nebraska Bill and quickly gained adherents among former Whigs and Democrats in all the Northern States. At first devoted to preventing the spread of slavery into the territories, it added to its platform, in 1860, advocacy of protective tariffs and free homesteads for settlers. It was later identified with the adoption of the Civil War amendments; the reconstruction of the Southern States; the maintenance of "sound money" through resumption of specie payments and, by 1900, the gold standard; high protective tariffs to aid American business and provide a "full dinner pail"; acquisition of territory outside the continent of North America; and a noninterventionist foreign policy. Throughout most of its existence it has been a sectional party with its strongest support among manufacturing interests, white collar workers, and farmers in the North and the West. It usually was successful in electing its candidates before 1932, but has been the minority party since that date.

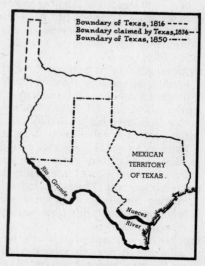

Disputed Boundaries of Republic of Texas

Republic of Texas. A former territory of Mexico with somewhat indefinite boundaries which became independent as a result of a successful revolution by American residents in 1836. It was annexed as a State of the Union in 1845. Its boundaries were settled by the Compromise of 1850, *q.v.*, in which the United States assumed the debt of the Republic of Texas in return for a reduction of Texan territory on the west and northwest.

repudiation. Refusal to honor an obligation; *especially:* persistent failure or refusal of a government to pay a debt in accordance with the terms agreed upon.

requisition. 1. A demand for supplies made by the commander of an invading force. **2.** A formal request by the head of a government, or by the governor of a State, for the surrender of a fugitive from justice.

reservation. 1. An area set aside for exclusive public use, as for military purposes or for occupancy by an Indian tribe. **2.** A special condition attached to a state's accession to a multilateral treaty or convention. **3.** A modification by the U.S. Senate of the draft of a treaty submitted to it for approval. When a reservation is added the President may drop the treaty, or may consult with the other state or states party to it. If agreement is reached on the reservation the President may proclaim the treaty in effect without again consulting the Senate.

reserved power. A power specifically withheld (as in the Tenth Amendment) or judicially interpreted as having been withheld, because not mentioned or reasonably implied in other powers conferred by a constitution or statute.

Reserve Officers' Training Corps. A student corps for training in military, naval, or air science and tactics maintained by the federal government in various American colleges and other educational institutions. Students who qualify after pursuing the course of instruction may become reserve officers.

residence. The place where a person habitually lives, though he may be temporarily absent or lodge elsewhere. *Compare* domicile.

resident commissioner. The representative of Puerto Rico (and formerly of the Philippines) at the national capital who has the privilege of speaking and serving on committees of the House of Representatives, but not the right to vote.

residual powers. The powers that are exercised by a component government in a federal system after other powers have been assigned specifically or by implication to another component government.

resignation. Relinquishment of an office by its occupant. Formal notice of a resignation is tendered to the person who has the power to fill the vacancy, and becomes valid only upon acceptance.

res judicata. A matter upon which a competent court of law has passed judgment and which it will therefore not re-examine.

resolution. A formal statement of legislative opinion or an exertion of legislative power. A *simple resolution* is a measure proposed or passed by a legislative house affecting some matter of internal organization (as the creation of a special committee) or expressing censure, thanks, condolence, or legislative opinion on some matter without having the effect of law. A *concurrent resolution, q.v.,* relates to some matter of interest to both houses, and does not have the force of law; but a simple or concurrent resolution can be used by Congress to recall a grant of discretionary authority previously made to the President. A *joint resolution, q.v.,* has the force of law when passed by both houses of Congress and signed by the President, or passed over his veto.

responsibility. 1. *Legal.* Accountability under the law for the proper performance of a duty, which may be enforced by judicial process and the imposition of penalties provided by law. 2. *Political.* Accountability of legislative and executive officers to the electorate, enforced in the United States by such means as popular election of officers, requirements for the publicity of proceedings, publication of reports, free access to public records, and provision for impeachment or recall, or for the initiative and referendum.

restraint of trade. An effort by one or more private persons or organizations to limit the free flow of trade, establish a monopoly, or reduce or hamper competition.

restricted district. An area in which the use of land for certain purposes is not permitted under zoning regulations.

restriction. A government restraint (as a statutory limitation on immigration) imposed upon former free, or relatively free, action.

restrictive covenant. *See Shelley* v. *Kraemer.*

resulting powers. Powers of the federal government derived, not from any single express or implied grant of powers in the Constitution but from a combination of several grants or the aggregate of power granted to the federal government.

Resumption Act. A law of Congress, Jan. 14, 1875, providing for gradual reduction in the amount of greenbacks outstanding and resumption of specie payments on Jan. 1, 1879.

retirement. Permanent withdrawal of a person from public employment in the civil or armed services as a result of advanced age, disability, or illness, usually with a retirement allowance or pension.

retorsion. A remedy under international law by means of which an injured state may retaliate in kind for harsh treatment of its citizens by another country.

retrenchment. Abolition of offices or curtailment of services in order to reduce expenditures.

retroactive legislation. Laws applying to conditions or circumstances before their enactment. The constitutional prohibition against ex post facto laws, *q.v.,* applies only to retroactive criminal laws which operate to the disadvantage of the accused. It does not apply to civil laws. The chief protection of the individual against retroactive civil laws is the constitutional provision that no State may impair the obligation of a contract.

returning board. A body, usually ex officio, which canvasses the votes cast at an election and announces the result.

returns. The result of an election as certified by the proper election officials.

revenue. A government's income from all sources, the principal one being taxation.

revenue cutter. An armed patrol boat used to pursue and investigate craft suspected of smuggling.

revenue tariff. A tariff which is enacted primarily for the purpose of yielding revenue from duties on goods imported. *Compare* protective tariff.

reversal. The action of an appellate court in rendering judgment in a case under review which has the effect of invalidating a judgment of a lower court or tribunal or of requiring a new trial. Such action is usually based on an error by the lower tribunal in interpreting the law applicable to the case.

review. 1. A re-examination of some matter (as the findings of a board or the valuation of property by an assessor) by a higher officer or tribunal. **2.** Reconsideration of applicable law in a judicial decision by a higher court.

Revised Statutes. 1. The collection of general and permanent laws of the United States, revised, arranged in order, and re-enacted by Congress, June 22, 1874. **2.** A similar body of permanent laws in force re-enacted in one of the States. *Compare* code 2.

revolt. A violent uprising against public authority, usually confined to a district or province, for the correction of wrongs, or to obtain autonomy or independence. *Compare* revolution.

revolution. The overthrow of a constitution or government as a result of armed rebellion of the citizens or other extra-legal means generally acquiesced in and the substitution of a different regime. *See* American Revolution.

revolving fund. A fund appropriated for some special purpose (as the provision of working capital for a public corporation) which is maintained without new appropriations, amounts paid out or loaned being returned to the fund without diminution.

Reynolds v. Sims. A case, 377 U.S. 533 (1964), in which the Supreme Court extended the principle of one man, one vote, *q.v.*, so as to invalidate the unequal apportionment of seats in both houses of the Alabama legislature. The Court advised against mathematical equality because it would be an invitation to partisan gerrymandering, and suggested following the boundaries of political subdivisions in creating single-member districts or the larger districts required for proportional representation.

RFC Reconstruction Finance Corporation.

Rice v. Elmore. A case in which, following the rationale of *Smith* v. *Allwright* (*see* Texas Primary cases), lower U.S. courts held that, even though South Carolina had repealed all constitutional and legal provisions concerning primary elections, party officials in the State were none the less exercising a public function when deciding who might vote in a party primary, and therefore violated the 14th and 15th Amendments when they discriminated against Negroes. The Supreme Court, 333 U.S. 875 (1948), denied an application for certiorari.

rich man's dollar. The gold dollar;—used as an epithet by advocates of greenbacks and the unlimited coinage of silver.

rider. An amendment which is added to a bill in the course of its passage in order that Congressional opponents and the President will have to accept the bill with its rider or do without the bill. Riders are most frequently attached to appropriation bills despite House and Senate rules prohibiting them.

Right. The conservative or reactionary element of any coalition or party, usually including all groups to the right of center;—derived from the custom in Continental European legislatures of seating members of conservative parties to the right of the presiding officer. *Called also* right wing.

right. 1. A legally enforceable claim or privilege. 2. A power, privilege, or immunity guaranteed under a constitution or the laws, or claimed as a result of long usage. *See* civil rights; natural rights; political right.

right of assembly. The right of the people under free or popular governments to assemble for the discussion of public or other questions and to petition the public authorities. The right is affirmed by federal and State constitutions in the United States and by basic public documents in British constitutional history. An assembly of three or more persons is unlawful if its express purpose is to commit an illegal act, and it becomes unlawful if its action involves a breach of the peace or results in riot or forcible resistance to public authority.

right of association. The right of persons to act together for some common purpose, without public grant or charter, whether transiently (as in peaceable assembly) or permanently (as by formal organization). It is protected against legislative encroachment by constitutional provisions, but is limited by the power of the government to preserve the public peace, health, morals, and safety. It is partly protected against private encroachments by statutory and common-law rules and by the conceded power of associations themselves to exclude and expel members.

right of asylum. 1. The right of a state, recognized by international law or custom, to provide a refuge for persons who are persecuted or accused of political crimes in another country, by admitting them to its territory or giving them sanctuary in its warships or its embassies abroad. 2. The sanctuary given to belligerent naval vessels or armed forces personnel in neutral territory.

right of discovery. A claim to sovereignty over territory based on its prior discovery by nationals of the state making the claim or by persons in its employ, such as England's claim to North America which was based on the explorations of John Cabot in 1497. To remain valid, a claim based on discovery must be supported by occupation of the territory.

right of innocent passage. The right of a foreign ship to proceed through the marginal sea of another state, subject to the ship's observance of navigational, sanitary, and customs regulations. Under certain circumstances crimes committed on board foreign merchant ships while in the marginal sea of another state may be tried in its courts. Warships of belligerents are forbidden to engage in battle in the marginal sea of a neutral state.

right of legation. The right of states to send and receive diplomatic representatives.

right of search. The right of a vessel to stop and examine the papers, and sometimes the cargo, of a vessel of a different nationality on the high seas when it is suspected of piracy or the slave trade in time of peace, or of carrying contraband in time of war.

right of way. 1. A prescriptive legal right of one or more persons to traverse property belonging to another. 2. A route acquired by a railroad or public utility as a result of a public franchise or through the power of eminent domain.

right to bear arms. The right of citizens under the Second Amendment to the Constitution to possess arms in order to provide a militia. The courts have held that this right is not infringed by the Federal Firearms Act, *q.v.*, or by statutes in most of the States which make unauthorized possession of lethal weapons a criminal offense.

right to counsel. A fundamental right of an accused person to be represented by an attorney at any stage of a criminal proceeding, including the rights to have an attorney assigned as counsel by the court if the accused is financially unable to pay counsel fees, to consult privately with counsel, and of counsel to have sufficient time to prepare the case. See *Gideon* v. *Wainwright; Miranda* v. *Arizona;* Scottsboro cases.

right-to-work-law. Legislation in more than a third of the States, endorsed and enforced by Section 14b of the Taft-Hartley Labor-Management Relations Act, which prohibits a union shop, *q.v.* Such laws are under continual attack from labor unions.

right wing. See Right.

rigid constitution. A constitution which sets up a complicated, involved, and difficult procedure for its formal amendment;—originally used by James Bryce, Viscount Bryce, in his *The American Commonwealth* (1888). *Compare* flexible constitution.

ring. 1. The inner circle of a party machine. 2. A group of spoilsmen who loot the public treasury for their own personal or political gain.

Rio de Janeiro Conference. A meeting at Rio de Janeiro, Brazil, Jan. 15, 1942, which resulted in all the Latin American states' either declaring war against, or breaking off diplomatic relations with, the Axis powers, *q.v.*

riot. The tumultuous disturbance of the peace by three or more persons unlawfully acting together for the accomplishment of some purpose by violence and terror.

Rio Treaty. The Inter-American Treaty of Reciprocal Assistance signed at Rio de Janeiro, Sept. 2, 1947, which provided enforcement machinery for the Act of Chapultepec, *q.v.* The signatory states obligated themselves to break off diplomatic and economic relations with any aggressor on vote of two-thirds of their number; but no state would be required to furnish armed forces without its consent.

ripper act. Any law making drastic changes in administrative organization or procedures, abolishing existing offices and creating new ones with slightly different titles and duties, increasing or decreasing the appointing and removal power of the executive, altering the terms of a city charter, or transferring authority to grant franchises from a city to a

State board, or vice versa, which is enacted from motives of obtaining partisan advantage or revenge, usually by a party recently come to power.

river and harbor bills. Bills making appropriations for the improvement of rivers and harbors, long the outstanding examples of logrolling and pork-barrel tactics in Congress.

road. A public way (as for the passage of vehicles, persons, and animals) constructed and maintained by federal, State, or local government. Early federal road construction (*see* Cumberland Road) ended abruptly with Jackson's veto of the Maysville Road bill in 1830. A system of free, hard-surfaced, interconnected highways was necessitated by the development of motor transportation, and was at first financed by State bond issues and special taxes on motorists. Various federal highway acts beginning in 1916 provided for grants-in-aid to be spent by State highway departments under the supervision of the Bureau of Public Roads, and for some direct federal expenditures on work relief projects. The Pennsylvania Turnpike, completed from Carlisle to Pittsburgh in 1940, was the first of several limited-access State toll roads. In 1956 Congress authorized the expenditure of $33.4 billion for a vast new highway system to provide major, arterial, high-speed north-south and east-west freeways. In spite of supplemental authorizations and appropriations the system is considerably short of completion. *See* post road.

Robinson-Patman Act. An act of Congress, June 19, 1936, which prohibits special or disguised discounts to purchasers of commodities or any price discrimination among such purchasers where it would tend to lessen competition or create a monopoly.

Rogers Act. An act of Congress, May 24, 1924, which consolidated the formerly separate diplomatic and consular services into one Foreign Service whose officers could be assigned on an interchangeable basis either to diplomatic or consular posts; and provided that appointments be made on the basis of merit to classes and grades in the Foreign Service, with promotion for merit and liberal retirement allowances. *See* Foreign Service; Foreign Service officer.

roll call. The calling of the names of members of a deliberative body to ascertain the presence of a quorum or for a record vote, *q.v.*

roorback. A campaign falsehood;—derived from the publication in 1844 of extracts from the supposed "Travels" of a fictitious Baron Roorback reflecting on James K. Polk.

Roosevelt Corollary. A policy developed by President Theodore Roosevelt in 1904 and 1905 that, since the Monroe Doctrine protects Latin America from European interference, the United States should protect European nations from flagrant wrongdoing on the part of a Latin American nation.

Roosevelt Doctrine. *See* stewardship theory.

Roosevelt Library. A library at Hyde Park, N.Y., in which are housed historical papers donated by President F. D. Roosevelt and materials acquired by the federal government which relate to his administration. It is supervised by the General Services Administration, *q.v.*

rooster. An emblem of the Democratic party dating from about 1842.

Root-Takahira Agreement. An executive agreement between the United States and Japan, Nov. 30, 1908, whereby each promised to respect the other's possessions in the Pacific, to preserve the independence and territorial integrity of China, and to respect the equal opportunity of all nations to trade with China.

rotation in office. Rapid turnover in the personnel of appointive offices, a characteristic of the spoils system introduced under President Jackson in 1829, and justified in Jackson's time as a means of educating a large number of citizens in political affairs.

ROTC Reserve Officers Training Corps.

rotten borough. A parliamentary constituency (as formerly in England) containing few voters;—sometimes applied to certain States or districts in the United States.

Roughrider. A nickname of Theodore Roosevelt, whose regiment in the Spanish-American War was familiarly so called.

royal colony. A colony governed by an appointive governor acting under strict instructions from the monarch. The governor is assisted by a council appointed by the monarch and by a popularly elected assembly which, by its controls over revenue, appropriation, and other bills, often secures a measure of self-government to the colony. *Compare* charter colony; proprietary colony.

RRB Railroad Retirement Board.

rubber stamp. An official or a public body with discretionary powers whose acts are said to be dictated by a superior officer or a political boss.

rugged individualism. Support of a laissez-faire economic policy; *also:* firm resistance to governmental collectivism or paternalism.

rule. 1. An authoritative regulation or standard to be followed; *specifically:* a regulation adopted by a legislative body to secure adequate debate, freedom of expression, full consideration, protection of the minority against surprise or fraud, and the orderly and prompt disposal of business. 2. A statement of an administrative agency, having general or particular application and future effect, designed to implement, interpret, or prescribe requirements to be followed in rate-making or in regulating financial structures, prices, services, and facilities.

rule-making power. 1. The power of a court to make regulations for its procedure or to devise a formula for the construction or interpretation of statutes. 2. The power of an officer or agency, derived from a constitution or statute to formulate, amend, or repeal a rule. It embraces the power to interpret and elaborate a statute and to determine when conditions exist that bring a contingent statute's provisions into effect.

rule of law. An Anglo-American doctrine that the law is supreme and that the rights of persons under the law are protected by the regular courts of justice from arbitrary acts of officers of the government.

rule of reason. A doctrine of the U.S. Supreme Court, first announced in 1911 in the American Tobacco and Standard Oil cases, 221 U.S. 106 and 221 U.S. 1, that the Sherman Antitrust Act applied not to large business combinations as such but to those which used their power for "unreasonable" restraints of trade.

Rule of 1756. A rule of international law that neutrals are not permitted in time of war to pursue trade with a belligerent which has been closed to them in time of peace.

Rules. *See* Committee on Rules.

ruling. An authoritative interpretation of a provision of a statute, order, regulation, or ordinance rendered by a superior administrative official, tribunal, or presiding officer. *Compare* rule.

rum fleet. Vessels of foreign registry engaged in smuggling liquors into the United States during the prohibition era.

rum, Romanism, and rebellion. *See* Burchard incident.

runoff primary. A second primary election between the two candidates who received the largest number of votes in the first primary, provided for in all the States of the Solid South except Virginia as a means of obviating nominations by a mere plurality.

Rural Electrification Administration. A unit of the Department of Agriculture, created in May, 1935, whose principal function is to make loans for the construction of electric power distribution systems in rural areas and improve telephone communication facilities.

Rush-Bagot Agreement. An agreement, in 1817, between the United States and Great Britain to maintain only token naval forces on the Great Lakes;—the first step toward the demilitarization of the 3,000-mile boundary between the United States and Canada.

Ryuku Islands. Some 64 islands in the Western Pacific, northeast of Formosa (Taiwan), which Japan, while retaining residual sovereignty, ceded to the United States at the end of World War II. The islands now constitute an important American base in the Far East. A high commissioner, representing the Secretary of Defense, supervises the local administration which consists of a locally-elected legislature and an appointed executive.

S

sabotage. Malicious waste, destruction of property, or other acts designed to hamper production by employees in a deliberate effort to weaken an employer or by rebels or fifth columnists to impede a nation's war effort.

Sacco-Vanzetti case. The case of two aliens who were convicted of the murder of a paymaster in Massachusetts on Apr. 15, 1920. The introduction of evidence showing their radicalism and certain questions of the prosecutor and remarks of the judge created a widespread impression that the defendants were being tried for their political opinions. After legal resources had been exhausted, Governor Fuller appointed a commission of laymen, who reported that the trial had been fair. Both defendants were executed on Aug. 22, 1927.

safe conduct. 1. A permit from a belligerent to make a designated voyage; *especially:* one of the papers carried by a vessel in time of war. **2.** A guard or convoy to insure unmolested passage through enemy territory or on the high seas.

safety appliance. Any mechanical device or other instrument, installation of which, often required by law, is intended to prevent accidents to operators of machines, or to workmen in mines and factories, or to insure safety of passengers and employees on airplanes, railways, and motor vehicles.

Sage of Greystone. A nickname of Samuel J. Tilden.

Sage of Monticello. A nickname of Thomas Jefferson.

St. Lawrence Waterway. A joint American-Canadian work which makes the St. Lawrence River navigable for ocean-going vessels as part of a deep waterway from the Great Lakes to the Atlantic and exploits the power resources of the river. It was projected by treaty in 1932, Congress appropriated the American share of the funds in 1954, and it was completed in 1959.

salary. Payment to an official or employee at fixed intervals for services rendered.

salary grab. An act of Congress, Mar. 3, 1873, which increased the salaries of members of Congress from $5,000 to $7,500 a year and made the increases retroactive to the Congress just expiring. It was repealed by the next Congress.

sales tax. A tax on the sale of commodities and services, usually a fixed percentage of the selling price, and normally paid by the purchaser at the time of the sale. Although opposed by some fiscal experts as regressive, sales taxes were imposed in many States in the 1930's and, by the 1960's, they had become normal sources of State and local revenue, with rates as high as 5 per cent in some taxing jurisdictions.

Salt River. A tributary of the Ohio River in the Kentucky backwoods, up which defeated candidates and parties are supposed to row to oblivion.

Samoan Islands. *See* American Samoa.

sample ballot. A facsimile of the official ballot distributed before an election for the information of voters.

sanction. 1. Approval or ratification by higher authority. 2. Coercive action authorized by a court to right a wrong, restore property, etc. (*civil sanction*). 3. That part of a law which is designed to secure enforcement by imposing a penalty for its violation or offering a reward for its observance. 4. *In international law:* suspension of normal economic relations, embargo of goods, and military intervention by one or several countries to discourage aggressive or inhumane acts by another.

Sand Lot party. A nickname of the California Workingman's party, opposed to Chinese immigration and monopolies, and organized by Denis Kearney, a labor agitator;—so-called because its almost nightly meetings were held on the sand lot that later became the site of the Civic Center of San Francisco.

San Francisco Conference. A conference of fifty nations held at San Francisco, Cal., Apr. 25–June 26, 1945, that drafted the Charter of the United Nations; *called officially* the United Nations Conference on International Organization (UNCIO).

sanitary district. A special district (as the Chicago Sanitary District, *q.v.*) set up by a State to provide sewage disposal service and protect water supplies of large metropolitan areas.

satellite city. A suburban area geographically and industrially a part of an adjacent metropolis but having a separate corporate existence.

satellite state. Any state (as Poland or Hungary) whose basic policies are determined by a more powerful state (as Russia) and are harmonized with its policies.

savings bonds and stamps. Obligations of the United States issued for purchase by the general public, to encourage direct lending by the citizen to his government and incidentally to promote thrift. Interest bearing bonds are issued in denominations of $25.00 and upward. In World War II stamps were issued in denominations as low as ten cents which bore no interest but in appropriate amounts were convertible into bonds.

S.B.A. Small Business Administration.

scalawag. A white Southerner who cooperated with radical Republicans in their reconstruction policies after the Civil War;—so-called by Bourbons, *q.v.*

***Scales* v. *United States*.** A case, 367 U.S. 203 (1961), in which the Supreme Court, in reviewing provisions of the Smith Act, *q.v.*, held that the First Amendment did not protect the speech or the privilege of association of an active member of a group (though ostensibly a political party) if the group advocated violent overthrow of the government; nor did the due-process clause of the Fifth Amendment protect an individual who was an active and knowing member of an organization which is conspiring to overthrow the government.

***Schechter Poultry Corp.* v. *United States*.** A case, 295 U.S. 495 (1935), in which the Supreme Court declared the National Industrial Recovery Act, *q.v.*, unconstitutional because it delegated powers, legislative in nature, to the President and attempted, under the guise of the inter-state commerce power, to regulate aspects of a business—in this instance the slaughtering and sale of poultry—which fell within the jurisdiction of the States.

schedule. 1. That part of a constitution which contains detailed arrangements for its becoming effective. 2. A section of a tariff law.

***Schenck* v. *United States*.** See clear-and-present-danger rule.

school district. A special district which has taxing and supervisory powers for the maintenance of public schools. Its governing body, usually a school board, constitutes a quasi corporation.

***School District of Abington Township* v. *Schempp*.** See Engel v. Vitale.

school lunch program. Congressional authorization of funds, June 4, 1946, which, when matched by equal amounts of State or other funds, were available to pay for lunches served in public or nonprofit private schools, the purposes being to safeguard the health of children and encourage domestic consumption of nutritious agricultural commodities.

Schuman plan. A supranational European community which seeks to maintain a common market for coal, iron, and steel among Germany, France, Italy, Belgium, The Netherlands, and Luxembourg. The treaty and institutional framework were largely the work of Jean Monnet and were announced by Robert Schuman, French Foreign Minister, May 9, 1950. *Called officially* the European Coal and Steel Community.

scientific assessment. The procedure in certain American cities of applying expert criteria and uniform valuation standards, based on actual prices received for comparable property, to the assessment of real estate for taxation.

Scopes trial. The trial in Dayton, Tenn., in 1925 of John Thomas Scopes, a high school teacher, who taught the theory of evolution in violation of a Tennessee statute (repealed 1967). William Jennings Bryan assisted in the prosecution and Clarence Darrow appeared for the defense. Scopes was found guilty and fined $100. The State supreme court rescinded the fine but upheld the constitutionality of the law. *Called also* the Monkey Trial.

Scottsboro cases. The cases of nine Negro youths tried at Scottsboro, Ala., for raping two white girls who were traveling on the same freight train with them, and later appealed to the U.S. Supreme Court. The Court held in *Powell* v. *Alabama*, 287 U.S. 45 (1932), that the guarantee of due process of law was violated by the failure of the lower court to make adequate provision for counsel for the defendants; and in *Norris* v. *Alabama*, 294 U.S. 587 (1935), that failure for a generation or more to summon qualified Negroes for jury service within the county was sufficient evidence of an intent to deny equal protection of the laws.

scratch. To strike out the names of one or more candidates on a party ticket and to insert the names of one or more candidates of another party.

scrip. 1. Publicly issued fractional paper currency. **2.** A substitute for legal currency issued in periods of emergency by clearinghouses and banks to be redeemed with legal currency when available.

Seabees. Construction battalions in the Department of the Navy which were assigned building and logistical tasks, especially the construction of airfields, runways, encampments and installations in the Pacific and elsewhere during World War II.

Seabury Commission. A legislative committee, of which Samuel Seabury was chief counsel, appointed to investigate maladministration in the government of New York City. Its disclosures resulted in the resignation of Mayor James J. Walker, Sept. 1, 1932, the temporary ousting of Tammany Hall from control of the city, and the adoption of a new city charter.

seamen. *See* impressment.

search. *See* right of search.

search warrant. Documentary authorization from a magistrate or court to a peace officer to enter and search designated premises and take into custody persons, papers, and other effects described in the warrant, which may be issued only when there is good reason to believe that the person or thing sought may be found on the premises to be searched. *See* unreasonable searches and seizures.

SEATO. An international agency for collective defense and the maintenance of peace and the international status quo in Southeastern Asia and the Southwest Pacific, signed at Manila, P.I., Sept. 8, 1954, by representatives of the United States, France, Australia, the United Kingdom, New Zealand, the Philippine Republic, Pakistan, and Thailand; *called officially* Southeast Asia Treaty Organization.

seat of justice. 1. A county seat. 2. A city or town in which courts of justice are located. 3. A court of justice.

S.E.C. Securities and Exchange Commission.

secession. A voluntary withdrawal; *specifically:* the action between Dec. 20, 1860 and June 8, 1861, of eleven Southern States in declaring themselves no longer members of the United States of America.

second chamber. A legislative house (as the British House of Lords) whose powers are inferior to those of the other house of a bicameral legislature. *Compare* upper chamber.

Second International. The international organization of Marxist parties founded at Paris in 1889 and known since 1921 as the Second and Labor International to which most moderate or gradualist socialist parties of the past half century, including the American, have nominally belonged.

second papers. An alien's formal application for naturalization, with supporting documents;—so-called because, under U.S. naturalization laws, they followed a formerly required (optional since 1952) declaration of intention to become a citizen.

second reading. The stage in American legislative procedure following next after the report of a standing committee.

Second War for Independence. Another name for the War of 1812.

Second War Powers Act. An act of Congress, Mar. 27, 1942, which extended the President's power to requisition tools, machinery and materials for war production; authorized priorities for machinery; extended wartime controls of transportation to motor and water carriers; and waived many formal requirements and procedures for the naturalization of aliens in the armed forces. *See* First War Powers Act.

secretariat. A permanent office, usually headed by a secretary general, with other officers and a corps of employees, that is responsible for administrative and clerical functions of a legislative body or an international organization.

secretary. 1. A head of an administrative department (as Secretary of State) of the federal or State government. 2. An administrative officer (as Secretary to the Governor) in certain States. *Compare* Secretary General.

Secretary General. The chief administrative officer of a public or semi-public body; *specifically:* the chief administrative officer of the United Nations, who is nominated by the Security Council and elected by the General Assembly.

Secret Service. A division of the Treasury Department established in 1860 which suppresses counterfeiting, protects the person of the President, and investigates embezzlement, thefts of government property, and the forging of government checks.

secret session. A legislative session at which the galleries are cleared and members are placed under obligation not to reveal the proceedings; *called also* an executive session because the U.S. Senate formerly conducted executive business in secret.

sectionalism. Excessive devotion to a geographical region to the prejudice of the unity of a country.

Securities Act. An act of Congress, 1933, which made it unlawful to sell securities in interstate commerce or through the mails without filing detailed financial and other statements concerning the companies issuing the securities; *called also* Federal Blue Sky Law.

Securities and Exchange Commission. An independent commission created in 1934 which enforces acts of Congress for the protection of the public against abuses in the issuance of stocks and bonds, regulates the conduct of trading on stock exchanges, supervises investment trusts and investment advisers, controls the use of credit, especially in margin transactions, and gives advice in bankruptcy proceedings when a substantial public interest is involved. It presided over the dissolution of highly pyramided public utility holding companies in the 1930's and 40's. *See* Securities Exchange Act; Investment Advisers Act; Investment Company Act; Trust Indenture Act.

Securities Exchange Act. An act of Congress, June 6, 1934, which created the Securities and Exchange Commission, *q.v.*, strengthened the Securities Act, *q.v.*, by requiring the filing of detailed reports by companies with the Commission and the exchanges, and the disclosure of stock holdings and security transactions of officers and directors, conferred on the Commission rule-making power concerning short sales, floor trading, and odd-lot dealings, and empowered it to fix minimum margin requirements.

Security Council. One of the principal organs of the United Nations consisting of representatives of the five permanent member nations (the United Kingdom, the United States, Russia, France, and the Republic of China) and, since 1966, of representatives of ten other nations five of which are chosen each year for two-year terms. Its chief responsibility is to discharge the duties outlined by the United Nations Charter for maintaining world peace and security. The concurrence of ten of the fifteen members is necessary to a decision, but on all substantive issues the five permanent members must concur; any non-concurring permanent member is said to have a veto of such council decisions.

security risk. A public employee who is unreliable or untrustworthy, or apt to yield to pressure to act contrary to the best interests of his country, or who has an association with a saboteur, spy, traitor, seditionist, or anarchist, or who advocates the overthrow of the government by violent means. By executive order of Apr. 27, 1953, federal security risks were made liable to dismissal if in sensitive positions.

sedition. Publications, utterances, or other activities, short of overt acts of treason, which are deemed to encourage resistance to laws or disrespect for government.

Sedition Act. 1. A law of Congress, July 14, 1798, imposing severe penalties for conspiracy against the Government or the writing or printing of false or malicious statements about the President or Congress. 2. An act, May 16, 1918, directed against anyone who hindered the prosecution of World War I.

segregated appropriations. *See* segregation 1.

segregation. 1. Determination, in minute detail, of the purposes for which monies appropriated by a legislature are to be spent. 2. The allocation of certain taxes or their proceeds to the use of local political subdivisions. 3. The practice prevalent in certain Southern States and formerly often required by statute in such States of providing separate but equal treatment for members of white and Negro races in educational, amusement, transportation and other public facilities. The Supreme Court declared separate but equal educational facilities unconstitutional on May 17, 1954, and ordered all States to integrate their public school systems. Other segregationist practices have since been held illegal by the courts. The existence of separate schools and other public facilities for Negroes and whites resulting from the residential concentration of the races in certain metropolitan areas is often called de facto segregation, *q.v. See* desegregation; equal protection.

seigniorage. 1. A fee charged by a mint for coining precious metal. 2. The difference between the value of the metal in a coin and its face value, representing a profit to the government.

select committee. *See* special committee.

Selective Draft Law cases. Cases arising from the refusal of persons to register for compulsory military service under the Selective Service Act of 1917. The Supreme Court, 245 U.S. 366 (1918), supported the compulsory features of the act, holding that Congress' power to raise and support armies is separate and distinct from its power to call the States' militia into federal service; that the power to raise armies includes the power to compel military service; and that compulsory service is an obligation of a citizen to his government, sanctioned by numerous precedents in American history. Subsequent cases have emphasized and extended this decision.

Selective Service System. The conscription or draft of persons into the armed forces established in 1940 and extended by later acts. Community draft boards of three or more members classify males of military age (*a*) as immediately available for military service or for limited service; (*b*) as deferred because of family obligations, engaged in, or preparing for an occupation essential to the national welfare, membership in the armed forces, the national guard, or the reserves; or (*c*) as mentally, physically, or morally unfit for service.

selectman. A member of the governing board of a New England town except in Rhode Island.

self-determination. *See* national self-determination.

self-government. 1. Government in which there is a substantial measure of participation by the generality of the citizens through a system of elections and representation. 2. The autonomy enjoyed by municipalities and local political subdivisions in the management of local governmental affairs.

self-incrimination. *See* incrimination.

self-liquidating project. A public work (as a toll bridge, dock, or electric plant) the income from which is sufficient to pay operating expenses and, within a stated period of years, amortize the cost of construction.

self-perpetuating board. A board with power to renew or maintain its membership indefinitely by electing new members to fill vacancies as they occur.

selling out. Abandoning one's party or political friends in return for an appointment or pecuniary reward.

semisovereign. Possessing limited or partial sovereignty.

senate. The upper legislative house of the federal government, of the States, and of many foreign countries. The U.S. Senate was designed to give the States, as such, equality of representation, and each State has two Senators. Under the terms of the 17th Amendment, adopted in 1913, Senators are elected by popular vote, and not by State legislatures, as formerly. The term is six years. Vacancies are filled by special elections, though the State legislatures may empower the governor to make temporary appointments until an election can be held. The Vice President is normally the presiding officer of the Senate, but he may vote only when it is equally divided. A President pro tempore, elected by the Senate from its own membership, presides when the Vice President is absent. The special powers of the Senate are to try impeachments, ratify treaties, confirm appointments, and, when no candidate for Vice President has received a majority of electoral votes, to elect a Vice President from the two receiving the highest electoral votes. A two-thirds vote is required for conviction after impeachment or the ratification of a treaty. The legislative power of the Senate is practically coordinate with that of the House of Representatives; for, though the House alone may originate revenue bills, the Senate may amend any part of such a bill after the enacting clause.

Senate's Conscience. A nickname of Senator John J. Williams of Delaware bestowed because of his numerous exposures of waste, corruption, and wrongdoing by officials belonging to both political parties.

Senator. A member of the Senate of the United States or of a similarly named chamber in a State legislature.

senatorial courtesy. A long-standing custom of the Senate that members of the majority party will refuse to approve nominations submitted by the President if the Senators representing the State in which the nominee resides, and belonging to the majority party, have not given their prior approval of the nomination. In effect the custom transfers to such Senators the distribution of patronage from their States. The custom does not apply to cabinet positions.

seniority rule. The custom, nearly always observed in both houses of Congress, that a member who has served on a committee in the preceding Congress is entitled to reappointment on it and to rank in accordance with his years of continuous service on the committee; and that the member of the majority party with the longest continuous service is entitled to be named as chairman of the committee.

sensitive position. A civil service position whose occupant has access to classified documents and other sources of information disclosure of which might imperil national security.

sentence. A judgment pronounced by a court of law; *especially:* the penalty imposed upon a convicted defendant in a criminal case.

separate but equal. *See Plessy v. Ferguson.*

separation of church and state. An historic policy, embodied in the First Amendment to the Constitution and in many State constitutions, which forbids public establishment and financial support of any religious confession, religious organizations being regarded as voluntary associations which, although enjoying the privilege of tax exemption, must seek support from their own members and not from the public treasury.

separation of powers. The allocation of lawmaking, law-enforcing, and law-interpreting functions of government to different bodies in order to preserve liberty from the tyranny thought to result from combining legislative, executive, and judicial powers in the same hands. Derived from European writers, especially Montesquieu, and supported by colonial experience, this theory, as applied in American State and federal constitutions, grows out of the assumption that the only effective restraints upon arbitrary governmental power—"paper guarantees" to the contrary notwithstanding—are those internal checks woven into the machinery of government itself. The separation of legislative, executive, and judicial powers becomes a convenient medium for establishing a check and balance system within the government. That this was the major objective behind the separation of powers theory is evidenced by the fact that nowhere is the separation complete; for each of the three departments does exercise powers logically belonging to the other two as a means of controlling them more effectively. The existence of numerous independent boards and commissions, each exercising combined legislative, executive, and judicial powers, apparently is contrary to the separation of powers theory, though it has not seriously impaired the efficacy of the check and balance system for which separation of powers became a convenient foundation stone.

sergeant at arms. An officer (though not a member) of a legislative body who is present at all sessions and executes its orders to compel the attendance of absent members, preserve order, make arrests, and serve subpoenas.

serial bond. One of an issue of bonds which mature at different specified dates, thus enabling the borrowing authority to redeem some of them each year without recourse to a sinking fund, *q.v.*

Servicemen's Readjustment Act. *See* G.I. Bill of Rights.

service rating. The opinion expressed by a supervisory officer, usually at intervals of six months, as to a civil servant's proficiency and character, which is used as a basis for promotion, retirement, or other action.

service record. 1. A continuing compilation of data about a civil servant's qualifications, performance, and status, maintained by the Civil Service Commission. **2.** The cumulative data pertinent to an enlisted man's service in the armed forces.

servitude. 1. Bondage or peonage, *q.v.* **2.** A restriction upon ownership or sovereignty. A *private servitude* qualifies ownership by a right enjoyed by a nonowner; a *state servitude* enables one state to use the territory of another for a specific purpose.

session. 1. The period during which a legislature or court is sitting. A session of Congress begins on a day fixed by the Constitution, by law, or by call of the President, and ends at a time fixed by concurrent resolution or when the terms of Representatives expire. 2. A sitting during one legislative day.

session laws. A collection of acts and resolutions of Congress which, before 1937, was published at the end of each session;—superseded by the *United States Statutes at Large, q.v.*, which, published at the end of each Congress prior to 1937, is now published at the end of each session.

Seventeenth Amendment. An amendment to the Constitution, proclaimed May 31, 1913, which transferred the election of U.S. Senators from the State legislature to the voters of the State qualified to vote for the more numerous branch of the State legislature, but provided that the legislature may empower the governor to make a temporary appointment to fill a vacancy until an election can be held.

Seventh-of-March Speech. An address by Daniel Webster in the U.S. Senate, Mar. 7, 1850, supporting the Compromise of 1850, *q.v.*, between North and South.

severance tax. A tax, levied either ad valorem or according to amount, on mineral or forest products at the time they are removed or severed from the soil and usually regarded as a form of property taxation.

Seward's Folly. *See* Alaska purchase.

sewerage district. A special district, which may include the areas of several cities, towns, or other local government units, established by a State to operate facilities for sewage treatment. *Compare* sanitary district.

shakedown. A forced contribution exacted by a political machine from underworld characters and others who have benefited from its special favors.

shaking the pear tree. Distributing the spoils of office.

shared tax. A tax which is assessed and administered by a higher unit of government, and from which a certain percentage or amount is distributed to a lower unit of government. It is commonly used by States for the collection and allocation of sales, income, motor vehicle, or other taxes; and its extension to federal-State relations is advocated by some tax reformers in order to avoid the overhead expenses of the grant-in-aid system.

share the wealth. A slogan taken from President F. D. Roosevelt's speech of acceptance in 1932 by Huey P. Long, Louisiana political boss and United States Senator, to describe his own social philosophy and his campaign against corporations and vested interests.

Shays Rebellion. An armed revolt led by Daniel Shays in western Massachusetts, 1786–87, which sought relief for the debtor class.

Shelley* v. *Kraemer. The case, 334 U.S. 92 (1948), in which the Supreme Court refused to validate enforcement of restrictive covenants (long-term private agreements which limit the right to own or occupy premises to certain races or groups of persons and exclude others, usually Negroes), on the ground that involvement of the State courts in the enforcement of such covenants amounts to State enforcement of a discriminatory policy against a group of its citizens and is, therefore, a violation of the equal-protection clause of the 14th Amendment.

Sheppard-Towner Act. A law of Congress, Nov. 23, 1921, providing for grants-in-aid to the States for the care and protection of mothers and their young children.

sheriff. The chief law-enforcement officer of a county who conserves the peace, attends sessions of courts, executes court orders, has charge of prisoners, usually has the duty of maintaining the jail and feeding its inmates, and in some States collects taxes. He is popularly elective in all States except Rhode Island and is often not re-eligible.

Sherman Antitrust Act. An act of Congress, July 2, 1890, which forbade "every contract, combination in the form of trust or otherwise, or conspiracy, in restraint of commerce among the several States," under severe penalties, and provided for its enforcement by injunction, criminal prosecution, confiscation of property used in the unlawful conspiracy, and the award of threefold damages to injured parties. It is the basic federal law on the subject of monopolies and has frequently been modified by later statutes and judicial interpretations.

Sherman Silver Purchase Act. An act of Congress, July 14, 1890, repealed in 1893, which required the Secretary of the Treasury to purchase 4,500,000 ounces of silver a month.

shinplasters. 1. Fractional paper currency issued by the United States, 1862–76. 2. Notes in small denominations formerly issued by private bankers.

shipping board. *See* United States Maritime Commission.

shipping subsidy. Public financial aid granted to private builders or operators of merchant ships either in the form of outright payments or as favorable contracts for carrying mails, for the purposes of building up a merchant marine, expanding foreign commerce, and having auxiliary vessels available for use in time of war.

shirt-sleeve diplomacy. The conduct of diplomatic relations by direct and relatively informal methods.

short-ballot movement. Agitation for the elimination of many elective offices with ministerial duties and making them appointive, to concentrate the attention of voters on legislative and policy-determining executive officers. The movement has succeeded in numerous State, municipal, and county reorganizations.

short-form bill. A legislative proposal in which the sponsor outlines the purpose and general provisions, leaving to a standing committee, if it approves, the function of drafting the bill in full. It was first used in Hawaii and later adopted in several other States.

short session. The session of Congress which, before the 20th Amendment, met on the first Monday in December of even-numbered years and ended the following March 3, when terms of members expired.

short-term paper. Bills maturing in less than one year or notes maturing in less than five years sold by the U.S. Treasury; *also:* any similar borrowing by others, usually at lower rates of interest than paid on long-term loans. Such obligations are not part of the government's funded debt.

Shreveport Rate case. A case, *Houston E. & W. Texas Ry. Co.* v. *United States,* 234 U.S. 342 (1914), in which the Texas Railway Commission was found to have fixed unreasonably low rates between distributing centers in Texas and points near the State's borders, to the disadvantage of distributors in other States. The Supreme Court ordered the Texas Commission to raise its rates to conform with those fixed by the Interstate Commerce Commission for interstate shipments.

sifting committee. A committee appointed in some State legislatures, or one branch, to determine the priority of bills.

silk-stocking district. An election district inhabited chiefly by people of wealth.

silver. A precious metal which in the early period of U.S. history had a fairly stable value in relation to gold, but which declined greatly following numerous discoveries of silver ore about 1860. Congress stopped the coinage of silver dollars in 1873; and a little later an insistent demand arose from advocates of cheap money for the remonetization of silver which, though partly satisfied by a limited coinage of silver after 1878 and the Sherman Silver Purchase Act, *q.v.,* of 1890, culminated in Bryan's campaign for the free and unlimited coinage of silver at the ratio of 16 to 1. His defeat temporarily settled the question, but in 1933 Congress remonetized silver and in 1934 in effect nationalized new production by requiring the Secretary of the Treasury to purchase silver until the total value held by the Treasury represented one-fourth of the total bullion reserve. In 1965 silver was practically eliminated from coinage.

silver certificate. United States paper currency formerly issued in varying denominations and based on equivalent value of silver bullion or silver coins held by the Treasury.

Silver Grays. The more conservative members of the Whig party who supported the Compromise of 1850 and Fillmore's administration.

Silver Shirts. A native American fascist movement of minor importance set up in 1933 and modeled on the Nazi storm-trooper organizations.

simple conference. A conference between legislative houses in which managers are bound by instructions of one or both houses.

simple resolution. A resolution, *q.v.,* passed by one legislative house.

sinecure. A public office providing a salary or other emolument but having no duties or only nominal ones.

sine die. Without fixing a date for reassembling.

single-member district. An electoral district which returns one member, chosen by a plurality, to a legislative assembly. In the United States such districts must be nearly equal in population.

single standard. A system of currency in which the value of the basic unit is a fixed weight of only one precious metal.

single tax. The proposal of Henry George and other economists that unearned increases in land value, as distinct from income from use of land or improvements thereon, should be diverted to the public treasury in the form of a tax, the proceeds of which, it was argued, would alone be sufficient to pay the cost of government.

single-transferable vote. See Hare plan; Ware plan.

sinking fund. A separate fund set aside out of revenues, usually at yearly intervals, to be invested and eventually, with accumulated interest, applied to the redemption of public debt or a certain bond issue.

sit-down strike. A work stoppage accompanied by occupation of company premises by workers attempting to compel employers to accede to their demands;—a frequent occurrence in 1937.

sit-in. A concerted effort to obstruct access to a building, bridge, or public way in order to call public attention to the grievances of the demonstrators and to secure redress by appropriate public action.

Sixteenth Amendment. An amendment to the Constitution, proclaimed Feb. 25, 1913, which permits Congress to tax incomes "from whatever source derived," thus nullifying the Supreme Court's decision in *Pollock* v. *Farmers' Loan and Trust Co.*, which had declared that an income tax was a direct tax, which would be constitutionally valid only if apportioned among the States according to population; *called also* Income Tax Amendment.

sixteen to one. A slogan of the Democratic party in 1896 to demand the free and unlimited coinage of silver at the value ratio of 16 ounces of silver to 1 of gold.

slander. The oral utterance or publication of a falsehood that is intended to defame a person or injure his reputation. *Compare* libel.

slate. A list of candidates informally agreed upon in advance of a primary election, convention, or election.

Slaughterhouse cases. Several cases in which butchers in New Orleans appealed for the protection guaranteed to citizens of the United States by the 14th Amendment against a discriminatory act of the Louisiana legislature passed under the police power of the State. In denying the appeal the Supreme Court, 16 Wall. 36 (1873), held that, though the amendment created a federal citizenship, the rights guaranteed against impairment were rights of federal, and not of State, citizenship; and that its adoption did not indicate any purpose to destroy the main features of the federal system. In later cases, however, the Supreme Court has gradually extended its protection over the field of personal and property rights against State impairment.

Slave labor law. An epithet applied by many labor leaders to the Taft-Hartley Labor-Management Relations Act, *q.v.*

slavery. A legal status of a person who is owned as a chattel by a master, subjected to the master's commands, and obligated to perform labor without consent or compensation. Slavery existed in all the colonies, but it had been abolished in the Northern States by 1804. Southern fears that the abolitionist movement would interfere with slavery in the South were partly responsible for the policy of keeping an even balance in admitting new States, 1820–1860, and for the doctrine of State sovereignty, secession, and the Civil War. Slavery was abolished in the United States by the Thirteenth Amendment, *q.v.*

slave trade. The transportation of persons for the purpose of selling them into slavery, which has been outlawed under numerous international agreements. Ships of all nations have the right to search vessels suspected of transporting slaves.

sliding scale. 1. A wage, tariff, or farm-support structure adjustable to change in prices. 2. A public utility rate structure in which a customer's rate base is reduced as his use of the utility's service increases.

slip law. A statute printed in pamphlet form for distribution to the public immediately after passage.

Slochower v. Board of Education. A case, 350 U.S. 551 (1956), in which the Supreme Court invalidated the discharge by the New York City Board of Higher Education of a tenure professor in one of the City's colleges, as required by New York State law, because the professor had invoked the Fifth Amendment's guarantee against self-incrimination in a Congressional investigation into Communist activity. The Court held that invocation of the self-incrimination clause of the Fifth Amendment is a procedural protection for the individual and a constitutional privilege, and does not imply, *ipso facto*, any violation of law or professional incompetence; and dismissal as in this case is a violation of due process and untenable under the 14th Amendment.

slowdown. A work stoppage or a deliberate decrease in the normal on-the-job activity by workmen, allegedly voluntary, but usually ordered by a union of which the workmen are members, designed to secure economic concessions from an employer when, for tactical reasons, the union does not consider a strike or other more formal economic sanction desirable.

slum clearance. Large-scale razing of outmoded, unsightly, and unsanitary dwellings and other buildings in the congested or slum districts of large cities and the construction on the cleared site of modern housing and community facilities for low-income families. Such activity is now encouraged by means of federal loans and capital grants to State and local public housing authorities which carry out the specific projects.

slush fund. A fund collected for bribing public officials or improperly influencing public opinion.

Small Business Administration. An agency created in 1953 to advise and assist small business ventures, to make certain that small businesses obtain a fair share of government contracts, to license and regulate small companies and extend loans to them, to improve their managerial direction, and to assist with loans and credit when they suffer from flood or other disaster.

small claims court. A special court which provides expeditious, informal, and inexpensive adjudication of small contractual claims.

small loan law. A law in effect in nearly all the States fixing the maximum legal rate of interest (normally from 2½ to 3 per cent per month) on short-term loans of $300 or less by banks and finance companies.

smear technique. The concerted effort of a group (often secretly sponsored by a party organization and not overtly identified with it), to destroy the reputation of an official or a candidate by distortion and misrepresentation of facts, impugning of motives, and innuendo.

smelling committee. A legislative investigating committee which is allegedly created from partisan motives to unearth unsavory facts about the conduct of an office for use in a political campaign.

Smith Act. An act of Congress, June 29, 1940, which required the annual registration of aliens and made it unlawful to teach or advocate the overthrow of government by force and violence, or knowingly to become a member of a group having such tenets, or to organize such a group. The act was upheld as constitutional when it was enforced in 1948 against eleven leaders of the American Communist party. *Called also* Alien Registration Act. *See Dennis* v. *United States.*

Smith-Connally Act. The War Labor Disputes Act, passed over President F. D. Roosevelt's veto, June 26, 1943, which compelled a union to delay thirty days before striking, required prior approval of a strike by secret ballot of union members, and authorized the President to seize any struck war plant.

Smith-Hughes Act. An act of Congress, Feb. 23, 1917, which provided federal grants-in-aid to States for vocational training in agriculture, home economics, trade, and industry.

Smith-Lever Act. An act of Congress, May 8, 1914, which supplied federal funds to the States, partly as grants-in-aid, to support extension work carried on chiefly by county agricultural agents under the joint auspices of the Department of Agriculture and State agricultural colleges.

Smithsonian Institution. An establishment for the "increase and diffusion of knowledge among men," created by act of Congress, Aug. 10, 1846, accepting the bequest of James Smithson, an Englishman, which now includes the National Gallery of Art, the National Collection of Fine Arts, the Freer Gallery of Art, the National Portrait Gallery, the John F. Kennedy Center for the Performing Arts, and certain scientific and technological centers and museums, such as the Museum of Natural History, the Museum of History and Technology, the National Air Museum, the Bureau of American Ethnology, the National Zoological Park, and the Astrophysical Observatory. It is governed by a board of regents consisting of the Chief Justice, the Vice President, three members each of the Senate and the House of Representatives, and six citizens appointed by joint resolution of Congress.

Smith v. Allwright. *See* Texas Primary cases.

smoke-filled room. A place where party bosses are commonly supposed to decide upon nominations prior to the formal choice by delegates to a party convention;—from a description of the circumstances preceding Harding's nomination in 1920.

smothering. An action, such as referring a bill to an unfriendly committee or abuse of power by a committee or its chairman, which prevents a bill from coming to a vote.

smuggling. Illegal and clandestine shipment of persons or goods into or out of a country in order to evade legal prohibitions against such shipments or the payment of customs duties.

Smyth v. Ames. An early rate-regulation case, 169 U.S. 466 (1898), in which the Supreme Court annulled maximum rates prescribed for railways by a public service commission in Nebraska as being so low as to be virtually confiscatory and suggested several different standards for the valuation of property of public utilities which legislatures and regulatory bodies might consider in computing the capital base for a fair return.

snap. Pertaining to a meeting called or a vote taken without sufficient notice to all those entitled to participate.

Snapper. A New York Democrat opposed to the renomination of Grover Cleveland in 1892. *See* Antisnapper.

soapbox oratory. Violent statements on public questions and criticism of the political and social order;—derived from the portable platform used by street corner speakers.

social contract *or* **social compact.** The supposed original covenant of each man with every other man living in a state of nature by means of which they voluntarily gave up some of or all the rights which they were supposed to enjoy in their natural state in return for certain advantages to be derived from organized society, especially the protection provided by government;—the starting point of many theorists of the 17th and 18th centuries in explaining the origin of civil society and establishing a rational basis for the exercise of the coercive powers of the state. The theories are all highly individualistic in that they assume the existence of unrelated individuals at the outset and make all social institutions the product of the deliberate contrivance of such individuals. The conclusions which are derived from these theories, however, vary from the individualism of Locke to the absolutism of Hobbes, for whom all individual rights (except that of self-defense) ceased to exist as soon as the contract had been made. As presented especially by Locke and his followers, social contract theories played a part in the creation of American State and federal Constitutions and in the rise of constitutionalism generally. *Compare* governmental contract.

social insurance. Insurance against the hazards of unemployment, accident, and sickness, and to provide for old age and the survivors of breadwinners, usually compulsory for all persons within a designated group, administered by government agencies, and financed from the proceeds of special taxes levied on employers, or on both employers and employees, and partly from general revenues.

socialism. Any of various doctrines of public ownership of the productive mechanism, and production for use instead of profit, especially as presented by Karl Marx and advocated by one or more minor parties in the United States since 1876.

Socialist Labor party. A union of several Marxist groups formed at Philadelphia, 1876, which rejects piecemeal reforms and cooperation with non-Marxists. Since the 1890's, it has nominated candidates and engaged in political campaigns, but none of its presidential candidates has received as many as 50,000 votes.

Socialist party. A minor U.S. party with progressive and moderate Marxian objectives which nominated candidates in presidential elections from 1900 to 1960. It cast more than 900,000 popular votes in 1912 and 1920. *See* socialism.

Socialist Worker's party. A U.S. party with only nominal voting strength, formed in 1938 by supporters of Leon Trotsky, which claims to have a more revolutionary program than Communists adhering to Joseph Stalin and his successors in power.

socialized medicine. Numerous proposals for public regulation of the services and fees of the members of the medical profession or for cooperative or governmentally subsidized projects to supply medical treatment to the public at little or no cost, which in 1965 resulted in the creation of Medicare, *q.v.*

social legislation. Laws relating to social insurance, public assistance, public welfare, protection of workers, consumers, and minority groups, land tenure, public housing, dependency, or training in specialized skills which are intended primarily to benefit persons in the lower income groups and those who lack the physical, intellectual, or emotional resources to help themselves. In the United States social legislation has been enacted under the police power of the States and under the commerce, taxing, or other powers of the federal government.

social science. Any organized body of knowledge which deals with man's environment, history, and political, economic, or other social institutions; *also*: such bodies of knowledge considered collectively. Traditionally the methodology of such sciences has been observational, historical, comparative, deductive, and descriptive, but increasingly analysis of behavioral data and application of statistical techniques characterize research in the social sciences.

Social Security Administration. A unit of the Department of Health, Education, and Welfare which administers the federal old-age, survivors and disability insurance (O.A.S.D.I.) and the federal credit-union programs which together provide partial replacement for earnings lost through old age and disability, encourage cooperative thrift, and make available small loans to members of credit unions.

Social Security cases. Two cases, *Helvering* v. *Davis*, 301 U.S. 619 (1937), and *Steward Machine Co.* v. *Davis*, 301 U.S. 548 (1937), in which the Supreme Court upheld the constitutionality of taxes levied by the federal government on employers and employees in certain establishments to finance the joint federal-State system of unemployment insurance, special assistance to wage earners and others, and the federal old-age insurance program of the Social Security Act of 1935. The Court held that Congress had properly regarded social insecurity as a national problem to be attacked nationally; that the cooperative federal-State features of the social security system did not violate the Tenth Amendment nor coerce the States into abandoning their appropriate governmental functions; and that the proceeds of taxes levied to support this program were spent in aid of the general welfare.

society. 1. A group of individuals united by common interests who possess a sense of corporate unity and discipline. 2. An organization to promote the common objectives of its members.

society of nations. Collectively the sovereign states of the world which are presumed to share certain common internal administrative characteristics and values and, under international law, to enjoy a status of equality in their relations with one another.

Society of the Cincinnati. An association of officers of the American Revolutionary army, formed at the close of the war and intended to be hereditary, which was influential in securing the adoption of the Constitution.

Softs *or* **Soft-shells.** The antislavery and reform wing of the Hunkers, *q.v.*, in New York about 1848.

soil bank. The agricultural program begun in 1956 under which the federal government compensated farmers who voluntarily reduced their planting of wheat, cotton, corn, and rice or who diverted land from tillage to forage crops or wood lots.

soil conservation. Any systematic effort to maintain soil fertility by crop rotation, use of natural or artificial fertilizers, prevention of erosion by reforestation, afforestation, and flood control, improved methods of tillage, or provision of increased water supply for arid lands. In the United States responsibility for encouraging and directing private owners of land in such activities is vested, for the most part, in the Soil Conservation Service of the Department of Agriculture acting in cooperation with State agencies. The Bureau of Land Management, *q.v.*, conducts soil-conservation practices in the public domain.

soldiers' ballot. *See* federal war ballot.

Solicitor General. An official of the Department of Justice who has charge of the business of the United States before the Supreme Court and represents it there in person. When requested by the Attorney General he may appear in any United States court or represent the interests of the United States before a State court. His approval is necessary before the United States may take an appeal to an appellate court.

Solid South. The States of Virginia, North Carolina, South Carolina, Georgia, Florida, Alabama, Mississippi, Louisiana, Texas, and Arkansas, in which, from 1879 to 1948, Republican opposition to the Democratic party was usually ineffective or negligible.

Sons of Liberty. Any one of several secret and informally organized groups of Americans who opposed the Stamp Act, 1765–66, and later oppressive acts of the British government, and who aided in enforcing non-importation agreements.

Sons of the South. Societies organized in Missouri after the passage of the Kansas-Nebraska Bill, 1854, to take possession of Kansas on behalf of slavery.

sons of the wild jackass. A nickname applied in 1929 to independent or insurgent senators by Senator George H. Moses of New Hampshire;— possibly derived from Job 24:5.

sorehead. 1. A defeated candidate who refuses to accept the result of a primary election or a convention. **2.** A disappointed office seeker who turns against his party.

South Americans. A nickname of the proslavery faction of the American or Know-Nothing party; *also:* a nickname of the American party after the North Americans, *q.v.*, seceded from it.

South Carolina* v. *United States. A case, 199 U.S. 437 (1905), in which the Supreme Court held that liquor dispensaries owned and operated by South Carolina were subject to federal excise taxes because the dispensaries were essentially business enterprises and not instrumentalities of government.

Southeast Asia Treaty Organization. *See* SEATO.

Southeastern Power Administration. An agency of the Department of the Interior which markets surplus power generated at reservoirs built by the Army Corps of Engineers in Virginia, the Carolinas, Georgia, Florida, Alabama, Mississippi, Tennessee, and Kentucky.

Southern Christian Leadership Conference. A civil rights organization founded by Dr. Martin Luther King and supported especially by Negro students, which in the 1960's staged demonstrations in several cities to direct national attention to the denial of the Negroes' civil rights.

Southern Confederacy. *See* Confederate States of America.

Southern Manifesto. The Declaration of Constitutional Principles signed by 19 Senators and 82 Representatives from Southern States and presented to Congress, Mar. 12, 1956, which stigmatized the Supreme Court's decision in *Brown* v. *Board of Education, q.v.*, as a clear abuse of constitutional power and decried its encroachment on rights reserved to the States and the people. The signers pledged themselves to use all constitutional means to secure the reversal of the decision.

Southwestern Power Administration. An agency of the Department of the Interior which markets surplus power generated at reservoir projects built by the Army Corps of Engineers at several sites in Arkansas, Missouri, and Oklahoma.

sovereign. 1. The person or body possessing legal sovereignty. 2. The body in whom political sovereignty is thought to reside.

sovereignty. As defined by Bodin in 1576, the "supreme power over citizens and subjects unrestrained by laws." Bodin ascribed to the concept the qualities of inalienability and indivisibility. Although he recognized certain limits upon sovereignty, his definition emphasized the obvious need for a center of final authority in the modern state. Later writers, notably Hobbes, practically discarded all limitations upon the sovereignty of the ruler or rulers and made the power of the state absolute. Today confusion can be avoided only by sharply distinguishing the concept of *legal sovereignty*, which is finality of legal authority, and *political sovereignty*, which is political supremacy; and by insisting that neither concept carries with it any necessary implication of ethical justification for the acts of the sovereign. In international law, sovereignty stands for independent statehood and complete freedom from direct external control.

space. *See* aerial domain.

Space treaty. A treaty signed Jan. 27, 1967, by some 80 nations, which outlines the principles governing exploration and use of outer space. It bars weapons of mass destruction in outer space (although not reconnaissance or spy satellites to check on armaments), and prohibits bases or claims of sovereignty on any celestial body. The treaty became effective several months later when ratified by the United States, the United Kingdom, the U.S.S.R., and other states.

Spanish-American War. A war largely resulting from hatred of Spain whipped up by newspapers, especially those controlled by Hearst and

Pulitzer, which began with a formal declaration by Congress, Apr. 25, 1898, and ended by an armistice, Aug. 12, 1898, and the Treaty of Paris, Feb. 6, 1899. As a result the United States gained Puerto Rico and Guam outright and the Philippines on payment of $20,000,000 to Spain, and for years assumed a virtual protectorate over Cuba whose independence Spain conceded.

span of control. The theoretical number of subordinates (as officers or employees) that in various circumstances can be effectively supervised by one administrative superior;—used in establishing gradations in an administrative hierarchy.

speaker. The presiding officer of the lower house of the legislature in English-speaking countries who conducts the business of the house in accordance with the rules, recognizes members who wish to speak, preserves order and decorum in debate, puts questions to a vote, authenticates by his signature all bills, resolutions, warrants and subpoenas of the house, and is the sole organ of communication between the house and persons outside it. The Speaker of the House of Representatives early became its political leader and at times exercised autocratic control over it largely through his power to appoint standing committees and his position as chairman of the Committee on Rules, powers that were taken from him by the Congressional Revolution of 1910–11, *q.v.* He may still affect the fate of measures through his powers of (*a*) recognition, especially in unanimous consent and suspension of the rules; (*b*) referring bills to committee; and (*c*) ruling on points of order; for though his references and rulings are subject to appeal to the floor, a partisan majority ordinarily sustains him. The Speaker retains all the rights of a member of the House, though he rarely participates in debate and may refrain from voting except to give a casting vote, *q.v.* Speakers in State legislatures usually possess the powers exercised by the Speaker of the House before 1910. The British speaker, who observes a studied nonpartisanship, has more power than American speakers to halt dilatory tactics.

special assessment. A levy upon the owners of property adjacent to a contemplated public improvement to defray the capital cost thereof. It differs from a tax in that it is levied for a specific purpose and in an amount proportioned to the direct benefit of the property assessed.

special committee. A legislative committee whose jurisdiction is limited to investigation, consideration, and report on a particular subject or bill; *called also* select committee. *Compare* standing committee.

special district. A political subdivision of a State established to provide a single public service (as irrigation, water supply, flood control, sanitation, or a school system) within a delimited geographical area.

special election. An election conducted in the interval between regularly scheduled elections in order to fill a vacancy, decide a question submitted on an initiative, referendum, or recall petition, approve a bond issue, adopt a new charter, or determine whether a suburb is to be annexed to a city.

special fund. Monies derived from unusual sources, obtained by special taxes, or reserved for special or extraordinary purposes.

specialized agency. An agency of the United Nations which conducts research on, or administers, a particular subject matter under the aegis of the Economic and Social Council, *q.v.* They are the Food and Agriculture Organization, Intergovernmental Maritime Consultative Organization, International Bank for Reconstruction and Development, International Civil Aviation Organization, International Development Association, International Finance Corporation, International Labor Organization, International Monetary Fund, International Telecommunication Union, United Nations Educational, Scientific and Cultural Organization, Universal Postal Union, World Health Organization, and World Meteorological Organization.

special legislation. Private bills, *q.v.*, passed for the relief or benefit of an individual or applying to a local government unit designated by name.

special order. 1. A legislative rule adopted for the consideration or disposition of a single measure or matter. A special order proposed by the Committee on Rules and adopted by the House of Representatives is the usual means of bringing a measure to the floor. 2. A military order applying to one or a few persons and not of general interest.

special session. An extraordinary session, *q.v.*

specie. Metallic money, especially gold or silver coins.

Specie Circular. An order of President Jackson, July 11, 1836, directing that government agents receive only gold, silver, or Virginia scrip in payment for public lands.

specific performance. The performance of the exact terms of a contract which may be required by a court of equity when an award of damages to the injured party at common law would be inadequate.

specific rate. A customs or other tax rate fixed upon articles according to their weight, volume, or other physical characteristics. *Compare* ad valorem tax.

speech and press. *See* freedom of speech and press.

speech of acceptance. An address before a party convention by a newly nominated candidate for high executive office, usually designed to create party unity and enlist enthusiastic support in the election campaign.

speeding. Operation of a motor vehicle or other conveyance at a rate of speed in excess of the maximum allowed by law.

speedy trial. A trial conducted without unreasonable delay according to the rules of procedure prescribed by law.

spellbinder. A charismatic orator who exercises great influence over a party convention or other meeting;—often used in a humorous or depreciatory sense.

sphere of influence. A politically backward, economically underdeveloped region, in which a powerful state claims, often with the concurrence of other states, special rights of economic exploitation, colonization, and possible ultimate annexation.

splinter party. A small party consisting usually of doctrinaire adherents which normally has little effect in elections, but which, proliferating in several European countries after World War I, effectively reduced the strength of established parties and prevented the creation of durable parliamentary coalitions.

split session. A legislative session, at one time required in several States, which consists of two parts: the first devoted to the appointment of committees and the introduction and reference of bills, after which an extended adjournment occurs for consultations between members and their constituents; and the second, to the consideration of bills already introduced or of new bills introduced only by consent of an extramajority vote.

split ticket. A ballot marked for candidates of more than one party.

spoils system. The practice of regarding appointive offices as booty for a party which comes to power, under the principle "To the victor belong the spoils of the enemy"; of turning out the incumbents; and of distributing offices, public contracts, and official favors to persons, regardless of their competence, who have worked for the success of the party; —opposed to merit system. *See* civil service.

sponsion. *International law:* an agreement made by a military commander or diplomatic agent when he is without power to act or acts in excess of authority. It is not binding on his state unless ratified by it expressly or by implication.

Square Deal. A slogan adopted by President Theodore Roosevelt to characterize his legislative and administrative policies, particularly those to limit the power of corporations and big business.

squatter. 1. One who settles on land to which he has no legal title. 2. One who, under former laws, settled on public land in order to acquire title to the land.

squatter sovereignty. The doctrine, 1854–61, that the settlers of a territory of the United States had the right when organizing a government to admit or exclude slavery as they chose.

S.S.A. Social Security Administration.

S.S.S. Selective Service System.

stabilization fund. The sum of about $2 billion which was the "profit" accruing to the U.S. Treasury from the devaluation of the dollar in terms of gold in 1933;—used by the Treasury to stabilize foreign exchange rates and the domestic money market.

staff. The portion of an administrative organization which has mainly investigative, advisory, or planning functions. *Compare* line.

stalking-horse. A candidate who is put forward by a party organization, or in the interest of another candidate, for the purpose of dividing the opposition, and who withdraws when the purpose is accomplished.

Stalwarts. The "regular" or "machine" faction of the Republican party who were responsible for many of the scandals of Grant's administration, 1869–77, who opposed the reform policies of President Hayes, and who in 1880 tried to obtain a third nomination for Grant.

Stamp Act. An act of Parliament, 1765, imposing taxes and requiring the affixing of stamps as evidence of payment on all legal and commercial documents and newspapers issued in the American colonies;—repealed in 1766 because of colonial and British opposition.

Stamp Act Congress. A meeting of delegates from nine North American colonies at New York, Oct. 7, 1765, which, though admitting the power of the British Parliament to make general regulations concerning the colonies, denied its power to tax them, insisting that only a colonial legislature could levy internal taxes.

stampede. A sudden tumultuous movement in a political convention when many delegates desert the candidates they have previously supported and concentrate their votes on the winning candidate.

standard metropolitan statistical area. 1. A county, or group of counties, which contains at least one city of 50,000 inhabitants or more or twin cities with a combined population of at least 50,000. **2.** *In New England:* contiguous cities and towns with a population density of 100 or more persons per square mile. *Compare* metropolitan area; metropolitan district.

Standards. *See* National Bureau of Standards.

standing army. The professional army of a country as distinguished from a volunteer, or temporarily conscripted, army or militia.

standing committee. A committee appointed at the beginning of a Congress or legislature, continuing throughout its existence, and having jurisdiction (unless discharged) over all bills which may be introduced concerning a certain subject matter.

standing order. A permanent legislative rule which is applicable in all appropriate circumstances during the life of a legislature and is normally adopted by succeeding legislatures.

standpatter. 1. A member of the conservative faction of the Republican party about 1900. **2.** Any conservative or reactionary in politics.

star-chamber proceeding. A secret proceeding in which a person is given inadequate or no opportunity to present his case or defend himself, and in which the proceedings are conducted and conclusions reached without observing usual judicial formalities;—from the Star Chamber, an ancient court (abolished by Parliament in 1641) which had no jury and was permitted to apply torture.

stare decisis. To stand by decided cases; a principle of Anglo-American jurisprudence that a precedent once established in the decision of a case should be followed in other like cases unless it is found to be in conflict with established principles of justice. *See* precedent.

Star Route Frauds. The establishment of unnecessary mail routes operated under extravagant contracts which was exposed in 1881.

Stars and Bars. 1. The first flag adopted by the Confederate States Congress consisting of two red and one white bars and a blue union containing a number of stars equal to the number of Confederate States. **2.** The battle flag with white stars representing the number of Confederate States on a blue St. Andrew's cross edged in white on a red field; *called also* Southern Cross.

Stars and Stripes. The Flag of the United States, *q.v.*, consisting of 13 alternate red and white stripes and a blue union containing a number of white stars equal to the number of States.

Star-Spangled Banner. 1. The poem composed by Francis Scott Key while detained on a British man-of-war off Fort McHenry in 1814, long used as a national anthem, and officially adopted as such by act of Congress in 1931. **2.** The Flag of the United States.

state. 1. A politically organized body of people permanently occupying a definite territory and living under a government entirely or almost entirely free from external control and competent to secure habitual obedience from all persons within it or specifically possessing both external and internal sovereignty. **2.** A component of the federal systems of the United States, Australia, and several Latin American republics.

State. *See* Department of State.

State aid. Subsidies or grants-in-aid made by a State to one of its subdivisions for educational or other purposes.

State central committee. The principal party committee within a State usually composed of one member from each Congressional district or of one member from each county.

State centralization. The process by which a State assumes direct control over subjects formerly administered by counties or other local subdivisions.

State constitution. The fundamental law of a State emanating from the people and vesting powers in the legislature and other departments and officers; together with limitations on the manner in which they may exercise their powers; a bill of rights (usually the first article); and provisions relating to local government, education, finances, suffrage, and elections. All the original States adopted written constitutions in the period, 1776–81, and every territory applying for statehood has been required to submit a draft constitution to Congress. The first State constitutions were brief documents recognizing the principle of legislative supremacy. They were replaced early in the 19th century by new constitutions which made executives and courts independent of the legislature. After the Civil War the Southern States were required, as a prerequisite for readmission to the Union, to adopt new constitutions incorporating guarantees of civil rights; and Northern States did likewise in order to expand their governmental organizations to meet rapidly growing social and economic needs. Since 1900 complete revisions have been relatively infrequent, and proposals of amendments have been incidents at every election in many States. Today most State constitutions are long, detailed, and prolix, with large admixtures and additions of a statutory nature, thus often making it difficult to determine what is the constitutional law of a State.

State examiner. A State official who inspects accounts of local governments or who examines applicants for licenses or for certificates to practice a regulated profession.

State Guards. A special militia established by act of Congress, Oct. 21, 1940, to serve as a substitute for the National Guard while the latter was in the federal service during World War II.

statelessness. The condition of being without nationality under the laws of any existing state.

state of nature. The condition of mankind assumed by many writers on political theory to exist before the establishment of organized government. It was a brutish existence, according to Thomas Hobbes, who wanted to establish strong governmental power; but an idyllic condition, according to Rousseau, who set out to show that "man is born free, and everywhere he is in chains."

state-of-the-Union address. A speech by the President at the opening of a regular session of Congress in which he performs his constitutional duty of informing Congress of the state of the Union and outlines a legislative program.

state of war. A legal condition (whether or not open hostilities are in progress), beginning with a declaration of war and ending with a treaty of peace or proclamation that war has ended, in which numerous usually dormant statutes to govern wartime conditions are in effect and in which rules of international law governing the conduct of belligerents and neutrals may be enforced.

state paper. A document emanating from a political department of a government or from one of its leading officials which relates to the government's domestic policies or its foreign relations.

State police. An organized professional police force maintained and directly commanded by a State authority for the enforcement of law, the suppression of disorder, the patrolling of highways, and the guarding of public property.

State's attorney. An officer, usually locally elective within a county, who represents the State in securing indictments and in prosecuting criminal cases; *called also* prosecuting attorney.

state's evidence. *Colloquial.* Evidence given by an accomplice against his confederates in crime in the hope of mitigation of his own sentence.

statesman. A political leader who consistently shapes public policy with foresight, or administers public affairs with wisdom and integrity.

State sovereignty. A doctrine of constitutional construction maintained by many writers before the Civil War that the States were sovereign before the adoption of the Constitution of the United States; that the Constitution was a compact among the States; and, sovereignty being inalienable, that the States retained the power through their conventions to secede from the Union or to nullify acts of Congress. *Compare* national sovereignty.

States' rights. 1. Rights not conferred on the federal government or forbidden to the States. 2. Rights claimed for the States under any of various theories of strict construction and interpretation of the Constitution ranging from State sovereignty to contemporary opposition to concentration of power in the national government.

States' Rights Democratic party. A minor party composed of Southerners who resented the civil rights stand of President Truman and the Democratic platform of 1948; *called also* Dixiecrats. Its candidate for President, J. Strom Thurmond, received 39 electoral votes and 1,169,000 popular votes out of a total of 48,400,000.

state succession. A change in sovereignty within a given area resulting from the absorption of a state into another or its division among two or more states. The successor state is normally expected to assume the financial and other obligations of the former state or states.

State use system. The system of employing prison labor in the production of articles exclusively for use in State institutions or by local subdivisions of a State.

statism. The policy of relying upon the centralized administrative structure and coercive power of government to secure social objectives instead of upon a pluralistic social structure and voluntary means.

status. A condition resulting from a privilege legally conferred upon a person because of his public position or profession, or imposed because of a person's minority, mental incapacity, sex, commission of a crime, or alienage, which may create special obligations to the state or limit legal relations with others, especially freedom to assume contractual obligations.

status quo ante bellum. The situation prevailing before the war;—a phrase used in treaties of peace restoring legal relationships temporarily altered by war.

statute. A formal written expression of the legislative will whether couched in the form of an act or joint resolution;—distinguished from unwritten or common law.

statute book. An official or privately published collection of statutes enacted by a legislature.

statute of limitations. A statute which fixes a period during which existing claims may be collected, judgments enforced, or crimes prosecuted and which, after the lapse of the prescribed period, serves as a legal bar to such actions.

Statutes at Large. See United States Statutes at Large.

stay-at-home voter. A voter who by remaining away from the polls tacitly aids an opposing party or faction.

stay law. A law declaring a moratorium on the payment of certain kinds of debts, preventing or delaying their collection or the application of a judgment against a debtor.

Steagall National Housing Act. An act of Congress, 1939, which authorized the issuance of insurance to the aggregate maximum of $3 billion to protect banks and other mortgage holders against loss on loans made to finance alterations, repairs, and improvements on existing dwellings.

stealing thunder. Appropriating an important issue or claiming credit for an accomplishment of another party or candidate.

steamboat inspection. The public inspection of steam plants, boilers, machinery, equipment, and hulls of commercial vessels, which is performed in the United States by the Bureau of Customs and the Coast Guard.

steam roller. A political force in a party convention which ruthlessly crushes opposition, often in disregard of established rules and precedents.

Stearns v. Minnesota. A case, 179 U.S. 223 (1900), in which the Supreme Court held that, when admitting a State, conditions imposed by Congress to protect a federal proprietary right within the State could be enforced. *Compare Coyle v. Smith.*

steering committee. A committee of each party's caucus, usually with the floor leader as chairman, which in the Senate makes assignments to committees and in the House of Representatives acts as a policy committee in trying to develop a program which all members of the party can support.

sterilization law. A law which empowers appropriate authorities to deprive feeble-minded or congenitally insane persons in public institutions of the power of reproduction.

Steward Machine Co. v. Davis. *See* Social Security cases.

stewardship theory. A theory, first enunciated by James Wilson and revived by Theodore Roosevelt, that the President may take any action in the general interest which is not interdicted by the Constitution or the laws.

still hunt. A canvass for votes or the support of delegates to a convention carried on unobtrusively or stealthily.

Stimson Doctrine. 1. A statement by Secretary of State Henry L. Stimson, Feb. 6, 1931, that recognition of a foreign government by the United States depends on the existence of three de facto conditions: (*a*) its control of the administrative machinery of the state, (*b*) the general acquiescence of the people in its rule, and (*c*) its ability and willingness to discharge its international obligations. This statement reversed the test of moral standards of Wilson and Bryan. *See* Wilson Corollary. **2.** A declaration on June 7, 1932, that the United States would not recognize the validity of any Japanese conquest in Manchuria or elsewhere in China or any Japanese violation of China's territorial integrity.

stockpiling. A federal program to accumulate reserve supplies of materials, especially minerals essential to national defense, in anticipation of a possible military emergency when access to such materials on the world market might become difficult or be cut off altogether. Stocks thus accumulated can be, and have been, used as a means of economic regulation, through government purchase and sale of reserve material. Stockpiling is carried on by the Office of Emergency Planning, the Departments of Agriculture and the Interior, and the General Services Administration.

storm troopers. The private army of a political party;—from the armed and uniformed group in the Nazi party that supported Hitler's rise to power in 1933.

straddle. 1. To take an equivocal position. **2.** To be on both sides of a question at the same time. **3.** To be noncommittal.

Straight-out Democrats. Democrats who, disapproving their party's endorsement of Horace Greeley in 1872, nominated Charles O'Conor for President. They cast about 30,000 votes.

straight ticket. A vote for all the candidates regularly nominated by one party. *Compare* split ticket.

strategic material. A material essential to national defense for the supply of which, in war, dependence must be placed in whole or substantial part on overseas sources. *Compare* critical material; stockpiling.

straw vote. An unofficial poll taken by a newspaper or private organization to forecast the result of an election.

strict construction. Any construction of a constitution, charter, or statute which is confined to the literal terms of the document. *See* construction; implied powers.

strike. A concerted work stoppage by employees in a plant or industry in an effort to compel the management to make concessions or redress grievances.

strike bill. A bill introduced in a legislative body for the purpose of extorting a payment from an individual or corporation which would be harmed if it were passed.

Stromberg v. *California.* A case, 238 U.S. 359 (1931), in which the Supreme Court narrowed somewhat its ruling in *Whitney* v. *California,* *q.v.,* by holding unconstitutional, under the due-process clause of the 14th Amendment, a statute which made it a felony to display a red flag or similar banner in a public place, as a symbol of opposition to organized government.

strong-mayor plan. A form of municipal government in which the mayor has effective control over the administrative services of a municipality and usually budget-making authority and veto power over municipal legislation, grants of franchises, and alienation of municipal property.

struck jury. A trial jury of 12 secured by having opposing counsel each strike out 12 names from a list of 48 veniremen and thereafter eliminate 12 more from the list by exercising the right of challenge.

stump. To make campaign speeches at numerous places in a constituency; —from the stump of a tree often mounted by campaign orators in frontier communities.

stump speech. A rough-and-ready campaign address.

Sturges v. *Crowninshield.* A case, 4 Wheat. 122 (1819), in which the Supreme Court held that a State might enact bankruptcy laws which, if they did not impair the obligation of a contract, would be valid until superseded by federal legislation. The limitation as to the effect of State bankruptcy laws on contracts was subsequently interpreted to include only contracts made before the enactment of a State law and not to later contracts.

subcommittee. A division of a standing legislative committee whose members are appointed by the chairman of the standing committee, and whose duties are to investigate (as by hearings) certain subject matters and report their conclusions to the standing committee.

subjugation. The process of compelling a people by force of arms to yield to the will of a conqueror.

sublegislative. Of or pertaining to a power of an administrative or local government body to issue regulations having the force of law. *See* ordinance power.

Submerged Lands Act. *See* offshore oil lands.

subpoena. An order of a court, tribunal, or legislative house requiring the attendance of a person as a witness under penalties for failure to appear.

subpoena duces tecum. A writ requiring a witness to produce in court certain specific documents or papers.

subsidiary coinage. Coins issued in denominations representing fractions of the monetary unit.

subsidiary motion. A motion proposed in a legislative body for the adoption of a particular method of considering or disposing of a measure or a matter.

subsidy. A gift of money or property by a government to assist a private person in the establishment or operation of a service (as a railroad, shipping line, or manufacturing establishment, or the production of foodstuffs) deemed beneficial to the public at large. In a controlled economy subsidies are often paid to producers in lieu of allowing increases in prices.

subsistence homestead. A plot of farm land with dwellings and other necessary buildings, production and income from which barely suffice to maintain a family. A few communities of such homesteads were publicly financed in the 1930's for families from congested or depressed areas.

substantive law. A branch of law which defines and prescribes the personal and property rights of persons in relation to each other, and the persons' corresponding reciprocal duties and responsibilities. *Compare* procedural law.

substantive right. A right to the enjoyment of fundamental privileges and immunities equally with others;—distinguished from procedural rights, *q.v.*

subtreasury system. The system of depositing funds of the federal government in the U.S. Treasury or in subtreasuries located in various cities, which was in use from 1840 to 1920, when federal reserve banks became the depositaries.

subvention. A subsidy, *q.v.*, to a private institution usually for educational, scientific, or literary purposes. *Compare* grant-in-aid.

subversive activity. Any organized effort intended to overthrow an existing government by force or to change it by methods characterized by fraud, deceit, or chicane.

Suez Crisis. An international crisis involving Anglo-French and Israeli attacks on Egypt following Egypt's seizure and nationalization of the Suez Canal in 1956. Egypt asserted that Canal tolls would be used to finance construction of the Aswan Dam which the United States had earlier promised to finance and from which promise it had withdrawn following Egypt's failure to fulfill certain obligations. The military attacks, which had penetrated into Egyptian territory, were suspended following intervention by the U.N. Security Council, supported by the United States and the Soviet Union. A compromise settlement maintained Egypt's control of the Canal's operations and provided international transit guarantees and compensation for private interests.

suffrage. 1. The privilege of voting for candidates for public office and on proposed constitutional amendments, initiated or referred measures, bond issues, and other questions; originally confined to landholders and a few others. *See* forty shilling freehold. In the early 19th century, extension of the suffrage was urged as a concession to taxpayers, as a proper recognition of past military service, as a natural right, and as a means by which an individual might find fulfillment as a man and a citizen. The States control the suffrage but they may not deny it on account of race, color, previous condition of servitude, sex, or non-payment of taxes. Idiocy, insanity, foreign citizenship, and insufficient period of residence are disqualifications in every State. The minimum voting age is 21 in 46 States, 20 in Hawaii, 19 in Alaska, and 18 in Georgia and Kentucky. Literacy or educational requirements are imposed in 20 States, almost equally divided among the Northeast, the South, and the Far West. 2. *Legal:* An exclusive franchise granted to certain described categories of individuals to participate in government.

suffragette. A woman who in the early 20th century advocated suffrage for women and the eligibility of women for political offices.

Sugar Frauds. Frauds in the weighing of sugar in the New York custom-house which were exposed in 1909.

suit. Traditionally any litigation following the rules and procedures of equity. *Compare* action.

summary. Descriptive of procedure (as in a police court or other court for the trial of minor offenses) which lacks usual judicial formalities.

summit conference. 1. *In World War II:* a meeting of Roosevelt, Churchill, and Stalin. **2.** *Since 1945:* a meeting of the heads of government of the principal countries of the world.

summons. 1. A judicial order addressed to a defendant in a civil action commanding him to appear and answer a complaint against him. **2.** An order by a court to appear as a witness or for jury service. **3.** An order issued by a police officer to a traffic violator or other petty offender requiring him to appear as defendant in a magistrate's or police court. *Compare* subpoena.

sumptuary legislation. Laws regulating the expenditures of persons in order to promote frugality and temperance and prevent ostentatious or vulgar display.

Sunshine Anthracite Coal Co. v. Adkins. See Bituminous Coal Code cases.

superannuation. The condition of being ineligible for employment because of the infirmities of age or because of having reached legal retirement age.

Superintendent of Documents. The sales agent for publications of the federal government.

superior court. 1. A court of record or general trial court in some States, superior to a justice of the peace or magistrates' court. **2.** In other States, an intermediate court between the general trial court and the highest appellate court.

supervisor. In some States the popularly elective chief administrative officer of a township, and a member, with other supervisors, of the administrative and fiscal board of a county.

supplemental appropriation. An appropriation made after the enactment of the regular appropriations for a fiscal period to defray unexpected or extraordinary expenditures.

supremacy clause. The clause of Art. VI of the U.S. Constitution which declares that all laws made in pursuance of the Constitution and all treaties made under the authority of the United States shall be the "supreme law of the land" and shall enjoy legal superiority over any conflicting provision of a State constitution or laws, and requires the judges of State courts to enforce the federal law. As applied by the Supreme Court, it has been important in establishing the ascendancy of the national government in the federal system.

Supreme Court. The highest court in the American federal system and the only one for which the Constitution directly provided. The number of justices was fixed by Congress at six in 1789; at five in 1801; at seven in 1807; at nine in 1837; at ten in 1863; at seven in 1866; and at nine in 1869, where it has since remained. Its original jurisdiction, as fixed by the Constitution, extends to "all cases affecting ambassadors, other public ministers, and consuls, and those in which a State shall be a party"; but, since the enactment of the 11th Amendment, not to cases in which a State is sued by a citizen of another State. Its appellate jurisdiction, as determined by Congress, has varied greatly and now extends to fewer subjects than formerly; but the popular impression that it is confined to cases involving the construction or interpretation of the Constitution (*see* judicial review) is erroneous. All cases in which a federal question is involved may be appealed from the highest court in a State, and cases in which a U.S. Court of Appeals declares a State law unconstitutional may be appealed; and others may be brought to the Supreme Court by writ of certiorari or under certification of division from circuit judges. A miscellaneous group of cases involving criminal law, certain decisions in which acts of Congress are held to be unconstitutional, determinations of commissions created under the interstate commerce power, etc., may be appealed if rights under the Constitution or national laws or treaties are asserted to have been denied or ignored. The Supreme Court sits from October to May and acts on about 2,500 cases annually, nearly all of them involving novel questions of constitutional or statutory interpretation. Decisions and opinions may be found in the *United States Reports*. The highest State courts are often called supreme courts; but the term is also applied to a lower court, as in New York.

supreme court of errors. The highest court in Connecticut.

supreme judicial court. The highest court in Maine and in Massachusetts.

Surgeon General. 1. The head of the Public Health Service, *q.v.* **2.** The chief medical officer of the U.S. Army and of the Air Force.

surplus. 1. An amount held in a treasury representing the excess of ordinary revenues over expenditures. **2.** A budgetary estimate in which anticipated revenue exceeds anticipated expenditures.

surrogate. A judicial officer in a county in certain States with jurisdiction over the probate of wills, the disposition of estates, and the guardianship of minors.

surtax. 1. A tax levied upon certain classes of taxpayers or goods in addition to the normal or general tax. **2.** An additional tax imposed after the enactment of regular tax rates.

surveyor of the port. A customs officer who determines the amount and value of goods arriving at a port of entry.

suspended sentence. An indefinite stay in the operation of a punishment prescribed by a court for a convicted offender;—often authorized in cases of first offenders or in connection with a system of probation, *q.v.*

suspending clause. A clause in a constitution, statute, or other public document identifying certain contingencies under which, temporarily, the document is not effective or some right or privilege granted in it may be withheld.

suspension. The action of an executive or administrative officer in barring a person from a position or employment pending final determination of his case by the authority which has power to remove him.

suspension of rules. The temporary abrogation of the rules of a legislative body for the consideration of a particular measure. In the House of Representatives the motion is usually "to suspend and pass" and requires a two-thirds vote.

suspensive veto. An executive veto which has the effect of suspending the operation of a proposed law until it is reconsidered by the legislature and repassed by a constitutional majority. *Compare* absolute veto.

suzerainty. A relationship between two states in which one is overlord of the other, although the vassal state may retain most of the prerogatives of an independent state. Prior to 1947, the British Crown was suzerain of the Indian native states.

sweating. 1. The employment of labor at low wages, for long hours, and under unsanitary conditions, including the employment of women and children on piecework to be done in their homes. 2. A method of extorting information or a confession from a prisoner or person held on suspicion of committing a crime by the use of threats and other forms of psychological pressure. *Compare* third degree.

Swift v. Tyson. *See Erie Railroad v. Tompkins.*

swing round the circle. An extensive speaking tour in which a President or candidate attempts to obtain popular support for his policies.

sympathetic strike. A strike called among workmen who themselves have no direct grievances but who wish to support a strike called in another plant or industry.

syndicalism. The socio-political theory of certain revolutionary labor movements akin to the Industrial Workers of the World, *q.v.*, which derives ideological inspiration from such writers as Bakunin and Sorel, normally eschews political weapons, stressing instead direct economic action (particularly the general strike), and seeks to replace the coercive state with a rather vaguely defined workers' cooperative commonwealth.

system. The relationship often existing between politicians and underworld characters or businessmen seeking special advantages from the public by underhand means;—used colloquially.

table. To suspend consideration of a pending measure. By means of a motion to lay on the table, a majority in a legislative body may lay aside a proposed measure thereby usually defeating it because, when a measure is tabled, a two-thirds vote is required to bring it to the floor again.

Taft-Hartley Labor-Management Relations Act. An act of Congress, June 23, 1947, amending the National Labor Relations Act, *q.v.*, which (*a*) outlaws the closed shop, but permits the union shop if the union represents a majority of the employees eligible to vote and if it gives equal rights to new members; (*b*) provides for a cooling-off period of 60 days (80 days in essential industries) before resort to strike or lockout; (*c*) increases the membership and the powers of the National Labor Relations Board, *q.v.*; (*d*) permits employers and unions to sue each other for breach of contract; (*e*) requires labor unions to file copies of their constitutions; (*f*) requires officers of unions to file affidavits that they are not members of the Communist party; and (*g*) forbids unions or employers to make direct or indirect contributions to party campaign funds. *See* Labor Reform Act.

Taft-Kutsura Memorandum. An agreement in 1905, by which the United States recognized Japan's "paramount interests" in Korea in return for Japan's assurance that she had no aggressive designs on the Philippines.

Tammany Hall. The regular Democratic organization of New York County;—so-called because from an early date until the 1930's it held its meetings in the hall of the Tammany Society, a benevolent society founded in 1789.

Tampico Incident. The arrest, April 20, 1914, by Huertista troops, of U.S. sailors who had landed their whaleboat at Tampico, Mexico, for supplies. They were released within an hour. Admiral Mayo demanded a 21-gun salute to the American flag, which Huerta refused unless a U.S. ship fired a simultaneous salute. Mayo stood firm and was supported by President Wilson who began preparations for war. On April 22, in order to prevent Huerta from receiving munitions from abroad, the United States occupied Vera Cruz, inflicting 300 Mexican casualties and losing 19 American lives.

tangible property. Property (as land, buildings, machinery, and furniture) which may be readily discovered and assessed for property and other taxes. *Compare* intangible property.

tariff. 1. A series of schedules or rates of duties on imported goods. Tariffs are *for revenue* if their objects are wholly or mainly fiscal; *protective* if they are designed to relieve domestic producers from effective foreign competition; *discriminatory* if they apply unequally to products of different countries; and *retaliatory* if they are designed to compel a country to remove artificial trade barriers against the entry of another country's products. The first tariff law of the United States, passed July 4, 1789, was designed partly to raise revenue and partly to protect certain industries, though the rates were so low as hardly to afford protection in fact. It was not until after the War of 1812 when many infant industries were threatened with extinction by foreign importations that Congress, in 1816, effectively applied the protective principle. Greater protection was afforded in the act of 1824 and in the "Tariff of Abominations," 1828, in which duties were so high as to bring about the nullification movement. A downward adjustment was made in 1832, and the Compromise Tariff of 1833 provided for further gradual adjustment downward over the next ten years. The law of 1842 generally restored the rates of the tariff of 1832; but the process was again reversed in the Walker Tariff, 1846, which introduced the principle of free trade, subsequently extended in the act of 1857. The Republicans, coming to power in 1861, reintroduced the protective principle in the Morrill Tariff, and continued it in later piecemeal revisions and in the act of 1883 and the McKinley Tariff of 1890. The revisions made by a Democratic Congress in the Wilson-Gorman Act of 1894 were disappointing to sincere free traders. In 1897, the Republicans passed the thoroughly protectionist Dingley Tariff and maintained the high rates, with only slight concessions, in the Payne-Aldrich Act of 1909. The Underwood Tariff, 1913, reduced duties in attempting to reach a point where foreign competition might be effective in curbing monopolies. The Fordney-McCumber Tariff of 1922 again raised duties, and further increases were made by the Hawley-Smoot Tariff of 1930; but reductions have since occurred through reciprocal trade agreements. *See* United States Tariff Commission. **2.** A rate of duty on a single product. **3.** A published statement of charges by a common carrier.

Tariff of Abominations. The generally unpopular tariff law of 1828 which South Carolina tried to nullify. It was modified by the act of 1832 and the Compromise Tariff of 1833.

task force. 1. A group of experts from several fields assembled (as by the Hoover Commissions, *q.v.*) to study and report on one or a few closely related problems. **2.** A temporary naval or combined service force used for the accomplishment of a particular mission in World War II.

Tasmanian dodge. An electoral fraud by which a vote buyer, having obtained a blank official ballot, marks it and gives it to a venal voter with instructions to cast it and return with a blank official ballot from the polling place, upon which he receives his bribe. The process is continued throughout election day. Many election laws seek to prevent this practice by providing a detachable numbered stub which can be compared with the number on the ballot cast by the voter.

Tattooed Man. A nickname of James G. Blaine, inspired by a cartoon by Bernhard Gillam in *Puck*.

tax. A compulsory contribution or payment, usually in the form of money, levied according to law upon a person for the support of government, or for defense, public works, promotion of social objectives, or for regulation. In the United States it must be for a public purpose and it must be uniform upon all taxpayers of a given class. It is levied without reference to the benefit which an individual receives from a government or his ability to pay, though consideration of both benefit and ability may strongly influence tax policies. Congress is forbidden to tax exports; to levy direct taxes (except income taxes) unless apportioned among the States according to population; to expend the funds raised by taxation for purposes other than the common defense or general welfare; or to show a preference among the ports of different States, which means in effect that taxes must be uniform throughout the States and incorporated territories.

Taxation without representation is tyranny. An American rallying cry in the period before the Revolution, based on the theory that taxes could be legally levied only by colonial assemblies.

tax avoidance. The action of a taxpayer in legally using alternative rates or methods of assessing taxes for his own advantage.

tax base. The basis used for levying taxes, such as a taxpayer's annual net income, the value of property of a decedent's estate, or the number, weight, volume, or value of items of a certain kind of property.

tax certificate. A document issued to the buyer of property at a tax sale by the officer making the sale which entitles the holder to the property thus purchased if it is not redeemed within the period provided by law.

tax code. A systematic compilation of the existing tax laws of a State revised and re-enacted by the legislature.

tax commission. A State fiscal body, consisting of three or more members, which supervises local tax officials, assesses public utility and other property, collects most taxes not collected locally, and often serves as a State tax equalization board.

Tax Court of the United States. An independent agency of sixteen members, created by Congress in 1924 as the Board of Tax Appeals, and called by its present name since 1942, which hears and decides cases appealed by taxpayers from the decisions of the Commissioner of Internal Revenue in which insufficient payment is alleged in income and other taxes. Its decisions in most matters may be reviewed by the regular courts.

tax credit. An amount which a taxpayer may deduct from taxes due in one State or locality on account of taxes he has paid in another; provided for in some State income tax laws for the benefit of people who work in one State while residing in another.

tax dodging. Tax evasion or tax avoidance, especially the practice of establishing a legal residence in a State or other area where tax rates are low.

tax evasion. Any illegal effort to escape the payment of taxes, as by failure to report taxable property or income.

tax exempt. Pertaining to property used for educational, religious, or charitable purposes which is ordinarily exempted by law from assessment for taxes; or to certain bonds issued by the federal government or a State or one of its subdivisions which, in order to secure ready marketability or a lower rate of interest, has relieved them from taxation. Interest on State and local government bonds is exempt from federal income taxation, and interest on bonds of the United States or its instrumentalities is correspondingly exempt from State income taxation. A long-established canon of constitutional construction that salaries of State and federal employees enjoyed a similar exemption was abandoned by the Supreme Court in *Graves* v. *New York* ex rel. *O'Keefe* and in *Helvering* v. *Gerhardt, qq.v.*

tax ferret. A private person who investigates and reports the existence of property or income on which taxes should have been paid by another person, and who may be rewarded by taxing authorities in proportion to the amount of taxes collected from the property or income reported by him.

Tax Legislative Counsel. *See* Office of Tax Legislative Counsel.

tax lien. A lien on real estate in favor of a State or a municipality which may be foreclosed for nonpayment of taxes.

tax limit. 1. The maximum tax rate which a subsidiary tax authority (as a political subdivision) may impose under a State constitution or laws. 2. Any constitutional or statutory limitation concerning the tax base or on the rate of taxation.

tax offset. Substitution of a particular amount paid to a State government for the amount of a tax imposed by the federal government; a means by which the federal government has sometimes induced the States to assume additional functions. Congress in 1926 provided that taxpayers could deduct from federal estate taxes up to 80 per cent of the inheritance taxes which they had paid to a State and in 1935 imposed a 3 per cent payroll tax with the proviso that employers could deduct from the amount due up to 90 per cent of the amount which they had paid into a State unemployment insurance fund. The States which had no inheritance tax or unemployment compensation provided for both, fearing to lose benefits which other States would enjoy. *Compare* grant-in-aid.

taxpayer's suit. A suit which, under the laws of nearly all the States (but not of the United States), may be brought by any taxpayer, with even a small pecuniary interest, to enjoin the illegal expenditure of public funds.

taxpaying qualification. A requirement that a person pay taxes in order to participate in elections, first introduced in Pennsylvania in 1777 as a substitute for the property qualification, and adopted by many other States before 1850. After disappearing before the manhood suffrage movement, *q.v.*, it was revived about 1890 by several Southern States to limit voting by poor whites and Negroes. It was prohibited, in elections of federal officers, by the 24th Amendment and later, in elections of State and local officers, by judicial determinations that it violated the 14th Amendment. *See Harper* v. *Virginia State Board of Elections.*

tax sale. Sale of property for nonpayment of taxes assessed upon it or upon the owner.

tax sharing. The use of the same tax by two or more taxing authorities one of which administers the tax and remits part of the proceeds to the other. Tax sharing differs from a grant-in-aid, *q.v.*, in that the amount remitted is not an appropriation and few or no conditions are attached to the use which may be made of the proceeds of shared taxes.

Taylor Grazing Act. An act of Congress, 1934, which sought to stop injury to public grazing lands by authorizing the Secretary of the Interior to set aside grazing districts and issue permits for grazing, with preference to persons who live near a district, landowners engaged in the livestock business, bona fide settlers, and owners of water or water rights.

Taylor v. Georgia. A case, 315 U.S. 25 (1942), involving the constitutionality of a Georgia statute which stipulated that a person who had been given an advance on a contract to render certain services and then had been unable to render those services should be compelled to remain at his employment until he had satisfied the debt. The Supreme Court held that the operation of such a statute amounts to peonage and violates the 13th Amendment.

teacher's certification. Issuance by a State department of public instruction, or equivalent agency, of credentials to an individual which formally establish that he has at least the minimum professional requirements and is qualified to teach in the public schools of the State.

teacher's oath. A sworn declaration required by the laws of several States of a teacher in a public or private school or college that he will uphold the Constitutions of the United States and of the State, and that he will neither teach subversive doctrines nor affiliate with organizations advocating them.

Teapot Dome. *See* Oil scandal.

technical assistance. Assistance and advice to underdeveloped countries in medicine, sanitation, education, communications, road building, government service, survey of resources, and long-range planning as outlined in President Truman's message to Congress, June 24, 1949. The U.S. program has been administered both directly and through a program of the United Nations, and consists not only in the sending of technicians and production goods, but also in scholarships for training in the United States of citizens of underdeveloped countries. Other countries, especially Russia, also conduct programs of technical assistance.

technocracy. Government by technologists; *specifically:* a scheme for supplanting the existing political and social order with one directed by scientists and engineers, which had a brief vogue in 1932.

Teheran Conference. A World War II conference of President Roosevelt, Prime Minister Churchill, and Premier Stalin at Teheran, Iran, November–December, 1943, to concert plans for concluding the war against the Axis powers and to draft armistice and peace terms.

Teller Resolution. A resolution, proposed by Senator Henry N. Teller of Colorado and passed Apr. 20, 1898, disclaiming any intention by the United States to exercise jurisdiction or control over Cuba when that island was freed from Spanish rule.

tellers. Persons appointed to count the members of a legislative body for or against a proposal as they proceed down the center aisle in separate files. A vote by tellers may be demanded by one-fifth of those present. It is not a record vote.

temperance. Habitual restraint in indulgence, especially in intoxicating liquors.

temporary chairman. A person appointed by a party committee to call a convention to order, deliver a keynote speech, and preside until a permanent chairman is elected.

Temporary National Economic Committee. A committee consisting of three Senators, three Representatives, and members of various federal administrative agencies, created by Congress in 1938 to make a comprehensive study of monopoly and the concentration of economic power in the United States. Results of the inquiry, including papers by many leading economists, were published in a number of monographs.

Tennessee Valley Authority. A corporation chartered by Congress in 1933 to construct dams and other works along the Tennessee River and its tributaries and promote the development of the Tennessee Valley, an area of some 41,000 sq. mi. The Authority maintains navigation and flood control works; generates electric power which is distributed to consumers at low rates through private utility companies, local governments, and cooperatives; manufactures and sells fertilizers; and produces nitrates for defense purposes. It is managed by a general manager under the supervision of a board of three directors appointed by the President and the Senate, has its own separate civil service system, and is now financed mainly by the sale of its own bonds and proceeds from the sales of its products and services.

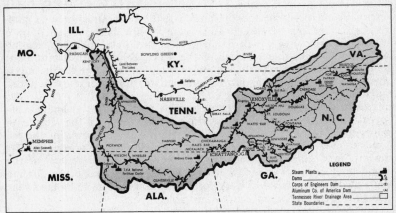

Tennessee Valley Authority

Tennis Cabinet. A group consisting of James R. Garfield, Gifford Pinchot, and other bureau chiefs with whom President Theodore Roosevelt played tennis, and who were influential in determining his conservation and other policies.

Tenth Amendment. An amendment to the Constitution, proclaimed Dec. 15, 1791, which provides that the powers not delegated to the federal government are reserved to the States or to the people. The absence of the word "expressly" which antifederalists wished to insert between "not" and "delegated" left in full effect the necessary-and-proper clause, *q.v.*, on which Chief Justice Marshall later built the doctrine of implied powers. The phrase "or to the people," negates the claims of States to the exclusive possession of reserved powers. Chief Justice Taney and conservative justices have used the Tenth Amendment in developing the doctrine of dual federalism, *q.v.*

tenure. The right to hold an office or to remain in public employment. The tenure of federal judges is during life or good behavior with provisions for voluntary retirement under the law. The tenure of merit system employees is during satisfactory performance of duties until a fixed age of retirement unless the position is discontinued.

Tenure of Office Act. 1. A law of Congress, Mar. 2, 1867, repealed Mar. 3, 1887, which required the approval of the Senate for the removal of an officer appointed by a President with the consent of the Senate. Alleged disregard of this act by President Andrew Johnson led to his impeachment. **2.** An act of like purport, passed July 12, 1876, applying to postmasters, which was declared unconstitutional in *Myers* v. *United States, q.v.* **3.** Another name for the Four-Year-Tenure Act, *q.v.*

term. The period for which a public official is elected or appointed.

terminal leave. The total of unused periods of leave which may be granted to a member of the armed forces or a civilian employee just before his discharge or retirement.

Terminiello **v.** *Chicago.* A case, 337 U.S. 1 (1949), in which the Supreme Court, by a majority of one, declared that the First Amendment's guarantees of freedom of speech and assembly had been breached by a municipal ordinance which defined, as a punishable offense, creating or assisting in creating a breach of the peace; this in turn having been defined by the lower court as speech which "stirs the public to anger, invites dispute, brings about a condition of unrest or creates a disturbance."

terms of trade. Conditions which determine the relative advantages enjoyed by a nation's trade in world markets, such as the degree of dependence upon export markets, the relative sophistication of the nation's economy, the value of its currency vis-à-vis that of other countries and of "key" currencies, and the stability of prices. In general, if the world price level of a nation's exports increases and that of needed imports declines, the terms of trade for that nation are said to be favorable; if the reverse situation obtains, unfavorable.

Terrapin War. The Embargo and Nonintercourse acts and the War of 1812;—from a derisive term applied by Federalists.

territorial courts. Legislative courts established in territories and some dependencies under the authority of Congress to make needful rules for the territories. Except in Puerto Rico, these courts have jurisdiction over matters which would ordinarily be determined by State courts, in addition to cases arising under federal laws.

territorial jurisdiction. The right of a state to exercise exclusive control over (*a*) all lands within its boundaries, (*b*) its territorial waters, *q.v.*, (*c*) an extensive portion of the air space over its territory (*see* aerial domain), and (*d*) all persons or things not covered by diplomatic immunity within any of the foregoing areas.

territorial waters. Waters within the jurisdiction of a state including (*a*) the marginal sea, *q.v.*, (*b*) inland rivers and lakes lying wholly within a state, (*c*) the waters of boundary rivers and straits up to the middle of the most navigable channel (thalweg), and (*d*) the waters of boundary lakes and bays as far as the middle point, measured from shore to shore, or as otherwise determined.

territory. 1. That portion of the United States which is not included in any State or the District of Columbia and to which the procedural guarantees of the Constitution may, or may not, apply. See incorporated territory; unincorporated territory. 2. A large area which Congress has carved out of the public domain and provided with a government consisting of an appointive governor and courts and a representative legislature (both houses elective after 1836) in order to promote its settlement and prepare it for eventual Statehood. 3. A relatively undeveloped area (as the Trust Territory of the Pacific Islands, q.v.) which is administered by the government of a more advanced state.

testimony. Information or evidence offered by witnesses under oath at a judicial or similar proceeding.

test oath. A declaration of past loyalty to the United States required of teachers, clergymen, and former public officials by certain State constitutions during the Reconstruction period following the Civil War. It was declared unconstitutional as both an ex post facto law and a bill of pains and penalties in Cummings v. Missouri, 4 Wall. 277 (1867).

Texas. See Republic of Texas.

Texas Primary cases. A series of cases in the Supreme Court concerning the right of Negroes to vote in primary elections of the Democratic party in Texas. Relying on the decision in Newberry v. United States, q.v., that a primary is not part of the election process, the Texas legislature by statute excluded Negroes from the Democratic primary. The Court voided the law, Nixon v. Herndon, 273 U.S. 536 (1927), declaring that it deprived persons of rights under the equal-protection clause of the 14th Amendment. A new law providing that the executive committee of the party might determine the eligibility of primary voters met a like fate in Nixon v. Condon, 286 U.S. 73 (1932), which held that when the executive committee excluded Negroes it had acted as an agent of the State. But when the State party convention, acting on its own motion, adopted a resolution excluding Negroes, the Court declined to interfere, Grovey v. Townsend, 294 U.S. 45 (1935), on the ground that the discrimination had been by private persons, a political party being a voluntary association under Texas laws. After United States v. Classic, q.v., had brought primaries under the scope of election laws, Grovey v. Townsend was reversed in a new test case, Smith v. Allwright, 321 U.S. 649 (1944), in which the Court held that Negroes were entitled, under the 15th Amendment, to vote in primary elections; and that their right to do so could not be nullified by a State through casting its electoral process in a form which permitted a political party to practice discrimination. In Terry v. Adams, 345 U.S. 461 (1953), the Court condemned the preliminary primaries of the all-white Jaybird party which for many years, with tacit State approval, had in fact chosen all candidates nominated in ensuing Democratic party primaries and elected to office in a Texas county. Compare Rice v. Elmore.

Texas v. White. A case, 7 Wall. 700 (1869), in which the Supreme Court denied the existence of the alleged right of secession and declared that "the Constitution, in all its provisions, looks to an indestructible Union composed of indestructible States."

thalweg. The middle of the deepest or most navigable channel of a boundary river, lake, or strait, which marks the exact legal boundary line unless an agreement between the riparian states stipulates otherwise.

theocracy. A state (as Geneva in the time of Calvin, or the Massachusetts Bay Colony) in which political authority is concentrated in the clergy, or in which the public officials are dominated by an ecclesiastical hierarchy.

third degree. The process of extorting a confession or information from a prisoner by prolonged questioning, the use of threatening words or gestures, or actual violence.

third estate. A former legislative house on the continent of Europe representing burghers and peasants.

third house. Any group of lobbyists that influence a legislature.

Third International. The international organization of Marxian Communist parties of various countries, often called the Comintern (Communist International), founded at Moscow in March, 1919, by Russian Soviet leaders to counter the successful efforts of moderate socialists elsewhere to revive the Second International established in 1889. The dissolution of the Comintern was officially announced in July, 1943, but its activities continued and, for all practical purposes, the Comintern was revived under the name of Cominform, *q.v.*, in 1947.

third party. A party, such as the Know-Nothing party, or the Progressive party of 1912, which occasionally rises in a two-party system and attains sufficient strength to have a decisive effect on the result of an election. *Compare* minor party.

third-term tradition. An unwritten custom of the American Constitution, begun by Washington and established by Jefferson and other early Presidents, that a President should not serve more than two terms. President Grant failed of a third nomination in 1880 though his friends argued that the tradition applied only to consecutive terms; and the same was true of Theodore Roosevelt in 1912 in spite of the additional argument that he had not already served two full terms. The tradition was broken by the re-election of President F. D. Roosevelt in 1940 for a third, and in 1944 for a fourth, term. In 1951, the limitation on Presidential tenure was made explicit by the Twenty-second Amendment, *q.v.*

Thirteenth Amendment. An amendment to the Constitution, proclaimed Dec. 18, 1865, which was designed to give constitutional sanction to Lincoln's Emancipation Proclamation and also to free slaves in the loyal slave States and elsewhere who were not declared free by the Proclamation. Its provision against involuntary servitude prohibits peonage and other compulsory service to fulfill the terms of a labor contract.

Thornhill v. *Alabama.* A case, 310 U.S. 88 (1940), in which the Supreme Court declared unconstitutional an Alabama statute which made peaceful picketing a misdemeanor on the ground that it violated a labor union's right to disseminate information concerning the facts of a labor dispute and thus the freedom of speech guaranteed in the First and Fourteenth Amendments.

three acres and a cow. A slogan of the Populists expressing their concern for the welfare of the poor farmer.

Three-fifths Compromise. A compromise between Northern and Southern States in the Convention of 1787 that in apportioning members of the House of Representatives and direct taxes among the States only three-fifths of the whole number of slaves were to be counted.

three-mile limit. The distance of one marine league or three miles offshore normally recognized as the limit of a littoral state's territorial jurisdiction. *See* marginal sea.

ticket. 1. A ballot formerly prepared at one party's expense for distribution to voters before an election, which listed only its own candidates. **2.** The candidates of one party collectively.

tidal wave. An overwhelming popular majority in an election.

tidelands oil. *See* offshore oil lands.

tied loan. A loan to a foreign country the proceeds of which may be used only for the purchase of the lending country's goods. *See* Export-Import Bank of Washington.

***Times-Mirror Co. v. Superior Court of California.* See Bridges v. California.**

tin box. The questionable source of a politician's income over and above his salary;—from the testimony of former sheriff Thomas M. Farley before the Seabury Committee, Oct. 6, 1931, that he obtained a large sum of money from a wonderful tin box.

Tippecanoe and Tyler too. A slogan of the Whig party in the campaign of 1840 in which the presidential candidate was William Henry Harrison, victor over Indians at Tippecanoe, Ind., and the vice-presidential candidate was John Tyler.

tissue ballot. A ballot printed on very thin paper. The depositing of several such ballots, folded together to look like one ballot, was formerly a favorite means of stuffing the ballot box.

title. 1. A preliminary part of a statute usually beginning with the words "An act for," followed by a summary of the statute's provisions. **2.** A subdivision of a code larger than a chapter.

T-Man. A law enforcement agent of the U.S. Treasury Department.

token coin. A coin with a face value greater than that of the metal it contains.

Toledo War. A boundary dispute between the State of Ohio and Michigan Territory, 1835, involving the town of Toledo which was settled by an act of Congress admitting Michigan as a State in 1837 with the addition of the Upper Peninsula and ceding the disputed district to Ohio.

toll bridge. A bridge, constructed with public funds or by a private company, for the use of which the public must pay a stipulated fee. Revenues thus collected amortize the cost of building the structure and help to maintain it.

Disputed Boundaries during Toledo War

toll road. A road for the use of which the public must pay a stipulated fee.

Tonkin Gulf Resolution. *See* Vietnam War.

tonnage. The weight or the internal cubic capacity of a vessel, which is the basis on which ships are registered.

too proud to fight. A phrase used by President Wilson in an address, May 10, 1915, and ridiculed by his opponents who desired a more vigorous foreign policy.

Torrens system. A system of registration of land titles under which, on payment of a fee, the purchaser of a tract of land may secure a valid title after a court hearing, and later claimants with valid titles are compensated in cash from an insurance fund created and maintained from the registration fees;—devised by Sir Robert R. Torrens and used in Australia, Canada, and several of the United States.

tort. A wrongful act, not including breach of contract, for which an injured party may bring a civil action against a wrongdoer.

Tory. 1. A member of an English political party, 1679–1832, which supported the royal prerogative and the Established Church;—still used occasionally to designate members of the Conservative party. **2.** An American who, during the period of the Revolution, adhered to the Crown or did not join the revolt against it. **3.** One who adheres to traditional or established beliefs, forms, and policies.

totalitarian. Pertaining to the quality of a government in which a dictator or an oligarchy exercises complete control over all aspects (as economic, social, intellectual, and moral) of individual and group activities by such means as monopolization of power in the hands of one official party, regimentation of industry, maintenance of captive labor and other organizations, intensive government propaganda, secret police, and concentration camps.

total war. Mobilization by a belligerent of all of its resources and manpower and the disregard of customary legal or moral limitations on the conduct of war, including the rights of neutrals and noncombatants. Those who wage total war ignore any distinction between military and civilian populations; sanction indiscriminate attacks upon heavily populated areas without regard to their strategic or direct military importance, justifying such attacks because they tend to discourage the will to resist; and support the use of chemical, bacteriological, and nuclear weapons. *See* war.

Toth v. Quarles. A case, 350 U.S. 1 (1955), in which the Supreme Court held that Congress by statute cannot require that a discharged serviceman be tried by a court martial for a capital crime allegedly committed during his service since such a requirement would lessen for the serviceman the constitutional safeguards enjoyed by other civilians when tried before the regular federal courts established under Art. III of the Constitution and encroach upon the jurisdiction of such courts.

town. 1. The principal unit of local government in New England except in more populous places which have been incorporated as cities. It is governed by a town meeting and administered by selectmen and other elected officers. 2. A subdivision of a county in some other States. 3. A small urban place whether incorporated or not.

town meeting. An assembly of the qualified voters of a town in whom all local governmental powers are vested. It is characteristic of New England but not limited to that section.

Townsend plan. The proposal (Old Age Revolving Pensions, Ltd.) of Dr. Francis E. Townsend in 1934 that the federal government pay a pension of $200 per month to all persons over sixty years of age on condition that the whole amount be spent within a month. The velocity of the circulation of money was expected to stimulate business recovery.

Townshend acts. Three acts of Parliament passed in 1767 when Charles Townshend was Chancellor of the Exchequer which levied duties on American imports of glass, paper, paints, and tea, created a commission to enforce trade laws, and suspended the legislature of the Colony of New York.

township. 1. A unit of local government comprising part of a county and often a mere subdivision of it, which is governed in a few States by boards of commissioners or trustees, in others, by one elective supervisor. The functions of township governments vary greatly in different States. 2. An area six miles square which is the unit of public land surveys in most of the area west of the original thirteen States; *called also* Congressional township.

Trade Agreements Act. An act of Congress, June 12, 1934, which authorized the President to enter into reciprocal trade agreements, *q.v.*, with foreign governments, thus permitting duties to be raised or lowered by as much as 50 per cent, and abolished many trade restrictions. *Compare* Trade Expansion Act.

trade association. A voluntary nonprofit association of competitors in a branch of industry for dealing with common business problems, such as accounting practices, trade promotion, and relations with organized labor, the public, and public officials.

trade barriers. Restrictions imposed by governments to limit competition from outside their boundaries and secure the home market for their own citizens. Internationally they have taken the form of tariffs, subsidies to domestic producers, preclusive buying policies, quotas, emigration control, exchange control, export and import licensing, and bilateral agreements for the exchange of designated goods. Interstate trade barriers have taken the form of discriminatory taxes and tax exemptions and laws passed ostensibly for the protection of health, morals, and safety, and for the prevention of fraud. The U.S. Supreme Court has held State action unconstitutional whenever it unduly burdens interstate commerce.

trade dollar. A U.S. silver coin, of slightly greater weight than the silver dollar, minted 1873–85 for use in trade with China and Japan. It was not a legal tender.

Trade Expansion Act. An act of Congress, 1962, which extended the principle of the flexible tariff, *q.v.*, by authorizing the President to negotiate additional reductions in tariff duties, or free entry for certain products of the Common Market, *q.v.*, and which resulted in the Dillon Round and the Kennedy Round, *qq.v.*

trademark. An emblem, symbol, trade name, or similar device used to distinguish the goods or services of a particular manufacturer or dealer. On payment of a fee, it may be registered with the U.S. Patent Office, but ownership and use of a trademark are regulated chiefly by the laws of the States.

trading. Mutual exchange of support for candidates or measures between rival politicians or party organizations. *See* deal.

trading-with-the-enemy act. Any statute passed after the outbreak of war prohibiting citizens from transacting business with enemy persons except under special license.

traffic court. A special municipal court which has summary jurisdiction over offenses against laws and ordinances regulating motor vehicle traffic.

transnational. Possessing jurisdiction beyond the frontiers of a single state;—a characteristic of a federal or supranational union or community, or even of a confederation because it has jurisdiction over one or more matters throughout the territory of member states.

Transportation Act. 1. A law of Congress, passed Feb. 28, 1920, shortly after the return of railroads from wartime government operation to private operation, which provided that railroad rates should be high enough to enable the companies to earn a reasonable return and that surplus earnings should be subject to partial recapture and use as a loan fund to aid needy companies; created a railway labor board; and planned for the eventual consolidation of the railroads into several large systems. **2.** An act of Congress, Sept. 18, 1940, extending the jurisdiction of the Interstate Commerce Commission to transportation on intercoastal and inland waterways in order to develop a unified rail, water, and motor transportation system.

treason. A violation of the allegiance which a person (whether a citizen or an alien resident) owes to the state under whose protection he lives. The Constitution, Art. III, Sec. 3, defines treason as overt acts levying war against, or aiding the enemies of, the United States and specifies the nature of the evidence required for the conviction of a person for treason. To be considered treasonable, there must be, at the least, an overt assemblage of persons with intent to overthrow the government or the laws. Neither a riotous resistance to officers nor a mere conspiracy to commit treason is treason; but supplying a public enemy with materials or information of military value does constitute treason. The penalty for treason, as fixed by Congress, may be death. The States may punish treason against themselves under the provisions of their own constitutions and laws.

treasurer. An officer of a State, municipal, or other local government who receives and is responsible for the custody of public funds, makes payments on the warrant of, usually, a comptroller, and sells and retires bonds and debt certificates. *Compare* Treasurer of the United States.

Treasurer of the United States. An officer of the Department of the

Treasury who is the official custodian of the public money and the keeper of financial accounts of the United States, who receives and disburses public funds, and who is fiscal agent for the payment of principal and interest on the public debt. Many of the functions nominally entrusted to him are performed through the Federal Reserve System.

Treasury. *See* Department of the Treasury.

treasury bill. A short-term obligation of the U.S. Treasury which is sold in order to meet immediate fiscal needs and usually matures in less than one year.

treasury note. 1. A piece of paper currency formerly issued in various denominations by the U.S. Treasury under the provisions of the Sherman Silver Purchase Act of 1890, and since retired. **2.** An obligation of the U.S. Treasury which matures in a period of from one to five years.

Treaties of Paris. The peace treaties between the United States and its allies, on the one hand, and Italy, Bulgaria, Hungary, and Rumania, which had been aligned with Germany in World War II, signed at Paris, Feb. 10, 1947.

treaty. A solemn agreement or compact between two or more sovereign states for the purpose of creating, defining, altering, or extinguishing mutual rights and reciprocal obligations. Treaties are made by negotiation, followed by formal ratification by the head of the treaty-making power. They may be ended by the accomplishment of the purposes for which they were made, by the expiration of a time limit, or by the creation of a new treaty. Denunciation, *q.v.*, by one state, unless provision is made for it in the treaty, may be regarded as a breach of faith. A war between states suspends, if it does not terminate, all treaties between them. For the enforcement of their provisions, treaties depend on the honor and interest of the governments which are parties to them. If these fail, an aggrieved state may make diplomatic protests, apply economic or other sanctions, or, as a last resort, declare war. Treaties are classified as *bilateral*, if only two states are parties; *multilateral*, if more than two accede; *executed*, or *transitory*, if they relate to a single matter which is at once disposed of; and *executory*, or *permanent*, if they relate to acts to be performed whenever the conditions specified in the treaty are present. In the United States, treaties are negotiated under the direction of the President and must be approved by a two-thirds vote of the Senate before ratification. A President often takes leading members of the Senate into his confidence during negotiations. According to the Constitution, Art. VI, "All Treaties made, or which shall be made, under the authority of the United States, shall be the supreme law of the land." In domestic law, they take precedence over State constitutions and statutes and are on an equal footing with valid laws of Congress. A treaty may render void the provisions of a prior federal statute and vice versa. But the action of Congress in passing statutes repugnant to the terms of treaties or in failing to carry out the provisions of a treaty is a violation of international obligations and may result in strained international relations. No treaty has been declared unconstitutional; and treaty making may increase the powers of Congress, as when the Migratory Bird Act, *q.v.*, to enforce a treaty with Great Britain was upheld as constitutional.

Treaty of Ghent. A treaty signed by representatives of the United States and Great Britain at Ghent, Belgium, Dec. 24, 1814, which officially ended the War of 1812. It provided that boundaries should remain as they were before the war but did not confirm American privileges in the North Atlantic fisheries, *q.v.*

Treaty of Guadalupe Hidalgo. The treaty signed Feb. 2, 1848, by Nicholas Trist, a former executive agent of President Polk, and representatives of Mexico. As ratified on May 30, it provided for ending the Mexican War, the cession of more than 500,000 square miles of territory to the United States, and the payment to Mexico of $15,000,000.

Treaty of Paris. 1. The treaty signed Feb. 10, 1763, which closed the French and Indian War, and by which Great Britain received Canada from France and Florida from Spain. **2.** The treaty signed Sept. 3, 1783, which ended the American Revolution, recognized the independence of the United States, fixed its boundaries, returned Florida to Spain, gave Americans certain rights to the North Atlantic fisheries, and provided that the United States should place no impediment to the collection of debts owed by Americans to British creditors. **3.** The treaty signed Dec. 10, 1898, which ended the Spanish-American War. Spain ceded Puerto Rico, the Philippines, and Guam to the United States on payment of $20,000,000 for public works in the Philippines, and relinquished her sovereignty over Cuba.

Treaty of Versailles. The treaty signed at Versailles, France, on June 28, 1919, between Germany and the Allied and Associated powers, following World War I. By its terms Germany lost her overseas possessions and ceded Alsace-Lorraine to France, parts of her eastern territory to the newly formed states of Poland and Czechoslovakia, Eupen and Malmédy to Belgium, and northern Schleswig to Denmark. She was compelled to pay reparations, to limit the size of her army and navy, and to agree to the demilitarization of much of the Rhineland. Part I of the treaty contained the Covenant of the League of Nations. The treaty was promptly ratified by all powers concerned except China and the United States, which signed a separate peace treaty in 1921.

Treaty of Washington. A treaty between the United States and Great Britain, signed at Washington, May 8, 1871, which provided for the settlement of the "Alabama" claims, *q.v.*, and a dispute over the San Juan Islands by arbitration, and allowed U.S. citizens certain privileges in the North Atlantic fisheries on payment by the United States of an amount to be determined by a joint commission. *See* Northwest boundary; Halifax Fishery Commission.

"Trent" affair. An international incident caused by the stopping and search of the British mail steamer "Trent" by the American ship "San Jacinto," Nov. 8, 1861, and the seizure of two of her passengers, James M. Mason and John Slidell, who were Confederate commissioners bound for London and Paris respectively. The British government insisted on their liberation, but responsible persons in both the United States and Great Britain acted to avert war, and the commissioners were subsequently put on board a British vessel.

trial. A judicial procedure for examining and deciding the merits of a controversy or establishing the guilt or innocence of a person accused of crime.

trial court. A judicial tribunal having original jurisdiction or the power to hear and decide cases or controversies in the first instance. *Compare* appellate court.

trial jury. A petit jury for the trial of a case. *See* jury.

tribal lands. Lands on an Indian reservation which have not been allotted to individual Indians in severalty but are for the common use of the whole tribe.

tribunal. A court or other body in which decisions binding on litigants are made.

tributary state. A state which has submitted to a stronger state by making payments in money, goods, or services in order to ward off threatened aggression and preserve the semblance of its sovereignty.

trimmer. A political opportunist who readily changes his opinions or loyalties for his own advantage.

Trinidad. An island, part of the British Commonwealth, lying off the northern coast of South America, on which the United States maintains an important naval base.

Trop v. Dulles. A case, 356 U.S. 86 (1958), in which the Supreme Court declared unconstitutional, as a cruel and unusual punishment forbidden by the Eighth Amendment, a provision of the Nationality Act of 1940 which automatically took away American citizenship from members of the armed forces when they were convicted of desertion in time of war.

truant officer. An employee of a board of education who enforces compulsory school attendance laws; *called also* attendance officer.

Truax v. Corrigan. A case, 257 U.S. 312 (1921), in which the Supreme Court declared unconstitutional the provisions of an Arizona statute that barred resort to injunctions in labor disputes, on the ground that denial of injunctive relief in labor disputes when such relief was continued in practically all other situations where equitable remedies were traditionally available, constituted an arbitrary and unreasonable legislative classification and violated the equal-protection clause of the 14th Amendment.

truce. A cessation of hostilities by agreement between military commanders in the field, usually for some specific purpose.

true bill. An indorsement made by a grand jury on a bill of indictment submitted by a prosecuting officer when the grand jury finds that sufficient reason exists to bring an accused person to trial.

Truman Doctrine. The policy announced by President Harry S. Truman in his address to Congress, Mar. 12, 1947, requesting $400 million for military and economic aid to Greece and Turkey for the reason that it was in the interest of the United States to provide moral and financial assistance to countries whose political integrity is threatened by Communism or totalitarian ideologies. The doctrine was the first practical application of the policy of containment, *q.v. See* North Atlantic Treaty.

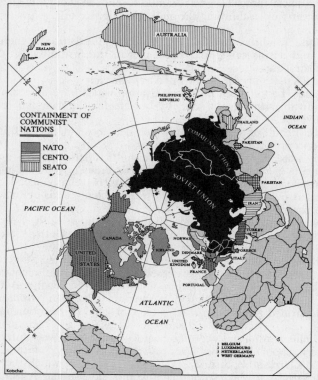

Truman Doctrine—Containment of Communist Nations

Truman Library. A collection of the public papers and memorabilia of the administration of President Harry S. Truman at Independence, Mo. It is under the jurisdiction of the General Services Administration.

trust. 1. A form of business combination, now illegal, by which stockholders of corporations or firms assigned their stock to a small board of trustees with voting or managerial powers, receiving in return trust certificates on which payments similar to dividends were made from time to time. **2.** *Colloquial.* Any cartel, pool, conference, or syndicate of companies, or any holding company or integrated corporation powerful enough to exercise monopolistic control.

trust busting. The vigorous prosecution of monopolies under the terms of the Sherman Antitrust Act, especially during the administrations of Presidents Theodore Roosevelt and William H. Taft.

Trusteeship Council. One of the major organs of the United Nations set up to supervise the administration by member states of trust territories, *q.v.*, and to promote the well-being of the inhabitants of such territories. Its membership must always include representatives of the five permanent members of the Security Council and of nations which administer trust territories, but half of the membership must always consist of nations not administering trust territories.

Trust Indenture Act. An act of Congress, 1939, which was designed to protect investors in certain types of bonds by requiring that the trust indenture include certain protective clauses and exclude certain exculpatory clauses, and that trustees should be independent of the issuing company.

trust territory. A colonial area surrendered by Italy or Japan after World War II, or a former mandate, *q.v.*, of the League of Nations, which is administered by a member state under the supervision of the Trusteeship Council of the United Nations.

Trust Territory of the Pacific Islands. Several island chains, the more important being the Marshall, Caroline, Marianas, and Gilbert archipelagoes, including more than 600 separate islands, mandated to Japan after World War I, which the Trusteeship Council of the United Nations awarded to the United States on Apr. 2, 1947, to be administered as a trust territory. The terms of the award permit the erection of fortifications.

Truth-in-packaging law. A law of Congress, 1966, which required accurate labeling of food, drug and cosmetic packages, forbade use of confusing terms, and authorized administrative officers to establish standards.

turnpike. Any road, such as the National Road, *q.v.*, or any of numerous roads built by States or private companies early in the 19th century, or any limited-access, high-speed superhighway built since the 1930's, whose construction, maintenance, and operation are financed from the collection of tolls;—so-called from the movable barrier formerly used to halt traffic until the toll was paid. *Called also* toll road.

T.V.A. Tennessee Valley Authority.

Tweed Ring. A group of spoilsmen, led by the notorious boss William Marcy Tweed, who were in complete political control of New York City from 1868 to 1871. They are estimated to have gotten more than $75,-000,000 through graft and outright thefts from the city.

Twelfth Amendment. An amendment to the Constitution, proclaimed Sept. 25, 1804, which altered the method of voting in presidential elections by requiring each elector to vote for President and Vice President on separate ballots instead of voting for two persons for President on one ballot as before. The Amendment was designed to prevent a recurrence of the situation in 1800 when Jefferson and Burr, Democratic-Republican candidates for President and Vice President respectively, received tie votes, and the election was decided, only after much intrigue and maneuvering by Burr's friends, by the House of Representatives in favor of Jefferson. In a broader sense, the Amendment was necessitated by the development of national political parties after 1789.

Twentieth Amendment. The so-called lame duck Amendment to the Constitution, proclaimed Feb. 6, 1933, which changed the beginning of Presidential and Vice-Presidential terms from March 4 to January 20, and of Congressional terms from March 4 to January 3, thereby eliminating the short session of Congress which had formerly convened early in December in even-numbered years, and in which a number of Congressmen sat who had not been re-elected to office. The Amendment also provided for Presidential succession in certain contingencies.

Twenty-fifth Amendment. An amendment to the Constitution, proclaimed Feb. 10, 1967, which provides that (*a*) the Vice President shall become President upon the death or resignation of the President; (*b*) when there is no Vice President, the President shall nominate a Vice President who shall take office when confirmed by a majority vote of both houses of Congress; (*c*) when the President is unable to discharge the powers and duties of his office he may voluntarily devolve them upon the Vice President by informing in writing the presiding officers of both houses of Congress of his inability, and may resume them by letter to the same officers; or (*d*) the Vice President may become Acting President when he and a majority of department heads, or other body designated by law, inform the presiding officers of both houses of Congress of the President's inability; but (*e*) the President thereafter may, by written statement to the presiding officers of Congress that no inability exists, resume the powers and duties of the presidency unless the Vice President and a majority of the heads of departments, or other body designated by law, within four days protest, and both houses of Congress by a two-thirds vote within twenty-one days thereafter, determine that the President is unable to serve.

Twenty-first Amendment. An amendment to the Constitution, proclaimed Dec. 5, 1933, which repealed most provisions of the 18th, or Prohibition, Amendment but prohibited the importation of intoxicating beverages into any State where delivery or use of such beverages violated the State's laws.

twenty-four-hour rule. The requirement that belligerent warships entering a neutral harbor for shelter, repairs, or supplies must leave within twenty-four hours unless a longer period is needed to render them seaworthy.

Twenty-fourth Amendment. An amendment to the Constitution, proclaimed Jan. 23, 1964, which prohibits federal or State denial or abridgment of the right to vote in any primary or other election for federal elective officers because of the prospective voter's failure to pay any poll tax or other tax. It was designed to render unenforceable in federal elections existing laws in Alabama, Arkansas, Mississippi, Texas, and Virginia which imposed a poll tax requirement for the suffrage. *Compare Harper* v. *Virginia State Board of Elections.*

Twenty-one-Day Rule. A rule of the House of Representatives, in effect 1949–50 and 1965–66, which permitted the Speaker to recognize a member of a standing committee for the purpose of calling up for floor consideration any bill previously reported by the committee for which the Committee on Rules had failed for 21 days to recommend a special order.

Twenty-second Amendment. An amendment to the Constitution, proclaimed Feb. 26, 1951, which prevents any person from being elected President more than twice, or, if he has succeeded to the Presidency before the midpoint of his predecessor's term, from being elected more than once. It restored permanently and legalized the usage limiting the President to two terms which had prevailed since Washington's retirement until broken by the third and fourth elections of F. D. Roosevelt.

Twenty-third Amendment. An amendment to the Constitution, proclaimed Mar. 29, 1961, which allots to the District of Columbia presidential electors, to be appointed as Congress directs, equal in number to those of a State of equivalent population but never more than the number of electors allotted to the least populous State. According to the census of 1960, the District was entitled to 1 elector for each 251,-317 inhabitants. In the least populous State, Alaska, the ratio was 1 elector to 75,300 people and in New York and California it was 1 elector to more than 391,000 people.

twilight zone. An undefined area along the boundary between subjects or jurisdictions, such as that lying between the constitutional powers of the States and those of the federal government.

Twining v. New Jersey. A case, 211 U.S. 78 (1908), in which the Supreme Court held that exemption from compulsory self-incrimination in a criminal proceeding is neither an immunity of national citizenship guaranteed against abridgment by the States under the 14th Amendment nor an exemption required of the States by the standards of due process; reversed in 1967.

twisting the British lion's tail. Political acts or statements against Great Britain generally made to gain applause and votes among certain elements of the American public.

two-party system. The condition which obtains when the political loyalties of the voters of a state are, for any considerable period of time, rather evenly divided between two great political parties, additional parties being nonexistent or relatively powerless to affect popular or representative decisions on public issues. The two-party system has been traditional in Great Britain, in some of the British dominions, and in the United States, although there have been periods in each of these countries when the system was seriously threatened by the rise of third parties. Because it facilitates the establishment of cohesive electoral and parliamentary majorities, disciplines political opposition, and simplifies the voters' problem in making electoral decisions, the two-party system is generally regarded as essential to stable popular government, or at least a means of effectively organizing political opinion in such a regime. *Called also* biparty system.

two-thirds rule. A rule of Democratic national conventions, adopted in 1832 and rescinded in 1936, which required that nominations of presidential and vice-presidential candidates be made by a two-thirds vote of the delegates.

tying contract. An agreement which requires distributors to maintain fixed resale prices, or to obtain supplies exclusively from one source, or to purchase goods of a specified quantity or quality in addition to those they actually wish to purchase. It is prohibited by antitrust laws.

tyranny. 1. *In classical antiquity:* government by a person who lacked legal or customary sanction for his position and who ruled with little regard for established law or custom, but who was sometimes regarded as a benefactor of the state. **2.** *In contemporary usage:* government by a despot which results in the arbitrary or capricious exercise of power in a state.

Tyson v. Banton. A case, 273 U.S. 418 (1927), in which the Supreme Court invalidated a New York statute limiting the resale price of theater tickets on the ground that ticket brokerage was not a business affected with a public interest and so its regulation was not a legitimate exercise of the State's police power.

U

Ullmann v. United States. A case, 350 U.S. 422 (1956), in which the Supreme Court upheld the constitutionality of an act of 1954 under which immunity from criminal prosecution could be granted to persons whose testimony was required by Congressional committees in national security matters. The Court declared that a person can be compelled to testify under such a grant even though such disabilities as loss of a job, denial of a passport, or public opprobrium might result, because the Fifth Amendment's protection against compulsory self-incrimination applies only to criminal proceedings.

ultimatum. 1. A final offer by one party in diplomatic or other negotiations, refusal of which by the other party results in the termination of the negotiations. **2.** A peremptory demand by one state of another, refusal of which may lead to a diplomatic rupture or possible war.

ultra vires. **1.** In excess of the constitutional powers of a legislature or an executive officer. **2.** Pertaining to acts of a public or private corporation which are void for want of legal authorization in the corporation's charter.

umbrella agency. *Slang.* A government unit created to coordinate and prevent overlapping and duplication of activities among a number of related agencies.

U.N. United Nations.

Un-American Activities Committee. Formerly a special committee but, since 1946, a standing committee of the House of Representatives which investigates un-American or subversive activities in the United States and occasionally makes recommendations for remedial legislation. At various times it has been accused of reckless and irresponsible action in bringing charges of Communism against public figures and for usurping functions of the Federal Bureau of Investigation.

unanimity. The agreement or consent of all members of a group.

unanimous consent. Consent, indicated by the absence of objection on the part of any member of a deliberative body, for proceeding contrary to a rule or rules. Unanimous consent is a time-saving device frequently used in a variety of minor matters and for expediting the passage of unopposed bills. *Compare* consent calendar.

Uncle Joe. A nickname of Joseph Gurney Cannon, Speaker of the House of Representatives, 1903–11.

Uncle Sam. A familiar personification of the government of the United States which originated about 1813.

Uncle Tomism. A contemptuous term applied by civil rights activists to the attitude of Negroes who regard education, training, and industry as the most substantial and permanent means of advancing the social and economic position of the Negro; or who are gradualists in their approach and who are accused of subservience to white leadership;—from the hero of Harriet Beecher Stowe's novel, *Uncle Tom's Cabin*.

uncommitted nation. A state which alone, or in informal association with other states, seeks to avoid identifying its international policies with post-World War II "power blocs," especially those headed by the United States or Soviet Russia.

Unconditional Surrender. 1. A nickname of General Ulysses S. Grant. 2. The terms announced at the Casablanca Conference of Prime Minister Churchill and President F. D. Roosevelt, 1942, for the capitulation of the Axis powers.

unconstitutional. 1. Repugnant to the provisions of a written constitution. 2. Contrary to the accepted principles and practices of a state.

underdeveloped country. A country in which, in greater or lesser degree, (*a*) the great bulk of the people depend on grazing and agriculture for livelihood; (*b*) power is largely supplied by men and animals, and tools are primitive; (*c*) the importance of a man depends on his family or class rather than his own productive efforts; (*d*) poverty and illiteracy abound; (*e*) public administration is mostly done at inefficient village and provincial levels; (*f*) medical and sanitary facilities are primitive; and (*g*) birth and death rates are high. Emergence from such conditions is slow because lowering of the death rate results in a population explosion, and consequently, per capita incomes improve little with the development of mechanization.

underground railroad. Organized secret assistance to fugitive slaves before the Civil War which often enabled them to escape to the North or to Canada.

under secretary. 1. An officer in most of the executive departments in the federal government ranking next to the Secretary. 2. *In the United Kingdom:* a political officer, assistant to a minister, who may represent his department in the house of Parliament to which the ministerial head of the department does not belong.

Underwood Tariff. A tariff law, Oct. 3, 1913, which substituted ad valorem for specific and compound duties, extended the free list, and reduced the rates on many manufactured articles to a point where foreign competition might become effective as a means of curbing monopolies.

undistributed profits tax. A graduated federal tax, ranging from 7 to 27 per cent, levied in 1936 upon corporate surplus (earnings above a certain percentage not distributed as dividends).

unearned income. Income derived from interest, dividends, gifts, certain types of royalties, or the like as distinguished from income derived from an employment, profession, or business.

unearned increment. Increase in the value of land which results, not from the owner's improvements, but from social and economic developments like the growth of population, industry, and transportation. Its recapture by the state is a basic tenet in single-tax, *q.v.*, theories.

unemployment insurance. A State-administered system whereby workers who meet qualifications receive a stipulated weekly income (unemployment compensation) from a tax-supported fund or reserve during periods of unemployment.

UNESCO United Nations Educational, Scientific, and Cultural Organization.

unfair labor practice. Any act by an employer or a labor union in violation of standards of union-management relations established by law.

unfair trade practice. Any deceptive or discriminatory business practice, such as a false or misleading advertisement, the misbranding of a product, or an agreement among business enterprises to fix prices, to discriminate among buyers of their goods or services, to divert business from competitors, or to establish monopoly conditions and restrain commerce. *Compare* restraint of trade.

unicameral. Pertaining to a legislature consisting of one chamber.

unified court system. The consolidation of courts of every degree and type of jurisdiction within a given area into a single tribunal with appropriate functional and regional divisions under the general supervision of a presiding magistrate, justice, or bench. Several large cities have unified courts and their adoption has been recommended in certain States.

Uniform Code of Military Justice. A comprehensive statement of the laws governing all the armed forces enacted by Congress in 1950, replacing the Articles of War and the Articles for the Government of the Navy, which also provides for a review of decisions of courts martial and for appeals to a newly created United States Court of Military Appeals, *q.v.*

uniformity. 1. A constitutional requirement that federal tax laws shall operate in the same manner upon persons and property in all the States of the Union. It applies also to the District of Columbia and incorporated territories. 2. Avoidance of discrimination or arbitrary classification in law or public policy.

uniform State laws. Model statutes drafted by the Conference of Commissioners on Uniform State Laws, *q.v.*, and enacted without amendment by all or several State legislatures, which are designed to substitute a series of uniform enactments on subjects like bills of lading, negotiable instruments, motor vehicle registration, and liability for accidents for conflicting laws of the States.

unincorporated territory. A territory or possession of the United States whose inhabitants, under the doctrine of the Insular cases, *q.v.*, can claim only the substantive rights of the Constitution and not such procedural rights as indictment by a grand jury or trial by a jury at common law. The constitutional requirement that taxes shall be uniform does not apply to such a territory.

union. 1. A joining of two or more states to form a single state. 2. An international organization (as a customs or postal union) formed usually for one purpose. 3. A labor organization. 4. *Colloquial.* The United States of America.

union calendar. A calendar of the House of Representatives which lists all revenue bills, general appropriation bills, and bills of a public character directly or indirectly appropriating money or property; *called officially* Calendar of the Committee of the Whole House on the State of the Union.

Union Labor party. A minor party organized in 1887 by various farm and labor groups and the remnants of the Greenback party. Its candidates received 146,897 votes in 1888.

Union League. A secret political organization founded in 1862 which, during the Civil War, countered the activities of Copperhead societies and other Southern sympathizers in Northern States and, in the Reconstruction period, was active in advancing the interests of freedmen in the Southern States.

union-maintenance clause. A clause in collective labor contracts stipulating that although nonunion men may be hired or continued in employment, all who are members of a union when the contract is signed or join voluntarily thereafter must maintain membership as a condition of employment. Under the Taft-Hartley Labor-Management Relations Act, *q.v.*, important restrictions are placed upon the operation of such a clause, the principal one being the requirement that the union demanding it must actually represent a majority of the workers eligible to vote in a collective bargaining election.

Union party. 1. A party formed in Ohio Valley States at the beginning of the Civil War by a fusion of Republicans and War Democrats, and later active throughout the Northern States. *See* National Union party. 2. A minor party in the election of 1936 composed of advocates of the Townsend plan, share the wealth, and other movements. Its presidential nominee, William Lemke, received 882,479 popular votes.

Union saver. A contemptuous epithet applied before the Civil War both in the North and South to an advocate of concessions and compromises as a means of averting the disruption of the Union.

union shop. A place of employment in which, if qualified union members are unavailable, nonunion workers may be hired on condition that they join the union within a specified period and continuously maintain their membership. *Compare* closed shop; open shop.

unitary state. Any state in which all the territorial subdivisions are constitutionally subordinated to the authority of the central government. *Compare* federal state.

United Labor party. A single-tax party which, with Henry George as its candidate, ran second in the New York mayoralty election in 1886. It cast 2,818 votes in the presidential election of 1888, after which it disappeared.

United Nations. An organization composed of nearly all the independent states of the world devoted to the settlement of international problems and the maintenance of world peace and security. The necessity for such an organization was recognized at the Moscow Conference, Nov. 1, 1943. Its structure was the subject of long discussions at the Dumbarton Oaks Conference which ended Oct. 7, 1944 and its Charter was brought to final form at the San Francisco Conference, which sat from April 25 to June 26, 1945. Membership in the U.N. is open to all peace-loving states which accept, and in the judgment of member states, are able to fulfill, the obligations of membership. New members may be admitted by a two-thirds vote of the General Assembly. The headquarters of the U.N. are in New York City. Its principal organs are the General Assembly, *q.v.*, in which all members are represented, each having one vote; the Security Council, *q.v.*, composed of five permanent and ten elective members; a Secretariat which keeps records and performs administrative functions; a Trusteeship Council, *q.v.*; an Economic and Social Council, *q.v.*; an International Court of Justice, *q.v.*; and specialized agencies, *q.v.*; fulfilling needs of the nations and inhabitants of the world.

United Nations Educational, Scientific, and Cultural Organization. An agency of the United Nations with headquarters in Paris, to which about 118 member states belong. Through recommendations to member governments and certain activities under its own direction, UNESCO advances cultural and educational standards throughout the world, promotes teaching, research, and the increase of knowledge, and stimulates the diffusion and exchange of ideas and information, especially through mass-communication mediums.

United Nations Institute for Training and Research. An autonomous unit within the framework of the United Nations which, in conjunction with universities and similar agencies, trains international civil servants drawn especially from developing countries for service within specialized agencies of the U.N. or in the civil servants' respective states of origin, and conducts research on the activities and objectives of the United Nations.

United Nations Monetary and Financial Conference. *See* Bretton Woods Conference.

United Nations Relief and Rehabilitation Administration. An international agency, created Nov. 9, 1943, which aided the people of regions liberated from the Axis powers by providing food, clothing, shelter, medical and sanitary assistance, and helping to secure the return of exiles and prisoners of war, and to restore agriculture, industry, and essential services. UNRRA was liquidated in June, 1947, but many of its activities were transferred to other international organizations.

United States Air Force Academy. An institution, established in 1954 near Colorado Springs, Colo., for training career officers of the Air Force.

United States Arms Control and Disarmament Agency. *See* disarmament.

United States Attorney. A federal attorney who, under the supervision of the Department of Justice, prosecutes criminal cases in the United States district courts and other lower federal courts.

United States Circuit Courts. Federal courts created in 1789 which were staffed by Justices of the Supreme Court, who rode circuit, and District Court judges, and which had original jurisdiction over cases involving diversity of citizenship and a limited appellate jurisdiction. The latter was transferred to the Circuit Courts of Appeals in 1891. The U.S. Circuit Courts were abolished in 1911. *See* United States Courts of Appeals.

United States Coast Guard. An essentially autonomous unit of the public forces of the United States, subject to the jurisdiction of the Department of Transportation in time of peace and of the Department of the Navy in time of war or national emergency. Although it is especially charged with the enforcement of the customs, navigation, and neutrality laws, it serves as a general law-enforcement agency upon navigable waters and the high seas and protects life and property at sea.

United States Code. A consolidation and codification of all the general and permanent laws of the United States in effect, classified by subject matter under 50 titles, prepared under the direction of the Judiciary Committee of the House of Representatives. A revision has appeared every six years since 1926, and a supplementary volume is issued after each session of Congress. Many of the titles have been enacted as law and, when all have been so enacted, the Code will constitute legal evidence of the law.

United States Commissioner. An official normally attached to a U.S. District Court who holds preliminary hearings in the case of persons accused of a federal crime and determines whether they shall be held for the federal grand jury.

United States Court of Claims. A special court consisting of a chief justice and four associates set up in 1855 with recommendatory powers only, granted jurisdiction in 1866 to decide claims against the Government arising under contracts, and empowered in 1946 to decide certain kinds of cases involving torts by government employees.

United States Court of Customs and Patent Appeals. A specialized court established in 1909 as the United States Court of Customs Appeals, given its present title and duties in 1929, and consisting of five justices, which reviews (*a*) decisions of the U.S. Customs Court on classifications and duties on imported merchandise; (*b*) decisions of the Patent Office on applications for, and interference with, patents and trademarks; and (*c*) legal questions in findings of the U.S. Tariff Commission concerning unfair practices in import trade.

United States Court of Military Appeals. A legislative court established by Congress in 1950 composed of three civilian judges appointed for fifteen-year terms by the President and Senate, which is required to review court-martial decisions affecting high military personnel or imposing the death sentence; and which may review other decisions imposing long prison sentences or bad-conduct discharges. Appeals from its decisions may be made to the U.S. Supreme Court.

United States Courts of Appeals. Intermediate appellate courts created
by Congress in 1891 and known until 1948 as United States Circuit
Courts of Appeals, sitting in ten numbered circuits and the District
of Columbia. Each court has from three to nine judges. Normally cases
are heard by divisions of three judges sitting together, but on certain
matters all the judges of a circuit may hear a case. Courts of Appeals
have appellate jurisdiction over nearly all cases decided by United States
District Courts, *q.v.*, and review and enforce orders of many federal
administrative bodies. Because few of their decisions are ever appealed
to the Supreme Court, the Courts of Appeals are said to have final
jurisdiction in most federal cases.

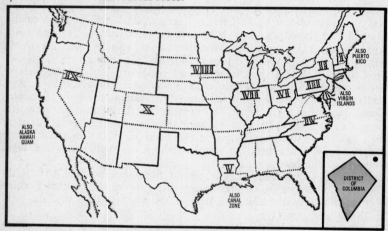

United States Courts of Appeals—Circuits and District of Columbia

United States Customs Court. A court created in 1890 as the Board of
United States General Appraisers and given its present title in 1926,
which consists of nine judges sitting in New York City, and which has
sole jurisdiction over the interpretation of tariff laws, the classification
of merchandise, and the determination of the dutiable valuation of
imported goods. In 1956 it was made a court of record under Article
III of the Constitution.

United States District Courts. Trial courts with original jurisdiction over
diversity-of-citizenship cases, and cases arising under U.S. criminal,
bankruptcy, admiralty, patent, copyright, and postal laws. There are 89
District Courts in the United States and Puerto Rico, each having
from one to twenty-four judges, a total of 303. Normally, one district
judge presides over each trial, but three-judge District Courts are necessary for the issuance of injunctions concerning certain subjects. From
District Courts the normal course of appeals is to a court of appeals,
q.v., but some decisions holding statutes unconstitutional, certain criminal cases, and the injunction orders of three-judge District Courts may
be appealed directly to the Supreme Court.

United States Employment Service. A public, nation-wide, job-placement service administered and maintained by the States largely with federal funds under the supervision of the Bureau of Employment Security of the Labor Department. In administering their respective services, the States must live up to the terms of the Wagner-Peyser Act, *q.v.* Other activities include obtaining employment for veterans, a system of inter-area recruitment of labor among the States, a placement service for employers and workers in agriculture, and an employment service for the District of Columbia.

United States Fish and Wildlife Service. A division of the Department of the Interior, dating from the consolidation in 1940 of the Bureau of Biological Survey and the Bureau of Sport Fisheries and Wildlife, which carries on research and wildlife conservation programs and is charged especially with the preservation of a vigorous fishing industry, the enforcement of international agreements relating to fur seals and commercial fish, and the conservation, for economic and recreational purposes, of various kinds of wild life.

United States Government Organization Manual. An annual official publication which contains information concerning the duties, functions, activities, and official personnel of all Administrations, Agencies, Authorities, Boards, Bureaus, Commissions, etc. of the Executive Branch of the federal government in existence as of the date it goes to press, with briefer accounts of the Legislative and Judicial branches. Appendices list, with brief notes, (*a*) Executive agencies and functions which have been abolished, transferred, or terminated since March 4, 1933; and (*b*) representative publications of departments and agencies of the federal government.

United States Information Agency. An independent unit established in 1953 which seeks to counteract Communist propaganda and present to the world a favorable impression of the political, economic, social, and cultural life of the United States by operating the Voice of America, *q.v.*, maintaining libraries and information centers in about 200 foreign cities, arranging for cultural exchanges, and distributing pamphlets and motion picture films.

United States Marshal. *See* marshal.

United States Military Academy. An institution at West Point, N.Y., established 1802, for the training of junior army officers.

United States Naval Academy. An institution at Annapolis, Md., established 1845, for training junior naval officers.

United States Reports. The official printed record of cases heard and decided by the U.S. Supreme Court which usually include a statement of the essential facts of each case, the opinion of the Court, concurring and dissenting opinions, if any, the disposition made of each case, and occasionally an abstract of counsel's briefs. Originally a series of *Reports*, with volumes numbered consecutively, was issued during the incumbency of each successive court reporter and these are cited as Dallas (1790–1800); Cranch (1801–1815); Wheaton (1816–1827); Peters (1828–1843); Howard (1843–1860); Black (1861–1862); and Wallace (1863–1874). By 1874, when the number of volumes so identified totalled 90, the practice began of eliminating the reporter's name and citing them as *United States Reports.*

United States Statutes at Large. An official compilation of the acts and resolutions of each session of Congress published by the Office of the Federal Register in the National Archives and Records Service, *q.v.* It consists of two parts, the first comprising public acts and joint resolutions, the second, private acts and joint resolutions, concurrent resolutions, treaties, and Presidential proclamations.

United States Tariff Commission. An independent federal commission of six members, not more than three of whom may belong to one party, appointed by the President and Senate for six-year terms, created in 1916. It studies the operation and effect of U.S. customs laws, conducts research in domestic and international commercial policy, supplies Congress and the President with pertinent information on tariffs and related matters, advises the President in the negotiation of reciprocal trade agreements and in the exercise of his discretionary power to raise or lower tariff duties, supplies the President with information on the effects upon specific industries that have been granted tariff relief and with the data required for the exercise of his statutory power to limit or otherwise regulate the importation of agricultural goods when such importation threatens benefits secured by law to domestic agriculture, and advises on the injury to American industry resulting from foreign or other unfair trade practices.

United States v. Brown. A case, 381 U.S. 437 (1965), in which the Supreme Court held that a provision of the Labor Reform Act of 1959, making it a crime for a Communist party member to serve as an officer or employee of a labor union, was unconstitutional as a bill of attainder; for, though Congress may legislate to prevent political strikes primarily designed to disrupt commerce and industry, it may not by legislation punish persons who belong to a party which might foment political strikes.

United States v. Butler. A case, 297 U.S. 1 (1936), in which the Supreme Court invalidated the first Agricultural Adjustment Act, declaring that coercive federal regulation of farm production and prices, contained in the act, invaded the reserved powers of the States; that the processing taxes, *q.v.*, levied under the act, were not bona fide taxes but an integral part of an unconstitutional program of regulation and hence themselves invalid; and that, in any case, the taxes could not be sustained under the general-welfare clause of the Constitution. *Compare Mulford v. Smith.*

United States v. Classic. A case, 313 U.S. 299 (1941), in which the Supreme Court upheld the power of Congress to regulate State primaries for the nomination of Representatives in Congress, declaring that the right of qualified voters to participate in such primaries was guaranteed by Art. I, Secs. 2 and 4, of the Constitution which establish the qualifications of electors of the House of Representatives and describe the extent of the regulatory power of Congress over elections. In holding that Congressional primaries are an integral part of Congressional elections and, as such, subject to Congress' control under the Constitution, the Court overruled an earlier decision in *Newberry* v. *United States, q.v.*

United States v. **Curtiss-Wright Export Corp.** A case, 299 U.S. 304 (1936), in which the Supreme Court upheld a statute authorizing the President to exercise broad discretion in issuing a proclamation to embargo a shipment of arms to foreign belligerents. Because of the plenary nature of the federal government's authority over international relations, the Court said Congress might exercise greater latitude in delegating power to the President over foreign affairs than might be permissible in delegating discretion to him over internal matters.

United States v. **Darby Lumber Co.** A case, 312 U.S. 100 (1941), in which the Supreme Court upheld the constitutionality of the Fair Labor Standards Act, *q.v.* The Court's opinion, sustaining the act's minimum-wage, maximum-hour, and other provisions, expressly overruled *Hammer* v. *Dagenhart* (*see* Child Labor cases); declared that Congress may prohibit the transportation in interstate commerce of goods made under substandard working conditions; and made it clear that the implications of this power to prohibit include the power to regulate conditions of manufacture.

United States v. **E. C. Knight Co.** A case, 156 U.S. 1 (1895), in which the Supreme Court held that the Sherman Antitrust Act was inapplicable to a merger of four sugar refineries in Pennsylvania. The Court viewed the merger as a monopoly of manufacture within a single State and held that the incidental effects upon interstate commerce did not warrant invocation of the Sherman Act. The Court later altered its view of the commerce power. *See* interstate commerce.

United States v. **Lovett.** A case, 328 U.S. 303 (1946), in which the Supreme Court held unconstitutional, as a bill of attainder, a statute (a rider to an appropriation act) which forbade payment of salaries to federal employees, mentioned by name in the act, whose conduct and political associations had incurred the displeasure of the Dies Committee. The Court held that the act, in effect, cut off the persons from federal employment and thus punished them in violation of Art. I, Sec. 10 of the Constitution.

United States v. **South-Eastern Underwriters Association.** A case, 322 U.S. 533 (1944), in which the Supreme Court reversed its decision in *Paul* v. *Virginia, q.v.,* and held that contracts of insurance between persons in different States were in interstate commerce and thus subject to federal regulation.

United States v. **Wong Kim Ark.** A case, 169 U.S. 649 (1898), in which the Supreme Court, interpreting literally the appropriate provision of the 14th Amendment, declared that a child born in the United States is a citizen of the United States even though his parents are aliens and ineligible for citizenship by naturalization.

unit instruction. A resolution of a party convention which requires all delegates to a higher (State or national) convention to vote in accordance with the decision of the majority of the delegation.

unit rule. A rule of Democratic national conventions that whenever a delegation is under unit instruction, *q.v.,* from its State party convention, its vote on the call of the States must be cast and counted as if it were unanimous, notwithstanding the existence of a minority within the delegation which desires to vote otherwise. Delegates chosen from Congressional districts by mandatory direct primary elections and not subjected by law to the authority of the State party convention may vote as individuals; and so may delegates who are not under unit instructions.

Universal Declaration of Human Rights. A declaration by the United Nations General Assembly, Dec. 10, 1948, which incorporates most of the contents of American and British bills of rights and in addition the rights to seek asylum from persecution; to a nationality; to marry and found a family; to seek and impart information and ideas by any medium, regardless of frontiers; to participate in the government of one's country; to social security; to work; to the free choice of employment; to protection against unemployment; to rest and leisure; to an adequate standard of living; to an education directed to the full development of the human personality; to participate in the cultural life of the community; and to an international order in which human rights can be fully realized. Efforts to make sections of the Declaration effective against governments by means of appropriate treaties have been unsuccessful, but it has had considerable influence on the content of bills of rights in various countries, judicial decisions, the standards of administration of colonial territories and, generally, as a moral standard for the freedom and privileges of the individual in organized society.

Universal Postal Union. A specialized agency of the United Nations, first created by a convention at Bern, Switzerland in 1874, which has the objective of establishing "a single postal territory for the reciprocal exchange of correspondence" among peoples living in different countries. A Congress of the Union meets every five years, and between sessions an Executive Council of 27 members conducts the Union's affairs. An International Bureau, supervised by the Swiss Confederation, furnishes statistics and information concerning services, rates, and costs.

unneutral service. *In international law of war:* the action of a neutral vessel in carrying contraband or transporting enemy troops or dispatches.

unofficial observer. A representative of the United States who attended meetings of commissions set up by the League of Nations.

unreasonable searches and seizures. Searches of persons and places and seizure of papers and effects without search warrants properly sworn to, issued by judicial officers, and particularly describing the places to be searched and the persons or things to be seized. Wiretapping and the use of a stomach pump are considered unreasonable searches; but blood tests for alcohol, and seizures made immediately after a proper arrest when objects wanted as evidence are in plain sight or danger exists that wrongdoers might escape, because of the delay necessary to obtain a warrant, are considered as not unreasonable. Since 1967, the courts have broadened the range of items that might be seized in a lawful search and used as evidence. The Fourth Amendment prohibits unreasonable searches and seizures, and the provision against self-incrimination in the Fifth Amendment prohibits the use of illegally seized articles as evidence against an accused person.

unreconstructed. A Southern attitude after the Civil War of refusing to accept in full the 13th, 14th, and 15th Amendments to the Constitution and Reconstruction acts of Congress.

UNRRA   United Nations Relief and Rehabilitation Administration.

unwritten constitution. 1. A constitution like that of Great Britain which, consisting largely of common law and custom, has never been comprehensively formulated as a single document. **2.** The usages and conventions which supplement and often modify the provisions of a written constitution.

unwritten law. 1. Customary law or law contained in judicial decisions which has never been reduced to statutory form. **2.** *Colloquial.* An understanding in some communities that a jury will not convict a person of a crime committed to avenge the seduction of a wife or daughter.

Uphaus **v.** *Wyman.* A case, 360 U.S. 72 (1959), in which the Supreme Court upheld, as consistent with the associational freedom and privacy guaranteed in the First Amendment and protected by the due-process clause of the Fourteenth Amendment, an effort of the attorney general of a State to compel a recalcitrant witness, through a contempt citation, to identify guests at a summer camp when the State had a "valid reason" to believe that such persons were subversives within the meaning of its anti-sedition act. Despite an apparently contrary ruling in *Pennsylvania* v. *Nelson, q.v.,* the Court insisted it was still permissible to legislate on the matter of sedition *against the state itself* and hence, *a fortiori,* to exercise appropriate investigatory powers.

upper chamber. A relatively small legislative house (as the U.S. Senate) which has powers approximately equal to, or greater than, those of the larger house of a bicameral legislature. *Compare* second chamber.

U.P.U. Universal Postal Union.

Urban Rapid Transit Act. An act of Congress, 1964, which authorized the expenditure of $375 million for up to two-thirds of the net cost of construction and improvement of public and private urban mass transit facilities, excluding highways.

urban renewal. A comprehensive program of slum clearance, relocation of some streets, redevelopment by subsidized construction of housing, public and private facilities, and mass transportation arteries, and rehabilitation of basically sound buildings which is carried on by cities with financial and technical assistance from the federal government.

usage. A long continued custom or convention (as the seniority rule in Congressional committees, meetings of the President's cabinet, or the relegation of the electoral college to an insignificant role) which supplements, or significantly modifies in practical application, the provisions of a written constitution or a statute.

U.S.C.G. United States Coast Guard.

U.S.E.S. United States Employment Service.

use tax. An ad valorem tax on the use, consumption, or storage of tangible property, usually at the same rate as the sales tax, and levied for the purpose of preventing tax avoidance by the purchase of articles in a State or taxing jurisdiction which does not levy sales taxes.

USIA United States Information Agency.

USMA United States Military Academy.

USNA United States Naval Academy.

U.S.S. United States Senate.

usurpation. The forcible seizure or arbitrary assumption of powers rightfully belonging to another person or branch of government.

usury. The lending of money at exorbitant interest. Nearly all the States limit interest rates by statute and penalize usury.

utopia. An ideal commonwealth or nearly perfect society;—from the *Utopia*, a book by Sir Thomas More first published in Latin, 1516.

U-2 Affair. The downing, 1200 miles within Russian territory, on May 1, 1960, of an American U-2 high altitude reconnaissance plane; followed by Russian disruption of a summit conference then in session in Paris, the admission by President Eisenhower that the United States had been gathering information to guard against surprise attack, the imprisonment of the pilot by the Soviet Union, and his eventual exchange for a Russian spy apprehended by the United States.

V

vacancy. An office temporarily unfilled because of the death, resignation, disqualification, or removal of the incumbent and the failure to provide an immediate successor.

vagrancy. The condition of a person without a fixed habitation or reputable means of self-support.

validating act. A curative statute, *q.v.*

validity. The quality of legal sanction or authority.

valuation. The process of appraisal used for determining rates, fair profits, taxes, or assessments, or for determining money indemnity due to owners as a result of destruction or alienation of property by eminent domain. Criteria used in the valuation process include current market value, replacement cost, original actual cost, prudent investment, and capitalized earnings or earning power. Although American practice purports to fix utility rates so as to insure a "reasonable rate on the fair value" of the property concerned, many economists argue that value is the product of earnings from rates charged, and hence cannot logically be used as the point of departure in determining fair rates.

Vandenberg Resolution. A resolution passed by the Senate, June 11, 1948, in favor of the establishment of regional self-defense arrangements by the United States and other countries under the United Nations Charter. It foreshadowed the NATO alliance and other regional pacts.

vassal state. A state apparently independent but actually subject to the overlordship of a more powerful state.

***Veazie Bank* v. *Fenno*.** A case, 8 Wall. 533 (1869), in which the Supreme Court upheld a federal tax of 10 per cent on the value of notes issued by State banks, thereby driving such notes out of circulation and making the note-issue privilege a monopoly of the newly created national banks. The Court upheld the tax as an exercise of Congress' constitutional power to provide a sound and uniform national currency.

Veep. An affectionate nickname of Vice President Alben W. Barkley developed by spelling out the initials of his office.

Venezuela Boundary dispute. A controversy of long standing between Great Britain and Venezuela over the western boundary of British Guiana. In 1895 President Cleveland served notice that, if the two countries would not agree to arbitration, the United States would determine the true boundary line. Great Britain later agreed to arbitration, and the award gave her most of the disputed territory.

venire *or* **venire facias.** An ancient writ for summoning jurymen.

venue. The locality (normally the county) in which a criminal trial or legal action takes place and from which the jury is chosen.

Vera Cruz seizure. *See* Tampico Incident.

verdict. The decision of the jury in the trial of either civil or criminal cases.

Versailles. *See* Treaty of Versailles.

Veterans Administration. An independent agency authorized by Congress in 1930 to consolidate all administrative units dealing with veterans' affairs. Under its head, the Administrator of Veterans Affairs, the V.A. administers laws providing for the hospital treatment, training, rehabilitation, pensions, death benefits, retirement pay, and institutional care of veterans or their dependents.

veteran's preference. Preferential treatment accorded under U.S. civil service laws to honorably discharged members of the armed services. They are exempted from the usual requirements of age and physical fitness and are entitled to have five points (ten points, if they are physically disabled) added to the rating they have earned. Widows of veterans who have not remarried and wives of veterans incapacitated for employment are also entitled to an addition of ten points. Similar preference is given under some State laws.

veto. 1. The return, to the legislative house in which it originated, of a bill unsigned and with objections in writing by a chief executive whose signature is necessary to complete the enactment of a law. The U.S. Constitution requires that every bill and joint resolution passed by Congress must be submitted to the President for his signature. If he returns it unsigned with his objections within ten days, it does not become law unless Congress passes it again by a two-thirds vote. If he fails to sign it and return it to Congress within ten days, it becomes a law without his signature; but if Congress adjourns before the end of such a ten-day period, the bill is lost (*pocket veto*). The governor has a veto power in all States except North Carolina. In all but a few States, he may veto items of appropriation bills, in some he may reduce items, and in one State he may veto sections of nonfinancial bills. The number of votes required to override a gubernatorial veto ranges from a majority to two-thirds of all members elected to a legislature. 2. The power exerted by one of the five permanent members of the Security

Council of the United Nations which, under provisions of Article 27 of the Charter, may prevent a decision on any important issue by refusing its concurrence.

Veto Mayor. A nickname of Grover Cleveland when mayor of Buffalo, N. Y.

vice. In place of; when prefaced to the title of an officer it usually identifies a deputy or substitute for the holder of the office, legally capable, under certain circumstances, of exercising some or all of the powers and duties of the office.

vice consul. An assistant or substitute officer stationed at a principal consulate.

Vice President. The officer who succeeds to the presidency in case of the death, removal, or resignation of the President, and who becomes Acting President in case of presidential disability, *q.v.* He is elected on separate ballot by majority vote of the electoral colleges; but if no candidate has a majority, the Senate, a quorum of two-thirds being present, elects from the two candidates having the highest electoral vote. The Vice President presides over the Senate except when the President is being tried on an impeachment; but he has no vote and little or no influence on its proceedings unless the Senate is equally divided. Since 1937, Vice Presidents have been actively engaged, by invitation of the President, in numerous important assignments in domestic politics and foreign affairs. Eight Vice Presidents, Tyler, Fillmore, Andrew Johnson, Arthur, Theodore Roosevelt, Coolidge, Truman, and Lyndon B. Johnson, have succeeded to the presidency on the death of the incumbent.

Vietnam War. A military struggle in which the United States became involved following the retirement of the French from Indochina in 1954 and the division of Vietnam at the 17th parallel, the northern half becoming the People's Democratic Republic of Vietnam (Communist), the southern area (South Vietnam) continuing as the Republic of Vietnam. An increasingly aggressive guerrilla campaign was mounted against South Vietnam after 1961 by North Vietnam regulars who assisted the Vietcong (South Vietnamese Communist guerrillas) and their political arm, the National Liberation Front. American assistance to the legal government of South Vietnam originally consisted of economic aid and the dispatch of military advisers and other specialists, but in 1962 troops were sent. Following an attack by North Vietnamese public vessels on a U.S. naval contingent in the Tonkin Gulf, Congress, by resolution, Aug. 11, 1964, authorized the President to take "all necessary measures" to check North Vietnamese aggression; and later several hundred thousand U.S. troops and forces from several of its allies were committed. Soviet Russia and the People's Democratic Republic of China actively supported the North Vietnamese, both diplomatically and with military equipment and specialists.

vigilance committee. A group of citizens in a frontier community who resort to direct action outside the law in order to punish wrongdoers and maintain a degree of peace and security.

village. A small compact community, larger than a hamlet (but not comparable to a town or city), which may, or may not, be incorporated.

Villa's raid. An attack on Columbus, N.M., by 400 Villista troops, Mar. 9, 1916, which resulted in the dispatch of a small U.S. Army into Mexico to defeat and disperse Villa's force.

Virginia Bill of Rights. A statement of legal and political rights, drafted mostly by George Mason from such sources as the English common law and the writings of political philosophers, which was adopted June 12, 1776, by the Virginia convention as part of the first State constitution of Virginia.

Virginia Dynasty. Three Virginians, Thomas Jefferson, James Madison, and James Monroe, who successively served as President, 1801–25.

Virginia Plan. A plan of union, largely the work of James Madison, which was submitted to the Convention of 1787 by Virginia's governor, Edmund Randolph. It provided for the popular election of the lower house of Congress, which would choose the upper house, and for executive and judicial departments chosen by Congress. It, rather than the Articles of Confederation, became the basis for the discussions and compromises which created the U.S. Constitution. *Compare* Paterson Plan.

Virginia Resolutions. Resolutions drafted by James Madison and adopted by the legislature of Virginia in December, 1798, which declared that the Constitution was a compact among the States, that the States should interpose when the general government attempted to exercise powers not granted in plain terms, and which invited other States to concur in declaring the Alien and Sedition acts unconstitutional. The resolutions were more temperate than the Kentucky Resolutions, *q.v.*

Virginia v. West Virginia. A long-drawn-out series of cases beginning in 1907 in which the Supreme Court ordered West Virginia to assume its proper share of the debt of Virginia as of the date of West Virginia's admission as a separate State. In case 246 U.S. 565 (1918), the Court suggested among other means of enforcing its judgment, that Congress might act, or that a writ of mandamus might be issued to the legislature of West Virginia. West Virginia's issuance of bonds to satisfy the judgment made further judicial action unnecessary.

Virgin Islands. An island group (St. Thomas, St. Croix, St. John, and small keys, total area, 133 sq. mi.) lying a few miles east of Puerto Rico, which was purchased from Denmark, Jan. 17, 1917, for $25 million. It is governed by an appointive governor and courts and a unicameral legislature of 11 elected members. The inhabitants have been U.S. citizens since 1927.

"Virginius." A vessel owned by Cuban insurgents and unlawfully registered in the United States which was captured on the high seas by a Spanish warship, Oct. 31, 1873, and taken to Santiago de Cuba, where the authorities executed 53 of her crew and passengers (including some American citizens) as pirates. Spain later surrendered the vessel, released the remaining prisoners, and paid an indemnity.

virtual representation. An 18th century British theory that all Englishmen, including those residing in overseas colonies, were represented in Parliament by members chosen by the electorates of shires and of the boroughs entitled to send representatives.

visa. A stamped or written endorsement on a passport by a consular officer prior to a traveler's journey, or by an immigration officer at the frontier, which permits the holder of the passport to enter a country. Visas are required by many countries in order to regulate the admission of foreigners.

VISTA. A corps of volunteers, created by the Economic Opportunity Act, who work in urban and rural hospitals, schools for the mentally ill or mentally retarded, Job Corps camps, and Indian reservations; who receive expense allowances and a small amount when their service ends; and who "typify the spirit of the war against poverty"; *called also* Domestic Peace Corps.

visit and search. The right of belligerent warships to halt and board neutral vessels to determine if they are carrying contraband, running a blockade, or rendering some unneutral service.

vital statistics. Data concerning births, marriages, sickness, deaths, and population mobility collected by State and local governments.

viva voce voting. Voting by word of mouth. *See* voice vote.

vocational education. Training for skilled and useful occupations. Beginning in 1917, federal grants-in-aid have been made to the States for vocational training under the supervision of the U.S. Office of Education.

Voice of America. Radio programs in more than thirty languages which are sent by shortwave transmitters from New York and from relay stations abroad. The broadcasts, prepared by the U.S. Information Service with the cooperation of the State Department, inform foreign peoples about the United States and its policies and encourage attitudes favorable to the United States.

voice vote. A chorus of voices by members of a legislative house voting for a motion (*ayes*) followed by another chorus of voices from those voting against it (*noes*), after which the presiding officer, judging from the volume of sound, announces the result; *called also* viva voce vote. *Compare* division; yeas and nays.

Volstead Act. An act of Congress, 1919, which provided for the enforcement of the 18th Amendment under stringent penalties and defined intoxicating liquors as those containing more than one-half of 1 per cent of alcohol by volume.

voluntary association. An unincorporated group of individuals (as a political party) acting in concert to achieve a common goal.

Volunteers in Service to America. *See* VISTA.

vote of no confidence. *In parliamentary governments:* a formal expression of the withdrawal of political support from the ministry by the legislative majority.

vote of thanks. A formal resolution of an assembly expressing gratitude for services rendered to the assembly or to the public.

voter. Any person legally qualified to cast a ballot or express a formal choice at a public election or referendum.

voting machine. A mechanical substitute for the paper ballot which has on its face a lever above the name of each candidate or referendum proposal and sometimes above the name of each party for straight ticket voting. The voter expresses his preference by pulling down appropriate levers and leaving them down. When he leaves the booth containing the machine, the levers spring back into place, and the machine automatically registers and counts the vote. After the polls have been closed, election officials, by unlocking the machine, may read at a glance the total vote for each candidate and for and against each proposal. Voting machines are in use in about three-fourths of the States.

Voting Rights Act. An act of Congress, 1965, which suspended all literacy and character tests for the suffrage in all States and counties where less than half the adult population were registered, and which provided for federal registration of voters where the Attorney General considered it necessary to enforce rights under the 15th Amendment.

Wabash, St. Louis, and Pacific R.R. Co. v. Illinois. A case, 118 U.S. 557 (1886), in which the Supreme Court decided that the States were without constitutional power to regulate the interstate rates of railways passing through their territory even in the absence of federal legislation on the subject. The ruling nullified the effect of earlier decisions in which the contrary had been held, thereby invalidating State laws which sought to regulate interstate rates and augmenting the demand for federal regulation. Such regulation began in 1887 by the enactment of the Interstate Commerce Act, *q.v.*

Wage and Hour and Public Contracts Division. A unit of the Department of Labor which administers the maximum-hour and minimum-wage provisions of the Fair Labor Standards Act, *q.v.*, and the Equal Pay Act of 1963; and enforces observance by government supply contractors of the Walsh-Healey Act's wage and related standards.

Wagner Act. An act of Congress, Feb. 10, 1931, which required each head of a department having construction agencies under his supervision to institute plans over a six-year period for the construction of public works.

Wagner-Connery Labor Relations Act. *See* National Labor Relations Act.

Wagner-Connery Wages and Hours Act. *See* Fair Labor Standards Act.

Wagner-Peyser Act. An act of Congress, June 6, 1933, which created the United States Employment Service, *q.v.*, and provided for the establishment and operation of employment offices in local communities in cooperation with the States.

Wagner-Steagall Act. The United States Housing Act, Sept. 1, 1937, which provided financial assistance to States and their subdivisions in eliminating unsafe and unsanitary housing conditions and in constructing dwellings for low-income families.

waiver. The relinquishment of some legal privilege, as of jury trial, or immunity from judicial process. A person possessing diplomatic immunity in some cases waives his immunity by becoming a plaintiff in a civil suit, thus risking the defendant's counterclaim.

Wake Island. A small American possession west of Hawaii with a military post and a station for trans-Pacific planes.

Walker Tariff. A tariff law, July 30, 1846, drafted by Secretary of the Treasury Robert J. Walker, and based on the principles of free trade and heavy taxation of luxuries.

Walsh-Healey Act. A law of Congress, June 30, 1936, which provided that government contractors should pay not less than the prevailing minimum wage, observe the eight-hour day and the forty-hour week, employ no convict labor and no person under 18 years of age, and allow no hazardous or unsanitary working conditions in their plants.

Walter-Logan Act. *See* Administrative Procedure Act.

war. Hostile operations conducted by one state against another whether or not such operations have been preceded by a formal declaration of war; *also:* an armed conflict between organized rebels and the *de jure* government of a state if the *de jure* government expressly or impliedly recognizes that the rebels have a belligerent status or if other states accord such a status to them. The outbreak of hostilities brings about a severance of diplomatic relations between contending states and automatically abrogates such mutual treaty engagements as have governed their political and commercial relations or any other such engagements not deemed to have established a permanent condition of affairs at the time they were entered into. Nationals of one belligerent who are in the territory of the other have the status of enemy aliens; and the respective belligerents may confiscate public enemy property discovered within their own territory and sequester or impose restrictions upon the private property of enemy nationals. Multilateral international conventions and international usage prescribe that warfare should be conducted according to certain rules. These relate to the use that may be made of certain weapons, to the status of the noncombatant civilian population, to the exemption of undefended localities from attack, and to the treatment of private property within the zone of combat or in the zone occupied by the enemy. They also govern the use of flags of truce, armistices, and capitulations; the right to quarter on the part of enemy forces which surrender; the treatment and exchange of prisoners of war; the duties and immunities of medical and hospital services; and the rights and duties of belligerents toward neutral states and the lives and property of their nationals. It is a principle of the traditional rules of war that belligerents ought not to direct hostile acts against the enemy's civilian population but rather against the enemy's public forces or strongholds. But contemporary methods of warfare make this distinction increasingly meaningless. Total blockade, expanded conceptions of contraband, bombing from the air, shelling from long-range guns, the use of nuclear and bacteriological weapons, including intercontinental and intermediate range missiles with nuclear warheads, and the mobility of mechanized armament inevitably jeopardize civilian lives and welfare. Contemporary belligerents resort to a complete mobilization of national life for war purposes. Labor is conscripted, civilians are inducted into a variety of paramilitary or defense agencies, and the entire national economy is geared to the needs of a community at war. Under such circumstances, it is difficult to distinguish between the practical military value of hostile acts against soldiers or fortifications on the one hand and against civilians and so-called undefended areas on the other. Bombing or other hostile operations against any part of the enemy's civilian population or any portion of enemy territory become logically defensible as having military value; and even the breaking of enemy civilian morale becomes a military objective to be achieved by any means whatsoever. *See* total war.

war against poverty. Efforts, especially by the federal government, to improve the condition of persons in the lowest income groups of the population. The phrase was frequently used by President F. D. Roosevelt and was popularized by President Lyndon Johnson.

war cabinet. An inner cabinet consisting of a small number of important officials which makes major decisions concerning policy in wartime.

ward. A municipal territorial subdivision for the election of one or more members of the city council and, in some cities, for convenience in the administration of certain public works and services.

War Democrat. A Democrat who supported the military policy of the federal government during the Civil War.

warden. A minor administrative official (as the warden of a penitentiary or a game or air-raid warden) with duties of guarding, conserving, or protecting persons or property or of law enforcement.

War Department. *See* Department of the Army.

ward heeler. 1. A local political hanger-on. 2. A minor professional politician in the entourage of a district leader or local political boss.

Ware plan. A system of preferential voting, *q.v.*, under which the weakest candidates are eliminated in order, and the votes cast for them are counted for other candidates as directed by voters in the second and later choices marked on their ballots. The Ware plan is also used in proportional representation.

war guilt. 1. The responsibility for having begun a war without sufficient moral or legal cause. A statement to the effect that Germany was so responsible for World War I was incorporated in the Treaty of Versailles. 2. The responsibility for having violated the laws of war or having committed crimes against humanity which were among the charges directed at Nazi German leaders at the Nuremberg trials, *q.v.*, and at Japanese military leaders of World War II.

war hawk. An advocate of war; *especially:* one of a group of young Congressmen elected in 1810 who wanted war with Great Britain or Spain in order to seize Canada or Florida, or a person who favored going to war with France in 1798. *Compare* jingo.

war horse. A party orator or leader who has participated effectively in many election campaigns.

War of 1812. A war between the United States and Great Britain resulting chiefly from American resentment at British commercial restrictions, impressment of seamen, and alleged stirring up of Indians in the North-west, which was declared by Congress, June 18, 1812, and was officially closed by the Treaty of Ghent, signed Dec. 24, 1814. The news of the treaty did not arrive in time to prevent the battle of New Orleans, Jan. 8, 1815.

war of nerves. Deliberate efforts to impair the morale of military or civilian personnel in another country by broadcasting or spreading by word of mouth false reports of disasters and threatened dangers.

war powers. Such powers as are constitutionally committed to the executive and legislative branches of government to wage war, raise, organize, equip, and command the necessary public forces, and to apply such regulations affecting personal liberty and the national economy as the exigencies of actual war or threat of war may require. When fully applied as a result of an emergency, the war powers are broader in scope and less affected by constitutional limitations than any other powers of government, especially of the general government in a federal system such as that of the United States.

War Production Board. A federal wartime agency created by executive order, Jan. 16, 1942, to control production and the procurement of supplies for military purposes; abolished on Nov. 3, 1945.

war profits tax. A tax the burden of which is intended to fall directly upon profits of private enterprise attributable to war contracts or to abnormal wartime demand for goods and services.

Warren Act. An act of Congress, Feb. 21, 1911, which authorized the Secretary of the Interior to sell to irrigation districts or private persons any surplus water not required for an irrigation project of the United States.

Warren Commission. A special commission, with Chief Justice Earl Warren as chairman, appointed by President Lyndon B. Johnson to investigate the circumstances of the assassination of President John F. Kennedy and of the murder of his alleged assassin. Its report, Sept. 27, 1964, contained principally material already known through newspaper sources.

warrant. A written order issued by a magistrate or court directing an officer to make an arrest or conduct searches or seizures. Constitutional restrictions prevent the issuance of a search warrant except for good cause, duly certified, and the warrant must describe the place to be searched and the person or property to be seized. *See* unreasonable searches and seizures.

war risk insurance. Insurance offered by the federal government to protect persons against wartime loss of vessels and property on the high seas, and death or injury while in the armed forces.

war to end wars. A catch phrase often heard during World War I.

Washington. The capital of the United States; a populous urban area whose boundaries coincide with those of the District of Columbia, *q.v.* Before 1871 it was a municipal corporation.

Washington Naval Conference. A meeting of delegates representing Japan, China, United Kingdom, France, Italy, The Netherlands, Belgium, Portugal, and the United States which began in Washington,

Nov. 12, 1921, to consider naval limitations and the settlement of problems in the Pacific and the Far East, and which resulted in the Five-Power and the Four-Power Treaties and the Nine-Power Pact, *qq.v.*

Washington's Farewell Address. A statement of President Washington, published Sept. 17, 1796, in which he renounced a third term and warned the people against the evil effects of domestic faction and unnecessary involvement in wars waged between other countries.

watchdog function. *See* oversight function.

watchdog of the treasury. A nickname given to a Senator or Representative who distinguishes himself by close scrutiny of items in appropriation bills and by protests against extravagance.

watcher. The representative of a party present at a polling place on election day to insure fair conduct on the part of election officials.

watchful waiting. President Wilson's characterization, Dec. 2, 1913, of his policy toward the Huerta government of Mexico.

water power. *See* Federal Power Commission.

water right. A legal right to use a lake or stream, or water flowing from it through a ditch or artificial channel, for such purposes as power, irrigation, or domestic consumption.

water supply. The collection and purification of an adequate supply of water and its distribution among the inhabitants of a municipality or other jurisdiction, a service originally, and to some extent still, rendered by a public utility company but usually supplied under municipal ownership or operation. Increases in population and in per capita consumption of water have resulted in the expansion of the area of many municipal watersheds and practical steps to prevent pollution, conserve water, and obtain additional supplies by desalination of sea water.

Watkins* v. *United States. A case, 354 U.S. 178 (1957), in which the Supreme Court limited the investigative power of Congress to matters in furtherance of a legitimate task of government and condemned excessive delegations of power to committees, and committee activities in excess of the powers granted to them.

waving the bloody shirt. Accusing the Democratic party of having caused the Civil War—a characteristic campaign device of the Republican party in the 1870's.

Ways and Means Committee. A legislative committee concerned with sources of revenue and taxes; *specifically:* a standing committee of the House of Representatives created in 1795 to supervise all financial legislation, which since 1865 has had jurisdiction over tariff, excise, income tax, and other bills disposing of public property.

weak-mayor plan. The system of municipal government in which the mayor lacked effective power over administration because officials were chosen by the municipal council or by popular vote, or, if appointive, were subject to confirmation by the council; his powers of removal and direction were limited by law or by the council; the council initiated the budget, awarded contracts, and granted franchises; and the mayor's veto could be overridden by the council. In the 19th century it was found in nearly all American cities. *Compare* council-manager plan.

Weather Bureau. An agency of the federal government, established in 1890 in the Department of Agriculture, and, since 1940, in the Department of Commerce, which is concerned with weather forecasting. More than 300 field offices of the bureau supply meteorological data for the general public and for a variety of private and public organizations including aviation and space agencies and private air transport companies. The bureau operates the space satellite system of weather observation, and disseminates resulting data throughout the world.

Webb-Kenyon Act. An act of Congress, Mar. 1, 1913, which divested intoxicating liquors of their interstate character when shipped into dry territory for use in violation of State laws.

Webb-Pomerene Act. An act of Congress, Apr. 10, 1918, which exempted associations solely engaged in export trade from the United States from the restrictions of the antitrust laws.

Wedemeyer Report. Recommendations of General Albert Wedemeyer, in the summer of 1947, that the United States grant Chiang Kai-shek greatly increased supplies of arms, provide American military personnel to train and direct the Chinese Nationalist armies, and set up, with other powers, a joint commission to prevent Chinese Communists from taking possession of Manchuria. The State Department suppressed the report, but its contents became known within the next two years.

Weeks Law. A law, Mar. 1, 1911, giving blanket Congressional consent to compacts which might be made among the States to conserve navigable waterways. It authorized appropriations for cooperation with the States in forest-fire protection and for acquiring lands at the headwaters of navigable streams, such lands to be permanently reserved as national forests.

welfare state. A state which promotes the economic security and expands cultural opportunities for the bulk of its citizens by such policies as subsidization of housing, provision for expanded educational opportunities and for medical and hospital care, assistance to indigent families and individuals, minimum wage legislation, pensions for the retired and the aged, and insurance against unemployment and job-connected accidents or illnesses.

Well-Born, The. A phrase sometimes used by John Adams and other Federalists which was seized upon by their Republican opponents as indicative of the aristocratic sentiments of the Federalist party.

Wesberry v. Sanders. A case, 376 U.S. 1 (1964), in which the Supreme Court, reversing the decision in *Colegrove* v. *Green*, invalidated the unequal apportionment of Congressional districts in Georgia on the ground that, since every voter is equal to every other voter, the districts from which representatives in Congress are chosen must be as nearly equal as practicable in population. *See* one man, one vote; *Gray* v. *Sanders.*

West Coast Hotel Co. v. Parrish. A case, 300 U.S. 379 (1937), in which the Supreme Court reversed earlier decisions (as in *Adkins* v. *Children's Hospital, q.v.*) by upholding the constitutionality of State legislation prescribing minimum-wage rates for gainfully employed women. *See* Fair Labor Standards Act.

Western Reserve. The northeastern part of the State of Ohio reserved by Connecticut for her own settlers when she ceded her rights to western lands to the United States. Connecticut gave up her title to the district in 1801.

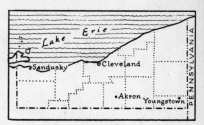

Western Reserve

West Florida. A strip of territory along the Gulf of Mexico east of the Mississippi River which was partly colonized by France and ceded to Great Britain in 1763. Great Britain erected it into a separate colony with boundaries extending eastward to the Chattahoochee and Apalachicola rivers and northward to the parallel through the mouth of the Yazoo River (32°28'). By the Treaty of 1783, Great Britain ceded both the Floridas to Spain and at the same time agreed that the southern boundary of the United States should be at the 31st parallel. Spain retained the post at Natchez and refused to relinquish

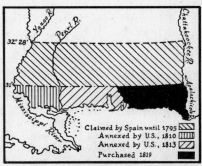

West Florida

her claim to the region as far north as the parallel of 32°28' until the signing of Pinckney's Treaty, *q.v.*, in 1795. When Spain in 1800 retroceded Louisiana to France, and when the United States purchased it in 1803, the United States claimed West Florida on the basis of early French exploration and settlement, formally asserting title to the district between the Mississippi and Pearl rivers in 1810 and occupying the district between the Pearl and Perdido rivers in 1813.

West Virginia Debt case. See *Virginia v. West Virginia.*

West Virginia State Board of Education v. Barnette. See Flag-Salute cases.

wet. An advocate of the manufacture and sale of intoxicating liquors. *Compare* dry.

wetbacks. Mexican agricultural laborers who illegally enter the United States by fording the Rio Grande or by crossing at other points; *called also* braceros.

Wheeler-Lea Act. An act of Congress, Mar. 21, 1938, which prohibited false and misleading advertising of foods, drugs, cosmetics, and devices for use in the prevention and treatment of disease; imposed criminal penalties for advertising articles the use of which may be injurious to health; and strengthened the enforcement powers of the Federal Trade Commission.

Whig. 1. A member of an English political party, 1679–1832, which supported the Protestant Succession and the House of Hanover. **2.** An

American who, before and during the Revolution, strove for the protection of American rights and for independence. *Called also* patriot.

Whig party. 1. *In England:* the party which, after 1680, supported the primacy of Parliament and which was largely responsible for the "Glorious Revolution" of 1688, the constitutional settlement which followed it, and the maintenance of the Protestant succession. In the 19th century the Whig party was succeeded by the Liberal party. 2. An American party, founded in 1834 by a combination of National Republicans, Antimasons, and various personal followings, which was dominated in the North by manufacturing, commercial, and financial interests, and in the South by the slaveholding class, and which advocated protective tariffs, the recharter of the Bank of the United States, and internal improvements. It won the presidential elections of 1840 and 1848. The Whigs' attempt to settle the slavery issue by the Compromise of 1850 alienated members in both North and South. After being soundly beaten in 1852, the party disintegrated.

whip. A member of a legislative body, designated by the party caucus, whose duties are to remind members of his party to be present when important votes are to be taken, to arrange pairs for members unavoidably absent, to conciliate members who are dissatisfied with the party program, and to keep his party leaders informed as to the attitude of members toward public questions.

Whisky Insurrection. Violent resistance in western Pennsylvania in 1794 to the collection of excise taxes on whisky imposed by the federal excise law of 1791. A force of 15,000 militia, ordered into the region by President Washington, overawed the rioters.

Whisky Ring. A combination of government officials and distillers in St. Louis which, it was disclosed in 1875, had defrauded the United States of $1 million annually in internal revenue taxes. The scandal forced several close friends of President Grant out of office.

whispering campaign. The circulation by word of mouth of false or scandalous statements concerning a candidate or party.

white backlash. *See* backlash.

white citizens' councils. Organizations founded in 1954, especially numerous in Mississippi, and usually affiliated with Citizen's Councils of America, Inc., which employ economic pressure or reprisals (as loss of jobs or withholding of credit) against both Negro and white advocates of integrating public education in accordance with the Supreme Court's decision in *Brown* v. *Board of Education, q.v.,* or who support compliance with recent federal civil rights legislation.

White House. 1. The official residence of the President of the United States in Washington, D.C. 2. The President and his immediate advisers.

White House Office. The staff of personal aides of the President which includes legal counsel, secretaries, and administrative assistants who handle executive relations with other branches of the government and with the public and undertake such duties as the President may direct. The Office is a division of the Executive Office of the President, *q.v.*

White League. A secret organization in Louisiana during the Reconstruction period which excluded Negroes from the polls by violence.

white man's burden. The supposed duty of members of the Caucasian race to spread their civilization to backward peoples. According to Kipling and other apologists for imperialism, this humanitarian responsibility, and not economic exploitation, was the prime motive for European penetration into undeveloped regions.

White Phosphorus Match Act. An act of Congress, Apr. 9, 1912, which levied a tax of two cents per hundred upon poisonous phosphorus matches, thereby effectively preventing their manufacture.

white primary. Formerly, a primary election in the South from which Negroes were excluded by State laws or rules of the Democratic party. *See* Texas Primary cases.

White Slave acts. Laws of Congress, 1910, which forbade aiding, causing, or inducing the transportation in interstate commerce of any woman or girl for immoral purposes.

white supremacy. The idea, held by many persons, especially in the rural South, that suffrage, office-holding and public affairs ought to be controlled by members of the Caucasian race, and that racial segregation ought to be continued.

whitewash. The report of a legislative or other investigating committee which, from friendly or partisan motives, exonerates a public official or party from charges of corruption or mismanagement.

Whitney v. *California.* A case, 247 U.S. 357 (1927), involving a prosecution under California's Criminal Syndicalism Act of 1919, the crime being defined, *inter alia*, as advocating, teaching, or abetting sabotage or effecting political change by force, violence, or terror. The Supreme Court sustained the statute as consistent with due process and equal protection. In a concurring opinion, Justices Holmes and Brandeis took the opportunity to refine Justice Holmes' clear-and-present-danger rule, *q.v.* Supporting a party advocating popular revolt in the distant future is protected by the 14th Amendment, they said; the danger flowing from speech cannot be deemed clear and present unless the evil apprehended is so imminent that it is likely to occur before there is full opportunity for discussion.

WHO World Health Organization.

who's who ballot. A ballot on which is printed a brief biographical statement after the name of each candidate.

Wickard v. *Filburn.* A case, 317 U.S. 111 (1942), in which the Supreme Court held that an Ohio farmer who planted 23 acres of wheat for his own consumption, in excess of the quota set by the Secretary of Agriculture, had exerted "a substantial economic effect on interstate commerce," and so had made himself liable for penalties imposed by the Agricultural Adjustment Act of 1938, *q.v.* This case is noteworthy as an extreme extension of federal power over commerce.

Wiener v. *United States.* A case, 357 U.S. 349 (1958), in which the Supreme Court held that the President could not constitutionally remove a member of the War Claims Commission because, unlike officials who are a part of the Executive establishment and hence removable at the pleasure of the President, a member of such a Commission exercises power intrinsically judicial, and its proper exercise requires absolute freedom from Presidential interference. *Compare Myers* v. *United States; Rathbun* (*Humphrey's Executor*) v. *United States.*

wildcat bank. A bank in the period before the Civil War with inadequate resources to redeem its circulating notes.

wildcat strike. A work stoppage by employees not authorized by the union of which the employees are members.

Wilderness Act. An act of Congress, 1964, setting aside 9,100,000 acres of public lands (to which more might be added) to be preserved against timber-cutting, extensive livestock grazing, or construction of permanent roads.

Wiley Act. An act of Congress, June 30, 1906, which prohibited adulteration, misbranding, and the use of deleterious ingredients in food or drugs and required the identification of narcotics used in food or drugs in interstate commerce.

Williams v. North Carolina. Two cases, 317 U.S. 287 (1942) and 325 U.S. 226 (1945), involving the application of the full-faith-and-credit clause of the Constitution to divorce decrees. In the first case, the Supreme Court overruled *Haddock* v. *Haddock, q.v.,* and held that the State of the marriage domicile must recognize an extra-State divorce if the divorced spouse had acquired a legal residence in the State where the divorce was granted. But this decision was practically canceled in the second Williams case in which it was held that the State of the marriage domicile could question the jurisdiction of the extra-State court granting the divorce and hence the divorce itself if it could be conclusively proved in its own courts that it was the intention of the divorcee to establish not a bona fide residence, but only a nominal legal residence, in the State in which the divorce was secured.

Wilmot Proviso. An amendment proposed by Representative David Wilmot of Pennsylvania to a bill appropriating funds to enable the President to make peace with Mexico, 1846, which would have prohibited slavery in any territory acquired from Mexico. It passed the House and was narrowly defeated in the Senate.

Wilson Corollary. A principle in American foreign policy initiated by Woodrow Wilson in 1913, especially in relations with Latin America, that the United States would refuse to recognize any government that had come to power as a result of violence and bloodshed. *Compare* Stimson Doctrine.

Wilson-Gorman Tariff. A tariff law, Aug. 27, 1894, in which a Democratic Congress retained many of the high duties of the McKinley Tariff, *q.v.*

Wilson v. New. A case, 243 U.S. 332 (1917), in which the Supreme Court upheld the constitutionality of the Adamson Act, *q.v.,* providing an eight-hour day and appropriate wage standards for interstate railway employees. The Court declared that, although Congress could not control or prevent collective agreement on wages on interstate railways or fail to enforce a voluntary wage agreement, the failure of employees and employers to agree establishes a condition which Congress may resolve by fixing wages or requiring arbitration, such authority being justified by Congress' responsibility for maintaining the uninterrupted flow of commerce.

wirepulling. Unethical conduct by individuals who secretly, or in ways not readily discerned by the general public, exert personal influence or other form of pressure upon public officials.

wiretapping. Clandestine listening-in to telephonic and other communications by wire. Although the Supreme Court has held that the constitutional prohibition of unreasonable searches and seizures does not extend to wiretapping, Section 605 of the Federal Communications Act, interdicting such activity, has been upheld by the courts and applied to evidence secured by federal and State officers. *See Olmstead* v. *United States.*

Wisconsin Idea. The reform program sponsored by Robert M. La Follette as governor of Wisconsin, 1901–05, which included statewide primary elections, conservation, safety regulations, workmen's compensation, a child labor law, and establishment of regulatory commissions.

Wisconsin Rate case. A case, *Wisconsin* v. *Chicago, B. and Q. Ry. Co.,* 257 U.S. 563 (1922), in which the Supreme Court extended the doctrine, first elaborated in the Shreveport Rate case, *q.v.,* that there is no invasion of a State's power over intrastate commerce if the Interstate Commerce Commission requires equalization of intrastate rates with interstate rates in order to overcome existing discrimination among shippers and make national control over interstate commerce effective.

witch hunt. A legislative or other investigation which, during a period of popular hysteria or fear, acts on rumors and irresponsible charges, with the result of indiscriminately condemning revolutionaries, critics of the established order, radicals, and persons who merely protest against the methods of the investigators. *See* Un-American Activities Committee; McCarthyism.

withholding tax. Deductions from wages and salaries, remitted by an employer to federal and State and local income tax collectors. Such deductions are credited against the current tax liability of the persons from whose income the deductions are made, in order to keep income tax payments nearly current and to provide greater certainty and speed in the collection of taxes. Congress first authorized withholding from federal income taxpayers in 1943.

witness. 1. An individual who gives evidence under oath in a court or other body as to what he knows about a pending case. 2. A person required to present himself at a transaction in order that he may subsequently be able to testify that it took place.

Wizard of Kinderhook. A nickname of Martin Van Buren, from his skill in State politics and his home at Kinderhook, N.Y.

Wolff Packing Co. v. Court of Industrial Relations. *See* Kansas Industrial Court.

woman suffrage. The right of women to participate in public elections on the same terms as men. Agitation for it began before 1850. In the United States, Wyoming Territory, 1869, pioneered in granting suffrage to women, followed by several other, principally Western, States. Nation-wide woman suffrage was achieved by the adoption of the Nineteenth Amendment, *q.v.* In Great Britain suffrage was granted to women over 30 in 1918 and to those between 21 and 30 (flapper suffrage) in 1928. On the European continent, most women were enfranchised by new constitutions adopted after the two World Wars.

Women's Bureau. A unit of the Department of Labor, created in 1918, concerned with research on the welfare of gainfully employed women.

Wool Products Labeling Act. An act of Congress, 1940, which requires the labeling of wool products to reveal the percentage of virgin, reprocessed, and reused wool and other materials used in manufacture.

Worcester v. Georgia. See Cherokee cases.

workhouse. 1. A county institution where those convicted of less grave offenses are confined and put to useful labor. 2. *In Great Britain:* a public shelter for transient vagrants or indigent inhabitants who are able to work.

Workingmen's party. An organization in New York about 1830 which later became identified with the Locofocos, *q.v.*

workmen's compensation. A system of social insurance financed by payroll taxes whereby workers employed in certain industries receive a money payment either as a lump sum or as regular monthly income in consequence of financial loss resulting from incapacity for normal employment due to industrial accident or occupational disease.

work relief. Employment furnished persons by a government or private social agency to alleviate distress and, by increasing purchasing power, to stimulate recovery in periods of economic depression. The federal government first engaged in direct work relief in 1933.

Works Progress Administration. A federal unit, 1935–39 (continued under the name Works Projects Administration, 1939–41), which administered a work program for employable needy persons, including writers, artists, musicians and other professional people.

World Bank. *See* International Bank for Reconstruction and Development.

World Economic Conference. 1. An international conference which met in Geneva in 1927 to study means of regulating international commerce by international agreement. 2. Another name for the London Economic Conference, *q.v.*

World Health Organization. A specialized agency of the United Nations, created in 1948, which coordinates international sanitary and health activities. In cooperation with other United Nations agencies and government officials, WHO seeks to advance knowledge and render technical and other assistance on health matters. Policies and programs are determined by the World Health Assembly, and the Secretariat, headed by a Director General, carries out programs through six offices located throughout the world. The organization has more than 100 members.

World Meteorological Organization. A specialized agency of the United Nations which promotes meteorological communications on a global basis, including the establishment of centers of meteorological services and networks of national and regional stations, standardizes observations and statistical measurements in the field, and stimulates research and the application and use of research findings in transportation, agriculture, and other activities.

World War I. A conflict, Aug. 1, 1914–Nov. 11, 1918, in which the Central powers, Germany and Austria-Hungary (later joined by Turkey and Bulgaria), were pitted against the Allied and Associated powers, an aggregation which ultimately included nearly all the other states of the world. Because of Germany's practically unrestricted submarine warfare the United States declared war against her Apr. 6, 1917, and against Austria-Hungary Dec. 7, 1917. German or Austrian armies overran Belgium, Serbia, and Rumania, penetrated deeply into France and Italy, and forced Russia to accept the harsh terms of the Treaty of Brest-Litovsk, Mar. 3, 1918. But by the autumn of 1918 the weight of Allied manpower and materiel on several fronts forced Germany to sue for an armistice which was granted Nov. 11. The Treaty of Versailles, *q.v.*, was signed June 28, 1919, but was never ratified by the U.S. Senate. On July 2, 1921, Congress passed a joint resolution declaring the war at an end, but reserving American rights. Subsequently Germany and the United States signed the Treaty of Berlin, Aug. 25, 1921.

World War II. The struggle between the Axis powers (Germany, Italy, Japan and certain satellite nations) and a coalition consisting of the United Kingdom, the British dominions, the United States, France, Soviet Russia, the Republic of China, and many of the remaining states of the world which began with Germany's invasion of Poland in September, 1939, and joint declarations of war on Germany by the United Kingdom and France as guarantors of Poland's territorial and political integrity. Italy entered the war June 10, 1940, and Russia, June 22, 1941. The surprise Japanese attack on Pearl Harbor, Hawaii, Dec. 7, 1941, brought the United States into the war, ranged Japan actively on the side of the Axis, and had the effect of merging Japan's war on China, which had begun with the seizure of Manchuria in September, 1931, with the global struggle. In the war's early phases, Germany overran most of the Continent of Europe, including a considerable part of European Russia, and Japan conquered much of the Far East. The tide turned against the Axis toward the end of 1942. Italy surrendered unconditionally on Sept. 8, 1943, and Germany on May 8, 1945. Japan signed surrender terms Sept. 1, 1945, following closely upon the first use, in warfare, of nuclear bombs which were dropped by the United States on Hiroshima and Nagasaki, Japan.

W.P.A. Works Progress Administration, or Works Projects Administration.

W.P.B. War Production Board.

writ. A formal written order, issuing from a court or tribunal having judicial authority, commanding an individual or individuals identified in the order to do, or abstain from doing, some specified act.

writing in. Voting for a candidate whose name has not been printed on the official ballot.

writ of assistance. A general search warrant, not specifying the place to be searched or describing the goods sought, which was issued prior to the American Revolution to authorize customs officers to seize smuggled goods. The constitutionality of British statutes authorizing this writ was widely debated in British North American colonies.

writ of error. An order issued by an appellate court to a lower court of record usually requiring the latter to send up the entire record of a proceeding after judgment in order that the appellate court may examine into errors allegedly committed by the lower tribunal and either affirm or reverse the latter's decision and judgment. *Compare* certiorari.

writ of execution. Process issuing from a court in a civil action authorizing the sheriff or other competent officer to carry out the court's decision in favor of the party who won the case.

writ of mandamus. *See* mandamus.

writ of prohibition. An order, issued by a superior court to a court of inferior grade, demanding that the latter refrain from exercising jurisdiction over some specific suit then pending before it.

writ of quo warranto. A writ issued on behalf of the state to inquire into the validity of the title by which a person holds an office or a public corporation its franchise, as the first step in legal proceedings to vacate the office or franchise.

written constitution. That part of the fundamental law of a state which sets forth in formal terms the organization of the government in its major organs and departments, defines the extent of their powers, and, by a bill of rights and other provisions, imposes limitations on the extent and methods of exercising power by officers of government. The written constitution, as distinguished from interpretations of its clauses by official bodies, especially the judiciary, and from customs and conventions which are regarded as fundamental, is made and can be changed only by the constituent power, *q.v.* In federal systems, the written constitution is regarded as a contractual agreement and usually includes some provision for judicial settlement of disputes between States or between a State and the general government. In the United States, a constitution is regarded as superior law which must be enforced over statutes which may be passed in conflict with its terms.

X.Y.Z. Papers. Documents sent to Congress by President John Adams in 1798 disclosing demands by agents of the French government for bribes and a loan to France as a price for making a commercial treaty with the United States. The letters X, Y, and Z were substituted for the names of the French agents.

Yakus v. United States. A case, 321 U.S. 414 (1944), in which the Supreme Court sustained the discretionary power of a federal administrator to enforce the Emergency Price Control Act of 1942. The Court declared that such authority was comparable to that given an administrative agency to fix fair and reasonable rates for a public utility and did not constitute a delegation of legislative power.

Yalta Conference. A conference of President F. D. Roosevelt, Prime Minister Churchill, and Premier Stalin held at Yalta in the Crimea, Feb. 3–11, 1945. Understandings were reached concerning the occupation of Germany after victory, the establishment of governments in liberated states, the delimitation of spheres of influence by the three powers represented, and the calling of a conference on world organization. *See* San Francisco Conference.

Yates v. United States. A case, 354 U.S. 298 (1957), in which the Supreme Court applied more generous tests of permissible speech and association under the First Amendment for members of the Communist party than were applied in other cases under the Smith Act, *q.v.* Mere advocacy of revolutionary philosophy, such as the Marxian, was not enough to convict a Communist party member under that Act. In order to convict, a member had to be proven guilty of advocating actual overthrow of the government and of prescribing the tactics involved. *Compare Dennis* v. *United States.*

Yazoo Land Fraud. The corrupt land grant by the legislature of Georgia in 1795 which the next legislature, 1796, rescinded. In *Fletcher* v. *Peck*, 6 Cr. 87 (1810), the United States Supreme Court declared the grant of 1795 a contract which the State could not impair by later legislation.

yeas and nays. A method of voting in a deliberative body or legislature by which each member votes for or against a measure as his name is called, and his vote is recorded. The Constitution requires that the yeas and nays shall be entered upon the journal when either house of Congress acts upon a measure vetoed by the President, and on any question when one-fifth of those present so demand.

yellow-dog contract. A contract between an employer and an employee in which the latter agrees not to join a labor union. By the Norris-LaGuardia Act of 1932, such contracts were made unenforceable in federal courts. *See Adair* v. *United States.*

yellow peril. The danger to the world supremacy of the Caucasian race discerned by some writers, race theorists, and rulers (as Emperor William II of Germany) in the rising political power and the vast numbers of the Japanese, Chinese, and Mongol peoples.

Yick Wo v. Hopkins. A case, 118 U.S. 356 (1886), in which the Supreme Court invalidated a laundry-licensing ordinance of the City of San Francisco on the grounds that it established an arbitrary classification of persons under the equal-protection clause of the 14th Amendment, and that the authority conferred by the ordinance had been administered so as to discriminate against Chinese laundrymen. The case is significant as a precedent in protecting the economic rights of non-Caucasians.

yield. 1. The net proceeds of a tax after expenses of collection and administration have been subtracted from the gross returns. 2. The return upon a government bond or any other investment.

Young Hickory. A nickname of James K. Polk, a Tennessee friend and fellow partisan of Andrew Jackson (Old Hickory).

Young plan. A revision of the Dawes plan, *q.v.*, of reparations payments by Germany after World War I, prepared by a commission of experts headed by Owen D. Young and signed at Paris, June 7, 1929. Total reparations, payable to the Allied powers over a period of 59 years, was fixed at 121 billion marks, and the Bank for International Settlements was established at Basle to serve as transfer agent. Because of the subsequent world-wide economic depression, the Allied powers, meeting at Lausanne in 1932, agreed to reduce Germany's total reparations to a token payment of 3 billion marks, provided the United States, as net creditor, agreed to the cancellation of all debts which she and the Allied powers had contracted with one another during the war. Though the United States agreed to a moratorium in 1931, it refused to cancel; even so, Germany paid no more reparations after the Lausanne meeting.

Youngstown Sheet and Tube Company* v. *Sawyer. A case, 343 U.S. 579 (1952), which arose out of President Truman's seizure of steel mills in an effort to avert a nation-wide strike, called in April, 1952. The existence of a broad Presidential power to act in this manner, in the absence of statute, was denied in unequivocal language by the Supreme Court. It found no such Presidential authority in the clauses in Article II of the Constitution, vesting the executive power in the President, or making him commander in chief, or imposing on him the duty to enforce the laws; nor, said the Court, can such authority be implied from the aggregate of these and other clauses.

Z

Zenger case. The case of a printer, John Peter Zenger, whose criticism of the administration of Governor Cosby of New York in 1735 resulted in Zenger's imprisonment on the charge of libel. At his trial the court ruled that evidence to prove the truth of the alleged libel was inadmissible; the jury, nevertheless, held Zenger not guilty. The precedent thus established is regarded as a milestone in the development of a free press in America.

Zimmermann Note. A note sent by the German government to its minister in Mexico, Jan. 19, 1917, proposing an alliance with Mexico and aid in reconquering "lost territory" in New Mexico, Texas, and Arizona if war occurred between the United States and Germany. The note was intercepted by British intelligence and made public, Mar. 1, 1917.

zoning. Regulation by statute or local ordinance of the use and occupancy of land in metropolitan areas. A zoning regulation usually subdivides the physical area of a city into specific zones or districts and determines whether the land in each district, and the buildings constructed upon it, shall be devoted primarily or exclusively to mercantile, industrial, or residential uses, or to some combination of these uses. The zoning regulations may supply numerous specifications affecting the design and construction of buildings in each district. The Supreme Court has upheld zoning ordinances as a legitimate exercise of the State's police power. *See Euclid* v. *Ambler Realty Co.*

Zorach v. Clauson. A case, 343 U.S. 306 (1952), in which the Supreme Court upheld New York City's public-school, released-time religious education program which allowed students, at the written request of parents, to secure religious instruction during school hours on premises other than school property. Construing the separation and establishment clauses of the First Amendment less narrowly than in *McCollum* v. *Board of Education, q.v.,* the Court held that the authors of those clauses never intended to establish an absolute separation of church and state and that, in any case, absolute separation would be impracticable and contrary to the tenets of a people whose institutions presuppose a supreme being.

THE FIFTY STATES

	Date Entered Union	Order of Entry	Order Present Const. Adopted	Capital	Population 1960	Rank	Reps. in Congress	Rank	Pres. Electors[1]	Area (sq. mi.)	Rank	Per Capita Income	Rank	Legislative Referendum[2]	Legislative Initiative	Const. Initiative	Recall of Officers
Alabama	Dec. 14, 1819	22	1901	Montgomery	3,266,740	19	8	19	10	51,609	29	1,910	47	—	—	—	—
Alaska	Jan. 3, 1959	49	1959	Juneau	226,167	50	1	50	3	586,400	1	3,375	2	X	—	—	X
Arizona	Feb. 14, 1912	48	1912	Phoenix	1,302,161	35	3	35	5	113,909	6	2,310	35	X	Direct	X	X
Arkansas	June 15, 1836	25	1874	Little Rock	1,786,272	31	4	31	6	53,104	27	1,781	49	X	Direct	X	—
California	Sept. 9, 1850	31	1879	Sacramento	15,717,204	2	38	2	40	158,693	3	3,196	8	X	Direct, Indirect	X	X
Colorado	Aug. 1, 1876	38	1876	Denver	1,753,947	33	4	33	6	104,247	8	2,706	19	X	Direct, Indirect	X	X
Connecticut	Jan. 9, 1788	5	1818	Hartford	2,535,234	25	6	25	8	5,009	48	3,390	1	—	—	—	—
Delaware	Dec. 7, 1787	1	1897	Dover	446,292	46	1	46	3	2,057	49	3,335	3	—	—	—	—
Florida	Mar. 3, 1845	27	1887	Tallahassee	4,959,560	10	12	10	14	58,560	22	2,420	28	—	—	—	—
Georgia	Jan. 2, 1788	4	1945	Atlanta	3,943,116	16	10	16	12	58,876	21	2,156	40	—	—	—	—
Hawaii	Aug. 21, 1959	50	1959	Honolulu	632,772	43	2	43	4	6,424	47	2,906	12	—	—	—	X[3]
Idaho	July 3, 1890	43	1890	Boise	667,191	42	2	42	4	83,557	13	2,338	34	X	Direct	—	X[3]
Illinois	Dec. 3, 1818	21	1870	Springfield	10,081,158	4	24	4	26	56,400	24	3,245	5	—	—	X	—
Indiana	Dec. 11, 1816	19	1851	Indianapolis	4,662,498	11	11	11	13	36,291	38	2,827	14	—	—	—	—
Iowa	Dec. 28, 1846	29	1857	Des Moines	2,757,537	24	7	24	9	56,290	25	2,595	24	—	—	—	—
Kansas	Jan. 29, 1861	34	1861	Topeka	2,178,611	28	5	28	7	82,264	14	2,692	20	X	—	—	—
Kentucky	June 1, 1792	15	1891	Frankfort	3,038,156	22	7	22	9	40,395	37	2,043	43	—	—	—	—
Louisiana	Apr. 30, 1812	18	1921	Baton Rouge	3,257,022	20	8	20	10	48,523	31	2,061	41	X	—	—	X[3]
Maine	Mar. 15, 1820	23	1820	Augusta	969,265	36	2	36	4	33,215	39	2,245	37	X	Indirect	—	—
Maryland	Apr. 28, 1788	7	1867	Annapolis	3,100,689	21	8	21	10	10,577	42	3,014	10	X	—	—	—
Massachusetts	Feb. 6, 1788	6	1780	Boston	5,148,578	9	12	9	14	8,257	45	3,023	9	X	Indirect	X	—
Michigan	Jan. 26, 1837	26	1964	Lansing	7,823,194	7	19	7	21	52,215	23	3,009	11	X	Indirect	X	X[3]
Minnesota	May 11, 1858	32	1858	St. Paul	3,413,864	18	8	18	10	84,058	12	2,682	21	—	—	—	—
Mississippi	Dec. 10, 1817	20	1890	Jackson	2,178,141	29	5	29	7	47,716	32	1,566	50	—	—	—	—
Missouri	Aug. 10, 1821	24	1945	Jefferson City	4,319,813	13	10	13	12	69,686	19	2,628	23	X	Direct	X	—

State	Date admitted		Capital													
Montana	Nov. 8, 1899	41	Helena	1889	674,767	41	2	4	147,138	4	2,409	29	X	Direct}Indirect	—	—
Nebraska	Mar. 1, 1867	37	Lincoln	1875	1,411,330	34	3	5	77,227	15	2,573	25	X	Direct	X	X
Nevada	Oct. 31, 1864	36	Carson City	1864	285,278	49	1	3	110,540	7	3,289	4	X	Indirect	X	X
New Hampshire	June 21, 1788	9	Concord	1784	606,921	45	2	4	9,304	44	2,570	26	—	—	—	—
New Jersey	Dec. 18, 1787	3	Trenton	1947	6,066,782	8	15	17	7,836	46	3,242	6	X	—	—	—
New Mexico	Jan. 6, 1912	47	Santa Fe	1912	951,023	37	2	2	121,666	5	2,227	39	X	—	—	—
New York	July 26, 1788	11	Albany	1894	16,782,304	1	41	43	49,576	30	3,242	6	—	—	—	—
North Carolina	Nov. 21, 1789	12	Raleigh	1868	4,556,155	12	11	13	52,712	28	2,028	44	—	Direct	—	—
North Dakota	Nov. 2, 1889	39	Bismarck	1889	632,446	44	2	4	70,665	17	2,304	36	X	Direct	X	X
Ohio	Mar. 1, 1803	17	Columbus	1851	9,706,397	5	24	26	41,222	35	2,816	16	X	Direct}Indirect	X	X
Oklahoma	Nov. 16, 1907	46	Oklahoma City	1907	2,328,284	27	6	8	69,919	18	2,236	38	X	Direct	X	—
Oregon	Feb. 14, 1859	33	Salem	1859	1,768,687	32	4	6	96,981	10	2,794	17	X	Direct	X	X
Pennsylvania	Dec. 12, 1787	2	Harrisburg	1873	11,319,366	3	27	29	45,333	33	2,728	18	—	—	—	—
Rhode Island	May 29, 1790	13	Providence	1843	859,488	39	2	4	1,214	50	2,817	15	—	—	—	—
South Carolina	May 23, 1788	8	Columbia	1895	2,382,594	26	6	8	31,055	40	1,838	48	X	Direct	—	—
South Dakota	Nov. 2, 1889	40	Pierre	1889	680,514	40	2	4	77,047	16	2,055	42	X	—	X	—
Tennessee	June 1, 1796	16	Nashville	1870	3,567,089	17	9	11	42,246	34	1,992	46	—	—	—	—
Texas	Dec. 29, 1845	28	Austin	1876	9,579,677	6	23	25	267,339	2	2,346	31	—	—	—	—
Utah	Jan. 4, 1896	45	Salt Lake City	1896	890,627	38	2	4	84,916	11	2,340	32	X	Direct}Indirect	—	—
Vermont	Mar. 4, 1791	14	Montpelier	1793	389,881	47	1	3	9,609	43	2,340	32	—	—	—	—
Virginia	June 25, 1788	10	Richmond	1902	3,966,949	14	10	12	40,815	36	2,392	30	—	—	—	—
Washington	Nov. 11, 1889	42	Olympia	1889	2,853,214	23	7	9	68,192	20	2,864	13	X	Direct}Indirect	—	X³
West Virginia	June 20, 1863	35	Charleston	1872	1,860,421	30	5	7	24,181	41	2,007	45	—	—	—	—
Wisconsin	May 29, 1848	30	Madison	1848	3,951,777	15	10	12	56,154	26	2,682	21	—	—	—	X
Wyoming	July 10, 1890	44	Cheyenne	1890	330,066	48	3	3	97,914	9	2,479	27	—	—	—	—

The data in this table have been secured mainly from *Statistical Abstract of the United States* (1966), pp. 12, 171, and 330; and from *The Book of the States* (1966-67), pp. 10, 12, and 32-34.

1District of Columbia has 3 electors.
2The legislatures of Georgia, Illinois, New Jersey, North Carolina, Vermont, and Wyoming may refer measures to the electorate.
3Except judicial officers.

Nicknames of the States

Aloha State	*Hawaii*	Hawkeye State	*Iowa*
Badger State	*Wisconsin*	Heart of Dixie	*Alabama*
Bay State	*Massachusetts*	Hoosier State	*Indiana*
Bayou State	*Mississippi*	Jaywalker State	*Kansas*
Bear State	*Arkansas*	Keystone State	*Pennsylvania*
Beaver State	*Oregon*	Last Frontier	*Alaska*
Beehive State	*Utah*	Little Rhody	*Rhode Island*
Big Bend State	*Tennessee*	Lone Star State	*Texas*
Bluegrass State	*Kentucky*	Magnolia State	*Mississippi*
Blue Hen State	*Delaware*	Mother of Presidents	*Virginia*
Bonanza State	*Montana*	Mother of States	*Virginia*
Buckeye State	*Ohio*	Mountain State	*West Virginia*
Centennial State	*Colorado*	North Star State	*Minnesota*
Constitution State	*Connecticut*	Nutmeg State	*Connecticut*
Corncracker State	*Kentucky*	Old Dominion	*Virginia*
Cornhusker State	*Nebraska*	Old Line State	*Maryland*
Cotton State	*Alabama*	Old North State	*North Carolina*
Coyote State	*South Dakota*	Palmetto State	*South Carolina*
Cracker State	*Georgia*	Panhandle State	*West Virginia*
Creole State	*Louisiana*	Peach State	*Georgia*
Dark and Bloody Ground	*Kentucky*	Pelican State	*Louisiana*
Diamond State	*Delaware*	Peninsular State	*Florida*
Empire State	*New York*	Pine Tree State	*Maine*
Empire State of the South	*Georgia*	Prairie State	*Illinois*
Equality State	*Wyoming*	Sagebrush State	*Nevada*
Evergreen State	*Washington*	Sage Hen State	*Nevada*
First State	*Delaware*	Show-me State	*Missouri*
Flickertail State	*North Dakota*	Silver State	*Nevada*
Free State	*Maryland*	Sioux State	*North Dakota*
Garden State	*Kansas, New Jersey*	Sooner State	*Oklahoma*
Gem State	*Idaho*	Sucker State	*Illinois*
Golden State	*California*	Sunflower State	*Kansas*
Gopher State	*Minnesota*	Sunshine State	*Florida, South Dakota*
Grand Canyon State	*Arizona*	Tar Heel State	*North Carolina*
Granite State	*New Hampshire*	Treasure State	*Montana*
Green Mountain State	*Vermont*	Volunteer State	*Tennessee*
	Wolverine State		*Wisconsin*

Presidents of the United States

No.	Name	Native State	Party	Term
1	George Washington (1732–1799)	Va.	Federalist	1789–1797
2	John Adams (1735–1826)	Mass.	Federalist	1797–1801
3	Thomas Jefferson (1743–1826)	Va.	Rep.-Dem.	1801–1809
4	James Madison (1751–1836)	Va.	Rep.-Dem.	1809–1817
5	James Monroe (1758–1831)	Va.	Rep.-Dem.	1817–1825
6	John Quincy Adams (1767–1848)	Mass.	Rep.-Dem.	1825–1829
7	Andrew Jackson (1767–1845)	S. C.	Democrat	1829–1837
8	Martin Van Buren (1782–1862)	N. Y.	Democrat	1837–1841
9	William Henry Harrison (1773–1841)	Va.	Whig	1841
10	John Tyler (1790–1862)	Va.	Democrat	1841–1845
11	James Knox Polk (1795–1849)	N. C.	Democrat	1845–1849
12	Zachary Taylor (1784–1850)	Va.	Whig	1849–1850
13	Millard Fillmore (1800–1874)	N. Y.	Whig	1850–1853
14	Franklin Pierce (1804–1869)	N. H.	Democrat	1853–1857
15	James Buchanan (1791–1868)	Pa.	Democrat	1857–1861
16	Abraham Lincoln (1809–1865)	Ky.	Republican	1861–1865
17	Andrew Johnson (1808–1875)	N. C.	Republican	1865–1869
18	Ulysses S. Grant (1822–1885)	Ohio	Republican	1869–1877
19	Rutherford B. Hayes (1822–1893)	Ohio	Republican	1877–1881
20	James A. Garfield (1831–1881)	Ohio	Republican	1881
21	Chester A. Arthur (1830–1886)	Vt.	Republican	1881–1885
22	Grover Cleveland (1837–1908)	N. J.	Democrat	1885–1889
23	Benjamin Harrison (1833–1901)	Ohio	Republican	1889–1893
24	Grover Cleveland (1837–1908)	N. J.	Democrat	1893–1897
25	William McKinley (1843–1901)	Ohio	Republican	1897–1901
26	Theodore Roosevelt (1858–1919)	N. Y.	Republican	1901–1909
27	William H. Taft (1857–1930)	Ohio	Republican	1909–1913
28	Woodrow Wilson (1856–1924)	Va.	Democrat	1913–1921
29	Warren G. Harding (1865–1923)	Ohio	Republican	1921–1923
30	Calvin Coolidge (1872–1933)	Vt.	Republican	1923–1929
31	Herbert C. Hoover (1874–1964)	Iowa	Republican	1929–1933
32	Franklin D. Roosevelt (1882–1945)	N. Y.	Democrat	1933–1945
33	Harry S. Truman (1884–)	Mo.	Democrat	1945–1953
34	Dwight D. Eisenhower (1890–1969)	Texas	Republican	1953–1961
35	John F. Kennedy (1917–1963)	Mass.	Democrat	1961–1963
36	Lyndon B. Johnson (1908–)	Texas	Democrat	1963–1969
37	Richard M. Nixon (1913–)	Cal.	Republican	1969–

Index Guide to the U. S. Constitution

PREAMBLE

ARTICLE I. The Legislative Department.
Organization of Congress and terms, qualifications, apportionment, and election of Senators and Representatives.
Procedure in impeachment.
Privileges of the two Houses and of their members.
Procedure in lawmaking.
Powers of Congress.
Limitations on Congress and on the States.

ARTICLE II. The Executive Department.
Election of President and Vice President.
Powers and duties of the President.
Ratification of appointments and treaties.
Liability of officers to impeachment.

ARTICLE III. The Judicial Department.
Independence of the judiciary.
Jurisdiction of national courts.
Guarantee of jury trial.
Definition of treason.

ARTICLE IV. Position of the States and territories.
Full faith and credit to acts and judicial proceedings.
Privileges and immunities of citizens of the several States.
Rendition of fugitives from justice.
Control of territories by Congress.
Guarantees to the States.

ARTICLE V. Method of amendment.

ARTICLE VI. Supremacy of the Constitution, laws, and treaties of the United States.
Oath of office—prohibition of a religious test.

ARTICLE VII. Method of ratification of the Constitution.

AMENDMENTS

I. Freedom of religion, speech, press, and assembly; right of petition.
II. Right to keep and bear arms.
III. Limitations in quartering soldiers.
IV. Protection from unreasonable searches and seizures.
V. Due process in criminal cases.
Limitation on right of eminent domain.
VI. Right to speedy trial by jury, and other guarantees.
VII. Trial by jury in suits at law.
VIII. Excessive bail or unusual punishments forbidden.
IX. Retention of certain rights by the people.
X. Undelegated powers belong to the States or to the people.
XI. Exemption of States from suit by individuals.
XII. New method of electing President.
XIII. Abolition of slavery.

   XIV. Definition of citizenship.
        Guarantees of due process and equal protection against State action.
        Validity of public debt.
    XV. Extension of suffrage to colored persons.
   XVI. Tax on incomes "from whatever source derived."
  XVII. Popular election of Senators.
 XVIII. Prohibition of intoxicating liquors.
   XIX. Extension of suffrage to women.
    XX. Abolition of "lame duck" session of Congress.
        Change in Presidential and Congressional terms.
   XXI. Eighteenth Amendment repealed.
  XXII. Limitation of President's terms in office.
 XXIII. Presidential vote for District of Columbia.
 XXIV. Elimination of tax-paying requirement.
  XXV. Presidential disability.

Constitution of the United States *

Proposed by Convention, September 17, 1787.
Effective March 4, 1789.

WE the people of the United States, in order to form a more perfect union, establish justice, insure domestic tranquillity, provide for the common defense, promote the general welfare, and secure the blessings of liberty to ourselves and our posterity, do ordain and establish this Constitution for the United States of America.

ARTICLE I

Section 1. All legislative powers herein granted shall be vested in a Congress of the United States, which shall consist of a Senate and House of Representatives.

Section 2. *1.* The House of Representatives shall be composed of members chosen every second year by the people of the several States, and the electors in each State shall have the qualifications requisite for electors of the most numerous branch of the State legislature.

2. No person shall be a Representative who shall not have attained to the age of twenty-five years, and been seven years a citizen of the United States, and who shall not, when elected, be an inhabitant of that State in which he shall be chosen.

3. Representatives and direct taxes[1] shall be apportioned among the several States which may be included within this Union, according to their respective numbers, which shall be determined by adding to the whole number of free persons, including those bound to service for a term of years, and excluding Indians not taxed, three-fifths of all other persons.[2] The actual enumeration shall be made within three years after the first meeting of the Congress of the United States, and within every subsequent term of ten years, in such manner as they shall by law direct. The number of Representatives shall not exceed one for every thirty thousand, but each State shall have at least one Representative; and until such enumeration shall be made, the State of New Hampshire shall be entitled to choose three, Massachusetts eight, Rhode Island and Providence Plantations one, Connecticut five, New York six, New Jersey four, Pennsylvania eight, Delaware one, Maryland six, Virginia ten, North Carolina five, South Carolina five, and Georgia three.

4. When vacancies happen in the representation from any State, the executive authority thereof shall issue writs of election to fill such vacancies.

5. The House of Representatives shall choose their Speaker and other officers; and shall have the sole power of impeachment.

Section 3. *1.* The Senate of the United States shall be composed of two Senators from each State, chosen by the legislature thereof,[3] for six years; and each Senator shall have one vote.

---

* *Spelling, punctuation, and capitalization have been modernized.*
[1] *See the 16th Amendment.*
[2] *See the 14th Amendment.*
[3] *See the 17th Amendment.*

2. Immediately after they shall be assembled in consequence of the first election, they shall be divided as equally as may be into three classes. The seats of the Senators of the first class shall be vacated at the expiration of the second year; of the second class, at the expiration of the fourth year, and of the third class, at the expiration of the sixth year, so that one-third may be chosen every second year; and if vacancies happen by resignation or otherwise during the recess of the legislature of any State, the executive thereof may make temporary appointments until the next meeting of the legislature, which shall then fill such vacancies.[1]

3. No person shall be a Senator who shall not have attained to the age of thirty years, and been nine years a citizen of the United States, and who shall not, when elected, be an inhabitant of that State for which he shall be chosen.

4. The Vice President of the United States shall be President of the Senate, but shall have no vote, unless they be equally divided.

5. The Senate shall choose their other officers, and also a President pro tempore in the absence of the Vice President, or when he shall exercise the office of President of the United States.

6. The Senate shall have the sole power to try all impeachments. When sitting for that purpose, they shall be on oath or affirmation. When the President of the United States is tried, the Chief Justice shall preside: and no person shall be convicted without the concurrence of two-thirds of the members present.

7. Judgment in cases of impeachment shall not extend further than to removal from office and disqualification to hold and enjoy any office of honor, trust, or profit under the United States; but the party convicted shall, nevertheless, be liable and subject to indictment, trial, judgment, and punishment, according to law.

Section 4. 1. The times, places, and manner of holding elections for Senators and Representatives shall be prescribed in each State by the legislature thereof; but the Congress may at any time by law make or alter such regulations, except as to the places of choosing Senators.

2. The Congress shall assemble at least once in every year, and such meeting shall be on the first Monday in December, unless they shall by law appoint a different day.

Section 5. 1. Each House shall be the judge of the elections, returns, and qualifications of its own members, and a majority of each shall constitute a quorum to do business; but a smaller number may adjourn from day to day, and may be authorized to compel the attendance of absent members, in such manner, and under such penalties as each House may provide.

2. Each House may determine the rules of its proceedings, punish its members for disorderly behavior, and, with the concurrence of two-thirds, expel a member.

3. Each House shall keep a journal of its proceedings and from time to time publish the same, excepting such parts as may in their judgment require secrecy; and the yeas and nays of the members of either House on any question shall, at the desire of one-fifth of those present, be entered on the journal.

4. Neither House, during the session of Congress, shall, without the consent of the other, adjourn for more than three days, nor to any other place than that in which the two Houses shall be sitting.

Section 6. 1. The Senators and Representatives shall receive a compensation for
[1] See the 17th Amendment.

their services, to be ascertained by law and paid out of the Treasury of the United States. They shall, in all cases except treason, felony, and breach of the peace, be privileged from arrest during their attendance at the session of their respective Houses, and in going to and returning from the same; and for any speech or debate in either House they shall not be questioned in any other place.

2. No Senator or Representative shall, during the time for which he was elected, be appointed to any civil office under the authority of the United States, which shall have been created, or the emoluments whereof shall have been increased during such time; and no person holding any office under the United States shall be a member of either House during his continuance in office.

Section 7. *1.* All bills for raising revenue shall originate in the House of Representatives; but the Senate may propose or concur with amendments as on other bills.

2. Every bill which shall have passed the House of Representatives and the Senate, shall, before it become a law, be presented to the President of the United States; if he approve he shall sign it, but if not he shall return it, with his objections, to that House in which it shall have originated, who shall enter the objections at large on their journal and proceed to reconsider it. If after such reconsideration two-thirds of that House shall agree to pass the bill, it shall be sent, together with the objections, to the other House, by which it shall likewise be reconsidered, and if approved by two-thirds of that House it shall become a law. But in all such cases the votes of both Houses shall be determined by yeas and nays, and the names of the persons voting for and against the bill shall be entered on the journal of each House respectively. If any bill shall not be returned by the President within ten days (Sundays excepted) after it shall have been presented to him, the same shall be a law, in like manner as if he had signed it, unless the Congress by their adjournment prevent its return, in which case it shall not be a law.

3. Every order, resolution, or vote to which the concurrence of the Senate and House of Representatives may be necessary (except on a question of adjournment) shall be presented to the President of the United States; and before the same shall take effect, shall be approved by him, or being disapproved by him, shall be repassed by two-thirds of the Senate and House of Representatives, according to the rules and limitations prescribed in the case of a bill.

Section 8. The Congress shall have power:

1. To lay and collect taxes, duties, imposts, and excises, to pay the debts and provide for the common defense and general welfare of the United States; but all duties, imposts, and excises shall be uniform throughout the United States;

2. To borrow money on the credit of the United States;

3. To regulate commerce with foreign nations and among the several States, and with the Indian tribes;

4. To establish a uniform rule of naturalization, and uniform laws on the subject of bankruptcies throughout the United States;

5. To coin money, regulate the value thereof, and of foreign coin, and fix the standard of weights and measures;

6. To provide for the punishment of counterfeiting the securities and current coin of the United States;

7. To establish post offices and post roads;

8. To promote the progress of science and useful arts by securing for limited times to authors and inventors the exclusive right to their respective writings and discoveries;

9. To constitute tribunals inferior to the Supreme Court;

10. To define and punish piracies and felonies committed on the high seas and offenses against the law of nations;

11. To declare war, grant letters of marque and reprisal, and make rules concerning captures on land and water;

12. To raise and support armies, but no appropriation of money to that use shall be for a longer term than two years;

13. To provide and maintain a navy;

14. To make rules for the government and regulation of the land and naval forces;

15. To provide for calling forth the militia to execute the laws of the Union, suppress insurrections, and repel invasions;

16. To provide for organizing, arming, and disciplining the militia, and for governing such part of them as may be employed in the service of the United States, reserving to the States respectively the appointment of the officers and the authority of training the militia according to the discipline prescribed by Congress;

17. To exercise exclusive legislation in all cases whatsoever over such district (not exceeding ten miles square) as may, by cession of particular States and the acceptance of Congress, become the seat of the government of the United States, and to exercise like authority over all places purchased by the consent of the legislature of the State in which the same shall be, for the erection of forts, magazines, arsenals, dockyards, and other needful buildings; and

18. To make all laws which shall be necessary and proper for carrying into execution the foregoing powers, and all other powers vested by this Constitution in the government of the United States, or in any department or officer thereof.

Section 9. 1. The migration or importation of such persons as any of the States now existing shall think proper to admit shall not be prohibited by the Congress prior to the year one thousand eight hundred and eight, but a tax or duty may be imposed on such importation, not exceeding ten dollars for each person.

2. The privilege of the writ of habeas corpus shall not be suspended, unless when in cases of rebellion or invasion the public safety may require it.

3. No bill of attainder or ex post facto law shall be passed.

4. No capitation or other direct tax shall be laid, unless in proportion to the census or enumeration hereinbefore directed to be taken.[1]

5. No tax or duty shall be laid on articles exported from any State.

6. No preference shall be given by any regulation of commerce or revenue to the ports of one State over those of another; nor shall vessels bound to or from one State be obliged to enter, clear, or pay duties in another.

7. No money shall be drawn from the Treasury but in consequence of appropriations made by law; and a regular statement and account of the receipts and expenditures of all public money shall be published from time to time.

[1] *See the 16th Amendment.*

8. No title of nobility shall be granted by the United States; and no person holding any office of profit or trust under them shall, without the consent of the Congress, accept of any present, emolument, office, or title, of any kind whatever, from any king, prince, or foreign State.

Section 10. *1.* No State shall enter into any treaty, alliance, or confederation; grant letters of marque and reprisal; coin money; emit bills of credit; make anything but gold and silver coin a tender in payment of debts; pass any bill of attainder, ex post facto law or law impairing the obligation of contracts, or grant any title of nobility.

2. No State shall, without the consent of the Congress, lay any imposts or duties on imports or exports, except what may be absolutely necessary for executing its inspection laws, and the net produce of all duties and imposts, laid by any State on imports or exports, shall be for the use of the Treasury of the United States; and all such laws shall be subject to the revision and control of the Congress.

3. No State shall, without the consent of Congress, lay any duty of tonnage, keep troops or ships of war in time of peace, enter into any agreement or compact with another State or with a foreign power, or engage in war, unless actually invaded or in such imminent danger as will not admit of delay.

ARTICLE II

Section 1. *1.* The executive power shall be vested in a President of the United States of America. He shall hold his office during the term of four years, and together with the Vice President, chosen for the same term, be elected as follows:

2. Each State shall appoint, in such manner as the legislature thereof may direct, a number of electors, equal to the whole number of Senators and Representatives to which the State may be entitled in the Congress; but no Senator or Representative, or person holding an office of trust or profit under the United States, shall be appointed an elector.

3. The electors shall meet in their respective States and vote by ballot for two persons, of whom one at least shall not be an inhabitant of the same State with themselves. And they shall make a list of all the persons voted for, and of the number of votes for each; which list they shall sign and certify, and transmit sealed to the seat of the government of the United States, directed to the President of the Senate. The President of the Senate shall, in the presence of the Senate and House of Representatives, open all the certificates, and the votes shall then be counted. The person having the greatest number of votes shall be the President, if such number be a majority of the whole number of electors appointed; and if there be more than one who have such majority, and have an equal number of votes, then the House of Representatives shall immediately choose by ballot one of them for President; and if no person have a majority, then from the five highest on the list the said House shall in like manner choose the President. But in choosing the President, the votes shall be taken by States, the representation from each State having one vote; a quorum for this purpose shall consist of a member or members from two-thirds of the States, and a majority of all the States shall be necessary to a choice. In every case, after the choice of the President, the person having the greatest number of votes of the electors shall be the Vice President. But if there should remain

two or more who have equal votes, the Senate shall choose from them by ballot the Vice President.[1]

4. The Congress may determine the time of choosing the electors, and the day on which they shall give their votes; which day shall be the same throughout the United States.

5. No person except a natural-born citizen, or a citizen of the United States at the time of the adoption of this Constitution, shall be eligible to the office of President; neither shall any person be eligible to that office who shall not have attained to the age of thirty-five years, and been fourteen years a resident within the United States.

6. In case of the removal of the President from office, or of his death, resignation, or inability to discharge the powers and duties of the said office, the same shall devolve on the Vice President, and the Congress may by law provide for the case of removal, death, resignation, or inability, both of the President and Vice President, declaring what officer shall then act as President, and such officer shall act accordingly until the disability be removed or a President shall be elected.[2]

7. The President shall, at stated times, receive for his services a compensation, which shall neither be increased nor diminished during the period for which he shall have been elected, and he shall not receive within that period any other emolument from the United States, or any of them.

8. Before he enter on the execution of his office, he shall take the following oath or affirmation:—"I do solemnly swear (or affirm) that I will faithfully execute the office of President of the United States, and will to the best of my ability, preserve, protect, and defend the Constitution of the United States."

Section 2. 1. The President shall be Commander in chief of the Army and Navy of the United States, and of the militia of the several States, when called into the actual service of the United States; he may require the opinion, in writing, of the principal officer in each of the executive departments, upon any subject relating to the duties of their respective offices, and he shall have power to grant reprieves and pardons for offenses against the United States, except in cases of impeachment.

2. He shall have power, by and with the advice and consent of the Senate, to make treaties, provided two-thirds of the Senators present concur; and he shall nominate, and by and with the advice and consent of the Senate, shall appoint ambassadors, other public ministers and consuls, judges of the Supreme Court, and all other officers of the United States, whose appointments are not herein otherwise provided for, and which shall be established by law; but the Congress may by law vest the appointment of such inferior officers, as they think proper, in the President alone, in the courts of law, or in the heads of departments.

3. The President shall have power to fill up all vacancies that may happen during the recess of the Senate, by granting commissions which shall expire at the end of their next session.

Section 3. He shall from time to time give to the Congress information of the state of the Union, and recommend to their consideration such measures as he shall judge necessary and expedient; he may, on extraordinary occasions, convene both Houses, or either of them, and in case of disagreement between them

[1] *This paragraph was superseded by the 12th Amendment.*
[2] *See the 25th Amendment.*

with respect to the time of adjournment, he may adjourn them to such time as he shall think proper; he shall receive ambassadors and other public ministers; he shall take care that the laws be faithfully executed, and shall commission all the officers of the United States.

Section 4. The President, Vice President, and all civil officers of the United States shall be removed from office on impeachment for and conviction of treason, bribery, or other high crimes and misdemeanors.

ARTICLE III

Section 1. The judicial power of the United States shall be vested in one Supreme Court, and in such inferior courts as the Congress may from time to time ordain and establish. The judges, both of the Supreme and inferior courts, shall hold their offices during good behavior, and shall, at stated times, receive for their services a compensation which shall not be diminished during their continuance in office.

Section 2. *1.* The judicial power shall extend to all cases, in law and equity, arising under this Constitution, the laws of the United States, and treaties made, or which shall be made, under their authority; to all cases affecting ambassadors, other public ministers, and consuls; to all cases of admiralty and maritime jurisdiction; to controversies to which the United States shall be a party; to controversies between two or more States; between a State and citizens of another State; [1] between citizens of different States; between citizens of the same State claiming lands under grants of different States, and between a State, or the citizens thereof, and foreign States, citizens, or subjects.

2. In all cases affecting ambassadors, other public ministers and consuls, and those in which a State shall be party, the Supreme Court shall have original jurisdiction. In all the other cases before mentioned, the Supreme Court shall have appellate jurisdiction, both as to law and fact, with such exceptions and under such regulations as the Congress shall make.

3. The trial of all crimes, except in cases of impeachment, shall be by jury; and such trial shall be held in the State where the said crimes shall have been committed; but when not committed within any State, the trial shall be at such place or places as the Congress may by law have directed.

Section 3. *1.* Treason against the United States shall consist only in levying war against them or in adhering to their enemies, giving them aid and comfort. No person shall be convicted of treason unless on the testimony of two witnesses to the same overt act, or on confession in open court.

2. The Congress shall have power to declare the punishment of treason, but no attainder of treason shall work corruption of blood or forfeiture except during the life of the person attainted.

ARTICLE IV

Section 1. Full faith and credit shall be given in each State to the public acts, records, and judicial proceedings of every other State. And the Congress may by general laws prescribe the manner in which such acts, records, and proceedings shall be proved, and the effect thereof.

[1] *See the 11th Amendment.*

Section 2. *1.* The citizens of each State shall be entitled to all privileges and immunities of citizens in the several States.[1]

2. A person charged in any State with treason, felony, or other crime, who shall flee from justice, and be found in another State, shall, on demand of the executive authority of the State from which he fled, be delivered up, to be removed to the State having jurisdiction of the crime.

3. No person held to service or labor in one State, under the laws thereof, escaping into another, shall, in consequence of any law or regulation therein, be discharged from such service or labor, but shall be delivered up on claim of the party to whom such service or labor may be due.[2]

Section 3. *1.* New States may be admitted by the Congress into this Union; but no new State shall be formed or erected within the jurisdiction of any other State; nor any State be formed by the junction of two or more States or parts of States, without the consent of the legislatures of the States concerned as well as of the Congress.

2. The Congress shall have power to dispose of and make all needful rules and regulations respecting the territory or other property belonging to the United States; and nothing in this Constitution shall be so construed as to prejudice any claims of the United States or of any particular State.

Section 4. The United States shall guarantee to every State in this Union a republican form of government, and shall protect each of them against invasion; and on application of the legislature, or of the executive (when the legislature cannot be convened), against domestic violence.

ARTICLE V

The Congress, whenever two-thirds of both Houses shall deem it necessary, shall propose amendments to this Constitution, or, on the application of the legislatures of two-thirds of the several States, shall call a convention for proposing amendments, which in either case shall be valid to all intents and purposes as part of this Constitution when ratified by the legislatures of three-fourths of the several States, or by conventions in three-fourths thereof, as the one or the other mode of ratification may be proposed by the Congress; provided that no amendment which may be made prior to the year one thousand eight hundred and eight shall in any manner affect the first and fourth clauses in the ninth section of the first article; and that no State, without its consent, shall be deprived of its equal suffrage in the Senate.

ARTICLE VI

1. All debts contracted and engagements entered into, before the adoption of this Constitution, shall be as valid against the United States under this Constitution as under the Confederation.

2. This Constitution, and the laws of the United States which shall be made in pursuance thereof, and all treaties made, or which shall be made, under the authority of the United States, shall be the supreme law of the land; and the judges in every State shall be bound thereby, anything in the constitution or laws of any State to the contrary notwithstanding.

[1] *See the 14th Amendment, Sec. 1.*
[2] *See the 13th Amendment.*

3. The Senators and Representatives before mentioned, and the members of the several State legislatures, and all executive and judicial officers, both of the United States and of the several States, shall be bound by oath or affirmation to support this Constitution; but no religious test shall ever be required as a qualification to any office or public trust under the United States.

ARTICLE VII

The ratification of the conventions of nine States shall be sufficient for the establishment of this Constitution between the States so ratifying the same.

Done in convention by the unanimous consent of the States present the seventeenth day of September in the year of our Lord one thousand seven hundred and eighty-seven, and of the independence of the United States of America the twelfth. In witness whereof we have hereunto subscribed our names.

[Names omitted]

Amendments

First Ten Amendments passed by Congress September 25, 1789.
Ratified by three-fourths of the States December 15, 1791.

Articles in addition to, and amendment of, the Constitution of the United States of America, proposed by Congress, and ratified by the legislatures of the several States, pursuant to the fifth article of the original Constitution.

ARTICLE I

Congress shall make no law respecting an establishment of religion, or prohibiting the free exercise thereof; or abridging the freedom of speech, or of the press; or the right of the people peaceably to assemble, and to petition the government for a redress of grievances.

ARTICLE II

A well-regulated militia being necessary to the security of a free State, the right of the people to keep and bear arms shall not be infringed.

ARTICLE III

No soldier shall, in time of peace, be quartered in any house without the consent of the owner, nor in time of war, but in a manner to be prescribed by law.

ARTICLE IV

The right of the people to be secure in their persons, houses, papers, and effects, against unreasonable searches and seizures, shall not be violated, and no warrants shall issue but upon probable cause, supported by oath or affirmation, and particularly describing the place to be searched, and the persons or things to be seized.

ARTICLE V

No person shall be held to answer for a capital or otherwise infamous crime, unless on a presentment or indictment of a grand jury, except in cases arising in the land or naval forces, or in the militia, when in actual service in time of war or public danger; nor shall any person be subject for the same offense to be twice put in jeopardy of life or limb; nor shall be compelled in any criminal case to be a witness against himself, nor be deprived of life, liberty, or property, without due process of law; nor shall private property be taken for public use without just compensation.

ARTICLE VI

In all criminal prosecutions, the accused shall enjoy the right to a speedy and public trial, by an impartial jury of the State and district wherein the crime shall have been committed, which district shall have been previously ascertained by law, and to be informed of the nature and cause of the accusation; to be confronted with the witnesses against him; to have compulsory process for obtaining witnesses in his favor, and to have the assistance of counsel for his defense.

ARTICLE VII

In suits at common law, where the value in controversy shall exceed twenty dollars, the right of trial by jury shall be preserved, and no fact tried by a jury shall be otherwise re-examined in any court of the United States, than according to the rules of the common law.

ARTICLE VIII

Excessive bail shall not be required, nor excessive fines imposed, nor cruel and unusual punishments inflicted.

ARTICLE IX

The enumeration in the Constitution of certain rights shall not be construed to deny or disparage others retained by the people.

ARTICLE X

The powers not delegated to the United States by the Constitution, nor prohibited by it to the States, are reserved to the States respectively, or to the people.

ARTICLE XI

Passed by Congress September 5, 1794. Ratified January 8, 1798.

The judicial power of the United States shall not be construed to extend to any suit in law or equity, commenced or prosecuted against one of the United States by citizens of another State, or by citizens or subjects of any foreign State.

ARTICLE XII

Passed by Congress December 12, 1803. Ratified September 25, 1804.

The electors shall meet in their respective States and vote by ballot for President and Vice President, one of whom, at least, shall not be an inhabitant of the same State with themselves; they shall name in their ballots the person voted for as President, and in distinct ballots the person voted for as Vice President, and they shall make distinct lists of all persons voted for as President and of all persons voted for as Vice President, and of the number of votes for each, which lists they shall sign and certify, and transmit sealed to the seat of the government of the United States, directed to the President of the Senate; the President of the Senate shall, in the presence of the Senate and House of Representatives, open all the certificates and the votes shall then be counted;

the person having the greatest number of votes for President, shall be the President, if such number be a majority of the whole number of electors appointed; and if no person have such majority, then from the persons having the highest numbers not exceeding three on the list of those voted for as President, the House of Representatives shall choose immediately, by ballot, the President. But in choosing the President the votes shall be taken by States, the representation from each State having one vote; a quorum for this purpose shall consist of a member or members from two-thirds of the States, and a majority of all the States shall be necessary to a choice. And if the House of Representatives shall not choose a President whenever the right of choice shall devolve upon them, before the fourth day of March next following, then the Vice President shall act as President, as in the case of the death or other constitutional disability of the President. The person having the greatest number of votes as Vice President shall be the Vice President, if such number be a majority of the whole number of electors appointed, and if no person have a majority, then from the two highest numbers on the list, the Senate shall choose the Vice President; a quorum for the purpose shall consist of two-thirds of the whole number of Senators, and a majority of the whole number shall be necessary to a choice. But no person constitutionally ineligible to the office of President shall be eligible to that of Vice President of the United States.

ARTICLE XIII

Passed by Congress February 1, 1865. Ratified December 18, 1865.

Section 1. Neither slavery nor involuntary servitude, except as a punishment for crime whereof the party shall have been duly convicted, shall exist within the United States or any place subject to their jurisdiction.

Section 2. Congress shall have power to enforce this article by appropriate legislation.

ARTICLE XIV

Passed by Congress June 16, 1866. Ratified July 28, 1868.

Section 1. All persons born or naturalized in the United States, and subject to the jurisdiction thereof, are citizens of the United States and of the State wherein they reside. No State shall make or enforce any law which shall abridge the privileges or immunities of citizens of the United States; nor shall any State deprive any person of life, liberty, or property, without due process of law; nor deny to any person within its jurisdiction the equal protection of the laws.

Section 2. Representatives shall be apportioned among the several States according to their respective numbers, counting the whole number of persons in each State, excluding Indians not taxed. But when the right to vote at any election for the choice of electors for President and Vice President of the United States, Representatives in Congress, the executive and judicial officers of a State or the members of the legislature thereof, is denied to any of the male inhabitants of such State, being twenty-one years of age, and citizens of the United States, or in any way abridged, except for participation in rebellion, or other crime, the basis of representation therein shall be reduced in the proportion which the number of such male citizens shall bear to the whole number of male citizens twenty-one years of age in such State.

Section 3. No person shall be a Senator or Representative in Congress, or elector of President and Vice President, or hold any office, civil or military, under the United States, or under any State, who, having previously taken an oath as a member of Congress, or as an officer of the United States, or as a member of any State legislature, or as an executive or judicial officer of any State, to support the Constitution of the United States, shall have engaged in insurrection or rebellion against the same, or given aid or comfort to the enemies thereof. But Congress may by a vote of two-thirds of each House, remove such disability.

Section 4. The validity of the public debt of the United States, authorized by law, including debts incurred for payment of pensions and bounties for services in suppressing insurrection or rebellion, shall not be questioned. But neither the United States nor any State shall assume or pay any debt or obligation incurred in aid of insurrection or rebellion against the United States, or any claim for the loss or emancipation of any slave; but all such debts, obligations, and claims shall be held illegal and void.

Section 5. The Congress shall have power to enforce, by appropriate legislation, the provisions of this article.

ARTICLE XV

Passed by Congress February 27, 1869. Ratified March 30, 1870.

Section 1. The right of citizens of the United States to vote shall not be denied or abridged by the United States or by any State on account of race, color, or previous condition of servitude.

Section 2. The Congress shall have power to enforce this article by appropriate legislation.

ARTICLE XVI

Passed by Congress July 12, 1909. Ratified February 25, 1913.

The Congress shall have power to lay and collect taxes on incomes, from whatever source derived, without apportionment among the several States, and without regard to any census or enumeration.

ARTICLE XVII

Passed by Congress May 16, 1912. Ratified May 31, 1913.

The Senate of the United States shall be composed of two Senators from each State, elected by the people thereof, for six years; and each Senator shall have one vote. The electors in each State shall have the qualifications requisite for electors of the most numerous branch of the State legislatures.

When vacancies happen in the representation of any State in the Senate, the executive authority of such State shall issue writs of election to fill such vacancies: *Provided,* That the legislature of any State may empower the executive thereof to make temporary appointments until the people fill the vacancies by election as the legislature may direct.

This amendment shall not be so construed as to affect the election or term of any Senator chosen before it becomes valid as part of the Constitution.

ARTICLE XVIII

Passed by Congress December 3, 1917. Ratified January 29, 1919.

Section 1. After one year from the ratification of this article the manufacture, sale, or transportation of intoxicating liquors within, the importation thereof into, or the exportation thereof from the United States and all territory subject to the jurisdiction thereof for beverage purposes is hereby prohibited.

Section 2. The Congress and the several States shall have concurrent power to enforce this article by appropriate legislation.

Section 3. This article shall be inoperative unless it shall have been ratified as an amendment to the Constitution by the legislatures of the several States, as provided in the Constitution, within seven years from the date of the submission hereof to the States by the Congress.

ARTICLE XIX

Passed by Congress May 19, 1919. Ratified August 26, 1920.

The right of citizens of the United States to vote shall not be denied or abridged by the United States or by any State on account of sex.

Congress shall have power to enforce this article by appropriate legislation.

ARTICLE XX

Passed by Congress March 3, 1932. Ratified February 6, 1933.

Section 1. The terms of the President and Vice President shall end at noon on the 20th day of January, and the terms of Senators and Representatives at noon on the 3d day of January, of the years in which such terms would have ended if this article had not been ratified; and the terms of their successors shall then begin.

Section 2. The Congress shall assemble at least once in every year, and such meeting shall begin at noon on the 3d day of January, unless they shall by law appoint a different day.

Section 3. If, at the time fixed for the beginning of the term of the President, the President elect shall have died, the Vice President elect shall become President. If a President shall not have been chosen before the time fixed for the beginning of his term, or if the President elect shall have failed to qualify, then the Vice President elect shall act as President until a President shall have qualified; and the Congress may by law provide for the case wherein neither a President elect nor a Vice President elect shall have qualified, declaring who shall then act as President, or the manner in which one who is to act shall be selected, and such person shall act accordingly until a President or Vice President shall have qualified.

Section 4. The Congress may by law provide for the case of the death of any of the persons from whom the House of Representatives may choose a President whenever the right of choice shall have devolved upon them, and for the case of the death of any of the persons from whom the Senate may choose a Vice President whenever the right of choice shall have devolved upon them.

Section 5. Sections 1 and 2 shall take effect on the 15th day of October following the ratification of this article.

Section 6. This article shall be inoperative unless it shall have been ratified as an amendment to the Constitution by the legislatures of three-fourths of the several States within seven years from the date of its submission.

ARTICLE XXI

Passed by Congress February 20, 1933. Ratified December 5, 1933.

Section 1. The eighteenth article of amendment to the Constitution of the United States is hereby repealed.

Section 2. The transportation or importation into any State, Territory, or possession of the United States for delivery or use therein of intoxicating liquors in violation of the laws thereof, is hereby prohibited.

Section 3. This article shall be inoperative unless it shall have been ratified as an amendment to the Constitution by conventions in the several States, as provided in the Constitution, within seven years from the date of the submission hereof to the States by the Congress.

ARTICLE XXII

Passed by Congress March 12, 1947. Ratified February 26, 1951.

Section 1. No person shall be elected to the office of the President more than twice, and no person who has held the office of President, or acted as President, for more than two years of a term to which some other person was elected President shall be elected to the office of the President more than once. But this article shall not apply to any person holding the office of President when this article was proposed by the Congress, and shall not prevent any person who may be holding the office of President, or acting as President, during the term within which this article becomes operative from holding the office of President or acting as President during the remainder of such term.

Section 2. This article shall be inoperative unless it shall have been ratified as an amendment to the Constitution by the legislatures of three-fourths of the several States within seven years from the date of its submission to the States by the Congress.

ARTICLE XXIII

Passed by Congress June 16, 1960. Ratified April 3, 1961.

Section 1. The District constituting the seat of Government of the United States shall appoint in such manner as the Congress may direct:

A number of electors of President and Vice President equal to the whole number of Senators and Representatives in Congress to which the District would be entitled if it were a State, but in no event more than the least populous State; they shall be in addition to those appointed by the States, but they shall be considered, for the purposes of the election of President and Vice President, to be electors appointed by a State; and they shall meet in the District and perform such duties as provided by the twelfth article of amendment.

Section 2. The Congress shall have power to enforce this article by appropriate legislation.

ARTICLE XXIV

Passed by Congress August 27, 1962. Ratified January 23, 1964.

Section 1. The right of citizens of the United States to vote in any primary or other election for President or Vice President, for electors for President or Vice President, or for Senator or Representative in Congress, shall not be denied or abridged by the United States or any State by reason of failure to pay any poll tax or other tax.

Section 2. The Congress shall have power to enforce this article by appropriate legislation.

ARTICLE XXV

Passed by Congress July 6, 1965. Ratified February 10, 1967.

Section 1. In case of the removal of the President from office or of his death or resignation, the Vice President shall become President.

Section 2. Whenever there is a vacancy in the office of the Vice President, the President shall nominate a Vice President who shall take office upon confirmation by a majority vote of both Houses of Congress.

Section 3. Whenever the President transmits to the President pro tempore of the Senate and the Speaker of the House of Representatives his written declaration that he is unable to discharge the powers and duties of his office, and until he transmits to them a written declaration to the contrary, such powers and duties shall be discharged by the Vice President as Acting President.

Section 4. Whenever the Vice President and a majority of either the principal officers of the executive departments or of such other body as Congress may by law provide, transmit to the President pro tempore of the Senate and the Speaker of the House of Representatives their written declaration that the President is unable to discharge the powers and duties of his office, the Vice President shall immediately assume the powers and duties of the office as Acting President.

Thereafter, when the President transmits to the President pro tempore of the Senate and the Speaker of the House of Representatives his written declaration that no inability exists, he shall resume the powers and duties of his office unless the Vice President and a majority of either the principal officers of the executive department or of such other body as Congress may by law provide, transmit within four days to the President pro tempore of the Senate and the Speaker of the House of Representatives their written declaration that the President is unable to discharge the powers and duties of his office. Thereupon Congress shall decide the issue, assembling within forty-eight hours for that purpose if not in session. If the Congress, within twenty-one days after receipt of the latter written declaration, or, if Congress is not in session, within twenty-one days after Congress is required to assemble, determines by two-thirds vote of both Houses that the President is unable to discharge the powers and duties of his office, the Vice President shall continue to discharge the same as Acting President; otherwise, the President shall resume the powers and duties of his office.

ARTICLE XXVI

Passed by Congress March 23, 1971. Ratified June 30, 1971.

Section 1. The right of citizens of the United States, who are eighteen years of age or older, to vote shall not be denied or abridged by the United States or any state on account of age.

Section 2. The Congress shall have the power to enforce this article by appropriate legislation.